HAYDN:
CHRONICLE AND WORKS

HAYDN: CHRONICLE AND WORKS
in five volumes by
H. C. Robbins Landon

★Haydn: The Early Years 1732–1765
★Haydn at Eszterháza 1766–1790
†Haydn in England 1791–1795
†Haydn: The Years of 'The Creation' 1796–1800
Haydn: The Late Years 1801–1809
(†previously published; ★in preparation)

HAYDN:
THE LATE YEARS
1801–1809

To
Karl and Irene Geiringer
with respect and affection

Haydn: Chronicle and Works

VOLUME V

HAYDN

THE LATE YEARS

1801–1809

H. C. ROBBINS LANDON

INDIANA UNIVERSITY PRESS

BLOOMINGTON   LONDON

First American edition 1977 by Indiana University Press

Library of Congress Cataloging in Publication Data

Landon, Howard Chandler Robbins, 1926–
    Haydn: chronicle and works.

    Includes bibliographies and indexes.
    CONTENTS
    v. 5. Haydn: the Late Years, 1801–1809
    1. Haydn, Joseph, 1732–1809.
ML410.H4L26   780'.92'4[B]   76–14630
ISBN 0–253–37005–1   1 2 3 4 5 81 80 79 78 77

Printed in Great Britain

Contents

LIST OF ILLUSTRATIONS

9

Preface

THIS VOLUME, THE LAST CHRONOLOGICALLY of the five which together constitute a complete biography of Haydn, is concerned with the composer's declining years: declining physically, but – as long as he continued to compose – not mentally. The old and much loved master stopped writing music when he himself felt that he was no longer up to the task physically, and thus we are saved from the embarrassing fate of having to apologize for music composed on the verge of senility. Haydn's last completed works are mostly choral – *The Seasons* and the last two Masses (*Schöpfungsmesse* and *Harmoniemesse* of 1801 and 1802, respectively), of which the former is now becoming appreciated as a giant monument of its composer's old age (whereas the latter was always highly regarded). In 1803 Haydn began his last Quartet (Op. 103, in D minor), but when he saw he could not finish it he cast the work aside; and if any large-scale sketches existed for its missing movements, they were probably destroyed.

The years under consideration were not a happy time for Haydn's fatherland. When this volume opens, we find the Austrians negotiating for a peace treaty at Lunéville, but in circumstances far from favourable to the *k. k. Monarchie*. On New Year's Day 1801, the Austrian representative at Lunéville, Ludwig, Count Cobenzl, writes – in French, as a matter of course between civilized men – to Franz, Count Colloredo-Wallsee, the Cabinet Minister in Vienna, as follows:

> Il n'échappera pas à la pénétration de V[otre]. E[xcellence]. que ce n'était pas, lorsque nos armées sont battues au-delà de tout ce que l'on pourrait craindre, que l'ennemi a pénétré jusqu'au cœur de la monarchie autrichienne, qu'il nous a obligés à un armistice tel que celui qui vient d'être fait, que j'aurais pu obtenir ici les Légations avec l'Adda et la retraite de l'armée de Moreau derrière l'Inn. Les propositions qui m'avaient été faites déjà par Talleyrand à Paris annonçaient les vues du premier consul, et si les discours familiers de Joseph Bonaparte ont pu faire espérer des conditions plus tolérables, la série de nos revers était bien faite pour remonter sur ses grands chevaux l'arrogant ennemi auquel nous avons à faire. Sans doute que les ordres de S[a]. M[ajesté]. m'autorisaient à tout; mais que V. E. se mette à ma place et juge de ma douleur, si, chargé de demander jusqu'à l'Adda, j'avais dû prendre sur moi de signer sur les propositions qui m'ont été faites par le plénipotentiaire français? . . . Soyez persuadé, Mr. le conte, que je ne perde pas courage. Vous avez vu, comme j'ai bataillé . . .

And a few days later, on the Feast of Epiphany (6 January), the losses sustained by the Austrians had made Cobenzl's stand even more untenable:

> Quelque accoutumés que nous soyons aux revers, j'avoue que les événements qui ont accompagné la reprise des hostilités, la nullité de notre armée et les progrès de l'ennemi passent toute croyance. Un peu de résistance de notre part et seulement

quelque égalité dans les chances nous auraient procuré des conditions très tolérables
. . . Mais lorsque les Français pénètrent de tous côtés dans les pays héréditaires,
qu'ils sont aux portes de Vienne, est-il étonnant qu'ils nous imposent les lois plus
dures? Est-ce par la voie de la persuasion qu'on peut attendre d'eux le moindre
avantage? Je crois n'avoir rien omis de ce qui dépendait de moi, soit du côté de la
fermeté, soit pour ce qui aurait pu d'ailleurs faire effet sur les Bonapartes. Malgré
mes scènes avec le premier consul, je ne suis pas mal avec lui. Mais qu'est-ce que
tout cela, en comparaison de leurs succès militaires? . . .[1]

In this volume we shall see that the French actually occupied Vienna on two
occasions, in 1805 and 1809. As Haydn grew older he was 'crushed' by the humiliation
which Napoleon inflicted on his fatherland, by the appalling battles that were raging
around Vienna as he lay dying, and not least by the state of affairs which had succeeded
the greatness of the Eighteenth Century, that monument of Enlightenment and
Civilization. Yet humanity was present in Haydn's actions (and in some respects in
those of the conquerors) to the very end: Haydn embraced a French officer who
knocked on his door and sang 'Mit Würd' und Hoheit' ('In Native Worth') from *The
Creation*, the officer then departing, in all probability to be massacred on the
battlefield. And a French guard of honour stood watch outside Haydn's little house in
the Kleine Steingasse, even as the confiscated newspaper, the *Wiener Zeitung* (with
whose reports readers of the earlier volumes of this biography are well acquainted),
informed the Viennese public that:

> The victories of Napoleon the Great are not only the astonishment and pride
> of the century, they are also the fortune and benefit of the nations. From the
> moment of victory, the conquered peoples are under the protection of the
> conqueror, those wise and brave men . . . [etc.]
>
> [*WZ*, 20 May 1809; report dated 18 May]

It all sounds depressingly familiar to us today. The report continues –

> The history of the war and its origins are, especially for the inhabitants of this land,
> of the greatest importance. Little is known about these origins; one must have had
> reasons for concealing with such great efforts the real motives for the war from the
> inhabitants of Austria . . .

– and so on, in the best *Völkischer Beobachter* style. In the confusion of the war and the
French occupation, Haydn's death passed almost unnoticed, but when the news
reached the ears of the French authorities a week after the event (Haydn died on 31
May; the news was officially registered on 6 June), they immediately published it on
the front page of the *Wiener Zeitung* as the leading news item. Haydn was still a figure
of international stature in Europe, and his death could cause even the inexorable
propaganda machine of the French military to cease its outpourings for an instant.

ACKNOWLEDGMENTS

As in earlier volumes of this biography, I am deeply indebted to many private
individuals as well as public institutions for the mass of material, and especially the
documents, which this last volume contains. My friends at the Országos Széchényi

---

1 *Vertrauliche Briefe des Freiherrn von Thugut, Österr. Ministers des Äussern. Beiträge zur Beurtheilung der
politischen Verhältnisse Europa's in den Jahren 1792–1801, ausgewählt und herausgegeben . . . von Alfred Ritter
Vivenot*, Vienna 1872, vol. II, pp. 358f, 362. A highly important series of original source material on the
Napoleonic Wars, as seen from the Austrian side (see Bibliography for other material by the same editor).

Könyvtár (National Library) in Budapest supplied documents, information, photographs and encouragement, and once again I thank them all for their hospitality, courtesy and assistance. The British Museum's Music Room (A. H. King and O. W. Neighbour) were helpful as always, and I owe the Museum thanks for sending the Elssler Catalogue of Haydn's music, which is here reproduced for the first time. In Paris, the Bibliothèque Nationale, now incorporating the Bibliothèque du Conservatoire de Musique, and my old friend M. François Lesure, furnished information and microfilms; and I should like also to thank my friends M. & Mme. Antonio de Almeida, who then lived in a marvellous *Directoire* house behind the Panthéon, and were my hosts on many occasions when I was working in the libraries. In Vienna, I must thank the Österreichische Nationalbibliothek, not least for the photographs of Haydn's legacy (here printed for the first time); the Archiv der Stadt Wien and the Stadtbibliothek for many favours; the Gesellschaft der Musikfreunde (Frau Dr Mitringer and Dr Otto Biba), especially for allowing us to photograph their rare reproduction of the Wigand painting of Haydn attending his last performance of *The Creation* in 1808 (the original painting disappeared in 1945); see colour plate III. The Bayerische Staatsbibliothek (Dr Robert Münster) has also been most helpful; it owns, among many treasures, the autograph of the great *Schöpfungsmesse* (in the acquisition of which I played a humble part, having found the right means to effect its removal from a Swiss antiquarian and its acquisition by the Library in Munich, in the operation of which Georg Henle and Professor Jens Peter Larsen played to perfection their respective roles of benefactor and travelling expert, thus placing in public hands a manuscript which was known to hardly anyone since it left its composer's library shelf). Once more, I should like to thank the then reigning Prince von Fürstenberg, who was my attentive host for a week in Donaueschingen Castle many years ago.

Among private colleagues, friends and strangers, who provided information of many and varied kinds, I must mention Mr Albi Rosenthal (London and Oxford), who copied out a valuable letter by Adalbert Gyrowetz about collecting Haydn's *The Seasons* and equally for copying out a Michael Haydn autograph letter, both hitherto unpublished. Professor J. M. Osborn, of New Haven (Connecticut), kindly sent photographs of an unpublished letter from Haydn to Dr Charles Burney (see Chronicle, 19 May 1804, *infra*). Dr Janos Harich of Eisenstadt was a helpful colleague, as he has been for many years, particularly as regards the personnel of the Esterházy choir and orchestra.

The Bibliography was first assembled in 1972 by Dr Alison Maitland (now Mrs Robert Shiel), who was then my efficient assistant; she also read through the manuscript of the fourth and fifth volumes.

The illustrations were supplied in generous fashion by the Kunsthistorisches Museum and the Historisches Museum der Stadt Wien, both of Vienna; the latter also furnished photographs of Haydn's autograph catalogue of his libretto collection, here reproduced for the first time. The Harrach Museum in Schloß Harrach, Rohrau, supplied a photograph of the magnificent lead bust of Haydn, and the Esterházy Administration (Eisenstadt), the Burgenländisches Landesmuseum (Eisenstadt), the Stadtbibliothek Leipzig, the Beethovenhaus Bonn, Mme F. de Cossette (Paris) and Mr Louis Krasner (Syracuse, N.Y.) sent photographs of one kind or another; the details may be seen in the list of illustrations on pp. 9–10.

The entire manuscript of the third, fourth and fifth volumes of this biography – *Haydn in England 1791–1795*; *Haydn: the Years of 'The Creation' 1796–1800*; and *Haydn: the Late Years 1801–1809* – was read by Mr and Mrs F. Gordon Morrill (Florence), whose astute comments and wide knowledge of eighteenth-century art and manners have been a constant stimulation for many years. Mr Charles Ford and Mr Mark Trowbridge were my editors for this biography, and no author was ever more fortunate in having such devoted and efficient assistance. The debt to my publishers is apparent in the handsome design and production of the volumes, but less obvious to the reader is the magnitude of the task involved in the preparation and processing of the quantity of textual and illustrative material contained in each volume, and not least the sympathy with which I have been treated by the management and staff of Thames and Hudson Ltd.

The third volume of this biography was begun in the autumn of 1969 and completed some two years later. The writing of the fourth and fifth volumes was completed at Buggiano Castello on 24 August 1973, but for a variety of reasons, it has taken a considerable time to produce, not least because of the printing complexities. I have brought up to date the more essential facts, and added the most important new publications to the general biography (see end of this volume); but otherwise I have left the manuscript with its occasional references to 'present writing (1972)' or whatever, if only because, as a historian, it seemed witless to change '1972' to '1976'.

This last volume is dedicated to my old teacher at Boston University, Professor Karl Geiringer, and his devoted wife, Irene, now Santa Barbara, California, in whose hospitable house my wife and I have spent many happy and rewarding hours.

Vienna, St. Nicholas 1976   H.C.R.L.

AUTHOR'S NOTE

Haydn's music

Vocal music is identified by title and, on the occasion of the first or major reference, by its number in Hoboken's *Haydn Verzeichnis* (vol. II, Vocal Works), Mainz, 1971.

Instrumental music is identified as follows.

Symphonies are referred to by their number in Mandyczewski's list for the publishers Breitkopf & Härtel, which numbering was taken over by Hoboken in his *Haydn Verzeichnis* (vol. I), Mainz, 1955. Symphony No. 95, for example, is I:95 in Hoboken's list.

String Quartets are identified by their opus number and, like all instrumental pieces, by the Hoboken number at the first and/or major reference.

Piano Sonatas are listed by their chronological numbering in the *Wiener Urtext Ausgabe*, edited by C. Landon.

Piano Trios are identified by the new chronological numbering in the *Complete Edition of Haydn's Piano Trios*, edited by H. C. Robbins Landon and published by Verlag Doblinger.

Other instrumental works are identified by their customary title (e.g. 'London Trios' and 'Overture to an English Opera') and by their Hoboken number.

The system of pitch notation used is based on middle C being represented by the symbol *c′*.

Instruments (in order of their customary appearance in the orchestral score) are abbreviated thus: Fl. – flute; Ob. – oboe; Cor ang. – cor anglais; Clar. – clarinet; Bsn. (Fag.) – bassoon; Contrafag. – double bassoon; Hr. (Cor.) – horn; Trbe. (Trpt) – trumpet; Trbn. – trombone; Timp. – timpani (kettledrums); V. – violin; Va. viola; Vc. – violoncello; Cb. (B.) – contrabasso (double bass); Cemb. – cembalo (harpsichord).

Documents

In all documents cited in the text the original orthography – whether in English, German, French or Italian – has been retained. Thus, accents have not been inserted where they were omitted in the original document, notably in passages from the Zinzendorf Diaries. The language of the original document is indicated only in those cases which require clarification. Bibliographical references will be found in an abbreviated form in the text, at the end of quotations and in the footnotes; the full titles of works cited are given on pp. 17–19.

The abbreviations 'k.k.' and 'I.R.' (meaning *'kaiserlich-königlich'*/'Imperial Royal') are used interchangeably. Austrian money is abbreviated thus: Gulden (gulden) = 'f.' or 'fl.' (or 'F.', 'Fl.'); Kreuzer = 'k.' or 'kr.' or 'xr.' ('K.', 'Kr.', 'Xr.').

ABBREVIATIONS OF
BIBLIOGRAPHICAL SOURCES

AMZ	*Allgemeine Musikalische Zeitung*, Leipzig, 1798 et seq.
Bartha	*Joseph Haydn, Gesammelte Briefe und Aufzeichnungen*, herausgegeben und erläutert von Dénes Bartha, Budapest-Kassel, 1965.
Bartha-Somfai	Dénes Bartha and László Somfai, *Haydn als Opernkapellmeister*, Budapest, 1960.
Beethoven-Handbuch	Theodor von Frimmel, *Beethoven-Handbuch*, 2 vols. 1926 (since reprinted).
Brand *Messen*	Carl Maria Brand, *Die Messen von Joseph Haydn*, Würzburg, 1941 (since reprinted).
Carpani	Giuseppe Carpani, *Le Haydine*, Milan, 1812.
CCLN	*Collected Correspondence and London Notebooks of Joseph Haydn*, translated and edited by H. C. Robbins Landon, London, 1959.
Crosse *Account*	*An Account of the Grand Musical Festival, held in September 1823, in the Cathedral Church of York . . .*, by John Crosse, F.S.A., F.R.S.L., York, 1825.
Da Ponte	*Memoirs of Lorenzo da Ponte*, translated from the Italian by Elizabeth Abbott, edited and annotated by Arthur Livingston; new edition, New York, 1967.
Deutsch *Freihaustheater*	Otto Erich Deutsch, *Das Wiener Freihaustheater*, Vienna, 1937.
Deutsch *Mozart, Dokumente*	Otto Erich Deutsch, *W. A. Mozart – Die Dokumente seines Lebens*, Kassel-Basel, 1961.
Dies	A. C. Dies, *Biographische Nachrichten von Joseph Haydn*, Vienna, 1810; new edition by Horst Seeger, Berlin, n.d. [1959]
Enciclopedia dello spettacolo	*Enciclopedia dello spettacolo* (11 vols.), Rome, 1954 *et seq.*
Farington	*The Farington Diary*, edited by James Greig, London and New York, 1923.
Gerber *NTL*	Ludwig Gerber, *Neues historisch-biographisches Lexikon der Tonkünstler*, 4 vols, 1812–14; new edition by Othmar Wessely, Graz, 1966.
Geiringer 1932, 1947, 1959 and 1963	Karl Geiringer, *Joseph Haydn*: Potsdam, 1932; New York, 1947; Mainz, 1959; Garden City, N.Y., 1963.
Griesinger	G. A. Griesinger, *Biographische Notizen über Joseph Haydn*, Leipzig, 1810; new ed. Franz Grasberger, Vienna, 1954.

Bibliographical sources

Grove, I, II, III, IV, V	Grove's *Dictionary of Music and Musicians*, first, second, third, fourth and fifth editions.
Hadden	J. Cuthbert Hadden, *Haydn*, London, 1902.
Hadden *Thomson*	J. Cuthbert Hadden, *George Thomson, the Friend of Burns: His Life and Correspondence*, London, 1898.
Hase	H. von Hase, *Joseph Haydn und Breitkopf & Härtel*, Leipzig, 1909.
Horányi	Mátyás Horányi, *Das Esterházysche Feenreich*, Budapest, 1959; English edition, *The Magnificence of Esterháza*, London, 1962.
HV	Thematic catalogue ('Haydn Verzeichnis') of Haydn's œuvre, for details see pp. 294f.
Landon *Beethoven*	H. C. Robbins Landon, *Beethoven: a documentary study*, London and New York, 1970.
Landon *Essays*	H. C. Robbins Landon, *Essays on the Viennese Classical Style*, London, 1970.
Landon *Supplement*	H. C. Robbins Landon, *Supplement to 'The Symphonies of Joseph Haydn'*, London, 1961.
Landon *SYM*	H. C. Robbins Landon, *The Symphonies of Joseph Haydn*, London, 1955.
Larsen *HÜB*	J. P. Larsen, *Die Haydn-Überlieferung*, Copenhagen, 1939.
MGG	*Musik in Geschichte und Gegenwart* (Allgemeine Enzyklopädie der Musik), ed. F. Blume, Kassel, 1947 *et seq.*
Mörner	C.-G. Stellan Mörner, *Johan Wikmanson und die Brüder Silverstolpe*, Stockholm, 1952.
Neukomm	Sigismund (von) Neukomm, *Bemerkungen zu den biogr. Nachrichten von Dies* (MS. in Pohl's hand, owned by Friedrich Matzenauer, Vienna; published 1959).
Olleson	E. Olleson, 'Haydn in the Diaries of Count Karl von Zinzendorf', in *Haydn Yearbook* II (1963–4).
Olleson *Griesinger*	E. Olleson, 'Georg August Griesinger's Correspondence with Breitkopf & Härtel' in *Haydn Yearbook* III (1965).
Parke	W. T. Parke, *Musical Memoirs*, 2 vols., London, 1830.
Plank	Plank's MS. Diary (Archives of Kremsmünster Abbey), printed in P. Altmann Kellner, *Musikgeschichte des Stiftes Kremsmünster*, Kassel, 1957.
Pohl *H in L*	C. F. Pohl, *Haydn in London*, Vienna, 1867; reprinted, New York, 1970.
Pohl *Denkschrift*	C. F. Pohl, *Denkschrift aus Anlass des 100-Jährigen Bestehens der Tonkünstler-Societät*, Vienna, 1871.
Pohl I, II, III	C. F. Pohl, *Joseph Haydn* (3 vols.): I, Berlin, 1875; II, Berlin, 1882; III (completed by Hugo Botstiber), Leipzig, 1927. All three vols. since reprinted.
Radant *Rosenbaum*	'The Diaries of Joseph Carl Rosenbaum 1770–1829', edited by Else Radant, *Haydn Yearbook* V (1968); also as a separate publication in the original German.
Rosenbaum	'The Diaries of Joseph Carl Rosenbaum 1770–1829' (MS. in Österreichische Nationalbibliothek, Vienna); see Radant above.

Schindler	A. F. Schindler, *Beethoven as I knew him*, ed. D. W. MacArdle, London and Chapel Hill, N.C., 1966.
Smart	*Leaves from the Journals of Sir George Smart*, by H. Bertram Cox and C. L. E. Cox, London, 1907.
Somfai	László Somfai, *Joseph Haydn. Sein Leben in zeitgenössischen Bildern*, Budapest and Kassel, 1966; also published in English, London, 1967.
Spohr	*The Musical Journeys of Louis Spohr*, selected, translated and edited by Henry Pleasants, Norman, 1961.
Thayer I	A. W. Thayer, *Ludwig van Beethovens Leben*, second revised edition (Deiters), vol. I, Berlin, 1901.
Thayer-Forbes	Thayer's *Life of Beethoven*, revised and edited by Elliot Forbes (2 vols.), Princeton, N.J., 1967.
Zinzendorf	MS. Diaries of Count Carl von Zinzendorf, in the Haus-, Hof- und Staatsarchiv, Vienna.

CHAPTER ONE

Chronicle 1801

OUR CHRONICLE, FOR THE YEAR 1801, will be concerned primarily with the first semi-public and public performances of Haydn's last Oratorio, *The Seasons*. The composer was still extraordinarily active for a man of sixty-nine years, delivering in this same year the great Mass known as 'Die Schöpfungsmesse' and continuing to conduct at charity concerts of various kinds. Among his many affairs of business, two publishers became increasingly important in Haydn's old age: Breitkopf & Härtel in Leipzig and his (relatively new) acquisition in Scotland, George Thomson of Edinburgh. More than five years after Haydn had returned to Austria, following his second visit to England, he (or his *bottega*) was still continuing to turn out settings of Scottish songs for the Edinburgh publisher (see *Haydn in England 1791–1795*, pp. 400ff., and *Haydn: the Years of 'The Creation' 1796–1800*, pp. 493ff.). Now, at the beginning of the year 1801, Thomson writes to Mr Straton, of the British Embassy in Vienna, who was acting as his agent there:

> Edinburgh 10th January 1801
>
> I shall be very happy to hear that Haydn has done the Ritornelles and accompaniments to the 25 Songs now in his possession and you will oblige me much by putting him in mind of them as you propose. I must further intreat you taking the trouble to send the other 5 to the Doctor, which are are here inclosed with a request that he will be so good as to do them immediately, at least that he will let me have the first three within a fortnight or three weeks. The 5 Airs which were inclosed in the Original of this letter, are: There came a young man to my daddie's door – in C for the Song of the Gaberlunzie man; Mary's Dream; The weary pund of Tow; Macpherson's farewell; The del's away wi' th' Exciseman . . .[1]

[Straton to Thomson in Edinburgh]

> Vienna Feb 3d 1801
>
> . . . Haydn has promised to send me his Composition in eight or ten days and it shall be forwarded to you by the first safe opportunity. . . .

---

1 Hoboken II, XXXIa: 46 *bis*, 1 *bis*, 129 *bis*, 182, 158. This letter and the answer to it are in the Thomson file in the British Museum; see also Pohl III, 172 (with mistakes). For the authoritative article on the subject, see K. Geiringer, 'Haydn and the Folksong of the British Isles', in *Musical Quarterly* XXV (1949), 2, 179ff. Bibliographically, the following articles by Cecil Hopkinson and C. B. Oldman, published in *Edinburgh Bibliographical Society Transactions*, are of the greatest value: 'Thomson's Collections of National Song, with special reference to the contributions of Haydn and Beethoven' (II, Pt 1, Session 1938–39, Edinburgh 1940, pp. 1ff.); 'Haydn's Settings of Scottish Songs in the Collections of Napier and Whyte' (III, Pt 2, Sessions 1949–50 and 1950–51, Edinburgh 1954, pp. 85ff.); and 'Thomson's Collections of National Song, with special reference to Haydn and Beethoven. Addenda et Corrigenda', *ibid.*, pp. 121ff. More recently, Georg Feder (*Haydn–Studien* I [1965], Heft 1, 43) was able to demonstrate that even for Napier's edition Haydn was given the musical lines to 'edit' without the words.

Extraordinarily, all Haydn's publishers – even Napier, when the composer was himself in London in the years 1791 *et seq.* – delivered to the composer only the melody of the songs, never (apparently) the words or even a précis, much less a translation. As if this were not detrimental enough to Haydn's attempts to fathom the secrets of Scottish – and later Welsh and Irish – folksongs, we now know that Haydn himself only supervised most of the work, giving it to his pupils. Probably Neukomm was responsible for most of the Thomson settings at this period. For this reason it seems useless to discuss the music in any great detail. As one might expect, the work is competently done, with some attractive details of form, harmony and melodic line (in the 'symphonies' that Haydn and his *bottega* added); but it is clear that the composer's heart was not really in this kind of hack-work, which he clearly did only for money. Such aspects of the continuing Haydn–Straton–Thomson correspondence, etc., as may be of interest to us from the biographical standpoint have, of course, been included in this Chronicle.

On 9 February the Treaty of Lunéville was signed, and the war was finished for Austria at the moment. In Vienna, the relief was general. '[I sent off some] peace proclamations. What a blessed word!', writes Rosenbaum (89). Although peace was not to be of long duration, the changed circumstances enabled the French and Austrians to re-establish commercial and cultural contacts, with interesting results for Haydn, as we shall see.

Meanwhile the old composer – he was nearing his sixty-ninth birthday – was using *The Creation* more and more for charitable purposes. On 16 January he gave a performance as a benefit for wounded soldiers. Rosenbaum noted in his Diary (88):

> Saturday, 17th: . . . There were 1,200 persons at *The Creation* yesterday. The Empress gave 1,000 gulden, the Queen of Naples 1,000 Gulden, Maximilian 1,000 gulden, Albert 100 gulden. In all, the receipts amounted to 6,683 Gulden, to which the Grand Duke of Tuscany added 500 gulden, increasing them to 7,183 gulden. –

Beda Plank of Kremsmünster Abbey was also present:

> On 16 January musical greed took me to the big k.k. Redoutensaal where the magnificent Oratorio *Die Schöpfung*, the *non plus ultra* of Herr Dr. mus. Joseph Haydn, was produced by several hundred musicians. Herr Dr. himself conducted. Herr Saal from the Court Theatre, his daughter and Herr Rathmayr, Professor at the Theresianum, sang the solo parts of the Angels and our First Parents [Adam and Eve] admirably. I noticed that the tempo, especially in the arias and also by the fugues, was rather moderate, and not as quick as we do it. Although one had heard the piece very frequently here, the crowd was so great that the very roomy hall was filled from top to bottom with people. The income was for the wounded Imperial Royal soldiers, and was 7,183 fl. 28 kr. [pp. 567f.]

Griesinger was also a witness and reported to Breitkopf & Härtel on 21 January:

> '. . . This music seems to have been made to help collect money for good works, and this time it in no way failed its purpose. Haydn himself conducted with youthful fire . . .' [Olleson *Griesinger*, 16]

Two weeks later Haydn was again asked to conduct at a charity concert, this time collaborating with Frau von Frank (the excellent singer better known to us under her maiden name, Gerhardi or Gerardi), the great horn virtuoso Punto, and Beethoven.

We have several contemporary reports on the concert, given in the Redoutensaal on 30 January:

[Zinzendorf's Diary] . . . au grand Concert en faveur des blessés dans la grande Salle de la redoute. J'y donnois f. 50, et me tine longtems contre l'Orchestre. Le cor de chasse de Punto n'a pu atteindre le fond de la Sale . . .   [Olleson, 59]

[Rosenbaum's Diary:] . . . Red[outen] Saal concert – rehearsal of Franck [*sic*]. I was introduced to Franck, a lively and nice little woman. Th[erese] received a ticket from Franck herself. . . . We visited Mme Rahl, stayed until 6 o'clock, and then went to Calvany [Magdalena Calvani-Willmann], with whom Th— drove to the concert. – I arrived to find the hall filled, and later there was quite a press in the hall and the gallery. – It was a fine company. Before the concert began, a lamp-trimmer provided involuntary entertainment by falling from the orchestra and pulling music stands and the barrier down with him. Franck *née* Gerardi, Willmann and Simoni sang excerpts from the operas *Morope* [*Merope*] by Nasolini and *Horasier* [*Gli orazii ed i curiazii*, 1796]. Beethoven played a sonata, Punto accompanying him on the hunting horn, Haydn conducted 2 of his own symphonies. The receipts amounted to more than 9,400 gulden. . . .
[Pohl III; Radant, 88]

[Beda Plank's Diary:] On 30 January at 7 p.m. there was a musical academy in the large k. k. Redoutensall and, like *The Creation* recently, it was dedicated to the wounded soldiers of the war; I couldn't miss it. Madame v. Frank, *née* Gerhardi, wife of the famous *Herr Doktor* of the Allgemeine Krankenspital [general hospital] here, was the principal vocal soloist and is the most famous lay singer in Vienna. Herr Simoni has also a pleasant tenor voice and distinguished himself, as did the soprano Madame Galvani. Two symphonies by Joseph Haydn, which began the second part of the concert, and which he himself conducted, were among the most beautiful products of the master and were applauded after every piece. Beethoven played a *Phantasiekonzert* on the fortepiano with as much expression as dexterity, and Herr Punto played on the hunting horn no less quickly and efficiently. Terzettes and Choruses were from the best operas. I thought on seeing the production of *The Creation* to have seen many people in the hall: today there were even more: and the income was 9,464 fl., that is, 2,281 fl. more than recently.
[pp. 568f.]

[*Wiener Zeitung* No. 11, 7 February:] The recently announced musical academy for the benefit of the wounded soldiers of the I. R. army was held on 30 January to the greatest delight of all listeners . . . the noble organizer, Frau Christiana v. Frank, *née* Gerhardi, earned by her rare vocal expression general admiration. Herr v. Bethoven [*sic*] played a sonata of his composition on the pianoforte, which was accompanied by Herr Punto on the hunting horn. Both entirely satisfied the expectation that the public entertained of these masters of their art. Frau Galvani and Herr Simoni likewise contributed to the excellence of this academy by their song, as did *Herr Kapellmeister* Pär [Paer] and Herr Conti through the direction of the orchestra. Finally the great Hayden [*sic*] took over the direction of two symphonies of his composition. . . . The receipts amounted to the respectable sum of 9,463 Guld. 11 Kr., to which Their Majesties the Emperor and Empress, the Queen of Naples and their R. I. Highnesses the Archdukes, and the Duke Albert, repeated their usual *largesse*.

From Pohl's notes (III, 170f.) we learn that Christine (as she is generally called) Frank had applied in writing to Prince Esterházy to request the participation of 'the greatest *Kapellmeister* in Europe'; of course, Haydn received permission – he hardly needed to ask it any longer for such a purpose – and promised 'to take over the direction of two lesser-performed symphonies'. Otherwise, it is clear from the above-mentioned diaries, etc., that Beethoven played two works: the horn Sonata, Op. 17, with Punto (his tone obviously being a very subtle one: *vide* Zinzendorf), and an improvisation ('Phantasiekonzert'). To conclude, we should add Rosenbaum's afterthought, 'Franck sang with much art and expression, much in the manner of Crescentini. It [the concert] went on rather a long time' (Pohl III, 171). The humorous Eipeldauer also had something to say:

> For the first time I went to hear a musical concert, which a good musical lady gave for the benefit of the wounded soldiers, and because this time a beautiful lady's voice could be heard, the attendance of the gallant world was much greater and there was an income of more than 9,000f. Never did I regret spending my 2 f.[1] less than this time. The famous musical artist, who did *The Creation*, wrote a new symphony and this turned out to be wonderful.
>
> [*Der wiederaufgelebte Eipeldauer* 1801, Heft 23, Brief No. 2, p. 19; Pohl III, 171]

Many of the musicians that night, not least Joseph Haydn, will have remembered that the famous composer of *Gli orazii ed i curiazii*, Domenico Cimarosa, had died some three weeks earlier, on 11 January, in Venice. Cimarosa was the greatest of the late eighteenth-century Italian operatic school, and had been adored by the Viennese in 1793 for his *Il matrimonio segreto*.[2] He and Giovanni Paisiello were indeed the only two composers of that once world-famous school to survive with any measure of permanent success the ravages of time and changing taste. Paisiello was to linger on until 1815, famous in his native Italy but half-forgotten north of the Alps. The passing of Cimarosa may indeed be said to mark the high watermark of *settecento* Italian opera outside that country; from this point, that music's popularity would begin to wane, and wane very swiftly.

A few days later Beda Plank from Kremsmünster went to hear a new work by Eybler at the Schottenkirche, the *Missa de sancta Elisabetha*:

> On 2 February I heard a brand new Mass by Herr Eybler, Choir Director at the Scottish Church, at 11 o'clock. The noisy passages, often contrasted with soft and quiet sections, made a curious effect. The frequently unexpected modulations, and the four-part solos in Et incarnatus and Benedictus, made a very pleasant effect. Before the 'Iudicare vivos et mortuos' there is a solo trumpet all by itself, and after a few bars the kettledrums come thundering in all by themselves. I would rather have heard a trombone there. [p. 569]

The martial effect of Haydn's *Missa in tempore belli* was having its profound influence on local church music. Naturally there is, as Warren Kirkendale has brilliantly pointed out, a much older tradition for Masses 'in tempore belli' with trumpet fanfares and kettledrum solos;[3] but it is clear that Haydn's 1796 Mass was the immediate impetus not only for Eybler but also for the Dona in the *Missa solemnis*.

---

1 *Wiener Zeitung* No. 7 announced: 'On the evening of Friday, 30 January, the famous *dilettante* of the art of singing, Frau v. Frank, *née* Gerhardi, will give a musical academy in the Imperial and Royal large Redouten Saale for the benefit of wounded soldiers of the Imperial and Royal Army.' An appeal was made: the price of admission was two gulden but it was hoped that more would be given: 'The price of admission, which however sets no limit on the generosity of friends of men, is two gulden'. (Olleson, 59; Rosenbaum, 89).
2 See *Haydn in England 1791–1795*, p. 126.
3 Warren Kirkendale, 'Beethovens Missa Solemnis und die Rhetorische Tradition', Beethoven Number (*Sitzungsberichte der Österreichischen Akademie der Wissenschaften, Philosophisch-historische Klasse*, Band 271), Vienna 1971, pp. 121ff., esp. 148. This is an essay of the first magnitude.

I   Joseph Haydn, portrait in oils by Isidor Neugass, signed and dated 1805 (the artist's request to the Esterházy administration for the acceptance of the picture is, however, dated '7 December 1806'). In the background (right) is seen a bust of J. S. Bach, and Haydn himself is shown holding in his left hand music from *The Creation* ('Nun schwanden'/'Now vanish' and 'Nun beut die Flur'/'With verdure clad').

II   Ludwig van Beethoven, portrait in oils by Isidor Neugass, *c.* 1806; the so-called Beethoven portrait of the Brunsvik House. Neugass executed two versions of this portrait; the other (in the possession of the descendants of Prince Lichnowsky, its former owner) is signed 'peint par Neugass Wienne 1806'.

III   Masked ball in the large Redoutensaal in the Hofburg, Vienna; coloured engraving by Joseph Schütz, *c.* 1800. In January 1801 Haydn conducted two charity concerts in this hall, followed on 29 May by the first public performance of *The Seasons*.

IV The famous performance of *The Creation* given in the hall of the Old University, Vienna on 27 March 1808 (cf. Chronicle); Haydn (centre) is shown seated, surrounded by members of the nobility and friends.

V   The Burgbastei, Vienna, 1809; aquarelle by Franz Jaschke showing damage resulting from the French bombardment of the city which occurred shortly before Haydn's death.

On 4 February the *AMZ* carried a notice about Haydn's proposed trip to Germany –
already postponed once because of the war:

> H a y d n is thinking of travelling next summer to north Germany, there to
> perform under his own direction *The Seasons*, now nearing completion, in the
> principal places. May he abide by his intentions and may a good fortune assist him
> in this plan! The most honoured and flattering reception is sure to await him
> everywhere.

As we shall soon see, the postponement of *The Seasons'* first performance in
Vienna and the composer's subsequent exhaustion prevented him from making this
journey, which might have done him much good; certainly it would have given him a
moral uplift.

Frederik Samuel Silverstolpe (the Swedish diplomat who was *chargé d'affaires* in
Vienna), to whom Paul Struck – Haydn's composition pupil – had dedicated a
Symphony in E flat, continued his correspondence with his family in Stockholm
about the young man. One passage in each of two letters is interesting. In a letter dated
Vienna, 11 February 1801, Silverstolpe thanks his brother Axel for being kind to
Struck and arranging some concerts for him. 'Thus far he doesn't know much of the
musical literature. He ought to know some other masters besides only Haydn, Mozart
and Gluck ...' (Mörner, 366). On 12 May, Gustaf Abraham Silverstolpe from
Stockholm writes:

> ... Struck certainly has genius, but his conceit will block his *perfectibilité*. His
> contempt for aesthetic culture, based upon the fact that Haydn had none, and the
> conviction that one cannot acquire it if one is properly to learn the rudiments of
> music, might easily turn him into a diligent music- and harmony-writer rather
> than a diligent composer: this is what I am afraid of . . . In case he returns to
> Vienna, encourage him to read partly in Sulzer, partly in Rousseau, Blair and
> Eschenburg, on general theories of the arts, and when he can, Kant [etc.]. . . .
> [Mörner, 377]

Where did Silverstolpe in Stockholm get the idea that Haydn had no 'aesthetic
culture'? Haydn was certainly not an intellectual writer, but considering how much he
is supposed to have read (every day, according to Elssler) it is curious to think of him as
a man without 'aesthetic culture'. Haydn's jovial exterior, apparently, did not help to
persuade his contemporaries that he could be one of music's severest intellectuals when
he wished; the dualistic nature of Haydn's art, as we see, confused many people then as
it does now.

On 11 February, Georg August Griesinger wrote to Breitkopf & Härtel about the long
delayed publication of *The Seven Words*:

11 February 1801

> With today's mail you will surely receive a letter from Father Haydn. When I
> delivered him the page of the Paris Journal he assured me that my visit was very
> welcome, because he has almost decided to let you have *The Seven Words*. Swieten
> himself has given his consent, after he had long persecuted him [Haydn] to issue
> the edition at his own expense; at his age and with his other affairs, he doesn't want
> to bother with it, and he wishes to return your many kindnesses with at least one.
> He will abide by the 50 ducats' fee but asks you that it remains between us. After

Haydn's earlier statements, this proposition was rather unexpected for me, and it will probably be equally so for you. I had no explicit instructions from you <u>still</u>, <u>today</u>, to negotiate about *The Seven Words*, but on the other hand I couldn't turn down anything on my own responsibility and didn't want to ruin anything by hesitating. Therefore I asked Haydn himself to write to you, thanked him meanwhile in your name and received the music. You will get it through Count Els [*sic*][1], who is leaving for Dresden in eight days at the latest to make his farewells – he is going to Madrid as Ambassador – from Dresden. In view of the great reputation that Hn. has here and abroad, you won't, I hope, lose anything by publishing it. . . .

To give this undertaking more authority I proposed to H. that it might be a good idea to preface the work with quite a short foreword which he would sign. Because he turns to the writing of letters only with difficulty, he suggested that I do it, and I shall send it to you with the next mail; it will contain only H's *ipsissima verba*. . . .

About Hofmeister's Bureau de Musique he laughed heartily, also about his [Hoffmeister's] idea to print sonatas by Sebastian Bach, 'which will and can be played by six ladies at the most'.

[Olleson, *Griesinger*, 17]

The *Allgemeine Musikalische Zeitung*, apropos the new wave of Bach publications, noted on 4 February that it was characteristic of the taste of the times 'that two music publishers have found it profitable to issue J. Sebastian Bach's works – Hr. Simrock in Bonn the famous Preludes [*Wohltemperiertes Clavier*] and the *Bureau de Musique* (Herren Hoffmeister und Kühnel) in Leipzig the *complete* works of this Father of German harmony' (III, 336). The Simrock edition was 'edited' by Beethoven's teacher, Neefe. A few months later, in May 1801, Hans Georg Nägeli of Zürich also announced a collection of 'Musical Works of Art in the Severe Style', including J. S. Bach's *Wohltemperiertes Clavier*. In supposing that this Bach Renaissance would not catch on, Haydn miscalculated the trend. Used as he was to works composed even thirty years ago being regarded as hopelessly old-fashioned, he could hardly imagine that there would very soon be a public eager for the *Passion according to St Matthew* and the Mass in B minor. In June, the *AMZ* reported a successful campaign to raise money for Bach's poverty-stricken youngest daughter, Regina Susanna. Beethoven (see his letter to Breitkopf & Härtel of 22 April 1801) suggested publishing a new work and giving Regina Susanna the income. Andreas Streicher, the Viennese piano-builder was also involved in raising money for the woman, and we note, in *AMZ*'s report, among the Viennese subscribers Baron van Swieten, Count Appony (Apponyi), Count and (separately) Countess Fries as well as Prince Lobkowitz (who gave 100 gulden). In all this campaign, Haydn's name does not figure at all; he was obviously out of sympathy with the project (*AMZ, Intelligenz-Blatt* No. IX, June 1801).

A few days later Griesinger again wrote to Leipzig:

21 February 1801

. . . Father Haydn couldn't write to you; he is again in bed with a fever [*Kopffieber*] which he caught from too much exertion. Now he is better. He said, as soon as he is well, that he must write to you about an Interlude that you will find in *The Seven Words*. If the execution of this decision takes as long a time as usual, I will ask Haydn to explain it to me personally and then I shall tell you. He wants to include

---

1 Probably the 'Elß' family also referred to in Beethoven's letter to his brother from Prague, 19 February 1796. Emmerich Joseph Philipp Johann Nepomuk, Count Eltz (*recte*), formerly Envoy at the Court of Saxony, was in Dresden in 1796 and Beethoven took letters to him. Landon, *Beethoven*, 91.

in the foreword a letter that they wrote him from Cadiz, when he was asked to do the composition of *The Seven Words*. The letter is with other papers in Eisenstadt. Moreau had *The Creation* performed in Salzburg, where one of Haydn's brothers lives. The applause was general . . .

. . . Count Eltz, who was supposed to have left for Dresden last week, did not leave till today. That's why you did not receive *The Seven Words* up to now . . .

[Olleson, *Griesinger*, 18]

The Cadiz letter is unfortunately lost. Griesinger reported on 18 March: 'Father Haydn is well again.' General Jean Victor Moreau commanded the French forces that had occupied Salzburg in the middle of December 1800.

A new production of Mozart's *Die Zauberflöte* at the Kärntnerthortheater excited much attention, though in the event it was only Therese Rosenbaum's Queen of the Night which was remembered. (She was engraved in the role; see *Haydn: the Years of 'The Creation'*, pl. 17.) The Emperor and Empress even attended the dress rehearsal on Monday, 23 February, and on the evening of the performance 'Th— caused a sensation' and on the 26th 'Mme Mozart sent word to Th— that in *Die Zauberflöte* Th— had offered her the fullest compensation for all the sufferings with regard to her husband's musical talents' (Radant, 90). It was the high-point in the career of Therese Rosenbaum, *née* Gassmann. A few days later, on 12 March, Philipp Schindlöcker the 'cellist, who was one of Beethoven's performing circle and a member of the Tonkünstler-Societät, came 'to see Th— during the morning, and asked her to sing in the 7 *Words* at the academy of the Society' (29, 30 March, *vide infra*). Two days later, on Saturday afternoon, the 14th, Therese and her husband went to visit Haydn:

. . . We spent a few hours with him and spoke, among other things, about [Therese] Saal. Haydn remarked about her as follows: she has four kinds of voices, one moment she sings high, the next moment down in the bass like a nun; she pulls faces and plays the coquette with the parterre, full of grimaces; she knows I do not care for her, for she will never be a great artist. I was not a little astounded at this description. He also asked Th— to take [Josepha] Hammer, the alto [from the Esterházy *Kapelle*, and a protégée of Haydn's], under her wing, to advise her on matters of dress, to deck her out, in short to improve her appearance. . . .

[Radant, *Rosenbaum*, 91]

On 16 March, Rosenbaum (91) informs us: '[I] went . . . to the Count's [Esterházy], where Quarin asked me whether Th— could sing at the 'Lower Jesuits' [Universitätskirche] after Easter. The work will be a Mass by Haydn.' On 25 March we have a long letter from Griesinger to Breitkopf & Härtel which, fortunately, has survived in its entirety and gives us *inter alia* a brilliant thumb-nail sketch of Baron van Swieten:

25 March 1801

Herewith I send you Haydn's signature, not without a secret joy over the successful completion of my negotiations, which, as you will see from the following circumstances, were rendered difficult. H. had the foreword for the last 4 weeks; during his illness I couldn't of course ask about it. After his recovery I reminded him of it. Now he proceeded to explain that he has considered the matter further and thinks it unnecessary to print a foreword, since he is not issuing *The Seven Words* himself. In vain I countered this objection with the most persuasive arguments. Finally I got him to the point where he agreed to abide by the decision of Bar. Swieten, and whatever he says, goes. Thereupon I set off at once to B. Sw. He did not disapprove of the foreword but asked to have his name, which I'd mentioned, omitted; and with Adelung[1] in his hand he insinuated to me that it would be better to write 'damahls' instead of 'damals', 'Adagio's' instead of 'Adagios', 'hangende' instead of 'hängende' (because it sounds fuller). I threw myself to his feet in submission of this purity, and brought him the next day the revised and castrated foreword, with which he was quite satisfied. Then I ran to H. and received that which I wanted. H. had asked me at the same time to ascertain Swieten's opinion about selling the plates of *The Creation*. Swieten is of the opinion that H. shouldn't get rid of them, they represent a capital that will bring in 50 to 60 ducats every year; H. should therefore demand either an annual rent or a sum of capital equivalent to it. H. won't be talked out of this decision of his oracle, though I saw at once that he is fed up with the business of being his own publisher. Up to now there haven't been 800 copies run off, the plates must therefore be in the best condition; now he is going to print eighteen *Riß*[2] worth of paper which he has received from Venice. 'Then I won't buy any more paper,' he added, rather annoyed. His costs have already exceeded 2,500 fl. and the return on the money is slow. He pays at the printer's 1 fl. 30 k. for each copy. The proposal with the 300 copies did not seem to please him, because he is afraid he will be stuck with them; he found some objections also because of Artaria, who up to now have seen to the shipping and who could be useful to him in many instances. Pleyel when in Leipzig wanted to buy the plates from H., but he received a negative reply, because H. does not gladly have anything to do with him.[3] Another case that shows the great influence that Swieten has over Haydn is the following statement which Haydn told me in confidence. Only by assuring him [Swieten] that he [Haydn] had received one hundred ducats for *The Seven Words* could he receive Swieten's permission to sell it. Nevertheless Sw. said to me: H. made a very modest demand.

I must select some notes from my visits àt Swieten's, each of which lasted about two hours. I am sure that this friendly information *will remain between ourselves*, and that you will be able to stand the criticism as soon as it is explained to you. Sw. seems to be quite outstanding among the persons of his rank here; he is a warm friend and patron of the Muses, and in many aspects one cannot deny that he has profound and clear views. He is a very careful and serious reader of the musical paper [*AMZ*]. Some articles pleased him; in many of the others he remarks a suburban tone *de cotterie*, lack of urbanity and true sensitivity for musical beauties. Thus one is told of the great success that an opera had in Neuwied, and in a warehouse at that, and moreover without wind instruments. Haydn was petulantly [*muthwilligerweise*] taken to task about some parallel fifths. (H. himself said to me on this subject: is it really worthwhile to cry to a writer during a great phrase that he had left out a comma? If he wanted to start criticizing, he could accuse Reichardt and many of the others of much more serious mistakes.)[4] A Haydn Motet is praised for its merits, with a side-look at *The Creation*; but this Motet is not by Joseph Haydn, it is by his brother [Johann Michael]. Knecht dared to wish to correct Handel, and in his improvement there are the most awful

---

1 A kind of eighteenth century 'Duden' *Stilwörterbuch* or guide to correct German usage.
2 = *Ries*, a measurement of paper in those days. English: 'a ream' – but this does not give the precise amount that the German term would have meant at this period.
3 Breitkopf was attempting to purchase the plates of the Oratorio, which in fact they finally succeeded in doing. Apparently they had suggested letting Haydn have 300 copies for potential subscribers. Concerning Pleyel, Haydn was perhaps still rather offended because of the first London visit, when Pleyel had come to London to act as Haydn's rival.
4 This is the famous *AMZ* criticism *inter alia* of the 'Clock' Symphony, which is quoted *in extenso* in *Haydn in England 1791–1795*, pp. 576ff.

mistakes (Haydn said: asinine lapses). Why did one have to read about Zumpfsteeg [*sic*] and other *diis minorum gentium*, and so little of the finest masters? A review about bad works of Girowetz [Gyrowetz] ended with the words: 'Buyers for such stuff can be found on the Danube.'[1] As if one knew less on the Danube than on the Pleiße what is good and bad music. Does there live a second Haydn in any town of Germany? Is there any place where more is done for music, than here? He does not in the least deny the greater culture of northern German in literary matters; but in respect of the arts, and especially in music and in matters of taste, southern Germany has unmistakable advantages. Recently Baron Lichtenstein engaged some singers for the theatre here, and announced to us a H[err] Neumann as the first tenor in Germany. In the northern provincial towns, such people can create a furore, but here where one is used to a higher standard they appeared very mediocre; and Mozart's *Zauberflöte*[2] was criticized for its bad casting of the roles of Tamino and Papageno (Neumann and Schüller); only through the singing of the regular Viennese members of the opera was it improved.

I told Sw[ieten] that for a long time you have been looking for a thorough correspondent in Vienna for the Musical Journal [*AMZ*]. He admitted that he could not name anybody who could write a good article, and he himself obeys the rule to do as much as possible and not to talk about it. But he did promise to give me information, partly about the Musical Society [Gesellschaft der Associirten] of which he is the founder and the soul, also about the *4 Seasons* as soon as the work is performed. I assured him that I would be glad to participate in this undertaking and that he would be doing your firm a very great favour. He did not answer your letter of July 1800 because he wanted to await the impression that the work might make after some rehearsals [the text of *The Seasons*, which the *AMZ* printed *in extenso* in the *Beylage* to its issue of 20 May 1801; III, 581ff. = *Beilage* XIX–XXVI]. He read me a part of 'Summer'; he adheres to the rhythm, that is the succession of iambuses, spondees, and so forth, with great strictness. He finds Kunzen's composition extremely cold, the text of Kunzen's *Creation* poetic but not musical.[3] All rhyme is ruinous for music and ought to be banned from it. – He hopes you will issue *The Seven Words* in score, for he cannot learn anything from piano scores. He seems to be well acquainted with Handel, Graun, Gluck, Bach and Mozart; but none of them has surpassed Haydn's spirit [*Geist*] and perception [*Empfindung*]; one could write a poem on every Haydn trio and quartet.

Haydn tells me that he has been meaning to write to you for several post-days[4] now; I hope he will not miss today's. He asks you to purchase for him in Leipzig a dozen East-Indian silk handkerchiefs of good quality; one can't get them here, and the ones he brought from England are beginning to tear. He doesn't care about which colour they are. Would you wash them and have them marked 'J. H.', otherwise he will have to pay duty on them. The costs you should subtract from the 50 ducats and send him the rest *in natura*.

On the 28th inst., *The Seven Words* will be performed at the National Theatre for the benefit of the musicians' widows. I look forward to it, for I shall hear it for the first time. *The Creation* will be performed in the Italian language at Prince Lobkowitz's. If you want to, tell the public through the Musical Journal, 'We have

---

1 Obviously quoted from memory. Griesinger writes: 'solches Zeug findet Käufer an der Donau', whereas in *AMZ* the words are 'Käufer finden sich ja doch wohl, zumal an der Donau', which is nastier: for our translation of the original, see *Haydn: the Years of 'The Creation'*, p. 492.
2 *Supra*, p. 27; only Therese Rosenbaum had made a real impression.
3 Friedrich Ludwig Aemilius Kunzen (1761–1817), who composed a setting of the 'Creation', *Halleluja der Schöpfung*, after Klopstock.
4 Those days on which the mail left for Germany.

just been informed by a friend travelling through Vienna that Haydn has completed the composition of the *4 Seasons* and soon after Easter it will be performed in the Palace of Prince Schwarzenberg. Expectations could not be higher, but Haydn will surpass them.'

Now, my friend, yawn a little. Your eyes must urgently need quiet and sleep.

Gr.

[Olleson *Griesinger*, 18–20]

Breitkopf & Härtel sent the silk handkerchiefs to Haydn as a gift, and Griesinger acknowledged their receipt on 5 June; Haydn promised to send a new song in return but we do not know if he ever did so (Olleson, *Griesinger*, 21).

We now turn to the interesting Diary of Beda Plank, who in the middle of March 1801 paid a visit to the man who had designed Prince Nicolaus I Esterházy's musical clocks. Haydn had composed the music for these clocks, several of which, fortunately, survive, as do most of the autograph manuscripts that Haydn gave to his friend, P. Primitivus Niemecz, the subject of the following entry:

On 20 March a friend took me to the suburb of Spitelfeld to the building of the Hungarian Noble Guards, in which P. Primitiv [Niemecz] now lives; he is from the Order of the Brothers of Mercy, and is famous because of his clockwork instruments. He showed us several of his products, which, when he winds them up, play whole pieces by Mozart and Haydn in the finest organ tones and with such precision that not the least appoggiatura or trill, or other ornament, is missed. Even the echo effect comes off excellently. I would only wish the bass a little stronger, and the *forte* and *piano* to be more distinctly differentiated. He works out the layout of the notes in a piece before he even starts so carefully that you don't see the tiniest gap of a misplaced pin on the cylinder. This priest is very happy in his work. The late Prince Esterházy took him to Esterház and left him a good pension, which he enjoys under the present Prince, who gives him a place to stay. For the present Prince he will soon complete a musical clock which will surpass the others in value and pleasantness of sound. [p. 570]

. . . On 31 March I persuaded the two Abbots [of Lambach and Kremsmünster] to walk to the handsome building of the Hungarian Noble Guards, to see and hear the mechanical clocks which so delighted my ear on the 20th inst. This most pleasant priest showed us today, apart from other clocks, that big musical machine which he had not quite finished recently. This machine, on pressing a button on the spring, plays the most excellent pieces all by itself. After each piece, another cylinder is inserted; there are six of them entirely finished, of which he chose two by Mozart, three by Haydn and one by Beethoven. One of the most difficult pieces from the newest quartets by Joseph Haydn, which the best violin players in Vienna could not master, was produced by this machine with such precision that neither the least appoggiatura, nor even the smallest note, is missed. [pp. 570f.]

The difficult piece from one of Haydn's newest quartets was probably the Finale of the 'Lark' Quartet, Op. 64, No. 5, which is also on the clock of 1793 and survives in Haydn's autograph (XIX: 30). Haydn was clearly fascinated by these musical clocks, which might be called eighteenth-century gramophones. In the *AMZ* for July 1801 (III, 736ff.) we read that Haydn also composed pieces for Strasser's 'Mechanical Orchestra' in St Petersburg. Johann Georg Strasser was a clockmaker and his orchestra was extremely complex, equalled only by the famous Mälzel 'Mechanical Trumpeter and Panharmonicon', for which Beethoven would later write 'Wellington's Victory', or the 'Battle Symphony' (Op. 91). Strasser's orchestra had fifteen 'barrels', of which, reported *AMZ*, 'eleven may be heard already':

1) *Ouverture de l'Opéra: la Flûte magique de Mozart.*
2) *Concerto pour le Fortepiano in F de Mozart* [K. 459].
3) *Allegretto du même Concert de Mozart.*
4) *Allegro assai du même Concert de Mozart.*
5) *Ouverture, Marche et Chorus de l'Opera: la Clemenza di Tito, de Mozart.*
6) *Concerto pour le Fortepiano in B* [Si ♭, K. 456?] *de Mozart.*
7) *Andante du même.*
8) *Allegro vivace du même.*
9) *Adagio, Allegro et Rondeau d'Eberl* (composed for this machine).
10) *Sinfonie militaire de Haydn.*
11) *Fantasie à 4 mains de Mozart* [K. 594?].
     The following barrels are in preparation:
12}
13} *Quintetto in B.* [Si ♭, K. 174?] *de Mozart.*
14}
15) *A large Pièce by Haydn*, composed for this machine by this great man.

The report in the *AMZ* notes that 'the barrels are prepared according to the scores of these pieces – without cuts . . .' Perhaps the 'large Pièce' by Haydn was the authentic arrangement for musical clock of Symphony No. 99's Finale (XIX: 32) of which the autograph has survived but which was never put on any of the known Niemecz clocks.

On 25 March Beda Plank went to a concert at which, apparently, Mozart's pupil Josepha von Auernhammer played the new Third Concerto for piano and orchestra (Op. 37) by Beethoven. Alas, it is the last of Beda Plank's diary entries which concern us here:

> On 25 March we again received an invitation to a musical concert [*Akademie*] in the evening at the National Theatre at the Burgthor. The Redoutensaal could not be used for it this time, because it is full of grain sacks which were deposited here from the remaining stores of the Imperial Royal Army Commissary, and is soon to be sent to help out the country above the River Enns. I did not want to deprive myself of the pleasures of this music, because I had the opportunity of hearing the best pieces by the Viennese composers. A symphony by Mozart opened the programme, then Mamselle v. Saal, a singer in the Court Theatre, did a *bravura* aria [*Forsarie*] which she didn't trill away, because trills seem to have gone out of fashion here, but which she did roll off with as much dexterity as pleasant grace. Then Madame von Auernhammer played on the pianoforte a very difficult concerto by Beethoven, whom they want to give the honour of being a second Mozart: she played excellently and, as the best lady pianist in Vienna, received unanimous applause. Then Herr Clementi [Clement] played a violin concerto, they say he is the most artistic violinist in Vienna. He was applauded, more for his artistry than for pleasing satisfaction, from all sides of the boxes and orchestra. Then came a wind-band quintet by Mozart with an oboe, a clarinet, a bassoon and two horns: a magnificent piece, as you would expect from such a master. The end was again a symphony by Joseph Haydn. Full of the most pleasant harmonious tones I went to bed today.   [pp. 572f.]

On this same evening, Punto, the great horn player, gave his benefit concert in the Freyhaustheater auf der Wieden (which he repeated on 31 March). At the

Leopoldstädter Theater there was *The Creation*, given as a benefit for the orchestral personnel of the theatre. Rosenbaum was there: '. . . I enjoyed myself well enough.'[1]

Rosenbaum also tells us of an important event on 27 March: the dress-rehearsal of Beethoven's new Ballet, *Die Geschöpfe des Prometheus*, of which the première, originally scheduled for 20 March, actually took place on the 28th:

> Friday, 27th: Cold and overcast. Completely black. I went early . . . to the office and to the rehearsal of the ballet *Die Geschöpfe des Prometheus* by Sala [*sic*] Vigano, the music by Bethoven [*sic*]. I went early to the Count [Esterházy] . . . then . . . to the rehearsal of *The Seven Words*. Haydn was exceedingly gallant to Th— . . . The ballet was not at all well received, the music little better. . . . At the end the ballet was more hissed down than applauded.   [Radant, 92]

Zinzendorf was at the première and wrote as follows:

> . . . Dela *au Spectacle*. [Schenk's] Le Dorfbarbier [revient] encore. Le nouveau ballet: *Les Hommes de Prométhée* est singulier. La musique de Bethoven [*sic*] ne me plut guère. Tout le Parnasse se trouve en evidence. Appolon immobile en haut d'un rocher Escarpé. Prom. fut danser ses hommes, cela n'avant pas, la musique les anime, la mise de la Europedie excite leur sensibilité et ferment semblant d'avoir tué Promethée. Vitement l[es] evolutions guerrières. Vigano a l'Épée et le boulet a la main. La Casentini lui declive une flêche. A la danse jusques vers 10^h . . . Lu dans Hegweisch de Gibbon.

The performers in the ballet were: Prometheus – Cesari; the Children – Casentini and Salvatore Viganó; Bacchus – Ferd. Gioja; Terpsichore – Mme Brendi. Despite the rather adverse comments by Zinzendorf and Rosenbaum (who by the way went to the work twice more, once with Johann Elssler on 11 April and again the following day), the ballet was a considerable success. It appeared in piano score at Artaria's (*Wiener Zeitung*: 20 June 1801), dedicated to Princess Lichnowsky, and was performed sixteen times during the same season and thirteen times in 1802. As for the music, it is in many respects the major orchestral work of Beethoven's formative Viennese years, perhaps even richer and certainly more varied than the otherwise much more famous First Symphony. In the Ballet, Beethoven experimented in writing instrumental pieces according to vocal forms, and we actually find large operatic finales transposed into the world of purely orchestral music. The instrumentation is in any case much more daring than in any of his symphonies or concertos of the period. We find (in No. 5) solo flute and solo harp used in a manner astonishingly like Bizet's *L'Arlésienne* music – could, after all, Beethoven's music have been Bizet's inspiration? – and there is one number (No. 14) with superb basset-horn writing for Johann Stadler, then the first clarinet of the Court Orchestra,[2] which for the first and possibly last time in Beethoven's career really exploits a clarinet-like instrument in all its registers, in particular the *chalumeau* which (as we have seen) was neither Haydn's nor Beethoven's speciality, otherwise. Indeed it is astonishing that this brilliant score – one of the finest works of Beethoven's so-called first period – should be almost unknown to the general public.

However, it was not unknown to Haydn, who attended the ballet and must have been highly interested to see the artful combination of his own style, Mozart's and the unmistakable features of his erstwhile pupil. We have a report of Haydn meeting

1 Radant 91; also Wenzel Müller's MS. Diary in the Stadtbibliothek, Vienna.
2 *Schematismus* for 1801, p. 361.

Beethoven afterwards, which has come down to us from the autograph collector, Aloys Fuchs:

> Aloys Fuchs reports in the *Wiener Allgemeine Musik-Zeitung* (No. 39, 1846) on Beethoven's meeting with Haydn:
>
> It has long been known, and especially proven by certain remarks by Beethoven against his equally artistic colleague Goethe, that Beethoven was very much aware of his position in the world of music, and on certain occasions knew how to take advantage of it, even if it meant running the risk of being harshly judged or misunderstood by lay persons. . . . When in 1801 Beethoven had written the music to the ballet *The Creatures of Prometheus*, he encountered his former teacher, the great Joseph Haydn, who immediately stopped him and said, 'Now, yesterday I heard your ballet and it pleased me very much.' Beethoven thereupon answered 'Oh, my dear Papa, you are very kind, but it is a long way from being a "Creation".' Haydn, surprised and almost offended by this answer, said after a short silence, 'That is true, it is not yet a "Creation" and I very much doubt whether it will ever succeed in being one.' Whereupon each of them, somewhat dumbfounded, took leave of the other. [Landon, *Beethoven*, 138]

The play on words, 'Geschöpfe' and 'Schöpfung', which Beethoven used to taunt his former teacher, does not come off in English; but even without it, the insult must have appalled the courteous Haydn. Relations between the two men were now deteriorating to the point of no return, and from the documentary evidence at our disposal, it is clearly Beethoven who wished to disassociate himself from Haydn, not *vice versa*. The next episode of this strange relationship between the two men – apart from the occasional encounter (as when Beethoven organized seats for the Brunsvik girls to *The Seasons*) – is the positively Kafka-like story of 'Polyhymnia' (1803–4), which shall be related *infra* (pp. 271, 289f.).

Haydn's exhaustion was causing some concern in Vienna. Silverstolpe believed that the first performance of *The Seasons* might have to be postponed until 1802. He writes to Stockholm:

> Vienna, 28 March 1801
>
> . . . Every day I think with great interest on the performance of *The Creation* [at Stockholm's] Ritterhaus on 3 April. I shall be pleased to hear (a) if the concert was a success and (b) how it was liked by the public and the connoisseurs. Yesterday evening I heard [*La*] *clemenza di Tito* by Mozart, given in a private house with full orchestra. The hostess, Demoiselle Sessi, formerly a singer in the theatre, had the principal part. She had left the theatre a year before my arrival and I had heard her only once before. Probably I will never hear her sing better. – Day after tomorrow I intend to hear Haydn's *Seven Words* performed under the master's own direction. This music always reminds me of the joy it gave to my late mother. My dear father noted this quite rightly in the very beautiful biography in her memory.
>
> I think that with these pleasures, musical events this year are at an end. Haydn's *Seasons* is finished, however, but a sickness which Haydn suffered postponed everything for so long that I think the performance will be put on next year. Too bad, for who can guarantee that the master will then be able to perform his work. He is old. His works can only lose if they later fall into strange hands. [Mörner, 367f.]

On 29 March, the Tonkünstler-Societät gave Haydn's *The Seven Words* under the composer's direction. The soloists were Therese Rosenbaum, Haydn's protégée

Josepha Hammer, Carl Weinmüller and Sigismund Hüller. The concert opened with a Grand Symphony by Eybler and in the middle of the Oratorio there was to have been a violin concerto by Aloys Tomasini jr. Rosenbaum's Diary (p. 92) informs us:

> A gloomy day . . . at about 6 o'clock I went into our box. Th— sang excellently, and Haydn paid her many compliments. Today Th— was given the part of Vitellia in [*La*] *clemenza di Tito* to sing at the benefit concert for the poor of the theatres.

At the last moment, it appears that Tomasini could not play and in his place, according to the *Wiener Zeitung* No. 29 (11 April 1801), was Anton Wranizky. The entire Court attended. When the concert was repeated on Monday the 30th, the concerto was the composition of, and was played by, the 'cellist, Philipp Schindlöcker. Rosenbaum informs us (p. 92):

> . . . In the morning Th— went . . . to the rehearsal of *Clemenza* . . . Th—, Hammer and I went home together along the bastion; Jean Haydn [Joseph's younger brother, the tenor] was waiting at home when we arrived . . . Mme Mozart came in the afternoon . . . Second performance of *The Seven Words* . . . Despite feeling sick, Th— sang excellently.[1]

Haydn's administrative work as *Kapellmeister* to Prince Esterházy continued, and he was obliged to deal with wearisome problems such as the following:

[To Haydn from Prince Nicolaus II Esterházy. *German*]
> To *Kapellmeister* Haydn:
> Concerning the request of Major Mayern from Györ, I would not object to his receiving old but still usable wind instruments for use abroad by the *Insurrections-Bataillon*, and I herewith instruct you to find a number of such instruments as soon as possible, and to suggest the best price to me beforehand; whereby, when the *Insurrections-Bataillon* is dissolved, the instruments could then be used again by my own band.
> Vienna, 30th March 1801. Exp.[2] Esterházy.
>
> [CCLN, 179]

The Italian translation of *The Seven Words* was the subject of the following letter from Griesinger to Breitkopf & Härtel:

3 April 1801

> Most valued Friend,
> Since I know nobody who is capable of organizing the Italian translation of *The Seven Words*, I turned to Bar. Swieten and asked his advice. He was most satisfied with the translation of *The Creation* by a certain Carpani (which also appeared at Artaria's), and I hoped that Swieten would give me his address. But Sw. said, Carpani is a wealthy and independent man to whom one couldn't make such an offer; he translated *The Creation* only because the Empress requested it; I should go to a Professor of the Italian language, Sarchi, who might do the work himself or could at least suggest a good man for the job. I will look up this Sarchi and report on it when the time comes. Sw. wishes to have the German text improved; it is by a priest from Passau and stuck together from church songs, and Sw. only changed something here and there. But you will hardly want to agree to this improvement because of the music which would perhaps also have to be changed. Do not count on Haydn's co-operation; he undertakes such things only

---

1 Pohl, *Denkschrift*, 66; *WZ* No. 29, 1801; Radant, *Rosenbaum*, 92.
2 'Exp.' = 'expedited for', i.e. actually sent. These late letters to Haydn are, of course, copies for the Princely files.

under protest, and recently he complained to me that Swieten wanted him to accommodate his music to *The Four Seasons* also to the Ital. and Engl. texts. – Sw. also told me that the Italian translator of *The Seven Words* would obviously have to have the score of the vocal parts in front of him, otherwise the work will end badly. The idea of the Latin text appealed to him. He was thoroughly satisfied with the last package of the musical journal [*AMZ*]. The articles about the formation of music in Germany in the 17th and 18th centuries [extract quoted in *Haydn: the Years of 'The Creation' 1796–1800*, pp. 589ff.] are masterly; he himself read me the brilliant [*geniale*] description of Haydn's 'Chaos' in No. 17. The man who felt it like that, said he, must himself be capable of composing a Chaos. He guessed Reichardt and asks you to let him know who wrote those articles and also the letter from Berlin. . . . [Olleson, *Griesinger*, 21]

As we have seen, the review of 'Chaos' was by Zelter, who later wrote the full-scale review of March 1802 (see *Haydn: the Years of 'The Creation' 1796–1800*, pp. 587f.). Haydn scholars have usually applied the following extract from a Griesinger letter to Leipzig to the full-scale review: '[Haydn and Swieten told me] that this reviewer wrote to them straight from the heart [*ganz aus der Seele*], and they would not be capable of describing better the feelings with which they were filled in writing the libretto and the music' (Olleson, *Griesinger*, 21). But surely Swieten cannot have approved of a review in which his part of the undertaking was brutally criticized; the passage can only refer to the 'Chaos' analysis, in which Swieten's role is, as it were, taken for granted but certainly not criticized. As is known, the Griesinger correspondence with Breitkopf & Härtel was destroyed during the Second World War and we are unable to ascertain the date of the letter from which the above extract is taken. – Carpani is of course Haydn's later biographer.

On Easter Sunday, Therese Rosenbaum started the day by singing in 'the first Mass written by the unfortunate composer Volkert' (Franz Volkert, organist of the Piaristenkirche in the Josephstadt suburb of Vienna). '. . . At about 6:30 there was a cantata by Weigl, *Das beste Geschenk*, in the Redouten Saal. A symphony by Haydn and a clarinet concerto by Anton Stadler preceded it . . . The cantata was not well received; the hall was empty.' Haydn had been asked to write a Cantata on the Peace for the directors of the Court Theatre. Griesinger adds that the composer turned it down, 'because he had enough to do with *The Four Seasons*.'[1]

A few days later, on 8 April, Griesinger reports on his progress with the Italian translation of *The Seven Words*:

> . . . I found in Professor Sarchi (he is at the same time a lawyer, notary and the son-in-law of the Court Printer Schmid) a very fiery and jovial man. Swieten's name obtained for me the most satisfactory reception, for [Sarchi] reveres him as a patron and father. He, too, knew of no good translator, but out of respect for Swieten he will take on the affair himself, and I doubt if we could do better, for Sarchi has a very lucrative job as a lawyer and works in the field of the fine arts only *con amore*. His conditions are as follows:
>
> 1) He can complete the translation only in a month;
> 2) He is a connoisseur and lover of music, but he doesn't play himself; therefore he has to rent a piano for a month and every day a *Capellmeister* has to play to him for several hours. This would mean an expenditure of 6 ducats.
> 3) If the translation prove to be successful, he would not refuse a discretion (that was his term); but he assured me that he would accept the undertaking more out of vanity than from any pecuniary gain.

1 Pohl III, 172; Radant *Rosenbaum*, 93.

Please be kind enough to let me know soon if these conditions are acceptable to you or not. And how are we to deal with the music, which really cannot be missed during the translation? I enclose a Strophe which Hofr[ath] Sommerfels [Joseph von Sonnenfels] wrote and Sarchi translated into Italian. . . .

[Olleson, *Griesinger*, 22]

Sarchi is known to us from the *affaire* Sieber-Haydn of January 1800 (see *Haydn: the Years of 'The Creation'*, pp. 538ff.): Schmid = Matthias Andreas Schmidt, who printed the original libretti of Haydn's last three Oratorios.

On 9 April Therese Rosenbaum sang a Haydn Mass, as she had promised to do (*vide* 16 March), at the Lower Jesuits:

. . . I went . . . to Mass at the Lower Jesuits [Universitätskirche], where the Mass by Haydn was done . . . Th— sang . . . At about 2 o'clock we came back into town and found the decree by Braun advising Th— in highly flattering form, of an increase in salary of 150 gulden effective April 1st. What threefold good fortune for her! ! !   [93]

Silverstolpe's father reported to his son in Vienna about the first performances of *The Creation* in Stockholm, put on for the benefit of the widows and orphans of Freemasons. 'With a deputation of Masons, of which I was one,' continues Father Silverstolpe in a letter from Stockholm of 7 April, 'the Duke himself received on Good Friday the reigning Queen and the Duchess, in the usual form.' The public adored the work, as usual, but Haydn's pupil Paul Struck, in a letter to Silverstolpe in Vienna written on 14 April, noted that there were those to whom the music was unattractive,

particularly Hr. Assessor Engmark. He didn't say it to me, but to others he made shameless remarks that there was no genius in *The Creation* but only *Mechanismus*, and before he even knew it he said to me: 'I doubt if I will like *The Creation*, because Haydn can't write for the voice.' But you mustn't imagine that the opinion of ignoramuses occasioned less applause for this music, for the public is beyond any description taken with it. . . .   [Mörner, 368–70]

On 15 April Griesinger had occasion to write to Leipzig:

. . . Father Haydn sends you his compliments and thanks you very much for the newspapers [*AMZ*]. . . . What he wanted to say about *The Seven Words* was something you'll know yourself, namely 'that the wind instruments before the word *Sitio* do not have to be complete and that he himself often performed it without [some of] the wind instruments'. . . . The Frères Erard in Paris have made Haydn a present of a handsome piano in the English manner, in mahogany with brass trimmings . . .   [Olleson, *Griesinger*, 22]

Haydn meant, about the *Introduzione* for wind band, that he often had to perform it without some of the instruments, or with strings substituting for some of the wind parts. Haydn was preparing for the première of *The Seasons* and postponed thanking Erard for the piano until after the first performances were over (*vide infra*, 28 May).

On 21 April was the first big rehearsal of *The Seasons*. That night, during a performance of *Die Zauberflöte* at the Kärntnerthortheater, Rosenbaum 'was backstage most of the time and heard [Therese] Saal whining that on Friday she will have no rehearsal for Eberl's opera, *Die Königin der schwarzen Inseln*, since she has to sing *The 4 Seasons* by Haydn at Schwarzenberg's that evening' (93). On 22 April Silverstolpe wrote that

. . . a death in the Schwarzenberg family has delayed the performance of Haydn's new Oratorio, *The Seasons*. Yesterday, despite that, I heard the first rehearsal; I am to hear the second tomorrow, and the day after tomorrow I shall attend the actual performance of this fine work. The subject is much more limited than that of *The Creation* but it is closer to Haydn's own taste . . .　　　　　　　　　[Mörner, 373]

And so, on 24 April (instead of the original date of the 15th) 1801, Haydn's final Oratorio, *The Seasons*, was given its first performance at the Palais Schwarzenberg in Vienna, with the same soloists as in the later performances of *The Creation*, viz., Therese Saal, Professor Matthias Rathmayer and Ignaz Saal. The orchestra was made up largely of members of the opera orchestras, and the chorus of various church choirs, etc. Apart from the illness in the Schwarzenberg family, there was also an operatic première which had to be staged before Haydn's Oratorio could be given. (Pohl [III, 176] reports that the new opera, *Bathmendi* by Lichtenstein, was hissed at the première.) For the first performance, which took place at 6.30 p.m., there were, of course, only invited guests; but for the preceding rehearsals, 'every honest man is permitted to attend' ('wobey jedem honnetten Mann der Zutritt gestattet war'). The Gesellschaft der Associirten paid for the costs, which amounted to 195 gulden for each member; Prince Schwarzenberg again paid for the police guard (to keep the traffic under control before the performances), for the costs of clearing the market stalls on the Neuer Markt, and for the illumination of the market place (Pohl III, 177).

It has been some time since we examined the situation of the two principal Viennese orchestras (Italian and German opera), many of the members of which participated in *The Seasons*. Since this work is the last which Haydn wrote for Vienna – the final two Masses were, of course, composed for the Esterházy chapel at Eisenstadt – readers will perhaps be interested in the constitution and quality of the performers at that time.

Of the soloists we have written before, but we might add a few words concerning the popular Therese Saal who, because of her youth, beauty and (despite Haydn's reservations) vocal abilities, had meanwhile become the toast of the city. In a report published in the *Zeitung für die elegante Welt* (No. 76, 1803), we read *inter alia*:

. . . Much is gained . . . by Mlle Saal's sweet-sounding, even and pleasant voice; it leaves only somewhat more strength to be desired, which it would doubtlessly have acquired had Mlle Saal not been urged to begin singing too early and too intensively . . . her simple, sincere and appropriate delivery show more feeling for art and more correct judgement than all the runs and embellishments so often and inappropriately interpolated . . . Mlle Saal has received a flattering demonstration of the universal esteem in which she is held. A serious illness brought her to the brink of the grave, and there was little hope that she would survive. She owes her recovery in large measure to the acknowledged skill of that universally respected physician, *Freiherr* [Baron] von Quarin . . . Everyone was most sincerely concerned, and the anteroom of the patient was filled from early morning until late at night by servants inquiring after her on their masters' behalf.
　　　　　　　[Translation from Radant *Rosenbaum*, 93f.]

In earlier volumes of this biography we have quoted long and rather interesting comments on Viennese orchestras and opera singers, mostly from *AMZ*. Now, in June 1801, *AMZ* printed another long report from Vienna, which must have been sent off shortly after *The Seasons'* première and which disagrees with the previous opinions of the *AMZ*'s Viennese correspondent. We include some extracts of this later report:

I do not know if there is another country in which the judgements of one part of the inhabitants concerning the other part are as different as the judgements of southern and northern Germany about each other. . . . As far as music is concerned, the *common* prejudice of the southern Germans is to admit that the northerners are good critics but are capable of nothing else and certainly nothing important; the *common* prejudice of the northern Germans admits that the southerners have an active sense of music and a by no means unsubtle gift especially for singing but are capable of nothing else and certainly nothing important . . . But if I am not mistaken, these . . . clichés have no little influence even upon the educated northern and southern Germans. The northern Germans can take care of themselves; I will attempt at least to begin a description of the southern Germans and especially the Viennese (since they have a decisive influence on south Germany, particularly in matters of art). . . .

[The correspondent draws attention to the previous 'Survey of the most important factors of all music matters in Vienna', published in the *AMZ* and quoted by us in *Haydn: the Years of 'The Creation' 1796–1800*, pp. 33f., 36f., 38f., with which the present correspondent differs in some cases. 'I will gladly ignore other articles of lesser importance in journals about the mode and others.']

Our *Italian Opera* is in *no* respect that which it used to be in the period, for example, when one could admire Gluck's[1] masterpieces; moreover, it is not at a very much lower level than in those times as far as singers are concerned – everyone is of one mind on these two points. . . . But one usually included without further ado the orchestra of the Italian theatre in this negative criticism. On this subject there is something to be said.

One cannot deny that the orchestra, though consisting of very clever individuals, does not constitute a good ensemble, and the operas are almost never played by it in such a way that the connoisseur leaves the theatre completely satisfied. The reason for this is not lack of good will, or unity, or love for art, but must be laid to quite another circumstance. In the times when the worthy Salieri was *Kapellmeister* at the Italian opera and – if I err not – Hr. Scheidlein leader of the orchestra, the members were (except for a few who perhaps have left) the same; and yet the operas were performed so that the severest critic could not ask for more. Clean intonation in all the instruments, proper ensemble and precision were only the smaller part of their advantages. The voices were accompanied with the greatest delicacy; true expression was never lacking. In those days the orchestra was unquestionably one of the first theatrical bands in Germany, the advantages of which were conceded by every connoisseur. When Salieri had to give up his position as *Kapellmeister* and Herr Conti became director, the orchestra sank step by step to the level it has now reached . . . Hr. Conti certainly lacks by far the qualities necessary for such a position . . . It is in fact incredible how this man could have been allowed to run this orchestra for so many years.

On the other hand, the leadership of Herr Paul Wranitzky (German Opera) has often been accorded unstinted and public praise. I cannot agree with this unstinted praise. I will not deny him the ability to conduct symphonies or concertos well, but that hardly makes him a good theatrical orchestra leader. It may be that he has all the necessary abilities to do so and the reason why he doesn't is possibly that he is either too lazy or that he does not care about the effect of foreign operas. He himself never plays during the rehearsals with the quartet [principal string players of the opera orchestra] but only at the last three full orchestral rehearsals; as a result he cannot possibly be informed of the spirit of the whole work. . . . One feels the difference in leadership most strongly in [Winter's]

---

1 Most proper names are letter-spaced (G l u c k); here ignored.

[*Das*] *unterbrochene Opferfest*. The first three performances were conducted from the violin by the composer himself. There was a precision and fire in the orchestra which greatly improved the music. At the fourth performance, which Hr. Wranitzky conducted, there was the body of the music (if I may be permitted the expression) but the soul which had filled the whole during the first three performances was wanting. From every standpoint the double basses of the orchestra are severely criticized. I must confess that I have not noticed the sinning in that quarter and find, as a matter of fact, the basses among the best elements of the band. . . .

It has often been said, and publicly (it is also true), that for some years there have been fewer casual concerts by *travelling artists* than there once were; but certainly not for the reasons that are usually given. The war is mainly at fault. No great artists are refused the theatre. Baron von Braun appreciates talent too much not to support it;[1] it requires therefore no intercession to secure the theatre from him. Rather he encourages artists to come to Vienna and promises them the theatre. That was the case with the Romberg brothers, whom he heard in Munich and there invited them to come and present themselves in Vienna. . . . [They] came from Italy and had not a single letter of recommendation. Their concert took place on a day, which, for various reasons, was the least satisfactory, and yet, after subtracting all costs, they took in close to six hundred gulden. . . .

The sojourn for the artist in Vienna is not at all dear. Never, according to the evidence of all foreigners, is there such hospitality as in this Imperial city. . . . In this respect the artist need not come loaded down with letters of recommendation. One single house is enough to secure other acquaintances within a week. . . . That is because in Vienna it is the *talent* of the artist which is *honoured* and not just the *letter* which he presents. . . . I never heard a foreign artist complain about Vienna. . . .
                                                                                    [III, 622–7]

. . . Among the composers who are most appreciated by the educated classes, Haydn stands at the top, and rightly; I defy anyone who has had access to the best houses to contradict me, if he can, when I say that Haydn's quartets, and those of some other valued composers of instrumental music, can nowhere be heard better, and in most important places not so correctly, deliberately and beautifully, as in Vienna. . . .   [III, 639]

It may be of interest to list the principal members of the Vienna Court Orchestra, as it is found in the *Hof- und Staats-Schematimus* for the year 1801.

K. K. Hofmusik
Hofmusikgraf.

Der Hoch und Wohlgebohrne Hr. Hr. Ferdinand des h. r. R. Graf von Kuffstein [*sic*], Sr. r. k. k. ap. Maj. wirkl. Kämmerer, Erbland Silberkämmer in Oesterreich ob- und unter der Enns, dann wirkl. Hofrath und provisor. Vize-Präsident der n. öst. Landesregierung, woh. in der Krugerstraße 1174.[2]

Hof-Kapellmeister.
Hr. Anton Salieri, woh. in der Spiegelgaße 1154.

---

1 For a contrary report, i.e. that it was very difficult to hire the theatre, see both Haydn's and Beethoven's cases: *Haydn: the Years of 'The Creation' 1796–1800*, pp. 457, 546.
2 We give this list in the original German so that students may see the type of official abbreviations, etc., with which such information was presented. Note that Salieri was in charge of the choir boys, who undoubtedly participated in *The Creation* and *The Seasons*, and who were under the direct leadership of Georg Spangler.

Hofkapelmeister [*sic*] Substitut und
Vorsteher der Hofsängerknaben.
Hr. Georg Spängler [*sic*], woh. in der Löwelstraße 17.

Kompositor.
Hr. Kozeluch zugleich Kammer-Kappelmeister [*sic*], woh: in der obern
Beckerstraße 812.
Hr. Tayber [*sic*], woh. in Burgerspital 1166.

Tenoristen.
Hr. Val. Adamberger, woh. beym Kärntnerthor 1102.
Hr. Albert Brichta, woh. in der Währingergaße 41.
Hr. Phil. Korner, woh. in der Leopoldstadt 40.
Hr. Jos. Simoni, woh. am Kohlmarkt 270.
Hr. Ignaz Spangler, woh. im Gundelhof 627.

Bassisten.
Hr. Jakob Wrabeczi, woh. auf der Mölkerbastey 84.
Hr. Jos. Hoffmann, woh. auf der Landstraße 283.
Hr. Anton Scharschmidt woh. bey St. Ulrich 38.
Hr. Ignaz Saal, woh. auf der Mölkerpastey [*sic*] 83.
Hr. Karl Weinmüller, woh. am Hohenmarkt 553.
Hr. Joh. Höller, woh. am Spitelberg 83.

Organisten.
Hr. Georg Summer, woh. in der Leopoldstadt 142.
Hr. Jos. Rusiczka, woh. in der Josephstadt 31.

Violinisten.
Hr. Anton Hofmann, Direktor, woh. in der Teinfaltstraße 75.
Hr. Jos. Scheidl, woh. im Burgerspital 1166.
Hr. Jos. Hofmann, woh. in der Leopoldstadt 289.
Hr. Karl Maratscheck, woh. in der Leopoldstadt 17.
Hr. Joh. Baptist Hofmann, woh. im Ledererhof 365.
Hr. Zeno Franz Menzel, woh. auf der Laimgrube 152.
Hr. Peter Fuchs, woh. am Stock im Eisenplatz 663.
Hr. Leopold Klemp, woh. am Spitalberg 13.
Hr. Jos. Millechner, woh. auf der Mölkerbastey 99.
Hr. Leopold Reinhard, woh. in der Naglergaße 320.
Hr. Jos. Schramb, woh. in der Strauchgaße 320.
Hr. Jakob Conti, woh. in der obern Bräunerstr. 1205.
Hr. Mathias Altmüller, woh. in der Naglergaße 316.
Hr. Franz Pösinger, woh. am Spitlberg 124.

Violoncellisten.
Hr. Jos. Orsler, woh. im Elend 222.
Hr. Jos. Weigl, woh. in der Himmelportgaße [*sic*] 1007.
Hr. Phil. Schindlecker, woh. in der Josephstadt 40.

Violonisten.
Hr. Jos. Sedler, woh. auf den Spitlberg 100.
Hr. Friedrich Holfeld, woh. im tiefen Graben 167.
Hr. Mich. Stadelmann, woh. auf der Gstäte 226.

Posaunisten.
Hr. Anton Ulbrich, woh. neben der Karlskirche 23.
Hr. Joh. Meserer, woh. am Platzl 6.

Fagotisten.
Hr. Ignaz Drobnat, woh. in der Josephstadt 37.
Hr. Franz Czerwenka, woh. in der Josephstadt 19.

Oboisten.
Hr. Georg Triebensee, woh. auf der Landstraße 287.
Hr. Johann Wend, woh. in der Josephstadt 26.

Klarinetisten.
Hr. Johann Stadler, woh. auf der Wien 45.
Hr. Georg Klein, woh. auf der Wieden 167.

Waldhornisten.
Hr. Martin Rupp, woh. in der Josephstadt 40.
Hr. Joh. Hörmann, woh. in der Rossau 104.

Trompeter.
Hr. Joh. Glaser, woh. in der Josephstadt 58.
Hr. Franz Jahnel, woh. am Rennweg 406.
Hr. Jos. Ruprecht, woh. im Ofenloch 467.

Paucker.
Hr. Fried. Kreit, woh. auf der neuen Wien 232.

Instrumenten Diener.
Joseph Federl, woh. auf den Platzl 22.

[*Schematismus* 1801, 359–61]

This group constitutes that which was later known as the 'Hofburgkapelle', including the world-famous 'Wiener Sängerknaben'. It will be noted that Salieri is still *Kapellmeister*, and the remarks about his no longer being so must apply to the opera theatre. The Wranizkys (Paul and Anton) are not listed at all, and Conti is far down the list of the violins. Obviously the two theatre orchestras (Italian and German opera) included many more musicians, but this nucleus must have formed the core of Haydn's orchestra for *The Creation* and *The Seasons*. The absence of flutes and violas has been noted elsewhere; of the fourteen violin players, probably three or four were actually violists. No less than four and possibly five members had played under Haydn in Eszterháza: the violinist Joseph Hofmann (Hoffmann),[1] though of him we cannot be certain; the violinist Peter Fuchs (Fux) (Eszterháza 1781–2); the famous 'cellist, Joseph Weigl (Eisenstadt 1761–9); the horn player Martin Rupp (Eszterháza 1776–81) and the second horn player Johann Hörmann (Eszterháza 1776–80). This fact has an immediate bearing on the celebrated horn solo in *The Seasons* (No. 10, 'Der muntre Hirt'): it was composed for a man whose capacities he knew intimately.

There are many eye-witness accounts of the first (and the following two) performances of *The Seasons*. On 25 April Griesinger wrote to Leipzig, telling Breitkopf & Härtel *inter alia* that he had been 'witness to the general enthusiasm with which the work was received. The voices which (for the most part only *a priori*) were contrary will have been converted . . . Haydn has learned the secret of the ancients,

---

1 The name Hof(f)mann being so extremely common, we cannot be certain that the Joseph Hofmann in the Vienna orchestra is the same musician who played under Haydn from 1775–87 and later (from 1790) in the Eisenstadt church choir as violinist. Janos Harich in *Haydn Yearbook* VIII, 21. Peter Fuchs (Fux): Bartha-Somfai, 172. Joseph Weigl: Pohl's article in Grove I, vol. iv, 432. Martin Rupp: Harich, ibid., 32. Johann Hörmann: Bartha-Somfai, 172f.

who knew how to make gold out of dirt [i.e. Swieten's libretto] . . .' (Olleson, *Griesinger*, 22). The *'a priori'* voices may perhaps be illustrated most graphically from the following report in *Moscowskije wedomosti* (No. 32, 20 April 1801):

> In the public foreign newspapers they write that the venerable *Kapellmeister* Hayden is now working on a new musical work which he calls *The Seasons*. We hope it will be a masterpiece by this composer; but many music connoisseurs have remarked that this subject is not very fitting for musical treatment. It enables one to present charming and delightful subjects, but not those suitable for higher art, e.g. deafening thunder claps, falling snowflakes, running brooks and streams, shining stars and all sorts of sunrises and sunsets. Perhaps some composer or other will undertake to compose the Four Corners of the Earth, and in this case will describe the Island of Teneriffa by the highest octave, the Dead Sea by semibreves and rests, the roaring of Asiatic lions and tigers, the straits at Suez by 36th [*sic*] notes, blacks and whites, yellow and copper-coloured Americans and cockroaches; what a huge field to display his talents![1]

The same newspaper had a correspondent in Vienna who sent off the following report after hearing the general rehearsal (23 April); he sent it, on the 25th, not only to the Moscow but also to the St Petersburg newspaper:

> On the 23rd inst. was performed for the first time, in the house of Prince Schwarzenberg, a musical work, *The Four Seasons*, by the celebrated *Kapellmeister* Hayden. The music connoisseurs expected much from the composer of *The Creation* which has been received with general praise throughout Europe, but the composer surpassed all their expectations. The power of expression with which the artist very vividly describes nature in all its guises surpasses any description . . . This whole affair lasts about four hours.
>
> [*Moscowskije wedomosti* No. 40, 18 May; Steinpress, op. cit., p. 98]

Count Zinzendorf was, of course, present and wrote in his Diary:

> . . . Le Commandeur Enzenberg me parla du Concert, il n'est pas du nombre des entousiastes du concert de la création. A 6^h.$\frac{1}{2}$ je me fis porter au Concert des Saisons. Il ne commença qu'a 7^h je me trouvois a coté de Me Mazzarelli [Muzzarelli?], ma voisine a gauche ne voulut pas decliner son nom. L'archiduc Ferdinand. l'Electeur [Maximilian Franz], le P^{ce} Starhemberg etoient la. Le Printems a de la musique douce, un Freudenlied et un Hymne qui plait. L'Eté exprime bien le langueur generale qu'occasionne le chaud. L'orage est rebattu. L'Automne est tres varié, un hymne au travail. Les noisettes, l'amour des champs, le limier, la chasse au lièvre, la chasse a courre, les vendanges, un tapage incroyable. L'Hyver, la chanson des fileuses, la romance d'Annette, de la morale et un Hymne. Cela est long . . .   [Olleson, 59]

Dies (181) reports on the first performance: 'The opinion of the public was divided: some placed the work above *The Creation*, others considered both works equal and still others contested both these opinions.'

Beethoven's great friend, Countess Josephine Deym, wrote to her sister about *The Seasons*, which was repeated at the Schwarzenberg Palace on 27 April and 1 May; she managed to get tickets to the last performance:

Vienna, 2 May 1801

> . . . Yesterday I heard the new work, *The Four Seasons* by Haydn, at Schwarzenberg's; it is superb, there were a lot of people there, Beethoven

---

1 See Boris Steinpress, 'Haydn's Oratorien in Russland zu Lebzeiten des Komponisten', in *Haydn-Studien* II (1969), 2, p. 98.

procured two tickets for us. Recently we too had charming music at our place: Punto, Beethoven, Schuppanzigh, Zmeskall. You can imagine that something good came out of that. Punto plays really enchantingly. They all lunched with us and then there was music the whole afternoon: the Sonata by Beethoven with the horn [Op. 17]. Then the new Quintet with piano [Op. 16] and several other beautiful things. . . .[1]

Possibly the most important contemporary criticism was that written by Griesinger himself, for the *AMZ*:

> Vienna, 2 May 1801.
>
> *The Seasons*, after Thomson, arranged by Baron Swieten[2] and set to music by J. Haydn, was performed in the rooms of Prince Schwarzenberg on 24 and 27 April and on 1 May. Silent devotion, astonishment and loud enthusiasm relieved one another with the listeners; for the most powerful penetration of colossal ideas, the immeasurable quantity of happy ideas surprised and overpowered even the most daring of imaginations.
>
> The very subject of this poem invites everyone to participate. Who does not long for a return of spring? Who is not crushed by the heat of summer? Who does not rejoice over the fruits of autumn? To whom is the numbing frost of winter not tiresome? The wealth of such a subject makes great demands on the poetry. But even if all are fulfilled, a special talent is required for judging musical effects, choosing the metre and for making a useful order out of the various sections, and this can only be accomplished by a poet who himself has penetrated the secrets of music. Since the reader may acquaint himself with the poem through this musical journal [footnote points out that the poem is printed as *Beylage* No. VII], he will be in a better position to see for himself just what Haydn had to do. That he did all this to perfection, however, is the unanimous opinion of the public here. Every word, under the hands of this musical Prometheus, is full of life and perception. Sometimes the melody of the voice delights, sometimes we are shaken, as a woodland torrent that bursts over its banks, by the mighty entrance of the orchestra; now one delights in a simple, artless expression; or one admires the sumptuous richness of swift and bright harmonies. From the beginning to the end the spirit is involuntarily swept along by emotions that range from the most touching to the most terrible, from the most naïve to the most artful, from the commonplace to the most sublime.
>
> From a work which must not only be heard but carefully studied, and which bears the stamp of genius in every line, it is not easy to select single passages as pre-eminent, for in relation to the whole and in their particular place all are excellent. The writer will therefore attempt to give an account, in a few broad strokes, of the impressions that he received in three performances. But: how poor are words!
>
> The Overture begins with a *unisono* of all instruments and lasts four bars. While wild storms are howling and masses of snow rolling from the mountains, here and there a gentle west wind makes itself felt, a warming ray of sun announces the reawakening of nature hitherto dead. – In the Chorus of the Country Folk, longing and hopeful trust that one's prayers will be heard are excellently expressed. – The Aria, 'Schon eilet froh der Ackermann', in which one hears the latter whistling the Haydn Andante from the 'Surprise' Symphony behind his plough, breathes the air of unaffected sprightliness. – The Prayer must move even a stone, and who is not delighted to see everything living again, everything soaring, everything in stir? The gambolling of the lambs, the darting fish, the bees swarming, the flutter of birds' wings – all this is very descriptively imitated in

---

1 La Mara, *Beethoven und die Brunsviks*, Leipzig 1920, p. 17.
2 Proper names are, as usual, spaced.

music, and without frivolity [*ohne Tändeley*]. – Sink to your knees and pray! Only in this spirit can one hear the chorus intoning 'Ewiger, mächtiger, gütiger Gott'. – The introduction to 'Summer' has a noble, slow pace. The harbinger of day is not concealed by the sharp tone of the oboe, and in the Aria, 'Der muntre Hirt versammelt nun', the horn sounds with a call which is the signal in every village for the herds to go out. An exceptionally brilliant and happily expectant chorus greets the rising sun. – Now the heavens are at high noon. Our breath is heavy and oppressed. Everything languishes. The faint noises fade away. The Aria, 'Welche Labung für die Sinne' is only for very experienced singers. – A storm rages frightfully. – The call of the quail, the sound of the cricket, the croaking of the frogs and the ringing of the bells are musical arabesques that announce the coming of evening. – 'Summer' closes with a quiet but powerful music. – With the moderate joy of a *tempo di minueto* 'Autumn' begins. The Duet, 'Ihr Schönen aus der Stadt' is the pure outpouring of a happy love; it comes from the heart and goes to the heart. – The hunt and the gathering of grapes are objects which have been often enough described; here they appears in a new and, through their truthful portrayal, most surprising guise. The usual hunting calls serve as the theme of the whole hunt. The originality and artistry of the master in portraying the gathering of the grapes is so extraordinary that I dare not say anything about it. – These pieces, because they are so easy and may be generally understood, will be received by every audience with shouts and enthusiasm. – Thick fog announces the coming of 'Winter'. – The Aria, 'Hier steht der Wandrer nun' describes fear, confusion and the cold that penetrates to the bone. – One only needs to hear the melody of the 'Spinning Song' once in order never to forget it. Also the 'Story' [*Märchen*] is a very simple movement without artful modulations. The laughter of young and old voices, as expressed at the end by alternating high and low notes, is the product of a most roguish humour. – The death of nature leads the poet to serious thoughts. But soon a ray of cheerful hope distracts his dark melancholy. The transition. 'Nur Tugend bleibt' is of unbelievable effect. – And now Haydn the giant collects his whole strength once more for the Double Chorus. The voice of the Almighty calls, the graves are split apart, the gates of Heaven are opened, spring reigns forever, virtue has conquered, she shines in the glory of God's Greatness. Amen!

The connoisseur will readily appreciate to which level of perfection the performance, under the direction of the composer himself, had to reach. Hr. Saal sang the role of Simon, his daughter the role of Hanne, and Herr Prof. Ratmayer [*sic*] the role of Lukas. All three received great and in every respect deserved applause. Also the orchestra gave in its playing laudable proof of its attention, accomplishment and adroitness.

One will perhaps ask if *The Seasons* as a piece of music is to be preferred to *The Creation*. To that must be said that each fully serves its particular poetic basis, and that Haydn remains everywhere great and exemplary.

I cannot possibly close without a word of respect and profoundest thanks towards those men who were initially responsible for Haydn's having composed *The Seasons*. For some years there has been in the Imperial city a society of friends of music, consisting of a small group of members who put on several concerts [*Akademien*] each year. The names Li[e]chtenstein, Esterházy, Schwarzenberg, Auersperg, Lobkowitz, Lichnowsky, Trautmannsdorf, Swieten, Czernin, Fries, Ap[p]on[y]i, Sinzendorf, Kinsky, Erdödy and Harrach lead one to great expectations. The results have outdistanced these expectations by far.

Yes, the annals of music will never forget that we owe our first thanks to this circle for two classical works, *The Creation* and *The Seasons*. In this circle, under the leading influence of Herr Baron v. Swieten (where the public speaks loudly, modesty dare not blush), only the finest is cultivated. In this circle Haydn's genius found love for Art, an educated and receptive audience, and an encouragement such as are not customary in Germany. Long may the taste of this school remain, may it spread, and may it continue to bring forth such fruits everywhere!

[*AMZ* III, 575–9]

Another interesting report, with some valuable quotations from Haydn himself, appeared in the *Zeitung für die elegante Welt*:

THE FOUR SEASONS BY HAYDN, PERFORMED IN VIENNA.

(Vienna, 25 April 1801.)[1]

While the educated society of half Europe is not yet tired of listening to Haydn's masterpiece *The Creation*, Vienna had the fortune to be able to admire a second similar work by this great master: *The Four Seasons*. It was given on 24 April at 6:30 p.m. in the rooms of Prince von Schwarzenberg, which are excellently suited to large performances of music. A subscription of the local aristocracy was organized to give performances several times a year of large works by Handel, Gluck, Haydn &c. The public was very numerous and mixed. The Archduke and the citizen, the Prince with the star and the modest scholar, were all together here. The performance was worthy of Viennese artists, the applause undivided and noisy.

It would be more than daring to wish to judge such a masterpiece on the basis of a single hearing; thus only a few general remarks here. Even during the composition, *Herr* Haydn stated that he would rather have composed another subject than the four seasons, for example the last judgement or something similar, because some ideas from *The Creation* involuntarily insinuated themselves [*einfielen*] into 'Spring'; also one noticed in the new work that some arias and choruses displayed a relationship, albeit a small one, with some [numbers] of *The Creation*. Who would want to blame the great master for that? *The Four Seasons*, instead, contained many passages which must move the coldest heart to the most gentle emotions, and many which are great, sublime, that sweep us along like a great river and excite one to the greatest enthusiasm. But the imitation of the cock's crowing at dawn, the gun's explosion during the hunt, seem to me to be a mistaken concept of tone-painting in music, perhaps even a degradation of this divine art.

On 27 April *The Four Seasons* will be given again.

[1. Jahrgang, 1801, pp. 427f.]

One of the most extensive contemporary criticisms appeared in the influential and widely read *Journal des Luxus and der Moden*:

Vienna, 10 June 1801

Two rehearsals of Haydn's *The Seasons* were held in the Palace of the Prince von Schwarzenberg, and every honest man was permitted to attend; whereupon a private performance was given there. Soon afterwards, at the request of the Imperial Court, the work was given there [at court] at a chamber concert and finally, after a general rehearsal, it was given in public at the Redoutensaal, at two gulden a ticket. The success it received, as might have been expected, was great and undivided. But great and undivided as this success really was, would it not have been even greater, had the material, which Haydn's art treated, not been musically more selective? It is not to be doubted that this subject is most suitable for the painter, then for the poet, and only after them for the composer. The fact that the

1 'Spaced' in the original. Proper names, 'Fürsten von Schwarzenberg', the first reference to 'die vier Jahreszeiten' in the article itself are also spaced (here ignored). All italics have been added.

present music is nonetheless excellent does not contradict my statement, since also in this case, at least up to a point, poetry and music are, each one, *sui generis*. There is a general instruction that one might give to the listener: the music as we have it would describe the four seasons – must do so – without any text, and would certainly produce the effect it does regardless of the words as they now stand. Music ought to describe only passions, emotions and objects that can be heard. It will be objected that I too severely restrict music's sphere of action by these restrictions. – Not at all! I would even propose the apparent paradox: that by these restrictions I enlarge its horizon; for when a tree is pruned of its excess branches, the tree thrives. If music concerns itself with the portrayal of passions and emotions, in many cases she gains more force of expression than the poet himself. Joys and sorrows, which the latter often deems inexpressible, can be portrayed by the composer completely and with all their delights and disasters. As far as the matter of natural objects [*Gegenstände des Gesichtes*] is concerned (which music so often attempts to portray and never ought to), I have to admit that – despite my objections to these visible objects – I have actually heard overtures, symphonies and even songs which, sometimes fully, sometimes partly, describe such objects and nevertheless delighted me; how to explain this disparity? – A small distinction will remove it completely. A composer may describe natural objects; but how? He should describe them, not as they are – their absolute appearance as physical nature – but only through the impressions they make upon us. He must describe them in the reaction that they produce in our souls, but made more beautiful as in a mirror. And only in this case can he ally himself with a poet; otherwise he should write chaotic symphonies – Haydn is to be excused on account of the badly selected material because the choice was not of his doing; for it is obvious how little suited for music the material really is. It offers neither passions nor emotions, even too few objects for the ear; the dominating objects of nature are not, in this case, seen by the poet in their reactions on our emotions but simply in their physical appearance as part of nature. Moreover, the syllabic division chosen is neither pure nor musical. The poet's preface to some of the introductions [*Ouvertüren*] is quite wrong; thus he requests, for example, in the introduction to 'Winter' that the music should express fog and vapours. Vaguely sad, depressing and fearsome it may be; but not to express fog and vapours. But not only this: the editor [*Verfasser*] of the text is responsible for other lapses: the hunt introduced into 'Autumn' is too common and goes into too much detail; the wine harvest is too long, and industry, allegorically described, is too abstract for musical composition. The final chorus (and some other single passages here and there, for example the Spinning Song in 'Winter', are further exceptions) is the only thing that expresses emotion [*Empfindung*]. But unmusical as the subject actually is, there would have been a way, at least in part, to make it more fit for musical setting. The poet should have held more closely to Thomson's excellent episodes (for the whole is taken from Thomson) and should have made them in some way the basis, as a result of which a certain amount of changing richness of emotions would have entered the picture. But the editor does not allow us to imagine that Thomson has included episodes in his poem; rather he has chosen to describe the whole physically. Perhaps this is the reason why the music, for all its descriptive excellence, does not quite reach that of *The Creation*. The orchestra was large and excellent and the three voices were sung in masterly fashion by Herr and D^{lle} S a a l and Herr R a t t m e y e r [*sic*].

[16. Band, Weimar 1801, p. 414; Pohl III, 371f., with wrong date]

Zinzendorf actually went to *The Seasons* a second time, on 27 April, but he was tired and only stayed a short while ('. . . Un instant au Concert. La chaleur me frappa les yeux, je causois avec Saurau . . .' – Olleson, 60). Zinzendorf was several years younger than Haydn, and one wonders how the composer, now in his seventieth year, could take the strain of conducting three performances in such proximity. But as we shall see, *The Seasons* took its serious toll of its composer's health.

Between the second and third performances, Haydn wrote to Hyde & Clementi in London:

[To Hyde & Clementi, London. *German*]

Vienna, 28th April 1801

Sir![1]

 Thank you for the hundred guineas which you sent to me, but I also hope to receive the rest of the money at your earliest convenience. For my part, I shall endeavour to serve you with 3 good pianoforte Sonatas by the end of the Summer.

 You received through Herr Artaria and Comp. two hundred and twelve (IN FIGURES: 212) copies [of *The Creation*]. I should now like to inform you that the music of my *Four Seasons* has been received with the same undivided approbation as was *The Creation*; in fact some prefer it to *The Creation* because of its variety. The words have already been translated into English and French. In hopes of a speedy answer, I remain, with every esteem,

Your most obedient servant,
Joseph Haydn [m.p] ria.

[postal stamp, indicating date of arrival: 'Foreign Office 1801, Ma[y] 19']

[Address:]   M[r] Hyde and Clementi.
N[ro] 26.
Cheapside.   London.   [CCLN, 179]

In the event, Haydn never wrote the Piano Trios (for this is obviously what is meant by 'Sonatas'), though he may have intended to do so. In fact the summer was to be taken up with the composition of the great penultimate Mass.

 The Edinburgh publisher Thomson now sent sixteen more airs for Haydn to arrange, and on 30 April Straton writes to Thomson that Haydn at first refused to touch them because the price paid was too low. But in the course of the conversation Straton learned that Haydn was writing to Thomson to ask him to procure a dozen India handkerchiefs, and it struck him that 'your making him a *present* of them might mollify the veteran into compliance respecting the sixteen airs'. Straton therefore took it upon himself to promise in Thomson's name that the handkerchiefs would be sent as a gift, and 'this had the desired effect to such a degree that Haydn immediately put the sixteen airs in his pocket, and is to compose the accompaniments as soon as possible on the same terms as the former'.[2]

 Haydn was now too old to have many composition pupils, but he still accepted a few if he thought they were particularly promising. Neukomm was still his pupil, and in Rosenbaum's Diary we hear of another one:

 Thursday, 30th [April] . . . we attended the concert too . . . The entertainment was pleasant and unconstrained. Young Lessel (a Pole, and a pupil of Haydn's) had a piece performed, a trio for pianoforte, horn and clarinet. It contains a few nice ideas but is rather a bore . . . and gives away the beginner.   [Radant, 94]

---

1 The letter is probably addressed to Clementi personally. Together with Haydn's autograph, an old, possibly contemporary translation has been preserved; it is in rather curious English – to say the least – and inaccurate in details.
2 Hadden, *Thomson*, 305f.

Franz Lessel (1780–1839) actually became one of Haydn's favourite pupils; when the young man returned to Poland in 1810 he carries with him the Haydn tradition which he passed on to Chopin and his generation.

On 4 May Haydn wrote to another former pupil, Ignaz Pleyel:

[To Ignaz Pleyel, Paris. *German, 'Du' form*]

Vienna, 4th May 1801

Dearest Pleyel,

I would very much like to know when your beautiful edition of my Quartets will appear, and whether or not you have received the copy of my *Creation* and also the portrait which Artaria sent to you.[1] Is it really true that one can buy *The Creation* in Paris, both the score and the pianoforte reduction? At the same time, please do tell me if it has been well received there, and whether there is any truth in the report that the entire orchestra has expressed a desire to offer me a gold medal. Please let me know about all these matters as soon as possible, because here in Vienna the whole thing is thought to be a wild exaggeration.

Last week they performed my new work, *The Four Seasons*, three times in front of the nobility, with an unparalleled success; in a few days it will be given for my benefit, either at the Theatre, or in the Large Redoutensaal.[2] We prefer performing *The Seasons* to the *Creation*, for it makes a pleasant change. It [*The Seasons*] has already been translated into French and English, after Thompson [*sic*], by our great Baron van Swieten. Everyone hopes for a speedy publication; but it will not appear for a little while, because I want to print the English and French words *a parte*, which will render the work easier to perform.

I send you my best regards, as always, and ask to be remembered to your wife. I am,

Dearest Pleyel,
Your most sincere friend,
Joseph Haydn.

P.S. My poor wife has been dead for a year now.

[Address:]   Monsieur Pleyel,
                    Compositeur très-célèbre
                              à
                           Paris.   [CCLN, 179f.]

Honours from all over Europe were beginning to arrive at the composer's house in the Kleine Steingasse in Gumpendorf. From Amsterdam came the following tribute:

[To Haydn from the 'Felix Meritis' Society,[3] Amsterdam, *Dutch*]

The Society of Merit, founded in Amsterdam under the motto 'Felix Meritis', wishes happiness and prosperity for each and everyone. Its primary purpose is to further the general well-being of this country's inhabitants; by a knowledge of true merits, and by encouraging and practising useful arts and sciences, it wishes to expand and increase this country's trade, its merchant marine, its agriculture, its factories, &c. Nothing can be more pleasing to the Society than to increase its membership by the constant addition of men of good will, capacity and ability.

---

1 See letter to Artaria of 3 September 1800.
2 *Vide infra.*
3 The files of the 'Felix Meritis' Society, of which photostat copies were placed at our disposal, show that Haydn's membership was proposed and agreed to on 30 March. The Secretary, A. Buijn, then asked Haydn if he would accept the membership, and upon receiving an affirmative answer, he thanked Haydn (see 25 July 1801) and sent him the official diploma and the Society's statutes. Haydn's formal note of acceptance was then written on 18 October 1801 (see *infra*). Pohl III, p. 182, thus requires correction.

To further this end, it has elected Joseph Haydn, Professor of Music, member of the Royal Swedish Academy of Music, and *Kapellmeister* in the actual service of H. H. Prince Esterházy, as an honorary foreign member of this Society, in the hope that said Joseph Haydn will assist them in their salutary intentions, and will live up to the flattering hopes they entertain of him.

As proof of his election, the majority of the members voted to send you the present open letter, signed by the commission appointed thereto, and affirmed by their seal.

Executed at Amsterdam this 4th of May 1801

<table>
<tr><td>Wragtendorp</td><td>Presiding Commissioner</td></tr>
<tr><td>Secretary</td><td>Jacques Breguet.</td></tr>
</table>

[CCLN, 180f.]

[To Haydn from the commission of the 'Felix Meritis' Society, Amsterdam, *Dutch*[1]]

The Commission chosen by the Philanthropic Society in Amsterdam, 'Felix Meritis'.

To Joseph Haydn, Teacher of Music, Member of the Royal Swedish Music Academy and *Kapellmeister* in the actual service of His Highness, Prince Esterházy.

Amsterdam, 4th May 1801.

Since the Society which we have the honour of representing always directs its aim towards fulfilling its primary purpose, as explained in the accompanying open letter, it is therefore a pleasure for us to offer you, in said open letter, our honorary foreign membership. Your numerous merits, so very well known, vouch for the Society's inclination, and remove from it every doubt that you will accept its offer, thereby assisting its name and its philanthropy: to which end we commend ourselves and enclose a copy of our statutes.

We remain, respectfully,

Commissioners of the above Society, and in its name and at its request:

Jacques Breguet,
M. Wragtendorp.

[CCLN, 181]

The most dramatic expression of Haydn's mood after completing and performing *The Seasons* is the fact that on 5 May he drew up the principal part of his first Will.[2] It is in many respects a most remarkable document showing, as it does, that Haydn's

---

1 A German translation of the year 1811 is in the Esterházy Archives.

2. The first date on the autograph manuscript, which serves as the basis for this translation, is clearly 5 May (Österreichische Nationalbibliothek, Handschriftensammlung, XXXIII, 109/6). Neukomm reports (*Bemerkungen*, 31) Swieten coming to visit Haydn and finding him 'busy with the fourth or fifth codicil.' 'That's right, Haydn', said Swieten, 'at our age we have to take care to put our house in order.' Griesinger, on the other hand, reports to Breitkopf & Härtel on 5 June: 'He was just writing his will when I came to see him', but probably Haydn was adding one of the many codicils. Pohl III, 179. Haydn's first will was published as 'Der erste Entwurf von Joseph Haydn's Testamente' in Zellner's *Blätter für Musik, Theater und Kunst* (Vienna) I (1855), 91, 93 and also in *Die Kultur* 1908, pp. 81ff. (ed. Mencik); in English it first appears in Lady Wallace's translation of Nohl, *Musikerbriefe (Letters of distinguished Musicians . . .* London 1867).

In the course of the following years, Haydn made many changes and additions to this will. There are in fact so many changes that the document would be best reproduced in facsimile, for a printed text cannot hope to convey all the subtleties of the manuscript, e.g. the sums, which Haydn often changed four or five times before arriving at the final figure. The female endings (e.g. 'Loderin' instead of 'Loder') and other local peculiarities ($\overline{m}$ for mm) have been normalized. The notes at the end correspond to the numbers of the will. We have tried to keep these notes to a reasonable length; readers who would like to know more about the members of Haydn's family mentioned in this and the final will are referred to Ernst Fritz Schmid's definitive book on the subject (*Joseph Haydn, Ein Buch von Vorfahren und Heimat des Meisters*, Kassel 1934).

preoccupation with money during and after his London journeys was exclusively motivated by a desire to leave his family, friends, and servants well provided for. This Will is also interesting in that it supplies hints, tenuous as they are, about the composer's past: who was 'Mademoiselle Catherine Csech, waiting woman to the Princess Graschalkowitz,' to whom Haydn originally left the large sum of 1,000 gulden? Geiringer (1947, 160) wonders if she might have been Luigia Polzelli's predecessor.

[Haydn's First Will; for notes see pp. 54f.]

N^{ro}		Fl.	
1	For Holy *Masses*	12	
2	To the *primary* school [*Normal* Schull]	5	[at first 3] +
3	For the poor-*house*	5	[at first 3] +
4	For the *Executor Testamenti*	200	[at first 100] + [Later:] and the smaller *portrait* by *Grassi*
5	For the clergyman [*Seelsorger*]	10	+
6	For the costs of a first-class burial	200	+
7	For my dear brother *Michael* in Salzburg	4,000	+
8	For my brother *Johann* in Eisenstadt	4,000	+
9	For my sister in *Rohrau* .... [This entry later crossed out and the following written underneath:] The children of my [added later: 'deceased'] sister	2,000 —	[at first 1,000] [Later:] †God rest her soul
10	For the seamstress in *Esterház*	500	+ Anna Maria Moser, *née* Fröhlich
11	For the seamstress in *Rohrau*	500	+ Elisabetha, married to Pöhein
12	For the second seamstress there .... [This entry later crossed out, and a new clause added on the bottom right-hand corner of the page:]	500	
12	The cobbler-mistress *Anna Loder* in Vienna .... [Further down, on this page, Haydn rewrote this clause as follows:] The present cobbler-mistress *Anna Loder* in Vienna 1 hundred. Her husband 100, and each child 100, that is 500 fl. in all. If she should [have lived in harmony with her husband until after my death, she may ask for 500 fl.] [This last sentence later cancelled.]	200	
13	For the cobbler-mistress there [the word 'there' later crossed out and 'Gerhaus' added]	500	+ *Theresia* Hamer, cobbler-mistress in Gerhauß.
14	For her son, the farrier	500	[at first 300] *Mathias Fröhlich*
15	For *Anna Wimmer*, the child of my late sister, at Nicolo in Hungary, and her husband and family [The 'her husband' etc. had a separate number '16', linked to 15 with a bracket; '16' later crossed out.]	500	[Later addition:]N^{ro} 16 For my niece [*Mumb*] Anna *née* Fröhlich, at present cobbler-mistress in Vienna 200 [at first 500; whole sentence later cancelled: see No. 12 *bis*]. If by any chance she should presume to come forward with a claim I wrote, I declare it to be null and void, inasmuch as I have paid more than 6 thousand Gulden of debts for her and her dissolute former husband, *Joseph Luegmayer*. If she should have lived in harmony with her husband until after my death, she may ask for 500 fl. [This latter sentence later cancelled.]

17	For her married daughter in *Koposwar* [*recte*: Kapuvár]	100	
18	For her other 3 children, together	300	
	[This entry later cancelled, and the following new clause added:] For the friends of my deceased wife, viz. [not filled in].		
19	For the married woman Düsseni, *née* Scheiger	300	[at first 200]
20	For her imbecile brother, Joseph	100	[This entry later cancelled.]
21	For her brother, Karl Scheiger, silversmith, and his wife, together	300	[at first perhaps '600'?]
22	For Frau v[on] Koller [later:] her son	300	[at first 200]
23	For her son [entry later cancelled]...........	100	
24	For the sister of my late wife, the former nun ..	50	
25	For my servant *Johan Elsler*	2,500	
	and also a year's salary	120	
	as well as a suit of clothes including waistcoat and breeches; cloak and hat		*Fidei comis* [trust fund]
			1,000
			1,500 for the cook
			600
			3,350 [*sic*]
26	For *Rosalia Weber*, who was in my service and will show my written certificate to that effect ..	300	
27	For my present maid-servant, *Anna* Kremnitz	1,000	[underneath are various smaller sums, heavily corrected]
	and also a year's salary at	46	
	[the sum originally read '36'] together with bedding and [later: '2 pairs of'] sheets which she uses on her bedstead. [Later addition:] Also 4 chairs, a table and the chest of drawers in hard wood; the clock, the mirror, the picture of the Blessed Virgin – all this is from her room. A flat-iron, earthenware kitchen utensils, a pail and other trifles.		
28	For my housekeeper *Theresia Mayer*.........	500	[at first 300]
	and a year's salary	20	
29	For the old gardener, Michel...............	24	
30	For the Princely choir [Chor *Music*] for my *obsequies*, to be divided equally among them ..	100	[sum erased]
31	For the clergy	12	[sum erased]
	[Later addition:]Nᵣ is valid		
32	For the parish clergy in *Eisenstadt* for a holy *Mass* [entry later cancelled]	5	
33	For his clerk [*vicario*]	2	
	[entry later cancelled]		
34	For the *P. Beneficiat*.......................	2	
	[entry later cancelled]		
35	For the priest in Möllendorf	2	
	[entry later cancelled]		
36	For the [priest] in *St. Georg*	2	
	[entry later cancelled]		
37	For the sexton [later cancelled]	1	
38	For the man who pumps the organ	1	
39	For the female singer, *Babett*	50	
40	For my relative [*Mumb*], the saddler's wife in *Eisenstadt*	50	
	For her daughter.........................	300	
41	For Mesdemoiselles *Anna* and *Josepha Dillim* [Dillin], together	100	

42	For the blind daughter of Herr Kraus, *Regens Chori* in Eisenstadt	100	[entry later cancelled]
43	For the 4 sisters Sommerfeld, daughters of the *wig-maker* in Pres[s]burg	200	
44	For *Nanet*, daughter of my neighbour, Herr Weißgrab	50	[entry later cancelled]
45	For Herr Ast, *merchant* in the Kleine Steingasse	50	
46	For the priest in *Rohrau*	12	
47	For the schoolmaster there.................	6	
48	For the schoolchildren	3	
49	For H[err] *Wamerl*, formerly *valet-de-chambre* to Count von Harrach	50	
50	For the present H[err] *Secretair* of Count Harrach	50	

[There follows a long series of rows of figures, much corrected, ranging from 17,478 fl. to 19,724 fl. – the sum total of all the sums from Nos. 1 by an unknown hand. Following No. 50 page one of Haydn's will ends. The following Nos. 51 and 52 were later crossed out.]

51	In order to implement the entire content of *articles* N.º 51 and 52, a capital of .... is to be deposited with Count v[on] Harrach, Lord of the Manor in Rohrau, at five percent, the *interest* of which is to be disposed of as follows:	6,000
51	I bequeath to the widow *Aloysia* Polzelli, formerly a singer in the service of Prince *Nicolaus Esterhazy* .... to be paid to her in ready money 6 weeks after my death. And each year, from the date of my death, she is to receive .... for life from the *interest* of the said aforementioned *capital*.	150
		150

      After her death, her son, Anton Polzelli, is to receive these 150 fl. for one year more, because he has always been a good son to his mother and a grateful pupil to me. N.B.: I declare the promise which I wrote in the Italian language, and which *Madam Polzelli* will produce, to be null and void; because otherwise so many of my poor relations, with greater claims, would receive too little. Finally: she, Polzelli, must be satisfied with the above-mentioned annuity. After her death, one half of the above *capital*, viz. 3,000 [Gulden], is to be divided in two parts, of which one part, 1,500, is to devolve on the Lords of the Manor in Rohrau, for the purpose of keeping in good order the *monument* erected to me by the count and also the *statue* which my late father caused to be placed at the door of the sacristy. The second part is also to be held in trust by the Count, and the annual *interest* of this sum, *viz.* 75 fl., is to be given to the two poorest orphan children in *Rohrau*.

      Finally

52	I bequeath to my niece [Mumb] *Anna Luegmayer*, the daughter of my dear sister .... payable 6 weeks after my death. She is also to receive the sum of .... annually so long as she and her husband are alive. On their demise, however, this annuity of 150 fl. is to go to their children until they come *of age*, at	100	fl.
		150	

which point 750 fl. of this invested *capital* is to be divided equally between them. Of the remaining 750 fl., 500 is to be given to my dearest Count v. Harrach, as the depository of this, my last will and testament; and 100 fl. are to go to his agent for his trouble. The remaining 150 fl., however, are to be given to my step-mother, and if she be no longer alive to such of her children as are alive. N.B. If she, Luegmayer, or her husband should perchance produce a document signed by me for a larger bequest, I wish it to be understood, as in the case of M[adame] *Polzelli*, that such a document is null and void, because both she, Luegmayer, and her husband, owing to my extraordinary kindness, squandered more than 6,000 fl. of mine during my lifetime, to which my own brother Johann as well as the whole population of Oedenburg and *Eisenstadt* will attest.

Within the period of one year and 6 weeks, all the *bequests* must be paid, using the *securities* which will be available after my death, the proceeds from the sale of the house, and likewise the sums which will accrue from the auction of my *effects* after all negotiations shall have been completed; all the other expenses shall be paid from the available ready money, for the disposition of which the *Executor Testamenti* should account to the heirs.

Nº	53	I bequeath to the poor widow *Theresia* Eder and her two daughters, *Anna* and *Aloysia*, lace-makers, resident in the *Magdalena* Grund Nº 36, together	150	fl.
NB	Nº 54	For my pupil, *Anton Polzelli*..............	100	f. [sum later cancelled]
	55	For the poor blind *Adam* in *Eisenstadt*	24	fl.
		For *Madam v. Liechtenthal* in *Eisenstadt*	100	[entry later cancelled]
	56	For my most gracious Prince, the gold commemorative medal from *Paris* and the letter that accompanied it, with the humble request to grant them a small place in the treasure chamber at *Forchtenstein* [Castle].		
Nº	57	For *Mademoiselle Catherine Csech*, waiting woman [*Kamerjungfrau*] to the Princess *Graschalkowitz* one thousand Gulden [sum later cancelled: underneath '500 fl.', also cancelled, and '*id est* 1,000 fl.', the figure later crossed out].		
Nº	58	For Miss *Anna* Buchholz .... because her grandfather lent me 150 fl. without *interest* when I was young and in great need; which money, however, I repaid 50 years ago.	100	

[To the right:]   1,000
        100 *Franci*
        100 *Polzelli*
         50
        100 Musi [? Music? No. 30?]
         <u>19</u>
       1,369

Nº	59	For the daughter of Herr Kandler, bookkeeper, my *forte piano* by the organ-builder Schanz.
N.	60	The smaller medal from Paris to Count v. *Harrach* together with the bust *à l'antique* by H. Grassi.

N.	61	For the widow *Wallner*, resident in the Schottenhof at the back, in the 2nd courtyard, next to the blacksmith............................	100	fl.
N.	62	For the Franciscan Fathers in *Eisen*[*stadt*]	50	fl. [entry later cancelled]
	62	For the *Pater Prior Leo* in *Eisenstadt* at the Brothers of Mercy [Barmherzige Brüder]	50	[later cancelled]
	63	For the Town Hospital for the poor in Eisenstadt	75	[entry later cancelled]

[Following No. 56, which was added later, are several totals, entered to the right of the signature and date, and ranging from 20,173 Gulden to 26,923 Gulden.]

To confirm the above, I have written and completed this my last will and testament entirely in my own hand, and would sincerely ask the worthy executory officials to consider it, if not as a proper will, at least in the light of a codicil, or to do all within their legal power to make it valid and binding.
Vienna, 5th May 1801.   Jos. Haydn mpria.

[Following the above paragraph are several additional clauses – Nos. 57–62 – which have been inserted in their proper chronological order, and a revised and much shortened version of No. 51 which, however, contains nothing not found in the first draft, and has therefore been omitted here. The provision for Anton Polzelli is cancelled in the final version, and the clause about the poor children in Eisenstadt now reads: 'After her [Polzelli's] death, however, half the *interest*, to wit 75 fl., is to go to the two poorest orphan children in Rohrau until they have come of age.' The second half of the interest is to go, as before, to keeping Haydn's monument 'and also the statue that my late father had put up in the *sacristy*, in good condition'.]

[Later additions:]
Should God unexpectedly call me to Himself, this present *testament*, although not written on franked paper, should be valid in all courts and the stamps paid tenfold to my monarch.
In the name of the Most Holy Trinity.
The uncertainty when it may please my Maker in His boundless Mercy to call me from this earth to Him has persuaded me, being of sound body and mind, to make my last will and testament concerning my few remaining worldly goods. My soul I consign to its merciful Creator, my body I consign, according to Roman Catholic custom, to consecrated earth to be buried in first-class ceremonies. For my soul I bequeath N^{ro} 1 [although on the last page, this paragraph is obviously intended as a preface to the will. It was, however, probably written later, as the following second date suggests:]

Joseph Haydn mpria
Vienna, the 6th of December 1801.
[Haydn's seal: 'JH']

[NOTES ON HAYDN'S WILL]
The numbers refer to those of the clauses in the Will.

4: Count Harrach.
9: Anna Maria married to Johann Philipp Frölich [*recte*].
10: Anna Maria, second daughter of Haydn's sister (9), married to Kaspar Moser.
11: Maria Elisabeth, eldest daughter of Haydn's sister (9), married to Michael Böheim [*recte*].
12*bis*: Anna Katherina, third daughter of Haydn's sister (9), married first to Joseph Alois Luegmayer – see *Haydn: the Years of 'The Creation' 1796–1800*, pp. 121f.

13: Therese, fourth daughter of Haydn's sister (9), married to Johann Michael Hammer.

14: Mathias, son of Haydn's sister (9).

15: Anna, daughter of Haydn's sister Anna Maria Franziska (usually known only as Franziska), married to Johann Michael Wimmer, inn-keeper.

16: see 12*bis*.

17: Anna Wimmer's (15) daughter, Josepha Anna, married to the surgeon, Joseph Apeller.

18: Anna Maria, Theresa Josepha, Anton Alois, children of Anna Wimmer (15).

19/21: relatives of Haydn's wife.

22: Maria Theresia Koller, daughter of Johann Kaspar Koller (Haydn's uncle), married to Johann Georg Stainer and, after his death, to the Eisenstadt saddler, Anton Nestmayer.

24: Therese Keller, Haydn's first love.

35, 36: Two villages near Eisenstadt.

39: Barbara Pilhofer, solo soprano in the Esterházy church choir.

40 = 22. Her daughter was Anna Nestmayer, married to Joseph Schmantz in Eisenstadt.

41: unidentified.

42: Carl Kraus: see also *infra*, p. 219.

43–5: unidentified.

51: Aloysia (=Luigia) Polzelli.

52: *vide supra*, No. 12*bis*.

53: unidentified.

55*bis*: Susanna Lichtenthal (*recte*), mother of Demetrius Lichtenthal.

58: Daughter of Anton Buchholtz [*recte*], one of the witnesses at Haydn's wedding on 9 November 1760.

59: Wenzel Kandler, Chief Bookkeeper of the Esterházy administration in Eisenstadt.

61: unidentified.

On 20 May Haydn finally found the time to write an appreciative letter to Erard in Paris, thanking them for the gift of the grand piano which the state of peace between Austria and France allowed them to send to Vienna.

[To Erard Frères, Paris. *German*.[1]]

Vienna, 20th May 1801

Monsieur!

It was not only a protracted illness but also the press of business that prevented me from sending you more promptly my overdue thanks for the wonderful *forte piano* you have shipped to me . . . [in the course of being transported from Paris to Vienna a certain amount of damage occurred, but the instrument arrived safely] except for one hammer, which is now in its proper place once again, and the sounding board, which is so warped, up to the tenor register, that if you play loudly a buzzing results; but as far as everything else is concerned, I must pay you the compliment that this *forte piano*, from its outward as well as its inner beauties, is the greatest masterpiece of its kind I have ever seen or heard.

Many cavaliers wish to know what the price of such an instrument is, and I would ask you to let me know.

Meanwhile I must thank you heartily for this costly gift, and as far as my powers allow, I shall not fail to show my gratitude to you [in the form of some composition, perhaps?]

I am [etc.]
Joseph Haydn.

1 Not in CCLN. The autograph was auctioned on 21 June 1971 by J. A. Stargardt, Marburg/Lahn, and is listed in their Catalogue, 'Autographen, Auktion am 20. und 21. Juni 1972' as item 624. The transcription in the catalogue is incomplete, but we were able to complete some of it by examining the autograph itself at Marburg, thanks to Messrs. J. A. Stargardt. The letter was first published in this more complete form in *The Listener* as part of our article, 'Haydn's Pianos' (20 July 1972, pp. 90ff.), from which article the subsequent information in this book is taken.

Haydn now had two impressive grand pianos, one by Longman & Broderip 'with the additional keys'[1] and with the *sopra una corda* pedal. Now he had another piano, combining all the mechanical excellence of British craftsmanship with Gallic taste; it, too, had the enlarged compass (up to *c''''*) and four pedals (lute stop, damper, piano stop, *sopra una corda*). Two important results of this noble present on Viennese musical life may be registered. One is that Walter, at least by 1802, began to construct pianos with the *sopra una corda* device. The other concerns Beethoven and his patron Prince Lichnowsky.

The man to whom the arrival of Haydn's Erard meant the most, apart from the recipient, was certainly Beethoven. Here was an instrument to stimulate the 'Waldstein' and 'Appassionata'. In November 1802, we find Beethoven writing to Haydn's and his friend, the Baron Nicolaus Zmeskall von Domanowecz, about a new piano, saying that Zmeskall should inform Walter that he, Beethoven, will not pay more than 30 ducats for a new piano . . .

> . . . I will give 30 ♯ [ducats] only if it is in mahogany, and I also want the register with the one string [*sopra una corda*]. If he won't agree, let me know *sub rosa* that I will choose one of the others [piano builders] and also take him *to Haidn* so that he [the builder] can see it [Haydn's Erard instrument, presumably]. (The complete letter in Thayer-Forbes[2] I, 308).

Beethoven's wish was apparently granted in a way different from what he expected, for the following year, 1803, he too received an Erard piano, as a result of which he immediately rewrote the Piano Concerto in C minor (Op. 37). That same year, 1803, Prince Lichnowsky purchased an Erard piano. Both his and Beethoven's have survived, which is important because in the event the composer found great difficulty in adapting his 'Walter' touch to the new Erard instrument. Beethoven was now becoming increasingly deaf, which must have contributed to his difficulties, but it is perhaps significant that Haydn also found the touch of his Erard too heavy. (Parenthetically Beethoven had the same difficulty in playing the Broadwood piano which he was given some years later. The action was too heavy for him, apparently.) Lichnowsky's Erard, which is in the family Castle at Grätz (now ČSSR), was not subjected to the severe alterations that Beethoven had made to his piano: by 1805 the composer had changed the mechanics twice, 'without [wrote Beethoven's friend, the piano builder Andreas Streicher of Breitkopf & Härtel] yet being able to deal with the piano properly'. Beethoven's (Streicher's) alterations were, it would seem, made to increase the tonal power – without success. The Lichnowsky instrument shows that Beethoven misunderstood the Erard piano; he seems to have wanted an instrument with the tone of a Walter or Streicher but with the strength of an Erard (and, of course, its extended range, *sopra una corda* device and the fact that it had foot pedals rather than knee pedals). The Erard that Beethoven owned – it is now in the Kunsthistorisches Museum in Vienna – was much more like the Longman & Broderip instrument which Haydn owned and which Beethoven must have played often: robust, brilliant, sturdy, but totally lacking the silvery, metallic delicacy of Walter's finest instruments.

---

1 Haydn's instrument – or an identical one – has now been rediscovered in a Salzburg attic and has been completely restored to playing condition; it is now in private possession in Vienna. On Haydn's pianos see also *Haydn in England 1791–1795*, pp. 414ff., and Horst Walter, 'Haydns Klaviere' in *Haydn-Studien* II (1970), Heft 4, pp. 256ff. Viennese pianos with six octaves were for sale at Leipzig in May 1803 (*AMZ Intelligenzblatt*).
2 German in Thayer II, 336.

As to the fate of Haydn's Erard, it is a sad tale to record. The instrument was put up for sale after Haydn's death at 200 Gulden (less than the Longman & Broderip, curiously enough) but at the last minute withdrawn by the heirs. It went to Rohrau and was last seen by a Haydn descendant who was interviewed in the early 1930s by the late E. F. Schmid; this descendant said he had seen Haydn's Erard 'in a desolate condition' in the attic of a house in Rohrau, its insides serving as a flour bin. Meanwhile it has disappeared entirely, making the rediscovery of Haydn's Longman & Broderip instrument all the more important.

On 20 May Haydn also wrote a letter in reply to a lost note from the father of one of Germany's best-known Romantic poetesses:[1]

[To Freiherr Max von Droste-Hülshoff, Münster. *German*]

Vienna, 20th May 1801

Nobly born Freiherr von Droste,
     The general and undeserved success of my *Creation* so inspired my 69-year-old soul that I have dared to compose yet another one, *The Seasons*, after Tomson [*sic*]. People here are very satisfied with this work, the composition of which was exhausting. If I should receive as much success abroad, perhaps I shall undertake to write something more (if my physical powers are equal to the task). Then, when I am in Heaven, I shall thank my Almighty God for having given me His blessing, and shall remember all those to whom I could render some little pleasure. I remain, Sir, most respectfully,

Your most obedient servant,
Joseph Haydn [m.p] ria.

[Address:]   An
          Den Freiherrn Max: Von Droste
          zu Hülshoff Hochwohlgeboren,
                         zu
                    Münster
Lives near the   in Westphalen
Lambertii Church
there.   [CCLN, 182]

On the same day Haydn also wrote to Ignaz Pleyel in Paris.

[To Ignaz Pleyel, Paris. *German, 'Du' form*]

Vienna, 20th May 1801

Dearest Pleyel[2]
     It is incomprehensible to me that I cannot manage to receive an answer to any of my letters, for I do think I deserve to be remembered, but perhaps the many things you have to do excuse you.
     Yesterday H[err] Pichl was with me, and he received from you the commission that he should have an announcement of [your edition of my] 80

1 Annette Elisabeth von Droste-Hülshoff (1797–1849).
2 Haydn had received no answer to his letter of 4 May (*vide supra*). The well-known composer Wenzel Pichl was one of Pleyel's correspondents in Vienna. Mollo = Tranquillo Mollo, who had been one of Artaria's partners and was now established in the music publishing business. Traeg = Johann Traeg, copyist and music publisher in Vienna. Our knowledge of the murky affair of Tost, Sieber and the string Quartets, Opp. 54, 55 and 64 (a total of twelve), is not materially added to by this odd request on Sieber's part: why should Sieber expect Haydn to make a statement that Tost had sold Sieber the Quartets in question? The public performance of *The Seasons* took place on 29 May (*vide infra*). The autograph of this hitherto unknown letter was sold as part of the Sacha Guitry Collection in Paris in the Autumn of 1974. A facsimile was printed in the Auction Catalogue (item 47). The address, not included in the facsimile, was included in the complete German transcription published by Hans Schneider in his Katalog Nr. 192 (1975), pp. 43f.

Quartets and *The Creation* printed in our newspapers; but since he made some difficulties about it, I took over this business, and next week it will be included in all the papers. I myself wish to subscribe to a copy, and you must tell me as soon as possible where and to whom I must deposit the money. It would seem to me that you don't want to have anything to do with Messrs. Artaria, if so turn to H[err] Mollo, or to H[err] Traeg and write to me soon. I would also like a copy of *The Creation*, and the piano score [*Clavier Auszug*] as well.

H[err] Sieber wrote to me recently, asking for a statement [*Attestat*] that he had purchased those particular 12 Quartets from H[err] Tost; but I shall never answer him. – Meanwhile I do hope to have a letter from you soon. On the 29th inst. my *Seasons* will be given in public. Adieu.

Yours sincerely
Jos. Haydn [m.p] ria.

[Address:]
Monsieur
Monsieur Pleyel compositeur
tres Celebre
     a Paris

[Not in CCLN; unpublished]

Three extracts from Griesinger's correspondence with Breitkopf & Härtel inform us of Haydn's many activities:

27 May 1801 : . . . The 7 Words [in the Oratorio] 'I thirst', &c. must remain in Latin, because the Italian Bible has no authority and Italian ears are accustomed to the language of the *Vulgata*. Today I received the vocal parts of *The Seven Words*. Swieten sends you both translations . . . [29 May] On the 24th the Empress sang *The Seasons* and on the 25th *The Creation* under Hn's direction but only in the presence of her family. (She has, according to Haydn, great taste and expression but a weak voice.) . . . [30 May] . . . Sarchi has finished half of the translation; he has many other things to do, and the *Capellmeister* cannot come every time he [Sarchi] would find it convenient. Here is the beginning, which I shall bring tomorrow to Baron Swieten to hear his opinion. [There follows some twenty lines of the Italian translation of *The Seven Words* almost exactly as printed.]

[Olleson, *Griesinger*, 23]

On 28 May the general rehearsal took place for the first public performance of *The Seasons* in the Redoutensaal. Rosenbaum went and 'saw Storace' – Nancy Storace, who had returned to Vienna for a visit. As before, the Gesellschaft der Associirten paid all the costs of the production, guaranteed a handsome honorarium (600 ducats) for Haydn and also turned over to him all the receipts of the box office, which in the event amounted to 3,209 Gulden (Pohl III, 178). The announcement in the *Wiener Zeitung* (No. 40, 20 May) read:

On the 29th of this current month will be performed *The Seasons*, composed by the Princely Esterházy *Kapellmeister* Herr Joseph Haydn, and performed for his benefit at the great hall of the Redout.

A few days later, on the 23rd, the announcement was repeated with the additional note: 'Price of admission as for the balls.'

After the triumphal first public performance of *The Creation* in 1799, Haydn must have expected a similar occasion for this public première of his latest masterpiece. He was mistaken. The report in Rosenbaum's Diary (95), despite its laconic words, tells the same story as he would record, twenty-three years later, for the Beethoven Ninth Symphony (and worse, for the nearly empty second performance): 'I went . . . to the

Redouten Saal: *The Seasons* in a benefit performance for Haydn. It was not too well attended, a little over 700 people' – the great hall hardly half filled! The ominous warnings – the nearly empty hall for the first performance (March 1800) of the Trumpet Concerto is one of the most spectacular – show that the fickle Viennese were slowly but surely turning away from their darling. We shall return to this subject, and Haydn's complaint about the lack of public enthusiasm, when the work itself is analyzed (*vide* p. 149). But the half-empty hall for such an event is one more thread in the strange story of the Viennese and their music.

One of Prince Nicolaus II's autocratic letters awaited *Kapellmeister* Haydn a few days later:

[To Haydn from Prince Nicolaus II Esterházy. *German*]
To *Kapellmeister* Haydn!
   Since I am not accustomed to receiving reports from anyone except from those who are directly responsible, through whom the material [*Verhandlungs-gegenstände*] is passed to me for my information, I do not see how the report of *Claviermeister* Fuchs concerning the petition of the trumpeter Martin Zech from the *Insurrections-*[*Batallion*] could be sent to me; for Fuchs is not in a position to act as your substitute. I shall therefore expect the necessary information directly from yourself, and return herewith the files on the subject to you.
Eisenstadt, 2nd June 1801.

Exp. Esterházy.
[CCLN, 182]

   A day later Griesinger reported that 'Swieten was very satisfied with Sarchi's specimen', and on 5 June he could add, '. . . Sarchi has finished the translation [of *The Seven Words* into Italian]; the day after tomorrow I will go with it to Swieten, and in a week it goes into the mail, because Sarchi wants to polish some things in it . . .' (Olleson, *Griesinger*, 23f.).
   On 18 June Emanuel Schikaneder's new Theater an der Wien was opened, and despite a chaotic general rehearsal (a triumphal float overturned, spilling two singers to the floor), the new opera – *Alexander von Indien* (music by Franz Teyber, libretto by Schikaneder) – was very well received, and various members of the royal family who were present were greeted with cries of *vivat*. 'The theatre itself found general approbation', wrote the *Wiener Zeitung* (No. 50). It is indeed a handsome opera house and together with the Redoutensaal may serve to remind one of Viennese musical life of the period; for those two buildings are the only ones of all the great eighteenth- and early nineteenth-century opera or concert halls in Vienna to survive. The rooms in the Mehlgrube of Mozartian fame, Jahn's rooms, the Augarten building, the old Burgtheater, the Kärntnerthortheater, the Freyhaustheater – all have disappeared forever.
   Griesinger was still busy with the Italian translation of *The Seven Words*, and reported on this and on a much more spectacular matter to Leipzig:

16 June 1801

. . . Do not yet begin printing *The Seven Words*; Swieten is now examining [it to see] if the Italian text is well fitted to the music, and Hdn. promised me that he would go through it himself, he regards this as his responsibility, &c. I hope you and the work will not suffer by this small delay. [Summary of the rest of the contents:] The wife of a Rhineland publisher had offered Haydn 1,000 ducats for

The Seasons. Her husband had adapted to music printing the lithographic process invented by Aloys Senefelder in 1798, which made it possible to take 2,000 prints off one plate.   [Olleson, *Griesinger*, 24]

The 'Rhineland publisher' was none other than J. J. André. Soon thereafter, Hoffmeister of Leipzig also made the composer an offer. The large sum of money involved made Haydn's negotiations with Griesinger/Breitkopf & Härtel considerably easier, and the composer, as we shall see, was easily able to obtain 4,500 Gulden from Breitkopf & Härtel for the Oratorio.

Meanwhile Breitkopf & Härtel announced their publication of *The Seven Words* in *Intelligenz-Blatt* XII (July 1801) of the *AMZ*:

Joseph Haydn,[1] who with admirable energy still devotes himself – and now perhaps more than ever – to the art for which he was born; who, in the case of those works where he has a free choice, has for some time specially concentrated his efforts on the monument which he has erected in his religious music, seeking to garnish it with new, never-fading wreaths; Joseph Haydn has done this in recent years also with a work which is long known to connoisseurs and amateurs and has been accounted by them as among those rare, original and profound products of genius over which time and fashion have no power; – with his

Seven Words of the Saviour on the Cross.

As is well known, this work was originally conceived as a great, descriptive instrumental piece and consisted of an Introduction, seven large movements (each dedicated to expressing one of the Saviour's Words) and after His death, the description of the earthquake as a conclusion. Later Haydn found that the critics were not wrong when they suggested that no matter how perfect these instrumental movements might be – in other words, if they were that which they are – , they would never (no instrumental work can) give the actual Words of the Saviour, in such a way as to be comprehensible without commentary to all. And then: seven slow instrumental movements in succession, despite the efforts of a most profound and experienced artist, will not awaken the necessary, desired attention and perfection in the listener who has no intellectual interest in the work but who would steep himself only in the impressions gained by listening to it.

The great artist, who quite rightly holds this work to be one of his most successful, countered these two, and all sorts of other possible criticisms by a completely new arrangement for vocal parts and by interrupting these movements in a dignified way. Although he retained much of the instrumental music, which could not be done better anyway, he had a cantata-like text written and composed it mostly for chorus but also with alternating soloists; he accompanied all this with the orchestral music; he added in front of each movement the Words of the Saviour, in the authorized translation for general public use, for *a cappella*, four-part voices in the spirit of the most noble, ancient chorales; he thus interrupted those principal movements, also by means of a most excellent, moving, large new piece for wind band alone; and in this wise he brought the work to a perfection which few pieces of music have attained; he lent to it, as a result, the possibilities of its being used as a sacred concert and for the church, thereby contributing to rectify the lack of truly good, new Passion cantatas, about which music directors have been complaining for some time.

This work, hitherto the *exclusive* property of the composer, has too much pure inner content, valid for all times; and the public has shown too much interest

---

1 Proper names spaced as usual in *AMZ*; not observed here.

recently in similar undertakings of importance, for us, trusting in both, not to dare to issue also this product *in full score*. We announce it herewith for speedy publication, a large part of it having already been printed. To the original German text will be added a useful Italian translation. The choral-like movements will contain, apart from the Luther translation, also the translation of the so called *vulgata*. A short foreword by Jos. Haydn informs about the interesting origin of the work.

Together with the full score appears a complete piano score by *Hr. Musikdirektor* Müller.

For those who wish to pay for the work in advance before *Michaelis* [29 Sept.], the prince of the score will be 4 Rthlr. (Saxon), that of the piano score 2 Rthlr. and for collectors the 5th copy is free. The list price after this date will be raised to: score – 6, piano score – 3 Thlr. We do not believe, moreover, that it is necessary to recommend this undertaking in further detail to the public, since the work itself and Haydn's name are sufficient guarantee. . . .

Leipzig, July 1801.   *Breitkopf und Härtel*.

While this message was circulating throughout the German-speaking world, Griesinger was writing to Breitkopf & Härtel with less happy news of the Oratorio:

1 July 1801

. . . What will you say when you hear that *The Seven Words* does not arrive with today's mail? As soon as they were ready and copied, they were brought to Baron Swieten; unhappily, he was taken ill; Haydn, Sarchi and I were not admitted, and meanwhile Hn. had to go with his Prince to Hungary, where he will pass the summer as usual; I wrote Bar. Swieten, asked for the work, and on the 28th sent it to Hn. in Eisenstadt. I hope to get it back soon, at least Hn. promised me before he left that he wouldn't delay it. . . . [In this same letter Haydn] spoke of Sonnleithner as of a 'filou' who lures the money out of people's pockets. . . .

[Olleson, *Griesinger*, 24]

Despite Haydn's objections, the Italian translation was printed more or less unchanged. About the middle of June Haydn went to Eisenstadt for the summer months, and at the beginning of July he wrote two letters to Griesinger:

[To Georg August Griesinger, Vienna. *German*]

Eisenstadt, 1st July 1801

Well born,
Most highly respected Sir!

I am really quite astonished to see how badly much of *The Seven Words* was translated, and also astonished at the delay. My dear Friend, I cannot possibly make the corrections myself at present, because of my Prince,[1] and I cannot think of any other solution than that Herr Härtel should find someone in Leipzig who can make the necessary improvements. Meanwhile Herr Hartl [*sic*] should publish the work as soon as possible in German. I hope that neither you, dear Herr von Griesinger, nor Herr Hartl [*sic*] will be angry at me, and remain, Sir, most respectfully,

Your most obedient servant,
Joseph Haydn [m.p] ria.
[CCLN, 182f.]

1 Haydn was about to compose the *Schöpfungsmesse*.

[To Georg August Griesinger, Vienna. *German*]
Well born,
Most highly respected Sir!

I have never doubted Herr Härtel's trustworthiness and integrity, and as a proof of my opinion he shall have the preference over all the others, provided that he agrees with what I now propose. First, in order to rid me of Herr André[1] and his female negotiator in Vienna, and so as to lose no time, Herr Härtel or you, Sir, as his business representative, must write me that Herr Härtel (I having demanded 6,000 fl. for *The Seasons*) is willing to pay me 5,000 fl. to have the exclusive rights thereof; which sum Herr André will never be able to give, the less so since I demanded cash from him. BUT OF COURSE THE AGREEMENT BETWEEN US FOR 4,500 FL. IN VIENNESE BANK-NOTES STANDS. Secondly, I ask for two thousand Gulden immediately upon signature of contract and delivery of the score, and the remaining 2,500 fl. within a period of 6 weeks following the Easter fair. On the other hand, I waive all further rights to the score and pianoforte reduction, except for two copies for my personal use; but Herr Härtel must agree to send 24 copies (which, however, will be paid for), as soon as the score shall have been printed, to the group of noblemen here,[2] either through me or through Herr Baron von Swieten. N.B.: This must take place a week or two before the official publication, but Herr Härtel can then publish both the score and the pianoforte reduction, as soon as this period of time expires. I shall not fail to correct said pianoforte reduction, but I cannot stop its being pirated in the Imperial and Royal States, since publication will take place abroad. Herr Härtel should not worry about this point, however, for our publishers here are quite incapable of undertaking anything of this size. At any rate, I hope that Herr Härtel will be satisfied with my proposal. I must add only one thing more: the autograph, like that of *The Creation* is to remain in the hands of Baron von Swieten, inasmuch as, after the Baron's death, both works, together with his own beautiful collection, will be left as mementos to the Imperial and Royal Library. Meanwhile I have had a clean, legible copy prepared in my house, under my own supervision, and have corrected it; this cost me 80 fl., but I do not require this sum to be repaid to me. I hope to have the favour of your early reply, and remain, Sir, with profound esteem,

> Your obedient servant,
> Joseph Haydn.

Eisenstadt, 3rd July 1801. [CCLN, 183f.]

The first letter concerning the Italian translation was in answer to the arrival of the score which Griesinger had sent on the 28th; the second letter concerns André's bid for *The Seasons*, which Haydn loyally reserved for Breitkopf & Härtel. Griesinger communicated the results of Haydn's letters to Leipzig, adding in one of his own letters (4 July) the information about the *four* quartets completed for Lobkowitz – the passage is underlined in the original – which we have considered *supra*, and the even more tantalizing news that Haydn then intended to compose a long-standing order of six quintets for Count Fries (Pohl III, 180), alas never written, of course. Leipzig approved all Haydn's stipulations and Griesinger wrote to Eisenstadt to confirm the whole affair. Haydn's answer is as follows:

---

1 The well-known music publisher, whose offices were at Offenbach-on-the-Main.
2 The group of noblemen who guaranteed the costs of the first performance and also Haydn's fee.

[To Georg August Griesinger, Vienna. *German*]
Well born,
Most highly respected Sir!

Two hours before I received the favour of your letter, containing the assurance that Herr Härtel had decided to pay me the sum of four-thousand-five-hundred Gulden for *The Seasons*, Herr Hofmeister[1] from Leipzig walked into my room and in all seriousness demanded the score of *The Seasons* from me; he agreed to pay cash at once, even if it cost five thousand Gulden. But I answered him that this very day I was expecting a letter from Herr Härtl [*sic*] with the assurance that Herr Härtel would pay me the five-thousand Gulden I demanded without hesitation. Scarcely a quarter of an hour after Herr Hofmeister had left my room, I received your letter, which I subsequently showed to Herr Hofmeister so that he could pass on its contents to the home office. At the same time I asked him to inform Madame N. N. von Offenbach[2] in Vienna that I had actually sold the work to Herr Härtel, so that she will no longer entertain any hope of getting it: in this way I got rid of both these plagues at once. Therefore I await the contract, and as soon as that is signed, I shall have my servant deliver the score to you, Sir. Meanwhile I remain, my dear Sir, most respectfully,

Your obedient servant,
Jos. Haydn.

Eisenstadt, 10th July 1801. [CCLN, 184f.]

We now come to two documents of great interest to our Chronicle: they are two authentic lists of musicians of the year 1801 from the Esterházy Archives: (1) a salary list, including all the musicians, dated 14 July 1801 and now, for reasons that cannot be ascertained at present, in the Burgenländisches Landesmuseum (*ex. coll.* Sándor Wolf); (2) a list of *personalia* and salaries for the Eisenstadt musicians of the year 1801, giving us all sorts of interesting information about each musician.

(1) 'Personal und Salarial / Stand / des Hochfürst. Eszterházy- / schen Majorats v[om] 14$\underline{\text{ten}}$ Julii 1801', tall folio.

HOF- und CENTRAL PERSONALE

[Namen]	[Character]	[Wohnort]	[Gehalt]	
Kammer und Chor Musique				
			fl	x.
Joseph Hayden	Capellmeister	Wien, Eisenst:	700	—
Aloys: Tomasini	Concertmeister	Eisenstadt	600	—
Aloys: Tomasini	Violinist	detto	450	—
Franz Pauer	detto	detto	379	15
Anton Tomasini	detto	detto	340	—
	[there follows page turn:]			
Jos: Dietzel	Violinist	Eisenstadt	420	—
Michael Ernst	detto	detto	174	—
Ignatz Manka	Violoncellist	detto	500	—
Thomas Düpe	Violonist	detto	329	15

---

1 In 1784, the composer Franz Anton Hoffmeister (*recte*) had opened a music-publishing business in Vienna. He subsequently published some Haydn and a good deal of Mozart for the first time, and after various vicissitudes sold most of his business to Artaria (1793) and then moved to Leipzig where with Ambrosius Kühnel, he formed the firm of 'Hoffmeister und Comp.', which later became the 'Bureau de musique', and still later C. F. Peters. Hoffmeister's Leipzig firm was about a year old at the time of present letter. See Alexander Weinmann, 'Wiener Musikverleger und Musikalienhändler von Mozarts Zeit bis gegen 1860' (*Festgabe der Akademie der Wissenschaften,* Band 230, 4th *Abhandlung,* Vienna 1956).
2 André's 'female negotiator' mentioned in the previous letter.

[Namen]	[Character]	[Wohnort]	[Gehalt]	
Anna Ruhmfeld	Discantista	detto	400	—
Barb: Pillhofer	detto	detto	232	52
Josepha Griesler	Altista	detto	100	—
Josepha Hammer	detto	detto	347	—
Johann Hayden	Tenorist	detto	199	15
Joseph Richter	detto	detto	450	—
Christian Specht	Bassist	detto	342	15
Johann Bader	detto	detto	92	30
Georg Fuchs	Organist	detto	318	20
Jacob Hirtel	Hautboist	detto	314	—
Jos: Elsler	detto	detto	314	—
Caspar Pezival	Fagotist	detto	319	15
Johann Michl	detto	detto	314	—
Anton Prinster	Hornist	detto	314	—
Michael Prinster	detto	detto	314	—
Georg Warlen	Clarinetist	detto	314	—
Gabriel Lendvay	Supernumer:	detto	221	—
Sebastian Binder	Trompeter	detto	27	—
Michael Altmann	detto	detto	27	—
Johann Pfann	detto	detto	27	—
Martin Zech	Musikansager	detto	144	—
Georg Rastetter	Orgeltretter detto [organ pumper]	detto	37	50

(2) The second document is 'Personal und Salarial Stand Numero I Anno 1801', from the Esterházy Archives, book in tall folio, listed under 'Eisenstäder Geistlichkeit und Kirchenstand', f. 2v. & 3 (r., v.), now Hungarian State Archives, Budapest; copied in 1959 by the late E. F. Schmid and kindly sent to us in 1960. We suggest that this document may be slightly later than (1), but in any case it contains later additions and is valid not only for the members who played in the *Schöpfungsmesse* (September 1801) but also for the *Harmoniemesse* of 1802.

Since this document has never been published, we do so for the first time here, giving first the original German which will be necessary for other Haydn scholars and following with our English summary.

Fürstl. Eszterhazÿscher 'Personal und Salarial Stand Numero I Anno 1801' (Buch in Gross —2°) Fol. 2^v/3^r unter 'Eisenstädter Geistlichkeit und Kirchenstand'.

[Die betreffenden Rubriken lauten: 'Dermaliger Dienst/Tauf. und Zuname/Gebürtig von/Gehalt samt Naturalien im Buchhaltereis Preis Fl. Kr/Alter./Dienstjahre./Verehligt./ Hat Kinder/Versteht die Sprachen und Rechte./Hat vorhin gedient als/Die Ursache seiner Transferirung von einer andern Station./Anmerkungen.' 'Zulagen' und 'Dienstaustritte' stets später eingetragen.]

[1] 'Schloß Schulmeister und Organist Georg Fuchs', geb. von Mattersdorf. Geh. samt Naturalien 318 fl. 20 xr; 63 Jahre alt; 23 Dienstjahre; Witwer; 3 Kinder; Versteht Sprachen: deutsch; vorher hat gedient als Schulm. in Forchtenau; Ursache des Dienstaustritts: Verbesserung; Anmerkungen: keine.'

[Fol. 3^v ff:] 'Eisenstädter Kammer und Chor Musique.'

[2] 'Capellmeister Joseph *Haÿden*; Rohrau; 700.—; 69; 39$\frac{2}{3}$; Wittwer; —; Deutsch, Französisch, Italienisch und Englisch; Kapellmeister bei Herrn Grafen Morzin; Verbesserung; —.'

[3] 'Concertmeister Aloisius *Tomasini*; Pesaro in Italien; 600.—; 59; 43; verh.; 9; Deutsch, Französisch, Italienisch; Kammerdiener bei waÿl. S^r. Durchlaucht Fürsten Paul Anton; obwaltet keine; —.'

[4] 'Violinist Franz *Pauer*; Pest in Ungarn; 379, 15 Zulage 50 Quartiergeld 40; 62; 31; verh; keine; Deutsch, Ungarisch; Waldhornist beim großwardeiner Bischof Patatitsch; Verbesserung; —.'

[5] 'Violinist Aloisius *Tomasini junior*; Eszterház; 450; 21; 5; nein [ledig]; — ; Deutsch, Italienisch; Nirgends; keine; —.'

[6] 'Violinist Anton *Tomasini*; Eisenstadt; 340 Zulage 100; 26; 5; nein [ledig]; —; Deutsch, Italienisch und mittelmässig Ungarisch; Kammer = Musicus bei Herrn Grafen Harsch; Verbesserung; —.'

[7] 'Violinist Michael *Ernst*; Eisenstadt; 174; 40; 27; nein [ledig]; —; Deutsch; Nirgends; keine; —.'

[8] 'Violinist Joseph *Dietzel*; Drautmannsdorf; 420; 55, 36; Wittib; 6; Deutsch; Musicus bei Herrn Grafen Hojosz; auf eigene Bitte; Ist in das Spital nach Forchtenau übersetzt worden. [Späterer Zusatz].'

[9] 'Violoncellist Ignatz *Mánker*; Wien; 500 Zulage 10; 30; 33; 6; nein; —; Deutsch; Musicus beim Herrn Fürsten v. Grasalkowitsch; auf eigene Bitte; —.'

[10] 'Violinist Thomas *Düppe*; Rothretsitz in Böhmen; 329; 15, 33; 6; nein; —; Deutsch, und Böhmisch; Musicus in Wien; Detto; —.'

[11] 'Fagottist Caspar *Petzival*; Jelenÿ in Böhmen; 319; 15 Zulage 60; 54; 30; nein; —; Deutsch und Böhmisch; Fagotist bei Herrn Grafen Bubna; Verbesserung; —.'
[Darunter ist später eingetragen der Fagottist Johann *Sommer* mit 409 fl.]

[12] 'Discantista Anna *Ruhmfeld*; Presbourg; 400; 20; 3¼; nein; —; Deutsch, etwas Französisch, und etwas Italienisch; Nirgends; obwaltet keine; —.'

[13] 'Discantista Barbara *Pillhoferin*; Schottwien; 232, 52½; 34; 13; nein; —; Deutsch; Nirgends; Detto; —.'

[14] 'Altista Josepha *Griesslerin*; Eisenstadt; 100 Zulage 50; 34; 18¾; ja; 1; Deutsch; Nirgends; obwaltet keine; —.'

[15] 'Contra Altista Josepha *Hammer*; Eisenstadt; 347 dann Zulage 47 fl Zulage 100; 24; 2½; nein; —; Deutsch; Nirgends; Detto; —.'

[16] 'Tenorista Johann *Haÿden*; Rohrau; 199, 15; 58; 29⅓; nein; —; Deutsch; Tenorist in Wien bei St: Stefan; Verbesserung; —.'

[17] 'Tenorista Jacob Jos: *Richter*; Kamnitz in Böhmen; 450; 26; in ersten; nein; —; Deutsch, Latein, Böhmisch; Nirgends; keine; —.'

[18] 'Bassista Christian *Specht*; Wien; 342, 15; 58; 32¼; ja; 3; Deutsch; Basist in Wien; Verbesserung; —.'

[19] 'Bassista Johann *Bader*; Gols in Ungarn; 50 Zulage 44, 30; 37; 3; ja; 3; Deutsch; Basist in der eisenstädter Stadtpfarr; auf eigene Bitte; —.'

[20] 'Hauboist Jacob *Hirtel*; Grems in Oesterreich; 314; 33; 4; ja; 1; Deutsch; Hauboist bei Herrn Grafen Franz v. Eszterházy; auf eigene Bitte; —.'

[21] 'Hauboist Joseph *Elsler*; Eisenstadt; 314; 32; 12; nein; —; Deutsch; Hauboist bei denen hochseeligen Fürsten Nicolaus und Anton; obwaltet keine; —.'

[22] 'Fagottist Johann *Michael*; Rakitzan in Böhmen; 314; 35; 4; ja; 2; Deutsch, Böhmisch; Fagotist bei Herrn Grafen Battÿanÿi; auf eigene Bitte; —.'

[23] 'Waldhornisten Anton *Prinster*; Wien; 314; 24; 4; nein; —; Deutsch; Waldhornist bei Herrn Grafen Franz v. Eszterházy; auf eigene Bitte; —.'

[24] 'Waldhornisten Michael *Prinster*; Wien; 314; 18; 2/12 [zwei Monate]; nein; —; Deutsch; Ebenallda; Detto; —.'

[25] 'Clarinetist Georg *Várlen*; Wallerstein in Schwaben; 314; 17; 2/12; nein; —; Deutsch; Clarinetist bei (Tittl.) Herrn Grafen Franz v. Eszterhazÿ; Detto; Ist aus dem Dienst getreten.'
[Darunter stehen noch mit je 314 fl. später zugefügt die Klarinettisten Franz *Finger* und Joseph *Hornick*.]

[26] 'III Trompeter
  a) Sebastian *Binder*; Mattersdorf; 300; 35; 1¼; ja; 3; Deutsch; Nirgends; keine; —.
  b) Michael *Altmann*; Eisenstadt; 27 Zulag 27; 46; 1¼; ja; —; Deutsch; Nirgends; keine; —.
  c) Johann *Pfann*; Eisenstadt; 27 Zulag 25; 36; 1¼; ja; 2; Deutsch; Nirgends; keine; —.'

[27] 'Supernumerarius Gabriel *Lendvaÿ*; Rechnitz; 221; 40; 6¼; ja; 1; Deutsch, etwas ungarisch; Beim hochseel: Fürsten Nicolaus, dann im Hoftheater, und beim Grafen Braschma[?]; Verbesserung; Ist aus dem Dienst getreten.'

In the following summary of this important document, a complete translation is unnecessary because the names and numbers remain identical. The information following a man's name was categorized on the original document as follows; born in/salary including emoluments reckoned out in money terms at fl. & kr./age/years of service [with Esterházy]/married status ('nein [ledig]' = no [single]; 'ja' = yes ('verheiratet' = married); 'Wittwer' or 'Wittib' (widower)/has children?/ understands which languages (the German originals are obvious)/why did he leave his previous post?/remarks: 'increase in salary' and 'left service' are noted separately.

[1] Fuchs 'served earlier as schoolmaster in Forchtenau, reason for leaving [that post]: increase in salary; no remarks.'

[2] Haydn . . . [reason for leaving:] 'increase in salary.'

[3] Tomasini . . . '*valet-de-chambre* to his late Highn. Prince Paul Anton'; 'obwaltet keine' ('none exists') under reason for leaving previous post.

[4] Pauer . . . 'Pest' (Budapest) . . . 'French-horn player for the Bishop Patachich [*recte*] at Gross Wardein [now Oradea Mare, Roumania]' . . . 'increase in salary' (*Verbesserung*) as reason for leaving previous post.

[5] Tomasini . . . 'Nirgends' (nowhere) previously engaged; 'keine' (no) transference from previous post.

[6] Tomasini . . . 'Hungarian fairly well' (*mittelmässig*) under languages.

[7] Ernst. [Had served in the Eszterháza marionette troupe in the 1770s].

[8] Dietzel: 'Drautmannsdorf' = Trautmannsdorf; 'auf eigene Bitte' (at his own request) for reason given when transferring to present job.

[9] Mánker: the variants of the name (without accent); see *Haydn: the Years of 'The Creation' 1796–1800*, 52, 525.

[10] 'Böhmen' = Bohemia, 'Böhmisch' = Czech.

[11] Underneath is the later addition of the bassoon player, Johann *Sommer*, with salary of 419 fl.

[12] 'Nirgends' ('nowhere') for previous position.

[16] Previous position: 'tenor at St Stephen's Cathedral in Vienna'.

[19] Ditto: 'bass in the Stadtpfarrkirche, Eisenstadt'.

[20] 'Grems' = Krems.

[24] 'Ebenallda' = also Count Franz v. Esterházy.

[25] 'Ist aus dem Dienst getreten' = left princely service. Underneath were added later the two clarinet players Franz *Finger* and Joseph *Hornick* at 314 fl. each *per annum*.

[26] The three trumpeters whose low salaries (in the case of II & III) are explained by the fact that they were only needed during the summer months. See *Haydn: the Years of 'The Creation' 1796–1800*, pp. 52, 326, 476f.

[27] Previous positions: 'With the late Prince Nicolaus, then in the Court Theatre, and at Count Braschma's[?]; left princely service.'

ANALYSIS

Salaries, etc.

The original salaries may be seen in the document of July. Several raises (*Zulage*) after the salary in (2) suggest that it continued in use after 1801. In [19], Bader's salary is the subject of some confusion. In (1) it is 92 fl., 30 kr., but that sum was patently added in a different ink. On the other hand, (2) lists his salary as 50 fl. with a raise (*Zulage*) of 44 fl., which makes 94. Case [26a] is also confusing: Binder's salary in the July list is, like those of the other trumpeters, 27 fl., but in (2) it is listed as 300 fl. Possibly as first trumpet of the group, he divided the 300 fl. among his colleagues. Either that, or the '300' is a mistake.

Size of Haydn's orchestra for the 'Schöpfungsmesse'

The orchestra included: 2 oboes, 1 clarinet (the second clarinet required by the score had to be engaged from 'outside'), 2 bassoons, 2 horns, 2 trumpets, kettledrums (could have been played by the superfluous third trumpeter or by Gabriel Lendvay [Lendway], a horn player.[1] Haydn's string players numbered six violins and violas (Anton Tomasini was known to be also a viola player), one violoncello and one double bass. The professional singers included two sopranos, two altos, two tenors and two basses. The original performance material shows that there must have been at least six violins, because there are two parts for each section; at a minimum, two players read from the first part and one from the second. But if all the violin players of our lists played violin in the *Schöpfungsmesse,* there would have been no violas. Therefore we

---

1 According to Dr Janos Harich, who found this information in the Esterházy Archives, Lendvay was engaged in 1793–4. Information about Anton Tomasini being also a viola player from Dr Harich.

have concrete proof that for the actual performance Haydn engaged (or persuaded to play *gratis*) several more string players, possibly from his friend Carl Kraus, *Regens chori* at the Parish Church (Stadtpfarrkirche) of St Martin. The total number of violins and violas might have been about 4-4-2 or 5-4-2, and there was probably another violoncello at least. The original number of vocal parts in the performance material also shows that Haydn had more than eight singers at his disposal; he probably added eight boy sopranos and altos (in addition to his four regular members; naturally in all these calculations, the soloists also sang in the tutti sections), two more tenors and two more basses. A suggested total might be: 7 or 8 sopranos, 5 altos, 4 tenors and 4 basses.

It is not known whether Haydn played the organ part (as the solo section in the Et incarnatus suggests) or whether he conducted from the violin (thus adding another man to that weak section).

There are two salaried members of the July list who do not, for some reason, appear in the other document: Martin Zech, the 'music announcer' – instead of programmes, this man announced each piece; and the organ pumper, Georg Rastetter.

Tenure

We have noted that Prince Esterházy dismissed his wind band sometime in 1798, leaving Haydn without wind players for the Masses of 1798 and 1799 (see *Haydn: the Years of 'The Creation' 1796–1800*, p. 326). In the Autumn of 1800, wind players were again engaged. Yet the 'number of years of service' given for these wind players in Document (2) suggests that some of them went on serving even during the 'lean' years 1798, 1799. For example the bassoon player and timpanist Peczival (other spellings are known) is listed as having thirty years of service (*vide* [11]) and Jacob Hyrtel [20] four years of service, which means he was engaged about 1797 (depending on whether the year 1800 is reckoned in the total or not; if it is, he was engaged in 1798); yet we have seen that he was one of the wind players engaged on 1 November 1799. Joseph Elssler (*recte*) [21] is listed as having twelve years of service, but he too was engaged on 1 November 1799. Johann Michael [22] and Anton Prinster [23] each list four years of service. Perhaps an explanation may be found in the archive description of Johann Michael, who is listed as 'musicus ad gardam', i.e. a member of the Grenadier Battalion (*Insurrections-Battalion*); in the 'Conventionale' for 1805, Michael is credited with eight years in service.

We now come to Michael Prinster [24] and Georg Várlen [25], who say they have been members for two months ($\frac{2}{12}$). The contract of 1 November 1800, referred to many times in our Chronicle, was for six 'neu aufgenommenen Chor Harmonie Individuen', viz. Hirtel (Hyrtl), Elssler, Michael (Michel), Várlen (Werlen), Anton and Michael Prinster. We suggest therefore that: (1) some of the musicians in this contract of 1800 had already been playing in the Grenadier Battalion's band; (2) some, such as Várlen and Michael Prinster, were newly engaged in November 1800 and had in fact been only two months in service by 1 January 1801; (3) the 'lean' years were therefore not only 1798 and 1799 but also 1800 as well (the name-day ceremonies for Princess Marie Hermenegild Esterházy having occurred in September).

We have seen that the French musicians participating in the performance of *The Creation* given at Paris in November 1800 had decided to strike a medal[1] in Haydn's

---

1 The large gold medal, *N. Gatteaux* [*recte*] sculpsit, was reproduced in *AMZ* IV, 79. Haydn left it to Prince Esterházy (see Will of 1801, item 56, *supra*).

honour. The elegant letter addressed to the composer which accompanied this medal reads as follows:

[To Haydn from 142 French Musicians, Paris. *French*]

> *De Paris, ce 1 Thermidor an 9 de la*
> *République Française.*
> [20 July 1801]

The French artists, gathered together in the *Théâtre des arts* to perform that immortal work, the *Creation of the World*, composed by the celebrated HAYDN, are filled with a just admiration for his genius, and beg him to accept the homage of their respect, of the enthusiasm which inspired them, and the medal which they have struck in his honour.

No year goes by in which a new product of this composer does not enchant the artists, enlighten their minds, contribute to the progress of the art, widen the immense spaces of harmony, and prove that its expanses are boundless if one follows the luminous torch with which HAYDN has brilliantly illuminated the present and which points the way to the future. But the imposing conception of the ORATORIO even surpasses, if such a thing be possible, everything which this wise composer has hitherto offered to an astonished Europe.

When in his work HAYDN imitates the FIRE OF HEAVEN, he seems to have portrayed himself, and thus persuades us all that his name will shine fully as long as the stars whose rays he seems to have absorbed.

P.S. If we here admire the skill and the talent by means of which Citizen GATEAUX has so well reflected our intentions in the engraving of the medal we offer to HAYDN, we must also pay tribute to the loftiness of his [Gatteaux's] sentiments, for he has been content to receive for his efforts merely the glory which is his today.

Rey, *chef de l'orchestre du théâtre des arts*. Segur le jeune. Auvray. Fr. Rousseau. Xavier. Rey 3me. Saillar. [etc., etc.] [142 signatures]

> [CCLN, 185]

The musicians took the medal and letter to Count Kobenzl (Cobenzl), the Austrian Ambassador in Paris, who forwarded it to Haydn. The whole affair was reported in the *Pressburger Zeitung* (we also include here a report on a strange new instrument which was seen *inter alia* by Haydn and Baron van Swieten), as follows:

Vienna:
Vice-Principal Zink, from Hessen-Homburg, has brought to Vienna a musical instrument of his own invention, which is attracting the attention of musicians. It is like a clavier in shape, and it is played like a clavier, but it has three keyboards. The instrument can be made to sound like an organ, a [glass] harmonica, a flute, a Forte-Piano, a simple clavier, and several other wind and string instruments; thus a single player can perform a whole score with all parts, which would otherwise demand several persons and instruments. The stops make possible more than one hundred changes in tone and register. Baron van Swieten and the Kapellmeisters Hayden, Salieri and Weigel have subjected the instrument to a thorough examination and, according to testimonials they have given, have found it to be the only perfect instrument of its kind.

> [No. 53, 7 July 1801]

Vienna:
On the same day of last year that the famous attempt was made on the life of First Consul Bonaparte, *The Creation*, that great masterpiece by Herr Joseph v. Hayden, Professor of Music, was performed to universal applause at the Théâtre

des Arts in Paris. A unanimous decision was made at that time to have a medal struck in honour of the composer. The medal was completed last month, and a deputation presented it, together with a letter couched in the most flattering terms, to His Excellency Count Kobenzel [the Austrian ambassador in Paris] who sent it to Vienna to His Excellency the Minister, Count Kolloredo. On the 5th inst. the latter despatched it to Herr Hayden in Eisenstadt. The medal weighs the equivalent of 50 ducats in value. On the obverse is the composer's likeness, and underneath is the name of the medallist, Gatteaux, who created the medal without fee; the reverse shows a lyre with various emblems and an inscription reading 'In honour of Hayden and dedicated to him by the musicians who performed the oratorio *The Creation* in the Théâtre des Arts in Paris, in the 9th year of the Republic, 1800.'

[No. 63, 11 Aug. 1801]

Vienna:
The letter written by His Excellency Count Ludwig v. Kobenzl to Herr Hayden, Doctor of Music, on sending the gold medal from Paris, reads in substance as follows:

[To Haydn from Count Ludwig von Cobenzl. *German*]

Paris, July 28th, 1801

Sir,
The Musical Society of Paris which performed your masterpiece *The Creation* in the Théâtre des Arts, to great applause and to the true pleasure and admiration of all connoisseurs of music, decided unanimously to have a gold medal struck as a token of the Society's deep reverence and admiration for the author of that work, who with it has attained the highest degree of perfection in the world of music. This a deputation presented to me with the enclosed letter, asking me to send both the medal and the letter to you. I am particularly happy to fulfil that request, for it gives me the pleasure of expressing, at the same time, my own admiration and respect for an art which has brought you full recognition at home and abroad. With this medal the Musical Society pays homage, in the name of all foreigners, to your outstanding services to music, and in honouring you has erected a monument to German music that will be the wonder of the present age and of posterity.

With true respect,
Count Ludwig Kobenzl

[No. 65, 18 Aug. 1801]

Vienna:
The commemorative medal presented to Herr Haydn by the Musical Society of Paris has an excellent likeness of the composer and the legend 'Joseph Haydn' on the obverse. On the reverse is Apollo's lyre; on its base is a bas relief of the god in contest with Marsias. Over the lyre burns a flame, the symbol of genius. The legend reads: Hommage à Haydn, par les Musiciens, qui ont executé l'Oratorio de la Creation du Monde, au Théâtre des Arts, l'an IX de la République Française, ou MDCCC.

[No. 71, 8 Sept. 1801]

Vienna:
The gold medal which Herr Kapellmeister Haydn has received from the Musical Society of Paris in recognition of his services to music, is now in the famous numismatic collection of the reigning Prince Esterházy, where the owner has placed it for safe-keeping. Haydn himself was ready to bring his illustrious career in music to an end with his last masterpiece, *The Four Seasons*; enjoined by his

closest friends and by Europe's finest musicians, rather than acting on his own volition, he has decided, however, to muster all his powers once more before his life's end, and to set the Last Judgement. He has already made noticeable progress. Experts who have seen the beginning of the work maintain that in every chord the composer has immortalized himself anew and has placed himself quite beyond reach.   [No. 77, 29 Sept. 1801]
[Translation: *Haydn Yearbook* VIII (1971), pp. 280f.]

What are we to make of the tantalizing remark about the 'Last Judgement'? Had Haydn really sketched, perhaps, the Overture (just as he had begun *The Creation* with 'Chaos')? Or is the whole report, as far as the new Oratorio is concerned, a journalistic exaggeration? We shall hear a good deal about this new Oratorio; this is to our knowledge the first time it was referred to in public.

A shorter report in the *Wiener Zeitung* (No. 69, 29 August 1801) refers to the arrival of the medal and a letter 'with the most flattering expressions' by Count von Cobenzl, but since it seems to be a reduction of the material in the *Pressburger Zeitung* – usually the reverse is true – it may be omitted here.

We have preferred to present this whole episode here, breaking our chronological rule for the sake of clarity. Returning to our Chronicle, we find two letters by Haydn, one to Griesinger about *The Seasons* and one to a schoolmaster in Bohemia which has become one of the composer's most famous documents:

[To Georg August Griesinger, Vienna. *German*]
Well born,
Most highly respected Sir!
    On the 18th[1] inst I duly received your kind letter together with the attached contract, and send you herewith the contract, which I find well drawn-up, and which I have signed. I cannot, however, allow the part of the public announcement which I have underlined, because no publisher should have reason to believe, or to suspect, that I have thrown away this large work, or have been obliged to give it away for a pittance, or that I shall receive some of the profits only in the course of time; for people might thus believe that our agreement concerning the 5 thousand Gulden, which I myself read to Herr Hofmeister from Leipzig, is not authentic. Therefore I wish you would omit this article altogether, and inform Herr Härtel about it while there is still time, for I don't want to lay myself open to criticism from all other publishers, and moreover Herr Baron von Swieten would never approve of it; I wish I could ask his advice about the matter. Herr Härtel should not put the subscription price too high if he wants to protect himself against anyone pirating the work. Because of its 4 sections, *The Seasons* are a good deal longer than *The Creation*; the choruses have just as many vocal parts. Meanwhile I am, Sir, most respectfully,

                                                          Your most obedient servant,
Eisenstadt, 21st July 1801.   Jos. Haydn.
                                                                          [CCLN, 186]

[To Charles Ockl, St. Johann near Plan, Bohemia. *German*. Only the signature and title autograph]
Nobly born and most respected Sir!
    I have duly received your two letters of the 29th May and 5th July with which you favoured me, and have noted their contents with pleasure. I was quite

---

1 In Mandyczewski's copy, the only available source, 'den 28th dieses', which we presume should read 'den 18th'. In Nohl, *Addenda*, p. LVI, 'den 20 ten'.

delighted to hear that my Oratorio was received by all the music-lovers in your district with the approbation which it has been fortunate enough to enjoy in almost the whole of Europe; but it was with considerable astonishment that I read of the curious happenings consequent on the performance, which happenings, considering the age in which we live, reflect but little credit on the intelligence and emotions of those responsible.[1]

The story of the creation has always been regarded as most sublime, and as one which inspires the utmost awe in mankind. To accompany this great occurrence with suitable music could certainly produce no other effect than to heighten these sacred emotions in the heart of the listener, and to put him in a frame of mind where he is most susceptible to the kindness and omnipotence of the Creator. – And this exaltation of the most sacred emotions is supposed to constitute desecration of a church?

Have no fears about the outcome of this affair, for I am convinced that an intelligent consistory will learn a good deal from this apostle of peace and unity: it is not unlikely that the listeners went away from my Oratorio with their hearts far more uplifted than after hearing his sermons. No church has ever been desecrated by my *Creation*; on the contrary: the adoration and worship of the Creator, which it inspires, can be more ardently and intimately felt by playing it in such a sacred edifice.

If, however, this affair – which sounds completely ridiculous to every intelligent person – is not settled by the consistory, I am willing to place it before their Imperial and Royal Majesties, for Their Majesties have never heard this Oratorio without being deeply moved, and are quite convinced of the value of this sacred work. I am, Sir, most respectfully,

Your devoted servant,
Joseph Haydn [m.p] ria.,
Doctor of Music.

[seal]
Eisenstadt, 24th July 1801.
[Address:]   A Monsieur
        MONSIEUR CHARLES OCKL
        Rector in Plan

a
⌒

PR. PILSEN   PLAN
                 NÄCHST MIESS
    Receipt to be collected

[CCLN, 186f.]

We forget that Haydn's prestige was really such that he could have gone to the Emperor about this ridiculous situation. Obviously Haydn did not answer the first letter and it was not until the *Rector*'s second letter that he decided to take some action.

1 The village of St. Johann near Plan intended to perform *The Creation*. Ockl, the local schoolmaster (*Rector*) and one of Haydn's admirers, applied *pro forma* to the consistory at Prague, and meanwhile all the necessary plans were made to perform the work in the parish church. Unexpectedly the consistory refused permission. The citizens then decided to perform the work in the open air, and erected a temporary platform which, however, proved hopelessly impractical. They therefore resolved to play the work in the church after all, and 'kidnapped' the 'rector', of whom they were fond, thinking that by removing him to another place he would not be present and would therefore have no responsibility. The priest misunderstood Haydn's name, and thought it was 'Heiden,' which in German means 'heathens'; he rampaged from the pulpit, accusing St. Johann of playing oratorios by heathens in the parish church. Ockl, fearing for his position, then wrote to Haydn. See *Allgemeine Musikalische Zeitung* 1874, No. 3, pp. 41f.

The first of the letters concerning the 'Felix Meritis' Society may be included at this point:

[To Haydn from A. Buijn, 'Felix Meritis' Society, Amsterdam, *Dutch*] [1]
To *Heer* Joseph Haydn.

Highly respected Sir,

I have duly received your letter, so very flattering to me, and see from it that you were gracious enough to accept the offer of the Society, and that you agree to become a member of it.

I thus fulfil a most pleasant duty in sending you the enclosed diploma and the membership rules of said Society, and wish you a happy future as a member.

It is with the utmost gratitude that I shall expect the 4 Seasons.[2]

I shall ask the Almighty to protect you, and subscribe myself, highly respected Sir, most respectfully,

Your most humble and obedient servant,
A. Buijn
op den dam tot Amsterdam.

Amsterdam, 25th July 1801.   [CCLN, 188]

On 28 July Haydn began the full score of the *Schöpfungsmesse* (the date on the autograph reads 'di me giuseppe Haydn mpria 1801 ai 28^{tro} di / Luglio'). Haydn was pressed for time, as he admits in his letter to Griesinger of 21 August, for the work had to be ready for performance by the middle of September.

On 30 July Rosenbaum and Therese arrived at Eisenstadt, and on the following day we read in his Diary:

Friday, 31st. Warm. Walther and Fuchs came early. At 9 o'clock we went to Th— who was just beginning to sing again, under Fuchs's accompaniment, for the first time. – Elsler [*sic*] and Stessel came to Therese. Then we went to look for Haydn in the castle but did not find him. – Fuchs let us hear the new organ and pianoforte instrument by Walther . . . Fuchs visited us [in the afternoon] and said that the Princess had told the Prince and Haydn to perform a Haydn Mass and to ask Th— to sing; he added that Haydn would visit us this afternoon. We remained at home until 6 o'clock, but Haydn did not come. At Fuchs's Th— sang the Motets she had brought along, then we went to Geyersberg in the castle and ate an ice . . .
[Brand, 411]

Fuchs (= Johann Nepomuk Fuchs, the composer and later *Vice-Capellmeister*) is one of the musicians *not* on either of the 1801 lists who obviously played in performances such as that of the *Schöpfungsmesse*. There are two Walthers in the above report, one is a member of the Esterházy administration and the other is the well-known piano-maker Anton Walter (the usual spelling): the new instrument has not survived; perhaps it was a combined piano and organ, such as the 'Claviorganum' which Mr Michael Thomas has brought back into fashion.[3]

Preparations for this previous Mass by Haydn – perhaps it was the 'Nelson' Mass with its brilliant soprano solo part – continued. We read in Rosenbaum's Diary:

August 1801. Saturday the 1st in Eisenstadt. Early, and the whole morning, rain . . . At 7 o'clock I went to the Prince. Walther announced me. I was received with

---

1 A German translation of the year 1811 is included in the Esterházy Archives.
2 Haydn obviously promised to send them his new Oratorio as a token of his respect.
3 An Irish claviorganum (upright harpsichord and organ) built by Woffington in 1785 was discovered by Mr Thomas and is now in the National Museum at Dublin. Mr. Thomas has recorded a selection of claviorganum music on the Oryx label – ORYX 507 (1967).

great goodness and condescension. He spoke at length about our disbursement office, about Th—'s art, about the difficulties with the theatre, about her salary; said that she would sing in Haydn's Mass, which is very charming; at the end he dismissed me with the remark that he was very pleased to have seen me and would I give his regards to Th—. At 8 o'clock breakfast and after 9 o'clock we went to Fuchs. Th— rehearsed Haydn's Mass. To my great dissatisfaction Th—'s voice was more hoarse than yesterday, and I was looking forward so greatly to hearing her, as always. Before 12 o'clock we came home and found already delivered the entrance ticket for the ball. Th— is so depressed and that made me so, too. – At noon she cheered up a little. – At lunch there was the same group as yesterday but without Haydn. At 4'clock we went to the castle for the benediction. Th— sang, too. Haydn took her arm going into the Berg Kirche and was extremely gallant. The *Rector* Burgerth took my arm and we entered the church in this way. . . . Th— got so overheated when going out, during the 2 Litanies, that she had little voice left. – This grieved me very much. – Haydn waited for Th— and paid her several compliments. . . . Th— was downcast and suddenly burst into a loud fit of weeping. This shocked me so much that I assured her she wouldn't have to sing tomorrow unless her voice was better. At 8 o'clock we went home; there was a cold wind. Th— drank *Boxhörndl* tea. . . .   [Brand, 412]

Sunday, 2nd. Windy. Elsler [*sic*] had breakfast with us. – At 9:30 we went to Fuchs and then with Th— to the old [Johann Georg] Fuchs. – Th— was so afraid that she had to drink camomile tea. . . . Th— sang better than anyone had anticipated. . . . After lunch [Anna] Rhumfeld and [Josepha] Hammer came . . . at about 5 o'clock we promenaded along the shooting range. – Haydn met us at the gate and walked with us . . . at about 10 o'clock we went to the Castle Ball. – It was a strait-laced occasion.   [Brand, 412; Rosenbaum, 97 (both with cuts)]

Wednesday, 5th: . . . In the morning we went to Oberberg to see Haydn at the castle, but we did not find him; then to Fuchs's, then home to lunch . . .
[Rosenbaum, 97]

Thursday, 6th: . . . Haydn paid a call shortly after 11. He showed us the gold medal [from Paris] with his bust and name on one side, on the other a lyre with the inscription 'To the composer of *The Creation*, performed at the Théâtre des Arts in the 9th year of the Republic (1800)'. The medal was accompanied by a letter containing the signatures of all the artists who had taken part. – He requested the Prince's permission to bequeath him the medal at his death, on condition that it be placed in the treasury at Forchtenstein.   [Rosenbaum, 97f.]

Saturday, 8th: . . . we went . . . to the castle, saw the Princess's new rooms . . . then to Haydn, who made a lot of flattering remarks to Th—. . . .
[Rosenbaum, 98]

The news of Haydn's honourable treatment from the Paris musicians had also reached Vienna, and we find Count Zinzendorf writing in his Diary (Olleson, 80) under date 9 August about a small dinner party he gave, to which Baron van Swieten was invited: '. . . Swieten y precha sur le Concert de la création, et la Medaille que les François envoyent a Haydn. . . .' Perhaps Swieten helped in the formulation of Haydn's answer to Paris, or perhaps Princess Esterházy was the one who gave the composer a helping hand. He could speak French with tolerable fluency, but he was obviously not up to the following document, the French original of which has survived in a contemporary print (broadside sheet) sold at auction in 1973 by J. A. Stargardt of Marburg/Lahn:[1]

[To the French Musicians, Paris. *French*. Answer to the letter of 20th July]

Vienna,[2] 10th August 1801.

Gentlemen,

It is the privilege of especially great artists to confer renown, and who can have greater claims to such a noble prerogative than you? You, who combine the most thorough and profound theory with the most skilful and perfect execution, who cast a veil over the composer's deficiencies, and who often discover therein beauties which the composer himself did not suspect. By thus embellishing *The Creation* you have earned the right to share in the approbation with which this composition was received. The public, too, echoes the just tribute which I must pay to you here: their appreciation of your talents is so great that your approbation ensures their own; and thus your approbation in some measure indicates to those on whom it is conferred the anticipated fame of posterity. I have often doubted whether my name would survive me; but your kindness inspires me with confidence, and the token of esteem with which you have honoured me justifies my hope that perhaps I SHALL NOT WHOLLY DIE. Yes, gentlemen, you have in one day rewarded the efforts of 60 years. You have crowned my grey hairs, and strewed flowers on the brink of my grave. My heart cannot express all that it feels, and I cannot write to you my profound gratitude and devotion. You will know how to appreciate them, however: you, gentlemen, who cultivate the arts from enthusiasm and not for gain, and who regard the gifts of fortune as naught, but fame as everything.

I am, &c.

Joseph Haydn.

[CCLN, 188f.]

The last entry in Rosenbaum's Diary during his trip to Eisenstadt which is of any significance for us occurs on the following day:

Tuesday, 11th August 1801: . . . Haydn sent [Johann] Elsler [*sic*] in the morning to invite us at 7:30 p.m. to the [*Gasthaus zum*] Engel again. – . . . it poured with rain all afternoon and evening. Haydn sent us the coach . . . to drive us to supper at the Engel inn. – [Luigi] Tomasini [Sr.], his wife and both sons dined with us. – It was a most enjoyable evening, and lasted until 11; Haydn was most exhilarated, drove with us into town and amazed us with his gallant compliments.

[Rosenbaum, 98]

Rosenbaum's mother lived in Eisenstadt and it is not at all clear from the documents whether the couple simply came on a social visit, during which Therese was casually asked to sing in a Haydn Mass, or whether she had been asked expressly to come to Eisenstadt for such a purpose. It is particularly strange that she was not asked

---

1 Item 626 of their Catalogue 'Autographen. Auktion am 20. und 21. Februar 1973'. The beginning is as follows: 'Lettre / du célèbre Haydn, / En réponse de celle que lui écrivirent les Musiciens qui ont concouru à l'exécution de l'Oratorio, en lui faisant hommage d'une médaille d'or. [text of letter:] Vienna, 10 Auguste 1801. Messieurs, C'est sur-tout aux grands Artistes qu'il appartient de dispenser la gloire; et qui, plus justement que vous, peut réclamer ce noble privilège, vous qui joignant la théorie musicale la plus profonde et la plus lumineuse à l'exécution la plus savante et la plus parfaite, jettez un voile sur les défauts des ouvrages des Compositeurs, et quelquefois y faites découvrir des beautés qu'eux-mêmes n'avoient pas soupçonnées?' etc. The writer of the Stargardt Catalogue assumes, no doubt rightly, that this print was organized by the Paris Opéra and issued in a very small edition. Another copy was sold at the Stargardt auction of 1–2 June 1976, item 636.

2 Haydn was actually in Eisenstadt, of course.

to stay on for the first performance of the *Schöpfungsmesse*; but perhaps she had previous commitments in Vienna. These little vignettes from Rosenbaum's invaluable Diary are particularly interesting to us, showing Haydn in his day-to-day life at Eisenstadt, composing his penultimate Mass (though of course Rosenbaum does not mention this), but also enjoying an active social life with his friends, giving small dinner parties rather frequently at the *Engel* (apparently his *Stammbeisel*, or regular restaurant-cum-tavern).

Haydn had now put the finishing touches on the copy of *The Seasons* for Breitkopf & Härtel and wrote the following note on the subject to Griesinger:

[To Georg August Griesinger, Vienna. *German*]
Well born,
Most highly respected Sir!
The short space of time I have in which to complete my new Mass [*Schöpfungsmesse*] does not permit me to write more than a few lines, to tell you that at last I now have the honour of sending you the complete score of *The Seasons*. I advise you to send it on to Herr Hartel [*sic*] as soon as possible; but please give our porter a receipt for it. Meanwhile I am, Sir, most respectfully,
Your most obedient servant,
Jos: Haydn.
Eisenstadt, 21st August 1801
[No address; on reverse side the following note in another hand: '1801/the 21st August' and to the right, 'Eisenstadt / Haydn'.]
[CCLN, 189]

During these days, Haydn had a pleasant visitor at Eisenstadt, the well-known composer Adalbert Gyrowetz, who had been a witness of the older composer's triumphs at London in 1791 and 1792. Haydn gave the (certainly very bulky) parcel containing *The Seasons* to Gyrowetz who took it back to Vienna. A few days later[1] Gyrowetz wrote the following letter to Breitkopf & Härtel:

. . . I am very sorry indeed that this time, too, I cannot fulfil your requests about reducing [for piano] the various operatic pieces. My own compositions require so much time that I cannot take on the reduction of other masterpieces.
During these past days I visited Herr Haydn in Eisenstadt. He gave me the parcel containing *The Four Seasons* to take to Vienna and deliver it to the place from which you will have received it. I congratulate you on this purchase and wish you in advance a great success with the undertaking, which certainly will not be wanting, if we take into consideration the enormous value of this great work and consider the possible sales. Our dear, great and good Haydn remains immortal. May God preserve him for many years to come. For the encouragement of Art, and for the joy of his admirers and his friends. . . .

News of Breitkopf & Härtel's acquisition travelled quickly, for those days. Anticipating the same kind of sensation with which *The Creation* was greeted in

---

1 This unpublished letter was sold by auction at Sotheby's (19 December 1960, lot 178, purchased by Hans Schneider); the Sotheby Catalogue dates the letter '30 August 1801' but in the transcription that our kind friend Albi Rosenthal made for us, the date is '20 August', though the figure in question is difficult to read, apparently. We suggest that 30 August is the correct date. This date is also suggested by a letter from Haydn to Swieten of 26 August. It appears that Haydn had borrowed the autograph of *The Seasons* which he needed to prepare the final version for Leipzig. We have only the date and contents: 'Eisenstadt, 26th August 1801. / Excellency!' [The letter accompanied the shipment 'by the diligence' of the score of *The Seasons*.] (CCLN, 190). Even the addressee's name is uncertain.

England, an enterprising German bookseller in Soho started to offer the forthcoming score and piano score even before the work was on the market:

> For the new musical piece of Haydn, intitled [*sic*] the Seasons, which is now publishing in Germany with the English and German text, Mr. Escher, German book-seller, in Gerard-street, Soho, takes subscriptions at 18*s*. a copy adapted to the harpsichord, and at 2*l*. 2*s*. a copy in score.
>
> [*The Monthly Magazine*, 1 January 1802, p. 545]

For some odd reason, Mr Escher obviously miscalculated the price, but in the event, English interest in the Oratorio was to be minimal.

Haydn now interrupted his quiet sojourn in Eisenstadt. On 28 August Griesinger wrote to Breitkopf & Härtel that Haydn's housekeeper expected him back in Vienna that evening. '. . . Haydn must be here by now. . . .'[1] Apparently the composer went to meet his brother, Johann Michael, who had been invited to compose a new Mass for the Empress Marie Therese. The *Missa sotto il titulo di S. Theresia* was completed on 3 August and, together with a Te Deum, was given a kind of general rehearsal at Salzburg on 25 August. Archduke Johann was present. Abbot Domenikus of St Peter's Abbey wrote: 'The music turned out to be masterly and won the great admiration of the Archduke and all those present.'

One of Michael's friends, the merchant, Georg von Reich, wanted to organize a consortium of friends to supply the composer with sufficient money to spend his declining years in Vienna; the sum necessary was left to Michael to decide. This time, the composer was accompanied by Pastor Rettensteiner, who later contributed to the first biography of the master and had been an intimate friend of long standing. Presumably Haydn met the friends in Vienna and took them back to Eisenstadt. There, the three Haydn brothers met for the first time in years. The *Stadtpfarrer* (parish priest) of Eisenstadt, Andreas Weghofer, invited the illustrious guests to lunch. Another time the two horn players of the Esterházy band, Anton and Michael Prinster, gave the Haydns an evening serenade. It is always asserted that Michael Haydn was present at the première of the *Schöpfungsmesse*, which is said to have occurred on Sunday, 13 September 1801, the Princess's name-day (St Mary's Day); in a letter to his wife, however, Michael states that he had an audience with the Empress on 9 September. We suggest that either he went to Eisenstadt first, returning to Vienna for the audience, or he went to Eisenstadt afterwards, in which case he certainly would have attended the new Mass. The sources do not give us further information. Rettensteiner has given us details of the audience. She: 'You haven't made the soprano part too difficult? I shall sing it myself. Oh, I know some of your compositions, and especially your *Requiem* [for Archbishop Schrattenbach's Death, 1771], which I know well and love.' In a letter to his wife, Michael relates this and other events:

> à Madame Madelaine Haydn, ma très cher [*sic*] Femme à Salzbourg / Vienna, the 24th of September, St Rupert's Day, 1801.
>
> Dearest Wife!
> I am well and hope the same of you and my good and true friends. Though I've found some new friends, there was no Georg v. Reich; I always miss him. But you mustn't fear at all that I shall stay here, for it is much too dear. Two single cords of wood cost my dear cousin v. Eybler 30 fl.
> On the 9th inst. I had an audience with Her Majesty the Empress. Her goodness, gentleness and condescension I found quite enchanting; and I had to

---

1 Olleson, *Griesinger*, 25; Pohl III, 189; Jancik, *Michael Haydn* (1952), pp. 235ff.

remind myself that I was talking with an Empress so that my tone would not become too familiar.

Yesterday morning at 10 o'clock was rehearsal for the Mass. At the beginning the Empress sang her solos rather shyly, but with gradually increasing courage, but especially the Et incarnatus est de spiritu sancto ex Maria Virgine (she did very well in all these) and the Benedictus was very correct and nicely done. That which pleased me the most was her satisfaction with my composition. One time after another: Bravo, beautiful; and her highest expression was: Haydn! Superb!

Don't be jealous. I have quite fallen in love with my gracious Empress. And she is a dear, lovely woman. The rest Pastor Rettensteiner will tell you in more detail; and he will also tell you what happened with my dear brother and a hundred other things. . . .

On 4 October 1801, Michael conducted the 'Theresa' Mass at Laxenburg Castle (the summer residence of the Court). It was certainly the spectacular success of the Mass, and its composer's visit to Eisenstadt, that prompted Prince Nicolaus, realizing that his own *Kapellmeister's* energies were waning, to offer a handsome job to Michael. In the event, as we shall see, Michael decided not to accept the offer, which he considered for some time. (As late as 7 April 1803 he wrote to Rettensteiner, 'With all this it will be difficult for me to enter Esterházy's service or I shall have to be late in doing so.') But at the beginning, Michael seems to have half-accepted[1] the offer, for the *AMZ* of November 1801 informs its readers that Prince Esterházy has now taken Herr *Kapellmeister* Michael Haydn into his service; *AMZ* further notes that Michael has few rivals in the church music style of really serious, religious music. In January 1802, *AMZ* continues its report, saying that Michael has received a very satisfactory contract with Esterházy and was mainly given the post so that his brother Joseph could enjoy the peace he wished for. It was not until April 1804 that *AMZ* finally denied the rumours and informed its readers that Michael would remain at Salzburg with a salary of 600 Gulden, a figure that *AMZ* found so low that they thought their readers would imagine it to be a printer's error (*AMZ* IV, 126, 264; VI, 450).

Two days before the first performance of the Mass, Haydn took the time to write a letter of recommendation to the son of his old friend, the 'cellist Joseph Weigl (whose eldest-born was Haydn's godchild).

[To Thaddäus Weigl,[2] Vienna. *German*]
Dearest Friend!

I consider myself fortunate to be able to do you a small favour by writing you a certificate, the more so since, without any flattery, you really do deserve this important position more than anybody else, because of your many and varied merits, and your understanding of the subject. I congratulate you, and very much

---

1 The Esterházy Archives provide us with positive information that Michael Haydn had at least agreed, in the Autumn of 1801, to supply some new church music to Prince Nicolaus, for in a letter dated Salzburg, 6 February 1802, Michael writes to the Prince that he has suffered a fall on the icy ground and sprained his right hand; he will try to supply the mass and the vesper by June or July. Michael wonders if he will receive the necessary permission to leave the Archbishop's service. Valkó II, 620.

It was on the occasion of this visit that Michael Haydn, together with Joseph Rettensteiner, went to see Joseph Haydn in his Gumpendorf house. Michael admired the canons hung on the wall and asked to have them copied, whereupon Joseph replied, 'Get away with you, you're capable of writing better ones yourself.' We have the story from Rettensteiner, who was a witness. Schmid, 258.

2 Thaddäus – or, as he called himself in later years, Thaddé – was born about 1774 and died in 1844. In 1801, he applied for, and received, permission to open a music-dealer's business (*Kunsthändlerbefugnis*), and Haydn's letter and certificate were obviously written to help Weigl secure the necessary permit from the Vienna City authorities.

wish I could write more, but I'm a poor old fellow because of my new Mass,[1] which I'm just finishing, and which is to be performed the day after tomorrow. Meanwhile I hope to see you soon in Vienna, and remain, my dearest Friend, with every esteem,

Your most willing servant,
Joseph Haydn [m.p] ria.

Eisenstadt, 11th September 1801.

[No address; Weigl notes: 'Father Haydn, from Eisenstadt / 11th Sept. 801/received 14th Sept. 801'.]

[CCLN 190]

[Certificate for Thaddäus Weigl. *German*. From an old copy]
Certificate
I, the undersigned, declare publicly and to all those whom it may concern that the music engraved under the supervision of Herr Thadäus [*sic*] Weigl distinguishes itself, over and above everyone else's, to his great advantage; which one would easily expect from such a man as Herr Thadäus Weigl, inasmuch as he himself is a composer, and possesses all the knowledge necessary to conduct such a business successfully. This is also to the obvious advantage of the state, since then it would no longer be necessary for our native composers to have their works sent abroad to be engraved.

At his request, and for his benefit, I have enumerated all these circumstances, which are entirely truthful, and set my hand and seal to this certificate.
Eisenstand [*sic*], 11th September 1801.

Joseph Haydn.
[CCLN, 190f.]

Our only knowledge of the festivities in connection with Princess Marie's name-day comes from the Hungarian newspaper *Magyar Hirmondó*:

. . . The name-day of Princess Esterházy was celebrated the day before yesterday. There arrived many guests even from Vienna, among them Cardinal Prince Albani, Muravief-Apostol the Russian Envoy Extraordinary, and also Prince Carl Schwarzenberg who had returned from St Petersburg. I do not feel competent enough to describe all the splendour, such as the dancing, the illumination of the ceremonial hall with eight hundred candles, the opulent dinners and suppers, the deafening roar of the cannon and the wonderful music in the evening.

[1801, II, 428–31; Horanyi, 171f.]

The high point of all these ceremonies was, of course, the great ecclesiastical service on Sunday morning, 13 September, at the Bergkirche, with the first performance of Haydn's great Mass for the occasion, the *Schöpfungsmesse* – so called because of a quotation from the Oratorio in the passage Qui tollis peccata mundi (*vide infra*, p. 204).

On 16 September the *AMZ* published a letter from Paris, in which the gold medal struck for Haydn is mentioned, as well as the letter from the 142 musicians (which *AMZ* quote quoted in the original French).

Perhaps [continues the report] it will amuse you, and no doubt also the Orpheus of Germany, if I relate to you the following about the last *concert de la Rue de Clary*. The members of this society, who insisted on paying tribute to Haydn, tried in vain to locate a bust of this great man, which they intended to erect, as a sort of crown, in the temple largely dedicated to him. The coronation followed

---

1 The *Schöpfungsmesse*.

the performance of one of his finest symphonies, given to a thousand-fold applause of a huge group of the most educated amateurs. In the general enthusiasm no one noticed that the bronze bust was hardly a real Haydn but a head of Cato from the antique, and on the pedestal of the bust one could read, in golden letters, 'To the Immortal Haydn'. We need not add that this noble homage was not a bit less heartfelt for that reason. Few people in France, various German artists living among us excepted, have had the fortune to meet Haydn personally. The medal is from a portrait of Haydn's, said to be a good likeness, that one ordered from Germany.   [III, 838f.]

On 18 September Griesinger reports to Breitkopf & Härtel:

. . . Haydn's brother from Salzburg had been here for some days; Brother Joseph must help celebrate birthdays and name-days for Esterházy. Yesterday his housekeeper assured me that he will certainly be here in a few days; then I will ask him about having Gyrowetz or Wranitz[ky] [do the arrangement of *The Seasons*], and if he allows I will get an impression of his medal in tinfoil and send it to you.

Once again my most profound and heartfelt thanks for your very noble present.

Your most grateful and most sincere
Griesinger.

[Olleson *Griesinger*, 25]

Meanwhile Gyrowetz had already turned down the offer and in the final event it was A. E. Müller who did the quintet arrangement *à la* Wranizky with the previous Oratorio. Breitkopf & Härtel had sent Griesinger a handsome present for his part in the successful negotiations to secure the rights of *The Seasons*.

In the midst of the celebrations at Eisenstadt, Prince Nicolaus found time to send to his *Kapellmeister* the following letter:

[*German*]
To Herr *Kapellmeister* Haydn:
I urge you to bear in mind that the members of the band[1] must appear at all times with their uniforms clean and neat, and with powdered wigs. Disobedience will result in the offender being dismissed from the band.
Eisenstadt, 26th September 1801.   [Exp. Esterházy]

[CCLN, 191]

On 1 October Haydn wrote to Griesinger:

[To Georg August Griesinger, Vienna. *German*]
Well born,
Most highly respected Sir!
I, too, regret that I did not have the honour of seeing you, Sir, in Vienna last time, but I hope to wait on you there very soon. Meanwhile I am sending you, Sir, the proof-impression you wanted of the medal,[2] and trust that Herr Härtel will be satisfied with it. As far as the arrangement of *The Seasons* for quartet or quintet is concerned, I think that Herr Wranizky,[3] [*Kapellmeister*] at Prince Lobkowitz, should receive the preference, not only because of his fine arrangement of *The Creation*, but also because I am sure that he will not make use of it to further his

---

1 A translation can hardly convey the arrogant German of 'Chormusik Individuen'; Esterházy also used this expression in the letter of 14 August 1802.
2 The gold medal sent by the Parisian artists.
3 Anton Wranizky, Paul's brother. Artaria had issued Wranizky's arrangement of *The Creation* for string quintet (2 V., 2 Ve., Vc.) in March (pl. no. 850).

own ends. In the near future you, Sir, will receive from Herr Baron van Swieten one or two sections of *The Seasons* with the English and French texts added. Meanwhile I have the honour to be, Sir, most respectfully,

Your most obedient servant,
Joseph Haydn.

Eisenstadt, 1st October 1801. [CCLN, 191]

And on 7 October the composer wrote to George Thomson, enclosing several changed violin parts to Scottish songs:

[To George Thomson, Edinburgh. *Italian*]

Eisenstadt, 7th October 1801.

Most esteemed Friend!

I send you herewith the violin accompaniment to the songs you requested, marked with the Numbers 1, 2, 3, 4, 5, 6, 7, 8, and trust that I have hit upon your taste. I have also altered the *ritornello* of No. 15, and added codas to Nos. 2, 9, 24 and 25, as you wished. I shall make every effort to satisfy you in the other songs, but you must be patient for a little while longer, and remember that I am now very old.

Send me the words of the 6 canzonettas, and I shall let you know in a short while how long it will take me to compose them; but I am not capable of composing the *Sonatine* for pianoforte and harp, for I am now too weak to do so.

I am eternally grateful to you for the handkerchiefs and for the beautiful snuff-box, which I treasure more than if it were made of gold. Please be good enough to mention to me someone in the Embassy who can take the place of Mr Straton in respect of our negotiations.

Meanwhile, esteemed Friend, I am, most respectfully,

Your indebted servant,
Joseph Haydn.

[CCLN, 192]

Breitkopf & Härtel had been offered Haydn's Masses, as we have seen, but they had refused; they then seem to have had second thoughts. We read in Griesinger's letter to the firm of 10 October:

. . . I shall certainly not forget about the Masses, but please be patient till I can speak to Hn. personally again. If we have to correspond about it, Hn. won't give anything away for nothing. There is no more talk of the trip to Paris . . . Haydn is going to take quarters in town this winter. . . .   [Olleson, *Griesinger*, 26]

Haydn had hoped to conduct *The Seasons* in Paris. The winter quarters proved too damp, and Haydn remained in his house in Gumpendorf. In this same letter Griesinger advises the Leipzig firm to send a copy of *The Seasons* to the Empress, 'as a great connoisseur and friend of music', though they can hardly count on payment.[1]

On 14 October, Count von Razumovsky returned to Vienna and presented his ambassadorial credentials to the Emperor 'with the usual ceremony and with a large following' (*Wiener Zeitung* No. 84, 21 October 1801). Although the Count has gone down in history as Beethoven's patron, we have seen that Haydn, too, played a by no means unimportant role in the Russian patron's artistic life; and Haydn must have been glad to welcome him back to the Austrian capital.

1 Olleson, *Griesinger*, 26; Pohl III, 191f.

Among the honours coming to Haydn from all over Europe, we have noted (p. 48f.) his membership in the Dutch Society 'Felix Meritis'. The composer now wrote them an official letter, thanking them for their attention. It is interesting that a shortened version of the Society's letter and Haydn's full answer were printed in the *Pressburger Zeitung* (No. 85, 27 October 1801).[1]

[To the 'Felix Meritis' Society, Amsterdam. *German*. Answer to the letter of 4 May]
Learned Gentlemen!

I regard the generous approbation with which the efforts of my small talents have been hitherto received almost everywhere as a most beautiful reward, but also the only one I could have promised myself up to now. But when a company of men, who are brought together by no title other than that of true merit, decides to elect me to its distinguished circle, then I cast my eye over 70 full years of uninterrupted devotion to an art which now, in my old age, proves to be such a rich source of honour and delight. Yes, Honourable Gentlemen, you fill my soul with the sweetest emotions, you revive an aged man and give him new strength; for you give me the flattering reassurance that, even if posterity does not cherish my works, my name, shining in the reflected brilliance of your own, will not wholly disappear in the stream of oblivion. As a result of this dignified public monument which you so nobly offer at the shrine of this art, posterity must ever be in your debt: for by your noble actions you awake sleeping talents. You show them the path, and also the reward which awaits them at the goal. Receive, therefore, the heartfelt assurance that my soul is filled with the deepest gratitude for the flattering marks of honour you have shown me. When my course is run, I shall pass on in complete peace of mind, filled with the happy thought that my place will never be empty, when true merits unite to guard and protect the art.

I have the honour to be, with every esteem,
Learned Gentlemen,
Your willing and obedient servant,
Joseph Haydn.

Eisenstadt, 18th October 1801.   [CCLN, 192f.]

The proofs of *The Seasons* now arrived. Haydn had expected them little by little and was rather alarmed at the prospect of correcting (as it would seem) some 400 pages of score. It is astonishing that Breitkopf & Härtel, who had received the score, *via* Gyrowetz and Griesinger, about the first week in September at the earliest could have engraved as much of the score as they apparently had in the short space of six weeks. (It may be that Breitkopf & Härtel were merely *announcing* the forthcoming arrival of the proof.) On 21 October Haydn writes to Baron van Swieten:

[To Baron Gottfried van Swieten, Vienna. *German*]
Excellence!

The great number of all sorts of works which had to be copied for the Princely band was responsible for the long delay.

I took the liberty of sending the whole score[2] to Your Excellency, because some of the things which I had added afterwards were not included, as Your Excellency will see by comparing the sign [left blank].

For rather a long time I have had no news either from Herr Hartel [*sic*] or from his business representative Herr von Griesinger, and I am very surprised at his

1 The interested reader may consult the original as well as a complete English translation in *Haydn Yearbook* VIII (1971), pp. 208, 281f.
2 This letter refers to *The Seasons*, the score of which Haydn had just sent to van Swieten.

announcement, for he promised to send the proofs to me, little by little, as they appeared. I would therefore beg Your Excellency to ask Herr von Griesinger to come to you, explain to him all the necessary points, so that Your Excellency will be satisfied. Next week I shall have the pleasure of waiting on you. Meanwhile I remain, with profound respect,

Your Excellency's most humble and obedient servant,

Joseph Haydn.

Eisenstadt, 21st October 1801.

[No address; in another hand the following notes (German): 'To the Baron van Swieten, Principal Imperial & Royal Librarian, and the author of the libretti of Haydn's *Creation* and *Seasons*'.] [CCLN, 193f.]

Baron van Swieten was not pleased at hearing these excuses by Haydn, who seems to have tried to shift some of the proof-reading on to the Baron's shoulders. Griesinger, writing to Leipzig on 24 October, informs us that Swieten maintains 'that it is just an *incuria* on Haydn's part, who on account of his (as they say last) Mass for Prince Esterházy has forgotten everything . . . Next week Haydn returns here . . .' (Olleson, *Griesinger*, 26).

On 25 October there was a celebration at St Stephen's Cathedral in honour of the fifty year jubilee of Cardinal Archbishop, Count Migazzi von Waal und Sonnenthurn, who had been Archbishop of Vienna since 1757 and had obviously watched Haydn's career with interest. After the *Te Deum* (composed, appropriately, by Haydn's teacher, Georg Reutter Jr., we read in the *Wiener Zeitung* (No. 87, 31 October 1801): '. . . The moving music [of the Mass] by Joseph Hayden, the festive atmosphere and the great dignity with which the whole ceremony was conducted, left a profound impression in all hearts.'

Possibly Haydn was on hand for this ceremony; the sources do not say; but he was certainly in Vienna two days later, for we find him writing to Thomson on that date:

[To George Thomson, Edinburgh. *Italian*]

Vienna, 27th October 1801.

Most esteemed Friend,
I now send you the arias you asked for, beginning with Number 14 and ending with No. 22. I sincerely hope that you will be satisfied with them. I could have made the *ritornelli* still longer, but the proportions of the songs do not allow it. I shall make every effort to complete all the others, and hope to send them in a little while. I would only ask you to designate another person to take Mr Straton's place. Meanwhile I am, dear Friend,

Your most sincere friend and servant,

[signature omitted].

[No address; Thomson's clerk notes: 'Haydn / Vienne 27th Octr. / 1801.— / With Symphs & Accpts to 9 Scottish Airs'.] [CCLN, 194]

Concerning these Scottish Songs, it may be (as we have noted earlier in this Chronicle) that Haydn's pupils wrote the actual songs, but it is probable that the sort of changes that Thomson was now requiring were made by Haydn himself: it was quicker and more certain to do such changes at once rather than send for a pupil and then, perhaps, have to correct his work. It is also obvious that Haydn actually wrote a certain amount of the songs himself, if only to show his pupils how the works should be fashioned.

Griesinger was now asked to procure the detailed list of Haydn's English subscribers (with exact addresses) for Breitkopf & Härtel's edition of *The Seasons*. But as we have seen, Haydn had only detailed addresses for those subscribers with whom he had corresponded personally. On 4 November Griesinger writes:

> . . . Hn. has no detailed list of subscribers in England. Salomon, Clementi and a Dr Burnet [Burney] took over that job for him . . . Prince Esterházy has taken his [Haydn's] brother from Salzburg into his service; church music is the Prince's passion. Concerning Swieten's plans (about which I wrote to you recently) Haydn knew nothing, eacn one puts the blame of *incuriae* on the other [*The Seasons'* corrections]. Apart from his Mass, Haydn has arranged twenty Scottish Songs for the Edinburgh publisher Thomson . . . I have made approaches about the Masses; Hn. thinks the publishers would make a good thing out of them, but Prince Esterházy won't even let the Empress have the newest ones; I couldn't get more out of him as he was just going out. . . . [Olleson *Griesinger*, 26]

Baron van Swieten's plan is revealed in another extract from this invaluable Griesinger correspondence; the Baron said he intended 'to arrange one more tragic and one more comic subject for Haydn, to convince the world of Haydn's all-embracing genius' (Pohl III, 179), and early in 1802 he told Griesinger that he 'was working once again on a new piece of work for Haydn'. The composer, however, was now most reluctant to set another Swieten libretto, for reasons which will be discussed *infra*, in connection with their stormy collaboration on *The Seasons*.

On 7 November the *Wiener Zeitung* printed Breitkopf & Härtel's announcement for the new Oratorio:

> Announcement of the publication of Haydn's *The Four Seasons* . . . The printing of the score and piano score is already completed, and before the end of the year we shall surely deliver them to the amateurs . . . Of the score and piano score two versions will be delivered, one with German and French texts, and one with German and English texts . . . The score and piano score will be embellished by an engraving of two of the most excellent German artists and will appear in a clean and highly elegant cover . . . The score will probably consist of over 100 *Bogen* [4 sheets], the piano of over 40 *Bogen* in large format . . . The subscription price of the score is 8 rthlr. (Saxon) or 14 fl. in Viennese currency, the piano score 3 rthlr. or 5 fl. 30 kr.
>
> Breitkopf & Härtel in Leipzig.

Subscriptions will be received by Johann Traeg, No. 957 in the Singerstraße.
[*WZ* No. 89.]

On 11 November we have a long letter from Griesinger to Breitkopf & Härtel (saved for posterity only because the late Dr Carl Maria Brand made a copy of it, as of many others, before the collection was destroyed in an air raid during the Second World War):

> . . . Father Haydn has a cold that has kept him in bed for several days; now he's better. The trip to Paris is not to be thought of yet; they encourage him greatly but without fixed commissions and without (as was the case with his trip to England) sending him a substantial sum in advance as an indemnity. I found the opportunity to make the proposal to him about the Masses and since I heard that the last one turned out to be particularly excellent I asked for that one. Hn. answered that Prince Esterházy would permit your announcement only after a few years have passed; the Empress asked him for it but he avoided the question and he will give it

only under the condition that the Empress gives him the Mass which Michael Haydn recently composed for her. Some of the earlier ones [by Joseph] are to be had; but since Hn. himself does not know which of them is in public circulation or which you have already, you should send him a catalogue of those church music works, *viz*. Masses, Te Deum, Salve, which are already in circulation so that he can make the right choice. He did not say if he would give them *gratis*; I left matters therefore with a gentle hint since the affair must be postponed in any case until your catalogue arrives. He would not advise publishing his *first* Masses, however, for they are not in today's taste; he mentioned a Te Deum which he composed two or three years ago for the Empress. It does not seem that you have any competition; Pleyel however will certainly consider the matter when, as it appears, the Catholic Religion is introduced into France again. He recently sent Hn. a copy of his magnificent edition of the quartets (an undertaking in which he dared to invest 40,000 fl.). Hn. is very satisfied with it not only because of the beautiful paper and print but because one can see his progress step by step in the art because of the clever [chronological] order. . . .

. . . You announced to me that you would send a copy of *The Seven Words* for the composer, but I have not yet received it. . . .   [Olleson, *Griesinger*, 27]

The Empress finally did receive the *Schöpfungsmesse*; her copy will be discussed *infra*. The significance of the remark '. . . two or three years ago for the Empress . . .' has been discussed in the context of the *Te Deum* of 1800 (see *Haydn: the Years of 'The Creation' 1796–1800*, p. 605). The earlier Masses to which Haydn refers are probably the two 'short' works (*Missa brevis* in F, *Missa brevis alla cappella* 'Rorate coeli desuper' in G) and presumably also the *Missa in honorem B.V.M.* ['Grosse Orgelmesse'] in E flat, none of which Breitkopf published. In Pleyel's edition were not only the very early Quartets known to us as Opp. 1 and 2 (with some horn parts omitted) but also the spurious Op. 3 (by Roman Hoffstetter – see *Haydn: the Years of 'The Creation' 1796–1800*, p. 597); thus Haydn's examination of the Pleyel set was probably somewhat casual, and moreover he hardly remembered many of those works composed half a century before.

The complimentary copy of the Oratorio arrived and Haydn was very pleased with it. Griesinger reports:

14 November 1801

. . . He was exceedingly pleased with its elegance, the engraving and your kind gift; he asked me to thank you most cordially. He lifted hmself from his simple bed with youthful good humour, forgot his pains, looked through the whole thing and found everything first-rate.

On the 18th we learn from Griesinger that 'Haydn got a relapse of his cold from going out too soon'; this is one more sign that the old composer's robust health had indeed suffered from constant overwork in the last few years. Ten days later, Griesinger was given the trombone parts to *The Seasons*, and also a page of missing percussion parts:

28 November 1801.

. . . Here, my friend, follows a new parcel from Swieten; but what will interest you more are the trombone parts to *The Seasons* which Haydn, Heaven knows why, has just sent, together with another page which must be inserted into the score. I remember that the triangle and tambourine made a surprising effect at this point. Moreover Haydn let me know that in *The Seven Words* the wind band piece has the tempo 'Largo' instead of 'poco Largo'. . . .

The missing parts for the Oratorio arrived too late to be put into the score in their proper places, and the publishers had to print the trombones as a supplement. In the drinking chorus (Autumn) the score reads 'von hier an, bis zu Ende des Chors, spielt Triangel und Tambourin mit', which was the best they could do at this late date. In *The Seven Words* the 'Introduzione' before No. 5 has, as the tempo, 'Largo è Cantabile', which should read 'Poco Largo è cantabile' – a hint not to take the sombre piece too slowly.

Despite all the precautions taken by everyone to prevent *The Seasons* falling into improper hands, a copy was smuggled out and Spehr of Braunschweig (Brunswick) soon announced that he would issue the work at the end of the year. Griesinger, writing on 3 December, said: 'The impudence of H. Spelz [*sic*] must be punished'. Within a few days, Haydn constructed a letter (see *infra*, 6 December) which established that Breitkopf & Härtel were the proper owners of the Oratorio. The publishers themselves issued a sharp denunciation of the whole venture under the title, 'Schlechte Spekulation', in the *Intelligenz-Blatt* No. II of the *AMZ* (November 1801).[1] Haydn thought that Hoffmeister, who in fact ordered eighty copies from Spehr and who announced the subscription for it in the *Wiener Zeitung* on 18 November, must have had a hand in the pirated edition (Hase, 32). Spehr's edition, which was not complete (e.g. all the choruses were omitted), was certainly real competition for Breitkopf, for the Braunschweig edition printed a subscription list with an advance sale of no less than 483 copies. Haydn may have flirted, earlier in the year, with other publishers: at one time he seems even to have offered the work to Bernhard Schott in Mainz, for Schott, writing on 13 June 1801 to his friend, the *Kanonikus* Batton, informs us that unfortunately he had to inform Haydn that, 'à Cause de la politique [the Treaty of Lunéville decreed that the left bank of the Rhine would remain French] et par raisons des difficultés techniques et personnelles', he could not publish *The Seasons*.[2] But now that Haydn had signed with Breitkopf & Härtel, his loyalties were entirely with the Leipzig firm.

Griesinger was soon able to tell his friend of some new Haydn works which would be eminently suitable for publication, the part songs (*Mehrstimmige Lieder*). At the beginning of December he wrote that Haydn 'has completed thirteen of them, which he showed to me. But now his work proceeds slowly and he needs texts, because (as he assured me) few poets write musically' (Olleson, *Griesinger*, 29ff.). Since negotiations for these part-songs continued for several years, we follow Olleson's good example and interrupt the Chronicle here to relate the rather amusing story of these works. Actually Haydn had completed these thirteen songs by 1799, but the composer wanted to make up a collection of twenty-five. 'Haydn won't negotiate until there are a full twenty-five, however, for 'if I am going to print something, it has to be rather big [in dialect: "ein bisserl groß"].' With texts you could do Haydn a favour, but nothing high-flown [*verstiegenes*] and no involved periods. . . . [Haydn said] the songs were just written *con amore*, in happy hours, without any commission.' Breitkopf & Härtel quite rightly doubted whether Haydn would write the missing songs and offered 300 Gulden. The composer accepted, though he said to Griesinger '. . . if Herr Härtel knew how my songs were composed, he would gladly admit that I should have earned more than 300 gulden for them.' On 15 January 1802 Griesinger wrote: '. . . With the three- and four-part songs by Haydn we are now rather in the

1 Reprinted in Hase, 31f.
2 Archives of the publishers Schott in Mainz, published in Hoboken II, 66.

clear . . . [He] said he was proud of [them].' At this point one of Beethoven's patrons, Johann Georg, Count von Browne-Camus, unexpectedly sent Haydn 500 gulden for twelve of the songs. 'This argument was too strong for Haydn to resist', and later (in 1805) the composer gave the autographs to the Count. Breitkopf & Härtel had to abandon the songs' publication for the moment.

Meanwhile an odd story set Haydn's fertile mind to work on other ways for realizing money on the songs. An Austrian courier had taken – 'at his own instigation and at his own risk' – a copy of the Grassi bust of Haydn for the Russian Tsar.

> . . . The Emperor [continues Griesinger] gave him a *tabatière* which is valued at 300 ducats. Old Papa was most annoyed that he hadn't made that speculation himself. But now he wants to entrap the Russian Emperor in another fashion and dedicate to him a work in the form of a swan-song. For this purpose he chose the songs which he had composed six months ago for Count Braun [*sic*] and for which 500 fl. were paid. Count Braun, from some unaccountable negligence, has not even sent to have the songs collected and has given up the plan he had made for them. Haydn, who hopes to collect another 500 fl. from a publisher, asked Count Braun if he would renounce the songs upon the money being returned to him. Braun was so polite as to answer that he did not want the money again but only a copy of the songs, and otherwise Haydn may dispose of the originals as he sees fit.
> . . .

Haydn intended to dedicate a printed edition to the Tsar, so that there would be the distinct possibility of a publisher's fee and a handsome present from the ruler, or rather from the Dowager Tsarina, Maria Feodorovna, who would have remembered Haydn from 1782, when she had taken some lessons from the composer. Thus Haydn again offered the songs to Leipzig; first they were refused, but then Breitkopf & Härtel changed their minds and bought them for 400 gulden. Griesinger drafted a letter for Haydn to obtain the Tsarina's approval of the dedication, which 'he only needed to copy out' (2 February 1803), but at the last minute Haydn had qualms of conscience. 'Because of a (to me quite inexplicable) sense of reticence, he has given up the idea of the dedication. He is afraid that the Prince and Swieten will accuse him of beggary if they learned that he had received a present.' The texts did not meet with unanimous approval – Haydn's choice of texts seldom did –, and Griesinger explained: 'It seems Haydn is predestined for bad texts; actually he is at fault because of his unscientific education. He never let me read the songs (except for one: "Der Augenblick"), but sent them sealed up either for you or for Swieten.' Finally the songs did appear, in the eighth and ninth volumes of the *Oeuvres Complettes* (1803). A presentation copy was sent to the Tsarina, and that excellent lady promptly sent Haydn a diamond ring. Haydn told Griesinger, 'Herr Härtel sent a really very nice letter about the songs.' Olleson, on whose research this whole section dealing with the part-songs is based, concludes: 'Griesinger no doubt observed that, instead of the original offer of 300 gulden for the songs, Haydn had received: from the publishers 400 gulden, from Count Browne 500 gulden, and from the Tsarina a valuable gift' (31) – not a bad profit for works written 'con amore'.

The following correspondence is self-explanatory:

[To George Thomson, Edinburgh. *Italian*]
Most esteemed Friend,
    I now send you the rest of the songs, and I am quite convinced that they could not better be done: for I have taken great pains to satisfy you, and to show the

world how far a man can progress in his art, especially in this *genre* of composition [*modulazione*], if he is willing to exert himself; and I wish that every student of composition would try his hand at this type of music. In time, the fruits of their efforts would surely be well rewarded.

I flatter myself that with this work I shall go on living in Scotland many years after my death. I would only ask you to send me a copy, when it is printed. In the hope of receiving your kind favour very soon, I am,

Dearest Friend,

Your sincere and most humble servant,

Giuseppe Haydn.

Vienna, 5th December 1801.

[Address:]   George Thomson. Esq[r]
        Trustees Office.   [Postal stamps indicating
        Edinburgh   date of arrival in England,
         North Britain.   and then in Scotland:
       [With Haydn's seal 'JH'] 'Foreign Office De[c.] 28,
                 1801' and 'De[c.] 31, 1801'

[Thomson or Thomson's clerk notes: 'Haydn/Vienna 5 Dec 1801/With more Scotish [*sic*]/Airs harmonized etc./by him – and mentioning HIS HOPE THAT HIS NAME WILL BY MEANS OF THESE AIRS LIVE IN SCOTLAND LONG AFTER HIS DEATH.']

[CCLN, 194f.]

[To Breitkopf & Härtel, Leipzig. *German*. Only the signature autograph]

I declare herewith that the firm of Breitkopf und Härtel in Leipzig is the only rightful publisher of my composition entitled *The Seasons* for the whole of Germany.

Joseph Haydn.

Vienna, 6th December 1801.   [CCLN, 195]

[Luigi Tomasini to Prince Nicolaus II Esterházy, passed on to Haydn for recommendation, with Haydn's answer. *German*]

[Vienna, *c.* 5th December 1801]

Your Highness!

The undersigned would certainly find it difficult to make this request, were not the greatly increased living costs – felt by everyone – such as to affect him and his family, and were he not in any case deprived of all extra benefits, also his usual winter trip which he has not been able to make for some years, and which used to be such a pleasant contribution to his well-being.

But convinced of his Prince's great generosity, judged merely by the many acts of kindness shown during these past years, and by the noble principle he has maintained in not letting anyone suffer: – convinced by all these noble-minded acts, he dares in all humility to request Your Highness in his graciousness to grant him a small increase in salary, which graciousness he will repay with gratitude and diligence to his duties.

Your Serene Highness'

most humble and most obedient

Luigi Tomasini.

[On the file's cover:]

To be sent to *Kapellmeister* Haydn for his opinion and report.

Exp. Esterhazy.

[Haydn's answer:]

Inasmuch as His Serene Highness, our Prince, blessed by God, has in his graciousness assisted almost all the personnel serving His Highness during these highly expensive times, I would ask that the old Luigi Tomasini be supported in some small measure.

Jos. Haydn [m.p.] ria.
[CCLN, 196]

[Prince Nicolaus Esterházy's decision:]
[Reverse side of Tomasini's petition:] In consideration of the present rise in basic costs of living, the suppliant is graciously granted herewith an increase in his yearly salary of one-hundred and fifty gulden.

Vienna, on 7th December 1801.
Nicolaus Prince. Esterházy mpria.

[To August Eberhard Müller,[1] Leipzig. *German*]
Well born,
Most highly respected Sir!

Again I admire your talent and the enormous energy which you have hitherto expended on such a difficult task. The arrangement is easy, and readily comprehensible throughout, especially the final fugue. But I must ask you to include the changes I have sent you, if at all possible. Apart from them, however, I rely entirely on your knowledge and your profound insight – even for improvements, should you perhaps still find a few small errors. I am too old and too feeble to be able to examine such a big work in detail, and the critics should therefore exercise a little forbearance. NOTHING IN THIS WORLD IS PERFECT. SED HOC INTER NOS.

N.B.: Since, because of the quick tempo, the storm in the 2nd part cannot possibly be played as it now stands, my suggestion would be to do it in the following way, so that the singers will find the right pitch more easily: *viz.* – you will see my suggestion on the enclosed sheet. I am so weak today that I cannot write more than this, but I hope soon to hear something from you, and also to see the results. I am, most respectfully,

Your wholly indebted servant,
Joseph Haydn [m.p] ria.

Vienna, 11th December 1801.

[Address:]   Monsieur
            Monsieur Müller Maitre
        de la Musique tres Célebre.

---

1 August Eberhard Müller (1767–1817), composer and *Kapellmeister* at Leipzig, did the pianoforte reduction of *The Seasons*. The present letter is Haydn's comment on Müller's arrangement. Müller foolishly showed the passage in the enclosed sheet, quoted above, to the editor of the *Zeitung für die elegante Welt*, who promptly included it in support of his criticism of Swieten's adapted libretto. Swieten was enraged, and Griesinger reported that His Excellency 'intends to rub into Haydn's skin, with salt and pepper, the assertion that he [Haydn] was *forced* into composing the croaking frogs.' See Hase, pp. 33f. The passage in question occurs in No. 18 (*Gesamtausgabe*, Breitkopf & Härtel, Ser. XVI, Band 6/7, p. 197 at the bottom).

[The enclosed sheet, or rather the corrected proofs, have not survived in their entirety, but they included the following remarks: 'No. 76, in the last line, the first bars should read as follows:

although they are not in the score. NB! This whole passage, with its imitation of the frogs, was not my idea; I was forced to write this Frenchified trash. This wretched idea disappears rather soon when the whole orchestra is playing, but it simply cannot be included in the pianoforte reduction.']   [CCLN, 196f.]

One day after this letter had been written, Griesinger had occasion to write to Breitkopf & Härtel and enclosed Haydn's letter to Müller with his own:

. . . Swieten has made such a fuss about his services in the matter of the English and French translations [for *The Seasons*] that you will have to make up your mind and write him a polite letter of thanks. He would like answers to the following two questions: (1) What would a special print of the English and French *vocal parts* cost, done as cheaply as possible? (2) What about a special print at least of the *fugues*? (If it is not too expensive for him, I presume he will organize the publication, out of enthusiasm for his work, of just the very text that he fitted under the music and which he sent to you.)

   Haydn just sent to tell me that he found many mistakes in the piano score [of *The Seasons*]; he will send me the proofs after lunch. If they arrive in time, I shall put them in a parcel of their own and mail them at once. Pray Heaven that you are not too far advanced with the printing!

   . . . The Emperor has allowed the citizens of Vienna to perform *The Creation* on Christmas Day in the Redoutensaal for the benefit of the Public Hospital. This gave the head of the orchestra the idea of doing the same with *The Seasons* as well as with *The Creation*, instead of performing *The Seven Words* for that purpose. Swieten and Haydn consider that their 'undertaking' [*Unternehmen*] can only profit by it, and they have nothing to fear in the way of thievery.

   Still in good time I have received the following letter from Haydn to H. Müller, whom we presume was responsible for the piano score, together with a page of music containing improvements. The single *errata* that Haydn found in the first twelve *Bögen* [sheets] I will place on the last page of Swieten's text; perhaps some of them have been discovered when your office read the proofs.

   I am pleased that I was able to anticipate your wish, that Haydn might say a few words [about the piano score]. . . .   [Olleson, *Griesinger*, 31]

The issue of the *Zeitung für die elegante Welt* containing the famous quotation came, of course, into Swieten's hands. Griesinger reports that the Baron 'was rather bitter' about it, as might have been expected; but, adds Griesinger, 'the storm is over now'.

The rather unclear reference to *The Seasons* means, quite simply, that organizations such as the Tonkünstler-Societät, the St Marx's Hospital (that is what is meant by 'Public Hospital'), etc. decided to place the new Oratorio in their repertoire for charity concerts, just as they had done with the eminently successful *Creation* and

Seven Words. We shall see that all three works continued to be very useful for bringing in quantities of money for the poor and needy.

Haydn's friend, the sculptor Anton Grassi, who had executed the successful bust of Haydn *à l'antique* in 1799, now asked for another series of sessions with the composer, and in December 1801 Grassi prepared two new porcelain busts of his friend: both are in contemporary costume, with wig, and are among the finest – and certainly technically the most perfect – of all the known Haydn busts. One, signed and dated 1802, is some forty centimetres high and has the inscription 'Blandus auritas fidibus canoris ducere quercus' (see pl. 2), while the other has the inscription 'Haydn' and is only about fifteen centimetres high. Many of these busts were sent abroad, and Grassi himself received from the King of Prussia 'the large golden medal for his bust of Haydn executed in bisquit'. Haydn owned several of Grassi's busts. The large bust with the Latin inscription, now in the Niederösterreichisches Landesmuseum, was badly damaged and has been painstakingly restored. Another version, with a different pedestal (inscribed 'J. HAYDN' in gold letters and with gold bands) is owned by the present writer: the pedestal and the bust proper are two separate pieces in all versions.[1]

On 22 and 23 December, Haydn conducted *The Seasons* for the Christmas concerts of the Tonkünstler-Societät in the Burgtheater. Double admission was charged, and the soloists were, as usual, Therese Saal, Matthias Rathmayer and Ignaz Saal. Rosenbaum went on the 22nd and wrote, laconically, 'It was not exceptionally effective.'[2] But Griesinger reported that the concerts were a great success and Haydn himself had received an enormous ovation. The French Ambassador, who attended the first performance, sent back immediately afterwards to get a ticket for the second performance, saying he had never heard anything more beautiful in his whole life.

Tributes continued to come from Paris, where at the end of his life Haydn was becoming a figure of national interest:

[To Haydn from the Institut National des Sciences et des Arts, Paris. French]
Institut National des Sciences et des Arts [letter-head]
à Paris, le 5 Nivose an 10 de la République
[Paris, 26th December 1801]

The President and the Secretaries of the
Institut National des Sciences et des Arts,
To Monsieur Haydn, celebrated composer of music in Vienna.
Monsieur,
L'institut National des Sciences et des Arts, in its plenary session held today, has voted to elect you a non-resident member of the section 'Literature and Fine Arts'.

We are persuaded that you will receive the notice of your nomination with pleasure, and we therefore hasten to inform you of it.

Please accept our sincere homage, Monsieur, and be assured of our profound respect,
La Porte du Theil, *Secrétaire*
Villat, *Secrétaire*

Vincent
Président.
[For Haydn's answer, see letter of 14 April 1802]
[CCLN, 198]

---

1 Pohl III, 195. Somfai 170 (both these later Grassi busts reproduced) and 216. *Historisches Taschenbuch . . . Dritter Jahrgang. Geschichte des Jahres 1803*, Vienna 1807, pp. 118f.
2 Radant, 98; Pohl, *Denkschrift*, 66; Pohl III, 192.

That same day also saw Griesinger writing to Leipzig:

. . . Also the request for the Masses has been very successful. Not one but two of them he intends to send you in score, so that you can choose; but he agrees at the moment to the publication of one only, as a test, to see if the public is anxious for the continuation. He thinks it would be better if you were to print the Mass not in score but every part *separate*, so that it can be performed at once. Haydn does not expect anything for the Mass; but we know his weak side, and the handkerchiefs gave him great pleasure; if you can find the opportunity to procure for him a small, not at all expensive, present – perhaps a waistcoat, or cambric for shirt-cuffs, or coloured silk stockings (for he doesn't wear white ones), or some other trifle –, and you will give the good Papa Haydn a happy hour. . . .

[Olleson, *Griesinger*, 32]

Haydn had sent authentic scores, probably made by Johann Elssler, of the *Missa Sancti Bernardi* and the *Missa in tempore belli*; the former was the first one in Breitkopf's series of Haydn Masses – for it did come to a whole series – and appeared in May 1802 in an edition of a thousand copies. As we have explained before, church music was never on the same footing, financially, as a composer's other works. Being for the glory of God (and in this case Princess Marie as well), copies were usually sold at a price which represented only the copying charges: this Chronicle has shown many instances. Thus Breitkopf & Härtel also received the works *gratis* (though in a few years Beethoven was able to collect a fee from them for the Mass in C).

On Sunday, 27 December 1801, Haydn conducted *The Creation* at the Redoutensaal for the benefit of the poor of St. Marx (the district where Mozart lies buried in an unknown grave). 'It was exceedingly well attended,' wrote Rosenbaum (98). The *Wiener Zeitung* had announced the concert, adding that 'the renowned author of the work, a man equally great as philanthropist and composer, Joseph Haydn, Doctor of Music and *Kapellmeister* . . . has offered to conduct the entire performance himself, so that every listener . . . may reckon with certainty with the pleasure of complete musical fulfilment.' The *Wiener Zeitung* No. 2 of 1802, reviewing the concert, said that there were such 'great numbers of charitable listeners in attendance, that the hall was not large enough to contain them.' The proceeds amounted to 6,088 gulden.[1] Griesinger had attended both *The Creation* and *The Seasons*; on 29 December he wrote to Breitkopf & Härtel:

. . . No preacher is capable of describing the greatness of the Creator, His works and His mercies with *such* decided strength, of filling our souls to *such* an extent with thankfulness and reverence, of lifting us above the spheres of our common material natures, as happens through the combined effect of word and music in *The Creation* and *The Seasons*. . . .

[Olleson, *Griesinger*, 32]

People were beginning to realize that the frail old man conducting these huge performances with such youthful fire would not always be with them, and Griesinger himself, it seems, also contributed the thoughtful review of these two Christmas-tide performances for the *AMZ*, with which our Chronicle for the year 1801 concludes:

Vienna, 29th Dec. 1801. On the 22nd and 23rd Dec. Jos. Haydn conducted his *Seasons* in the Court Theatre with 200 musicians, and on the 27th *The Creation* in

---

1 Hanns Jäger-Sunstenau, 'Beethoven als Bürger der Stadt Wien', in *Colloquium Amicorum*, Bonn 1967, p. 135.

the large Redoutensaal. It is not necessary to say anything about the latter, for in this, as in no other, work it can be said that

> In all the lands resounds the Word,
> Never unperceived, ever understood.

Also *The Seasons* is an evergreen laurel in the wreath on Haydn's brow. In what multiplicity do we see, following the poem's plan, cheerfulness, satisfaction, hope, fear, prayer, extravagant joy, joking whim and profound seriousness succeed one another! And what truth there is in the musical expression of all these conditions of the soul! How the composer, through the magic of his melodies and harmonies has described and brought the feelings of the listener nearer to that which the poet occasionally expresses in only a few words! As a result, this work, too, earns great approbation everywhere. Perhaps it is not superfluous at least to suggest the influence that such musical works can have on the aesthetic and moral education of a nation. No preacher [etc., very similar to the thoughts of the letter of 29 December] . . . The performances were for the benefit of two local charitable organizations.

[*AMZ* IV, 263f.]

CHAPTER TWO

Works of 1801

Die Jahreszeiten / The Seasons
(XXI: 3)

I. THE LIBRETTO: SURVEY OF THE MATERIAL

(1) James Thomson's poem and Gottfried van Swieten's adaptation
On 11 February 1794, the day following the first performance of Haydn's Symphony
No. 99 at the Hanover Square Rooms in London (see *Haydn in England 1791–1795*, pp.
233ff.), the *Oracle* – in its review of the concert – stated:

> We must of necessity be brief. And after all it may be best, when the *chef d'oeuvre* of
> the great HAYDN is the subject.
>   'Come then, expressive SILENCE, muse his praise.'

No doubt one of Haydn's many English friends would have told him then that the
quotation was the last line of the 'Hymn' that concludes Thomson's huge epic poem,
The Seasons. Indeed, the poem was, in the 1790s, enjoying not only continuous but if
anything an increased popularity. James Thomson (1700–48) had first published his
poem between 1726 and 1730, but the quarto edition of 1730 had assembled all four
cantos together for the first time. From the very outset, the poet struck a responsive
chord in his readers' hearts. In a twentieth-century appreciation of the poem, Hans
Hammelmann writes:[1]

> If a census had been taken some time in the eighteenth century to discover the
> most widely read poem, Thomson's *The Seasons* might well have topped the list.
> In an age which, by preference, expressed its thoughts and feelings in verse, the
> Scottish poet's chief work was among the first in the English language – and
> certainly one of the longest – to take nature for its theme. Hitherto there had been
> little attempt to apply real observation to life in the country; appreciation of
> natural scenery is something one looks for in vain in writers and painters of the
> preceding age.
>   James Thomson, a country boy from a Roxburgh manse, set himself to
> describe what he had seen and experienced as a youth in his little village, following
> eventually the whole cycle of the seasons in their effect on nature and, through
> nature, on man. He would hardly have been a true child of his age, however, had
> his descriptions of the beauties of nature not constantly moved him to speculations
> and ideas philosophical, scientific, political and social whose relevance to the
> progress of the seasons is often more than tenuous. What is worse, when he found
> that the first part of his poem, *Winter*, was having a ready welcome among
> readers, Thomson saw fit to enlarge upon his subject. He added still further

1 *Country Life Annual*, London 1970, pp. 52ff.

didactic reflections and allusions ranging from flora and fauna not merely to geology and mineralogy, but to optics and astronomy and even mercantile expansion and prison reform, until the whole became a strange patchwork of direct observation and landscape painting, moralising, sententious anecdotes and pseudo-scientific gossip. What is to be thought of these corrections, re-corrections and insertions has perhaps been said once and for all by Samuel Johnson. 'Thomson had a true poetical genius, the power of viewing everything in a poetical light,' he declared one evening, according to Boswell. 'His fault is such a cloud of words, sometimes, that the sense can hardly peep through.'

What does come through, fortunately, is the poet's gentle and genuine affection for the country, his enjoyment of the simple pastimes and diversions of peasant life, and the charm of his descriptions of the rural scene. It is this idyllic innocence of *The Seasons* which must have contributed, in a measure, to the gradual emergence of the new taste for rusticity in Georgian England and the belief in the perfection of a pastoral life. People began to look at the country with fresh eyes, and discovered beauty and sublimity where they had seen nothing but crudity before. The liberating effect of this new vision on the arts, and particularly on painting, was striking – and never again altogether lost.

During Haydn's years in England, several handsomely illustrated editions of *The Seasons* were issued: two came out in 1793, another one (with illustrations by Conrad Metz) in 1794, and in 1797, two years after Haydn had left England for the last time, Francesco Bartolozzi engraved the illustrations, after designs by William Hamilton, for what Dr Hammelmann describes as 'the ambitious luxury folio' edition. Even Henry Fuseli could not resist the poem and provided two plates for the 1797 edition. In 1802, *The Seasons* was reprinted in New York, thus coinciding by chance with Haydn's publication of the work at Breitkopf & Härtel's.[1]

There is also a strong feeling of deism in the poem, and this aspect probably appealed to Gottfried van Swieten, whose choice of the subject for Haydn's music was, however, motivated rather by the descriptions of nature which, the Baron no doubt rightly considered, would fire the composer's imagination. Whatever the defects of the poem – and its verbosity and 'fragmentation' are, alas, all too obvious – Swieten was right to choose it for Haydn and, as we shall see, very clever in his adaptation. It is strange to think that Thomson's poem, once so celebrated, is known to many people in the second part of the twentieth century only because of its association with Haydn.[2]

Readers of the Chronicle in this biography have noted the Baron's insistence to leave his name out of libretti, scores, and even criticisms not only of *The Creation* but also of *The Seasons*. In the case of the former, he was simply adapting an Oratorio which already existed. In the latter, his work was perhaps more extensive, but nevertheless his model existed and not only the English model but also an old German translation.

We have seen that Thomson's poem was first published complete in the quarto edition of 1730; but the author continued to revise it at great length, and the final

---

1 The New York edition, 'Printed and Sold by George F. Hopkins. *At Washington's Head*' contains 'The Life of the Author by Patrick Murdoch' and 'An Essay on the plan and manner of the poem by J. Aiken, M. D.'. This octavo book, which contains pretty engraved illustrations by 'Roberts sc. N. York' as well as several vignettes, runs to no less than 217 pages. The luxurious British editions were also voluminous in size.

2 For two recent defences of the poem, see Ralph Cohen's two works: *The Art of Discrimination: Thomson's 'The Seasons' and the Language of Criticism* (Baltimore 1964), and *The Unfolding of 'The Seasons': A Study of Thomson's Poem* (Baltimore 1970).

'authentic' version was not published until fifteen years later. In that same year (1745) there appeared a remarkable edition in Hamburg, where the complete English text was printed but also with a line-for-line German translation by B. H. Brockes, who had furnished Handel with the text of a German Passion (known nowadays as the 'Brockes-Passion'). Swieten knew this Brockes translation of the Thomson poem and made use of it for his own adaptation. This was yet another reason why the Baron was firm in not allowing his name to be used as the author of the text, for the simple reason that not even the German translation was wholly his own. Apart from the rather odd mixture of Thomson-Brockes-Swieten, we must not forget that the Baron also used a poem by Bürger and another by Weisse (both in the 'Winter' section), of which we shall examine the circumstances later. Thus there were no less than four other authors materially connected with Swieten's adaptation, and he was being realistic and sensible as well as modest in keeping his own name in the background. He would have been the first to describe his own rather curious position in the libretto as that of a compiler. We shall see, however, that he also added several sections wholly his own.

If the latest theory regarding Swieten's treatment of *The Creation*'s English libretto is correct – i.e. the supposition that Swieten left many sections of the original English unchanged[1] – one would be tempted to look for a similar procedure in the Baron's adaptation of Thomson's poem. But the *modus operandi* in the later work was entirely different. *The Creation* was already a libretto intended for Handel by the time Swieten came to 'edit' it for Haydn, whereas Thomson's poem had to be completely recast – not to speak of the drastic excisions necessary – before it could be made into a word-book. Swieten had to recapture the essence, the spirit, of *The Seasons*, and in creating his libretto only the occasional line proved useful. Swieten also perceived that Thomson's poem suffered from disorganization, and the Baron felt obliged to regroup some of the material in order to make his libretto tauter and more logical.

Thus Swieten was forced to re-translate his new German adaptation into English when composer and librettist decided to print the work not only with its original German text but also French and English translations. Swieten's knowledge of English was not up to this task, and both the French and English translations (if indeed he was also responsible for the French) are very unhappy. We have drawn attention,[2] following Edward Olleson, to one particularly drastic example. Sometimes Swieten was able to use a whole phrase from Thomson's original English, but in many places he could not do this and was forced to make a new translation, which in the event did no good service to the work's dissemination in English-speaking countries. The faulty English may have been one of the reasons for the Oratorio's total non-reception in England, a subject which we shall discuss in connection with '*The Seasons*' Progress' at the end of this analysis.

A typical example of Swieten's beneficial effect on the libretto's organization occurs at the very beginning of the work. Thomson opens with his hymn to Spring:

> Come, gentle SPRING! ethereal Mildness, come,
> And, from the bosom of yon dropping cloud,
> While music wakes around, veil'd in a shower
> Of shadowing roses, in our plains descend.

1 See *Haydn: the Years of 'The Creation' 1796–1800*, pp. 345ff.
2 Op. cit., p. 348.

Seven lines later, Thomson suddenly brings in winter.

> And see where surly WINTER passes off,
> Far to the north, and calls his ruffian blasts:
> His blasts obey, and quit the howling hill,
> The shatter'd forest, and the ravag'd vale:
> While softer gales succeed, at whose kind touch
> Dissolving snows in livid torrents lost,
> The mountains lift their green heads to the sky.
>
> As yet the trembling year is unconfirm'd,
> And WINTER oft at eve resumes the breeze, [etc.]

Swieten begins with an Overture designed to show the passage from winter to spring, and the first words of the Oratorio, spoken by one of the three peasants whom Swieten has chosen to relate the story, describes the 'surly winter' passing off. Without wishing to begin any musical analysis here, we might point out that to make this transition clear, Swieten has the solo voices pass from bass to tenor to soprano, the latter describing the advent of the south wind, and the arrival of Spring. Then Swieten adapts the opening 'Come, gentle Spring' hymn but includes in the middle a reference to the 'trembling year' as yet unconfirmed:

> Frohlocket ja nicht allzufrüh!
> Oft schleicht, in Nebel eingehüllt,
> Der Winter wohl zurück . . .
>
> (Do not rejoice too soon!
> Often winter, cloaked in fog,
> creeps back again . . .)

Swieten then returns, more or less, to the point where Thomson, after his interruption about Winter, continues with the advent of Spring.

> At last from Aries rolls the bounteous Son,
> And the bright Bull receives him.

In the libretto, this thought (though not the words) is set as a recitative, to be followed by an aria, based on Thomson's lines

> Joyous, th'impatient husbandman perceives
> Relenting Nature, and his lusty steers
> Drives from their stalls, to where the well-us'd plough
> Lies in the furrow, loosen'd from the frost.
> There, unrefusing, to the harness'd yoke
> They lend their shoulder, and begin their toil,
> Cheer'd by the simple song and soaring lark.

Swieten's adaptation is not only shorter but much more direct:

> Schon eilet froh der Ackermann
> Zur Arbeit auf das Feld.
> In langen Furchen schreitet er,
> Dem Pfuge flötend nach.
>
> (The husbandman, content, hastens
> to his work in the fields.
> He whistles as he follows the plough,
> making long furrows.)

The middle part of this Aria (No. 4) contains the adaptation of

> While thro' the neighb'ring fields the sower stalks,
> With measur'd step; and liberal throws the grain
> Into the faithful bosom of the ground:
> The harrow follows harsh, and shuts the scene.

Swieten rewrites these lines as follows:

> In abgemessnem Gange dann
> Wirft er den Samen aus.
> Den birgt der Acker treu und reift
> Ihn bald zur gold'nen Frucht.
>
> (With measured step,
> he scatters the grain.
> The harrow follows true
> and ripens it soon to golden fruit.)

Allowing for our prose translation, Swieten's adaptation of these four lines is in many ways typical. He has made prose out of the poetry, completely losing the charm of such phrases as 'into the faithful bosom of the ground' or 'The harrow follows harsh' (for which 'Den birgt der Acker treu' – literally 'the harrow vouches faithfully for it' – is not a very subtle adaptation).

The recitative 'Der Landmann hat sein Werk vollbracht' is followed by a Trio (soloists) and Chorus entitled in the libretto 'Bittgesang' (Prayer), 'Sey nun gnädig'. Again, Swieten has effected a sensible transposition of Thomson's

> Be gracious, Heaven! for now laborious man
> Has done his part. Ye fostering breezes, blow!
> Ye softening dews, ye tender showers, descend!

In the libretto, Swieten has isolated the thought of the 'laborious man', expanded it, and turned it into a short recitative, while the chorus with soloists (No. 6) starts with the 'Be gracious' ('Sey nun gnädig') thought but expands it later with the addition of a prayer

> Uns sprießet Überfluß
> Und deiner Güte Dank und Ruhm.
>
> (Bounty is given to us,
> Praise and Thanks for Thy goodness.)

This may be an adaptation of a slightly later passage in the original

> So, with superior boon, may your rich soil,
> Exuberant, Nature's better blessings pour
> O'er every land. . . .

The following Recitative (No. 7) combines two passages of the poem:

> The north-east spends his rage; he now shut up
> Within his iron cave, th'effusive south
> Warms the wide air, and o'er the void of heaven
> Breathes the big clouds with vernal showers distent.
> . . .
> Thus all day long the full-distended clouds
> Indulge their genial stores, and well-shower'd earth
> Is deep enrich'd with vegetable life.

97

No. 8, 'Freudenlied' (Song of Joy), has the soloists and also a chorus of young men and girls. Swieten was now faced with his most difficult task hitherto. Thomson's poem contains, at this point, a huge catalogue of life on this planet, ranging from herbs to the 'glaring lion' and from 'the tulip race' to the 'wishing bosom' of the virgin; there are long descriptions of nature interspersed with remarks on 'Britannia's weal' and the 'amazing frowns on utmost Kilda's shore' which, a footnote informs us, is 'the farthest of the western islands of Scotland'. Swieten uses his alternating chorus of young girls and boys to tell us of the joys of green thickets, of lilies, roses, lambkins, fish, bees, and so forth. The libretto does not escape the original poem's tendency to a catalogue, but it shortens Thomson's descriptions so severely that hardly a phrase of the original remains. In the midst of this Finale to 'Spring', Swieten very freely adapts

> Hail, SOURCE OF BEING! UNIVERSAL SOUL
> Of heaven and earth! ESSENTIAL PRESENCE, hail!
> To THEE I bend the knee; to THEE my thoughts,
> Continual, climb. . . .

to

> Ewiger, mächtiger, gütiger Gott!

It will be noticed that throughout the libretto, Swieten has turned Thomson's vaguely deistic thoughts to direct prayers to God. The final part of 'Spring', in the libretto, is almost entirely Swieten's work:

> Ehre, Lob und Preis sei dir,
> Ewiger, gütiger Gott!
>
> (Honour, praise and thanks to Thee,
> everlasting God of goodness!)

Swieten passed over the opening of Thomson's 'Summer' and began with the words

> And soon, observant of approaching day,
> The meek-ey'd Morn appears, mother of dews,
> At first faint-gleaming in the dappled east . . .
> Rous'd by the cock, the soon-clad shepherd leaves
> His mossy cottage, where with *Peace* he dwells;

This is set as an accompanied recitative, and there then follows an Aria and Recitative (No. 10), which continues Thomson's text:

> And from the crowded fold, in order, drives
> His flock, to taste the verdure of the morn.

Swieten adds a section describing the shepherd, leaning on a knotty club and watching the sun rising; this is not in Thomson. The recitative is based on the following passage in the poem:

> But yonder comes the powerful King of Day,
> Rejoicing in the east. The lessening cloud
> The kindling azure, and the mountain's brow
> Illum'd with fluid gold, his near approach
> Betoken glad . . .

The Sunrise Trio-Chorus (No. 11) is based on the direct continuation of the above lines:

> . . . Lo! now, apparent all,
> Aslant the dew-bright earth, and coloured air,
> He looks in boundless majesty abroad;
> And sheds the shining day, that burnish'd plays
> On rocks, and hills and towers, and wandering streams.
> High-gleaming from afar. Prime chearer Light!
> Of all material beings first, and best!
> Efflux divine! Nature's resplendent robe!
> Without whose vesting beauty all were wrapt
> In unessential gloom; and thou, O Sun!
> Soul of surrounding worlds! in whom best seen
> Shines out thy Maker! may I sing of thee?

In Thomson's poem, the section dealing with the sun continues for many lines, culminating in the effect of the strong midday heat.

> 'Tis raging Noon; and, vertical, the Sun
> Darts on the head direct his forceful rays.
> O'er heaven and earth, far as the ranging eye
> Can sweep, a dazzling deluge reigns; and all
> From pole to pole is undistinguished blaze.

Swieten actually managed to use some of these original words in his English translation ('Tis noon; and, vertical, the Sun darts all his fire). This section is set as an accompanied recitative, preceded by the reapers at work in the cooler morning hours:

> Now swarms the village o'er the joyful mead . . .
> Wide flies the tedded grain; all in a row
> Advancing broad, or wheeling round the field,
> They spread their breathing harvest to the sun . . .

The 'heat' section is concluded by a *Cavatine* (No. 13), based on these lines:

> . . . Distressful nature pants.
> The very streams look languid from afar;
> Or, thro' th'unshelter'd glade, impatient, seem
> To hurl into the covert of the grove

Although Swieten's verses are a very free adaptation

> Dem Druck erlieget die Natur;
> Welke Blumen,
> Dürre Wiesen, ,
> Trockene Quellen,
> Alles zeigt der Hitze Wut,
> Und kraftlos schmachten Mensch und Tier
> Am Boden hingestreckt.

> (Nature is prostrated by this force.
> Withered flowers,
> parched fields,
> drained fountains,
> all show the heat's fury.
> And prostrate, man and beast
> exhausted lie on the ground.)

he could nevertheless use the opening words of Thomson's original, 'Distressful nature fainting sinks', for his English translation.

No. 11, an accompanied recitative, is based on this section:

> Welcome, ye shades! ye bowery thickets, hail!
> Ye lofty pines! ye venerable oaks!
> Ye ashes wild, resounding o'er the steep! . . .
> Around th'adjoining brook, that purls along
> The vocal grove [etc.] . . .

Swieten introduces buzzing insects, the smell of fragrant herbs, and finally the sound of a shepherd's pipe. After the Air (No. 15)

> Welche Labung für die Sinne!
> Welch' Erholung für das Herz!
> Jeden Aderzweig durchströmet,
> Und in jeder Nerve bebt
> Erquickendes Gefühl.
> Die Seele wachet auf
> Zum reizenden Genuß,
> Und neue Kraft erhebt
> Durch milden Drang die Brust.
>
> (Which comfort for the senses!
> What relief for the heart!
> Streaming through every vein
> and beating in every heart
> is a revived feeling.
> The soul awakes
> to delightful pleasures,
> and new force
> gently enlivens the breast.)

Swieten now makes a gigantic cut in the poem, omitting some of Thomson's most abstruse references (hippopotamuses, Montezuma, 'the swelling Nile', 'the Nubian rocks', Christopher Columbus, Caesar, Cato, Vasco da Gama, etc., etc.) and going straight to the spectacular thunderstorm, which Swieten introduces first by a recitative and then by a chorus. His source in Thomson was this passage:

> . . . A boding silence reigns.
> Dread thro' the dun expanse; save the dull sound
> That from the mountain, previous to the storm,
> Rolls o'er the muttering earth, disturbs the flood,
> And shakes the forest-leaf without a breath. . . .
> 'Tis listening fear, and dumb amazement all:
> When to the startled eye the sudden glance
> Appears far south, eruptive thro' the cloud;
> And following slower, in explosion vast,
> The Thunder raises its tremendous voice.
> At first, heard solemn o'er the verge of heaven,
> The tempest growls; but as it nearer comes,
> And rolls its awful burden on the wind,
> The lightnings flash a larger curve, and more
> The noise astounds: till over head a sheet
> Of livid flame discloses wide; then shuts. . . .

Swieten has taken this atmospheric piece of blank verse and reworked it as if the local population were pleading for help ('Ach, das Ungewitter naht! Hilf uns Himmel!') and crying 'Weh uns' (literally: 'woe to us'). The Baron now makes another huge cut in Thomson's poem and in order to link up with the beautiful description of a summer's evening approaching, Swieten provides a short passage telling of the end of the storm (beginning of the Trio with Chorus No. 18). He then does another summary of Thomson's section about the evening, but whereas Thomson was content to have the occasional descriptive line about bird or beast ('While the quail clamours for its running mate'), Swieten has Noah's Ark, cows returning to be milked (Thomson described, instead, the 'ruddy milk-maid'), the quail, the cricket, the frog; then the church bell, tolling Vespers, and signalling that which Thomson (but alas not Swieten) so prettily describes as the beginning of the night:

> Among the crooked lanes, on every hedge,
> The glow-worm lights his gem; and, thro' the dark,
> A moving radiance twinkles. *Evening* yields
> The world to *Night*. . . .

Swieten has, instead, the star winking in heaven and calling us 'to soft repose' ('zur sanften Ruh').

> Mädchen, Burschen, Weiber, kommt!
> Uns erwartet süßer Schlaf.
> Wir geh'n, wir folgen euch.
>
> (Come, girls, boys, women!
> Sweet sleep awaits us.
> We're coming, we'll follow you.)

It is not exactly inspiring poetry!

The beginning of Thomson's 'Autumn' is much more abstract than the similar passage in Swieten. Thomson's beginning reads:

> Crown'd with the sickle and the wheaten sheaf,
> While AUTUMN, nodding o'er the yellow plain,
> Comes jovial on; the Doric reed once more,
> Well-pleas'd, I tune. Whate'er the Wintry frost
> Nitrous prepar'd; the various-blossom'd Spring
> Put in white promise forth; and Summer suns
> Concocted strong, rush boundless now to view,
> Full, perfect all, and swell my glorious theme
> . . . [22 lines omitted]
> Extensive harvests hang the heavy head.
> Rich, silent, deep, they stand; for not a gale
> Rolls its light billows o'er the bending plain:
> A calm of plenty! till the ruffled air
> Falls from its poise, and gives the breeze to blow,
> Rent is the fleecy mantle of the sky;
> The clouds fly different; and the sudden sun
> By fits effulgent, gilds th'illumin'd field,
> And black by fits the shadows sweep along.
> A gaily checker'd, heart-expanding view,
> Far as the circling eye can shoot around,
> Unbounded tossing in a field of corn.

By this time in his adaptation, Swieten was beginning to adhere less and less to the actual words of the original poem; rather, he took the essential spirit and rewrote it in German, whereby he had to take into account the (perhaps in the first place dubious) presence of his three peasant soloists. Thus we have, after the orchestral introduction (which 'indicates the husbandman's satisfaction at the abundant harvest'), the following recitative:

> Was durch seine Blüthe der Lenz zuerst versprach,
> Was durch seine Wärme der Sommer reifen hieß,
> Zeigt der Herbst in Fülle dem frohen Landmann jetzt.
> Den reichen Vorrath fährt er nun auf hochbelad'nen Wagen ein.
> Kaum faßt der weiten Scheune Raum, was ihm sein Feld hervorgebracht.
> Sein heit'res Auge blickt umher, er mißt den aufgetürmten Segen ab,
> Und Freude strömt in seine Brust.

> (What Spring has promised with its blossoms,
> What Summer has ripened by its warmth,
> Autumn displays to the husbandman in all its richness.
> He now drives in the rich harvest on his heavily laden waggons.
> The wide barn can scarcely contain that which his fields have yielded.
> His pleased eye looks about, he measures his rich blessings
> And joy stirs within his breast.)

As earlier, Swieten has made the abstract personal, and the husbandman figures much more prominently than ever in Thomson's setting. Perhaps the most curious – and, as we shall soon see, to Haydn most repellent – transformation of Thomson's world comes in the following passage, which has come to be known as the Chorus (with soloists) 'In Praise of Industry' (*Lob des Fleißes*). Thomson writes

> These are thy blessings, INDUSTRY! rough power!
> Whom labour still attends, and sweat, and pain,
> Yet the kind source of every gentle art,
> And all the soft civility of life:
> Raiser of human kind! . . .
> . . .
> But this the rugged savage never felt,
> Even desolate in crowds; and thus his days
> Roll'd heavy, dark, and unenjoy'd along;
> A waste of time! till INDUSTRY approach'd,
> And rous'd him from his miserable sloth;
> His faculties unfolded . . .
> Taught him to chip the wood, and hew the stone,
> Till by degrees the finish'd fabric rose;
> Tore from his limbs the blood-polluted fur,
> And wrapt them in the woolly vestment warm.
> Or bright in glossy silk, and flowing lawn;
> With wholesome viands fill'd his table, pour'd
> The generous glass around, inspir'd to wake
> The life-refining soul of decent wit:
> Nor stopp'd at barren bare necessity;
> But still advancing bolder, led him on
> To pomp, to pleasure, elegance, and grace;
> And, breathing high ambition thro' his soul,
> Set science, wisdom, glory in his view,
> And bade him be the *Lord* of all below.

Thomson's dissertation on the merits of industry (equals progress) continues for many lines, touching on 'imperial justice', the joys of commerce, praise of the Thames and the British navy ('whence ribb'd with oak, / To bear the BRITISH THUNDER, black, and bold, / The roaring vessel rush'd into the main'). From there, we turn back to nature, the autumn crops, the reapers, and so on. Swieten has adapted this 'Praise of Industry' as follows:

> So lohnet die Natur den Fleiß;
> Ihn ruft, ihn lacht sie an,
> Ihn muntert sie durch Hoffnung auf,
> Ihm steht sie willig bei;
> Ihm wirket sie mit voller Kraft.
>
> Von dir, O Fleiß, kommt alles Heil.
> Die Hütte, die uns schirmt,
> Die Wolle, die uns deckt,
> Die Speise, die uns nährt,
> Ist deine Gab', ist dein Geschenk.
>
> Du flößest Tugend ein,
> Und rohe Sitten milderst du.
> Du wehrest Laster ab
> Und reinigest der Menschen Herz.
> Du stärkest Muth und Sinn
> Zum Guten und zu jeder Pflicht.
>
> (Thus does Nature reward industry.
> It calls, it smiles at us,
> It encourages us through hope,
> It is always at our side;
> And exerts all her power.
>
> From thee, O Industry, comes every blessing.
> The hut that protects us;
> The wool that clothes us;
> The food that nourishes us;
> – All is thy gift, thy grant.
>
> Thou encouragest virtue,
> And rude manners are tamed by Thee.
> Thou preventest wickedness
> And cleansest the heart of mankind.
> Thou strengthenst mind and will
> For goodness and for every duty.)

Swieten, of course, realized that Thomson's original verses, attractive though many of them are here, were singularly unfitted for musical treatment. The Baron's own verses are obviously much better from the metrical standpoint, but the whole idea of suggesting a large hymn of which the key word was 'Fleiß' (a less attractive word in German than 'industry' in English) was mistaken. How was a composer to set lines such as 'The hut that protects us; the wool that clothes us; the food that nourishes us'? As any admirer of Haydn's music knows, the old composer achieved a great and moving – indeed an almost epic – piece of musical composition here: a miracle in view of the unpromising words.

For the rest of 'Autumn', however, Swieten had to depart almost completely from the original, which is particularly disjointed and chaotic. From the end of the section on industry, we proceed (after the autumn crops and the reapers, to which we have alluded) to the story of 'lovely young LAVINIA', a poor girl living with her widowed mother, and 'The pride of swains / PALEMON was, the generous, and the rich; / Who led the rural life in all its joy / And elegance, such as Arcadian song / Transmits from ancient uncorrupted times.' After considerable difficulties and in the course of many lines, Lavinia gets her Palemon,

> Who flourish'd long in tender bliss, and rear'd
> A numerous offspring, lovely like themselves,
> And good, the grace of all the country round.

Swieten thought that this love story might be too obscure and perhaps too comical for his Viennese audience, and so he changes the whole scene, as follows:

No. 21 (Recitative)

Seht, wie zum Haselbusche dort
Die rasche Jugend eilt!
An jedem Aste schwinget sich
Der Kleinen lose Schar,
Und der bewegten Staud' entstürzt
Gleich Hagelschau'r die lock're Frucht!

Hier klimmt der junge Bau'r
Den hohen Stamm entlang, die Leiter flink hinauf.
Vom Wipfel, der ihn deckt,
Sieht er sein Liebchen nah'n,
Und ihrem Tritt entgegen fliegt
Dann im trautem Scherze die runde Nuß herab.

Im Garten steh'n um jedem Baum
Die Mädchen groß und klein,
Dem Obste, das die klauben,
An frischer Farbe gleich.

(See, how to the hazelnut tree,
the youth hastens.
On every branch swings
the small and merry group,
and shaking the branches,
a shower of nuts falls to the ground.

A young peasant climbs
up to the tree's top, on his ladder.
At the top, hidden from view,
he sees his sweetheart coming,
and at her feet he hurls,
in well-loved sport, a round nut.

Round every tree in the orchard
stand the girls, great and small,
their fresh colour like the fruits
which they gather.)

Swieten then constructs a duet (No. 22), extolling the advantages of country girls, whom he calls nature's daughters, and especially his Hannchen (Jane). The subject is remarkably like the extraordinary Aria, 'Chi s'impaccia di moglie cittadina', from Haydn's *L'infedeltà delusa* (1773), the autograph of which was in Haydn's 'archives' when *The Seasons* was being drafted.

Duet (No. 22)

Ihr Schönen aus der Stadt, kommt her;
Blickt an, die Töchter der Natur,
Die weder Putz noch Schminke ziert.
Da seht mein Hannchen, seht!
Ihr blüht Gesundheit auf den Wangen;
Im Auge lacht Zufriedenheit,
Und aus dem Munde spricht das Herz,
Wenn sie mit Liebe schwört.

Ihr Herrchen süß und fein, bleibt weg!
Hier schwinden eure Künste ganz,
Und glatte Worte wirken nicht;
Man gibt euch kein Gehör.
Nicht Gold, nicht Pracht kann uns verblenden,
Ein redlich Herz ist, was uns rührt;
Und meine Wünsche sind erfüllt,
Wenn treu mir Lucas ist.

Blätter fallen ab,
Früchte welken hin,
Tag und Jahr vergeh'n,
Nur meine Liebe nicht.

Schöner grünt das Blatt,
Süßer schmeckt die Frucht,
Heller glänzt der Tag,
Wenn deine Liebe spricht.

Welch' ein Glück ist treue Liebe!
Uns're Herzen sind vereinet,
Trennen kann sie Tod allein.
Liebstes Hannchen!
Bester Lucas!

Lieben und geliebet werden,
Ist der Freuden höchster Gipfel,
Ist des Lebens Wonn' und Glück!

(You ladies from the city, come here;
behold a daughter of nature,
who knows neither powder nor paint.
Here, look at my Jane!
health blooms on her cheek;
satisfaction is in her eye.
And from her lips speaks the heart
when she swears her love to me.

You gentry, sweet and fine, away with you!
Your gifts can find no place here,
and smooth words carry not;
no one will heed them,
Neither gold nor pomp can blind us:
a true heart is what moves us;
and my wishes are fulfilled
if Lucas be true to me.

Leaves must fall,
fruits will wither,
day and year disappear;
only not my love.

The leaf is greener,
the fruit tastes sweeter,
the day gleams brighter,
when your love speaks.

What a fortune is true love!
Both hearts are fast united,
only death can part them.
Dearest Jane!
My best Lucas!

To love and be loved
is the greatest gift of life,
is life's joy and bliss.)

These verses have come a long way from Thomson; they are pure Viennese *Volkskomödie*, and have their ancestry not only in *L'infedeltà delusa* but also, very strongly, in Haydn's Hanswurst opera, *Das abgebrannte Haus* (*Die Feuersbrunst*, *c.* 1776), and of course in the Papageno-Papagena scenes in *Die Zauberflöte* (1791). In view of Haydn's predilection for this kind of an aria, one wonders if in fact it was the composer who suggested the idea to his librettist.

If there is such a point in Thomson's poem, it is the love story of Lavinia and Palemon, as we have said. In the original 'plot', we now have another storm scene, such as Thomson had already introduced in 'Summer'; the second storm was wisely omitted by Swieten, who proceeds to the following vignette which links what has gone before with the great hunting scene.

Recitative (No. 23)

Nun zeiget das entblößte Feld
Der ungebet'nen Gäste Zahl,
Die an den Halmen Nahrung fand
Und irrend jetzt sie weitersucht.
Des kleinen Raubes klaget nicht der Landmann,
Der ihn kaum bemerkt;
Dem Übermaße wünscht er doch nicht ausgestellt zu sein.
Was ihn dagegen sichern mag,
Sieht er als Wohltat an,
Und willig fröhnt er dann zur Jagd,
Die seinen guten Herrn ergötzt.

(Now the stripped field shows
a host of self-invited guests,
who had found food in the corn-stalks
and now frantically run about and seek it further.
The husbandman objects not to the small loss,
which he hardly notices;
but he wishes to be preserved from excesses.
That which can assure him
he regards as a favour,
and thus he willingly joins the hunt
that so delights his good landlord.)

This latter section is pure Swieten, and so is the detailed construction of the hunting scene. Thomson's hunt is followed to the extent that, like Swieten's, it is divided into various sections: one dealing with birds, one dealing with the hare, and then one dealing with the stag. It was this particular order that Haydn received from the Baron. Since the words are entirely Swieten's we may abstain from a detailed quotation. No. 24 (Aria) is the hunt for winged game, of which Thomson thoroughly disapproved ('. . . the steady tyrant Man, / Who with the thoughtless insolence of power / Inflam'd, beyond the most infuriate wrath / Of the worst monster that e'er roam'd the waste, / For sport alone pursues the cruel chase . . .'), while No. 25 (Accompanied Recitative) is about the hunting of hares (Thomson also thought very little of that 'sport': 'Poor is the triumph o'er the timid hare!'). This leads into the famous 'Hunting Chorus' (No. 26), which coincides with Thomson's stag hunt. Here, Swieten also follows one detail of the original: the stag 'in speed . . . puts his faith; and rous'd by fear',

> Gives all his swift aerial soul to flight;
> Against the breeze he darts, that way the more
> To leave the lessening murderous cry behind:
> Deception short! . . .

Swieten has 'Jetzt hat er die Hunde getäuscht' (now he has deceived the hounds), but of course in the end, the hunters and the hounds surround him. Thomson writes, pathetically:

> . . . but fainting breathless toil,
> Sick, seizes on his heart; he stands at bay;
> And puts his last weak refuse in despair.
> The big round tears run down his dappled face;
> He groans in anguish; while the growling pack,
> Blood-happy, hang at his fair jutting chest,
> And mark his beauteous checker'd sides with gore.

Swieten, however, has taken over practically none of this nostalgic regret for the dying stag; instead he has the chorus acting both as story-tellers and hunters, explaining how the animal is now surrounded and 'Sein nahes Ende kündigt an' (Swieten's own English: 'His gasping agony proclaim'), the sound of the last horn call and the chorus yelling out 'Ha-la-li'. There were too many passionate hunters in Austria (Haydn and Swieten included) for them to be able to resist the delights of *la chasse*, in both libretto and music.

The final scene of 'Autumn', and musically, at least, one of the most brilliantly successful numbers of the whole Oratorio, concerns the wine harvest. This scene, of course, is only briefly described in Thomson's poem, which continues (after the reference to 'the fuddled foot', the 'mutual swill' and the reeling talk) with a series of long descriptions of such varied objects as 'brown October', the autumn fogs (which Swieten saves for the beginning of 'Winter'), Lapland, Caucasus, the Andes, the Rhine, the Hebrides, Prime Minister Pitt ('thy country's early boast'), British Youth, etc., etc. With immense gusto Swieten and Haydn tell us, in No. 27 (Recitative) and No. 28 (Chorus) of the 'juicy grapes' and the 'ready tubs and vats', concluding in the riotous 'drunken' Chorus. This part, too, is thoroughly Austrian.

Swieten's winter setting begins with an orchestral introduction in which Haydn was to 'paint the thick fogs at the beginning of winter' (No. 29). Thomson writes:

> See, WINTER comes, to rule the varied year,
> Sullen and sad, with all his rising train;
> *Vapours*, and *Clouds*, and *Storms*. Be these my theme. . . .

Again Swieten follows only the thought, not the word:

> Nun senket sich das blasse Jahr
> Und fallen Dünste kalt herab.
> Die Berg' umhüllt ein grauer Dampf,
> Der endlich auch die Flächen drückt,
> Und am Mittage selbst der Sonne matten Strahl verschlingt.
>
> Aus Lapplands Höhlen schreitet her
> Der stürmisch düst're Winter jetzt.
> Vor seinem Tritt erstarrt
> In banger Stille die Natur.

> (Now sinks the pale declining year [Swieten's English]
> And cold vapours fall on us.
> The mountains are covered with grey mists,
> that gradually descend on the plains
> and at noon even swallow up the sun's weary rays.
>
> From Lappland's caves now comes
> the stormy, dark winter.
> At his approach,
> nature, appalled, freezes still.)

From an idea in Thomson, 'vital heat, light, life, and joy, the dubious day forsake', Swieten begins his next, very short *Cavatine* (No. 30), which also uses the basic message of

> . . . This Winter falls,
> A heavy gloom oppressive o'er the world,
> Thro' Nature shedding influence malign,
> And rouses up the seeds of dark disease.
> The soul of man dies in him, loathing life,
> And black with more than melancholy views.

Swieten's words are

> Licht und Leben sind geschwächet,
> Wärm' und Freude sind verschwunden.
> Unmuthsvollen Tagen folget
> Schwarzer Nächte lange Dauer.

> (Light and life have weakened,
> warmth and joy have disappeared.
> Sullen days are followed by
> dark nights of great length.)

Similar telescopings occur in the following Recitative (No. 31), which bring us to the heart of winter and deep drifts of snow. Only here and there can we find a phrase in Swieten that might be said to derive from Thomson, such as 'The cherish'd fields put on their winter robe of purest white' (Swieten: 'Die Felder deckt, die Thäler füllt ein' ungeheure Flockenlast'). On the other hand, the libretto faithfully follows the idea of someone (Thomson has a 'swain', Swieten a 'wanderer') getting lost in the snow (Aria No. 32).

> . . . the swain
> Disaster'd stands; sees other hills ascend,
> Of unknown joyless brow; and other scenes,
> Of horrid prospect, shag the trackless plain.
> . . .

> . . . Now sinks his soul!
> What black despair, what horror fills his heart!
> When for the dusky spot, which fancy feign'd
> His tufted cottage rising through the snow,
> He meets the roughness of the middle waste,
> Far from the track, and blest abode of man
> . . .

> . . . On ev'ry nerve
> The deadly Winter seizes, shuts up sense,
> And o'er his inmost vitals creeping cold,
> Lays him along the snows a stiffen'd corse,
> Stretch'd out, and bleaching in the northern blast.

Swieten has, however, made a radical and characteristic change. In his version, the wanderer suddenly finds a friendly house.

> Jetzt sinket ihm der Muth,
> Und Angst beklemmt sein Herz:
> Doch plötzlich trifft sein spähend Aug'
> Der Schimmer eines nahen Lichts.

> (Now courage begins to forsake him,
> and fear grips his heart:
> but suddenly his eagle eye
> finds the gleam of a nearby light.)

In Thomson's poem there is another gigantic digression, involving 'The Jail Committee, in the year 1729' (footnote to 'the generous band'), Socrates, Greece, Sparta, Rome, 'The British Muse', the 'MORAL SCENE' and so on – all part of a winter evening as spent by the philosophers. Earlier in the poem (line 134 of 'Winter') we have a thought

> Even as the matron, at her nightly task,
> With pensive labour draws the flaxen thread . . .

which Swieten expanded into one of the most satisfactory sections of his libretto. After a Recitative (No. 33) describing the 'warme Stube' (the warm room) in a village, we hear of 'easy work and merry talk' (also taken from a later passage in Thomson – 'Heard solemn goes the goblin story round . . . Rustic mirth goes round . . .') and there then follows an interpolation, the 'Spinnerlied' (Spinning Song) by Gottfried August Bürger, whose poetry Haydn is known to have liked. There next follows a bit of 'rustic mirth', a Recitative (No. 35) leading to another highly successful interpolation, a *Lied mit Chor* (No. 36) known variously as a 'Romance' or 'Fairy Story'. The song started life as a French 'Romance' by Madame Favart, whose husband, Charles Simon Favart, had written *Les trois sultanes* (1761), for a German translation of which Haydn had composed incidental music which has come down to us embedded in Symphony No. 63 ('La Roxelane'). Madame Favart's song was incorporated into Johann Adam Hiller's *Singspiel* entitled *Die Liebe auf dem Lande* (1768), the German translation having been prepared by Christian Felix Weisse.[1] Swieten and Haydn placed this story, 'Ein Mädchen, das auf Ehre hielt', in the middle of 'Winter' to introduce a lighter element into a serious section. While the Spinning Song is simply a description of the spinning wheels 'whirring', the Romance is the story of a girl who outwits a licentious noblemen – once again a favourite theme of Haydn's that we know from *L'infedeltà delusa* (where, however, the nobleman and the nobleman's drunken German servant are both parodies, being Vespina, the heroine, in disguise: the basic theme, nonetheless, is the same).

Another Recitative (No. 37) describes the earth in the grip of icy winter; again, it is a paraphrase of several hundred lines in Thomson:

> Vom dürren Osten dringt
> Ein scharfer Eishauch jetzt hervor.
> Schneidend fährt er durch die Luft,
> Verzehret jeden Dunst
> Und hascht des Tieres Odem selbst.
> Des grimmigen Tyranns,
> Des Winters Sieg ist nun vollbracht,
> Und stummer Schrecken
> Drückt den ganzen Umfang der Natur.

> (From the dry East
> an icy blast now presses.
> It cuts sharply through the air,
> destroying every breath,
> even that of living souls.
> The grim tyrant,
> Winter, has now conquered all
> and dumb terror
> now spreads over the earth.)

Swieten now takes up Thomson's metaphor of man's life ending like winter:

> 'Tis done! dread WINTER spreads his latest glooms,
> And reigns tremendous o'er the conquer'd year.
> How dead the vegetable kingdom lies!

---

1 Madame M. J. B. Favart's work was entitled *Annette et Lubin* and was composed in 1762. A German translation (and reworking) of Madame Favart's Operette was produced by Johann Joachim Eschenburg in 1763 as a *Singspiel* entitled *Lucas und Hannchen*. See Julien Tiersot, 'Le Lied, "Ein Mädchen, das auf Ehre hielt" et ses prototypes français', in *Zeitschrift der Internationalen Musikgesellschaft*, 12. Jg., 1910–11, pp. 159ff; Max Friedlaender, *Das deutsche Lied im 18. Jahrhundert*, Band II (Stuttgart-Berlin 1902), pp. 113f., 137. Also Pohl III, 368.

How dumb the tuneful! Horror wide extends
His desolate domain. Behold, fond man!
See here thy pictur'd life! – Pass some few years,
Thy flowering Spring – thy Summer's ardent strength,
Thy sober Autumn fading into age –
And pale concluding Winter comes at last,
And shuts the scene. Ah! whither now are fled
Those dreams of greatness? those unsolid hopes
Of happiness? those longings after fame?
Those restless cares? those busy bustling days?
Those gay spent festive nights? those veering thoughts
Lost between good and all, that shar'd thy life?
All now are vanish'd! VIRTUE sole-survives,
Immortal, never-failing friend of man,
His guide to happiness on high.

In the libretto, Swieten actually used, for his English translation of the last sentence of
the Recitative, the words ''Tis done' (coinciding with our 'The grim tyrant' etc.), and
for the ensuing Aria & Recitative (No. 38) he adheres rather closely to the original
poem:

[Aria]
Erblicke hier, betörter Mensch,
Erblicke deines Lebens Bild!
Verblühet ist dein kurzer Lenz,
Erschöpfet deines Sommers Kraft.
Schon welkt dein Herbst dem Alter zu,
Schon naht der bleiche Winter sich
Und zeiget dir das off'ne Grab.

Wo sind sie nun, die hoh'n Entwürfe,
Die Hoffnungen vom Glück,
Die Sucht nach eit'lem Ruhme,
Der Sorgen schwere Last?
Wo sind sie nun, die Wonnetage,
Verschwelgt in Üppigkeit?
Und wo die frohen Nächte,
Im Taumel durchgewacht?
Verschwunden sind sie wie ein Traum.
Nur Tugend bleibt.

[Recitative]
Sie bleibt allein und leitet uns,
Unwandelbar, durch Zeit und Jahreswechsel,
Durch Jammer oder Freude
Bis zu dem höchsten Ziele hin.

For the concluding number (No. 39, Trio with Double Chorus), Swieten begins
with Thomson's lines following 'His guide to happiness on high', quoted above:

. . . And see!
'Tis come, the glorious morn! the second birth
Of heaven and earth! awakening nature hears
The *new-creating word*, and starts to life,
In every heighten'd form, from pain and death
For ever free.

Van Swieten's German –

> Dann bricht der große Morgen an,
> Der Allmacht zweytes Wort
> Erweckt zum neuen Daseyn uns,
> Von Pein und Tod auf immer frey.

– may be compared with his own English translation of the paraphrase:

> Then comes the great and glorious morn,
> The new-created word
> Awakes to second life us all,
> From pain and death for ever free.

This is of course much better than some of the Baron's English (e.g. No. 37: 'Fiercely roring [*sic*] throughout the sky, it seizes ev'ry wet, and self the breath of living souls') but it shows the whole difficulty in providing a new English text to Swieten's German adaptation. From this point to the end, Swieten proceeds with a moralizing pseudo-prayer which he considered a more fitting conclusion than either the somewhat flat ending of Thomson's actual poem or the lengthy 'Hymn' which rounds off the whole cycle, Swieten has a series of questions and answers divided up between the soloists, Chorus I and Chorus II:

> Die Himmelspforten öffnen sich,
> Der heil'ge Berg erscheint.
> Ihr krönt des Herren Zelt,
> Wo Ruh' und Friede thront.
>
> Wer darf durch diese Pforten geh'n?
>
> Der Arges mied und Gutes that.
>
> Wer darf besteigen diesen Berg?
>
> Von dessen Lippen Wahrheit floß!
>
> Wer darf in diesem Zelte wohnen?
>
> Der Armen und Bedrängten half!
>
> Wer wird den Frieden dort genießen?
>
> Der Schutz und Recht der Unschuld gab!
>
> O seht, der große Morgen naht!
>
> O seht, er leuchtet schon!
>
> Die Himmelspforten öffnen sich,
> Der heil'ge Berg erscheint.
>
> Vorüber sind,
>   verbrauset sind,
> Die leydenvolle Tage,
>   des Lebens Winterstürme!
>
> Ein ew'ger Frühling herrscht;
> Und grenzenlose Seligkeit
> Wird der Gerechten Lohn!

Auch uns werd' einst ein solcher Lohn!
Laßt uns wirken, laßt uns kämpfen!

Laßt uns kämpfen, laßt uns harren
Zu erringen diesen Preis!

Uns leite deine Hand, o Gott!
Verleyh' uns Stärk' und Muth!
Dann singen wir,
                     dann geh'n wir ein
In dieses Reiches Herrlichkeit. Amen.

(The Heavenly gates open,
the holy mount appears,
crowned by the Lord's tent,
where peace eternal dwells.

Who may enter these gates?

He who avoided evil and did good.

Who may climb this mount?

He from whose lips came truth.

Who may dwell in this tent?

He who helped the poor and needy.

Who will enjoy peace there?

He who gave protection and law to the innocent.

See, the great morning approaches!

See, it begins to shine!

The gates of Heaven open,
the holy mount appears.

Passed away,
               and forgotten
the cruel days
               of life's winter storms!

Here there is ever spring,
and endless bounty
will be the reward of the righteous!

For us, too, there will be such a reward!
Let us participate, let us battle!

Let us battle, let us hold out for
this great reward.

Lead our hand, O God!
Give us strength and courage!
Then we shall sing,
                     then we shall enter
in the glory of this kingdom. Amen.)

By now the reader will have some idea of the methods by which Baron van Swieten produced his by no means unclever adaptation of Thomson's poem. Of course there were elements in Thomson that Swieten could hardly translate, given his concept of having living persons tell the story. Thomson's audacity in constructing the poem precisely *without* such living persons, i.e. without sustained narrative action, was what interested Swieten least; the Baron was much more attuned to the nature-poetical aspect of the poem, and indeed chose largely – though as we have seen not exclusively – from this side of Thomson's work. Yet Swieten, and Haydn in particular, understood one element of the Scottish poet's work which has, until recently, been largely overlooked: the subtle range of encounter between inanimate nature and human life in *The Seasons*. There may be no narrative, and by including one (at least occasionally) Swieten may have coarsened Thomson's delicate wash of linguistic colour, but both the composer and the librettist understood that one of the most rewarding things about the poem was the interplay between animate and inanimate objects. In a way, this quiet perception in Thomson has its climax in the final section of 'Winter', where man himself is likened to the fading year.

Swieten also could not translate Thomson's felicitous diction, with its (then brilliantly new) reliance on Latin-derived words and its compact organization of the blank verse into paragraphs rather than linear thoughts, a Miltonian concept which Swieten well knew, among other things, from *The Creation* libretto, as well, of course, as from its original, *Paradise Lost*. Basically Swieten thought in prose rather than poetry, and when he had to devise verses of his own – as was quite frequently the case in *The Seasons* – the result is hardly ever inspiring either as poetry or as stimulating intellectual thought. It is too rooted in German *Pietismus*, on the one hand, and on an age-of-Enlightenment motivation to 'educate', on the other. Griesinger's idea, that *The Creation* and *The Seasons* would be beneficial to the *moral* tone of Austro-Germanic society is certainly an echo of the Baron's, perhaps also of Haydn's, aesthetic principles. That is why *The Seasons* ends with the heavenly gates rather than Thomson's philosophical ruminations on Power and Wisdom ('why heaven-born truth, and moderation fair, wore the red marks of superstition's scourge'); also, perhaps, Haydn and Swieten were still smarting under the criticisms of *The Creation* as being fundamentally Masonic, too much rooted in the Josephinian Enlightenment, somewhat deistic in places, and not fitted for use in the Church. Thomson's poem never had the leanings towards direct religious beliefs that we find inserted in the Oratorio at strategic places; Swieten and Haydn made a semi-religious work out of what was basically a secular poem (whose deistic leanings they, in any case, almost entirely removed).

Swieten's adaptation cannot be called a great libretto. It falls far below *The Creation* in strength of language, unity of concept and especially in organizational planning. But Haydn made almost superhuman exertions and managed to create a work which, by the stunning power of its music, has long been placed alongside the earlier Oratorio. *The Seasons* is a brilliant success despite, and not because of, its libretto; but although Swieten's language is not inspiring, his organization slipshod and his choice of detail dubious, the libretto as such has many good points. The long 'Finale' is rather well thought out, with its antiphonal choral disposition and the use of the three soloists as a third vocal element. Some of the arias were ideally suited to Haydn (particularly the cavatinas), and the descriptions of the animals, the thunderstorm, and so on were all calculated to fire the septuagenarian's still vivid imagination.

(2) The Swieten Autograph

Formerly owned by Max Friedlaender, the Swieten autograph libretto now exists only in fragmentary photographs and in a transcription by E. F. Schmid (*vide infra*, p. 123) published by the Haydn Institut.[1] The original title of the autograph was 'Die Jahrszeiten' (not 'Jahreszeiten'). As in the case of *The Creation*, there are a few small differences in the libretto between this autograph and the final published score and the first published libretti of 1801. As in the earlier oratorio, Swieten offered advice to Haydn, much of which the composer accepted. We follow the plan here of citing Swieten's advice; the numbers and page references refer to those of the score published by Philharmonia (W. Ph. V. 28; textually based on the critical score edited by Eusebius von Mandyczewski for Breitkopf & Härtel, *Haydns Werke*, Ser. XVI, Bände 6/7, 1922).

No. 1 (p. 1) 'The Introduction describes the passage from Winter to Spring.' [Swieten's comment:] The style [*Züge*] is suggested by the text of the Recitative [pp. 26ff.], and it should serve as the accompaniment to it. [Haydn followed this suggestion.]

No. 8 (pp. 104ff.). [Swieten's comment:] Up to the point where the vocal basses enter [p. 125, 'Laßt erschallen'], it would be good to have only violoncelli in the bass section of the instrumental accompaniment. [Haydn ignored this comment and had double basses throughout.] At the entrance of 'Ewiger &c.' [p. 127] I think that a key remarkably different from that of the preceding Song of Joy would create a good effect and would greatly bring into prominence the solemn and devotional aspect of the [choir's] cry. [Haydn followed this suggestion and wrote the first part of the movement in A major and the 'Ewiger' in B flat major.]

Then I would like to have the melodic line of the words 'Ewiger' &c. used either as the theme or as the countersubject of the fugue which is to enter with the words 'Ehre, Lob' &c. [p. 135], and to this end the words 'Ewiger' &c., after the whole chorus is repeated, have been appointed once again in the three principal [solo] parts [see p. 134], each one of them, so that the beginning of the fugue 'Ehre, Lob' &c. can be clearly realized. [Haydn ignored this suggestion.]

No. 9 (pp. 154ff.). [Swieten's comment:] The Introduction should describe morning twilight, as the succeeding Recitative says, and should serve as its accompaniment. [Haydn followed this idea.]

The twilight must continue, just as the approaching day must grow up to sunrise, as is indicated in the second Recitative. The Introduction therefore could end with the sound of the screech-owl, since in the Recitative it is not to be heard any longer. [Haydn did not describe the sound of the 'screech-owl' but instead set the tone of 'gloomy night' and the mournful sound of night-birds.] [p. 156].

No. 10 (pp. 159ff.). [Swieten's comment:] This Aria, the accompaniment of which must continue to describe the morning-twilight, ought therefore to be short and should not much exceed the usual length of a *Cavatina*.

The sound of the shepherd's pipe to gather together the flocks should make a good effect after the end of the Recitative, and might serve as the ritornello. [Haydn wrote a relatively short Aria which merges with the following Recitative, but he used not the

---

1 Max Friedlaender, 'Van Swieten und das Textbuch zu Haydns Jahreszeiten', in *Peters Jahrbuch* 1909, pp. 47ff. See also p. 120, note 1.

shepherd's pipe but the French horn, in a traditional 'call' that summoned the shepherds and their herds to go forth to the fields in the early morning.]

No. 11 (pp. 167ff.). [Swieten's comments:] After the end of the Recitative, when the chorus expresses its vivid joy, it would seem that the Song of Praise [*Lobgesang*, 'Heil! o Sonne, Heil!' pp. 170ff.] might well be construed as a solemn expression of respect, which could turn into thankful feelings upon the listing of the various benefits. [Haydn started the number slowly, speeded up to allegro at the Song of Praise, and used alternating soloists and choir; at p. 181, he introduces a middle section, andante, to the words 'Dir danken wir'.]

At the words 'Dir jauchzen' &c. [pp. 186ff.] there could be introduced with good effect a fugue which, while not exactly strict, could well be based on a running theme. [Haydn followed this suggestion.]

No. 14 (pp. 204ff.). [Swieten's comment:] The words, 'Des Schäfers Rohr' (shepherd's pipe), are placed there to prepare, in the accompaniment, the presence of an oboe for the following aria, whereby in the rest of the orchestral accompaniment I would like to hear also the murmuring of the brook, the humming of the flying insects, so that the picture given in the Recitative may be fully realized. [Haydn used the oboe at the end of the Recitative and in the following Aria No. 15. For the descriptions requested by the Baron, however, Haydn used only the strings, though the beginning of the Recitative also includes one flute, two bassoons and two horns.]

No. 16 (pp. 225ff.). [Swieten's comments:] Muffled roll of the kettledrums [after 'in schwarzes Dunkel ein', p. 226]. Perhaps the part of the Recitative in which Jane sings [p. 227] could be taken in tempo and accompanied with short accented or pizzicato notes, so as to have the stringed instruments ready for the lightning. Lightning and thunder. [Haydn used pizzicato strings in tempo, poco adagio, but preferred the flute to express the lightning on p. 228.]

No. 17 (pp. 228ff.). [Swieten's comments:] The 'Ach' of the choir requires a penetrating expression of sudden terror, which must manifest itself as suddenly as a thunderclap. [Haydn used the orchestra, and especially the *ff assai* kettledrum stroke, to express this shock.] Lightning [bar 9, triplets in upper woodwind]. Thunder [bars 11f., timpani roll with *fz* inserted in the middle].

The 'Hilf uns, Himmel' [p. 237] of the women can be embedded in the song of the other voices and then brought into prominence by means of sharply dissonant notes. [Haydn ignored this suggestion.] The storm rages for a while still; then it recedes, little by little, and finally disappears entirely [pp. 258ff.].

No. 25 (pp. 370ff.). [Swieten's comments:] Here [after 'Die Hasen aus dem Lager auf'] the [orchestral] accompaniment could enter and describe the running about of the hunted hares, and perhaps also the sound of shots as well. [Haydn had the orchestra enter as Swieten suggested but ignored the suggestion of gunshots.]

The Recitative does not have to end with a cadence but can be interrupted with the horn call – *Lancé* – and thereafter the chorus should enter at once. [Suggestion followed.]

No. 26 (pp. 373ff.). [Swieten's comment:] The 'Halali' [pp. 405ff.] of the hunters, which they sing by themselves at the beginning, must again appear importantly in the following Chorus of the Peasants, and in such a way that the middle syllable of the

'Ha–la–li' is at the end very extended. [Haydn mixed up the choruses of the hunters and peasants but extended the middle syllable of 'Halali'.]

No. 28 (pp. 418ff.). [Swieten's comments:] [The Baron obviously planned a double chorus, dividing the forces into 'Männer und Burschen . . . Tenori, Bassi' and 'Weiber und Mädchen . . . Canti, Alti'. Then:] All. When *all* sing, the second chorus should enter to reinforce 'Juch-he' [pp. 427f.; Haydn ignored this comment and wrote for one chorus. At the words 'Nun tönen die Pfeifen und wirbelt die Trommel', pp. 436ff., Swieten requests:] These instruments, when they are mentioned, must also be heard, and heard until the last entrance of the chorus. But since they are not grouped in one place but are spread throughout in various groups, they must have differing melodies and differing rhythms and come forth with the one or the other melody. Thus the fiddles could have the German *waltz*, the drums and pipes the 'Juch-he', the lyre and bagpipes could sometimes be heard in the *waltzes*. The *Contratempi* should be useful in suggesting the varied places of the instruments. [Swieten thought of several orchestras, as in the ball scene in *Don Giovanni*, but Haydn ignored this plan, and also Swieten's complicated suggestions for bringing in the various instruments so as to suggest depth and different physical locations. Haydn brought in the 'Turkish' instruments towards the end, pp. 457ff.]

No. 29 (pp. 466ff.). [Swieten's comment:] The thick fog must serve as the accompaniment [when the voice enters]; perhaps long-held low notes would be useful. [Haydn solved this problem in his own fashion.]

When *Jane* has the words, the accompaniment stops, so that the *Cavatina* or the *in Tempo*, which should be accompanied, stands out more. [Haydn ignored this suggestion.]

No. 31 (pp. 475f.). [Swieten's comment:] [At the words 'Der Erde Bild ist nun ein Grab', p. 476] Here the long-held low notes of the accompaniment could enter, to describe the monotonous, sad face of the earth. [Haydn had the orchestra enter, after the secco accompaniment, but not with the music of the Introduction.]

No. 33 (p. 493). [Swieten's comment:] At the last four verses ['Am Rocken spinnen die Mütter'] the whirring of the spinning wheels could enter as the accompaniment, and at the end of the Recitative the Spinning Song with the choruses of women and girls could enter immediately. [Haydn followed Swieten's suggestion precisely.]

No. 36 (p. 512). [Swieten's original title was 'Romance', changed to 'Das Mährchen'.]

No. 38 (p. 540). [Swieten's comment:] At the words 'wie ein Traum' the instrumental accompaniment should disappear upwards. The end of the Aria occurs at the first four words of the Recitative ['Wo sind sie nun', p. 539] and the vocal part should be without accompaniment and have a recitative-like cadence, finishing with the full orchestral accompaniment, even the timpani (which therefore should not be used in the Aria), and with big notes [*mit vollen Noten*], to suggest the resolution of the word virtue [*Tugend*]. Whereupon the simple Recitative with the words 'Sie bleibt allein' [p. 541] should enter. [Haydn disregarded most of this suggestion.]

No. 39 (pp. 560ff.). [Swieten's original plan was to conclude with a double fugue, as follows:]

Doppelfuge

I^{ter} Chor
Thema: 'Uns leite deine Hand, o Gott';
Contrasubject: 'Sie lehr' uns deinen Weg'.

2ter Chor
Thema: 'Auf dich, o Herr, vertrauen wir';
Contrasubject: 'Verleyh' uns Muth und Kraft!'

[This plan was later abandoned, and Haydn composed a fugue for single choir.]

The composer was not enchanted with the libretto. We have several authentic reports, of which three may find a place here. The most interesting is perhaps from G. A. Griesinger's biography (pp. 39f.):

> Baron Swieten, then nearly seventy years of age, was a man interested in the arts and sciences, whose opinion was considered very weighty in the circle of the great in whose presence he moved. The rules according to which works of taste were to be judged were not foreign to him; but in his own productions he fell into all the lacunae and mistakes that he would have severely objected to in others. The best in his poetry was not that which he actually wrote but that which he imagined, and it was curious that his works were not distinguished by any of those beauties which, according to his intentions and his feelings, they should have contained.
>
> Haydn often complained bitterly about the unpoetic text of *The Seasons*, and how hard it was for him to wax enthusiastic over such things as 'Heysasa, Hopsasa, es lebe der Wein! es lebe das Faß, das ihn verwahrt! es lebe der Krug, woraus er fließt!', etc. When he came to the section 'O Fleiß, o edler Fleiß, von dir kommt alles Heil!' he remarked that he had been an industrious man his whole life long, but it had never occurred to him to set industry to music. Haydn attributed the weakness which grew ever more marked from this time to the effort which composing *The Seasons* cost him. Shortly after having completed the work, he was seized with a brain fever, and at that time he described it as his greatest martyrdom how his fantasy was continually occupied with notes and music.
>
> Once it was decided to set to music a libretto of this kind, Haydn certainly did all he could, and only a composer of genius could succeed in rendering less conspicuous, by means of an attractive façade, the unattractive aspects of the material. Thoughts which were expressed in dull and often vulgar prose were really ennobled and idealized by the magic of the musical poetry. . . .

A. C. Dies, Haydn's garrulous biographer, adds several interesting details:

> Since *The Seasons* succeeded *The Creation* so quickly, and Haydn was still older by several years, and at that age wanted to bring to pass the bold enterprise of a work which should overflow with youthful energy, it is easy to believe that he overexerted himself, as he had already said [17 August 1806, after making several mistakes at the piano, Haydn exclaimed: '. . . You can hear for yourself, it's no good any longer! Eight years ago it was different, but *The Seasons* has brought this misery on me. I never should have written it! I overworked myself in doing so!']
>
> Moreover, there arose several small annoyances between him and the *Freiherr* van Swieten because of the text. Haydn was frequently annoyed about the many descriptive passages or imitations in *The Seasons*; he was especially displeased by the croaking of the frogs. He sensed the baseness and tried to conceal it from the

auditor. Swieten criticized him on this account and produced an old piece by ★ ★ ★ [Grétry] in which the croaks were displayed prominently, and attempted to make Haydn imitate it. . . .

Swieten criticized the Aria in *The Seasons* in which the husbandman goes behind the plough and whistles a melody from the 'Surprise' Symphony's Andante. He wanted to persuade Haydn instead to use a song from a rather popular opera and named two or three such operas. This request was really insulting. Haydn realized it and answered with confidence: 'I won't change a thing! My Andante is as good as any song from those operas.'

Swieten took offence at this and no longer visited Haydn. Twelve days went by. Then Haydn went to Swieten but had to wait half-an-hour in the anti-chambre. Finally he lost his patience and was about to leave, when he was called back and admitted. Haydn could not at once conceal his rage and said to the *Freiherr*: 'You called me back at the right moment. I almost saw your anti-chambre for the last time.'

Haydn said about *The Seasons* that in order to lift it out of the eternal monotony of imitations, he hit on the idea of representing drunkenness in the final fugue [of 'Autumn']. 'My head,' he said, 'was so full of that mad business "Es lebe der Wein, es lebe das Faß"', that I let everything go to pieces in it, and that's why I call that final fugue the drunken fugue.'   [Dies 137, 180f.]

Neukomm, commenting on this passage, writes as follows:

. . . In this role [that of a 'Protecteur' of both Haydn and Mozart] he [Swieten] persecuted his protégé in a quite appalling way when H. was composing *The Seasons* and he often said so in confidence to me, sighing, especially about the leathery [*ledernen*] text which H. through his magic notes drew up from the swamp. Swieten in all seriousness demanded of Haydn that instead of the well-known Andante he should use a disgusting [*jämmerlichen*] street song from the Schikaneder and Heibl [*sic*] Opera, *Der Tyroler Wastl*! His Excellency the Ambassador had no idea of the people's poetry [*Volkspoesie*], or of the people's language – he was of the time when the word 'people' was synonymous with 'canaille' – and therefore the prosaic Hanna, Lukas and Simon as 'personae dramatis'; therefore the silly toasts 'es lebe der Krug', 'es lebe das Faß' etc. *Jam satti*! I heard every note of this wonderful series of tone-paintings (for *The Seasons* is not, and cannot be, an Oratorio) in their newest newness tête-à-tête with Haydn at the piano, as my great teacher dragged his cross past every act of martyrdom, pointing it out, like a Catholic Mount of Calvary. But his critics can have not the faintest idea of all these stones and thorns; those critics about whom he would sometimes say, in his humorous way, 'Yes, yes, these gentlemen have pointed and witty pens; but when they have to compose eight bars, then their ears stand out, more pointed and wittier than their pens.' – In this connection a criticism of M. Berlioz in his feuilleton in the *Journal des débats* occurs to me, wherein he preaches *ex cathedra* about H's *Creation* and calls the descriptive recitatives 'les niaiseries du bon homme Haydn'. – Who cannot help but think of the fable by La Fontaine, 'le lion mourant'? *Difficile est satyram non dicere!*   [Neukomm, 31]

To these authentic anecdotes may be added a contemporary note in the *Neue Teutsche Merkur* of 1801, a journal edited by C. M. Wieland, in which an anonymous Viennese correspondent writes about Lichtenstein's *Bathmendi* and Haydn's *The Seasons*. According to this report, Swieten forced on the composer 'all kinds of pictures, often of the most common variety', so that Haydn's victory over the word was difficult.[1]

It is hard to see why the descriptive passages in *The Seasons* gave Haydn so much more trouble than those in *The Creation*, which he obviously composed with relish. Perhaps, however, he really was feeling his age; perhaps, too, the Baron's autocratic manner did not improve with time and closer proximity; but most of all, Haydn may have realized that the critics would seek out just those passages for contempt, as indeed they had done with *The Creation*. The prosaic quality of much of *The Seasons* cannot be denied, however, and it does no good to blame it on Thomson, as Horst Walter of the Joseph Haydn Institut has recently tried to do. 'The weaknesses of the text', he writes, 'manifest themselves especially in those places where the poet follows the dry and schoolmasterish character of the original source'[2] – a statement that presupposes Herr Walter to have a knowledge of English poetry in general and Thomson in particular which we somehow beg leave to doubt he possesses. The dryness and schoolmasterishness are largely the work of the stiff Baron; whatever natural charm, especially in the descriptions of nature, that the libretto contains must be credited, as the reader will have been able to see for himself even in this brief exposé, to James Thomson and hardly to Gottfried van Swieten. The fact that *The Seasons* has survived is as much due to Haydn's genius as the survival of *Die Zauberflöte* is to Mozart's (whereby Schikaneder, in his pandering to popular taste, at least had the great advantage of understanding such taste from within, as it were). Nevertheless, if it had not been for the Baron's persistence, we should be the poorer for a great masterpiece. Haydn may have considered that '*The Seasons* broke my back', but it is doubtful if without the Baron's pressure Haydn would have written much more after 1802, *Seasons* or no. And after Swieten's death, Haydn could never find another libretto on the grand scale which he was willing to compose; there is even the possibility that, had Swieten lived a few more years, he might have beaten, bribed and coaxed yet a third great Oratorio out of Haydn.

II. THE SKETCHES

In contrast to the rich legacy of sketches for *The Creation*, we have only one set of sketches for *The Seasons*. It belonged formerly to Felix Mendelssohn-Bartholdy and is now in the Preussische Staatsbibliothek in Berlin. The sketch consists of four pages, of which pages one and four are blank, while pages two and three contain drafts to Nos. 33 (Recitative) and 36 (Song with Chorus). The first page is reproduced in Geiringer 1932, p. 145, and also in *Musiker Handschriften von Palestrina bis Beethoven* (edited by Walter Gerstenberg, Zürich 1960, No. 98). The music of the sketch has been well transcribed by Georg Schünemann ('Ein Skizzenblatt Joseph Haydns', in *Die Musik* VIII [1908/9], Heft 16, pp. 211ff.), including differences between the sketch and the final version, and we refer interested readers to this publication.

---

1 Horst Walter, 'Gottfried van Swietens handschriftliche Textbücher zu "Schöpfung" und "Jahreszeiten"', in *Haydn-Studien* I (1967), Heft 4, p. 246.
2 Ibid.

III. THE MUSIC

(1) List of the Numbers and their Orchestration

All numbers refer to the Philharmonia miniature score No. 28. The principal soloists in the work are: Hanne (soprano); Lucas (tenor); Simon (bass).

DER FRÜHLING

No. 1 *Einleitung und Rezitativ. Die Einleitung stellt den Übergang vom Winter zum Frühling vor.* G minor, *Largo, alla breve*; *Vivace*→V of G. Soloists: Hanne, Lucas, Simon. The Recitative changes tempo to *Adagio*. 2 fl., 2 ob., 2 clar. in B♭, 2 fag., contrafag., 2 cor. in B♭, 2 *clarini* (trpts.) in C, 3 trbns. (alto, tenor and bass), timpani, str. 'Seht wie der strenge Winter flieht'.

No. 2 *Chor des Landvolks* (S-A-T-B), G major, *Allegretto*, 6/8. 2 fl., 2 ob., 2 fag., contrafag., 2 cor. in G, str. 'Komm, holder Lenz!'

No. 3 *Rezitativ (secco)* Simon. 'Vom Widder strahlet jetzt'.

No. 4 *Arie* (Simon), C major, *Allegretto*, 2/4. piccolo, 2 ob., 2 fag., 2 cor. in C, str. 'Schon eilet froh der Ackermann'.

No. 5 *Rezitativ (secco)* Lucas. 'Der Landmann hat sein Werk vollbracht'.

No. 6 *Terzett und Chor* (S-A-T-B). Soloists: Hanne, Lucas, Simon. F major, *Poco Adagio*, 3/4. 2 fl., 2 ob., 2 clar. in C, 2 fag., contrafag., 2 cor. in F, 3 trbns., str. 'Sey nun gnädig'.→*Un poco più moto*.

No. 7 *Rezitativ (secco)* Hanne 'Erhört ist unser Flehn', leading to *Andante*, 2/4, A major *(accompagnato)*, 'Sie häufen sich'.

No. 8 *Freudenlied, mit abwechselndem Chore der Jugend* (S-A-T-B). Progressive tonality: A major, *Adante*, 2/4→B flat, *Maestoso*, leading to *Poco Adagio*→*Allegro*. 2 fl., 2 ob. 2 clar. in B♭, 2 fag., contrafag., 2 cor. in B♭, 2 trpts. in B♭, 3 trbns., timp., str. 'O wie lieblich ist der Anblick'.

DER SOMMER

No. 9 *Einleitung und Rezitativ. Die Einleitung stellt die Morgendämmerung vor.* C minor, *Adagio*, 4/4→V of C major. 1 ob., 2 clar. in B♭, 1 fag., str. Soloists: Lucas, Simon. 'In grauem Schleier'.

No. 10 *Arie und Rezitativ.* Arie (Simon), F major, *Allegretto*, 6/8. 1 fl., 2 ob., 1 fag., 1 cor. in F, str. 'Der muntre Hirt' leading to Recitative (Hanne) 'Die Morgenröthe'→D major.

No. 11 *Terzett und Chor* (S-A-T-B). D major, *Largo*, 4/4→*Allegro*→*Andante*→*Allegro*. Soloists: Hanne, Lucas, Simon. 2 fl., 2 ob., 2 fag., contrafag., 2 cor. in D, 2 trpts., 3 trbns., timp., str. 'Sie steigt herauf, die Sonne'.

No. 12 *Rezitativ (secco)* Simon. 'Nun regt und bewegt sich alles umher', leading to *accompagnato*, no tempo→[*Larghetto*]. Lucas. 'Die Mittagssonne brennet jetzt in voller Gluth'. Str. A→E major.

No. 13 *Cavatine* (Lucas), E major, *Largo*, 4/4. 1 fl., 1 ob., str. 'Dem Druck erlieget die Natur'.

No. 14 *Rezitativ (accompagnato).* Hanne. C major, *Poco Adagio*, 4/4. 1 fl., 1 ob., 2 fag., 2 cor. in C, str. 'Willkommen jetzt'.→B flat major.

No. 15 *Arie* (Hanne). B flat major, *Adagio*, 3/4. 1 fl., 2 ob., 2 clar. in B♭, 2 fag., 2 cor. in B♭ [*alto*], str. 'Welche Labung für die Sinne'→*Allegro assai*, 4/4.

No. 16 *Rezitativ (secco)* Simon (later Lucas) 'O seht! Es steiget in der schwülen Luft'→ *(accompagnato)*, D flat, 3/4 (Hanne) 'In banger Ahndung' leading to V of C. Str., timp. solo.

No. 17 *Chor* (S–A–T–B), C minor, *Allegro assai*, 4/4→*Allegro, alla breve*. 2 fl., 2 ob., 2 clar. in B♭, 2 fag., contrafag., 2 cor. in C, 2 trpts. in C, 3 trbns., timp., str. 'Ach, das Ungewitter naht!'

No. 18 *Terzett und Chor* (S–A–T–B), F major, *Allegretto*, 2/4→E flat major, *Allegro*, 3/4. 2 fl., 2 ob., 2 clar. in B♭, 2 fag., contrafag., 2 cor. in E♭, 2 trbns., str. Soloists: Hanne, Lucas, Simon. 'Die düstren Wolken trennen sich'.

DER HERBST

No. 19 *Einleitung und Rezitativ. Der Einleitung Gegenstand ist des Landmanns freudiges Gefühl über die reiche Ernte.* G major, *Allegretto*, 3/4; leading to Recitative (*accompagnato*) Hanne. 'Was durch seine Blüthe'. Str.; leading to *secco* (Lucas, Simon). 'Den reichen Vorrath führt er nun'.

No. 20 *Terzett mit Chor* (S–A–T–B). C major, *Allegretto*, 4/4→*Più Allegro*. Soloists: Hanne, Lucas, Simon. 2 fl., 2 ob., 2 fag., contrafag., 2 cor. in C, 2 trpts. in C, timp., str. 'So lohnet die Natur den Fleiß'.

No. 21 *Rezitativ* (*secco*). Hanne, Lucas, Simon. 'Seht, wie zum Haselbusche dort'.

No. 22 *Duett* (Hanne–Lucas). B flat, *Allegretto*, 2/4. 1 fl., 2 ob., 2 clar. in B♭, 2 fag., str. 'Ihr Schönen aus der Stadt'.

No. 23 *Rezitativ* (*secco*) Simon. 'Nun zeiget das entblößte Feld'.

No. 24 *Arie* (Simon), A minor, *Allegro*, 4/4. 1 fl., 2 ob., 1 fag., timp., str. 'Seht auf die breiten Wiesen hin'. Twice the tempo changes to '*Più moto*'→A major.

No. 25 *Rezitativ* (*secco*, then *accompagnato*) Lucas. Progressive tonality, from VI of E minor→D major. 2 ob., 2 fag., str. 'Hier treibt ein dichter Kreis'.

No. 26 *Chor* (*Landvolk und Jäger*, S–A–T–B). D major, *Vivace*, 6/8. 2 fl., 2 ob., 2 clar. in B♭, 2 fag., contrafag., 4 cor. in D, later E♭, 3 trbns., str. 'Hört das laute Getön'.

No. 27 *Rezitativ* (*secco*) Hanne, Lucas, Simon. 'Am Rebenstocke blinket jetzt'.

No. 28 *Chor* (S–A–T–B), *Allegro molto*, C major, 4/4→*Allegro assai*→G major (E minor)→C major. 2 fl., 2 ob., 2 clar. in C, 2 fag., contrafag., 2 cor. in C, 2 trpts. in C, 3 trbns., timp., triangle, tambourine, str. 'Juchhe, Juchhe! der Wein ist da.'

DER WINTER

No. 29 *Einleitung und Rezitativ. Die Einleitung schildert die dicken Nebel, womit der Winter anfängt.* C minor, *Adagio ma non troppo*, 4/4. 2 fl., 2 ob., 2 clar. in B♭, 2 fag., 2 cor. in E♭, str. Recitative (*accompagnato*) Simon–Hanne. Progressive tonality: C minor→A major. 'Nun senket sich das blaße Jahr'.

No. 30 *Cavatine* (Hanne). F major, *Largo, alla breve*. Str. 'Licht und Leben sind geschwächet'.

No. 31 *Rezitativ* (*secco*, then *accompagnato*) Lucas. Progressive tonality: D flat major→dominant of E. 'Gefeßelt steht der breite See'.

No. 32 *Arie* (Lucas). E minor, *Presto*, 4/4. 2 fl., 2 ob., 2 fag., 2 cor. in E, str. 'Hier steht der Wand'rer nun'.→E major, *Allegro*.

No. 33 *Rezitativ* (*secco*, then *accompagnato*). 4/4→6/8, *Allegro*. Progressive tonality:→A major→V of D. Str. Lucas, Hanne, Simon. 'So wie er naht'.

No. 34 *Lied mit Chor* (Hanne, S–A–T–B Chorus). D minor, *Allegro*, 6/8. 1 fl., 2 ob., 2 fag., 2 cor. in D, 3 trbns., str. 'Knurre, schnurre'.

No. 35 *Rezitativ* (*secco*) Lucas. 'Abgesponnen ist der Flachs'.

No. 36 *Lied mit Chor* (Hanne, S–A–T–B Chorus). G major, *Moderato*, 4/4. 2 fl., 2 ob., 2 fag., str. 'Ein Mädchen, das auf Ehre hielt'.

No. 37 *Rezitativ* (*secco*) Simon. 'Vom dürren Osten'.

No. 38 *Arie und Rezitativ* (Simon). E flat major, *Largo*, 3/4→*Allegro molto*, 2/4. 2 fl., 2 ob., 2 clar. in B♭, 2 cor. in E♭, str. 'Erblicke hier, bethörter Mensch'. Recitative (*accompagnato*) 'Sie bleibt allein'→C major.

No. 39 *Terzett* (Hanne, Lucas, Simon) *und Doppelchor* (S-A-T-B). C major, *Allegro moderato*, 4/4. 2 fl., 2 ob., 2 clar. in B♭, 2 fag., contrafag., 3 cor. in E♭ and C *alto*, 3 trpts. in C, 3 trbns., timp., str. 'Dann bricht der große Morgen an'.

(2)   The Authentic Sources

(a) The sources of the libretto are:

A. Autograph by Baron Gottfried van Swieten, formerly owned by Max Friedlaender. Partial photograph and transcription by Ernst Fritz Schmid owned by Joseph Haydn Institut, Cologne.

B. Original Libretto: 'Die / Jahreszeiten / nach Thomson. / In Musik gesetzt / von / Herrn Joseph Haydn, / Doktor der Tonkunst, / der Königl. Schwedischen musikalischen Akademie Mitglied / und / Kapellmeister in wirklichen Diensten Sr. Durchlaucht des Hrn. Fürsten von Esterhazy. / Wien, / gedruckt bey Mathias Andreas Schmidt, / k. k. Hofbuchdrucker. / 1801'. Copies: Österreichische Nationalbibliothek, Vienna; Alan Tyson, London. In this form, with slight variations, the libretto was printed in the *AMZ* III, Beilage VII (20 May 1801), pp. XIX–XXVI.

C. Original Libretto for the first public performance: 'Die / Jahreszeiten / nach Thomson. / In Musik gesetzt / von / Herrn Joseph Haydn, / Doctor der Tonkunst, und Kapellmeister in wirk- / lichen Diensten Sr. Durchlaucht des Herrn Fürsten / von Esterhazy, und der königl. Schwed. Musi- / kalischen Akademie Mitglied. / Aufgeführt / im kais. kön. National-Hof-Theater / von der hiesigen Tonkünstlerge- / sellschaft zum Vor- / theile ihrer Wittwen und Waisen. / Wien, / Gedruckt mit v. Kurtzbek'schen Schriften.' Copy: Gesellschaft der Musikfreunde, Vienna.

(b)   The sources of the musical score are:

A.   Copy of the lost autograph by Johann Elssler and assistants in four volumes in oblong format (without the wind instruments, for which there was no room on the paper) from the Tonkünstler-Societät, Stadtbibliothek, Vienna. Twelve-stave paper.

A[1]   The original performance material, also from the Tonkünstler-Societät Archives and now in the Stadtbibliothek; with many holograph additions in Haydn's hand. A[1] was prepared by Johann Elssler and assistants. This original performance material shows the large forces which Haydn used at the public performances of 1801 *et seq.* Source A[1] was discovered in 1952 by the present writer.

A[2]   Authentic parts, Esterházy Archives (National Széchényi Library, Budapest, Ms. mus. 0,15).

B.   The authentic first edition of the score, for which Haydn sent the manuscript (probably an Elssler copy), Breitkopf & Härtel: 'DIE JAHRESZEITEN / nach Thomson, / in Musik gesetzt von / JOSEPH HAYDN. / PARTITUR. / [large illustration] / Originalausgabe. / Bey Breitkopf & Haertel in Leipzig.' Two volumes. There were two editions: (1) German-French and (2) German-English. Both were published in 1802, with a list of subscribers. Copies are in most of the major libraries; we used the one owned by the British Museum (*ex. coll.* Prince of Wales, later George IV, R. M. 14.d.25).

Modern critical edition: as Series 16, Band VI/VII of *Joseph Haydn Werke*, Breitkopf & Härtel 1922, edited by Eusebius von Mandyczewski from source B, but including in the *Revisionsbericht* the uncut Introductions to 'Autumn' and 'Winter' as well as the original version of the Introduction to 'Summer' (*vide infra*, pp. 150ff.). The problem of the *contrafagotto* (double bassoon) has not, however, been solved in this edition. Although C undoubtedly represents the musical text Haydn chose to send into the world, certain details of the earliest authentic manuscripts (A and A¹) were *not* incorporated into it.

The Overture (Introduction to Spring), provided with a concert ending, and the uncut Introductions to 'Autumn' and 'Winter' have been published in score and parts by G. Schirmer, New York, 1973, edited by the present writer.

The Breitkopf & Härtel full score served as the basis for the Philharmonia miniature score (No. 28), which in turn has been reprinted by Edition Peters (659) and Edition Eulenburg (987).

(3) The general Form and Style

Perhaps the first feature of Haydn's *The Seasons* that strikes the modern listener is its sense of profound humanity. The composer may have objected to some details in Swieten's libretto, but there were many things in it which not only allowed Haydn's imagination full sweep but even seemed to be specially created for the purpose of illustrating his attitude towards life: his deep love of nature and his understanding of it, his relish of the hunt, his quiet certainty of God's presence in everything – Swieten found countless features, great and small, which took into account Haydn's peculiar aptitudes. And over it all floats, serene and secure, the old composer's unfailing sense of humanity and compassion. Perhaps we sense this particularly, as indeed did Haydn, because he is describing things – the first glow of dawn on the horizon, the hazy heat of midsummer, the ripe fields of autumn – which will soon retreat beyond his grasp. And this brings us to another fundamental characteristic of this Oratorio – the panoramic sweep of its style. We look back to the gay earlier years of the 'Symphony with the hornsignal' (No. 31, 1765) when we hear the rousing horn calls of Haydn's hunting scene in 'Autumn'. Janus-like, we also peer far into the future, almost to the Wagner of *Tristan*, in that extraordinary Introduction to 'Winter', whose chill chromatic lines announce not only nature's dying but also man's. That Haydn identified 'Winter' with himself is shown clearly in a remark he made to Neukomm, who had expressed his admiration for the bass Aria No. 38 (the text of which Neukomm, interestingly, quotes 'Erblicke nun, bethörter Mensch'; perhaps the 'nun' is an earlier, discarded version). Haydn said: 'That Aria refers to me'. Neukomm continues:

> In this wonderful masterpiece, he really spoke from the very innermost part of his soul, for he became seriously ill when composing it and one had to assume that this was the decisive point in which the Lord giveth, the Lord taketh away, closing Haydn's glorious career and allowing him to see 'his life's progress and his open grave' [referring to the text of the Aria].   [Neukomm, 30]

Haydn had remained faithful to a number of musical principles throughout his life, for example to the all-embracing concept of motivic development. Yet his style, as such, underwent vast changes from *c.* 1750, when he first began composing, to these final works, of which *The Seasons* is the great culmination. The second subject of the Introduction to 'Spring' (bars 55ff.) may be the essence of Haydn, but the beginning might be the work of the young Weber, or another member of the German Romantic school. Haydn's style was never at a standstill for very long, and part of the difficulty in assessing his contribution to the history of music is (a) because it is in itself so vast and (b) because his style was constantly, or very nearly constantly, in a state of flux. If we have, in *The Seasons*, a sense of looking back across Haydn's whole career, we are equally faced with other stylistic elements that are as new as any of the composer's previous innovations.

If the Oratorio is steeped in the great humanistic tradition, it is also a last and particularly successful tribute to the popular Viennese style, in the creation and perfection of which Haydn had been so intimately involved. The *Volksstil* of *The Seasons* is just as apparent, and just as profound, as in *Die Zauberflöte*; and, as in Mozart's many-sided work, the 'popular style' in Haydn also exists on several levels. We have the Papageno-like simplicity (and the Papageno key of G major) of No. 36, 'Ein Mädchen, das auf Ehre hielt',

which transferred the world of German comic opera (and Haydn's own instrumental music) to Oratorio. (The hand of the great craftsman may be observed, in the above musical example, in the two *fz* markings, which give a certain 'flair' to the theme by accentuating the obvious, *viz.* the identical note *d″* of both phrase-endings; but Haydn never repeats this device in the whole number.) If No. 36 represents one side of this *Volksstil*, another is seen in the Chorus, 'Komm, holder Lenz!', which like the Andante of the 'Surprise' Symphony or the Allegretto of the 'Military' Symphony, was 'born famous'. In that Chorus, it is the lilting six-eight metre and the great sense of melodic contentment (also the harmonic peacefulness of the slow-moving bass line, with its many pedal points) which among other things give the piece its genuinely popular cast. Being of a much more relaxed formal construction than *The Creation*, and having a much more 'earthy' subject, Haydn fills *The Seasons* with melodies as popular as the above-quoted No. 36. The opening melodies of such sections as No. 18 or No. 22 have a very strong taste of the popular semi-slow movements in Haydn's quartets and symphonies (e.g. Symphonies 82 or 85), and it is certainly no accident that both the two numbers from the Oratorio and the two movements from 'L'ours' and 'La Reine' are all marked allegretto – that comfortable tempo of no less than six numbers of *The Seasons* (Nos. 2 and 4 of 'Spring', Nos. 10, 18 and 20 of 'Summer', No. 22 of 'Autumn'). Allegretto gradually disappears as the seasons grow less comfortable and it is significant that it never appears in 'Winter' at all.

A dramatically graphic illustration of the proximity of the *Volksstil* of *The Seasons* to Haydn's own popular style of the earlier instrumental music is, of course, Simon's Aria No. 4 ('Schon eilet'), where the music effortlessly merges into the second movement of the 'Surprise' Symphony, speeded up from its original andante to the allegretto tempo of Simon's ploughing and whistling. Perhaps in no other large-scale work did Haydn so successfully merge the light melodies of the Viennese popular classical style with the heaviest orchestration of the period – about which more later – with numbers on a large scale, and with pieces of an entirely different style. In the hands of a less skilled master, this plethora of forms, styles and moods would be bewildering rather than versatile; it is, for example, almost a stylistic prestidigitation to move from the deadly serious Introduction to 'Winter', with its leaden-footed atmosphere of frozen life, to the saucy *Lied*, 'Ein Mädchen, das auf Ehre hielt'; and from the swirling, heavily accented Spinning Song in D minor to the brilliant C major conclusion of the whole work, with its bright horns in high C – echoes of those sensational C major symphonies and vocal works with high horns and kettledrums which were so much a feature of the Eszterháza years.

Ever since the 821 bars of the Gloria in the *Missa Cellensis in honorem B. V. M.* (1766) and the 822 bars of Act I's Finale in *La fedeltà premiata*, Haydn had shown great interest in larger vocal forms, and in the various devices necessary to preserve their unity without compromising their diversity. In *The Seasons* we may observe many such devices to preserve unity in a work of great length and thirty-nine separate numbers. In *La fedeltà premiata* not only the Finale to Act I but also that to Act II, though slightly less complex, consisted of a vast ensemble, broken down into various units ranging from one to half-a-dozen or more vocal parts. *The Creation* had introduced not only many 'ensembles' but had combined soloists and chorus as well; now, in the later Oratorio, we find ensemble numbers on an equally large scale. Nos. 6, 8, 11, 18, 20, 34, 36 and 39 are all numbers with one or more of the three soloists together with the chorus and orchestra. Some of the complicated methods which Haydn uses to cement together these large forms will be discussed below, and here we can only provide one or two typical examples.

In No. 1, describing the passage from Winter to Spring, Haydn employs all three soloists. They enter in the order: Simon, Lucas, Hanne, or bass-tenor-soprano, symbolizing the passage of heavy winter to lighter spring, from 'dark' to 'light'. This process is accompanied by a shift from G minor to G major (*via* sundry related keys), and by a general lightening of the orchestration: the entire brass section and the timpani drop out as Simon enters, the clarinets disappear just before Hanne enters. Out of the melodic climax of the main theme –

Haydn segregates the interval of the sixth, and each soloist enters with an upward jump of a sixth, culminating in Hanne's section, where not only the interval of the sixth but the next phrase is used:

The listener has the feeling that, notwithstanding the 248 bars, he is witnessing a highly organized piece that, moreover, even manages to act as the introduction to the first Chorus (No. 2), which may be considered the logical conclusion of all the foregoing material. The whole of *The Seasons* is full of similarly organic entities created from extreme diversity. Anke Riedel-Martiny[1] has pointed out that even the recitatives display this same subtle ability to convey a sense of unity within diversity. In No. 27, the entry of each of the three soloists follows a similar pattern as he or she appears, and this repetition of the modulatory plan and the melodic curve automatically convey a comforting sense of organizational unity.

1 'Das Verhältnis von Text und Musik in Haydns Oratorien', *Haydn-Studien* I (1967), Heft 4, pp. 205ff.

Of course, *The Seasons* contains many delightful descriptions of nature. Nowadays, the argument about Haydn's right to compose such pieces of *Thonmahlerey* has become so stale as to be almost non-existent; these vignettes contain many of the work's most touching moments. Only the careless listener would, however, imagine that Haydn's symbolism is limited to *Thonmahlerey*; it is far more comprehensive than that, as even our brief analysis of one aspect chosen from No. 1, discussed above, reveals. Symbolism is not only darting strings to illustrate buzzing insects, it is also in No. 39 (conclusion) equating the kingdom of Heaven with C major, the key of earthly princes and pomp, the key of Empress Maria Theresa (Symphony No. 48, Symphony No. 50) who was, in turn, the defender of the faith and the leader of a kingdom. The final number of *The Seasons*, representing 'the holy mount of heavenly bliss', is also in the key that for many faithful Austrians represented church music *par excellence*: a glance at any thematic catalogue of an Austrian monastery in the second part of the eighteenth century – Melk or Göttweig or Herzogenburg or Kremsmünster – will reveal that three-quarters of all solemn 'figuraliter' Masses are in C major. The sun rises in D major, as it did in *The Creation*, but 'The Heavens are telling' and No. 29 are in C. We shall discuss further aspects of tonality below.

We have seen that Haydn equated the great E flat Aria in 'Winter' with his own decline. Throughout *The Seasons* we find nostalgic references to Haydn's fifty years of unceasing activity in music, and not only to his own. In that very same E flat Aria No. 38, the most poignant reference, perhaps, in the whole work comes when the text refers to 'dein kurzer Lenz' (thy short Spring), and then 'erschöpfet deines Sommers Kraft' (exhausted thy Summer's strength). The music that accompanies these words is a quotation from the slow movement of Mozart's Symphony in G minor (K. 550), written in the Summer of 1788: the passage in question is quoted *infra* (p. 181). Setting to music 'dein kurzer Lenz', Haydn unconsciously remembered the short spring and 'summer's strength' of music's greatest loss – the spontaneous tribute from music's finest craftsman to music's greatest genius.

In some respects *The Seasons* was intended from the beginning to display as many sides as possible of Haydn's talent, to provide the listener with a summation of his abilities. In this versatility, too, the Oratorio shows a strong spiritual affinity to *Die Zauberflöte* – the Mozart opera Beethoven admired above all others because in it he found the widest variety of forms and styles. Many of Haydn's earlier works provided him with spiritual nourishment when composing *The Seasons*. In the middle of 'Summer' Haydn felt constrained to repeat one of his most difficult tasks: the setting of a series of slow movements, as in *The Seven Words*. Here we have a Recitative, in itself a slowish piece in the German language, which ends larghetto and is then followed by largo (No. 13), poco adagio (No. 14), adagio (No. 15), finally changing, in the middle of No. 15, to allegro assai. We even recall Symphony No. 8 (*Le Soir*), with its final 'La tempesta', when hearing the huge storm scene in 'Summer': Haydn's symbol for lightning (the flute) has not changed in forty years.

Another integral aspect of this looking-back is Haydn's use of the fugue, by now part and parcel of his musical thinking also in the oratorio form. Of all the many excellent fugues in *The Seasons*, perhaps the most masterly is the famous 'Drunken Chorus', which shows the peasants so inebriated that they cannot really sing their entries properly; the piece therefore becomes an orchestral fugue accompanied by the tipsy singers. The fine fugal tradition of *The Creation* and *The Seasons* kept alive the form for a whole generation which might otherwise have forgotten it except in a historical concept or in church.

And thus we return to the extraordinary Janus-like aspect of this great work, encompassing as it does many hallowed traditions, yet peering into a limitless future. In *The Seasons* Haydn summed up, but he also left the road open to anyone who had the heart and mind to pursue it.

(4) The general Key Structure and Problems of Tonality

The Seasons is in progressive tonality: it begins in G minor and ends in C major, and thus it 'progresses' as do the seasons themselves. The individual four seasons are also in progressive tonality, 'Spring' (G minor to B flat) and 'Summer' (C minor to E flat) being third-related, while 'Autumn' (G major to C major) and 'Winter' (C minor to C major) gradually settle in the key of C, in which the work ends. A brief survey of the key structures within each of the four main sections may prove useful:

Spring

G minor→V of G:	G major	C major	F major		A major → B flat major
(No. 1 ------)	(No. 2)	(No. 4)	(No. 6)		(No. 8 ------)

Summer

C minor→	F major→	D major	E major	C major→	B flat major
(No. 9)	(No. 10)	(No. 11)	(No. 13)	(No. 14)	(No. 15)
C minor (major)		F major→E flat major			
(No. 17)		(No. 18 ----)			

Autumn

G major	C major	B flat major	A minor→major	D major→E flat major
(No. 19)	(No. 20)	(No. 22)	(No. 24 ---)	(No. 26 ------)
C major				
(No. 28)				

Winter

C minor→A major		F major	E minor→major	D minor	G major
(No. 29 ---)		(No. 30)	(No. 32 --)	(No. 34)	(No. 36)
E flat major	C major				
(No. 38)	(No. 39).				

Some of Haydn's tonal symbols are perfectly clear: G major, as we have said above, is the Papageno key, the *Volkstonart* of Hanne's little Song and also the gentle opening Chorus of 'Spring'. It represents, moreover, the equally unaggressive and contented opening of 'Autumn', the 'sound' of a rich harvest successfully gathered. C major is also clear: it is the church key of the ending, the merry sound of the happy farmer ploughing and whistling the 'Surprise' Symphony's slow movement. Haydn may have been willing to speed up his famous tune, but being possessed of perfect pitch he could do nothing else but write the whole Aria in C major. Apart from serving as the key of restful, shady groves (No. 14). C major is also the key for the Chorus in Praise of Industry (No. 22), which Haydn soon begins to treat in the same manner as 'The Heavens are telling'. C minor serves a function similar to that in *The Creation*; for Haydn it was the key that symbolized the world before light. Therefore it is used at the beginning of 'Summer' to describe the pre-dawn and later the storm during which the heavens are darkened. The lightless beginning of 'Winter', and the symbol for old age, is also expressed by C minor.

D major, of course, is Haydn's old hunting key. He wrote three symphonies (Nos. 31, 72, 73) on 'chasse' motifs and one *Cassatio* in D (Hoboken *deest*) with four horns.[1] There is a special twist to the hunting chorus in *The Seasons*, however, because the music shifts from D to E flat. D major, the key of sunrise in *The Creation*, is also the key for the rising sun in *The Seasons*, but otherwise it is never used, except in passing. The surprising shift from D major to E flat illustrates the stag deceiving the hounds, but it is not the first time in the work that Haydn has given us such a modulation. In No. 8 we begin in A major and end in B flat – the surprising modulation was one of van Swieten's ideas – but the great *Maestoso* B flat section, followed by the fugue, reminds us that Haydn's last three Masses are in B flat (also the key in which *The Creation* ends). The angels sing in C, and so does man when he approaches the gates of heaven, but otherwise Simon, Lucas and Hanne, with their friends, address God in the more subdued B flat.

We may illustrate Haydn's subtle sense of keys in one section, 'Winter'. Here we have a steady downwards progression from the beginning, in C minor, through A major, F major, and E minor-major, to D minor (the 'Spinning Song'), *viz.*

D is the dominant of G, and G is the dominant of C, but between G and C we pass through the third-related key of E flat, the fatal moment of Haydn's *verità*, always moving downwards. Winter is equated with old age and expressed in keys that descend. It is a masterly and yet highly delicate way of illustrating winter / old-age sinking slowly into ice / dotage.

(5) The Orchestration

The symphony orchestra had been stabilized, when Haydn stopped composing symphonies in London in 1795, at pairs of flutes, oboes, clarinets, bassoons, horns, trumpets, kettledrums, with the usual strings and occasionally 'Turkish' instruments for special effects (cymbal, triangle, bass drum). With *The Creation*, this 'standard' orchestra was considerably enlarged by three flutes (instead of two), a double bassoon and three trombones. It might have been thought that these additional instruments were added only for the special occasion of that Oratorio. With *The Seasons*, it was clear that the symphony orchestra, in Haydn's hands, was now permanently expanded and included, at maximum, piccolo, two flutes, two oboes, two clarinets, two bassoons, double bassoon, four horns, three trumpets, three trombones, timpani, extra percussion and strings. It was this orchestra that, with small alterations (two flutes, no piccolo, two trumpets, no extra percussion), Beethoven was to use for the *Missa Solemnis*, but it would be some time before he succeeded in enlarging the orchestra for purely instrumental symphonies (trombones were not used until the Fifth Symphony).

This very large orchestra is used with the same brilliance as in *The Creation*, though there is hardly anything in *The Seasons* to approach the modernity of 'Chaos', except possibly the Introduction to 'Winter'. Here we have the bleakest orchestral sound

---

1 Edited by the present writer for Doblinger's series, 'Diletto musicale', No. 66.

Haydn ever produced ('Chaos' has a wildly eccentric – even a 'dangerous' – sound but certainly not a bleak one); he achieves it by very low string notes (contra C in the double basses, which were, as always in Haydn, C-oriented, not E-oriented, instruments) and by the peculiarly thick and yet transparent use of his wind choir (flutes, oboes, clarinets, bassoons, horns). Several times, too, the bleak sound is produced by stopped notes in the horns. Nowadays, with valved instruments, this effect disappears. Haydn's horn notes (E♭ horns)

'fall' when the note *b*, which must be produced by hand-stopping, follows the *forzato* open note *c*. The same occurs at the end (bars 28f. of the 'final' version).

The most original orchestral sound in *The Seasons* is the extraordinary beginning of No. 39, for unsupported wind band, whose 'heavenly boldness and radiance' (Tovey)[1] are produced, among other things, by having only the first trumpet and, incredibly, the double bassoon play *forte* as against the *piano* of everyone else. Altogether No. 39 is most instructive about Haydn's late orchestration. It is fastidious on the one hand and as massive as Bruckner on the other (the very end). The clarinets start out in B flat, the horns in E flat. This is so Haydn can use them in an excursion into E flat major, at bars 32–4 (describing the man whose life was incorrupt); they are not used at all before then, and after the E flat section, they are instructed to change their instruments (clarinets from B♭ to C) or their crooks (horns from E♭ to C *alto*) and join the general proceedings only at bar 61. At that point the trombones enter for the first time, too. One other detail which strikes the eye is the use of stopped notes not only for the horns (as in 'Winter') but in No. 39 also for the second trumpet – a feature of earlier Haydn works such as Symphonies Nos. 86 and 95, also the 'Nelson' Mass (see *Haydn: the Years of 'The Creation' 1796–1800*, p. 442). Here, at bars 53ff., we find

The bracketed portion must be stopped. Since it is difficult to imagine the trumpeter being able to insert his hand into the bell of his instrument – natural trumpets being some 75 centimetres (30 in.) long in those days – perhaps he had a 'slide' or some such mechanical device. Bar 55, with its strong dissonances in the trumpet parts, is the kind of detail that one encounters throughout the work. As for the double bassoon, Haydn uses it with his usual combination of conservatism and modernity. One particular passage in No. 39 may be singled out, when the soloists are supported only by two bassoons and the double bassoon ('He that to want and grief lent aid!' in the Baron's translation); 'and grief' (German original 'Bedrängten') is illustrated by syncopations:

1 *Essays in Musical Analysis*, vol. V, London 1937, p. 161.

Of course, Haydn was setting 'Bedrängten', which means also 'squeezed', 'pushed' – thus the syncopations.

This brings us directly to the problem of the double bassoon, for in the Breitkopf & Härtel score, something appears to have gone wrong. We have learned, in the Chronicle (*supra*, p. 84), that Haydn seems to have forgotten to include the parts for the trombones and the extra percussion when he sent the score to Leipzig. These parts, and another missing sheet, were delivered to Griesinger later ('Heaven knows why') and sent on to Germany on 28 November 1801. The score that Breitkopf & Härtel published included two trombones (alto, tenor) in the score but placed the third trombone at the end of the score (pp. 486–96). Something similar seems to have happened to the double bassoon, which does not play until No. 17 (the storm chorus), although it obviously plays earlier in *The Seasons*. Examination of the authentic parts[1] in Vienna and Budapest revealed the astonishing fact that the genuine double-bassoon part for Nos. 1–17 has never been printed at all. We include it here. There are also discrepancies between the double-bassoon part from No. 17 to the end as found in the Breitkopf & Härtel (and Philharmonia, etc.) scores and as Elssler copied it. It is, of course, hardly possible to reconstruct the way in which the editors of the first

1 The set of authentic orchestral parts of *The Seasons* in the Tonkünstler-Societät Archives, now preserved in the Stadtbibliothek (Vienna), in fact contain parts for *two* double bassoons, marked 'Contra Fagotto I^{mo}' and 'Contra Fagotto II^{do}', which differ radically from each other. No. II is essentially the part found also in the Esterházy Archives and reproduced here. No. I plays much more frequently. Obviously we cannot at this time perform the function of an editor for the future volume of the *Gesamtausgabe* in which *The Seasons* will appear, and we can only indicate the differences roughly. We should like to thank Dr Fritz Racek, Director of the Music Division of the Stadtbibliothek, for many kindnesses in the past, and for his help on this particular problem as well. Here is a brief summary of the difference between the two parts.

		Contrafagotto	
Part	Number (Philharmonia score)	I	II
I	1 Einleitung & Recit.	yes	yes
	2 Chorus 'Komm, holder Lenz'	yes	yes
	4 Aria 'Schon eilet'	yes	no
	6 Terzett 'Sei nun gnädig'	yes	yes
	8 Freudenlied 'O wie lieblich'	yes	no
	'Ewiger, mächtiger . . .'	yes	yes
II	11 Terzett & Chorus 'Sie steigt'	yes	yes
	17 Chorus 'Ach, das Ungewitter'	yes	yes
	18 Terzett & Chorus	yes	yes
III	19 Einleitung & Recit.	yes	no
	20 Terzett & Chorus 'So lohnet'	yes	no
	26 Chorus 'Hört das laute Getön'	yes	yes
	28 Chorus 'Juchhe'	yes	yes
IV	29 Einleitung-& Recit.	yes	no
	(incl. bars 55f., 58f.)		
	34 Spinnerlied 'Knurre, schnurre'	yes	no
	36 Lied 'Ein Mädchen'	yes	no
	38 Aria & Recit. 'Erblicke hier'	yes	no
	39 Terzett & Double Chorus	yes	yes

There are several remarks that must be made about this situation. Firstly, the forces used in the Tonkünstler-Societät performances were enormous, requiring at least two, and possibly even four, double bassoons (two on each part). A similar organization, often entered in the parts in Haydn's own hand, controls when the various numbers of flutes, bassoons, and so forth, are to play and when not ('Solo' and 'Tutti'). The second part, which is the only one to be found in Haydn's own orchestral material, is obviously the *second* part of the large-scale performances and the *first* part for those with a smaller band. It will be a difficult problem for the editors of the new Collected Edition to know what to print of all these doubling parts; we would suggest printing *both* parts in the score, and indicating, for the information of conductors, which are for larger, and which for smaller, forces.

Breitkopf score went wrong, but probably it had to do with the arrangement of Haydn's autograph score, which must have been written in two sets of volumes, one for the voices and strings and one for the woodwind, brass and timpani. But even in this presumed second score there would hardly have been room for everything; possibly the double bassoon was included in the bassoon stave to save space. Probably it arrived in Leipzig in an incomplete state.

Conversely, the double-bassoon part for No. 20 is not found in all the authentic parts; perhaps Haydn added it after the original parts had been copied; or perhaps it was added by the editors of Breitkopf & Härtel. It would seem a curious procedure to have omitted it in the first place, and we see no particular reason to doubt its authenticity.

The differences between the authentic double bassoon part and that of the Breitkopf score are also characteristic; Haydn's part is, of course, more idiomatic and usually at a lower tessitura. All this suggests still another explanation. The sketches to *The Creation* included the autograph of the double bassoon part; perhaps Haydn wrote out a similar part for *The Seasons* and merely left a kind of 'cue' part in the score.

It is a sobering thought to consider that for 170 years we have been hearing *The Seasons* everywhere except in Vienna (where the Tonkünstler-Societät went on using the original MS. parts until the end of the nineteenth century) without the authentic double bassoon part for the first half of the work, and with a slightly bowdlerized part for the remainder.

Die Jahreszeiten | The Seasons   Joseph Haydn

Contrafagotto

Der Frühling

No. 1 Einleitung

* Elssler MS. (Budapest)

No. 2 Chor

* Elssler (Budapest)

No. 3 *tacet* / No. 4 *tacet* / No. 5 *tacet*

No. 6 Terzett und Chor

No. 7 *tacet*

No. 8 Freudenlied, mit abwechselndem Chore der Jugend

DER SOMMER

No. 9 *tacet* / No. 10 *tacet*

No. 11 Terzett und Chor

* Elssler (Budapest)

Changes vis-à-vis the Philharmonia score (Nos. 17–39)

No. 17

No. 18

No. 26 Chor

No. 28 Chor

No. 39 Terzett und Doppelchor

The rather fastidious use Haydn made of his wind instruments may be admired in many places throughout *The Seasons*. His use of the trombones is a case in point. If we examine No. 6, we may observe that they do not slavishly double the chorus. They enter with the chorus at bar 13, but they provide, as it were, only a skeletal outline of the choral pattern. They appear, in the first part of No. 6, only in bars 13–18, 45–50 and 66–8. On the other hand, when the fugue enters at 'Un poco più moto', the trombones immediately have a much larger role. Again, however, they do not double the actual vocal lines but rather its contours ♪ ♪ ♪ | ♪. ♪♪ ♪ ♪ ♪ | ♩. ♪ ♩ in the vocal line is supported by ♩ ♩♩ ; ♩ ♩♩ ; ♩ ♩♩ in the third trombone (bars 74ff.). A particular joy of Haydn's (and of course Mozart's) trombone writing is the high tessitura of the alto trombone, on which *c″* is easily playable. Today, when alto trombones hardly exist apart from Vienna, where the tradition has been preserved intact since Haydn's time, these obsolete instruments present a serious problem, for their highest range is very difficult to attain on a tenor instrument. Perhaps, with the current revival of authentic performances of Baroque music, alto trombones will return permanently to the orchestra.

Another typical illustration of Haydn's delicate use of the wind group may be seen in No. 26 (the hunting chorus). We note that the score includes two clarinets in B♭, but there is no sign of them so long as the piece is in D major. When the music swerves to E flat, however, at bars 83ff., the horns (or rather two of them) have re-crooked their instruments to E flat and the clarinets enter for the first time, continuing to the end. Haydn obviously associated B♭ clarinets with flat keys, and particularly with such passages as bars 133ff., where the female voices of the chorus are accompanied only by two clarinets and strings (describing the stag's exhaustion).

The appearance of the 'flauto piccolo', or in modern Italian terminology 'ottavino', in Simon's Aria No. 4 is, as far as can be determined, the first in Haydn's music. It, too, is brought in for a special purpose, to show Simon's whistling the air from the 'Surprise' Symphony. Cleverly, Haydn does not use the piccolo until the actual air enters at bar 17. In the whole Aria, the piccolo appears only in conjunction with the 'Surprise' tune, and this means that the instrument is silent from bar 42 to bar 110. Haydn patently considered its tone too high-pitched and exotic to use except very sparingly. Throughout *The Seasons*, the astute student of late eighteenth-century Viennese music will note that altogether Haydn's orchestration, despite the vast array of instruments at his disposal, is invariably more ascetic than that of Mozart's. Even in this late period, one never finds the richness, not to speak of the erotic use, of Mozart's orchestration and in particular his writing for the woodwind. All that gorgeous panorama of colour and passion, those sensuous clarinet passages, those extravagantly rich chords for solo wind band, are foreign to Haydn's far more puritanical nature. On the other hand, it will be noted that Beethoven, with a few obvious exceptions (such as the Quintet, Op. 16), took over Haydn's orchestral palette rather than Mozart's. This is partly because, in a sense, Mozart had in his own music exhausted his new orchestral style, his sense of different woodwind colour. He had, especially in *Die Zauberflöte*, taken it as far as it could go. With the larger apparatus at Haydn's disposal (the four horns, which Mozart had used, in the mature operas, only in *Idomeneo*; the three trumpets; the double bassoon), Beethoven saw that his former teacher, with his fastidious scores, had opened a whole new world that might be immeasurably enriched by someone less rooted in the ideas of *le bon goût* as viewed by a man of the *ancien régime*. Haydn had hardly used, for example, the dynamic marking *fff* except at the end of *The Seven Words*. It is the same with his orchestration. Even in the late Oratorios, which were played with a vast orchestra (180 members), i.e. with tripled woodwind, brass and drums and a huge violin section, the scores eschew loud effects *per se* or exotic colour except as special effects.

It was not only Beethoven who took over the Haydn orchestra, but also Weber and the young German Romantic school. Schubert had a delightful flirtation with the Mozartian scoring in Symphony No. 5 in B flat, but the later vocal and instrumental works (Masses, operas, incidental music) are written in the train of *The Creation*, *The Seasons*, and of course Haydn's last six Masses. Indeed, the influence of those two Oratorios was so enormous that it has never been properly assessed. But anyone who has examined the parish church archives of the old Austro-Hungarian monarchy, and the monastery and castle libraries, will have been astounded at the countless arrangements of the Oratorios as church pieces, for wind band of various sorts (usually octets, such as pairs of oboes, clarinets, bassoons and horns), and even as cantatas. For thousands of people in the provinces, Haydn's Masses and Oratorios formed the taste of a whole generation of young men and woman in the first three or four decades of the nineteenth century and the new and large orchestra required in both Oratorios set a standard that was to prevail for many decades.[1]

(6) Analytical Notes

No. 1 *Einleitung* and Recitative (*accompagnato*)
The slow introduction (largo) consists of four notes

played in unison by the strings with a curious addition: the bassoon, viola and timpani playing *g* three times and then *d* in the drums and *a* in the viola, bassoons and double bassoon. The final chord, a unison *d* except for that strange *a* peering forth from the lower strings, is oddly unsettling. The use to which these four notes is put is one of Haydn's great *tours-de-force*. The main theme itself is in canon and includes the first transformation of the four notes:

They then appear as a unison figure

---

1 The first recording of *The Seasons* was made, after performances in January (Rome) and June (Venice), in 1943 for the Italian firm of Cetra (LPC 1202) with Gabriella Gatti (sop.), Francesco Albanese (ten.) and Luciano Neroni (bass), conducted by Vittorio Gui, who kindly supplied these details in a letter of 16 April 1973. The first LP of the work was issued by the Haydn Society in 1950 with Trude Eipperle (sop.), Julius Patzak (ten.), Georg Hann (bass), the Chorus of the Vienna State Opera and the Vienna Philharmonic Orchestra conducted by Clemens Krauss.

shortly thereafter altered to

and then, more like their original state, to

As we proceed to the relative major the four notes appear in the following guise:

While the arrival at B flat major shows the four notes as follows:

In the second theme, a derivation of the figure is used in the first violins:

And in the development section, as might be expected, the four notes become, if anything, even more important to the total structure, e.g.

In the recapitulation, the figure is also used in chains but moving downwards:

Nothing could be more fitting to describe the inexorable forces of nature: the four notes are mutable but their basic shape remains, clearly perceived, throughout. But as winter gradually changes to spring, the four notes lose their force and turn into a new pattern (see the quotation *supra*, p. 126). Despite the fact that much of this severe movement sounds like the product of a composer writing at the time of *Der Freischütz*, the technique is Haydn's and as recognizably personal as one of the famous Berensonian fingerprints by which anonymous Italian Renaissance artists are identified. This introduction, indeed, is as forceful and energetic as the symphonies composed in the late 1750s for Count Morzin, and it is difficult to believe that it was the work of a near-septuagenarian.

No. 2 Chorus

The first of the many genuine *Volksstücke* in this work, 'Komm, holder Lenz!' is in the great pastoral tradition: the key (G), the lilting six-eight time, the held notes in the bass (approximating the 'drone' of bagpipes), the folk-tune-like melody – all these things were part of an old and loved heritage. As in many parts of the Oratorio, Haydn has provided us with a magnificent summing-up: here, we feel, is the essence of spring in the country. The form is appropriately simple, a large tripartite pattern with a middle section branching out to a long excursion in the subdominant (C), the subdominant minor and then, in turn, its relative major, E flat. Whereupon we have arrived at yet another of Haydn's flirtations with third-related keys, though here the flirtation is of short duration; within a few bars we move gracefully back to the recapitulation. Even in this popular and pastoral chorus, learned passages are quietly introduced:

The whole chorus is filled with the tenderness of 'the trembling Year', as yet 'unconfirmed'.

No. 3 Recitative

The first *secco* recitative in *The Seasons* brings us to a knotty problem of interpretation, namely, when should appoggiature be sung and when not. As the eighteenth century waned, many composers simply wrote in the appoggiature, as we have seen in such a work as Beethoven's 'Ah! perfido' (see *Haydn: the Years of 'The Creation' 1796–1800*, p. 68). But many did not. In *The Seasons* we have a rather perplexing situation in this regard. On the one hand, Haydn actually writes out an appoggiatura that he considered essential (e.g. the beginning of No. 27) –

– while on the other he uses an old abbreviation or shorthand to indicate an initial appoggiatura in No. 3, as follows:

The little notes (which in modern editions are written in wildly improbable values, even ♪ – a 'short' grace note) simply mean that the note to which the grace is attached must be dropped entirely, *viz*.

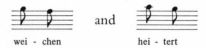

For this old rule we have a celebrated passage in Haydn's 'Applausus' letter to Zwettl Abbey (see CCLN, 10) with a musical example which makes this point absolutely clear.[1] And Haydn uses many of these little 'cancelling' notes in the recitatives; but did he permit his singers to insert other appoggiature? We have, alas, no contemporary evidence, but presumably the occasional mutation of a third drop to a second, as in the above examples, was permitted even if the little 'cancelling' note were missing. Apart from this problem, the recitatives should be accompanied by a fortepiano (*Hammerklavier*), violoncello and double bass, as we know they were in *The Creation*.

As in the earlier Oratorio, these *secco* recitatives in *The Seasons* are remarkable for their brevity: in most cases, their only *raison d'être* seems to be that of providing a wide contrast between the instrumental vocal numbers, some of which are heavily orchestrated. The bland sound of the *secco* recitative gives the ear a short but necessary respite from the otherwise large apparatus.

No. 4 Aria (Simon)

On the whole, the arias in *The Seasons* have not achieved the enormous popularity of those in *The Creation*. There are several decisive reasons for this, but the most cogent one is that many of *The Seasons*' arias are intimately bound to the particular place in which they were inserted and either do not hold up as separate entities or else break off and are thus unfitted for concert purposes. In the first category might be placed the beautiful little Cavatine – No. 13 'Dem Druck erlieget die Natur' – from 'Summer', which is very moving in context but perhaps unsatisfactory as a concert aria; while into the second we might put such a section as the Aria and Recitative No. 10 from 'Summer', 'Der munt're Hirt', which turns into a recitative and modulates to D in preparation for the sunrise.

---

1 Also Haydn's sketches for *The Creation*; see *Haydn: the Years of 'The Creation' 1796–1800*, p. 387.

An exception in all this is Simon's Aria about the ploughman whistling the 'Surprise' Symphony. Hoboken's Catalogue (II, 64) lists seven early prints of the number, a popularity rivalled, strangely enough, only by No. 10 (six prints), which amateurs probably ended at bar 61, and by No. 30 (also six prints). Simon's Aria is indeed irresistible: full of optimism, with the greatest 'hit tune' of Haydn's life in it, and written for the bass voice with Haydn's customary virtuosity, it could hardly fail to please. Here, the bassoon is used, doubling the viola, to express 'eilet froh' ('rushes happily', would be a modern translation). The piece is in the usual three parts, with a middle section moving from C minor to E flat and back to C minor. It ends *pp*, describing 'flötend nach', the whistles dying away in the distance. The scoring is very light, to match the subject: piccolo, oboes, bassoons[1] and horns, with the usual strings.

No. 5 Recitative

A very short (nine-bar) *secco* leading to:

No. 6 Trio (Soloists) with Chorus: Prayer

This is the first time in *The Seasons* that the soloists are used together with the chorus and orchestra. The number is in two parts, a beautiful and reverent Poco adagio which then turns into a fugue after 73 bars. The entire piece might be from a late Haydn Mass. It is held together by a delicate system of note transfers such as we have observed in other works of Haydn's maturity.

becomes

and later in the fugue the accompaniment, or more precisely the top part of it; the rest of the accompaniment derives from the semiquavers which gradually assume an ever more important role in the first part. The particularly striking semiquaver pattern in the bass line that accompanies 'Laß deinen Thau die Erde wässern' (Let Thy dew water the earth)

becomes the pattern for the bottom part of the fugue's accompaniment, which therefore gives the strongest impression of growing organically from the preceding material. Here is the beginning of the fugue:

[1] In the Tonkünstler-Societät MS. parts, also double bassoon.

Tovey was perhaps the first to remind us of the extraordinary debt that this fugue owes to the 'quam olim Abrahae' of Mozart's *Requiem*, which begins as follows (Tovey's reduction, *op. cit.*, 152):

'The fugue subject', writes Tovey, 'is, of course, an inevitable tag; but the figures of the orchestral accompaniment, though equally conventional, make a combination the resemblance of which is beyond coincidence. Also, the beautiful hush towards the end seems to ask for Mozart's blessing upon this work of Haydn's old age.'

   Although the trombone parts of this section of the *Requiem* are by Süssmayer, Haydn would have heard the work, and studied it, in the form as we know it today. In any case, even the Mozartian-Süssmayerian sound is reflected in Haydn's spacious fugue, not to speak of the omnipresent 'leading notes' (three quavers leading to a crotchet). It is the first, but not the last, time in *The Seasons* that Haydn paid a final musical tribute to Mozart. In No. 6, the key word to the quotation seems to be 'Überfluß', 'abundance' – a word that obviously turned the old man's thoughts to Mozart. Of course, this reference, as well as that to the Symphony in G minor, would have been perfectly clear to a large majority of Haydn's Viennese audience (and indeed to many throughout Germany as well, the *Requiem* having been published by Breitkopf & Härtel in 1801 and having caused a profound impression[1]).

No. 8 Song of Joy, with Trio (Soloists) and Chorus

This is the concluding number of 'Spring', planned and executed on a large scale (296 bars) and reminding one of an operatic Finale. The choir is called 'Chorus of youths' by van Swieten ('girls and lads' in the Baron's English translation). The rather complex formal scheme is as follows:

| Andante A major | Maestoso B flat | Poco Adagio B flat | Fugue (Allegro). (B flat) |

The A major section is the one most like an operatic construction. It is 'durchkomponiert' but self-developing, using fragments of the material presented by Hanne in her seventeen-bar(!) opening statement – these seventeen bars are broken into the following subsections: five + six + six – which is repeated by Lucas. We say like an operatic construction, and in fact the opening of the Finale to Act I of *La fedeltà premiata* could have served as Haydn's unconscious model. Even Amaranta's opening phrase is irregular: six + two + six; and the music develops out of itself in a very similar

---

1 See the long review in *AMZ* IV, 1–11, 23–31. It is, one feels, symbolic that the last page of this review faced the announcement of *The Seasons'* publication by Breitkopf & Härte! (*Intelligenz-Blatt* No. I, October 1802).

way. In the operatic Finale, after Amaranta's initial statement, the music settles into a characteristic pedal point in quavers:

And in *The Seasons*, the music follows very much the same course:

In the review of the première of *The Seasons* in the *Zeitung für die elegante Welt* (*vide supra*, p. 45), Haydn is quoted as saying that in 'Spring' some ideas from *The Creation* had insinuated themselves. This is, of course, true, and not only in 'Spring'. In 'Summer' there is a sunrise and although the composer took great pains not to copy his sunrise in *The Creation*, the parallel was obvious to everyone. By the year 1801, not many people, apart from the Viennese (who had heard *La fedeltà premiata* in 1784) knew that opera, and the above-quoted parallel probably escaped most of them. But we must not forget that *The Seasons* does represent a great summing-up, even if an unconscious one.

As the piece proceeds, in the form of a 'dialogue' between Hanne and Lucas, Haydn has to deal with a catalogue of natural phenomena, some of which, of course, cannot be described at all (the lily, the rose, 'the flowers all'). The chorus enters in a most dramatic way. In the process of describing Thomson's

> Groves, meadows and the landscape all;
> Land's surface, waters and the lucid air;

Haydn brings the music round from A minor to C major, and in C major the strings and woodwind rush up the scale (bars 8of.) and settle quietly into the key, the chorus entering with a magical *piano* thrust from the altos (musical example overleaf: bar 82). The key of C major remains for twenty bars, and the chorus continues to use material previously expounded by Hanne and Lucas. By now we can see Haydn's grand tonal scale – one of the boldest and most imaginative of his larger pieces in this period. From C major we move slowly to D minor, E minor, B minor, D major, and then for the

next choral entry into G major, where the music again settles (with some minor excursions) for the rest of the opening section. To move forward for a moment, the section is halted on the dominant of G, so that the principal tonal relationships of the number are third-related, *viz.* A major to C major, G major to B flat.

Here, too, occur the first major series of *Thonmahlerey*.[1] It is hard, after the passage of one and three-quarters centuries, to understand the outcry that these modest, humorous and witty descriptions raised with Haydn's contemporaries. The lambkins gambol and the woodwind enters with little 'gamboling' figures:

the fishes dart to rapid clusters of demisemiquavers; the bees swarm to chattering sextuplet woodwind and 'buzzing' string figures; the birds flutter down the scale in a long pattern of the old Baroque 'sighing' motif. We have now gone far away from A major, and those among the first audience with perfect pitch or good relative pitch will have wondered where Haydn was leading them. The answer comes in a stunning outburst for the full orchestra, including trombones and horns (silent all during No. 8 hitherto) as well as the trumpets and kettledrums (silent since the Introduction), in B flat major, marked Maestoso and with the old dotted rhythm of the French Overture. It is the prayer 'Ewiger, mächtiger, gütiger Gott!' The text and music, apart from the extraordinary tonal manipulations described above, prepare us for this joyous outburst in a striking way. For the first time in all these proceedings of No. 8, Simon, the bass, enters, Haydn has saved him for Thomson's lines

> What is this mighty Breath . . . ?
>
> . . .
>
>   . . . What? but God!
> Inspiring God! who boundless Spirit all,
> And unremitting Energy, pervades,
> Subsists, adjusts, and agitates the Whole.

Simon enters, and who is not reminded of the bass voice in *The Creation* announcing life itself in that passage of boundless inspiration so often quoted ('Be fruitful, all' . . .)? Or of the great entrance by Raphael (bass), 'Du wendest ab dein Angesicht' from 'Zu dir, O Herr' / 'On thee each living soul awaits' from the previous Oratorio? Indeed, it is certainly No. 8 that Haydn meant when he said that 'Spring' included some involuntary borrowings from *The Creation*; the similarity of the middle section of 'By thee with bliss' to No. 8 of *The Seasons* is evident. In the earlier work we have the same references to the 'purling fountains', 'ye plants', 'ye flowers', 'ye birds', 'ye, that swim the stream'. We must bear all this in mind when considering Haydn's marvellously successful efforts in avoiding duplication (no matter what he himself said).

The majestic slow introduction leads us to a middle section in a slow three-four, with beautiful woodwind writing to usher in the praying soloists. Twice the chorus interrupts with its cries 'Mächtiger Gott!' etc., the second time, ominously, in B flat

---

1 For Haydn's earlier use of 'painting in sound' in *The Creation*, see *Haydn: the Years of 'The Creation' 1796–1800*, pp. 403ff.

minor, with the timpani hammering out the martial rhythm of the *Missa in tempore belli*:

It is, again, not a literal quotation but part of the panoramic summing-up discussed above.

The big fugue that concludes 'Spring' is built upon the following subject:

Note how Haydn prolongs the word 'ewiger' ('forever'). In the course of the fugue's development, there are whole series of augmentations, e.g.

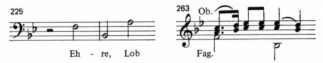

both being derived from the first two or three notes of the fugue itself. Towards the end, the sopranos soar up to high *b flat* to illustrate 'ewiger'

and during the final cadence we have one of the most prophetically Beethovenian series of *fz* markings in all Haydn: off-beat, thrusting syncopations of a kind that Viennese audiences would soon hear, magnified greatly, in a very few years:

It is an astonishing look into the future.

This virile fugue, which unfolds before us so effortlessly, was in fact the product of six weeks' exhausting work. We have a revealing report from the hand of Vincent Novello, who was talking to Haydn's (and Beethoven's) friend Streicher, the piano builder.[1]

> [Swieten] also prepared the words of *The Seasons* for Haydn, who did not think he could do much with them . . . After the first performance of *The Seasons* Streicher called upon Haydn to congratulate him upon having accomplished another great work. [Haydn said] that the words of *The Creation* had inspired him, as he had to make the Angels sing. *The Seasons* cost him more labour than *The*

1 'Haydn much admired the pianoforte playing of Madame Streicher (she is still an excellent performer)', notes Novello. *A Mozart Pilgrimage*, pp. 195ff.

Creation, one fugue alone (the one in B flat [at the end of 'Spring'] . . .) cost him 6 weeks' work – and yet nobody seemed to think anything of it. Haydn was much hurt with the ill-natured remarks and criticism that were made upon this Oratorio – and scarcely ever afterward felt inclined to exert himself for so ungrateful and tasteless a set as the generality of the Viennese in matters relating to music.

Haydn was delighted when Streicher told him how highly he esteemed this work and threw himself in his arms.

The Viennese, however, were not being ungrateful when they failed to single out this fugue. Haydn had blessed them with far too many great fugues, not a few of them in B flat and even rather similar in tone (as in the *Missa Sancti Bernardi* or 'Theresienmesse'). On the whole, as Tovey said, 'It is perhaps not without practical grounds that *Spring* is the best-known part of Haydn's *The Seasons*.' It is one of the shortest, it is fabulously organized (remember that detail, dropping the trumpets and timpani from the end of the Introduction to the Maestoso section of No. 8), and contains at least two instantaneous 'hits', the opening chorus and Simon's aria. Other parts of *The Seasons* contain, no doubt, bolder thoughts and tauter intellectual music, but 'Spring' has something comfortably relaxed about it. Probably this impression has to do with the fact that Haydn wrote it first, shortly following *The Creation*; and while the final fugue seems to have given him much trouble, the rest of it, at least on the surface, does not reveal any inner tensions. (Perhaps all those off-beat *fz* in the final fugue are a hint as to Haydn's inner state of mind when composing it.) It is significant that the first attempt to perform any part of the work in England was, as we shall see, in 1817, 'when a selection of *Spring* was brought forward at Birmingham . . .' (Crosse, 398). On all counts, 'Spring' is a most successful accomplishment.

No. 9 Introduction and Recitative (Lucas, Simon)

We now come to the first of three important changes made in the introductions, respectively, to 'Summer', 'Autumn', and 'Winter'. When Haydn made the changes cannot be determined, but since the original versions are to be found in Elssler's copy of the lost autograph, we may presume that they were made after the first performance or performances. The altered passages are found in the earliest MS. parts. Two of the changes are rather substantial cuts, in the introductions to 'Autumn' and 'Winter', and while we may very much regret the beautiful music removed, there is no doubt that *The Seasons* is a very long work and that the cuts were well advised. When the pieces in question are performed in the concert hall, the uncut version is to be preferred. But in the original version of the Introduction to 'Summer' Haydn discarded one of his most original and beautiful orchestrations for no apparent reason. Instead of the full string orchestra, Haydn entrusted the grey of dawn to the violas, 'cellos and double basses, sometimes dividing the violas and 'cellos into two parts. The effect is of a mysterious and magical summer morning, with the light as yet uncertain ('in a grey veil the gentle morning light increases'). Now there seem to us to be two reasons why Haydn abandoned this breathtakingly modern and original instrumentation. One is that he felt it too close to the 'Be fruitful' section in *The Creation* – but the two passages are greatly dissimilar in message. The other reason may have been a grimly practical one: possibly the violas could not negotiate this extremely long solo passage, in which they are for the most part entirely unsupported. On careful consideration, this would seem to be the more likely explanation, and if it is the right one, we must speedily restore Haydn's magnificent and daring orchestration. Here is the original version, followed by the later one for the full string orchestra.

[*The Seasons*: original version of the Introduction to 'Summer', from the Elssler MS.
(Tonkünstler-Societät; Stadtbibliothek, Vienna)]

zu düstren Höhlen flieht

der Lei-chen - vö - gel blin - de

Schaar,   ihr dumpfer Kla-ge-ton   be-klemmt das bange Herz   nicht mehr.

[*The Seasons:* final version of the Introduction to 'Summer']

DER SOMMER
Die Einleitung stellt die Morgendämmerung vor
[The introduction represents the idea of morning-twilight]

No. 9 EINLEITUNG UND REZITATIV

In grauem Schleier rückt her-an das sanf - te Morg - en-licht;

mit lah - men Schritten weicht vor ihm die trä - ge Nacht zu-rück.

The entrance of the full string orchestra, after the long introduction with only the lower instruments, is yet another reason to adopt Haydn's original orchestration. This entrance occurs at bar 28 and coincides with the shift from C minor to C major; it is immediately followed by the famous crowing of the cock, which Haydn gives to the solo oboe in a passage which is at the same time touching, brilliant and of an almost Stravinskyan texture. Simon now takes over the recitative, which leads directly to the horn solo of No. 10. The first few bars are apparently the traditional call heard in Austrian villages at dawn, to summon the peasants to their fields (see the *AMZ* criticism, *supra*). Times had changed since the great horn-solo works of Haydn's youth – the Trio in E flat of 1767, the 'Hornsignal' Symphony No. 31 of 1765 and Symphony No. 72 of about 1763, not to speak of Symphony No. 51 in B flat, the slow movement of which includes a horn solo that (like the Trio) rises to written *f'''*. In those days, the first horn players possessed what might be called a 'clarino' technique, and their speciality was the fearfully high tessitura that we find in all those works of the 1760s enumerated above. In *The Seasons* Haydn was writing for a different kind of horn and a different kind of technique: the music never surpasses written *g''*. But from the kind of music, we can also get quite a clear idea of the tone and technique of Haydn's first hornist, Rupp, whose speciality must have been a beautiful tone in the register from *g'* to *g''*. The Aria is very lightly scored, including (among the woodwind) only a short bassoon passage. The Aria slides unobtrusively into an accompanied recitative; the woodwind come in, once alone, to describe the rosy-tinted clouds that announce the coming sunrise. And now we see why Haydn has been so fastidious in his scoring of Nos. 9 and 10: he is saving everything for:

No. 11 Trio (Soloists) with Chorus.

It must have been a fearsome problem to have to compete with the celebrated sunrise in *The Creation*, but Haydn managed even this apparently insoluble question. In *The Creation*, we were given the first sunrise in musical history, and Haydn wrote one of his most miraculous pieces. Here in *The Seasons*, the sunrise is a happy occasion but not *unique* (as it is in *The Creation*): the peasants pause in their work for a moment to watch the great spectacle, but of course it is one with which they are familiar. The mystery involved is almost non-existent. The soloists start out singly, one joining the next, then the chorus and some of the woodwind enter, then the brass, timpani and everyone *ff*. The passage is constructed with the greatest economy but the results are spectacular. The 'flaming majesty' is greeted not only *ff*, but with the sopranos reaching an extended high *a''* and the brass and timpani blazing through the strings in demisemiquaver triplets. Haydn has treated all this as a kind of slow introduction:

Largo (introduction)	—	*Allegro*	—	*Andante*	—	*Allegro*
D major (8 bars)		(bars 9–57)		(bars 58–69)		(bars 70–117).

This is a difficult movement not only for the chorus but also for the soloists. The short Andante is a kind of miniature slow movement without chorus, and the final Allegro a shortened and altered repetition of the opening quick movement; it is here that we find one of the most taxing passages for the soloists, of which we give the soprano part as an example:

No. 12 Recitative (Simon, Lucas)

A brief *secco* recitative leads to one accompanied by muted strings. This is the beginning of Haydn's great *tour-de-force* describing the summer heat and its effects on man and beast – four slow movements (or parts of movements). Once again he returns to an earlier language to depict the parched fields in this recitative, for with the Larghetto (bars 17ff.) we seem to be in the midst of a symphonic slow movement of the early 1770s.

No. 13 Cavatine (Lucas)

With its fastidious scoring (one flute, one oboe, muted strings) and concise form, this beautiful Cavatine is a model of a late Haydn aria in slow tempo. The woodwind, entering in quiet syncopation, seem to give us the essence of 'tyrant heat' and its effect on 'drooping flowers' and 'singed meadows'. Later, when Haydn sets the word 'kraftlos' (without strength), the music literally droops, and the syncopations thereafter suggest panting in a vivid way. The last word, 'hingestreckt' (stretched out), introduces only a 'stretched out' note in the first violin, but the mutes of the strings are lifted. It is a gentle way of preparing us for the 'shady groves' of the next number,

No. 14 Recitative (Hanne)

which is an *accompagnato*, starting lazily in C major and moving with exquisite slowness to B flat. A few of the details are magnificently accomplished. The murmuring of the ash, faintly stirred by the summer wind, which Haydn presents with sextuplet violins, tracing slow, undulating curves over a slow bass line; then a whole series of *pp* demisemiquavers which first describe a brook and then the humming of insects. Into this idyllic drone of sound enters the solo oboe, 'the shepherd's warbling reed', which climbs to the dizzy heights of *e flat'''* and leads us to:

No. 15 Aria (Hanne)

In some respects this well-known Aria has a certain spiritual affinity with the F major Aria for soprano ('Auf starkem Fittige'/'On mighty pens') that opens Part II of *The Creation*. Both are bravura pieces, and both are to some extent more conventional than the other arias with which they are surrounded. In 'Welche Labung', the piece under examination, there is a very long slow introduction which is undoubtedly the finest part. In both sections, the oboe has such a prominent part that the whole Aria might be described as a work for soprano, obbligato oboe and orchestra. The other woodwind do not enter until the quick section (flute, two clarinets); two horns are used also in the slow section, and ought to be in B flat *alto* (as they are in 'With verdure clad' in *The Creation*) rather than *basso*, as they are in B flat choruses with the trumpets (such as the end of 'Spring'). The triplets and sextuplets introduced in the Adagio also figure largely in the fast section; they are in this case a unifying device. In the Allegro assai, we note that after fifteen bars a new thought emerges:

This is to introduce 'und neue Kraft erhebt' ('and new strength raises'). It is one of the few points in the rather flat text that might inspire a composer.

No. 16 Recitative (all Soloists)

If No. 15 was one of the more conventional numbers in the work, both this recitative and the following chorus are not only original but (in the chorus) of massive power. We are approaching a summer thunderstorm of frightening proportions, and the *secco* is interrupted by a soft timpani roll marked 'Solo ad lib.', and as at the beginning of the 'Drum Roll' Symphony, the player was expected to create his own dynamic marks (perhaps a 'hairpin'?). There are parts of this recitative that sound like Schubert, and we note (a) that Haydn has written out the piano part, rather than giving it figures, when he thinks it necessary, and (b) has added dynamic marks, something that composers hardly ever did in *secco* recitatives. This passage of Schubertian power leads directly to the famous section with pizzicato strings that announce the first raindrops breaking the oppressive silence:

No. 17 Chorus

Descriptions of storms are a genre which goes out of date more quickly than almost any other aspect of the art. Today we smile at the storm in Holzbauer's Symphony *La tempesta del mare* in E flat, and even at *La tempesta* which concludes Haydn's Symphony No. 8 ('Le Soir'). In storms, the large orchestra plays a decisive role, and inevitably the terrifying sound of Wagner's gigantic orchestra at the beginning of *Die Walküre* (eight horns, two sets of kettledrums, and so on) makes it difficult for us to be other than amused at eighteenth-century *tempeste*. But this Storm Chorus in Haydn's Oratorio is the first 'modern' storm scene, that is, the first to use a really large orchestra and to make it evoke the terrors of thunder and lightning. As such, this piece is the father of the famous storm scene in Beethoven's 'Pastoral' Symphony, in Berlioz' *Les Troyens*, and in many other nineteenth-century works. Haydn remains true to his symbols. In Haydn's early symphony – 'Le Soir' – composed forty years before, the flute represented lightning – as we have pointed out above – and it is the flute darting down in triplets that lets loose the fearful storm. The first unison is marked *ff*, all except for the kettledrums, which have *ff assai*, a marking which we have never heard to be observed in any performance; it is the same with the *ff assai* (just before the coda), in Mendelssohn's *Midsummer Night's Dream* Overture, which is also hardly ever observed.

In the next bar, all the remaining instruments (bassoons, trombones) and the chorus enter. It is interesting to see how Haydn disposes his huge orchestra. The contrabassi and double bassoons provide a sixteen-foot pedal on Contra C (below the bass clef), supported by a continuous roll on the drums. The woodwind and brass have chords, following the basic shifts of the chorus, while the rest of the strings repeat a pattern of alternating semiquavers. If we examine this 'layout' carefully, we see that there are several of Haydn's earlier scores that served – consciously, or perhaps unconsciously – as models. The earliest is the fire scene (end of Act I) from *Die Feuersbrunst*, also in C minor and for chorus; another is the Madrigal *The Storm* (with soloists, chorus and orchestra), composed in London in 1792 and revised later. In each of these earlier models, Haydn had a rather better text, even considering the German dialect of the Opera. Swieten's idea of the countryfolk cowering under the storm really smacks of baronial ignorance – 'Whither shall we flee? Help us, Heavens!' But Haydn kept a straight face and wrote storm music of really spectacular proportions. Here is a page that will illustrate the imaginitave brilliance of the scoring (notice the different techniques in first and second violins) and the crushing power of the woodwind and brass, hammering out those repeated *c*s (see musical example overleaf). Later we have a graphic portrayal of 'schmetternd krachen Schlag auf Schlag' ('crashing peal after peal of thunder') with huge chords in the violins and the horns, trombones and timpani in sharp crotchets (bars 61ff.). The 'schmetternd krachen Schlag auf Schlag' also returns in a fugue which relieves Haydn of having to continue endlessly with descriptions of thunder, lightning, and so on; at bars 100ff. we have 'schmetternd', etc. accompanied by four bars of repeated *c*s in all the brass and timpani (crotchets in *alla breve*), and we realize that this is a transformation of bars 45ff. quoted above. Even the harmonic context is the same (the repeated *c*s, in both cases, being the background to a progression in F minor with a modulation towards the dominant of G). Similarly, the triplet 'lightning' pattern of the flute in the first part becomes the accompaniment to the fugue in the second). In all this mass of sound, the timpani are used with a force and a sense of their power which was unknown in music hitherto except, perhaps, in the Finale to Act II of *Don Giovanni* and in *The Creation*. We have a spectacular *crescendo* to the last climax of the work (bars 141ff.) which recalls the drama of the 'Military' Symphony's second movement: in the Oratorio this marks the moment after which the storm recedes, the flute's triplets disappearing into a quiet cadence, *pp*, for the strings. As a whole, the movement represents a new aspect in Haydn – the exploitation of the orchestra to create an atmosphere of cataclysm. We

have had a few earlier cases in Haydn's earlier works, one being the Finale to Act IV of *L'anima del filosofo*, when the bacchanti drown, but the storm scene in *The Seasons* goes, perhaps, a step further in pure, naked power.

No. 18 Trio (Soloists) and Chorus

The trumpets and timpani now disappear from the scene, and the scoring (apart from an occasional special effect) is lightened considerably. The melody, too, is almost like an operatic 'couplet', reminding one of such 'couplets' in *La vera costanza* (e.g. in the Finale of Act I). The storm passes away and low over the horizon the sun shines once more. The cows, heavy with milk, return to the stalls and are depicted by Haydn so realistically that we almost hear the bellow : this is achieved by a series of figures –

to which the sudden appearance of the double bassoon and trombones adds a realistic note. We are then treated to the sound of the quail, the improbably dissonant notes (Tovey called these 'Straussian') of the cricket, the (in)famous croaking of the frogs, into which the bells of eventide intrude, summoning the peasants home from the fields. The tempo shifts from allegretto to allegro and in a beautifully worked finale, Haydn describes the evening star and the peace of the sleeping village. The music slips away to a *pianissimo* close, and one has the feeling that, 'Frenchified trash' (*französischer Quark*) or not, all these rustic scenes were not only part of Haydn's long memory but also close to his heart ; that for him the village life had a Wordsworthian poetry and a dignified place in the universe – *vox populi, vox Dei.*

No. 19 Introduction and Recitative (all Soloists)

The Introduction, like that to 'Winter', was originally longer, but Haydn shortened it after the first performance or performances. The music is surprisingly archaic, almost like an old Haydn symphony of the 1770s, with a small orchestra (flutes, oboes, bassoons, horns) and the ancient dotted rhythm of the French Overture. It is possibly the first time in this long Oratorio when we have a sense of Haydn's falling back on a conventional language, in a word the first time when it might be said that his powers showed signs of failing. It is also hard to see how this Allegretto is supposed to 'indicate the husbandman's satisfaction at the abundant harvest'. The music moves into an *accompagnato*, then a *secco*, telling us of the good harvest and the farmer's joy at seeing it.

No. 20 Trio (Soloists) and Chorus

This is the Chorus 'in Praise of Industry', to the words of which Haydn objected. But the results are magnificent, suggesting that the composer's dictum was always 'prima la musica, poi le parole'. No. 20 also provides us with a spectacular example of Haydn's architectural construction, of the constant increase, in size and scope, of the material at his disposal. We begin with an interesting orchestral score : no clarinets and no trombones ; the first are perhaps omitted because they were regarded as instruments too sensuous for 'industry', and the second are omitted to lighten the orchestral texture and provide a different sound from that heard in the other large choruses, such as the storm in 'Summer'. But the double bassoon is included,[1] though it does not enter until the chorus makes its appearance. The work starts with one soloist, and very light scoring. We modulate to the dominant and there are two soloists, and the music remains a long time in G major. Then the third soloist joins the proceedings. As we move into E flat, the same procedure is repeated: one, two, then three soloists, and the third-related key of E flat is also well established (bars 78–93). The chorus and full orchestra enter unexpectedly as we are proceeding back to C major, and then we settle into C major again. Suddenly the words 'Die Hütte, die uns schirmt', etc. – 'the house that lodges us, the wool that covers us, the food that nourishes us' – acquire an immense and personal dignity, expressed, as so often in late-period Haydn, by a long pedal point. Haydn had nearly starved as a young man in Vienna, and the deep humility and goodness of this passage must have struck many in the audience that evening in April 1801 to whom Haydn's early history was known. To hold this very large form together, the composer has recourse to various strategies that bind the various sections one with another in such a way that the listener feels the unity unconsciously, while the analyst may see the ingenuity with which this unity is accomplished. The beginning of the number contains a series of playful figures in the woodwind:

In that marvellously dignified passage referred to above (bars 106ff.), the woodwind figures from the beginning act as the unifying factor (see musical example opposite and overleaf). The second part is a fugue, based upon a subject that grows out of the previous material: the fourth plays an important role even as early as the first solo passage.

and so on. The choral entry concludes with the soprano's

and later leads to this:

<hr />

1 Though perhaps a later addition: *vide supra*, p.132.

The fugue subject is answered by a note-for-note derivative of the example given on p. 162:

The tempo is speeded up to 'più allegro' for this fugue, and it is in this accelerated motion that we arrive at yet another variant of the pedal point quoted above. Now, we have the same pattern in the woodwind and soloists but the chorus shouts interjections between the soloists' statements (see musical example overleaf).

The whole chorus is a mighty triumph on Haydn's part over what is basically an uninspired text. Again and again we find the composer illuminating some small detail with his genius. The text describes the 'full force' ('mit voller Kraft') with which industry excites the farmer, and when the word 'Kraft' appears for the first time, the music swerves into E flat and horns, trumpets and timpani come in, the trumpets and drums for the first time in No. 20, with a stunning single note, *g*. In another detail, Haydn twice takes the sopranos up to high *a''* in the climactic end of the fugue, the first time holding the note (and the whole surprising chord, A major, with a fierce dissonance, *g*, in the kettledrums) by means of a fermata. The second time that Haydn approaches the *a*, the chord is subtly different, having *g* as the bass and introducing, just as the sopranos reach the difficult *a*, a blazing entrance for the brass and timpani, *ff*. The first time, the crucial word was 'Fleiß', the second time 'Heil' (blessing), thus the mitigating harmonies the second time and the illumination of the brass and kettledrums. The chorus is a great achievement and one more reason to thank the Baron for his perseverance in forcing the old composer to such heights of brilliance and enthusiasm. Perhaps, after all, the bland opening orchestral Introduction to 'Autumn' is part of Haydn's grand architectural plan, in which there is a delicate sense of stress and relaxation over long periods. From the beginning of 'Autumn' to the end of No. 20 is one such line, a psychological *crescendo*.

No. 21 Recitative (Hanne, Lucas)
Here we begin another cycle which starts as blandly as possible, *viz.* with a *secco*, and concludes in the brilliant 'drunken fugue'. The *secco* leads into:

No. 22 Duet (Hanne-Lucas)
Here again we approach the style and, as we have said earlier, even the content of a love duet in Haydn's own operas. It is delicately scored (only a flute, oboes, clarinets and bassoons). One is at first surprised that even the horns are omitted, but this is all part of Haydn's grand scheme, for the horns are being saved for their grand entry at the beginning of the hunting chorus (No. 26). It is a detail typical of the care which Haydn lavished on this huge score.

The theme itself might be from one of Haydn's comic operas:

and has all the lightness of the popular Viennese comic style; but the overall form is very large (306 bars) and the whole is stamped with the composer's customary ability to think 'large'. The middle section, Adagio, is in C major. 'Only death can separate us', and at the word 'death' ('Tod') we hear a faintly ominous knocking, given to – of all instruments – the clarinet (bars 212f.):

But death is a remote thought from the enchanted lovers' minds, though not from Haydn's; and it is only casually that we note the music passing into C minor, soon to be the symbol of winter – and death. The third part returns to B flat and two-four time, but allegro rather than the earlier allegretto. It is as if we were hearing a scene from *La vera costanza* or *La fedeltà premiata* in the Eszterháza opera house, and one more aspect of the panoramic display of Haydn's whole career in the Oratorio.

No. 23 Recitative (Simon) and No. 24 Aria (Simon)

We now enter the hunting section of 'Autumn' and the aria tells of the hunting dog following a scent, something Haydn accomplishes with marvellous realism. As the scent becomes 'hotter', the music speeds up no less than twice, and by the time the second 'più moto' arrives, the whole string orchestra is tearing along, as it were, beside the frantic dog:

When the dog points, the music drops to a standstill ('as still as a stone'), then shifts into A major as the bird attempts frantically to escape, rises into the air (all this graphically described), is shot (crash from the woodwind and *ff* timpani) and plummets to the ground (a mighty skip, in the voice, from *e'* to *g*). It is all most delightfully accomplished but it is to be feared that Haydn's obvious relish for the hunt in all its aspects will not be everywhere appreciated today.

No. 25 Recitative (Lucas)

describes the hares frantically running in all directions – again, tellingly portrayed in the score – but soon fallen (the music scrambles down the scale, instrument by instrument) and laid out, as the Baron's translation reads, 'in showy files'. Into the last word of Lucas, four horns suddenly enter and with

No. 26 Chorus (Peasants and Hunters)

we are in the midst of a great Austro-Hungarian *battue*. Students of Haydn's earlier hunting works know that he actually used then well-known 'calls'; one of these, with the characteristic octave skip upwards, appears not only in the famous 'Hornsignal' Symphony (No. 31) but also in the *Cassatio* in D (Hokoken *deest*) for four horns and strings which the present writer discovered at Prague. In *The Seasons* Haydn has reunited a whole series of hunting calls (pls 13–18), mainly French but occasionally Austrian, which distinguish the various important moments of the *battue*. Recently an Austrian expert on the subject, Dr Ernst Paul, published a fascinating résumé of Haydn's use of these old hunting calls;[1] with this knowledge, No. 26 appears like a catalogue of the eighteenth-century hunting calls, and its effect must have been far more immediate on European audiences of 1801 than it is on us today.

According to Dr. Paul, the *par force* hunting signals of the courtly hunt as practised throughout western and central Europe were primarily French, but by the year 1801 their significance was gradually becoming forgotten, the melodic shape changed or, especially in the Austro-Hungarian territories, combined with local signals. Haydn has presented us with a typical hunting scene from beginning to end. He starts with a 'search' call, the 'Cornure de quête', which is to be found in several variants in French sources of the period:

This is followed by two signals for the dogs ('Tons pour les chiens'):

At bars 33ff. the 'search' call that we recall from the opening bars is repeated, but to it is added the famous old signal, 'Le Lancé', signalling that the game has been flushed:

The signals listed here always precede the words of the hunters (chorus); here they sing 'Schon flieht der aufgesprengte Hirsch', or in Swieten's English, 'Here starts the fear-aroused stag'. The repeated notes

1 In Hoboken II, 67f. Other literature on the subject includes Carl Clewing, *Musik und Jägerei*, Kassel 1937, and Alexander L. Ringer, 'The Chasse as a Musical Topic of the 18th century', in *Journal of the American Musicological Society* VI (1953), No. 2. Swieten himself, in an early comic opera entitled *Colas toujours Colas*, used two of the signals that are found in No. 26 of *The Seasons*: the *Lancé* and the final 'call' in the chorus. E. E. Schmid, in his study 'Gottfried van Swieten als Komponist' (*Mozart-Jahrbuch* 1953, p. 20), analyzes the Opera and its relationship to *The Seasons*. Two of the calls also appear in the Finale of Carl Stamitz's Concerto in D for viola d'amore and orchestra.

which appear here and at the end are the concluding formulas of many Austrian signals. They are used now to separate 'Le Lancé' from another signal, 'Le Débouché'

The next fanfares,

and

are part of a signal called 'Le Volce-l'est' and show that a new scent has been found (text, afterwards, describes the stag breaking out of a thicket). And 'fresh scent' is illustrated by Haydn in a sudden modulating to D minor (bar 75). Note that he has tacked an Austrian ending to the call beginning at bar 58 ('concluding formula'). We now shift the whole music from D to E flat, which is symbolically a change from the French *cor de chasse* in D to the Austrian *Jagdhorn in Es* (or E flat), and also describes the hounds losing the trail for a moment. The following fanfare that announces the switch to E flat

is taken from 'Le Rapproché' but then Haydn adds an old Austrian (or rather Lower Austrian) call for the 'search' which exists in several variants:

This Austrian 'search' signal continues for several pages. But the next call is again French, the 'Réponse à l'appel':

We now approach the climax of the hunt. The stag is at bay, and Haydn turns to an Austrian 'signal of the dead game' (*Wildtodsignal*), preceded by the cries of 'Ho, ho' and concluded by 'Tajo, tajo, tajo':

The next fanfare is French, 'Halali sur pied', and is used in part and then *in toto* by Haydn; we quote the 'total' version:

This 'Halali' signal, which appears to have been composed by the Marquis de Dampierre, is also used in Nicolas Méhul's Overture to *Le jeune Henri* (1797). This catalogue of French and Austrian horn calls closes with a quotation from the 'Retour de la chasse', to which Haydn adds the favourite Austrian 'concluding formula' of repeated (written) *g*s:

This is the melody that Baron van Swieten also uses in his comic opera, mentioned above.

We have, then, in this remarkable hunting chorus another of Haydn's historical panoramas: we have had fugues, reminiscences of Mozart, tunes that seem to come from Haydn's earlier operas, and now we have a catalogue of *la chasse* 'as a musical topic' in eighteenth-century Austro-French aristocratic life: even then, the great *battue* was a fading dream, linked to earlier times, and Haydn, of course, shows his age and an old man's fondness for reminiscences in this chorus. It carried not only Haydn's, but many other men's, memories back to the great Esterházy hunts of the 1760s, when their return had been greeted by Haydn and the orchestra in the 'Hornsignal' Symphony, accompanying a sumptuous repast served by dozens of men in Esterházy *livrée*. It recalled the pungent smells of an Austro-Hungarian autumn more poignantly, perhaps, than any painting.

No. 27 Recitative (all Soloists)
This *secco* transports us to the Austrian vineyards and possibly the greatest *tour-de-force* in *The Seasons*:

No. 28 Chorus
We may first examine the way in which Haydn holds together this complicated and lengthy (225 bars) movement, with its various subdivisions. The chorus opens with its praise of wine, 'Juch-he! der Wein ist da' (No. 1 of the music example below), which is later shortened (No. 2) and then is altered in various ways (e.g. No. 3). Even when an apparently new theme is introduced in the next section (Allegro assai, No. 4), it has the intervallic and harmonic feeling of the previous material. In turn, we have the 'drunken' fugue, whose tipsy subject, with its crazily off-beat accents (No. 5) still continues to have a certain relation to what has gone before (a skeletal reduction of the *Urlinie* as No. 5a). When the extra percussion instruments enter, near the end, the chorus sings a less swaying version of the fugue theme (No. 6), and to show that all this

has one melodic, harmonic and intervallic father. Haydn even brings in a note-for-note quotation of No. 2 (see No. 7). For example

in No. 4 becomes the syncopated top line of No. 5 and the basis for No. 6. Naturally the listener is not expected to digest all this rather complex relationship on a first, or even a second, hearing, but he feels the unity which is the relationship's *raison d'être*.

The chorus starts out in a gay Allegro molto, and it is instructive to see Haydn's accurate timing for the wine to start to take effect. The music closes in the dominant, there is a double bar, and we move into a quicker tempo (Allegro assai) and a different time (six-eight). This is a German dance such as Haydn himself composed, but never with such a huge orchestra. 'es wirbelt die Trommel' coincides with a massive *cresc.-decresc.* in the timpani. The bagpipes are then described with relish, taking back to that delectable and justly famous Trio from Symphony No. 88 (where, too, the bassoons growl in open fifths, as they do at bars 101ff. in this chorus). The men with their girls or wives are now beginning to feel the effects of that strong red wine from the

Burgenland, and the music becomes increasingly hectic. Figures are at first slurred

or but at bar 121 Haydn switches to to match the swaying couples. There is a 'new' *deutscher Tanz* in F major (bars 134, upbeat, etc.), charmingly scored for oboe and strings marked *ff* against the timpani, marked *p*. Some of Haydn's pretty effects cannot really be assimilated the first time, such as the octave jumps in the lower strings (bars 129f.) to suggest the men jumping ('laßt uns springen!'). We are suddenly in the middle of a fugue, and the crowd's state of inebriety is cleverly suggested by the fact that the music is in two keys at once, G major and E minor (see No. 5 of the previous music example). The people are so drunk that they cannot sing the rather complicated fugue, they can only lurch out scraps of it:

The bitonality, the syncopations, the 'reeling' *fz* (which collide at intervals of a quaver, as at bar 154 in the example) all combine to produce a hilariously drunken uproar. Throughout the course of this fugue, the brass instruments and timpani are silent, so that their entrance later will be spectacular. At bars 185ff. the bassoons and contrabassoon, together with the lower strings, produce obscene belches and in a few bars the music dives into C major, introducing horns, trumpets, trombones, timpani, triangle and tambourin. With the gigantic size of Haydn's orchestra, and the brass instruments all raised high above the rest of the orchestra, the effect must have been spell-binding. It should be even today. There is one huge hiccough, where the sopranos stagger up to high *b flat* (bars 211f.), supported by a host of other instruments including several that stagger up an octave. There is one huge drunken reel in the trombones that sounds particularly offensive (bars 217ff.) and this incredible movement closes with a last shout of 'juch, juch!' from the completely intoxicated chorus. It a scene of Breugelian realism and one of Haydn's most brilliant achievements.

No. 29 Introduction and Recitative (Simon, Hanne)

The saddest cut that Haydn ever had to make in his music – and he was ruthless when necessary, especially in his earlier operas and in such a work as *Il ritorno di Tobia* – occurred in this Introduction; but in its context he was right to do so. In the analysis of *The Creation* we have noted the uncanny look into the future (*Tristan*) that occurs in 'Chaos'. Another pre-Wagnerian passage occurs in this desolate and bleak Introduction to 'Winter'. The harmonic language of the violins is astonishing in itself, and the rich chromaticism is balanced by the gaunt *forzato* sound in the horns, with the stopped notes discussed above. The beautiful but as usual 'economic' scoring for the woodwind may also be seen in this example, both when the flute, oboes, clarinets and bassoons rise out of the orchestra and later when they are unsupported (see overleaf). Simon enters, telling of 'the pale year', while the music continues with motifs from the Introduction. In two *ff* chords which sink to *p*, the woodwind and strings describe the icy blasts from Lapland, introducing Hanne, who then sings:

No. 30 Cavatine (Hanne)

This is one of the most beautiful and moving parts of the Oratorio; as the title implies, it is a very short aria, accompanied only by strings. She tells us of light and joy receding, of 'sullen days' followed by 'black nights'. It is the first of Haydn's own farewells, and the quiet postlude, describing 'lange Dauer' ('of long duration'), sounds almost like a benediction. With the exception of an occasional excursion to a related key, the whole Cavatine remains in the tonic, putting the many chromatic turns of phrase into high relief.

No. 31 Recitative (Lucas)

Beginning as a *secco* and ending as an *accompagnato*, this recitative tells us, *via* Lucas, of the lake and waterfalls frozen. 'The face of earth appears a grave', in the Baron's translation. The harmonic sweep of this recitative is surprising. The Cavatine ended in F, while the recitative begins abruptly in the flattened submediant, D flat (the piano part is written out here). Within a few bars we are in F sharp major (avoiding G flat) so that Haydn can arrive, for his *accompagnato*, at A major and then the dominant of E, the key of No. 32.

173

[No. 29]

[No. 29: original version of Introduction (cf. caption p. 177)]

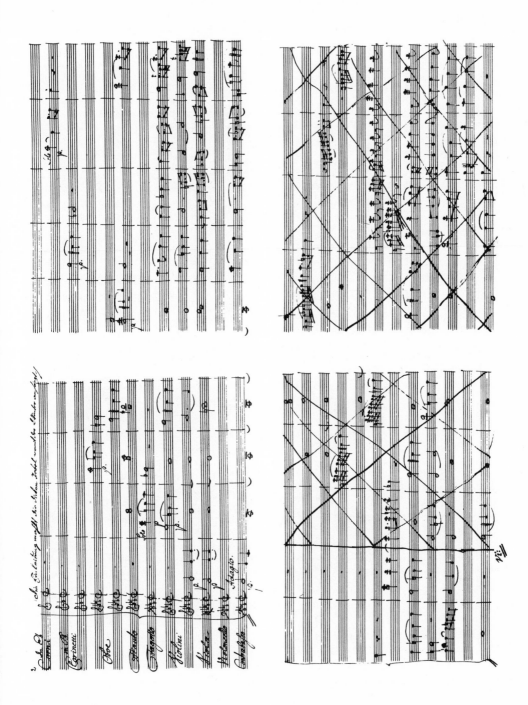

[No. 29: original version of Introduction – *cont.*]

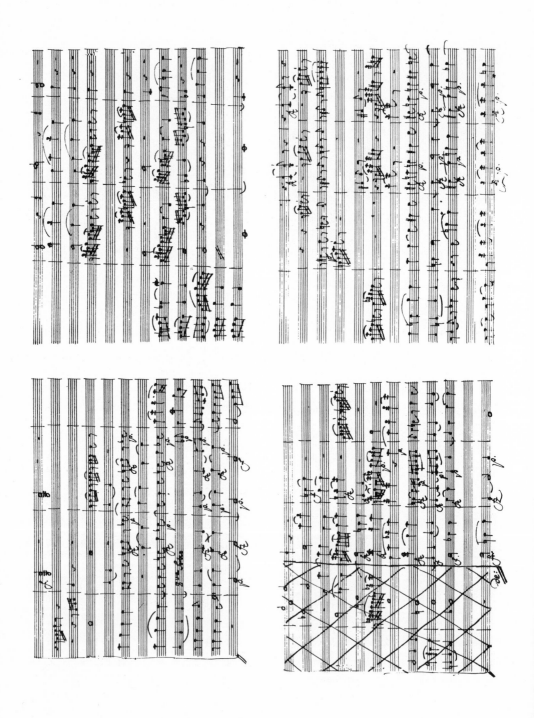

[No. 29: original version of Introduction – *cont.*]

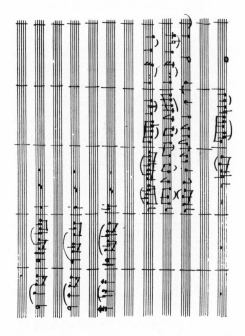

The Seasons

The Introduction to 'Winter' in its original version, from the full score (used by Haydn when conducting the work) copied by Johann Elssler and his assistants. Here is shown the original version of the Introduction (copied by one of the assistants), with only the beginning and end of the deleted passage crossed out; the pages between the cancelled passages were concealed by being sewn together and were thus left uncancelled. From the Archives of the Tonkünstler-Societät; Stadtbibliothek, Vienna.

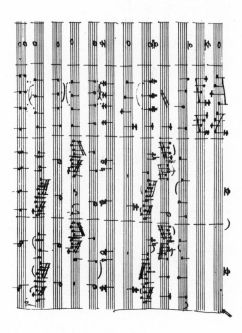

No. 32 Aria (Lucas)

The Aria, starting in E minor and ending in E major, describes the lost traveller (see above, p. 109). There is a haunting portrayal of fear gripping his heart as he pushes through the snow (syncopated strings), and the repeated quavers suggesting frost is in the long tradition of Austrian music; it can be found in Leopold Mozart's *Musicalische Schlittenfahrt* (MS. in the Thurn und Taxis Archives, Regensburg), where there is an amusing description of a woman shivering with cold, also expressed in repeated quavers. In the Aria, Haydn illuminates the word 'plötzlich' ('suddenly') with a *f*, the first one in many bars (bar 104). The weary traveller has 'suddenly' seen a nearby light. The music moves to Haydn's radiant key of E major: the traveller is saved. Several times, the text is graphically illustrated: 'starr und matt' ('stiff and tired') has a stiff, drooping accompaniment in two unharmonized lines (bars 134f., and even more dramatically at bars 165ff.). 'Freude' is sung by Lucas with a little turn suggesting someone jumping for joy; 'eilt' ('hurries') is given a whole series of quavers in the vocal part, one of the very few *bravura* passages for the voice in 'Winter'.

No. 33 Recitative (all Soloists)

describes the warm room inside and prepares us, in an *accompagnato* which introduces in quiet *unisono* for the strings, the 'spinning' motif of:

No. 34 *Lied* with Chorus (Hanne)

This is the first of the two famous 'set pieces' in 'Winter', the other being, of course, 'Ein Mädchen, das auf Ehre hielt'. Bürger's *Spinnerlied* is set in severe D minor, the lower strings with their rushing semiquavers and *fz* accents, suggesting the whirring wheels in a wonderful way. The six-eight metre is also perfectly adapted for the accented forward movement Haydn wants. The text passes from the chorus to Hanne and back again. The modulation to C major is another look into the future; the normal thing would have been from D minor to its relative major (F). The D minor section returns only once again to yield to C major; but the end of the piece turns back to D minor again, and in a miraculous way Haydn brings the spinning wheels to a stop, the music dying away and slowing up without any change of tempo:

This Spinning Song had a profound influence on the nineteenth century. Tovey (159) says 'its rustic modulations to C major and E minor foreshadow in mere picturesqueness the most heartbreaking features of Schubert's "Gretchen am Spinnrade"', and traces of Haydn's music may be found, as Geiringer (1947, 321) points out, even in Wagner's *Der fliegende Holländer*, a work composed forty years afterwards.

No. 35 Recitative (Lucas) and No. 36 *Lied* with Chorus

This short *secco* leads to the second famous 'set piece' in 'Winter', written as a strophic song with chorus and orchestra. It is lightly scored, with only flutes, oboes and

bassoons, apart from the strings. (The Spinning Song included horns and trombones.)
The organization of the 'Song with Chorus' is as follows:

> Hanne: [Summary:] A girl who believed in honour once loved a nobleman and
> he, already attracted by her, met her alone. 'Come,' he said, 'kiss your lord.' 'Ah,'
> she answered, much shocked, 'gladly.'

> Chorus: Ha, ha, and why not?

> Hanne: 'Be quiet,' said he, 'my dear child, and give me your heart, for my
> intentions are pure, not trifling or in jest. I shall make you happy. Take this
> money, the ring and the gold watch. And if I have anything else you might like,
> just ask.'

> Chorus: Ha ha, that sounds fine.

> Hanne: 'No,' said she, 'that would be too much. My brother might see it and if he
> tells my father, what would happen to me? He is ploughing much too near us –
> otherwise it might well happen. Look, you can see him ploughing on that hill.'

> Chorus: Ho, ho, what will happen now?

> Hanne: While the Junker goes and looks, the girl jumps on his horse and flies
> away, swifter than the wind. 'Farewell, gracious Sir,' she said, 'that's my revenge
> for your shameful proposals.' The lord gapes, open-mouthed, as she disappears.

> Chorus: Ha, ha, and serve him right!

This rather silly tale has, of course, sexual overtones as overt as those in *Le nozze di
Figaro*. 'Otherwise it [*sic*] might well happen' ('sonst könnt' es wohl geschehn') is set
with a malicious series of staccato quavers in the violins, and the whole passage is
couched in G minor: from 'No' to the chorus's 'Ho ho, what will happen now?' The
irony is, of course, the girl's getting on his horse and riding away. Usually 'it might
well happen'. This couplet-song ends with a laughing chorus ('ha-ha-ha-ha, das war
recht fein') which is, among many other things, the father of the laughing chorus in
Weber's *Der Freischütz*. Once more we are in the realm of German *Märchenkomödie*, a
real German *Volksstück*; that epithet sounds incongruous if we consider the French
origins of the text (*supra*, p. 110). We must remember, however, that although French
culture dominated not only garden, *chasse*, Jacobin thoughts, dress and philosophical
speculation throughout Europe, yet its chansons were incorporated into the *Singspiel*
sufficiently early in the second part of the century for the German product to develop
its own style and sink its own roots. 'Ein Mädchen, das auf Ehre hielt', as far as its
musical content is concerned, owes no more to French musical culture than does *Die
Zauberflöte* or *Entführung*. Like the Spinning Song, 'Ein Mädchen, das auf Ehre hielt'
was of enormous and lasting influence.

No. 37 Recitative (Simon) and No. 38 Aria (Simon)

Another admirably short *secco* now leads us to the celebrated piece in which winter is
likened to our old age. It is composed in Haydn's favourite key of E flat major, a key in
which he had written a host of great music – quartets, piano sonatas, piano trios,
symphonies, a mass, and countless numbers from operas and religious music. As we
have seen, Haydn in this austerely beautiful Aria expressed his innermost thoughts on
the subject. It was *his* spring that was 'verblühet', and the musical illustration is a *pp*
series of repeated demisemiquavers – like the soundless trembling of those curiously
opaque and off-green trees that grow along the Danube between Vienna and

Pressburg. And then we come to the great quotation from Mozart's Symphony in G minor, K. 550: 'Erschöpfet deines Sommers Kraft' ('exhausted thy summer's strength').

We see that Haydn has utilized not only the downwards group of notes – like a person whose breath is painfully short – but also the other pattern from Mozart (bar 105, for example, of K. 550's slow movement:

[woodwind in octaves]

We quote from the recapitulation. Mozart's score exists in two authentic version, one in which the downwards pattern is given to the woodwind and one, made to simplify the woodwind writing, in which it is given to the strings; we reproduce the string version, which is in some ways closer to Haydn's layout (only for strings – can the Mozartian string version have been the one commonly played from MS. parts in those days?):

[Mozart: Symphony No. 40 in G minor (K. 550), second movement: Andante][1]

The tempo changes to allegro molto, and the music enters well off-tonic and moves thereafter to E flat minor, F minor, D flat major and only reaches the tonic after some fifty bars. It is perhaps significant that in Mozart's movement, also in E flat, there is an extremely wide tonal spectrum which inter alia places us squarely in – D flat major even during the exposition, and just during the first presentation of the downwards pattern quoted above when it comes in the recapitulation (see K. 550/II, bars 29ff.). In fact, Haydn does not reach the tonic permanently until about thirty bars before the Aria's conclusion. 'Where are they, now?' (those wild nights, etc.) – gone like a dream, and a halo of solo woodwind floats like a *fata morgana* and fades away. 'Nur Tugend bleibt', sings Simon after the vision of the dream has disappeared. 'Bleibt' ('remains') is

1 From the edition of the *Neue Mozart Ausgabe*, Serie IV, Werkgruppe 11, Band 9, edited by the present writer.

extended in a long *b flat*, across which the orchestra has a strong cadence, leaving the voice to 'remain' after the instruments are silent.

Six bars of accompanied recitative lead to:

No. 39 Trio (Soloists) with Double Chorus

The concluding number of *The Seasons* is a complicated chorus which, with its three soloists and two choirs (did Haydn divide them up, and if so, when did the regrouping take place?), has elicited much praise. Tovey found it 'as moving as anything in *The Creation*' (160). The original orchestration has been discussed above. The concluding fugue subject contains a surprising *b flat*, which turns to *b natural* as the next voice enters. Notwithstanding the glories of Haydn's orchestra and the contrapuntal skill of this final fugue, we may detect a certain conventionality in this conclusion. Haydn was now a very weary old gentleman, and in this echo of past C major pageantry for kings and princes and empresses, the originals (such as the Finale of *L'infedeltà delusa* or Symphony No. 56) perhaps shone more brightly. For the last time in his life, the old C *alto* horn joins the trumpets at the end in what is really the most stirring fanfare of *The Seasons*: first in unison, then in thirds, then in triads, the horns and trumpets rise up, culminating in the (for the horns) cruelly difficult *g''*. The music comes to a massive and very loud (*ff*) 'false' cadence, on F major. And the end comes suddenly, in four bars that Tovey (161) thought was one of the 'most overwhelmingly energetic closes' he had ever heard; while Geiringer (1947, 321) calls these four bars 'more significant than many similar pieces of much greater length'.

The effort involved in the composition of *The Seasons* left Haydn weary and exhausted; after this huge undertaking there would follow only two other major works – both settings of the Mass – in the composer's creative output during his late years.

THE PROGRESS OF 'THE SEASONS'

Little more than a year elapsed between the first performance of *The Seasons* (April 1801) and its appearance in full score (Breitkopf & Härtel, May 1802), a much shorter time than in the case of *The Creation* (April 1798–February 1800). Therefore we have found it opportune to add a short note here on *The Seasons'* dissemination throughout Europe, rather than interrupt the ensuing Chronicle of 1802. This course seems the more justified because, in Germany, manuscript copies were circulating by the end of 1801 and the first performance at Leipzig took place on the Fourth Sunday after Advent.

> Haydn's [Oratorio] [writes Tovey (146)] has suffered from the hard things he was the first to say about it. . . . It is the more unfortunate for the reputation of a great work that his self-criticism should amount exactly to what any fool can say beforehand. It is much more true that the obvious defects are the most negligible aspects of Haydn's qualities. The 'französischer Quark' was forced upon him largely in consequence of the success of what is now becoming priggish to condemn in the word-painting and animal-painting of *The Creation*. It is an automatic function of his sense of humour, which, as is now proverbially known, was never so irrepressible as when he rejoiced in the goodness of God.

Haydn's 'hard things' have already been the subject of the Chronicle, and we have noted his remark to Streicher about the angels (*supra*, p. 148). The comparison between *The Creation*'s angels and *The Seasons'* peasants seems to have become a *bon mot* with the old Haydn. We find it in two other impeccable contemporary references. In Dies's biography (182) we read the following:

> It will not displease the reader to learn Haydn's own view in a few words. The Emperor Franz asked him, on the occasion of a performance of *The Seasons*, which product of his art he preferred, *The Creation* or *The Seasons*. '*The Creation*,' replied Haydn. 'And why?' – 'In *The Creation*, angels speak and tell of God, but in *The Seasons* only Simon talks.'

To another friend, Giuseppe Carpani, Haydn said something similar.

> The best of the criticisms was made by *Haydn* himself. I was present the first time this *Oratorio* was given in the house of Prince *Schwarzenberg*. The applause was general, cordial and without end. But I, astonished that two parts [of the work] containing such variety, quantity and excellence could spring from one brain [*una testa sola*], hastened at the end of the *concert* to find my *Haydn* and convey to him my most lively and sincere congratulations. *Haydn*, as soon as I opened my mouth, cut off my conversation and said the following memorable words: 'Ho piacere che la mia musica sia piaciuta al pubblico; ma da voi non ricevo complimenti su di essa. Sono certo che capite voi stesso che dessa non è la *creazione*. Lo sento io, e dovete sentirlo ancor voi; ma eccovene il perchè: in quella i personaggi erano angioli, nelle *quattro stagioni* sono contadini.' One could print tomes about a comparison between the two *oratorios*, but it could never be said better than in those few words of the composer himself. [Carpani, 212]

Undoubtedly some of Haydn's self-criticism is reflected in the early contemporary notices that followed the first few Viennese performances; for example, in the following notice from the *Historisches Taschenbuch* for 1802:

> For the benefit of the widows and orphans of our [Viennese] musicians Haydn's *The Seasons* was given in the Court theatres; the public understood and admired many very beautiful and brilliant details here, but on the whole one preferred *The Creation*, that magnificent flowering of musical Romanticism, in which sublime grandeur is reflected in its clear beauty. . . .
> [*Historisches Taschenbuch . . . Zweyter Jahrgang. Geschichte des Jahres 1802*, Vienna 1806, pp. 204ff.]

The first performance outside the Austrian monarchy was, as far as can be determined, that given at Leipzig on the Fourth Sunday in Advent, 1801. The following report in *AMZ* concerns not only the actual performance but also the work itself.

> [Leipzig]
> . . . Jos. Haydn's *Four Seasons* was performed in public here for the first time in the Theatre, on the 4th Sunday after Advent, conducted by Music Director Müller, and in order to satisfy in some measure the expectant public the work was repeated a few days later.
> The publication of the work will soon take place, and we dare not anticipate the future reviewers of the work in this Journal; but a few short remarks may be allowed now. From *The Creation* and the well-known text of this, its companion, one already realizes what the two men, both friends, had in mind here. Appearances of nature, as many as ever possible, were to be seized and expressed in music – that was their purpose. The poet thereby sacrificed himself entirely; he did not want to *write poetry*[1] at all, but only to give the composer sufficient

---

1 Letterspaced words in the original are given here in italics, and likewise in other quotations from *AMZ*.

opportunity to fulfil that purpose and to indicate to the listener that which the composer then offers us. A view of the work from afar gives us an uplifting and at the same time a depressing view: one sees with admiration and pleasure the giant steps with which instrumental music has proceeded along its course; one sees with regret how far vocal art, by comparison, has remained behind, so that [instrumental music] is obliged to seek new paths wherein it will not be hindered by vocal art but, on the contrary, supported by it. Far be it from us to repeat that which has been said in, after and because of Engel's well-known publications[1] about the painting of objects [*Objektmahlerey*], the faults of which have been, and mostly with reason, exposed. But we would like to ask all the same: *since things have arrived at this stage*, should we not allow instrumental music to enjoy some matters which, if things had not arrived at this stage, it would not be allowed to enjoy because there would be no necessity? Would we do well, if we had a new Correggio, to find fault with him and in the end make him unsure of himself, because – like the old [Correggio] – he could enchant with his colours but in the general plan of his works, in his choice of subjects and in his designs, etc., etc. he was now and then more successful than his predecessor? –

Artists and amateurs generally ask, upon the appearance of a new, important composition, above all else the following: What can we, and the art itself, win by it? And then: which effect does it have on a large, *mixed* audience? *The Seasons* provides the artists (and thus also the art itself) with a rich harvest, if one judges it as a trial by which one may learn what, in particular, the present instrumental music *can* do in this particular category. The problem is to be regarded as completely resolved, for it was *Haydn* who raised and solved it; and in none of his works, not even in *The Creation*, does he work towards that goal, out of the fulness of his spirit and experience, with such unremitting persistence. The effect of the work on a large, mixed audience *must* be very lively, if only because of the inexhaustible richness and exceptional variety in the content and its treatment, which in itself reaches the extremes, and though which *every* listener, however educated (in music) he may or may not be, receives something dear to him. We will not deny that just this variety adversely influences the total impression. If only it would have occurred to the poet to take all these appearances and perhaps in this fashion weld them into a unity: – he should have changed the principal protagonists into active persons, something that happens only occasionally; and he could have arranged and consolidated the work as far, dramatically, as was the case in Part III of *The Creation*.

To say at least a few words about single sections, we may be permitted to single out those movements in 'Spring' and 'Summer' which pleased us particularly and never lacked for the finest effects. 'Summer' is perhaps the most successful part of the work altogether, though 'Autumn' is composed with an even richer expenditure of intellectual energy and care. The Chorus, 'Komm, holder Lenz!', is a yearning, insinuating invitation. The movement 'Sey uns gnädig, milder Himmel' is indescribably moving, also the *Mahlerey* therein is most excellent. The final chorus, 'Ewiger, mächtiger, gütiger Gott', is staggering [*erschütternd*], great; it then dissolves the senses in a comforting and endlessly joyous devotion. The Overture to 'Summer', short as it is, is most significant; the small movements that follow thereafter are in themselves very nice [*artig*] but also provide a good introduction to the scene when dawn breaks, and finally the sun rises. This latter scene is treated quite differently than such a well-known sunrise as that in *The Creation*, and is much more nobly conceived and executed. The Song of Praise, 'Heil, o Sonne, Heil!', is so enthusiastic that the listener attempts to join

1 Johann Jacob Engel (1741–1802), author and, from 1786 to 1794 director of the Berlin National Theatre.

in with his entire being. But with the entrance of the *accompagnato* in the Recitative, 'Nun regt und bewegt sich alles umher', there begins the preparation for the powerful storm scene which, with this extremely tense preparation, is in our opinion the greatest and noblest masterpiece in the whole work. How heavy and crushing and choked one feels in the excellent Aria, 'Dem Druck erlieget die Natur'. – The following accompanied Recitative, 'Willkommen jezt [*sic*], o dunkler Hain' and the Aria, 'Welche Labung für die Sinne', are in wise moderation so constituted that again one dares to breathe more freely; but one is not delivered from the secret, fearsome expectation. Now appear the closer envoys of the storm, gradually, and marvellously calculated; one awaits the storm, but Haydn still holds the listener firmly in the fearsome stillness of nature, during the short, simple but unsurpassed movement, 'In banger Ahndung stockt das Leben der Natur' – until a strange, highly descriptive [*mahlerische*] and really deceiving figure for the flute (a trial piece for *secure* flute-players) unexpectedly enters; and now with the choir's entrance, 'Ach, das Ungewitter naht', everything is offered – the most sublime spectacle of nature, in all its great moments and in its single details – to enchant the attentive listener. After the (in relation to the whole, rather too quick) storm's abatement, the calm of evening descends and the music seems, like nature itself, gradually to slumber; with which 'Summer' concludes.

It will be permitted us to be brief about the performance. We gladly avoid the *appearance* of small-town-mindedness, which often and with delight praises that which it already has; and in this case we would have much to praise. [Extols the performance, carefully prepared by August Eberhardt Müller; forty voices from the *Thomanerchor* made up the upper parts of the chorus; the solo soprano was Demoiselle Weinmann from Halle.]   [*AMZ* IV, 239ff.]

One of the most controversial and widely read criticisms appeared in the *Zeitung für die elegante Welt* on 31 December 1801.[1] It will be recalled that A. E. Müller, to

1 There is another short review in the *Zeitung für die elegante Welt* in this same year (1. Jahrgang, 1801, pp. 1051f.), the tone and style of which suggest that it, too, was written by A. G. Spazier. We are much indebted to our colleague, Dr Robert Münster, of the Bayerische Staatsbibliothek, Munich, for photographing a number of criticisms from this newspaper, and for many courtesies altogether.

Music
The Seasons by Haydn.

The Breitkopf-Härtel music publishers, which have helped us come nearer to the spirit of many a great composer by the inexpensive publication of their most important works, has just arranged for the publication of the score and piano reduction of Haydn's *The Seasons* – a work which created a very great sensation in Vienna and must do so everywhere. The music (except for some playful tone-paintings, for the presence of which the composer is least to blame) is on an incomparably greater scale, is richer, more finely worked and has more *artistic glow* than *The Creation*. One only has to study the score to be convinced that the composer has used his intellect far more than merely relying in a comfortable fashion on the suggestive powers of his imagination [*Genies*]. How much more, then, must a fortunate and large-scale performance make us aware of the artistic greatness which is impressed on this work – in so far as the *composer of the libretto* (at whose hands, despite only copying Thomson's *The Seasons*, the text, alas, often enough comes to grief) has allowed the *poet of the music* to make that impression. *The Creation* created a sensation in half of Europe (because, among other things, of the matter's novelty, the fortunate combination of circumstances, the desire on the part of cities and nations to emulate each other, the prejudice for the subject's mystical greatness, &c.); that must be even more the case with *The Seasons*, a much more self-integrated work, provided that all the circumstances are equal, as in the case of *The Creation*. If so, a similar artistic drama, with just the same effort and just the same success, will be played out.

The action of the above-mentioned music publishers therefore deserves the most active support, and there is no doubt that it shall be found for such a work, especially under such inexpensive conditions. There will be two editions of the score and piano reduction, both of which are in the presses . . . [conditions, price, &c.]. – May in this case, as always, our nation honour itself by strong support of the products of its leading artists, and never lag behind foreign nations! [Spaced words here reproduced by italics.]

whom Haydn had written on 11 December 1801, showed A. G. Spazier, the journal's editor, the famous passage about Frenchified trash. The use to which Herr Spazier put this piece of news may be seen in his review:

The advantage of the first and at the same time successful public performance of the great new product of Haydn's genius was given to Leipzig. After the music had been given in part in the concert in the Thomasschule – which concert, under the very noble auspices of the worthy *Herr Prokonsul Einert*, a great friend of the arts, was recently given by *Herr Mus. Director Müller* – the latter conducted the work on the 20th of the month in complete order, with short intervals, at our local theatre, and with great success; and on the 2nd Christmas Holiday [Boxing Day] this music was, to the joy of the public, repeated there.

A theatrical decoration cannot really be termed very satisfactory for the effect of this music; but despite this, *The Seasons* – performed by the combined orchestras of the concert and theatre, by Dem. Weinmann from Halle and, with great effort and precision, by the gallant music pupils of the Thomasschule – produced a very great effect. To appreciate such a work is rather more than one can expect, obviously, from the majority of the public; yet even for the general taste there must have been a hint that extraordinary things were happening and that a work had been born which has much to give, both to the ear and to the imagination.

And so it is, indeed. *The Seasons*, judged as a musical work of art, is more of a piece, even considering the much greater variety and freshness (except for some boring stretches, e.g. the beginning of 'Autumn', where the composer obviously did not know what to do with the appalling and dry verses), and is altogether by far above *The Creation*, which, the world will learn with sceptical astonishment, Haydn himself holds only in *little regard*, as one learns from his handwritten remarks. It may be, all the same, that the intellect, and with it the inseparable and, in many of life's situations, dangerous partner, the *pure taste*, may object seriously to certain passages. It may be that one damns the treatment of the text, especially in the recitatives, and altogether protests against the whole undertaking in which things are described that actually cannot be described: nevertheless the work has, and will continue to have, incomparable beauties, wonderfully and grandly produced passages and tone-paintings; true artistic diligence, especially in the choruses, which manifests itself at the same time in an entirely new accompaniment. Because of all this, the work will be distinguished for all time.

One need not produce that unpleasant critical sense that, like a bookkeeper, is forever asking why and wherefore, and would measure the play of fancy as if it were a fortress. Much less should one lend an ear to the artistic pedant who up to the point of self-nausea would confine the boundaries of music – an art that most of all reaches the world of the spirits – and prefers conventional barracks of music-buildings to an *English garden of notes*. Such persons have no voice when it comes to free creations of genius, and besides, one can give many an answer even to these gentlemen.

Firstly, the composer obviously had less of a share in the jesting than did the writer of the text, who gave the tools out of which the former fashioned the music. The whole plan is mistaken: peasants sing the most sublime and the most ridiculous, rise to lyrical heights and sink to platitudinous depths, and so forth. – *Secondly* Haydn, thanks to his better instinct, escaped the trap more brilliantly than another with the most careful calculations (how he did so belongs in a musical journal). *Thirdly*, the music in *The Seasons* has pushed to the last degree that which belongs in the realm of the *pictorial* by using the association of ideas. And *finally*, no one has to be so genteel as not to participate a little in the village market. Autumn, with its hunt and wine-harvest, has the most comedy in it, but I want to see the grumbling connoisseur who does not share the joy of the shouting orchestra and is not amused about the fresh, fine life!

But for all those who would wish to burden with their textbooks the distinguished old man with his perenially young imagination, I will provide a self-confession of this great artist, which he recently said and which is as much to his honour as it forces back into the bounds of modesty those severe gentlemen who find criticism easier than improvement.[1] 'This whole passage' – he writes – 'with its imitation of the frogs, was not my idea. *I was forced to write this Frenchified trash. This wretched idea* disappears rather soon when the orchestra is playing, but it simply cannot be included in the pianoforte reduction.'[2] 'May the critics' – he said on another occasion – 'be not too severe; I am an old man and cannot read through all that again.' Glory and honour to the worthy Haydn.   [Pohl III, 365–7]

We have seen earlier that Baron van Swieten was extremely annoyed about this criticism and intended to 'rub it into Haydn with salt and pepper' that he had been *forced* to write the 'Frenchified trash'. In the Chronicle for 1802 we shall see that there must have been considerable comment about the review in Vienna altogether, for we shall find Griesinger wondering where the *Zeitung*'s editor, A. G. Spazier, got his information about Haydn's deprecatory remarks on *The Creation*, remarks which, of course, Haydn never made (*infra*, p. 214).

Berlin followed Leipzig, and we read the following notice in the *AMZ*:

> Berlin, End of Feb. [1802]. By far the most interesting event of the concerts given here since my previous letter was the performance of *The Seasons* by Haydn in the Royal Opera House, given by the *Kapelle* for the benefit of its institute for widows and orphans. Some difficulties before the performance seemed to place it in question. Herr *Kapellm.* [J.F.] Reichardt, who was entrusted with the direction, received the sad news that his son, so full of promise, had drowned in the Elbe at Magdeburg and rushed from us to comfort his wife; Dem. Schmalz suddenly became ill. *Kammermusikus* Gürlich [Joseph Augustin Gürrlich, 1761–1817], also popular as a composer, took over the direction and the solo parts were sung by Herr [Ludwig] Fischer (Simon), Herr [Friedrich Franz] Hurka (Lukas) and Mad. [Margareta Louise] Schick; the chorus was made up of public choirs from the local schools [*Gymnasien*] and from the private organization of the Cantor, Herr Adelung. The very numerous audience, gathered together in the greatest expectations, was quite delighted by several scenes; and if it did not find its way in some of the others, the fault lies, as far as I am concerned, not only in the persons but also in the material. As proof may be cited the poetic (I mean by that, in metric verses) or unpoetic remarks and criticisms with which everything that is new here, whether important or not, is greeted, and of which the public newspapers printed something.   [*AMZ* IV, 397]

In November 1802, the *AMZ* reviewed a new publication, *Musikalisches Taschenbuch auf das Jahr 1803*, edited by Julius and Adolph Werden (Penig bey Leipzig, 1802), wherein there is a short passage concerning Haydn's Oratorios. The comments of the *AMZ* are given in brackets.

> They [Haydn's Oratorios] are proof of his indefatigable, ever youthful spirit; but are these completely beautiful works of art? The truthful description in both

1 [Original footnote:] It goes without saying that the artist [Kunzen] who recently (Num. 50 [of the journal, see *Haydn: the Years of 'The Creation' 1796–1800*, pp. 599ff.]) delivered a severe criticism of *The Creation*, and who himself produces works of genius, must be excluded from this category.
2 See Haydn's letter to A. E. Müller of 11 December 1801 which also contains a paraphrase of the second quotation.

products is admirably great, and truth and beauty in their *highest potential* [*AMZ*: must mean in their deepest roots or something like that] are completely one. A work of art is beautiful alone through its truth, true only through its beauty; the one without the other is neither truth nor beauty. But there is a high, divine truth, and a subordinate, deceitful one. [*AMZ*: a *deceitful truth*, that will not do; an 'earthly' one, perhaps.] Not the latter but the former is the rule of beauty, and its representation, connected with the natural material, is the purpose of art. Through the imitation of the dependent, earthly truth works are produced which excite our interest only through the art by which the raw elements of nature are represented, without its being attached to the divine. The truth of representation in *The Creation* and in *The Seasons* tends more to the raw elements of nature than to the high, divine truth. Both works are therefore interesting, but are not completely beautiful. [*AMZ* V, 118f.]

In May 1804, Zelter's large and influential review appeared in the *AMZ*.

> *The Seasons after Thomson. Set to music by Joseph Haydn. Score, two parts, 496 pages, with a title engraving by Kinninger and Böhm.* Leipzig, bey Breitkopf und Härtel. (Two editions, the one with German and French, the other with German and English texts. Subscription price 8, retail price 12 Thaler.)

The reviewer of the Haydn Oratorio, *The Creation*, has hoped in vain, since the publication of that review in the fourth year of this journal, for a review of *The Seasons* by another hand, because he well knows how few musical critics then were of his opinion concerning that work. Since then, however, no other reviewer has been found for the work, and he considers himself the more competent to judge it since in an existing critical–musical journal, an important lacuna must occur if such an important work were to be overlooked; and the reviewer has not yet found any reason to change his opinion about *The Creation*. On the contrary, he admits that his admiration for the great Haydn has been increased by the present work, and increased in such measure as during this time he [the reviewer] might have increased his knowledge of art and his ability to judge.

If there were anything to stand in the way of a total impression of Haydn's *Creation*, it was the perennial concept of the name 'oratorio', in so far as it is taken to mean the poetical and musical representation of a religious subject. This concept could not be brought into connection with the actual results, as was shown at that time [in Zelter's review]. This hindrance does not occur in *The Seasons*, and the greatest wrong one could do to this work would be to introduce a particular form of action into the unembarrassed delights of the piece – though the libretto of *The Seasons* manifests all the same mistakes found in the libretto of *The Creation*. Thus there are again persons indicated who, as such, have no grounds either to act or to speak, and to whose names attaches no importance, in so far as no personal character etc. is thereby intended.

The whole consists of four sections, describing the course of the seasons and thus does not presuppose any mood on the part of the hearer. Rather, the most general of all happenings is the theme, and through a free play of the art, the one or the other idealized appearance is caused to happen and passes before us as the artists will it.

It need hardly be added what a terrific task for a composer this is: he must combine the most free caprice with already existing rules, only through a reciprocal recognition of which can an understanding be reached, because without understanding no art of communication can be established; and we would have our composers in a field where there are more dangers than laurels.

One could be quickly enough finished with a judgement of this important work if one were to subject it to that theory according to which music is supposed to be nothing else but the language of feelings [*Sprache der Affekten*] when it wishes to communicate them. The result would have to be unfavourable to the work of our master, and the criticism would be finished except for one detail, which cannot be explained according to this theory. Let us suppose that the music of *The Seasons* were an offence against all the previous rules of lyrical art: whence comes, then, the absolute pleasure in this work, against which we cannot really defend ourselves? Should one not admit that, many though our rules and theories are, and many though our objections to them have been, we seem not to have enough of them, for in our art do we not miss completely – a criterion to judge this work? And that is the situation! Haydn's *Seasons*, like his *Creation*, requires a new criterion to be understood, and whoever is not willing or able to provide one must obviously forfeit his opinion.

The total impression of *The Seasons* is like a gallery, a suite of paintings, where the various pictures of physical objects are exposed to a simultaneous inner reflection. The words do not wish to say more than – 'that might be it!'; 'you might at first think it was so!' 'here it comes!' – The whole intention is therefore sensuous [*sinnlich*], is supposed to act sensuously and to disappear from the senses even as it appeared; it is a higher play for the ear and may be compared to a shadow-play and with fireworks, without taking objection to it as long as one does not cross the magic circle which poet and composer have clearly drawn, or ask for something they did not intend.

It cannot be doubted that from this concept arises a problematical situation that renders more difficult the reviewer's task. He who is only used to praise or criticize, without explaining the one or the other to himself – is he supposed to solve puzzles, provide theories, steep himself in a new productivity? Where should the many critics find the time and the will for it? Another factor renders a judgement of the work difficult. For some time, the misuse of musical tone-painting [*Malereyen*], added to the frequent employment thereof by ignorant composers, have placed in a bad light anything that resembles the tone-painting of objects, rendering it suspicious. Our judgement must be isolated in this instance, must be independent of use and misuse, habit and manner; otherwise we cannot penetrate our work.

If it is true (and it is true!) that since the almost incredibly great perfection of instrumental music, the lyrical tendency of vocal music has been reduced to lifelessness, so that almost no sign can escape the pure breast without its being destroyed by a blast of the trumpet; no feeling on the part of the singer can be awakened without its being crushed by the burden of the orchestra; if, especially in theatrical music, this misuse has become so general that the good production of the human voice has become ever more rare and has sunk to a play of figures [*Figurenspiel*] of this or that favourite instrument; if the whole theory of impression is built upon an arbitrary explosive effect [*Knalleffekt*], which removes all gradation and destroys the impression of what is right; one might then ask: what have we won by the perfection of instrumental music, since it only hinders, trumps the expression and therefore renders impossible any impression? Since it speaks a language which cannot be that of nature, because it reminds us of no object in nature; and can be no real art, because it leads to no peace, but has rather a thoroughly unsteady, revolutionary tendency.

But the perfected instrumental music is there, despite its misuse; it took place, therefore it was necessary; and the question now arises, how is it to be used, how is it used, and should it *remain*?

The question will answer itself if one raises this instrumental music to the potency of a genre. For what *is* there must *be* something, and here, too, we meet Haydn on his own ground and property. If, moreover, this instrumental music is to be combined with vocal or choral music, without the latter being destroyed, it must be subordinated to artistic wisdom; if it were to dominate, the vocal parts become subordinate to it and we have a work like Haydn's *Seasons*, wherein the text is, and can be, nothing but the vehicle, the date, the exercise, which the composer wishes to solve; in short, we have another genre, and at the same time the criterion by which it must be received and judged: for how should one judge a work of art which one does not understand and the intentions of which one has not in the least penetrated? But on what level of art will this genre be? With a genre one cannot use these concepts: it is as if one were to ask which is higher, masculine, feminine or neuter.

We called the present work, earlier in this review, a gallery of pictures, and we use it as the basis for the entire piece; we even use it as the basis for the cycle in which this artistic genre is and must be cast, if it is to live and be lively.

The Overture is in G minor and describes winter. There is enough to be said against a task such as painting winter by musical means, and if a composer were asked to fulfil such a task he could certainly protest and the entire world would agree with him. 'Music can only speak to the senses [*Empfindung*], she cannot speak without melody, or without warmth and fire, without idealistic good-health [*Wohlseyn*]. How should one be able to paint winter? How should one depict frost and cold, snow and ice, discomfort and objections to dead nature, which man precisely through his education manages to conquer by artificially clothing his body, by warming his atmosphere so that his love, his hate and all his necessities may survive the winter? How should the warmest of all the arts describe such a condition? How could she, even if she wanted to, describe it without wrongly overstepping the boundaries of the art? The art which we, out of necessity, gladly enclose with our body and bring into safety?' – All this a composer could rightly object to; but there the work is, and we cannot demonstrate it out of existence, even as winter itself; and now arises the question once again: what is there? and what should we make of it?

Firstly, the following questions must be answered. Is this Overture a good, artistic work of genius? Does it excite the imagination, and does it speak a language which sounds in such a way that we can understand it? Does it indicate something that forces or encourages us to contemplation? All these questions we answer with a yes! And if we place opposite to it the concept of an artificial description of winter, the skin prickles in front of the warming fire, we imagine the snowflakes with pleasure, hear the howling of the winter storm, and if such a description does not unpleasantly remind us of something foreign, we let it all pass before us like a pleasant spectacle.

The Overture starts with a *Grave* of four long notes proceeding downwards from *g, f, eb, d*; no key can be determined. The composer purposely set out to avoid any fixed tonality, and in these four successive notes no third of a tonic or dominant appears, and on the last note only the empty, dead, terrible fifth. The character of the following *Vivace* is raw, dark seriousness; cold and grim, it displays icy talons which seize that which cannot flee from it. A crackling and raging assail our ears only, for all sensible people have found safety; and this tone-painting turns into an excellent piece of Romanticism of its kind, which we receive, not without the greatest, most luxurious and most delicate sense of delight, the more gladly the more we approach with understanding the fresh source from which so much foreign and piquant have streamed towards us.

The genre would be proved, though at the same time we may not at all approve of its weaker imitation and continuation: such a unique thing dare appear but once, just as there is only one Haydn, one Michelangelo, one Achilles, though history is not lacking either in good artists or heros. Art is as rich and endless as nature, and brings forth many a new fruit to the taste of which our senses must first become accustomed, and which will not please everyone equally; but the connoisseur learns to appreciate them, otherwise he *is* no connoisseur.

After this Overture there follows the transition to spring; partly constructed from fragments of winter and finally becoming a mild thing. Spring itself begins with the Chorus, 'Komm, holder Lenz!' which breathes the real air of spring. A yearning sense of budding and pain animates the piece, which reminds us, completely and irresistibly, of our loveliest hopes and youthful feelings. The ploughman appears, almost like a picture, as he hastens to his field, striding behind his plough and the long furrows, whistling, sowing his seeds in steady rhythm. The plough receives them, cares for them lovingly and turns them to golden fruit. A prayer for mild heavens, fruitful rain and sunshine: a pre-taste of thankfulness for, and satisfaction over, rewarded industry and certain pleasure; a song of joy by the happy youth when regarding the colourfully sprouting earth; it turns into active movement. The shoal of fish, the buzzing of the bees, the flutter of the birds are interrupted by the youths, happy and eager to work; and in the songs we imagine all the strength of flowering youth, like a fresh flame in the ether.

Although all these pieces are in very different forms, the whole is nonetheless one flow of strength and mastery. In it, physical objects are idealized by figures, but so perfectly that the impression of a lovely spring is not interrupted by anything foreign, and reveals a serious intent throughout. A finely fugued chorus on the words 'Ehre, Lob und Preis sey dir' concludes Spring.

Summer begins with an eight-bar introduction describing dawn and the lazily retiring night. One hears the last notes of the disturbed night-birds. The cock crows in the new day. But which words would be sufficient to portray the indescribably delightful-sounding shepherd's horn, with which the merry shepherd calls his herd to pasture, and in which we hear all the peace and all the joy of the pastoral life? The sun rises in its majesty. The chorus of all nature celebrates its appearance in a truly high-minded song: all is gratitude and joy, all rejoice, all pray.

Midday approaches. The sun pours its mighty fire through the cloudless air in full streams upon the earth. Man and beast are prostrated by the press of nature and seek a cool, dark grove. Bedded on soft moss, at the side of a clear, airy brook, they breathe herbs and balsamic air; Zephyr rustles across the gently waving branches of the trees. But on the sticky horizon, from the mountain ridges, arises a pale mist and clothes the heavens in black darkness. A muted roar, through swirling dark clouds, threatens the undefended men and herds with death and destruction. That which grows and lives on the earth stands solemnly awaiting the dread judge, the near thunder. In trembling fear, life is at a standstill, no leaf moves, and the stillness of the grave spreads its secretive wings over field and flower. A bolt of lightning strikes down, followed by a clap of thunder and suddenly the whole heavens are a mighty fire. 'Ach! hilf uns Himmel', 'wo fliehn wir hin?' The storm rages furiously, thunderclap crashing on thunderclap, back and forth. The earth shakes perilously, the ocean's depths yawn. The storm grows, it howls, it roars, it moves towards us – it is over.

It would be an idle undertaking to analyze the force of this heroic piece, for that which is otherwise admired in masterworks – the orderliness of composition, the proper preparation, the right gradation, the adding of the mighties to the mighty, the careful execution, the harmonic and metric treatment of thoughts and melodic form, even exceptionally fine fugal passages – all this almost disappears before the brilliant [*genialen*], great organization and shaping of this enormous

191

body of power [*Kraftmasse*], which was never approached by any of its known predecessors in the history of the art. One is astounded about this fantastically grand picture of furious nature, which is preceded by a long row of colourful, small and attractively designed pictures of the smallest and most varied objects of nature: these roll off playfully and finish in such a triumph of art. – Everything about this piece is free and natural; nothing is daring or affected, nothing violates the old rules. Modulation, orchestration, song – it is all here, as it was throughout the whole work. The art of the predecessors, whereby a thunderstorm gradually approaches in all its terror and grows to a climax, is not even employed once. The thunderstorm is there all at once, in its full distance from human weakness. Nature is in revolt with herself, and the chorus behaves against the orchestra like two worlds fighting each other. The crashes do not reach only the ear; the very depths of the human heart are shattered. The profound impression of disability and weakness opposed to eternity and complete power is awakened; the proud, brave heart is uplifted and worships.

The day draws to a close. The distant sun, sinking, sheds its grace once more on field and flower. Evening comes. The contented herd returns, slow paced, to the village. The quail is heard, the cricket, the frog. The evening bells ring. From above the host of stars beckons, inviting to sweet repose; and so closes Summer.

Good as this order of Summer is, which the poet opens with the beginning of day and closes with a beautiful evening, and excellently though the condition of quiet after the storm is described by the composer, this condition is self-evident, since such an unheaval of nature presupposes this conclusion. Therefore it would have been better to close the summer with the storm.

Autumn opens with an introduction describing the joyous feelings of the husbandman about the rich harvest. A song of praise is dedicated to noble industry; country life is extolled. But in all these matters the poet is enormously behind the composer. Not only that he freights the composer with unimportant details that are really not suitable for an interesting portrayal, but he also heaps upon him a whole mass of excessively prosaic words which would have clearly embarrassed any other composer. Our master, however, has once more shown what he alone is capable of bringing forth from within himself, and the Praise of Industry, judged by itself, is a rich masterpiece of dignity, clarity and genius.

The hunt appears. The hunting dog chases through the grass, looking for the game's spoor along the ground. Greed speeds him forward. He hastens to point, stops dead and immovable right in front of his prey. The shy bird, sensing his enemy, flies up in fright; we have a flush, an explosion, and he falls dead to earth.

It is unparalleled how perfectly clearly, tellingly and seriously this little occurrence is described *en passant* and portrayed in a lively fashion; and now follows a picture of the large hunt. The small game has been killed, a tribe of hare lies stretched out in rows. The horns sound loudly in the forest. The dogs attack. The flushed stag is in flight, dogs and riders in pursuit. How he races and jumps, out of the bushes and across field and thicket! His pursuers stop, confused, dispersed, his spoor lost, looking frantically hither and yon. Tajò, ho! ho! The hunter's cry, the horns gather them once again. With doubly renewed vigour the group together takes up the hunt again. Reached by his pursuers, the agile beast collapses, exhausted. He is taken prisoner and killed. The hunter's song of joy, the horns' victory signal, announce to the forest the call of the kingly stag. The hunt is finished.

One can say that in the light, happy hunting life of this picture there is manifested an overpowering longing for the hunt and freedom, against which the very finest painting with brush and colours, only depicting a moment, cannot compete; and however clear and certain in its contours, it is only a weak imitation of that which appears to an awakened imagination through this music. The easy melodic forms of the various instruments, which *en masse* surround the well-known hunting signals of the horns, form a drama of a higher plane that passes in front of us like the most beautiful vision.

The happy life of the vineyards and the wine harvest follow. Juchhe! [etc., paraphrase of the text]. . . . This section, too, has its own characteristic flavour of lightness, youthful life and friendliness. It is a truly moralistic bacchanalia[!], a natural tangle of youths full of life, strength and health.

Winter opens with a description of a tenaciously foggy November. The raw outer air forces men of soft body away, just as the sap of the tree hides in the earth's lap and all forms of life automatically avoid nature's destruction; thus man retires to the safety of his house. The field is empty and lifeless, and raw winds whistle over grass and bush. The wanderer stands, confused; the path, the trail where human steps fall, is drifted over, covered in snow. The dark, long night approaches him [etc., paraphrase of the text; he sees a distant light and] finally reaches the peaceful ale-house and the warm oven where the village neighbours are sitting about the fire, knitting, carving and spinning. A spinning song delights the ear. Stories are told about the lords of the manor, about the servants [*Gesinde*] and other such village topics. The Romance of Hanne is a real masterpiece of village story-telling: she sings and tells the story of a country girl who fools a young and noble seducer and preserves her innocence by her wit; the chorus of peasants comments in between with its naive, rustic remarks. One can call the whole of the piece a work of antique art, though the occasion is from modern country-life. The life-like, naive, peasant-phlegmatic truth of this scene (for it is a scene) is made clear and interesting by such a genius; so that despite its subaltern nature it must enchant and delight every educated heart which is not ruined by genteel aversion and thus incapable of such pleasure.

After this piece, which is the principal moment of Winter, the poem takes a moralistic turn once again and ends with a fugue which is the best part of it.

Before we conclude our investigation of this work, it might be well to face the reproach which appears to be arriving from outside, as it were, and concerns the musical style of this work: the reproach of a wrongful mixture of the comic and the serious. We could escape easily enough by placing the blame on the poem, if this reproach were made. But no. The reviewer is as persuaded as anyone can be that this beautiful work, as far as the music is concerned, can only be judged as the product of a genius and not speculatively; he feels himself certain and strong enough to defend this work against any reproach of mistaken comical expression or comedy wrongly placed in the serious parts. And though he [the reviewer] personally would never stoop [*unterziehen*] to idealize croaking frogs, chirping crickets, the quail's call, etc., by musical means, this circumstance in Haydn's *Seasons* is by no means proved to be repellent. It can only appear – as indeed the most serious moments – comical to a person of a comical disposition, for whom this comical tendency would at once disappear if one took away the words and let the music continue by itself. Our master may have known beforehand, or not, what he actually wanted to represent: in the whole of his work everything transitory is treated as transitory, and Genius herself may have guided him. If he has treated a *transitory* object as *permanent* and composed frog-, cricket- or quail-arias, then he would truly have fallen into a mistaken comical idiom, which we would have defended as little as we are inclined to allow compromises in art.

Hitherto we have sought to analyze single sections of *The Seasons* as such, and to characterize their ability to portray; now we shall investigate if and how these single pieces together create a whole.

It was said that there is nowhere in this work any reference to human affections and their known or discernible motives – love, hate, anger, etc. Rather the purpose is, without any prejudice to the intellect, to allow the senses the freedom of a well-appointed park, where there is no promise or certainty of an intellectual delight but where everything is unexpected, fabulous and should strike us as something never before experienced. – We stress again the principal tendency of the work because it displays a clearly defined artistic purpose, and not to force our opinion on the complacent observer but rather to persuade him that we have arrived at our judgement not for reasons that lie beyond the realms of art.

In *The Four Seasons* there are four principal moments: spring, summer, autumn, winter, which constitute a cycle. Each of these four *principal moments* has been provided by the composer with a *principal movement* [*Hauptmasse*]: in the first part, the Overture; in the second, the storm; in the third, the hunt; and in the fourth, life at home [*Stubenleben*]. One might ask: why is the principal movement of Spring the Overture, which describes winter? one could even say that there are two winters, and that Spring is treated in too cursory a fashion, since it is wanting a spring-like principal movement. – We will not defend the poem from this reproach. It was absolutely unnecessary to start the whole thing in winter. The poet could have commenced his piece very grandly and nobly with the general idea of resurrection and changing of all living things, and in this way Spring would have had a great and worthy principal movement. But this did not happen. The composer needed a dark foreground, and thus we have this Overture which on the one hand merges into a friendly spring but on the other is attached to winter and, as such, can and must be regarded as the key-stone of the entire work. The composer at any rate has produced something really great with this Overture, to which the poet contributed nothing. However faulty the poem may be as far as its artistic execution is concerned, yet the subject of the seasons, considering its total generality for the whole earth, is a truly poetical subject for art and one which lends itself particularly to musical representation.

This musical representation, however, by our great *Joseph Haydn*, must, considering its four principal movements (to which the smaller parts surrounding them are episodically attached), be regarded as a whole new opus which in its totality was not yet known to the art; with all the objections which critics may find today or tomorrow, it will survive the passage of time. In its quality it ranks among the Oratorios of all time and of its kind it has nothing above it save Handel's *Messiah*, which is more firmly constructed and altogether was conceived and executed at a higher power.

The score of *The Seasons* is printed with great typographical beauty but has many printing errors, which can be easily noted. . . .   [*AMZ* VI, 513–29]

That same month, May 1804, the correspondent from Breslau wrote about *The Seasons* in the *AMZ*:

[Breslau, in May 1804.] We closed our numerous Winter Concerts with Haydn's *The Seasons* and *The Creation* in the Easter week. . . .

If *The Seasons* in repeated performances does not draw the audiences which a masterpiece, exhausting as it does almost the art itself, ought to, it may perhaps depend on the fact that *The Creation* is usually given during the same week. Most people here are accustomed to hearing a religious piece on Maundy Thursday; and families with several children find such a double expense too dear, while the elegant world during those days crowds into the beautiful Aula Leopoldina, to see and be seen. All this, however, was of no consequence to the entrepreneur.

I take the liberty of expressing my opinion about *The Seasons*, too, without wishing to intrude too closely on the opinions of others, or to pretend that mine is more than the result of my feelings. I have heard *The Seasons* several times in concert, and each time I have returned home with the innermost satisfaction. My feelings were excited and prepared to receive every beauty: but the same sympathy, on the part of a human soul, for the most sublime – Prayer to the Almighty – as for the most tipsy joy of a drinking bout, or the merry conversation[1] during the dry telling of a fairy-story at the spinning wheel – that is not to be thought of. Pity for the wasted art in the thrilling, staggering choruses! Pity for the charming picture of spring, and so on! If we could at least ho-la, ourselves, in the merry hunting scene or could really laugh together with the lusty laughing of the farmers! We do laugh with them, but the heart takes no part in it. It is the embarrassed smile of a child who has suddenly stopped crying because it has been given a new toy and would like to be pleased about it. . . .

The Creation gave us again the great delight that a good performance of this masterpiece must give. . . .   [*AMZ* VI, 573ff.]

If the Breslau correspondent was slightly embarrassed by *The Seasons*, very soon embarrassment was to turn to disgust, as may be seen in the following devastating criticism of the work in the *Musikalisches Taschenbuch auf das Jahr 1805*, edited by F. Th. Mann:

> On 12 Dec. in Leipzig was the yearly benefit concert for the poor and sick members of the orchestra. Haydn's *The Seasons* was performed. The opinion of the educated judge of art concerning this work was that from its text it is a vulgar imitation of nature in detail, unworthy of a great artist, and for this very reason it is no complete entity – on the contrary, it is easily tiresome and cannot produce a *pure and single artistic effect*. The singers, too, performed as inartistically as possible and tried, especially in the choruses, to display their vulgar joy [*Jubel*]. The beautiful and noble choruses stand isolated in this work and do not belong to that description of the Seasons.   [Pohl III, 372]

We have called this section 'The Progress of *The Seasons*'; but unlike *The Creation*'s triumphal journey through Europe, the later Oratorio was hardly noticed in France and not noticed at all in England. Part of the difficulty was the ghastly translations that the Baron had made into French and English and which were, in a bewildering error of judgement (was there *no one* in Leipzig capable of warning Breitkopf?), printed in the first edition. Carpani (212f.) says, drily, 'fu stampato, e tradotto barbaramente in varie lingue'. The French avoided the problem by bringing out a new edition, in French and Italian, of the principal pieces. The publisher Porro announced the work on 23 Germinal an X (14 April 1802) in the *Journal de Paris* as 'Les Saisons avec accompagnement de piano . . . traduit scrupuleusement sur sa Musique, en vers français & italiens, par P. Porro et L. Balochi'.[2] But even with the new edition, *The Seasons* was hardly performed in France.

The situation in England was even more incredible. What had happened that Haydn, darling of London only a few years before, was now of such little interest to the English that no one, literally no one, ever performed *The Seasons* anywhere in the British Isles during the composer's lifetime? There are possibly three reasons for this grotesque state of affairs. (1) *The Creation*, as we have seen, was a highly controversial work in England; it excited much admiration but an equal amount of perplexity and, very soon, scorn and anger that Haydn should have dared to match himself against the

---

1 *AMZ* has 'Konservation', patently a printer's error for 'Konversation'.
2 Hoboken II, 60. Porro published twelve numbers.

inimitable Handel whose Oratorios, being deemed perfect, could brook no opposition whatever. (2) If Swieten's (or rather Anonymous's) English in *The Creation* may have appeared old-fashioned and often difficult to understand, the English of *The Seasons* was really 'tradotto barbaramente', and may have proved a real stumbling-block to the work's dissemination in English-speaking countries. (3) A now little-known affair concerning the author of *A School for Scandal* and the composer of *The Seasons* which rocked London society in the very month, May 1802, that the full score of the new Oratorio left the press at Leipzig, and which caused Haydn's name to be vilified throughout England.

The prelude to this strange episode may be seen in a small newspaper announcement a few days before Christmas 1801:

> HAYDN, the Musician, it is said, is personally canvassing at Paris, for the election to the *National Institute*, in opposition to Mr. SHERIDAN.
>
> [*Morning Herald*, 21 December 1801]

Haydn may have read of this silly controversy in a publication edited anonymously (but actually by Carl Bertuch) in Weimar, entitled 'London und Paris'. In the fifth *Jahrgang* (No. 1, 1802, pp. 10–15), the situation is caustically reported and a number of the poems quoted.[1]

Richard Brinsley Sheridan, the brilliant author and later politician, had been proposed for membership of the *Institut National de France*, but in the event Haydn was elected (*supra*, p. 90), much to the rage of the English (who despite a long war with France found such an honour irresistible). Sheridan and his many friends of the English Press thereupon mounted a verbal attack on Haydn such as had never before been seen other than in the world of politics. The following letter[2] gives an idea of the passions aroused.

Jan. 1802

Sir,

As by your insertion of certain French Epigrams you have commenced what I conceive to be a very scurrillous attack on a French National institute for electing Mr. Haydn, the celebrated musician, as the representative of the Literature of Europe in Preference to one Sheridan, who, whatever may be said of his Writings Wit or Eloquence, I am credibly informed cannot support a Part in a Glee even at the Prince's Table, I beg you will follow that sound[3] rule of Equity – audi alteram Partem. Epigrams if I may so call them, which, I am assured do full justice to Mr. Haydn, tho' from my Ignorance of the English Language I cannot judge of them, and am ever obliged to trust this communication to a Translator.

Yours with great consideration

Jan Caspe Spreinck   Titchfield Str.

Epigrams
for the Morning Chronicle
National Institute of France
Haydn versus Sheridan
The two Candidates proposed by the Primary Electors for the Class of Literature and the Fine Arts

---

1 For the sake of completeness, we list the first lines of the poems quoted: (1) "Haydn l'emporte donc sur Sheridan l'unique!'; (2) 'L'Institut dans son sein avoit peu de génie'; (3) 'Haydn successful!'; (4) 'Pass by wit, eloquence and poetry'; (5) 'Haydn a pious dirge compos'd'; (6) 'Time was when Pindars sacred fire'.
2 *The Letters of Richard Brinsley Sheridan*, ed. Cecil Price, II, 1966, 167ff.
3 [Original footnote:] ev. 'sacred' as in *The Courier* version.

Haydn successful!
>The wise decision all admire
>Twas just beyond dispute[1]
>Sound Taste! which to Apollo's Lyre
>Prefferr'd – a German Flute!

another Haydn Loquitur

N.B. as Mr. Haydn, the foreign Representative of Literature and the fine arts of Europe in the national institute of France supposes [?] himself to be only a very eminent *composer* of Musick it would be extremely unjust in any of our readers to be hypercritical with respect to a few trifling errors which may occure in the metre or rhythm of this his first attempt at *Literary* composition indeed we have ourselves taken the Liberty of correcting in many Places the Grammar and Spelling of this little practical jeu d'esprit both in the original German of Mr Haydn and in the Translation which his English Correspondent Mr. Florio has so obligingly furnish'd us with.

>Haydn to Florio a distinguish'd Performer
>on the German Flute
>The wond'ring World has heard with admiration
>my Fine English Oratorio call'd Creation Indeed
>it succeeded greatly beyond my expectation.
>And since the Days of Handel
>I may say it without Scandal
>No such Piece of Messiah has been heard in this their Nation
>But now the *national institute* of France
>have thought proper this humble Servant to advance
>And member of that Institute *created* me
>in spite of Sheridan's presumptuous Claim
>To all that Genious can derive from Fame
>For Wit and Eloquence and Poetry.
>I be only fearful in my new Station,
>that this the Institutes *Creation*
>if it be not in truth a Blunder
>may cause more admiration
>And create more wonder
>Than did my said delightful Oratorio. –
>Pray tell me what you hear dear Florio
>>yours Haydn.

>Foreign Representative of the Literature and fine Arts of Europe –
>Another Pass by Wit Eloquence and Poetry
>Give way to Claims of higher Place
>Give way to – Tweedledum and Tweedledee
>Make room make room, for Thorough Bass
>Another
>Time was when Pindars sacred Fire
>And bold Alcaeus' Song
>And gay Anacreon's festive Lyre
>Assumed the homage of the human heart.
>Yet gave to 'concord Sweet' its praise and Part
>Time was when music was the Poets Tongue.
>Then modest melody, thy Task and Praise

1 [Original footnote:] Sheridan adds alternative 'And worthy of the institute'.

> Follow'd the Bard and his inspiring Lays
> A gentle helpmate by his side you stood
> Watch'd his commanding Eye and own'd the Muses God.
> [Poet] that time is past – subdue thy pride[1] –

We may sum up this war of words by quoting the *AMZ*, which carried the following article in its issue of 9 June 1802:

> It indicates the level at which London's art-lovers, art-experts, critics and Maecenases operate nowadays; it reveals a by no means uninteresting view of English cultural history, that which we are about to relate; and *therefore* we relate it – but not with the detailed attention, including some all too silly and dirty documents, which our correspondent devotes to it; we offer it in as brief a form as is necessary for the purpose.
>
> Nowadays it is in London the custom to attack 'the God of the ponderous Germans', 'the man whose name, like the whole language of his nation, can only be pronounced by them', etc.; to abuse our worthy Jos. Haydn, not only in – fine society but also in newspapers and brochures, some coarser than others. In the package of epigrams and unsubtle [*armsdicker*] jokes of all sorts and kinds, which we have before us, there is not one single uncoarse and really witty notion – and how little it is to ask that he who attacks a great man be at least witty. On the contrary, we hear the more frequently of a plumply fashioned German flute, even of 'the German fiddler', etc. And why all this? *Admitted by them all*, for the sole reason that the Parisian National Institute has first chosen Haydn as one of their members and has preferred him to the Englishman Sheridan – Sheridan, 'that first of geniuses, that unique orator and poet, that [here is the clue][2] Member of Parliament.' What about this Herr Sheridan? There can be just as little discussion of him in his role as Member of Parliament as there can be about him as a theatre director. Also the Opposition Orator had better been left out of the affair. Artist against artist: – what has he in fact created? According to the opinion of his admirers, excellent things: a *Pizarro*; Kotzebue's *Rolla*, imitated and made even worse; an opera, *The Duenna*, which is somewhat better, and the moralizing comedy, *A School for Scandal*, which does contain many excellent things but which can only be said to usurp, or secretly size, the role of a poetic work. And now Haydn? But we do not wish to perpetrate an eye for an eye, or to denigrate Chloe by praising Doris! So we shall not continue but rather conclude the story. After the newspapers had tried for a time to trump each other, at last there appeared an artistic judge who in one of the leading newspapers investigated the matter seriously and pronounced the following verdict of British criticism: 'The French National Institute, in its choice of Haydn as a foreign member for the class of fine arts, has committed a blunder. Haydn, it is true, is a great musician [really?]; but music is only the handmaiden of poetry and should not do more than serve it. [Now we have it! That's what music is for – and we helpless Germans have been wringing our hands to find it out. But he knows how to make it even more plausible and continues:] To place a musician at the head of the fine arts is about the same thing as giving the prize to the weaver who made the canvas or the carpenter who made the frame instead of the great painter who alone made the painting.' – Enough!   Editorial Staff.
>
> <div align="right">[<i>AMZ</i> IV, 602–4]</div>

---

1 [original footnote:] Continued with other verses in different order, in *The Courier*. There are twelve further lines in Mr. S[heridan]'s hand (and cancelled) in the manuscript.
2 *AMZ*'s interjections are in parentheses, which we have changed to brackets throughout. Letterspaced words have been italicized.

The combination of these various circumstances seems to have prevented even Haydn's old friends such as Salomon and Dr Burney from attempting to produce *The Seasons*. Crosse, in his *Account* (398ff.), has this to say about the work:

> Upon its first appearance, *The Seasons* was criticized by the Italians as too masculine and harsh, and the commencement, in which a northern spring, partaking largely of the horrors of the winter, is described, gave occasion to the sarcastic remark, that there were two winters in the German year. It was also objected to, as containing few airs, and being in fact a piece of instrumental music, with a vocal accompaniment.
>
> *The Seasons* was published in this country, in the year 1813, adapted for voices and the piano-forte, by Mr. Clementi, previous to which it was scarcely known except by name; nor can it yet be said to be very popular, as it requires three good voices to execute it, and some little relish for, at least, if not acquaintance with, the mysteries of musical composition. We are not aware that any portion of it was ever publicly performed in England until 1817, when a selection from the 'Spring' was brought forward at Birmingham. . . .

And so we come to the curious ending of *The Seasons'* progress, its non-performance in England: a circumstance that neither Haydn nor, indeed, anyone else could have imagined possible. It was in fact the dramatic beginning of Haydn's fall from grace with the British public, a fall accelerated, perhaps, by the ridiculous Sheridan episode but one as inexorable as had been Wren's own oblivion after his death.[1] *The Seasons'* complete failure in England (for non-performance is the most complete failure a composer can suffer) is one more indication of the fate that was in store for Haydn's music within the next few years.

Missa ('Schöpfungsmesse') in B flat major
(XXII: 13)

Basic scoring: 2 oboes, 2 clarinets in B♭, 2 bassoons, 2 horns in B♭ and E♭, timpani in B♭-F, strings, organ (used as solo instrument in the Et incarnatus), soli (maximum SSATTB; usually SATB), choir (SATB).

I Kyrie (*Adagio – Allegro moderato*): full scoring.
II Gloria –
   (a) Gloria in excelsis Deo (*Allegro*): full scoring.
   (b) Miserere nobis (*Adagio*): full scoring.
   (c) Quoniam (*Molto vivace*): full scoring with soli (SSATTB).
III Credo –
   (a) Credo in unum Deum (*Vivace*): full scoring.
   (b) Et incarnatus est (*Adagio*): full scoring, solo organ.
   (c) Et resurrexit (*Allegro*): full scoring.
   (d) Et vitam venturi (*più Allegro*): full scoring.
IV Sanctus (*Adagio – Allegro*): full scoring.
V Benedictus (*Allegretto*): full scoring.
VI Agnus Dei (*Adagio*): full scoring;
     Dona nobis pacem (*Allegretto moderato*): full scoring, without soli.

---

1 'As so often happens immediately after the death of a great man, a reaction against Wren's baroque style set in which lasted until the hero-worship of Robert Elmes in the early nineteenth-century began a Wren revival.' – Harold F. Hutchison, 'Sir Christopher Wren', in *History Today*, April 1973, p. 237.

Martin Chusid's proposed scheme for dividing the Mass into three vocal symphonies[1] is as follows:

Vocal Symphony No. 1

MVT.	TEXT	TEMPO AND NO. OF BARS	METRE	KEY
I	Kyrie	as *supra* = 28 bars plus	3/4 –	B flat→B flat minor→V→
		111 bars	6/8	B flat major
II	Gloria	as *supra* = 160 bars	alle breve	B flat major[2]
III	Miserere	as *supra* = 63 bars	3/4	E flat major
IV	Quoniam	as *supra* = 119 bars	4/4	B flat major

Vocal Symphony No. 2

MVT.	TEXT	TEMPO AND NO. OF BARS	METRE	KEY
I	Credo	as *supra* = 59 bars	4/4	B flat major
II	Et incarnatus	as *supra* = 41 bars	3/4	G major→G minor→V
III	Et resurrexit	as *supra* = 78 bars	4/4	B flat major→ B flat minor→V
	Et vitam	as *supra* = 45 bars	4/4	B flat major

Vocal Symphony No. 3

MVT.	TEXT	TEMPO AND NO. OF BARS	METRE	KEY
I	Sanctus	as *supra* = 18 bars	4/4	B flat major→ F minor→V
	Pleni	as *supra* = 29 bars	4/4	F minor→B flat
II	Benedictus	as *supra* = 123 bars	6/8	E flat major
III	Agnus Dei	as *supra* = 47 bars	3/4	G major→V
IV	Dona	as *supra* = 123 bars	alla breve	B flat major

Critical edition: Reihe XXIII, Band 4, Messe Nr. 11, in 'Joseph Haydn Werke' (Haydn Institut), edited by Irmgard Becker-Glauch, 1967. This full score was later reduced in size and printed as a miniature score by Bärenreiter-Verlag, Kassel. A piano-vocal score, edited by the present writer, is published by G. Schirmer, New York (1973).

The principal sources for the work are (a) the autograph, owned by Breitkopf & Härtel and sold to Erasmus-Haus in Basel from which, at our instigation, it was purchased by Dr G. Henle and given to the Bavarian State Library in Munich. A complete facsimile was published by the Haydn Institut in 1957; (b) the authentic first performance material, Esterházy Archives, Eisenstadt, copied by Elssler and his assistants; (c) the authentic parts, by Elssler and his assistants, copied for the Hofburgkapelle and containing the change in the 'Qui tollis' that Haydn made for the Empress Marie Therese; (d) the authentic parts, by Elssler and his assistants, for the Lobkowitz Archives, now in the National Museum, Prague; (e) the first edition, by Breitkopf & Härtel, in full score, issued in 'Typendruck' in an edition of 1,024 copies (Brand, 130) as 'Messe . . . N° IV' (1804).

The first gramophone recording was made in June 1962 for 'Musica Sacra' (Lumen in Paris, Schwann in Düsseldorf, AMS 35) by Maria Taborsky (sop.), Julia Falk (alto), Erich zur Eck (ten.), Carlo Schmidt (bass), the Salzburg Radio and Mozarteum Choirs and the Mozarteum Orchestra (Salzburg), Robert Kuppelwieser (org.), conducted by Ernst Hinreiner.

---

1 'Some Observations on Liturgy, Text and Structure in Haydn's Late Masses', in *Studies in Eighteenth-Century Music* (Geiringer *Festschrift*), p. 133; reprinted by permission of George Allen & Unwin Ltd.
2 The final nine bars in E flat and overlapping with Miserere.

The then-famous *Singspiel* composer, Johann Adam Hiller (1728–1804), who held the venerable position of Cantor of St Thomas's Church in Leipzig, wrote on his copy of the 'Schöpfungsmesse' in huge block letters 'Opus summum viri summi J. Haydn'. He considered it the greatest of all Haydn's Masses. The work has something of the same reputation among connoisseurs as Symphony No. 102: that symphony has never been one of the really popular ones such as the 'Surprise', the 'Clock' or the 'London', but many consider it Haydn's finest achievement in the genre. Hiller's remarks, which were quoted in the *AMZ* (VI, 857f.), were also incorporated into Dies's biography (101n.) and thereby received more attention than they might otherwise have done. Both Griesinger and Dies cite Haydn in connection with the 'Qui tollis', where *The Creation* is quoted. Griesinger (62f.) writes:

> In the Mass which Haydn wrote in the year 1801, it occurred to him at the 'Qui tollis'[1] that weak mortals sinned mostly against moderation and chastity only. So he set the words 'Qui tollis, peccata, peccata mundi' entirely from the passage in *The Creation*, 'Der thauende Morgen, o wie ermuntert er'. In order that this profane thought should not be too conspicuous, however, he let the 'Miserere' enter right afterwards with the full chorus. In the copy of the Mass that he made for the Empress, he had to change this passage at her request.

We have seen that the Empress's copy has survived in the Hofburgkapelle Archives; both the Henle and Schirmer editions offer the altered version as an Appendix. The situation, as related by Dies, is confusing and even contradictory; we have quoted the relevant passage in our introduction to the last six Haydn Masses (see *Haydn: the Years of 'The Creation' 1796–1800*, p. 124). As with all such anecdotes in Dies's biography, truth is inextricably intertwined with fiction. Haydn 'could not suppress' his joy 'but gave vent to [his] happy feelings and wrote *miserere* [recte: 'Qui tollis'] in *tempo allegro*'. Undoubtedly the composer did discuss this controversial passage with Dies, and the interesting thing about it all is that it reveals Haydn's slightly guilty feelings about the already famous quotation from the 'dew-dropping morn'. 'Qui s'excuse, s'accuse', and one actually begins to wonder if he would have incorporated the change for the Empress in the printed score (Breitkopf & Härtel) if he had been consulted, which he was not, the Leipzig publishers having procured a pirated manuscript of the work. Nowadays, of course, the passage hardly raises any objections, even from the Church; but perhaps it is not one of his most successful attempts at humour.

The mighty Kyrie starts quietly and starts, moreover, with a note-for-note quotation from the *Theresienmesse* (1799); but after three notes the music pursues a different course. We note that Haydn has invented a new kind of accent; previously he used *fz* (which he continues to use, for strong accents), and then in London he turned to the 'modern' accent ($>$), which he confusingly placed below the note rather than above it, so that copyists, unfamiliar with the new sign, often turned it into a *decrescendo* sign: this confusion was to persist as late as Schubert's symphonies, where final accents were idiotically turned into *decrescendo* signs in the old *Gesamtausgabe* (e.g. end of the first movement of the 'Unfinished' Symphony). Now Haydn followed an idea he had developed in the *Te Deum* (1800?), where at bars 134f. he had added personally accents to the violins in the Eisenstadt performance material. But in the 'Schöpfungsmesse' they are placed above the note, like the modern sign for an

up-bow, *viz.* . After this accent, not adopted generally, there is usually a *p*.

---

1 Griesinger writes, wrongly, 'Agnus Dei, qui tollis peccata mundi'.

There is a long (28 bar) slow introduction, which contains many hints of the future Allegro moderato, with which the movement concludes. The first *f* (bars 5f.) includes a marching rhythm in the accompaniment which steadily increases in importance, appearing just before, and as an accompaniment to, the first choral entrance (bar 13) and with striking force in B flat minor, where however the actual key is never actually played. The ominous feeling of this passage (bars 18ff.) is greatly heightened by the focal point of *g* flat in the lower parts. A great many bars later (114f.), shortly before the end of the quick section, this passage is re-introduced, complete with the returning *g* flat in the lower voices (marked *ff*, to drive the point home) and the marching rhythm in the violins. It is precisely the technique we know from the first movements of Symphonies 97 and, especially, 103. But the unity in this extraordinary Kyrie operates at another level, too. This dotted rhythm, of a nearly Wagnerian *Leitmotiv* importance, is much more omnipresent than we at first realize. The first vocal entry, an alto solo, begins

the *Urlinie* of which is strongly felt when the *Allegro moderato* begins:

The progression from *b* flat to *c* is, of course, retarded in the second example, but later Haydn returns to the initial treatment, first in the dominant (bar 41); but later we have it in the tonic:

By now the listener realizes the tight motivic web of the movement and the vital significance of the march rhythm. But there is another outcome of this emphasis on B flat minor. In the middle of the Christe, we again turn to B flat minor and modulate to the relative major, where we remain so thoroughly that it is obvious Haydn is making a point: to remind us that B flat minor appears at three crucial points (matching the symbolic division of three in the text): at the end of the slow introduction, in the middle of the Christe, and near the end. The unity is once again stressed, in this Christe section, by a clear use of *Urlinie*. If we examine bars 119f., quoted above, we may see a progression *b* flat – *c* – *d*. This *Urlinie* is the basis for the following as well:

It remains to be said to what unexpected use Haydn puts the six-eight time, making it a powerful, driving and yet very dignified, even 'fervent', metre such as we could never imagine from the 'Clock' Symphony's opening movement or, especially, from the many finales that make use of the metre. In a characteristic way he has robbed the metre of its 'unchurchly' lightness.

This particularly involved use of *Urlinien*, rhythmic motifs, etc. was considered necessary because of the new kind of form adopted in this Kyrie. The basic scheme is as follows:

	Adagio		Allegro moderato		
Introduction	A	B		A¹	Coda
1–28	29–66	67–92		93–119	120–139
B flat→B♭ minor	B♭→F→V	B♭ minor→		B♭ major→	tonic
→V	of tonic	D♭ major→		V of tonic	
	(end *fermata*)	V of tonic		(end *fermata*)	

The symmetry, latent in itself, is accentuated by the almost identical fermate ending the 'A' sections, and by the B flat minor excursions mentioned above. But this is a new kind of Kyrie form and one that, as Haydn considered, required various structural devices to cement it together. We have drawn attention to several, but there are others (e.g. the use of triplets and where they occur) equally interesting.

The first part of the Gloria, up to the quotation from *The Creation*, is also in a new kind of form using one of the oldest devices in eighteenth-century music – the ritornello. In this case the key figure is a fanfare for unaccompanied wind band and timpani, in which the bottom note of the bassoon (*b* flat below the staff) stands out. It opens the Gloria and reveals a whole new concept of nineteenth-century sound: both the present work and the *Harmoniemesse* of 1802 employ a world of sound very distant from that of Haydn's youth. The wind band is not as large as that of the last Oratorios, and we have seen, for example, that the cautious clarinet writing in the church works of 1796–7 reflected the level of the Eisenstadt band at that time. The new wind band seems to have been of a generally high standard, and no doubt the increased technical ability of the wind instruments mirrored a general rise in technical ability all over Europe. We can see this in the beautiful clarinet writing which abounds in the 'Et in terra pax' section. This is the first subsidiary section of this rondo-like structure and it is in B flat minor; the ritornello wind-band fanfare returns to usher in the Laudamus te. The second subsection is the 'Gratias' which is in G minor; the ritornello then announces the 'Domine Deus. The horns change crooks, from B flat to E flat, and the dew-dropping morn' is introduced in its original key (E flat). The musical example overleaf will show the first version of this section, as in the autograph and Eisenstadt performance, to which is added Haydn's change made for the Empress Marie Therese. The 'Miserere' enters in the middle of this quotation and turns out to be another of Haydn's spacious slow movements (adagio), beginning with the chorus (see the example overleaf, where the first bar of the new section is included to show this transition) and continuing with an alto solo. The 'Qui tollis' text is actually repeated by her. During the long passage for all four solo voices, there is a most original sound at bars 178ff., where the oboes and first clarinet have long chords, supported only by the soft tap of the timpani and the accompanying strings, and the soloists enter in syncopation one after the other. This figure

203

[*Schöpfungsmesse*: Gloria – Qui tollis]

is later given to the chorus in the tonic, with a similar but slightly more involved accompaniment (bars 210ff.). Throughout, one notices the interplay between the oboes and the clarinets (bars 192ff.), an airy orchestration that does not conceal the clear and logical development of the 'Miserere' fragment quoted above. It began its life as part of a cadential figure (bar 175), was continued in the passage discussed briefly above (see quotation, 178f.), becomes

[suscipe] de - pre - ca - ti - o [nem]

for the alto solo and, in turn,

for the solo soprano. At the end the figure quietly attaches itself to the violins and the movement ends *pp*.

The 'Quoniam tu solus sanctus' operates as a very fast introduction, with a dazzling display of violin semiquavers and a cascade of fanfares from brass and timpani, leading to an even faster fugue on the following unusual subject:

In the course of this robust fugue there appears a vision of heavenly benevolence for the solo woodwind (bars 272ff.):

This peculiarly comforting and lovely figure later returns, greatly expanded, to grace the concluding 'Amen'. Once again, too, we have another strange foretaste of Beethovenian unruliness in the slashing *fz* accents that accompany the unison progression to V and the final cadence of the movement:

It is one of the most stirring choral fugues in late Haydn, and its formal freedom, coupled with its original orchestration, were to colour the thinking of many in church as well as in composition class (and not a few proceeding simultaneously along both lines).

By 1801, Haydn's friends must have been used to the curiously old-fashioned rhythmic structure of his Credos. The bass figures such as we find here

recur in almost all the opening sections of these late Credos, even in the *Harmoniemesse*. The retrospective elements are so marked that one is tempted to seek a symbolic explanation: the Nicene Creed, being the Rock of Faith for the Mother Church, is ageless (though dateable); therefore Haydn's music is deliberately unmodern and ageless (though dateable). The sturdy, four-square construction, with its Baroque overtones, denotes the solid basis of the Church itself: of the last six Masses, every Credo is in four-four (or cut time).

The old symbolism which we know from all Haydn's Masses is at work here, too. 'Et invisibilium' drops to a *piano* and all the winds disappear. A long digression into G minor leads back, at the words 'Genitum, non factum', to a wind band fanfare and a tremendous tutti (*ff*) to match our return to B flat major and the words 'consubstantialem Patri . . .'. 'Qui propter nos homines' introduces another *p*, and only the clarinets shine through the strings. 'Because of us men' (the new literal translation) must weaken the Divine strength, men being feeble. And of course 'descendit de coelis' awakens Haydn's sense of imagery, as it always does: here, the 'descendit' is a multi-levelled affair, first with the chorus in crotchets and the upper strings in repeated semiquavers, then with the chorus in crotchets. It is all in the best Baroque tradition.

The Et incarnatus illustrates an even older symbolism. Dropping to the soft mediant key of G major, the orchestra at first consists only of a solo bassoon, strings, and a *concertante* organ part, the right hand of which is marked 'Flauto' in the autograph and 'Flautino' in the first edition – meaning that a four-foot 'flute' register is requested. Geiringer (1932, 130) described the effect of this register as 'ein zartes Trillern und Zwitschern', to which Brand (435) took extreme objection. But the 'gentle trilling and twittering' is indeed precisely what Haydn intended when he sought, by the flute register of his organ (there being no flute in his orchestra!), to paint for us the fluttering of the doves that, since time immemorial, have been the symbol of the Holy Ghost. The delicate pastel colours of Haydn's fluttering doves was, no doubt, one of the models for the trilling flute in the Et incarnatus est of Beethoven's *Missa Solemnis*.[1] The organ part of the *Schöpfungsmesse* is in itself as old fashioned (but dateable) as similar stylistic elements in the Credo's beginning. Here, in the organ part, Haydn seems to look back to the innocence of his own organ concertos, composed forty years before; to the 'Positiv' (i.e. pedal-less) layout and the delicate, rococo passagework that made those early products of Haydn's art so popular at the time.

The organ solo drops out as the 'Crucifixus' begins, and there is an astounding modulation to B flat ('Sub Pontio Pilato'), bringing in the whole wind band and timpani (the horns and trumpets still being crooked in B flat). The death symbol, the tremolo, as old (almost) as the violin itself, whispers behind 'passus et sepultus est': our tonal basis has imperceptibly shifted from G major to the 'Dorian' D minor (Crucifixion), to B flat major (Pontius Pilate) to the V of G (never resolved: He died

---

1 See again Warren Kirkendale's remarks in 'Beethovens Missa Solemnis und die Rhetorische Tradition' (*op. cit.*, 133f.).

and was buried . . .). The whole movement effects an enormous sweep of emotion and seems to encompass the whole of Haydn's career: for not only do we hear, in our mind's eye, the organ concertos of the 1750s but during the 'passus', the second-beat chords of the woodwind are strikingly reminiscent of just this passage in the *Missa in tempore belli*: but there, we had a full cadence, whereas here the wind chords fade away, unresolved, after two 'breathless' quavers, *pp* (expiring breath, symbolically).

The Et resurrexit bursts upon us with its brilliant orchestration and solid choral layout. Surprisingly, the clarinets do not play for the first four bars, but when they enter, in long lines, they symbolize Heaven ('et ascendit in coelum') together with the age-old Haydnesque rhythm ♫♩♫ ♩ , which first appears in the kettledrums alone ('secundum Scripturas') and then leads us, bar after bar, as we hear 'And He ascended to Heaven and sitteth at the right hand of the Father'. That same fanfare then returns to colour 'judicare', entering in the middle of a blazing D flat major chord, and later the words 'simul adoratur, et conglorificatur'. Another fragment is used with much affection

in conjunction with the first clarinet. Later (144ff.) the clarinet has this figure by itself, together with the alto solo's 'qui ex Patre Filioque procedit'. The two places in the text for death symbols, 'vivos et mortuos' and 'et exspecto resurrectionem mortuorum', are as usual treated with ancient symbolism. In the first instance (bars 125ff.), apart from the sudden modulation to A flat, the clarinet has a curious, syncopated octave drop; whereas in the second (bars 173ff.) we even have the old symbol of a diminished seventh and, naturally, the customary dynamic reduction to *p*. The Et vitam is a kind of rapid fugato; the tempo is speeded up and the voices enter more in the fashion of a canon than a fugue. It is another of Haydn's 'rabble-rousing' fugues, of short duration – everything in the Mass is, if we examine it closely, relatively short – but worked out in the longest possible sense of sweep and drama. The way in which the wind instruments are used, in a slow-moving pattern against the bustle of the violins and the canonic structure of the voices, is typical. The horns and clarinets move in stately minims; the violins have themselves a tight canonic structure over all this (see musical example overleaf).

Astonishingly, it will be noted that here even the various wind groups are in canon with each other. Later the slow moving trumpets and horns outline the large contours as we move with quick inner voices and slow outer harmonies from G minor to E flat (bars 190ff.). The 'Amen' is celebrated in various ways: in a stunning tutti (bars 200ff.) where all the upper strings have semiquavers and the chorus and wind instruments sound out the music with colours as vivid as an early Fra Angelico; then in a huge cadence, culminating in the soprano's high *b* flat (a note always used with the greatest effect in these B flat Masses), and working its way down the scale in a long series of syncopations (bars 204ff.). The off-beat orchestral syncopations, to the effect of which the *fz* contribute a further accent, again sound tellingly prophetic of Beethoven (bars 207, 218, 220) and bring this wonderfully vigorous movement to a close of explosive power.

[Et vitam venturi]

The orchestral sound of the Sanctus's beginning is breathtakingly original. Against a background of steady, repeated quavers, which proceed, light-footed (because marked with tall staccati), through this entire Adagio, a triplet pattern is established:  , first in the violins, then echoed by solo second horn and kettledrums. It is a very odd sound. At bar six, the voices begin to enter, first the bass, then the tenor, then the whole chorus; and always this triplet pattern glittering in the background. We burst into *f* as we modulate *via* G minor to the dominant, and the trumpets enter, doubled by the horns an octave lower. The modulation continues, and we enter Haydn's old 'Passione' key of F minor: the second horn and timpani now sound curiously muffled, each being in their lowest tessitura (low 'f'). The Pleni breaks into this pattern, still in F minor. The solo soprano sings 'Osanna in excelsis', followed by the chorus and the brass choir. Later the strings develop a dancing pattern of semiquavers () and with this jubilant accompaniment the movement closes: jubilant, but always of a slightly reticent nature. This is not the ecstatic excitement of the 'Nelson' Mass, and in this work, even the trumpets are not allowed to dominate: when the horns, towards the end of the Osanna, have

the trumpets are allowed no more than

supported by the timpani, and it is not till the very end that the brass and drums thunder out in Haydn's usual manner.

The pastoral Benedictus is another very Austrian movement of its kind, pastoral in its easy six–eight motion and the Allegretto tempo, Austrian in its melodic shape: who but an Austrian would have dared to introduce the old 'contradanse upbeat' in the first violins and support the whole by the first horn, each note of the latter being marked by a slight accent (*poco forz.*)? The beginning will illustrate the atmosphere of the whole, and will also show a clear example of Haydn's strange new accents that look like indications for up-bows (see overleaf).

As in the *Missa Sancti Bernardi*, Haydn retains the trumpets in B♭ and kettledrums in B♭–F. Throughout this radiantly happy movement one notes the juxtaposition between the solo voices – often used as a quartet – and the chorus. Formally, we have an interesting new device. If we may call the orchestral introduction followed by the vocal entries 'A', this section follows the usual pattern of modulating to the dominant. But we end on a V[7] chord and at bar 57 we begin again in the tonic with the principal subject. This middle section (A[1]) modulates differently: to C minor and then, *ff* and with a cascade of sextuplet semiquavers as accompaniment, into D flat major. At bar 61 we have what might be termed a recapitulation (A[2]). The ending, in E flat, has the curious effect of the trumpets and drums piercing through with repeated *b* flats (because of the fact that they are still pitched in that key).

[Benedictus: opening]

The authentic sources are contradictory about the vocal beginning of the Agnus, but Frau Becker-Glauch, who edited the work for the new critical edition (*Haydn Werke* XXIII/4), was undoubtedly right in starting the movement with the soloists and having the chorus enter at bar 34. Continuing the tradition of Haydn's full maturity, the movement is in the submediant major, G. There is an astonishing modulation to B flat, when the wind instruments, and also the horns, trumpets and timpani, enter for the first time. The single note, *b* flat, in brass and drums is as daring an orchestral and harmonic gesture as Haydn ever made. This excursion to B flat brings us to D minor and back to a repetition of the opening material in G major. Now we modulate, again without wind instruments, and in a similar pattern (but softer: *pp*) but this time to F: once again a single note, *f*, in brass and drums, and the woodwind enter, this time to remain with us as we return, a last time, to G major and the opening thematic material.

The Dona is of enormous power, beginning with a kind of intrada: the chorus enters not only unexpectedly but in off-tonic. Soon a free fugato develops, broken off several times by homophonic sections. The whole is in a kind of tripartite form in that bars 120ff. operate as a kind of recapitulation. Among the many fascinating details of this potent Allegro moderato, the ending, a kind of transfigured coda, is perhaps the most impressively prophetic moment in a late Haydn choral work. The B flat minor tutti (bars 145ff.) dies away to a *piano* and the motion almost stops, to be succeeded by an ending of gigantic power, *fortissimo*, the chorus striding down in unison crotchets against a tightly rhythmic pattern in the strings and a series of syncopations in the wind band. Here is the whole language and concept of middle-period Beethoven being foretold to us with Isaiah-like clarity and persuasion. Even the organ has that, for Haydn, exceedingly rare marking 'pleno Organo'. Beethoven may have told his friends that he never learned anything from Haydn; he may even – so vain is the human frame – have believed it, at least a little. But anyone with eyes and ears would have heard the lie in such a passage as this – a noble ending to one of Haydn's greatest Masses:

CHAPTER THREE

Chronicle 1802

ON 2 JANUARY 1802, Haydn continued his correspondence with George Thomson on the subject of settings of Scottish songs:

[To George Thomson, Edinburgh. *Italian*]
Most esteemed Friend!

I trust that you will have now received the remaining songs which I sent in two separate letters some time ago. I send you herewith the favorite song, THE BLUE BELL OF SCOTTLAND[1] [*sic*], and would like to have this little song printed all by itself and dedicated in my name to the celebrated Mistriss Jordan, as a tiny, tiny token of my esteem for her; for although I have not the honour of her acquaintance, I have the most profound respect for her great virtue and reputation. I did not want to compose a more brilliant accompaniment, for that might have overpowered the expressive and beautiful voice of so delightful an artist.

I am very grateful to you for the handkerchiefs, which are most beautiful. Send me the words[2] as soon as possible, one after the other, so that I can give you a speedy reply whether I shall be able to satisfy you. Meanwhile I am, dear Friend,

Your most devoted servant,
Giuseppe Haydn.

I received the last package containing the rest of the songs.
[The following line is crossed out:] To tell you the truth, I am tired[3] of this work.
Vienna, 2nd January 1802.

[Address:] Georg Thomson Esqu[r]
Trustees office,
Edinburgh.
North Britain.
[With Haydn's seal 'JH']

[Postal stamps indicating date of arrival in England: 'Foreign Office Fe[b.] 1, 1802', 'Feb. 1, 1802', *etc.*]

[Thomson's clerk notes: '2[d] Jan of 1802/ Haydn/ with Symph[s]. Accomp[s]./ & Variations to the/ Blue bell – / And desiring Eng: Verses to be sent to him as proposed –'.]   [CCLN, 198f.]

---

1 'The Blue Bell of Scotland' first appeared in Thomson and later also Preston's Volume III. The original title page read 'Fifty / Scottish Songs, / with / Symphonies & Accompaniments, / wholly by / Haydn. / Vol. III. / Edinburgh: / Printed for G. Thomson, York-Place, / by J. Moir. / 1802.' 'The Blue Bell' was No. 35. Later it was issued separately, with the dedication that Haydn wanted, in a set of 'Six Admired Scotch Airs' (Preston, 1805), of which No. 1 is entitled 'The Blue Bell of Scotland. / Arranged & Dedicated to M[rs] Jordan / by D[r] Haydn'. A still later arrangement by Haydn, in his autograph, is in the British Museum, signed and dated 'D[r] Haydn mpria 6[ten] Febr. 8̄0̄5̄'. Hoboken XXXI a, No. 176 (see Vol. II, 532f.). Hoboken has, wrongly, '8̄0̄6̄'.
2 The words to songs which Thomson wanted Haydn to compose.
3 The Italian word is clearly 'stanco'. It was misread by us as 'vanto' (= proud) in CCLN.

Haydn was obviously bored to tears by this work, but he reconsidered what he had written and crossed out the postscript; the lure of good Scottish pounds sterling was strong, and his pupils were willing to continue.

That same evening, Prince Esterházy held a *soirée* at his Palais on the Wallnerstrasse. Count Zinzendorf went 'Après 9ʰ chez le Prince Esterházy. Il y avoit encore peu de monde. Le Prince me parla de son introduction aux Etats. Le jeune Paul me plut beaucoup et son gouverneur Görög. Froid et le soir de la neige.' A few days later the Count notes in his Diary (9 January): 'Au grand souper au Pᶜᵉ Eszterházy, il y avoit beaucoup de monde, plus que l'autre jour. Je jouois au Whist avec Pauline Schwarzenberg, M. Ferguson et le jeune Furstenberg. La partie ne finoit pas avant le souper, et Sickingen s'en chargea. Mᶜ Czernin y etoit, Mᶜ Rotenhamm.' There is hardly ever a mention of music at such Esterházy affairs, but it is possible that the new wind band, which had recently played in Haydn's *Schöpfungsmesse*, entertained the company with such music as arrangements from Mozart's operas.[1]

The criticism concerning *The Seasons* (*supra*, pp. 185ff.) in the *Zeitung für die elegante Welt* of 31 December 1801 reached Vienna in January and caused some astonishment. Griesinger writes to Leipzig on 13 January:

> ... Who told H. Spazier [editor of the *Zeitung für die elegante Welt*] that Haydn 'himself only holds *The Creation* in little regard'? Haydn is modest but not stupid and cringing [*dumm-demüthig*]. ... Haydn thinks the Mass [either the *Missa in tempore belli* or the *Missa Sancti Bernardi de Offida*, which he had sent to Leipzig] would sell better if it were printed in parts, because one could put it right on the music-stands; the number of students is not large enough and they can take the trouble of putting the parts into score. That is what he himself saw Mozart do with his [Haydn's] quartets.   [Olleson *Griesinger*, 33]

As we have seen, Breitkopf & Härtel published all the Masses in full score, and in large editions. The times had changed and many more people now preferred to have such works in score rather than parts.

Griesinger now began another delicate operation: purchasing the rights, for Breitkopf & Härtel, of the Mozartian arrangements of Handel's Oratorios. Constanze Mozart had made a contract with Johann Anton André for the publication of her late husband's manuscripts (see *Haydn: the Years of 'The Creation' 1796–1800*, p. 499), but the Handel arrangements which, said Griesinger, 'are supposed to be orchestrated with quite exceptional care', belonged to Swieten. Delivery of the copies that Swieten intended to make was retarded because of the cold in the Baron's library. We read in Griesinger's correspondence:

> 15 January 1802
>
> ... When I asked Swieten recently for *Alexander's Feast* he said ponderously: 'my – word – is – sacred – and – I – have – given – it – to – you'. ... [Haydn is] annoyed and upset over an old illness which has appeared again, namely a polyp in the nose, and as a result of this he hasn't been able to leave his rooms for eight days. ...

> 17 January 1802
>
> ... Between ourselves: Swieten will write you this week. Mozart's widow explained to Swieten that she has made a contract with André according to the terms of which she is to deliver to him not only all the surviving manuscripts of her late husband but also those which might turn up later; in these circumstances she cannot accept any fee. Swieten finds this attitude not only delicate but also

1 Several of such arrangements, in contemporary MSS., survive in the Esterházy Archives at Eisenstadt.

correct; he nevertheless agrees to let you have the Handel-Mozart works, his own property and paid for, in return for which he will suggest a present of some music from you to Mozart's son. The original MSS., however, will not be sent to Leipzig, but copies are to be prepared here. . . .   [Olleson, *Griesinger*, 33f.]

Haydn had meanwhile finished another ten 'ariettas' for Thomson:

[To George Thomson, Edinburgh. *Italian*]

[Vienna, middle of January 1802][1]

Most esteemed Friend,

    Again I send you ten ariettas, and will deliver the rest in a little while. I also trust that you will fulfil your promises, and am,

Your humble servant
Giuseppe Haydn [m.p] ria.

I AM PROUD OF THIS WORK.

[Address:] George Thomson Esq[r]
          Trustees Office
          Edinburgh
          North Britain.
  [With Haydn's seal 'JH']

[Postal stamps indicating date of arrival in England, 'Foreign Office, Fe[b] 8, and then in Scotland: 1802', 'Fe[b] 11', *etc.*]

[Thomson, or Thomson's clerk notes: 'Jan ./. 1802 rec[d]. 11 Feb[y]. / Haydn/W[t]. Symph[s] & Accom[s]. to 10 Airs – & ment[g]./ THAT HE IS PROUD OF THIS WORK! HE SAYS, MI VANTO DI QUESTO/LAVORO.']

[CCLN, 199]

On 20 January Griesinger reports to Leipzig on Haydn's activities, including these Scottish songs. Of course it will always remain a mystery how many Haydn himself did and how many his pupils wrote, but it is safe to guess that the older Haydn became, the less he himself did the arrangements. On 19 November 1800 Griesinger had written to Breitkopf & Härtel about the songs, 'sometimes he does six to eight in a day, sometimes he studies one for eight days'. Now we read:

20 January 1802

. . . Hn. is again working on a new Mass [the *Harmoniemesse*] for Esterházy and is arranging some Scottish songs for Thompson [*sic*] in Edinburg [*sic*]. But they are supposed to be the last ones. Over a hundred are printed and Haydn has arranged 250 in all. Haydn finds a value in them; the melody is harsh, often shocking, but through the accompaniment he provides them and with a little assistance, these remains of old national songs are very enjoyable. . . .

    . . . The business with the plates for *The Creation* still has Haydn's complete approval, but sending them is a slow affair, and it's not my fault. . . .

[Olleson, *Griesinger*, 34]

Griesinger's hopes were, however, soon dashed by the arrival of the following letter from Haydn:

[To Georg August Griesinger, Vienna. *German*]

[Undated: Vienna, *c.* 20th January 1802]

Most esteemed Herr von Griesinger!

Yesterday evening I received a letter from Herr von Wassler concerning the transport of the plates and copies of *The Creation* to Herr Hartel [*sic*] in Leipzig. I am very sorry to have to report that at present I cannot serve Herr Hartel, because of a

---

1 The date of the letter can be judged from the postal stamps noting its arrival in England.

political reason which I could not foresee, and that the whole affair will have to be postponed. Meanwhile I am sending you the Mass, which I would like you to return to me in due course. Yesterday I also received a letter from Music Director Herr von Müller, who would also like to have one of my masses. If Herr Hartel can give it to him, I should be glad; if not, I am sorry but I cannot help him. Meanwhile I am,

> Your most indebted servant,
> Giuseppe Haydn.
>
> [CCLN, 199f.]

The procrastination over the plates probably derived from Swieten's disapproval of the procedure. Apparently the Baron thought it would be degrading for Haydn to give up selling the work himself. Breitkopf & Härtel did not get the plates until the summer of 1803. Griesinger tried repeatedly: '. . . I had to give in if it were not going to appear that I was holding a knife to his throat. . . .' Later, when a ray of hope appeared, we read '. . . perhaps Herr Härtel can get the plates yet.'[1] The Mass that Haydn delivered was probably the *Missa Sancti Bernardi de Offida*, the first of the Breitkopf series, already announced in April 1802.

Three days later, we have another letter from Griesinger to Härtel with news of Haydn:

> 23 January 1802
> . . . Still on that same evening when I wrote you my last letter I betook myself to Haydn to discuss with him 1) on account of the *Zeitung für die elegante Welt*; 2) the plates to *The Creation*; 3) the Masses. . . . As to the third point I received quite a satisfactory answer. This morning Haydn now sends me the following note together with the Mass. Hn. received a four-page letter with a 1 page postscript from Müller, but read only the end, wherein he asks for a Mass. Müller wants to have a Mass by Haydn as a relic to be kept in the Thomasschule, and this Mass would also be performed on the great feast-days. The old Hiller is always revived when he hears something by Haydn &c &c. Haydn excused himself to Herr Müller by saying that business prevented him from not answering now (that means, in Haydn's case, *ad graecas latendas*!). On the 25th the Mass will be put on the mail carriage. Please have it copied soon and treat with Müller in this regard as you see fit. Hn. leaves you a free choice. . . .   [Olleson, *Griesinger*, 35]

The day before, 22 January, the *Pressburger Zeitung* carried an announcement from Russia:

> St. Petersburg:
> Two days ago *The Creation* by Haydn was performed to an audience of some 1,000 people; the performance will be repeated on the 25th. The orchestra numbered 200 musicians and the chorus 50; the Oratorio was excellently played and sung, although the music could not have its full effect in a hall that was too small and too crowded. The words were translated into Italian for the sake of the singers.

The incredible statement of a four-to-one ratio between orchestra and chorus seems to have been accepted as quasi-normal, though Haydn's own chorus was, of course, much larger. It is interesting that performances of *The Creation* abroad were still considered to be news in Austrian newspapers.

---

1 Olleson, *Griesinger*, 34f. Hase, pp. 14ff.

Another letter from Haydn to Edinburgh follows:

[To George Thomson, Edinburgh. *Italian*]
Most esteemed Sir!
 Today, the 29th of January 1802, I received your letter of the 28th of December 1801, containing another 15 *canzonetti*, which – like the others – I will make every effort to correct in the near future. I trust, however, that you will have received thirty-two *canzonetti* by now, which I have sent at various times. There now remain eight; these are finished, and I shall put them in the mail today; you ought to have them in 4 weeks.
 You would do me a great favour if you would be kind enough to arrange payment for them at once, a total of FORTY GUINEAS, which is FOUR-HUNDRED FLORINS in Viennese currency. With this hope, I remain, Sir, with every esteem,

Your most humble and devoted composer
and servant,

Vienna, 29th January 1802.   Giuseppe Haydn.

[Address, in Johann Elssler's hand:]

N°. 3

George Thomson Esqr	[Postal stamps indicating date of
EDINBURGH	arrival in England, and then in
North Britain.	Scotland: 'Foreign Office Fe[b]
Joseph Haydn	16 1802' and 'Fe[b] 19, 1802', *etc.*]
Gumpendorf N^{ro} 73 kleine steingasse	

[seal]

[Thomson, or Thomson's clerk notes: '29 January 1802/Haydn/Of his having received / the 15 Scottish Airs/last sent & that he/will soon add Symph:/ & Accompts to them – / and desiring a remittance for those unpaid.']

[CCLN, 200f.]

Haydn's Swedish friend, F. S. Silverstolpe, asked the composer to help in the selling of Johan Wikmanson's Quartets, issued by his daughter Christina. Haydn's reply is as follows:

[To F. S. Silverstolpe, Vienna. *German*]
Well born,
Most respected Herr von Silverstolp!
 I take the liberty of enclosing 10 fl. for the kind *Mademoiselle*, and would ask you, my dear Herr von Silverstolp, to send it to her as a small token of my gratitude for the Quartets[1] she dedicated to me. At the same time, however, I regret to have to tell her that I can not fulfil her wish as far as selling the other copies to amateurs is concerned; for two very wealthy cavaliers (whose name I am ashamed to mention, and to whom I sent the first violin part so that they could look it over) said that they would not buy these Quartets until they had played through them.
Since they have refused me, and because it is a delicate matter with these gentlemen, I am afraid I shall have to forgo helping the kind Mademoiselle. I remain, Sir, most respectfully,

Your most obedient servant,
Joseph Haydn [m.p] ria.

[Vienna] From my home,
6th February 1802.   [CCLN, 201]

1 Johan Wikmanson (1753–1800), *Tre Quartetter för Trå Violiner, Alt och Violoncelle Tillägnade Joseph Haydn . . . Op. 1, Stockholm,* issued posthumously by his daughter Christina. See Mörner, pp. 188ff., 385ff. Title page reproduced on p. 189, Christina's dedication to Haydn on pp. 189f.

Breitkopf & Härtel were being offered pirated scores of Haydn's Masses, but of course they preferred to have authentic copies, particularly since Haydn seemed willing to supply them gratis. On 10 February 1802, Griesinger asks Härtel to 'write me if the Mass which you have received is one of the unknown ones. . . .' At the same time, Griesinger's interest had been aroused by seeing, on Haydn's piano, music with the title *Die wüste Insel*:

> . . . What is that? 'Someone sent me a German translation of an Opera by Metastasio, *L'isola disabitata*, which I wrote in 1785 [*recte*: 1779]. The work is done diligently and since I have the text, I've orchestrated all the recitatives; I must only change something of the Finale, a Quartet, because it's too long, and here and there some of the notes don't fit the German text.' Was the Opera ever printed? 'Never.' Won't you let Härtel have it? 'Certainly.' What will you ask for it? 'Herr Härtel can give me what he thinks fit; the Opera lasts about 2 hours; my operas are not known, but I would like to appear with this one. Fifty ducats are perhaps too much?' [Olleson, *Griesinger*, 35]

A certain Schaum from Hirschberg in Silesia had prepared the translation, from one of the many MS. copies which had circulated throughout Europe in the 1780s and 1790s. Johann Traeg owned the autograph, and we shall soon see Haydn trying to purchase it from him; Traeg offered the whole score in MS. copies for sale in his famous catalogue of 1799, and one such copy, in Schloss Namest (Náměšť), is probably such a Traeg score. Fortunately, the German copy of the piano score that was sent to Haydn still exists: it is in the Berlin State Library and contains some corrections in Haydn's own hand. The autograph of the changed Finale, signed at the end 'Fine G: H: mpria', was in the collection of the late Dr A. Wilhelm in Basel. Haydn made huge cuts in the Finale, for example forty-three bars of the opening ritornello, so that the final result contains only 158 rather than the original 365 bars (Hoboken II, 392f.). This cut version has never been published. We shall see that Breitkopf & Härtel agreed to purchase the Opera, but in the event they never published it.

The following correspondence between the famous German playwright August von Kotzebue (1761–1819), the one-time rival of Goethe's, was until recently known only from the summary in Griesinger's biography (pp. 41f.); but in 1960, Russian scholars published Haydn's answer, the autograph of which is now in the Central Historical Archives, Moscow.

[To Haydn from August von Kotzebue, Weimar. *German*]

Weimar, 8th February 1802

[Contents:]

Kotzebue wants to increase the value of his patriotic play, *Die Hussiten in Naumburg*, by having each chorus set to music by a different composer (Weber, Reichardt, Danzi, Schuster, Vogler &c.[1]), and asks Haydn if he would write the final chorus of the first act. [CCLN, 202]

[To August von Kotzebue, Weimar. *German*]

Most highly respected Herr von Kotzebue,

Since my youth and for many years it has been my dearest wish to set to music something of your sublime poetry, but now that I am a seventy-year-old fellow [*Knabe*] and always sickly, I do not dare to enter into musical competition with

---

1 The young Carl Maria von Weber (1786–1826), J. N. Reichardt (1752–1814), Franz Danzi (1763–1826), Joseph Schuster (1748–1812), Georg Joseph (Abbé) Vogler (1749–1814).

those great masters indicated to me (in which I might easily be conquered); so I must regretfully but completely abstain from my wish and from you, noble Sir, I must ask for pardon that I cannot serve you in this and meanwhile I remain with the utmost respect

Your most obedient servant,

Joseph Haydn mpria.

Vienna, 24th February 1802.

[Bartha, *Gesammelte Briefe . . .*, 396]

In earlier chapters of our Chronicle, the Russians' admiration for Haydn has often been noted. We now print an extraordinary report from Russia, which appeared in the *AMZ* on 17 February 1802 and was entitled 'Letters about the present condition of music in Russia'. The letter really seems to be the transcript of a personal missive from the writer to an unstated friend in Germany (Austria?).

Some days ago I received your admirable present, the bust [probably Grassi's] of the immortal *Joseph Haydn*;[1] it arrived undamaged, as if it had made the long trip from your hand to mine on the wings of a Zephyr, not on the axles of a freight waggon. My joy was very great. Here I have the beautiful bust of the respected, lively, even still fiery old man next to me; the man whose inexhaustible spirit is admired from Lisbon to Petersburg and Moscow, across the ocean and in the Arctic, and to whom thousands of men thank for the enjoyment of the sweetest hours of life. I may gaze at his bust or on his new works; I find in both an affirmation of the old truth, that through the consacration of sciences and the arts, the spirit and life of a sensible, moderate, true scholar and artist, may achieve a long-lasting, full and rich flowering. Euterpe, his mother, smiles from the wall at this her son, her darling. I understand her smile, and soon she will see such a one beneath her, in proper genealogical fashion, on a foreshortened pillar; and because of it my little music room will be raised to a music temple. Yes, friend, it now deserves this name: for since I own Haydn's bust, the local male and female amateurs as well as musicians of both sexes make pilgrimages to it. From many a lovely breast escape sighs that go to Heaven, praying for the continuation of this great man's life and reverently I add, Amen. One of our local graces, an intellectual lady and one of the first virtuosi on the fortepiano, placed a wreath on that respected brow, which her beautiful hand had made and wound of myrtle, laurel and everlasting leaves. I send you a laurel leaf from it, which will certainly be as remarkable to you as if I had plucked it from a tree over Virgil's grave. . . .

[*AMZ* IV, 346f.]

On 3 March Haydn's old colleague Carl Kraus, *Regens chori* of the Parish Church of St Martin at Eisenstadt, died, aged 79.[2] Haydn must have known that Kraus owned a considerable number of music manuscripts. Some of these were copied for the parish church and ended in their archives, but an equally important part was the property of the estate; and Haydn arranged to have these purchased by the Esterházy Archives. Among the works by Haydn, there is a copy of the *Missa Cellensis* ('Mariazellermesse') composed in 1782.

---

1 Name letterspaced in original.
2 The *Totenprotocoll* reads: '1802 März 3 Perillustris D[omi]nus Carolus Kraus, S. R. Imperii Eques, Interioris Ordinis Senator item Chori uti et olim Scholae Rector, subsque autem hujatum Scholarum Nationalium Capitalium Director. – 79 Jahre alt – Vir plenus Meritorum utpote Cujus indefesso labori Collectionem sic dictorum Musicalium Ecclesiae Chorus et Cujus . . .'. In a document in the Esterházy Archives, the purchase of music from the Kraus estate is recorded: *vide infra*, 20 Dec. 1802.

Breitkopf & Härtel had meanwhile written to Griesinger about *L'isola disabitata*, and Griesinger went to see Haydn about it and other matters:

3 March 1802

. . . Since I specially told Hn. that you already owned the Opera and it was a question only of copying charges, I thought I could expect him to propose a reduction of the 50 duc. to a smaller sum. But he didn't say a word about it! – I then arranged matters at least so that he had to promise to give me the great Mass in C and the other of which you sent me the theme. He agreed to this gladly and if they are not among his papers here, he will have them sent from Eisenstadt. I told him that you owned both works already and that you were concerned about an accurate copy. [Olleson, *Griesinger*, 35f.]

The Mass in C is the *Missa in tempore belli*, No. 2 of the Breitkopf series, and the other one is presumably the 'Nelson' Mass, No. 3. The following day Prince Esterházy wrote a letter to Haydn, the first of a series.

[To Haydn from Prince Nicolaus II Esterházy. *German*]
Herr Kapellmeister Haydn!
    Since Katharina Krines[1] of Eisenstadt, who has requested me to assist her while she is studying singing, has – according to the report of the tenor Haydn,[2] who was designated to examine her in this capacity – a most beautiful alto voice, and could become a right excellent alto singer, I expect from you a written report as to which sum one might give her, and with whom she might pursue her singing lessons.
Vienna, 4th March 1802.

Exp. Esterhazy.

[CCLN, 202]

[To Prince Nicolaus II Esterházy's Administration. *German*]
    Whereas His Serene Highness has ordered my brother to examine the musical talent of Catherina Krines, and he has found it very good, my humble opinion and request would be to give her, in view of her alto voice of such rare beauty, and also my brother, for his efforts up to now in teaching her, the sum of 4 fl. per month.

Joseph Haydn.

[Vienna], 10th March 1802.

[In the hand of a clerk: 'vid. No. 592. 1802', referring to a parallel file.] P.S. I shall undertake as soon as possible to find another clarinet player to take the place of Werlam.[3]

[CCLN, 202f.]

[Prince Nicolaus II Esterházy's answer to the above petition. *German*]
    To the Director's Office: Since Katharina Krines, who is the suppliant of the enclosed petition, has already been examined as to the possibilities of her musical talent, and has been found capable of developing into an alto voice, the tenor Haydn will give her lessons, and see to it that she becomes a real alto singer as soon as possible, for which he is to be given four Gulden per month, which sum shall be issued to him by my Director's Office.
Vienna, 13th March 1802.

Exp. Esterhazy.

[CCLN, 203]

1 Katharina (or Catharina) Krines' name does not appear on any of the musicians' lists known to us.
2 Johann, tenor in the Esterházy choir.
3 His name appears variously as Georg Warlan or Varlen.

[To Prince Nicolaus II Esterhazy. *German*]

[Vienna, March 1802]

Inasmuch as the alto singer Josepha Hammer[1] has made such musical progress in a year that she is able to sing almost everything correctly *a prima vista*, and since apart from this she has an alto voice of such rare beauty, in my humble opinion Your Highness should graciously grant her request.

Joseph Haydn [m.p] ria,
Kapellmeister.
[CCLN, 203]

[To Haydn from Prince Nicolaus II Esterházy: Answer to above petition. *German*]

As a special act of grace, and taking into consideration all the other circumstances, the suppliant Josepha Hammer is granted – apart from her yearly salary – an additional sum of one-hundred Gulden, which is to be paid to her by my chief cashier.

Vienna, 24 March 1802. Nicolaus Fürst Esterházy m.p.
[CCLN, 203]

In one of the letters from Griesinger to Leipzig – their loss (except for the extracts here quoted) is one of the tragedies of Haydn scholarship – we learn of a new project. Antonio Salieri came to Haydn and asked for permission to perform *La vera costanza*, one of the composer's operas that was still being performed, usually in German translation as *Die wahre Beständigkeit*. Salieri wanted to mount the work at the Court Opera in Vienna, for which Haydn had composed it about 1778 or 1779 (the story of the work's being withdrawn because of intrigues with the singers, and then staged at Eszterháza in 1779 is well known). This would have been a long-delayed triumph, similar to Haydn's membership in the Tonkünstler-Societät; but the composer refused. Salieri intended to give the main role (Rosina) to the popular soprano, Irene Tomeoni, whose name has figured often in our Chronicle (*inter alia* in the concert of 8 January 1796 at which Haydn conducted and Beethoven played a piano concerto; see *Haydn: the Years of 'The Creation' 1796–1800*, p. 93). Tomeoni, according to Haydn, was not the right person for the part; one needed an innocent girl like Therese Saal to make Rosina convincing. And so *La vera costanza* was once again withdrawn from the Vienna Court Opera, no doubt to its composer's great regret (Pohl III, 196).

The winter concerts were now in full swing. Silverstolpe refers to them briefly in a letter to Stockholm of 13 March:

> . . . The concerts are at their height and one enjoys them partly gratis and partly with paid tickets. At Count Fries good things are now and then given, on Mondays; but here all the concerts are very mixed. All too often one is served Aria Buffa: thanks to my temperament, these are always impossible for my ears. . . .
> [Mörner, 388]

Griesinger, a few days earlier (10 March), had told Leipzig that they might expect 'the Mass in C and the other one of which you sent the theme, together with the *Isola disabitata*. I shall have to remind him several times, for otherwise Hn. forgets – or at least he pretends that he has forgotten.' Probably Griesinger had no idea of the heavy

---

1 Josepha Hammer, from Pressburg, had made her début in Haydn's *Missa in tempore belli*, at a performance in Eisenstadt given in honour of the Archduke Carl on 29 September 1797.

administrative work connected with the Esterházy *Capelle*, of which only a part was written down. Ten days later, Griesinger had good news to report:

> Yesterday I turned over to the mail coach the parcel with the score and the piano score of *Isola disabitata* together with a Mass. Here is Haydn's receipt. Hn. will have written to you himself that he would like to have the Opera printed with the original text, i.e. the Italian. What he has crossed out should not be included; for his old Prince, for whom he had to compose this Opera, nothing was too long; the final Quartet is quite new. Hn. believes this Opera to be a good example for would-be composers, on account of the recitatives: it's a little work that, in its present form, can be performed in every private theatre. Hn. has composed two Masses in C, a larger one that lasts for two hours and a smaller one. Both are in Eisenstadt. He promised me that I should have the latter before my departure (on the 24th of April), also his newest Te Deum which he wrote for the Empress. But don't let us triumph before we have them, for the correspondence with Eisenstadt and organizing the copy (the Te Deum Hn. has only in parts, which one may need any time at Eisenstadt) require a little while. . . .
>
> . . . Artaria will postpone the edition of the two Haydn Quartets until such time as Hn. has composed the third, a task to which Hn. will now devote himself. Afterwards there's a new Mass for his Prince. . . .   [Olleson, *Griesinger*, 36]

Breitkopf & Härtel seemed to have asked Griesinger about Haydn's older C major Masses, and the composer means, of course, the huge *Missa Cellensis in honorem B.V.M.* of 1766 and the 'Mariazellermesse' of 1782. Griesinger intended to leave in April for Störmthal, Count Schönfeld's country house a few kilometres south-east of Leipzig and intended to deliver the music to Härtel personally. Breitkopf & Härtel published the Te Deum at once. Artaria in the event published the two Quartets, Op. 77, without waiting for the third, a D minor work ('Op. 103') which Haydn began in 1803 but never finished.

On 25 March there was a charity performance of *The Creation*, at which, the *Wiener Zeitung* (No. 31, 17 April) informs us, Mad. Willmann and Herr Teemis sang *gratis*. In the *Pressburger Zeitung* (No. 31, 20 April) we read:

> Vienna:
> On the 25th of last month *The Creation* . . . was performed in the Theater an der Wien to benefit the Children's Hospital. The entrepreneur was Doctor Gölis, Director of the hospital. . . . Herr Haydn, who is as widely known for his charity and kindness of heart as for his genius, which is the wonder of the greatest nations, conducted the performance of his masterpiece himself, to the thunderous applause of a large audience. . . .

On 31 March (or 1 April, depending on the source) Haydn celebrated his seventieth birthday in typical modesty: there is no mention of the event in any of the newspapers, nor is there any hint of an official celebration.

On 6 April Paisiello's *I filosofi immaginari* was given at the Kärntnerthortheater, and it is a sign of the new taste that Rosenbaum went and wrote that it was 'an utter failure' (Radant, *Rosenbaum*, 100); but a few days before, on 23 March, Cherubini's *Lodoiska* had been given by Schikaneder, and Rosenbaum thought it was 'lovely music' (ibid.).

Breitkopf & Härtel were now preparing to launch the Haydn Masses and sent Griesinger the proofs of an announcement (probably the one for the *AMZ*, which appeared in the *Intelligenz-Blatt* No. IX, attached to the issue of 10 March 1802):

No one who has even a small interest in the most important affairs of music will remain indifferent to the news that the great Haydn has decided to make generally available also the finest products of that which from the treasury of his intellect he has laid in all stillness on the altar of Religion. If his other works for the voice may be misunderstood or misinterpreted by some persons (since actually they require a special attitude and thus admit of a wrong one), this is certainly not the case with those works where the heart of a religious man overflows, and where he expressed in his fashion that which every religious person feels, and must find, therefore, in works where the artist is not distracted by a text which goes into too much detail but, on the contrary, is one that already contains certain predisposed outer forms (the basic, large outline). In Haydn's Masses on the whole there does not predominate the dark spirituality and the sense of constant repentance and bigotry that we find in the Masses by the great men of the past, especially Italy; rather we find a cheerful, reconciled devotion, a gentle melancholy, and a blessed sense of awareness of heavenly goodness. He who wishes to have detailed examples need only take the movements Et incarnatus – Crucifixus – and Et resurrexit from the present Mass, the mention of which leads us nearer to the announcement of the present undertaking.

Joseph Haydn will allow those of his sacred works which he wishes to preserve for posterity to appear in full score under our auspices. The first of these Masses (mainly in B flat, with almost all the customary instruments) is almost completely printed from his own autograph and was not announced by us previously so that the publication of *The Seasons* would not be disturbed. It [the Mass] is one of his most recent and is surely one of Haydn's greatest works in this genre.

The appearance of this series of works is entirely the same as with the Mozart scores in our edition – e.g. Mozart's *Requiem*. The single volume costs 1 Thaler 12 Groschen (Saxon) for subscribers, the fifth copy is free. The format etc. is as for the other works. In order not to hasten unduly the prospective participants, we have set the terminal date for subscribers at the end of June; after this date the price will be doubled. The first of these Masses, on which the discussion now centres, will surely appear before the Easter Fair and will consist of one volume. We rely in this project on the public's support, which has been, to our satisfaction, so forthcoming in similar projects and which has so benevolently supported the wider dissemination of newer music.

Leipzig, in March 1802. *Breitkopf* and *Härtel*.

Griesinger (36) wrote to Leipzig on 7 April, '. . . I won't show the announcement of the Masses to Hn., because I well know that he won't like it on account of his Prince', which means, of course, that Griesinger knew that Esterházy was very jealous of 'his' church music and anxious to keep it for himself. On the other hand, Haydn could (and undoubtedly did) explain to his Prince that pirated copies of these Masses were circulating all over Germany and that no one was in a position to stop, say, Breitkopf & Härtel from issuing the works even without the composer's approval. It was the same with his symphonies. Griesinger (37) writes, '. . . Haydn does not object to your issuing his symphonies, and he will undertake the revision if he has some advantage from it.' But he could do nothing even to prevent publishers from issuing textually corrupted editions, and when Le Duc of Paris sent Haydn their wretched edition of his symphonies, Griesinger (37) wrote to Härtel, '. . . he could hardly understand how one could send him such a corrupted and falsified piece of bungling [*Machwerk*], for he is ashamed to place such products among his music. . . .' Altogether Haydn was not overtly anxious to undertake large revisions of this kind.

'. . . He said neither yes nor no, but it was easy to see that he considered this work among the *odiosis . . .*' (ibid., 37).

In one of these letters (7 April) we learn the interesting fact that '. . . Haydn praised your good and correct payment in front of Beethoven. . . .'[1]

On 9 April 1802, Johann Michael Haydn conducted a performance at Salzburg of his brother's Oratorio, *The Seven Words*, which proved to be a resounding public success. The forces used were 7 sopranos, 6 altos, 5 tenors, 7 basses, 18 violins, 4 violas, 3 violoncelli, 3 double basses, 2 oboes, 2 bassoons, 1 serpent [instead of the double bassoon], 2 trumpets, 2 trombones and timpani.[2] It is interesting once again to note the small size of the chorus compared to the big orchestra; also to note that Michael Haydn was obliged to omit the flutes, clarinets and horns that the score requires.

On Palm Sunday (11 April) and the day following, Haydn conducted *The Seasons* for the Tonkünstler-Societät (soloists: Therese Saal, Mathias Rathmayer and Ignaz Saal). Rosenbaum (100) notes that it was 'overcast and cool' on the 11th. 'Schindleker [the 'cellist] sent tickets for *The Seasons*, in the *parterre noble* . . . the theatre was crowded. . . .'

The following is Haydn's letter of thanks to the *Institut National* in Paris in answer to that body's letter of 26 December 1801 (*supra*):

[*French*. Only the signature autograph]

Vienna, 14th April 1802.

Joseph Haydn to the Citizen Vincent, President, and to the Citizens La Porte du Theil, and Villat, Secretaries of the *Institut National des Sciences et des Arts*, Paris.

Citizens,

The signal honour which the *Institut National des Sciences et des Arts* has shown me, by electing me a NON-RESIDENT MEMBER of the section 'Literature and Fine Arts', is a reward so great that the value of my works – even considering the approbation which the public has seen fit to bestow on them – can never, in my opinion, be such as to deserve it.

I am keenly aware how flattering it is to have been admitted to a group which is so universally revered, and which has been so justly celebrated for so long a time. My future efforts will have no other goal than to justify this honour, and thus I wish to proffer to the Society, who has taken me into its illustrious ranks, the emotions of respect and gratitude with which my heart is filled.

I beg you, Citizens, to convey my respects to our colleagues, and to accept yourselves the assurance of my most profound esteem and most sincere regard.

Joseph Haydn [m.p] ria.

[At the top left, Villat's notice:] to be communicated to the other two classes. – 8 floréal an 10. – Villat, scre [secrétaire] 1.

[CCLN, 204]

On 21 April, Griesinger wrote a long letter to Leipzig which, fortunately, has been preserved almost in its entirety.

21 April 1802

. . . Widespread and large-scale revisions of older symphonies are things you can't expect from Haydn, who is now working on a Mass and afterwards, if God wills, wishes to undertake another large work . . . I shall bring also the Te Deum and another composition, called *The Storm* that Hn, if I err not, wrote for

1 W. Hitzig, 'Beethoven und das Haus Breitkopf & Härtel', in *Der Bär*, 1927, p. 24.
2 Hans Jancik, *Michael Haydn, Ein vergessener Meister*, p. 207.

Schwarzenberg.[1] On the 25th we leave. . . . Haydn told me yesterday that from all quarters he had received much praise of his *The Seasons*. The Empress and many other persons, too, are urging him to *undertake one more large work*, and he would be very much inclined to do so if he only knew of a useful text. I assured him, thinking of your earlier proposal, that you could well be of assistance here; he should only tell me of the poet in which he had the most confidence. He said – *Wieland*. If it is possible to win this veteran for the editing of the text, you would win for your presses by the combination of these two excellent talents an immortal monument. Haydn leaves the choice of the subject to the poet; but he does not want anything dramatic but an Oratorio that should have at most the length of *The Seasons*. He thinks that the Last Judgement would offer rich material, namely in the first part death, in the second the resurrection, in the third hell and heaven. The thought seems Baroque, but in the hands of genius it might turn out to be very successful. A young local poet, who started to treat the subject, but could not continue for lack of support, had, for example, a God-fearing man, a pretty girl, a villain each die in the first part, and so on. Should such a subject be quite impossible and allow of no aesthetically sublime treatment? Haydn would work at it *con amore*, the more so since it would be fulfilling a favourite idea of the Empress. Haydn also wishes that Wieland would send the text direct to the Empress with a request to Haydn to compose it. It would certainly be well received, and the Empress would feel herself flattered to participate in such a work and, what for local conditions is of no little account, the *Baron* [van Swieten] and his bungling would have to stay at home. Haydn also asks, in order not to violate the poet's intention, for a *very detailed* commentary on the text, and also remarks where the poet would find a duet, trio, allegro, ritornello, chorus, &c. most fitting. Through it the composer's work is made easier, and the poet is forced to write *musically*, a thing that so seldom happens. Haydn's trust in Wieland is partly because of the beautiful strophe which Wieland wrote about *The Creation*, and which I formerly sent to you for the musical journal [*AMZ*].

[Olleson, *Griesinger*, 37]

Alas, Wieland, who was himself an old man, could not be persuaded to write the text. Apparently Haydn was not satisfied with another treatment of the subject, proposed by an Austrian priest, of which the libretto is in the Esterházy Archives (Ha. I. 11, from Haydn's legacy): 'Das / Jüngste Gericht / Ein Gegenstück zur Schöpfung, / In Musik gesetzt / von / Herrn Joseph Haydn / Doktor der Tonkunst und Kapellmeister / in wirklichen Diensten S[r]. Durchlaucht / des Herrn Fürsten v. Esterhazy, und / der k. Schwed. Musik. Akademie / Mit=/glied / Meistens nach Schriftstellern verfasst / v. / I. Ignatz Scheiger / Pfarrer zu Kirchberg am Wagram.'

Luigi Tomasini Jr., a violinist of great talent, is the subject of the following letter from a very annoyed Prince Nicolaus Esterházy:

[To Haydn from Prince Nicolaus II Esterházy, Vienna. *German*]
Dear *Kapellmeister* Haydn:
     You are to intimate to the young Lougi [*sic*] Tomasini[2] that – inasmuch as his sojourn here is not only completely useless, but apart from that affords him the possibility of pursuing a frivolous existence – he is to proceed at once to Eisenstadt,

1 It was in fact composed in England in 1792 but revised (with larger orchestra) and translated into German for the Schwarzenberg concerts.
2 Aloysius (Luigi) Tomasini, son of the leader Luigi, was born on 10 July 1779. He and his brother Anton were engaged in 1796, when the Esterházy band was reconstituted, Luigi Jr. as violinist, Anton as violinist and viola player. See Pohl II, 382 (correcting the information found in I, 263f.). Luigi Jr. managed to stay in the band this time, but eventually he married a singer without the Prince's permission and found it better to leave Eisenstadt. J. Harich, 'Das Haydn-Orchester im Jahre 1780', in *Haydn Yearbook* VIII, 16ff.

where he is to take up his duties, unless he wishes, by his obstinacy and prolonged absence, to provide the reason for his no longer being regarded as a member of my music personnel; for no special prerogative attaches to his person, and he is under obligation to fulfil his duties in the same way as the other members of the music personnel.   Exp. F[ürst] Esterhazy m.p.
Vienna, 30th April 1802.   [CCLN, 204]

It is believed that the following undated letter by Haydn, in the Esterházy Archives, refers to Aloysius (Luigi) Tomasini Jr.:

[To Prince Nicolaus II Esterházy. *German*]
    In order properly to support the *rare* genius of the suppliant (which, because of an accidental illness and the resulting lack of money, has been rather shaken up), it would be my humble opinion that through the grace of Your Serene Highness a yearly addition of 100 fl. or at least 50 fl. would force him to even greater efficacy in his services.

Joseph Haydn
Kapellmeister.
[Not in CCLN; Pohl I, 264, and III, 219]

Haydn was deeply attached to the whole Tomasini family: he had stood as godfather to several of the children and had watched their careers with pride and affection. Indeed, it was a highly talented family.

Meanwhile Griesinger had departed for Leipzig, carrying with him a number of Haydn's scores for publication. Thus Haydn was obliged to write directly to Härtel in the following matter:

[To Gottfried Christoph Härtel, Leipzig. *German*]

Vienna, 8th May 1802.
Kindest Friend!
    Since I must accompany my Prince to Hungary at the end of this month, I should very much appreciate it if I could have the promised two-thousand-five-hundred gulden[1] from Herr Kunze beforehand. Hoping to receive an answer in the affirmative I am, with my kindest regards to Herr von Griesinger, most respectfully,

Your most obedient servant,
Jos: Haydn.
[CCLN, 205]

There is some question how often Haydn went to the theatre those days; but he may have been an astonished witness at a performance of Mozart's *Die Entführung aus dem Serail* at the Burgtheater, on 28 May 1802, with a new singer (Madame Gley) as Constanze, which Rosenbaum attended. His comment was: 'The theatre was empty. . . .' The Viennese audience was really one of the most unpredictable in Europe.

Griesinger's next letter is written from Störmthal and concerns the proposed libretto on the Last Judgement:

[Störmthal] 1 June 1802.
. . . Haydn cannot divest himself of his first idea; this proposed poem [by I. I. Scheiger, title page quoted above] is not that which he, the Empress and the already conceived idea [*sic*] have in mind, and he will not discuss anything else. Wieland also knows how to create musical rhymes; he [Haydn] has heard of a

1 Payment for *The Seasons* (the first 2,000 gulden had been paid upon signature of contract, in July 1801).

piece of this kind which is supposed to have been composed by Kunze in Weimar,[1] and he would like to have the libretto of that and also of the *Alceste*,[2] which he [Wieland] had arranged to be printed some time ago, so that he [Haydn] can study them.

What is to be done? It will be difficult to make Haydn change his mind; he believes in Wieland, and in articles of faith everyone likes to retain his own opinion.

Couldn't you obtain that libretto which Haydn mentions?...

[Olleson, *Griesinger*, 38]

The birthday celebrations of the Empress Marie Therese were this year combined with the tenth anniversary of the Coronation of the Emperor Francis; at Pressburg, Haydn's *The Creation* was given on 6 June in the Town Theatre, with free entry for everyone (*Wiener Zeitung* No. 47 of 12 June 1802). It seems that among the high personages at Pressburg was the Grand Duke of Tuscany, Ferdinand III, a brother of the Emperor, who was married to Luise, daughter of the King of Naples. Ferdinand had a fairly complete collection of Haydn Masses at Florence but wished to have all of them.

[To Haydn from Prince Nicolaus II Esterházy. *German*]

[?Eisenstadt, *c.* 7th June 1802]

To *Herr Kapellmeister* HAYDN:

You will be able to see from the enclosed sheet, on which the first bars of each piece are noted, which of your own Masses the Grand Duke of Tuscany already owns. I expect a further report from you, indicating which additional scores of your own compositions you had thought of giving to His Royal Highness, so that I can inform His Royal Highness thereof.

Exp. F[ürst] Esterhazy [m.p.].

[CCLN, 205]

[To Prince Nicolaus II Esterházy, Pressburg. *German*]

Most Serene [Prince],

From the list of music which the Grand Duke of Tuscany sent, I see that His Highness lacks only two of my Masses: i.e. one of the earlier works and the last one,[3] which I wrote a year ago. But since Your Highness decreed that no one should have a copy of this Mass, I dared not to send it to him without previously informing Your Highness. Therefore I await your command whether I should have both these works copied and sent to Pressburg, where unfortunately they will be performed in my absence and thus (because they will lack finesse) lose much of their effect – and this will be greatly to the detriment of my industry, and will be most unpleasant for me. Meanwhile I am labouring WEARILY on the new Mass,[4] though I am ANXIOUS whether I shall receive any applause because of it.

Your most humble servant,

Vienna, 14th June 1802.   Joseph Haydn.

[CCLN, 205]

---

1 Friedrich Ludwig Aemilius Kunzen [*recte*] or Johann Friedrich Kranz; the latter really was *Kapellmeister* in Weimar. Haydn thought little of Kunzen's work (undated letter by Griesinger).
2 Wieland's *Alceste*, composed by Anton Schweitzer in 1773.
3 The *Schöpfungsmesse* of 1801; the earlier one is probably the *Missa Sancti Nicolai* (G. Feder, in *Haydn Yearbook* IV, p. 132).
4 The *Harmoniemesse*.

[To Haydn from Prince Nicolaus II Esterházy, Pressburg. *German*]
To *Herr Kapellmeister* HAYDN:

I do not deny that it would be very difficult – especially in the case of new works – to perform music without the personal direction of the composer; but on the other hand, you need have no fears, particularly about the finesse, because in view of the worldwide fame of your celebrated works, you may be assured that these Masses will not lose their value in the eyes of the connoisseurs. Apart from this, I leave it to your own discretion what sort of answer should be given to a Grand Duke's request of this kind. But since there really seems to be no way to refuse his wishes, there is nothing to do but to have both Masses copied and sent to me at Pressburg.

By the by, since I have had no news from your brother, I would ask you to let me know if and when he will be coming from Salzburg.[1]

Pressburg, 21st June 1802.   Exp. F[ürst] Esterhazy, m.p.

[CCLN, 206]

On Tuesday, 6 July, Rosenbaum and his wife went to Eisenstadt:

. . . We arose at about 6 o'clock, and drove off about 8 . . . to Eisenstadt . . . We arrived at our mother's at about 3:30.

In Eisenstadt

Elsler [probably Joseph Elssler, the oboist] came immediately after our arrival. Th— put our belongings in order. Elsler and I had coffee, then we marched . . . through the menagerie in the castle grounds, saw the unsuccessful water machine, looked at the glass-house and the childish lay-out of the English garden from the River Inn (now the Casino) to Pölt's; one hardly gets the impression of an English garden.   [Radant, *Rosenbaum*, 102]

Haydn was still in Vienna, as we see from the following letter to his old friend, the *Regens chori* of Baden:

[To Anton Stoll, Baden. *German*]

Vienna, 30th July 1802.

Dearest Friend!

Yesterday evening I had the pleasure of seeing my Prince in my humble cottage; he asked me to go to Eisenstadt next week, in order to rehearse under my direction various pieces of new music, *inter alia* two Vespers and a Mass by Albrechtsberger and a Vesper by Fuchs. Therefore I regret that I cannot go to Baden at present, and moreover, I am expecting the installation of an Assistant *Capellemeister* in the place of my brother. I do not yet know who this will be. I

---

1 In 1801, Michael had been offered the post of Assistant *Kapellmeister* (*supra*, p. 77). Esterházy had subsequently written to him on 18 January 1802 (Esterházy Archives, Acta Musicalia 1914): 'Since I do not doubt that you have already made most of the preparations incident to your coming and settling here without further delay, I shall await your arrival with pleasure; and as a sign of your attention, I expect to receive from you, by August at the latest, a *Missa Solemnis* and a *Vesper de beata*.' On 6 February Michael wrote that he will ask permission to leave Salzburg in June or July, to enter the Prince's service in August. In fact he was too attached to Salzburg to leave it.

thank you very much all the same for your kind offer to put me up at your house, and with a hearty kiss to your wife, I am, dearest Friend,

Your sincere servant, Jos: Haydn

P. S. Herr von Albrechtsberger received a princely reward for his composition, and I was very pleased about this.

[Address:]   Herr v. Stoll
Regens Chori
in
Baden.

[CCLN, 206]

Johann Nepomuk Fuchs, who had composed the Vesper, was in fact to become Assistant *Kapellmeister*, as we see from the next letter:

[To Haydn from Prince Nicolaus II Esterházy. *German*]
To *Kapellmeister* HAYDN:

Since, in view of his previous service to me, I have decided to appoint *Claviermeister* Fuchs as Assistant *Kapellmeister* of my orchestra and church music, I wish to bring this fact to your attention, and at the same time ask you to introduce the newly appointed Assistant *Kapellmeister* to the assembled band and music personnel; except for Lougi [*sic*] Tomasini Senior[1], they are all ordered to defer to him with the proper SUBORDINATION.

Just as the said Assistant *Kapellmeister* is now entrusted with the direction of the orchestra and church music in your absence, so the leader Lougi Tomasini is to assume the direction of the chamber music. Together with you, both of them, according to these circumstances, are to ensure that all the individual members of the band[2] show the proper obedience; whereby I insist that there will be no case of insubordination, and that the various duties be performed in an exemplary manner: this includes personal appearance, care of uniforms, and other tokens of good behaviour.

In this connection, the personnel is instructed to obey the following order: the whole band – male and female singers, without exception – is to hold a weekly rehearsal; their superiors will decide on which day it is to be held. They are likewise responsible for the music, and should draw up a CATALOGUE under your supervision: the Assistant *Kapellmeister* the church music,[3] and the leader Lougi [*sic*] Tomasini the chamber music, with the stipulation that no one – under the most severe penalty – is to be allowed to copy or print either scores or other pieces which are part of our MUSICAL COLLECTION; a special room will be designated for this purpose.

For the rest, I have observed, not without displeasure, obvious proof of negligence of duty among certain members of the band: in future, a monetary punishment will be levied on any member of the band who absents himself from the [church] service; namely, one Gulden per person concerned, which is to be collected from anyone not having a proper excuse for being absent. The supervisors will be responsible for collecting such monetary punishments, and they will report to me about it from time to time.

Exp. F[ürst] Esterhazy, m.p.

Eisenstadt, 14th August 1802.
[CCLN, 207]

---

1 The leader and violinist Luigi [*recte*] Tomasini, who had been engaged in 1762.
2 'Musik Individuen': see comment to the letter of 26 September 1801.
3 This part of the catalogue, beautifully written on small octavo paper and bound in red, is preserved in the Burgenländisches Landesmuseum, Eisenstadt, *ex coll.* Sándor Wolf.

Haydn was now in Eisenstadt, occupied with the final pages of the *Harmoniemesse* and immersed in the usual administrative work. On 22 August he wrote a letter to Breitkopf & Härtel which, unfortunately, has not survived (see Hase, 28). A few days later the composer wrote his pupil Anton Polzelli,[1] who was living in the house at Gumpendorf.

[To Antonio Polzelli, Vienna. *German, 'Du' form*]

Eisenstadt, 28th August 1802

Dear Polzelli,
    Please be good enough to send me the fugal Quartets by Gallus[2] which he dedicated to me, and which you know. They are lying on my pianoforte in the bedroom, or opposite, in the other room, on the cabinet. Also my calendar for this year, which my Johann[3] and I both forgot to take along with us; but take care that no piece of paper or memorandum drops out. Just tell my cook, to whom I send my regards: you must pack it very carefully and seal it up, and then give it to the driver Härtl. Lessel[4] wrote me yesterday that you are well and go to see him often: I'm glad to hear it, and please give him my regards. I hope that your Mama, too, is well; all the best to her. Today I also heard that everyone in my house is well. Please mail the enclosed letter on this coming Wednesday, for which I am your debtor and

Your sincere teacher,
Joseph Haydn.

Please also send me the German libretto of
The Seasons, if you can find it.
[No address]   [CCLN, 208]

The summer of 1802 was the driest in years. In a copy of the *Kais. Königl. Österreichischer Provinzialkalender für das Jahr Jesu Christ, 1802* (Wien im Verlage der v. Kurtzbekischen Buchdruckerey, in der obere Breunerstrasse Nro. 1202, im ersten Stock) there is the following MS. note opposite the month of November: 'Nach 6 sehr trockenen Monathen fiel den 3ten November der erste ergiebige Regen' (After 6 very dry months the first proper rain fell on 3 November). Eisenstadt, always a dusty town, must have been covered with a fine light-brown powder, and the incoming carriages must have raised clouds of dust in the castle courtyard. For this season of 1802 we are fortunate in having an interesting eye-witness account of the name-day festivities for Princess Marie Hermenegild at Eisenstadt. It comes from Ludwig, Prince Starhemberg, in Austrian diplomatic service and then Ambassador to the Court of St James. On 13 July 1802 he returned from London to Vienna and on 7 September he accepted an invitation by Prince Esterházy to visit Eisenstadt.[5] The diplomat was a passionate music-lover, who in his youth had played the flute; his wife was an excellent performer on the pianoforte. When in London he held weekly concerts or theatrical evenings in which the host and hostess participated. He had been one of the

---

1 Luigia Polzelli's youngest son, born at Eszterháza in 1783. It was rumoured that Haydn was Antonio's father, but if this be true, neither Luigia nor Haydn ever admitted it.
2 Johann Gallus (Mederitsch) (1752–1835), composer and member of the Vienna Court Theatre Orchestra. The works dedicated to Haydn were 'Trois Quatuors ou Fantaisies pour deux Violons, Alto et Violoncello', Op. 6 (Artaria, pl. no. 1570), published in August 1802.
3 Johann Elssler.
4 Franz Lessel (1780–1838), a Polish pupil of Haydn's (see *Haydn: the Years of 'The Creation' 1796–1800*, p. 335).
5 A. J. Graf Thürheim, *Ludwig Fürst Starhemberg*, Graz 1889, pp. 115–7; Brand, 454.

few to appreciate Mozart's talents. Consequently his Diary entry concerning the first performance of the *Harmoniemesse* on the Feast of the Birth of the Virgin, 8 September, is particularly valuable.

> Mercredi 8 Septembre. C'était le jour de fête de la Princesse, en conséquence de 10 heures nous allâmes chez elle dans le grand uniforme d'Eisenstadt, puis en grand cortège de beaucoup de voitures à la Messe. – Messe superbe, nouvelle musique excellente du fameux Haydn et dirigé par lui (il est toujours au service du Prince). – Rien de plus beau et de mieux exécuté; après la messe retour au château et cour plenière des souverains pour leurs nombreux sujets, qui vinrent les complimenter. (C'est réellement comme à St. James.) Ensuite diner immense et magnifique, aussi excellent que nombreux, musique pendant le repas. Santé de la Princesse portée par le Prince, et répondue par les fanfares et canons, – plusieurs ensuite, telle que la mienne, et celle de Haydn dinant avec nous et proposée par moi.
>
> Après le diner on se mit en frac pour le bal, qui fut réellement superbe, comme un bal de Cour, la princesse Marie l'ouvrit par un menuet à quatre avec sa fille. On ne fit ensuite que valser. . . .
>
> Jeudi 9 Septembre. On partit à 9 heures pour la chasse, après avoir réveillé par les cors . . . nous eumes ensuite un concert superbe dirigé par Haydn et composé des plus beaux morceaux de la messe de la veille. Après le souper je pris congé des habitants d'Eisenstadt, et revint fort content de mon voyage, à 4 heures du matin, chez mon père en ville, et me couchai.

Here is a picture quite different from that of even a few years earlier. Haydn, we see, is now dining at the same table as the *Herrschaften* while the musicians (under Fuchs, perhaps) play *Tafelmusik*; and a distinguished diplomat proposes the toast to Haydn. Within his lifetime, then, he had seen the complete transformation from a servant in livery, literally kissing the hem of the Prince's garment, to a distinguished artist asked to dine with the Prince, the Princess and their guests, and the object of affection and adulation. Haydn had accomplished this transformation modestly but no less thoroughly; and it must have been a source of quiet satisfaction to the son of the Rohrau wheelwright and the castle cook.

Except for a march and the unfinished Quartet ('Op. 103') this performance closes the long chronicle of Haydn's new works.

Haydn may have told the Prince that this latest Mass had cost him untold effort and that it would probably be his last. Esterházy, whose gradual mellowing *vis-à-vis* his world-famous *Kapellmeister* was partly the work of his wife, Princess Marie Hermenegild, and partly the result of Haydn's own tact, now did a charming act of homage to his old and faithful servant. In the documents of the Esterházy Archives we read:

> To my First Wine Steward Springer
> Since I have herewith decided to issue to my *Kapellmeister Hrn* Haydn a *gratis* annual amount of six Eimer of princely table wine from the first inst., this information is hereby given to my First Wine Steward Springer and to the further cognizance of the Cellar Assistant Graf.
> Vienna, 12th December 1802. exp. Esterházy.
> [Valkó II, 622]

Although the document is dated December 1802, it seems clear that it was the resounding success of the *Harmoniemesse* that produced this generous *pourboire* (in the words's ancient and literal sense).

During the time that Haydn was at Eisenstadt, his brother wrote a letter to Sigismund Neukomm:

[*German. 'Sie' form*]

Salzburg, 16th September 1802.

My very dearest Cousin!

You have given me such pleasure with your work, so excellently produced in every respect, that I do not know how to begin to thank you nor how to end, either. The Quartets[1] will bring you the greatest honour also in the far, far future, because you have been able to put such a fully orchestrated work as *The Seasons* into four single voices without the finest connoisseur being able to miss anything. The piano reduction[2] is masterly, but has also turned out to be very difficult (without even mentioning anything of the fugues, it is enough to look at page 154); but a diligent, fiery player will not give up until he has mastered all the difficulties; and for the other, lazy persons you won't have written it. Do you know that I owe you another very great debt of thanks for the most favourite rondo variations in F from *The Creation*? A few days ago I came across them by accident and since then I can hardly play them enough, so delighted am I with them. Finally I must tell you that I asked your worthy father to lend me *die letzte Nacht*. In this piece you have shown that you are a man and a master, and I congratulate you from my heart for your increased knowledge.

If I can serve you with any of my works and if they could be of use to you, I shall be pleased to do so at any time.

My compliments to the whole Milder family, especially my very best Mademoiselle Nanett, and live well and happily!

I am with the most complete respect,

Your sincere Friend,
Joh: Michael Haydn.[3]

[Address:] De Salzbourg
a Monsieur
Monsieur Sigismond
Neukom͞, Maitre de la
Musique e mon très-cher ami
à Vienne
Abzugeben auf der
Wien in der Jägergasse
No. 20

[Neukomm's hand:] Received on 19th September [*Herbsten*] 802. Ans'd 23rd——.

Haydn did not tarry this year in Eisenstadt, and by 22 September[4] he was back in Vienna; on that day he wrote a long letter which has subsequently become one of the composer's most famous documents.

---

1 Neukomm's arrangement of *The Seasons* for quartet was issued by Artaria of Vienna (later Mollo); in the German edition, by Simrock, we read 'par S. Neukomm, approuvés par l'Auteur' (Hoboken II, 61). The Viennese edition was announced in June 1802.

2 Neukomm's piano score was also issued by Artaria, in July 1802.

3 This letter, auctioned at Sotheby's, is now owned by Mr Albi Rosenthal, London and Oxford, who kindly supplied me with a complete transcription. The letter is unpublished.

4 Two Haydn letters are dated Vienna, 22 September 1802. Yet Griesinger, when he returned from his long sojourn in Störmthal, wrote a letter to Breitkopf & Härtel dated Vienna, 23 October, in which he reports that Haydn is still in Eisenstadt. There would seem to be two explanations for this discrepancy: (1) the two letters, being in the nature of 'official' rather than personal documents, were signed and dated Vienna so as not to confuse the recipients (Haydn's principal correspondence obviously took place from the Kleine Steingasse in Vienna and not from the Esterházy Castle in Eisenstadt); (2) Haydn came up to Vienna for a few days on or about 22 September and later returned to Eisenstadt; this procedure obtained in 1801, for example, when he went up to Vienna to fetch his brother Johann Michael from Salzburg.

[To Jean Phillip Krüger on behalf of the members of the *Musikverein* in Bergen, on the Island of Rügen, North Germany. *German*. Only the signature autograph]
Gentlemen,

It was indeed a most pleasant surprise to receive such a flattering letter from a part of the world where I could never have imagined that the products of my poor talents were known. But when I see that not only is my name familiar to you, but my compositions are performed by you with approval and satisfaction, the warmest wishes of my heart are fulfilled: to be considered a not wholly unworthy priest of this sacred art by every nation where my works are known. You reassure me on this point as regards your fatherland, but even more, you happily persuade me – and this cannot fail to be a real source of consolation to me in my declining years – that I am often the enviable means by which you, and so many other families sensible of heartfelt emotion, derive, in their homely circle, their pleasure – their enjoyment. How reassuring this thought is to me! – Often, when struggling against the obstacles of every sort which oppose my labours: often, when the powers of mind and body weakened, and it was difficult for me to continue in the course I had entered on; – a secret voice whispered to me: 'There are so few happy and contented peoples here below; grief and sorrow are always their lot; perhaps your labours will once be a source from which the care-worn, or the man burdened with affairs, can derive a few moments' rest and refreshment.' This was indeed a powerful motive to press onwards, and this is why I now look back with cheerful satisfaction on the labours expended on this art, to which I have devoted so many long years of uninterrupted effort and exertion. And now I thank you in the fulness of my heart for your kindly thoughts of me, and beg you to forgive me for delaying my answer so long: enfeebled health, the inseparable companion of the grey-haired septuagenarian,[1] and pressing business, deprived me till now of this pleasure. Perhaps nature may yet grant me the joy of composing a little memorial for you, from which you may gather the feelings of a gradually dying veteran, who, even after his death, would fain survive in the charming circle of which you draw so wonderful a picture. I have the honour to be, with profound respect.

Your wholly obedient servant,
Joseph Haydn [m.p] ria.

Vienna, 22nd September 1802.

[Address:]   de Vienne

    [in another hand:] Portstrasse 21
              b Dammas
  A Monsieur
  Monsieur Jean Phillip Krüger
  Doctor Medicinae und königl. Assessor
  des Collegii Sanitatis in Stockholm.
           a
          Bergen
          auf der
         Insel Rügen
     IN SCHWEDISCH POMMERN

[CCLN, 208–10]

Nohl, when he published this letter (*Musiker-Briefe*, Leipzig 1867, p. 168), found the son of one of the men who had been responsible for the 'flattering letter' which had

---

1   On the left-hand margin, someone has written 'geb[oren] 1732'.

been sent to Haydn. When the local music society of Bergen performed *The Creation* for the first time, the effect was great and Dr Krüger toasted Haydn afterwards to general applause, especially when he proposed to write a letter of thanks and gratitude to the composer; which letter was immediately written and mailed.

The second letter written by Haydn on 22 September was addressed to Frau Naumann in Dresden:

> [To Frau Naumann,[1] Dresden. *German.* Only the signature and postscript autograph]
> Well born,
> Most esteemed Frau von Naumann!
>
>   Above all, I must beg your forgiveness a thousand times for the fact that my answer to your kind and esteemed letter arrives much later than duty and politeness would normally allow. My enfeebled state, and likewise pressing duties for my Prince, deprived me of this pleasure; perhaps I am now branded in your eyes as a heartless friend. Certainly, my esteemed lady, I feel to the depths of my heart the loss which you and the sweetest of all the arts have suffered in your husband's death, and irreplaceable is the position in which this noble priest served this beautiful godhead, to general applause. The whole of Europe had but one voice, and that was the praise and approbation which your late husband's undeniable merits inspired in everyone. It would be presumptuous of me to imagine that my voice could possibly add anything to the deceased's fame; it would be an echo of the opinion which every connoisseur and expert has already expressed about the immortal works of Naumann. This opinion founded his deserved reputation, and ensures that your late husband will continue to live forever. The general voice of opinion is the voice of God, and is more important than that of an individual, especially when the latter is in agreement with the general voice of opinion. The biographer has enough material to erect a worthy monument to the deceased without requiring my opinion; this monument will be based on the truth and the agreement of all the experts. I have the honour to be, with every esteem,
>
> Your wholly obedient servant,
Joseph Haydn [m.p] ria.
>
> Vienna, 22nd September 1802.
>
> P. S. Her Majesty the Empress has demanded to see that most magnificent Opera, *Aci und Galatea*.[2] I will tell you more about this in my next letter.
>
> [CCLN, 210f.]

On 30 September we read in Rosenbaum's Diary the following: 'Windy. Today there is a benefit performance of *The Creation* for Schuppanzigg [*sic*] at 12 noon in the Augarten; admission 2 gulden . . .' (Radant, *Rosenbaum*, 103). Schuppanzigh also inserted an advertisement about the concert in the *Wiener Zeitung* (No. 77, 25 September 1802).

Early in October, the Parisian *Concert des Amateurs* reminded Haydn of a promise he had made (perhaps verbally, through one of his colleagues such as Steibelt) to compose a new symphony for the organization. In the event, he sent them a parcel of valuable church music (see letter of 11 January 1803, *infra*).

---

1 The widow of Johann Gottlieb Naumann, who had died at Dresden in October 1801. She had asked Haydn to contribute an essay to Naumann's biography in the form of a musical judgement of his works.
2 The full title of the Opera is: *Aci e Galatea, ossia, i cyclopi amanti.*

[To Haydn from the *Concert des Amateurs*, Paris. *French*]

Paris, 7th October 1802.

Monsieur,

The six months which have elapsed since our concerts of the past winter have not been able to make us forget the success which we gained by performing your sublime compositions, nor the promise you were kind enough to give us, that you would go to the trouble of writing a symphony for us, to the execution of which we would devote the care proportionate to our gratitude. It would be difficult indeed for us to pass over in silence a favour which would bring us such honour. The whole of Paris will soon know that you have flattered us with this hope: a hope which permits us to extend invitations to all those who wish to participate, and to those who ardently wish to attend. Consider, *Monsieur*, how many people you would delight if you were to respond to this universal enthusiasm by offering to the public, as the overture of our next concert series, a new *chef d'oeuvre* which would reassure them, and no less ourselves, as to the state of your health. We await a favourable answer with keen expectation.

Please forgive, *Monsieur*, this insistence, which would perhaps appear indiscreet if it were not the result of our love for that which counts the most in the art which is our profession, and the expression of our veneration for your genius.

We have the honour to be, with the highest esteem,

Monsieur,

The members of the committee of the
Concert des Amateurs.

de Bondy	Frederic Rousseau
Brollet [?] [Grasset?]	Bréval [Brevas?]
Plantade	Frederic Duvernoy

[CCLN, 211]

The long war with France was beginning to have a very detrimental effect on the Austrian currency – a situation which would, after Haydn's death, lead the State to bankruptcy. We read in Rosenbaum's Diary:

Friday, 8th October ... The government bonds are sinking day by day; today the 5% banknotes at a loss of $10\frac{1}{2}$%. The 12 Kreuzer notes are often exchanged for 10 Kreuzer, but only until 20th Oct., then they go down to 9 Kreuzer. Unpleasant prospects! – The inflation becomes greater every day, and with it the lack of ready money. – With the metamorphosis of the 12 Kreuzer notes down to 7 they are scarcely able to cover the most basic needs. [Radant, *Rosenbaum*, 103]

The steadily increasing inflation was, of course, the reason that so many of the Esterházy musicians petitioned for higher salaries, or rather 'additions' (*Zulagen*); usually Haydn was asked for his opinion and invariably he asked the Prince to increase the payments.

Meanwhile Haydn's popularity in Paris had reached that of London in the early 1790s. At the end of October, the Berlin composer and pianist, Friedrich Heinrich Himmel (1765–1814), came to Vienna after a trip to London and Paris; he went to visit Haydn, and Griesinger reports:

... He is not satisfied with London but he cannot grow tired of telling of the enthusiasm with which Haydn's works are received and performed in Paris. He is using all his powers of persuasion to talk Haydn into a trip to Paris. Pleyel has produced a very elegant pocket edition in 8vo of Haydn's Quartets. And can you imagine why? The dilettanti and professionals stick them in their pocket and read them in concerts. [Olleson, *Griesinger*, 40]

Here we have the first miniature scores, an idea that Pleyel was clever enough to invent, at least on a large commercial scale. We shall see that he hastened to send Haydn some samples (see letter of 6 December 1802 from Haydn to Pleyel, *infra*). Griesinger's meetings with Haydn were still concerned with the Last Judgement. Breitkopf & Härtel sent a sample from an opera libretto by Friedrich Rochlitz, editor of the *AMZ*; but Haydn was determined to have his way and refused the Rochlitz text.

10 November 1802.

. . . A libretto for the Last Judgement is still very close to the Papa's heart. Haydn wants to have a word on the subject said to Wieland and Göthe [Goethe], and he intends to use for this purpose his pupil Kranz, who was here recently, and is now *Capellmeister* at Weimar.[1] The text should be rich in pictures but not too long, so that the performance should not last at the most $1\frac{1}{2}$ hours. Haydn would have liked H[err] Rochliz [*sic*] to have done the work [of seeing Wieland and Goethe]. Could he perhaps still be persuaded? It will be easy for him to ascertain if the muses in Weimar are willing to undertake the matter. He hasn't to expect anything for the text from Haydn; but he should refer to Haydn's proposal and send it straight to the Empress, and should dare to find out if his work should carry off the prize among the competitors. Haydn intends to compose [*bearbeiten*] the text that the Empress sends him. . . .

. . . Haydn asks you to send back the last sheets of *The Storm* and the original scores which you have in hand and no longer need. . . .   [Olleson, *Griesinger*, 39]

Meanwhile Swieten had read the announcement of the Mozart arrangement of *Messiah* (in the *AMZ Intelligenz-Blatt* IV of 1802), wherein we read *inter alia* that Mozart had been requested to undertake the work by the Baron, 'that connoisseur and famous protector of all that is excellent in the Arts and especially in Music . . .', etc. Years before, the Baron had, according to Griesinger, 'wrapped himself icily in the cloak of his own convictions' (10 March 1802) and on an even earlier occasion had said 'everyone has his way and he lets each one enjoy it' (21 October 1801). But now, in that same letter of 10 November 1802, we read:

. . . He would have liked that in the announcement of the Handel *Messiah* his name had not been mentioned at all. But he especially forbade it to be mentioned in the Musical Journal [*AMZ*] in connection with *The Seasons*. The text to *The Creation* has been so badly criticized that the good man seems to think that nothing good will come out of his second product. Nevertheless he gave me (I am not exaggerating) a more than one-hour apology about the plan, the execution, the poetry, &c. of that so-called poem. Spare him, if you can, one of the bitterest insults. Would it not be better to review *The Seasons* only as a musical product and leave the text out of it, just as one reviews masses without mentioning the Credo, Miserere, etc.?   [Olleson, *Griesinger*, 39]

Public opinion, which had found the text of *The Creation* admirable in 1798, had now fallen in line with that of the severe German critics; the Viennese knew that they were far behind their German colleagues as far as literary taste and experience was concerned – the Imperial and Royal censor saw to that – and by now Swieten's texts to both Oratorios were in low repute. Added to the Baron's insults was the clear plan, organized by no less a personage than the Empress herself, to bypass him in the choice of the next libretto text for Haydn. The composer and his friends may have tried to keep the plan a secret, but there is little doubt that in a scandal-mongering city like Vienna someone must have passed on the plan to the Baron.

1 Johann Friedrich Kranz who, in fact, had left his position in June.

At the end of November Haydn sent his last completed instrumental work, the 'Hungarischer National Marsch' (VIII: 4), to an oboist of the Princely *Feldharmonie* with the following interesting letter about its performance:

[To Jacob Hyrtl (Hiertl),[1] Eisenstadt. *German*]

Vienna, 28th November 1802.

Dearest Hiertl,

Yesterday I sent you a new military March[2] by my copyist Elsler,[3] but forgot to write you that in case the following passage

should prove too difficult, you can play it as follows

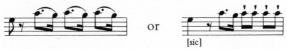

I leave it to your judgement, and recommend a good rehearsal; but you mustn't change anything in the clarinet part.

Meanwhile I remain your obedient servant,

Jos: Haydn.

[Address:] [Haydn's seal 'JH']
Monsieur
Monsieur HIERTL Musicien de
S: Alt: Monseig. le Prince Esterhazy
a
Eisenstadt.

[CCLN, 211f.]

Breitkopf & Härtel were now preparing the third Haydn Mass of their series, the *Missa in angustiis* ('Nelson' Mass), and having procured a pirated copy, they were obviously surprised to see the elaborate solo organ part and the lack of wind instruments (except for the three trumpets and kettledrums). They urged Griesinger to find out about the matter, and they now received the following reply:

4 December 1802.

Most excellent Friend!

Haydn told me that in the Mass you wrote about he actually put the wind instruments into the organ part, because at that time the Prince Eszterházy had dismissed the woodwind players. He advised you, however, to take everything which is obbligato in the organ part and transfer it to the wind instruments, and to print it in that way . . . [Olleson, *Griesinger*, 40]

As we have seen, Breitkopf printed the work in the manner Haydn had suggested, but apart from that, their edition is very faulty from the textual standpoint (see *Haydn: the Years of 'The Creation' 1796–1800*, pp. 429f.).

1 Jacob Hyrtl oboist in the Princely 'Feldharmonie' (hunting wind-band).
2 The autograph is in the Esterházy Archives, Budapest.
3 Johann Elssler [*recte*].

On 6 December Haydn had occasion to write to his old pupil, Ignaz Pleyel, in Paris:

[To Ignaz Pleyel, Paris. *German, 'Du' form*]

Vienna, 6th December 1802.

Dearest Pleyel,

The bearer of this letter is one of my pupils in composition, by the name of Haensel,[1] a charming young man of the best character, and also a good violin player. He has asked me to introduce him to you, so that if necessary you can lend him a helping hand. You will see how talented he is by examining his three new Quartets.[2] He is in the service of the Polish Princess Lubomirsky, and for that reason I suggest that you treat him kindly. Incidentally, I am much obliged to you for the exceptionally beautiful edition of the Quartets[3] which you sent by Herr Pichl:[4] because of their beautiful engraving, the paper – and the fact that they are so correct – as well as their general appearance, you will be remembered for them forever. It's only a pity that two sheets of the quartet version of *The Seven Words* in the small format, which I bought from Pichl for 52 fl., are wanting. I therefore asked Herr Pichl to write and ask you to replace the missing sheets. Recently I received still another proof of your industry from Herr Himmel[5] in Berlin: 3 Quartets and one Sinfonia in E flat in pocket size.[6] One can't imagine anything more beautiful and elegant; Heaven reward you for your pains! You thus increase my musical talent, and yours! I only wish I could brush away 10 years of my old age, so that I could still send you some new compositions of mine – perhaps it will happen yet! Meanwhile farewell, and love your old Haydn, who was always your friend, and always will be. Amen.

Joseph Haydn.

My compliments to your kind wife.

My Prince will arrive in Paris towards the end of this month: go and see him. Please go and retrieve the letter, addressed to me, which has been sitting in the post-office for a long time, and send it to me here.

[Address][7]

[CCLN, 212f.]

In the Chronicle of the past year, it will have been noted that Beethoven's name hardly figures any longer in Haydn's life. But Beethoven's enmity had, if anything, grown; in a letter from Griesinger to Breitkopf & Härtel of 8 December we read: 'He [Beethoven] did not have the common education of many of his colleagues and is incapable of selling for the second time a manuscript for which he has been paid once. Papa Haydn has prostituted himself enough in this respect. . . .' (Günter Thomas, 'Griesingers Briefe über Haydn', *Haydn-Studien* I [1966], Heft, 2, p. 100). This is, of

---

1 Peter Haensel (1770–1831), whose chamber music, published by Artaria and others, achieved considerable fame in his lifetime.
2 Probably Artaria's Op. 8 (pl. no. 865), in F minor, C and G, published – with the composer's portrait – in 1801.
3 Pleyel's collected edition of Haydn's Quartets in parts.
4 Wenzel Pichl (1741–1805), a prolific composer whose works were frequently confused with Haydn's. See Landon *Sym.*, Appendix II, Nos. 1, 61, 72, 85, 106 – five spurious Haydn Symphonies written by Pichl.
5 Friedrich Heinrich Himmel. He had conducted a performance of *The Creation* there on 5 January 1801.
6 Pleyel issued two Haydn Symphonies in miniature score: Nos. 99 and 103. Probably Haydn saw the latter, which was the first of Pleyel's series. It is hard to say which of the Quartets Haydn received.
7 Address: this letter, on exhibition in the Maison Pleyel, Paris, is framed so securely that we could not, without destroying the frame, remove the letter to see the exact address. It is probably similar to that of 4 May 1801.

course, a classic case of the pot calling the kettle black; but at this point, and in 1803, Beethoven's animosity towards his old teacher was at its zenith. But if Haydn was (as we shall see in the Chronicle for 1803) genuinely hurt by this bizarre attitude, he must have been genuinely impressed by the list of Beethoven's works published in 1802 (*WZ = Wiener Zeitung*; all dates 1802 unless otherwise stated):

Op. 19 piano Concerto in B flat (*WZ* 16 Jan.)
Op. 20 Septet (*WZ* 24 July)
Op. 21 Symphony No. 1 (*WZ* 16 Jan.)
Op. 22 piano Sonata (*WZ* 3 April)
Op. 23 Sonata for piano and violin (*WZ* 28 Oct. 1801)
Op. 24 Sonata for piano and violin (ditto)
Op. 25 Serenade for flute, violin and viola (Spring)
Op. 26 piano Sonata (*WZ* 3 March)
Op. 27/1 piano Sonata (*WZ* 3 March)
Op. 27/2 piano Sonata (ditto)
Op. 28 piano Sonata (*WZ* 14 Aug.)
Op. 29 string Quintet in C (Dec.)
Op. 30 Three Sonatas for piano and violin (*WZ* 28 May)

[From the Kinsky-Halm *Verzeichnis*]

It is a formidable list, containing as it does some of Beethoven's most popular works (Septet, 'Moonlight' Sonata, First Symphony) and which established him, together with the old Haydn, as the leading composers in Europe. Although Beethoven did not realize it, from 1803 he was to be alone; Haydn's life-work was now finished and he was no competition to Beethoven at all. But it would take several years for that fact to become public.

We hear more about Haydn's proposed Paris visit in a letter from Griesinger to Härtel:

. . . I already told you that Himmel tried to persuade Haydn to undertake a trip to Paris; in the heat of the discussion Haydn said he would go if the travelling costs were covered. Himmel took this seriously, wrote to Paris and in a few days Haydn received an invitation from an amateur concert and a transfer of 4,400 fl. for the trip. He won't accept it but the ardour of the French flattered him. . . .

Haydn gave Prince Esterházy, who is leaving for Paris in a few days, a Mass to deliver to the Conservatoire[1] which sent him a medal. . . .

On 20 December 1802 Haydn submitted a bill (*Specification*) to the Esterházy administration for various expenses incurred in the past few months:

---

1 Actually *Concert des Amateurs*: see letter of 11 January 1803, and footnote, p. 252.

[To Prince Nicolaus II Esterházy. *German*]
Specification
Various expenses which I have had in the service of His Serene Highness for the
year 1802 (see attached list), *viz.*:

The cost of copying my last new Mass together with that for 8 voices by my brother Michael, together[1]	71 Fl.	10 xr.
A new March for the wind players[2]	1 Fl.	—
For the music of the late Rector in Eisenstadt[3]	60 Fl.	—
For the trip to Eisenstadt and back by the Extra Post	22 Fl.	—
Total	154 Fl.	10 xr.

Vienna, 20th December 1802.   Joseph Haydn mpria
Kapellmeister

[There follows Prince Esterházy's approval, dated 26 December and underneath
Haydn's receipt for payment:]
I hereby certify that I have received the above-listed sum of 154 Fl. 10 xr. from the
Princely General Disbursar correctly and in cash

Joseph Haydn mpria
Kapellmeister
[not in CCLN; from Bartha, 417]

On 22 and 23 December, Haydn conducted the Christmas concert of the
Tonkünstler-Societät: on this occasion *The Seasons* was given with the same soloists as
in April (Saal, Rathmayer, Saal). Rosenbaum (104) went twice, and so did Zinzendorf
(Olleson, 61). On 23 December the Count adds a rather cryptic reference to a friend
named Kinigl (or Künigl?): '. . . A 7$^{h.}\frac{1}{2}$ passé au Concert des Saisons. J'assistois avec
plus de connoissance de cause, ayant Kinigl dans la loge. la Chasse, la Vendange, la
fui pathétique, la difficulté de l'execution. . . .'
A few days later there was a benefit performance of *The Creation*. We learn from
Rosenbaum (104): 'Sunday, 26th [Dec.]: St Stephen's day . . . From 12 until 2 o'clock
The Creation was performed in the Redouten Sall [*sic*] under Haydn's direction, a
benefit performance for the townspeople of the St Marx district.' The *Wiener Zeitung*
(No. 10, 2 February 1803) noted that 'there was an exceptionally large number of
generous patrons, and the income . . . grew to a very considerable sum.' The income
was 4,505 fl., the costs for the lighting 230 fl.[4] A Russian visitor, Andrei Ivanovich
Turgenev, was present and wrote to his brother, Alexander: 'Yesterday, my dear
brother, I heard *The Creation* here which Hayden [*sic*] himself conducted. With the
greatest pleasure I heard, felt and understood all that the music expressed.' The
brothers had a regular exchange of correspondence, and A. I. Turgenev, who was
studying at Göttingen, kept a diary. He heard a 'mignature' performance of the work
at Göttingen and remembered how much more impressive the work had been in
Moscow 'when in that half-lighted, gigantic Rotunda the creative word "It was
[light]" thundered forth'. In November he heard *The Seasons* and thought 'not only
the music but also the poetry are glorious [*wunderschön*] – et ceux, qui l'ont executé de
même.'[5] It took a Russian to find the libretto equal to the music . . .

1 The *Harmoniemesse* and Michael Haydn's *Missa Solemnis*, mentioned in the letter of Prince Esterházy
dated 21 June 1802.
2 The 'Hungarischer National Marsch' (see letter of 28 Nov., *supra*).
3 Carl Kraus (*supra*, p. 219).
4 Hanns Jäger-Sunstenau, *op. cit.*, p. 134.
5 Boris Steinpress in *Haydn-Studien* II/2, pp. 91f.

1 Joseph Haydn, life-size lead bust (c. 1800), attributed – by Haydn's biographer, Dies – to Anton Grassi and, recently, to F. C. T(h)aller, who modelled the famous wax busts of the composer (reproduced in *Haydn: the Years of 'The Creation' 1796–1800*, pls. I, 1 and 2). This lead bust was bequeathed by Haydn to Count Harrach, and is still preserved in the Harrach family's castle at Rohrau, the village where Haydn was born.

2 Joseph Haydn, bust in unglazed porcelain by Anton Grassi, 1802; height, c. 40 cm. (16 in.). Cf. p. 90.

Opposite, above
3 Joseph Haydn, engraving by David
Weiß (1810), after a wax medallion
by Sebastian Irrwoch (or Irwach),
c. 1803. The engraving was used by
Dies as the frontispiece to his authentic
biography of Haydn (Vienna 1810),
and the portrait was also considered a
good likeness by Georg August
Griesinger. One of the medallions by
Irrwoch, signed 'Irwach sc. 1803 Vienna',
was in the possession of Haydn's friend
Frederik Samuel Silverstolpe and is
now in the family castle at Näs,
Sweden; another, now lost, was
owned by Haydn himself.

Opposite, below
4 Joseph Haydn, miniature by Christian
Horneman, *c.* 1803 (lost); cf. p. 274.

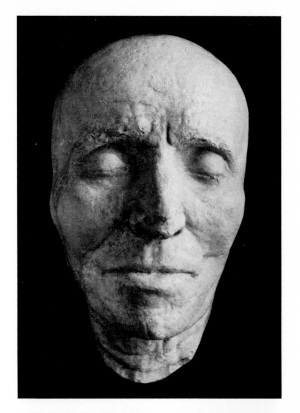

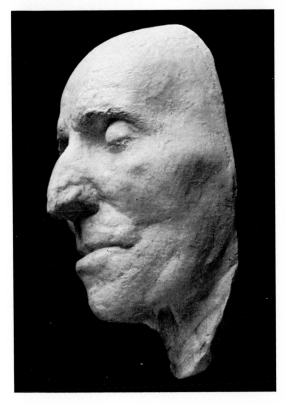

5, 6 Joseph Haydn, front and profile
views of the death-mask (1809) by
Johann Elssler.

7 The Kaiserliche Hofbibliothek (Imperial Court Library), Vienna; coloured engraving by Carl
Schütz, 1798. The square depicted, which still exists, was subsequently renamed the Josephsplatz and,
shortly before Haydn's death, a large equestrian statue of the Emperor (Francis I; cf. pl. 26) was erected
there. This engraving shows the famous Redoutensaal (on the right-hand side of the main building).
Haydn's patron and librettist, Baron Gottfried van Swieten, was Court Librarian.

8 Haydn's house in the Kleine Steingasse, in the Gumpendorf suburb of Vienna; lithograph, after a
drawing by Berndt, 1840, from the *Denkschrift* published on the occasion of the twenty-fifth anniversary of the founding of the Gesellschaft der Musikfreunde, Vienna.

9, 10 Eisenstadt: view of the town (above), seen from the roof of the Esterházy Castle (below); photographs taken in 1909.

The town of Eisenstadt changed little in the hundred years following Haydn's death, and in 1909 most of the houses in the main street leading from the castle into the town remained much as Haydn had known them.

11 Autograph of a letter from Haydn to G. A. Griesinger, written at Eisenstadt, 1 July 1801 (for translation see p. 61).

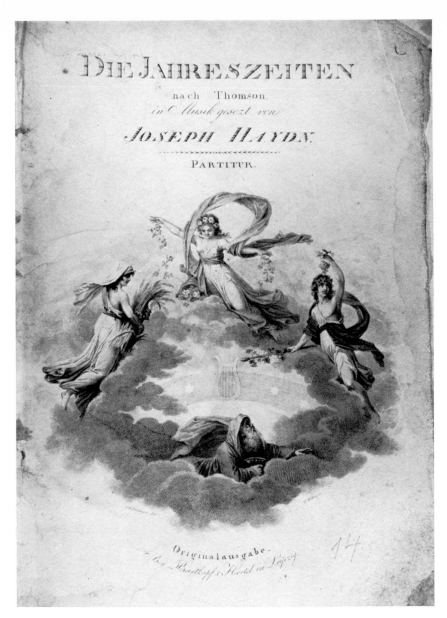

12 Title page of the first edition in score of *The Seasons*, published by Breitkopf & Härtel, Leipzig, in 1802.

13–18 The first six music plates, showing hunting calls, from M. de Changran's famous *Manuel du Chasseur*, published in Paris in 1772 and reprinted in 1780 and 1785. Many of the horn calls used by Haydn in the hunting chorus of *The Seasons* may be observed here, some almost note for note, some in a local (Austrian?) variant form; cf. pp. 167–77. The final example, 'L'Ancienne Vue', was used by Haydn in the Overture to *La fedeltà premiata* (1780) and in its derivative, the Finale of Symphony No. 73 ('La Chasse').

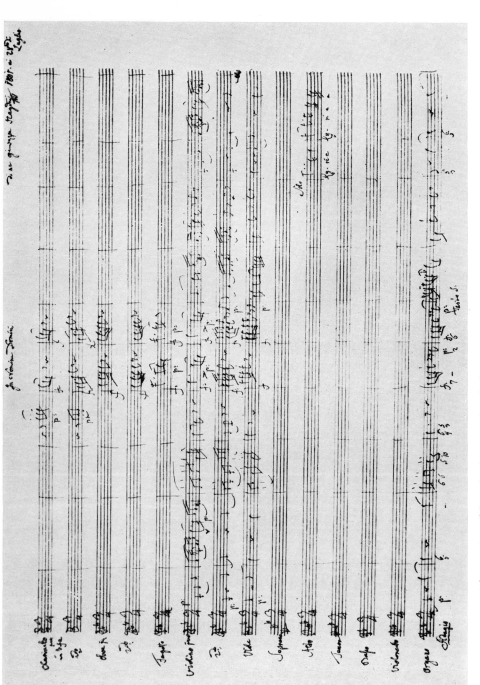

19 The opening of the *Schöpfungsmesse* (1801), from Haydn's autograph; the parts for horns, trumpets and kettledrums were written on separate sheets because there was no room for them on the page.

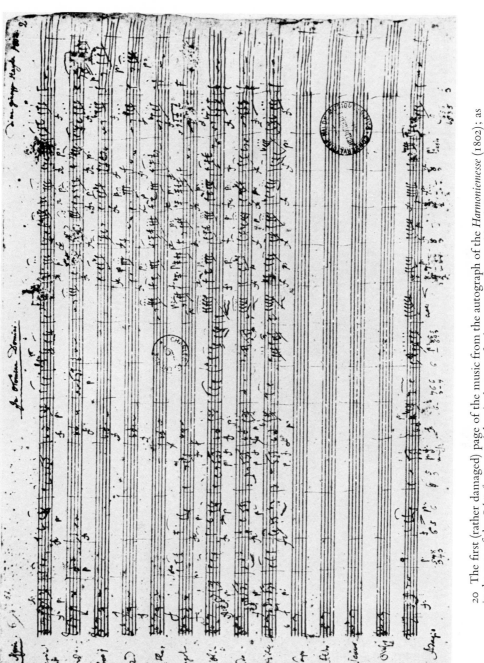

20 The first (rather damaged) page of the music from the autograph of the *Harmonienmesse* (1802); as in the case of the *Schöpfungsmesse* (pl. 19), the parts for horns, trumpets and kettledrums were written on separate sheets.

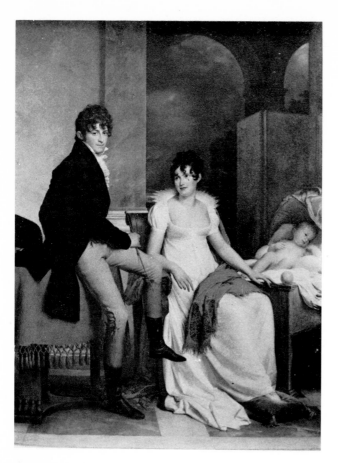

21 Moritz, Count Fries, and his family; painting in oils by François Gérard.

22 Soirée at the Palace of Moritz, Count Fries, in Vienna; drawing by J. Fischer, 1800. Haydn often participated at such soirées; his unfinished String Quartet in D minor ('Op. 103') of 1803 was dedicated to the Count.

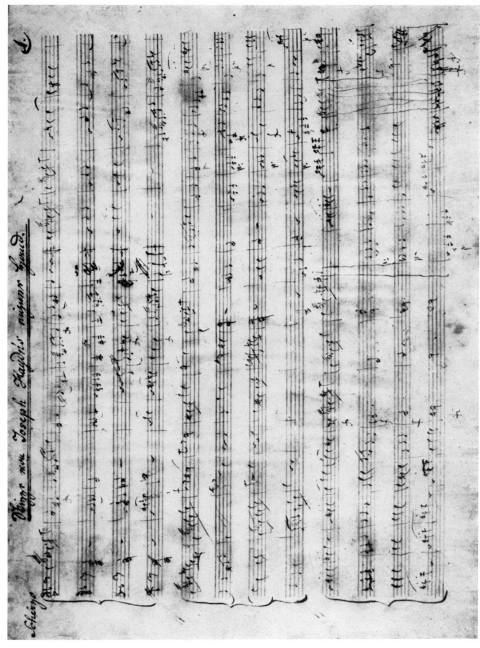

23 The unfinished String Quartet ('Op. 103'); Haydn's sketch in full score for the beginning of the Minuet. The title 'Scherzo' and the words 'Skizze von Joseph Haydn's eigener Hand' have been added in an unknown hand.

Opposite, above
24 Paul Wranizky, who led the
orchestras in the first performances
of Haydn's late Oratorios;
engraving by Heinrich Philipp
Boßler.

Opposite, below
25 Christian Fürchtegott Gellert
(1715–69), anonymous miniature
(oils on copper); Gellert was
Haydn's favourite German poet,
and the composer set many of
his poems to music.

Above
26 Franz (Francis) I, Emperor of
Austria, portrait in oils by Peter
Krafft, formerly owned by
Emperor Franz Joseph of Austria.

27 Archduke Carl of Austria,
portrait in pen-and-ink and wash
heightened with white, by
Vincenz Georg Kininger, *c.* 1797.

28 Luigi Cherubini, who first met Haydn in Vienna in 1805 (cf. pp. 335, 343); anonymous stippled engraving published by Artaria & Co., 1805.

29 Antonio Polzelli, youngest son of Luigia Polzelli (Haydn's former mistress) and pupil of the composer; stippled engraving by F. Dirnbacher, after a drawing by Lanzadelli. Cf. pp. 230, 358.

CHAPTER FOUR

Works of 1802

Hungarischer National Marsch
(VIII: 4)

Critical edition: *Joseph Haydn – Sämtliche Werke für Blasinstrumente – Märsche*. Scores, edited by the present writer, Verlag Doblinger, Vienna-Munich, 1960 (Diletto Musicale No. 34). Based on the autograph manuscript, signed and dated 'Jos: Haydn mpria 8̄0̄2̄', in the Esterházy Archives of the National Széchényi Library, Budapest, Ms. mus. I. 43 [a]. Complete facsimile in *Haydn Compositions in the Music Collection of the National Széchényi Library, Budapest, Published on the Occasion of the 150th Anniversary of Haydn's Death (1809–1959)*, Budapest 1960, pp. 48–51 (also in Hungarian and German with different pagination). Scoring: 2 oboes, 2 clarinets in B♭, 2 bassoons, 2 horns in E♭, 1 trumpet in E♭.

Haydn was always inclined to allow his players to make small – or even larger – changes in his pieces for the *Feldharmonie*. It is extraordinary to observe all the changes in his Marches for the Derbyshire Cavalry Regiment (London 1795). In No. 1 (p. 8 of our publication, *supra*) the changes between autograph and first edition are so great that we could not even include them as footnotes, a procedure which was possible in No. 2 (ibid., p. 9). Almost all the changes concern changes of instrumental colour (e.g. the trumpet's crotchets changed to minims, which means it sings through the texture as it did not before: see No. 2, bar 5). Thus when Haydn allows his oboe player to simplify the difficult passage in the 'Hungarian National March' (bar 26), he was only following an old Haydnesque tradition. In fact, the amusing thing is that the passage as quoted in the letter (*supra*, p. 237) is the (transposed) version of the clarinet; the oboe has already a simplified version, *viz.*

It is interesting to note that Haydn allowed nothing in the clarinet part to be changed. We are witnessing, here, the last dying echoes of that improvised performance practice that flourished in Baroque times, and where the performer was allowed to make such changes as he found necessary or desirable.

Haydn's last independent instrumental work is orchestrated with all the panache and attention to the colour of the instruments, separately and together, which have been hallmarks of the composer's style for half a century. Enough to remark on the way he writes for the trumpet, giving him his top notes (*b* flat″) in the first half, and precisely at bars 3, 8, 9 and 11, and otherwise only once, at the beginning of the second part (bar 16): Haydn is characteristically saving the trumpeter's lip and giving him the hard notes when he is still fresh. The fine use of the horns in their lowest tessitura, always as a pedal point, may also be briefly noted. It is unusual that there is no serpent part, but that instrument was perhaps becoming obsolete in Austrian military bands.

The Hungarian aspect of this short March can be seen in two characteristic figures: the cadential pattern

which happens twice (bars 4 and 12), and the 'Gypsy' snap

The figure marked with an arrow appears several times and culminates in the bar Haydn quoted in his letter (which also happens to be the *ff* climax of the little work). Haydn was the first great composer to introduce Hungarian (Gypsy) elements into his music and it is fitting that this, his last completed instrumental composition, should be a final tribute to the country in which he had passed the greater part of his adult life.

Missa ('Harmoniemesse') **in B flat major**
(XXII: 14)

Basic scoring: 1 flute, 2 oboes, 2 clarinets in B♭, 2 bassoons, 2 horns in B♭, 2 trumpets in B♭, timpani in B♭-F, strings, organ, soli (maximum: SSATTB, usually SATB), choir (SATB).

  I Kyrie (*Poco Adagio*): full scoring.
 II Gloria –
    (a) Gloria in excelsis Deo (*Vivace assai*): full scoring but only soprano solo.
    (b) Gratias (*Allegretto*): full scoring.
    (c) Quoniam (*Allegro spiritoso*): full scoring.
III Credo –
    (a) Credo in unum Deum (*Vivace*): full scoring but only tenor and bass soli.
    (b) Et incarnatus est (*Adagio*): full scoring.
    (c) Et resurrexit (*Vivace*): full scoring but no soli.
    (d) Et vitam venturi (*Vivace*): full scoring (with maximum soli).
 IV Sanctus (*Adagio–Allegro*): full scoring.
  V Benedictus (*Allegro molto*): full scoring;
    Osanna (*Allegro*): full scoring but no soli.
 VI Agnus Dei (*Adagio*): 2 oboes, 2 clarinets, 2 bassoons, timpani, strings, organ, soli (SATB);
    Dona nobis pacem (*Allegro con spirito*): full scoring.

Martin Chusid's proposed scheme for dividing the Mass into three vocal symphonies is as follows:[1]

Vocal Symphony No. 1

MVT.	TEXT	TEMPO AND NO. OF BARS	METRE	KEY
I	Kyrie	as *supra* = 130 bars	3/4	B flat major
II	Gloria	as *supra* = 70 bars	4/4	B flat major
III	Gratias	as *supra* = 178 bars	3/8	E flat→G minor
IV	Quoniam	as *supra* = 93 bars	4/4	B flat major

Vocal Symphony No. 2

MVT.	TEXT	TEMPO AND NO. OF BARS	METRE	KEY
I	Credo	as *supra* = 79 bars	4/4	B flat major
II	Et incarnatus	as *supra* = 61 bars	3/4	E flat major
III	Et resurrexit	as *supra* = 70 bars	4/4	C minor→V of G minor
IV	Et vitam	as *supra* = 63 bars	6/8	B flat major

Vocal Symphony No. 3

MVT.	TEXT	TEMPO AND NO. OF BARS	METRE	KEY
I	Sanctus	as *supra* = 28 bars	3/4	B flat major
	Pleni	as *supra* = 38 bars	3/4	B flat major
II	Benedictus	as *supra* = 105 bars	4/4	F major
	Osanna [2]	as *supra* = 33 bars	3/4	B flat major
III	Agnus Dei	as *supra* = 43 bars	3/4	G major→V of G minor
IV	Dona	as *supra* = 168 bars	*alla breve*	B flat major

Critical edition: Reihe XXIII, Band 5, in 'Joseph Haydn Werke' (Haydn Institut), edited by Friedrich Lippmann. This full score was later reduced in size and published as a miniature score by Bärenreiter-Verlag, Kassel. A piano-vocal score, edited by William Herrmann, is published by G. Schirmer, New York (1966).

The principal sources for the work are (a) the autograph, given by Haydn to his pupil Sigismund Neukomm in 1809 and then part of the Conservatoire de Musique (now Bibliothèque Nationale, Paris). The trumpets, drums and horns were written on extra sheets and attached to the back of the autograph proper; (b) the authentic first performance material, Esterházy Archives, Eisenstadt, copied by Elssler and his assistants; (c) the authentic MS. parts by Elssler and his assistants (with two trombone parts, added later), copied for the Hofburgkapelle in Vienna; (d) the authentic parts, by Elssler and his assistants, for the Lobkowitz Archives, now in the National Museum, Prague; (e) the first edition, by Breitkopf & Härtel, in full score, issued in 'Typendruck' in an edition of 600 copies (Brand, 130) as 'Messe . . . Nº VI' (1808).

The first gramophone recording was made in April 1949 for the Haydn Society of Boston with soloists, the Mozarteum Choir and the Mozarteum Orchestra of Salzburg conducted by Joseph Messner (from a tape recording made at the Salzburg Festival in August 1947).

The *Harmoniemesse* has always commanded great respect. It was one of the first Haydn Masses to be reprinted in the twentieth century, in a heavily edited score by Georg Göhler published in 1910 (Rieter-Biedermann, later Peters and Böhm). Although its large wind band (from which the work received its name) prevented frequent performances in the Viennese churches during recent years – such works as the 'Mariazellermesse' or the 'Nelson' Mass were preferred, having a more economical

---

1 Chusid, op. cit., pp. 133f.; reprinted by permission of George Allen & Unwin Ltd.
2 Same material as in the 'Pleni' of the Sanctus.

orchestration – it was one of the few Masses by Haydn to receive a regular performance at the Salzburg Festival (see recording mentioned above).

Haydn did not make things easy for himself with his last completed composition of any size: he begins the Mass with an enormous slow movement, a surging Poco Adagio which rolls on like some mighty river. Here is an entirely new kind of Kyrie: mystical, slow-paced, exalted, but also filled with a sense of nostalgia. This is the real *Spätstil*, a genuine farewell to music. Formally we may discern a faint, sublimated echo of the concerto and sonata forms: the opening is like the orchestral ritornello of a concerto, which leads to an exposition, a middle section, a recapitulation and a kind of coda. But the whole structure of the movement is possibly Haydn's most complex display of interrelated motivic unity. The music develops from itself continually, and this lends the strongest sense of unity to the whole. Since the entire Kyrie is so full of this motivic development, we will only show one characteristic motif. In bars 3/4, the orchestra has

a figure that is given to the solo soprano in bars 22/3. When we reach the dominant, the chorus has a little fugato based on the motif, as follows:

The figure in the tenor part also assumes a role of great importance. The most immediately striking effects of the movement are the choral entrances at the beginning and at the recapitulation: in the beginning it enters in a totally unexpected fashion, not only off-tonic (actually a diminished seventh chord) but where no one could expect it, while in the recapitulation it is 'falsely' prepared by a long series of cadences in the mediant major. The recapitulation is reached simply by moving up the D major triad to B flat

The effect of the first choral entrance (bar 17) must have been stupendous, because in the autograph we read, at the bottom of the page and under that bar:

'NB fortissimo' (the timpani ♩ 𝄾 must, of course, be interpreted ♩ ♩ as elsewhere in Haydn's compositions). In this Mass, we may also see an attempt to link different parts of the work together motivically: the octave skip in the Kyrie, which may be seen in the above example (bar 84) also turns up in the middle of the Gratias, where it is given to the word 'suscipe' (deprecationem nostram), showing that the link is to demonstrate the two sections' emotional similarity and underlying textual closeness: both are two aspects of prayer. The troubled chromaticism of the Kyrie's beginning, with its dense harmonic ambiguity, gives way at the end to a close of great peace: Haydn believed that our prayers are answered.

The soprano solo begins the Gloria with a tune that sounds like a folk melody but is, of course, a characteristic side of the Viennese classical style:

(It has its stylistic antecedents in the Kyrie of the 'Mariazellermesse' where, in the quick part, the solo soprano has a folk-like melody of similar grace and charm.) The chorus now takes over, in the Gloria, supported by a jubilant orchestra with those shining B flat trumpets that give this music such a peculiarly individual timbre. Speaking of the harmonic structure of this Mass, William Herrmann, the editor of the Schirmer edition, writes:

> It will be noted that the chief element of surprise in each of these passages [in the Kyrie] is harmonic. Haydn's harmonic genius, the outstanding characteristic of his late works, is nowhere more evident than in this Mass. In his modulations as well as the key relationships between movements, in his increasing exploitation of dissonance and chromatic alteration, and above all in his use of harmony as a dramatic force, Haydn clearly foreshadows the Romantic century.

When the chorus enters softly with the words, 'Et in terra pax', the score displays one of these forward-looking modulations. In smooth lines, Haydn takes us from the dominant of C via A flat (unison) to F major, then to E flat, C minor, the dominant of D minor, G minor and finally via F major back to the tonic; where we are treated to an angelic concert of woodwind to usher in the words 'Adoramus te'. It is a Renaissance picture of the Heavenly Host surrounded by 'the joyful music-making of the angels' (Brand, 480); we immediately think of the Isenheimer Altar or of Bellini. The end of the movement is swift: Haydn thought it was too swift and added the two bars of orchestral postlude to the finished conclusion in the autograph manuscript.

The moderately quick Gratias, with its three-eight time, has a long and distinguished tradition in earlier Haydn Masses. We find such movements in the *Missa in honorem B. V. M.* (Great Organ Mass) and in the 'Mariazellermesse'; but perhaps the most striking similarity occurs in the *Missa Cellensis in honorem B. V. M.* of 1766 (formerly known, wrongly, as the *Missa Sanctae Caeciliae*). There we have a Gratias in allegro three-eight, starting with an alto solo, then a tenor solo, then a bass solo, then all three together; the entries are separated by orchestral interludes. In the *Harmoniemesse* we have:

> *Ritornello* (12 bars)
> Alto Solo (27 bars)
> *Ritornello* (6 bars)
> Soprano Solo (22 bars)
> *Ritornello* (5 bars)
> Tenor Solo (11 bars)
> Tenor and Bass Solo (10 bars)
> *Ritornello* (9 bars)

The bar lengths are only approximate because of overlapping, but the similarity to the earlier Mass, also in the general style, is striking: the proportions of the 1766 Mass are much longer – it was a so-called 'Cantata Mass' of huge proportions – and the orchestra is much simpler, but otherwise it may have been even a conscious model for the Gratias of the *Harmoniemesse*.

The chorus enters with the words 'Qui tollis' in F minor, Haydn's old key of the Passion. Brand (483) sees in this turbulent passage the scourging of the Saviour. After the long F minor interlude, we modulate to A flat and there appears the 'Suscipe' quotation of the Kyrie referred to earlier. The chorus then continues the 'Qui tollis' music but in G minor and to the words 'Who sitteth on the right hand of the Father'; and in G minor this complex and fascinating middle part of the huge A-B-A form of the Gloria ends.

The third (C) part is the 'Quoniam tu solus sanctus', which flares up in martial grandeur, soon turning into a magnificent double fugue ('In gloria Dei patris' and 'Amen' are the words of the subject and countersubject, respectively). These late-period Haydn fugues are always stirring and splendid, the golden harvest of the great European contrapuntal tradition; how thrilling the entrance of brass and timpani after forty-two bars of rest (they enter, with dazzling *ff*, at bar 315), and how beautifully worked out the interruption of the four soloists just before the closing pages (bar 332), where the kettledrums thunder out the bass of the final cadence! In the interrupted cadence, another detail from the autograph manuscript is significant: to support the unexpected modulation to G minor, Haydn instructs the organ to play 'ff pleno org[ano]'.

The first part of the Credo is once again in that extraordinarily conservative, neo-Baroque manner, with bass patterns

that could be from a work a hundred years earlier. This extreme conservatism is obviously a reflection of Haydn's attitude towards the Credo – see our remarks *supra* in connection with the *Schöpfungsmesse* – and one is reminded of Mozart's letter to his father:

[Vienna, 12 April 1783]

. . .When the weather gets warmer, please make a search in the attic under the roof and send us some of your own church music. You have no reason whatever to be ashamed of it. Baron van Swieten and [the Viennese composer Joseph] Starzer know as well as you and I that musical taste is continually changing – and, *what is more*, that this extends even to church music, which ought not to be the case. Hence it is that true church music is to be found *only* in attics and in a worm-eaten condition. . . .[1]

We find the same 'word-painting', as in the other late Masses (ascendits; descendits; etc.), the same use of dynamic marks to underline the text (et invisibilium has a murmuring string figure, *piano*), and the same careful attention to large structural masses. The climax of this relatively short 'A' section – like the Gloria, Haydn separates the Credo into three movements, fast-slow-fast – is a gorgeous wash of colour, marked *ff*, to symbolize the words 'Deo vero de Deo vero', with the kettledrums slashing through the texture in that rhythm ♩ ♫ ♩♩ which has marked Haydn's timpani writing for forty years and is one of those unmistakable, Berensonian 'fingerprints' by which we may identify an artist's style. (In Mozart, of course, it is rather the marching ♩ ♩.♫ ♩ ♩ which is typical for his brass and timpani writing.)

It was Johann Christian Bach who, it seems, invented the glorious sound of clarinets with orchestra in E flat, as early as 1763 in his Opera *Orione ossia Diana vendicata*; but we tend to associate the concept with Mozart, as no doubt Haydn did, too. The Et incarnatus of the *Harmoniemesse* begins with a clarinet solo of four bars, a sort of ritornello. If we examine the structure of this movement and the one that follows, we will see that Haydn has worked out a kind of *scena* in which tonality, orchestration, and choice of the voice, play a vital role. First we have the proud Virgin Mary (soprano, also note the beautiful woodwind writing at bars 11–13, used to announce the words 'ex Maria virgine'). As she tells us 'et homo factus est' solo horns enter, and later soft trumpets and kettledrums, coinciding with the first important modulation, from E flat to B flat. But the triplets in the orchestra grow restless, as if hinting at the Saviour's fate, and in a strange modulation we find ourselves in G flat major, with the other three soloists (alto, tenor, bass) repeating the words 'et homo factus est'. It is a very uneasy passage and leads directly to the first choral entrance with the words 'Crucifixus', the music shifting in a weird modulation: G flat major, A flat minor, B flat minor, C major. The lower three soloists again appear with the words 'passus et sepultus est', and the music sinks from C minor to E flat. Having reached, after all these wide excursions, the home key, Haydn also reintroduces the solo soprano and the solo clarinet; she repeats 'passus et sepultus est' and at the end is joined by all the other soloists; in the final cadence, the bass soloist symbolizes 'sepultus' by dropping to low E flat.

But Haydn's range is longer than we think. His tonal scheme still continues to develop as the third part of this grand A-B-A plan is put into operation. The Et resurrexit begins vivace in C minor, without horns, trumpets or kettledrums. The words and the music ascend to Heaven (sopranos up to *a* flat), also 'shown' by a wind-band chord which floats serenely across half-a-bar (117) and brings us to E flat. In a modulation of enormous impact, Haydn brings in his brass and timpani to illustrate the judgement of 'the quick and the dead':

1 *The Letters of Mozart and his Family*, ed. Anderson, II, 843.

[Credo, bars 158ff.]

Haydn's tonal scheme is still unfolding slowly: 'cujus regni non erit finis' is in F minor, 'Et in Spiritum Sanctum' in F major moving to G minor, and it is not till bars 185ff. that we move in slow majesty into the tonic ('simul adoratur et conglorificatur, qui locutus est per prophetas'). The passage 'Et unam sanctam catholicam' is set like plainchant, reminding us of a similar treatment in the 'Nelson' Mass. We have again left the tonic and are heading for a cadence on the V of G minor, which Haydn matches with his vivid description of 'Et exspecto resurrectionem mortuorum', the last word being a sudden drop to *piano*.[1] The 'Et vitam venturi' is set as a large-scale fugue, the subject of which enters in the middle of the bar until the fifth entry (bar 231), which is set backwards half-a-bar. It is during this fugue that Haydn brings in six rather than four soloists. The ending is short, as always in Haydn's Masses.

The Sanctus opens with the four soloists in a rapt and solemn atmosphere. The chorus enters majestically at bar 7. Formally, this slow section is worked out rather like A – A[1]. The infinite variety of the work's tonal regions may be seen here *en miniature*. In A[1] the soloists begin as they did at bar 1, but the music suddenly goes in quite a different tonal direction (towards C minor rather than E flat). In the swift section our attention is automatically centred on another prophetic passage:

The abrupt change of harmony at bar 56, the off-beat orchestral *forzati*, and indeed the whole language are like middle-period Beethoven.

What are we to make of the Benedictus? It is marked Allegro molto and starts *pp* like that pre-Mendelssohnian scherzo movement, the Andante più tosto Allegretto of

---

1 This *p* is, oddly enough, totally missing in the Schirmer edition; it should be inserted at bar 205 in all the voices and the orchestra.

Symphony No. 40. The editor of the Schirmer score is clearly embarrassed; he writes: 'The present editor feels . . . that the style of the movement suggests something closer to Allegro moderato'. It is original almost to the point of being bizarre. Not only does the music flash past us, but the whole is pure sonata form, with a luscious second subject in the dominant:

In our example, we have not shown the woodwind, which warbles delightfully with the voices, but the reader may nevertheless see that the whole passage is as Rococo as Vierzehnheiligen or Wilhering Monastery. Once again, we are reminded of a work from Haydn's past: the 'Mariazellermesse', in which the Benedictus contains a second subject of similar richness. That Benedictus was lifted from Haydn's comic opera, *Il mondo della luna*; ours from the *Harmoniemesse* is not from an opera, of course, but it is decidedly not a piece of religious gloom. The Osanna that concludes the movement uses the same music as in the Sanctus.

No one has ever pointed out the similarity between this Agnus Dei and that of Mozart's 'Coronation' Mass (K. 317, of which Haydn's choir owned a set of manuscript parts). It is another Rococo piece, with rich woodwind soli over pizzicato strings: when the four soloists enter the first violin turns to a semiquaver *coll'arco* accompaniment. The choir is silent throughout. Certainly the most famous part of the Mass is the stunningly dramatic transition to the Dona. William Herrmann, writing of this part in the Preface to the Schirmer edition, points out a similar change in the Kyrie and adds: 'Electrifying indeed is the way in which the D and F of the trumpets are made to hang in the air ambiguously for three [bars] until the timpani's B flat triumphantly affirms the true tonic: a dazzling stroke of genius.' In the Dona movement, the writing becomes increasingly contrapuntal for the voices, though there is no strict fugue. At the end there is a dramatic drop to *piano* and we find an extremely ominous harmonic shift to *ff* and angry *g* flat murmurings from the string basses (bar 191) before Haydn brings the music to an unexpected fermata: peace in Austria, and indeed in all of Europe, was the great blessing of 1802, with its Treaty of Amiens; but everyone sensed that the peace was a false one and not destined to last. Perhaps this thought crossed Haydn's mind when writing this strange mood of foreboding just before the triumphant ending, where the sopranos and tenors rise up to high *b* flat and the orchestra brings this last great work to a triumphant close.

Haydn's handwriting on his scores had become very small, very neat, and slightly shaky by this time. But he did not forget to begin this Mass with the words 'In Nomine Domini' and to close the last page with his private note of thanks, 'Laus Deo'.

CHAPTER FIVE

Chronicle 1803

PRINCE NICOLAUS II ESTERHÁZY had gone to Paris, it will be remembered, with a parcel of music for the *Concert des Amateurs*. That institution's reply to Haydn was as follows:

[To Haydn from the *Concert des Amateurs*, Paris. *French*]
Concert des Amateurs
We, the administrators of the *Concert des Amateurs*, declare that His Highness *Monseigneur le Prince* d'Esterhazy had the kindness to deliver to us a letter and a sealed package containing a Mass, an *Offertorium*, and a *Te Deum*[1] composed by the celebrated Joseph Haydn; and that these three works will be deposited in our archives as a souvenir, attesting to the token of esteem which the learned composer has been kind enough to proffer our Society.
Paris ce Vingt un Nivôse an 11 [11 January 1803], de Sorie, Plantade, Brevas [Bréval?] Frederic Duvernoy. de Bondy. Fr. Rousseau.   [CCLN, 213]

What must have been a very interesting correspondence, over the years, between Joseph and his brother Michael Haydn has disappeared, except for the following:

[Draft of a letter to Haydn's brother, Johann Michael, in Salzburg. *German. 'Du' form.*]

Vienna, 22 January 1803[2]
Thank you heartily for all the kind wishes which you once again showed me in your recent letter. I, too, wish it would be within my power to fulfil your wish about my wretched health, which has plagued me for so long. For the last 5[3] months I have been subject to a continual nervous weakness which renders me quite incapable of doing anything. You can easily imagine how terribly this sudden change of health has depressed me, but I am not entirely desperate and hope to God that, when the weather changes, my previous health will be restored to at least half of what it once was.
Your decision, of which you wrote me, concerning His Royal Highness the Archduke and my Prince, is well thought out and bold, but it must cause not only me but the whole world regret.[4] Neither side can reproach you for having done

---

1 Haydn received a medal from the *Concert des Amateurs* (*infra*, p. 255). The music was probably the autograph of the *Schöpfungsmesse* (1801) and the autographs or parts of the *Offertorio in stylo a capella* 'Non nobis Domine' and the great *Te Deum* in C of about 1799. See Brand, p. 413f. (We do not believe that the *Schöpfungsmesse* can have been sent to the *Conservatoire*, which would certainly have kept it in their archives until the present day. But if he sent it to the *Concert des Amateurs*, it is quite likely that the autograph came into private possession after the *Concert* was disbanded. Breitkopf & Härtel bought it at a Paris auction in the middle of the nineteenth century.)
2 The date, 'Vienna. 22 January 1803', suggests that Haydn started to write an Italian or an English letter and then used the space to draft the above letter to Michael.
3 Haydn originally wrote '7'.
4 Both Esterházy and the Archduke of Tuscany offered Michael Haydn lucrative and honourable positions. See also *supra*, p. 77.

anything wrong. Both are great, but the Archduke's love and understanding for music are greater than those of my Prince: your heart and your brain must make the decision here, to which of the two you give the preference. Meanwhile I wish you happiness, whichever choice you make, and I hope to hear your final decision as soon as possible. Till then, and as always, I am [end of draft].   [CCLN, 214]

News still travelled slowly, and it was some time before the rest of Europe realized that Michael Haydn had refused the excellent offers of the Grand Duke and Prince Esterházy. In the *AMZ* of 4 April 1804, there is a report from Salzburg which concludes:

> By chance I have just now found in a number of the musical paper [*AMZ*] of last year a report from Vienna that Michel [*sic*] Haydn, who was at that time on a trip to his brother, was to stay in Vienna. This report is not true: the excellent man has remained ours and receives 600 gulden as a salary. [Footnote by the editor of the *AMZ*:] The writer of this article writes quite clearly: six hundred gulden. But if one takes into consideration the present costs of living in that part of the world and considers that the subject is Michel Haydn, that means an artist who, foremost as a church composer, shines as one of the *first*; then one most imagine that the figure is a slip of the pen.   [*AMZ* VI, 450]

Alas, it was no slip of the pen, and Johann Michael's declining years were passed with the spectre of poverty close to him, partly due to the various French invasions but mostly because of growing inflation. Joseph did what he could to help, and there were flattering commissions from the Empress Marie Therese; but Michael's determination not to leave Salzburg made outside help rather problematical.

In preparing works for inclusion in the Haydn *Oeuvres Complettes* Breitkopf & Härtel now drew up thematic lists of the material they had in Leipzig. Haydn began to look through these carefully, and we shall see that soon he saw the speedy necessity of a proper catalogue of his works, compiled from material at his disposal in Vienna and Hungary. Early in January, Griesinger was able to tell Breitkopf about a number of piano compositions: 'No. 8 [piano Trio XV: 3] is by Haydn's brother. N°s. 17, 18, 21 and 26 he doesn't think are genuine [piano Trios XV: C1, D1, piano *Divertimenti* XIV: C1, G1], at least he cannot remember them from the themes. All the others [*Divertimento* XIV: 4, Trios XV: 1, 4, 5, 33–38, 41, the piano Sonatas XVI: 5–14 and the Variations XVII: 7] are genuine Haydn and mostly from his very early years'.[1] Haydn was now contemplating Clementi's request for more music to publish. He searched through his old scores and found three pieces, but the following quotation indicates that it was more convenient to offer them to Griesinger for Breitkopf & Härtel than to Clementi:

> [undated] . . . 1. An Andante and Finale for piano [Sonata No. 61, XVI: 51], which Haydn composed for a lady [Therese Bartolozzi] in England who kept the original and gave Haydn instead a copy in her own hand. 2. An Aria (Adagio) on an English song wherein Mistress Hunter (daughter [*recte*: wife] of the famous surgeon) takes leave of Haydn ['O tuneful voice']. 3. A certain *Harrington, Dr.* of music at Bath, sent Haydn a song of praise set to music, whereupon Haydn

---

1 Günter Thomas in *Haydn-Studien* I (1966)/2, 92. The letter was dated 7 January 1803. The Trio XV: 3, omitted from the new Doblinger complete edition, is one of two actually composed by Ignaz Pleyel. See A. Tyson in *Music Review* XXII (1961), 21ff.; H. Schwarting in *Archiv für Musikwissenschaft* XXII (1965), 170ff. What little information we have about the authenticity of these very early keyboard pieces comes mostly from Pohl's old notes (Gesellschaft der Musikfreunde, now on loan to A. van Hoboken) on this series of *incipits* sent from Haydn to Leipzig and *vice versa*.

answered with the words: 'What Art expresses and what Science praises, Haydn the Theme of both to Heaven raises', set first as an Adagio for one voice, then with a Tutti, then a small set of variations and then for one voice again [*Dr. Harington's Compliment*] . . .   [Olleson, *Griesinger*, 41]

Haydn wanted twenty-five ducats for the three pieces, a sum which Griesinger thought too high. But 'it is the marrow from my bones', said Haydn; 'today I would not be capable of doing something similar for ten times the price.' We shall continue this correspondence with a letter of 6 June *infra*.

Other prospective publishers received a polite but negative answer, for example the Silesian publisher Barth:

[To the publisher Barth, Breslau. *German*]
                                                           Vienna, 3rd March 1803
. . . You, Sir, did me the honour of sending me the *Blumenlese*, for which I am much indebted to you. I find in this journal, which is so important for music, nothing which is unworthy of the art, and I should very much like to be numbered among the competitors; but my age of 72 years [*sic*], and a rheumatic nervous fever which I have had for quite some time, deny me the necessary strength to do so. I am barely able to do even those services which my Prince requires for his establishment.

I do not yet disqualify myself from earning the laurel wreath which all the composers (especially, however, KNECHT)[1] deserve. God grant that my body be strengthened, and that nature will not extinguish in me those qualities with which she was hitherto so generous! . . .   [CCLN, 214f.]

Haydn was now physically much reduced and turned down almost every offer. In February we read in the *Pressburger Zeitung* that 'The Princely Esterházy *Kapellmeister* Joseph Haydn has received an invitation from an amateur concert in Paris together with a bank transfer of several thousand Pf. for travelling costs. Haydn, because of concern for his health, did not, however, accept this invitation' (*PZ* 10, 8 February 1803). It was probably the information that Griesinger had forwarded to Leipzig on 18 December 1802 (*supra*) but it was, no doubt, not an isolated case in point.

From this period we have a short note to Griesinger:

[To Georg August Griesinger, Vienna. *German*]
Most esteemed Herr von Griesinger!
    For various well-considered reasons, I have declined to send my songs[2] to the Russian Empress,[3] so that Herr Härtel, by publishing the works soon, can make his profit more quickly; please therefore inform him of this at your earliest convenience.
    To you, kindest Herr von Griesinger, I must express my gratitude a thousand fold for all the pains you have gone to on my account, and am, most respectfully,
                                        Your most obedient,
                                        Joseph Haydn.
[Vienna], 13th March 1803.   [CCLN, 215]

---

1 Justin Heinrich Knecht (1752–1817) was an organist and composer. He edited a musical periodical entitled *Die Schlesische Blumenlese*, which included songs etc. by leading composers of the day. Knecht had tried repeatedly to induce Haydn to write a piece for the *Blumenlese*, but without success. Barth was the publisher of the journal.
2 The three- and four-part songs with pianoforte accompaniment which Breitkopf & Härtel were about to publish.
3 Maria Feodorovna: see also letter of 15 February 1805.

Frederik Samuel Silverstolpe, one of Haydn's interesting foreign friends, had left Vienna to return to Stockholm. '1803, the 7th of February, a Monday, at 9 o'clock in the morning I left Vienna in deep snow but on wheels . . .' (Mörner, 397). From a letter of 15 March by Paul Struck, Haydn's pupil, we hear warm words of praise for the Swedish diplomat:

> . . . He [Haydn] assures you [Silverstolpe] that he could have earned the acquaintance of such a man as you only through the greatest respect, and that he does not consider himself worthy of the mark of attention that you showed him through me, at the time of your departure. – His nerves are so weak that he now works at the clavier [clavichord?] because the fortepiano is too noisy for him . . .
>
> [Mörner, 398]

We hear, then, that Haydn is working, though at what appears to be a clavichord (or a *Tafelklavier*, a small square piano?). The work was probably the last, unfinished String Quartet ('Op. 103') for Prince Lobkowitz, the autograph of which is dated 1803, and which was later dedicated to Count Fries.

On 29 March 1803, Baron Gottfried van Swieten died, aged 69. In his biography, Dies (182) informs us that 'Haydn had lent the original scores of *The Creation* and *The Seasons* to the *Freiherr* van Swieten for revision. He kept them a long time and put them in a drawer of his desk. Shortly before the *Freiherr*'s death they were seen there. Afterwards Haydn sent for them, but the scores had disappeared and were never again found.' Neukomm, commenting on this passage, describes how Swieten came to visit Haydn as the latter was putting the fourth or fifth codicil on his will:

> 'That's right, Haydn,' said Sw., 'at our age we have to take care that our affairs are in order.' Nevertheless, [continues Neukomm] soon thereafter the very rich, very miserly old bachelor died of a sudden and mortal stroke – without leaving any will behind him, & the laughing heir, as executor, dismissed from the house, unmercifully and without recompense, the poor servants, some of whom had served the *Freiherr* for some forty years and more. At the moment when H. received the news of Swt's death, I was there. H. asked me to go at once to the heirs and request in his name the original score of *The Seasons*, which H. had vainly requested many times before from Sw.: this score could not be lost and *had* to be among Sw's papers. But despite all our useless searching it has not been found to the present day and the thief or thieves enjoy, still undiscovered, this lawless possession! [Neukomm, 31]

The two scores have in fact completely disappeared, as surely as the autograph manuscripts to Beethoven's First, Second, and Third Symphonies.

On 2 April we learn from a letter by Griesinger to Leipzig that '. . . The Concert des Amateurs, rue Clery, recently sent Hn. a small gold medal (7 ducats in weight) for some Masses [!] he sent to them; they also sent a friendly letter' (Olleson, *Griesinger*, 41). The following day, 3 April, Haydn wrote the famous note to Neukomm, famous, because it clearly indicates the role his pupils played in preparing the Scottish Songs.

> [To Sigismund Neukomm, Vienna. *German*]
> Dearest Friend, [Vienna, 3rd April 1803[1]]
>   Your servant Jos. Haydn urgently requests you to do the enclosed two Songs as soon as possible, and to tell my servant on which day he may come and get them – I hope perhaps the day after tomorrow.
> [Address:]   To my dear Neukom [*sic*]. [CCLN, 215]

1 The date in Neukomm's hand.

When Silverstolpe became *chargé d'affaires* in St Petersburg, he met Neukomm and became friendly with him. Neukomm told Silverstolpe that he had written accompaniments for *seventy* Scottish Songs; the Swedish diplomat adds, 'this perhaps explains why they have been so often criticized' (Mörner, 404). In an article by Rochlitz in the *AMZ* for 1813, we read *inter alia*:

> About his last works, especially *The Seasons*, H. [Haydn] spoke with N. [Neukomm] not as with a pupil but as with a faithful artistic house-friend; and Father H. allowed, no doubt, several smaller commissions that were offered to him at this time, and which were of lesser importance [*weniger zu Sinne*] and would have taken away the time for the larger works, to be entirely written by N. and only occasionally added something of his own – this was especially the case, for example, with the often difficult and delicate harmonic arrangements of the well-known and rich collection of old (and not so old) Scottish, Irish and English ballads, folk-songs, etc. This information may be admitted openly since it is no more against Haydn's credit than the same procedures practised by Rubens and other great painters of old times; nor is it contrary to N's honour.
>
> [*AMZ* XV, 233f.]

A clearer series of statements could hardly be imagined. We would go (as the attentive reader of the foregoing Chronicle gathers) even further: it is entirely possible that most of the Scottish Songs which Thomson and others published under Haydn's name are in fact compositions of various pupils. We suspect that Haydn himself gladly began the work and did all the first arrangements himself – not only those in London, of course, but also the first for Thomson in 1799 *et seq*. We very much doubt, however, if after 1803 the composer did more than re-copying pupils' work and 'editing' the results.

Since we first registered our doubts about the authorship of the Scottish Songs that Haydn sent to Edinburgh, Rudolph Angermüller has discovered the autographs of twenty-three Scottish Songs by Neukomm which were then copied by Elssler and sold to Thomson as by Haydn; two more songs in this particular series copied by Elssler also seem to be by Neukomm, who is now thought to have written at least forty-three Scottish Songs 'für Vater Haydn'. Of the twenty-three songs surviving in Neukomm's autograph, none is contained in the Elssler Catalogue of 1805 (at least Haydn did not go that far!). The total of forty-three songs was composed between February 1803 and November 1805, when Neukomm was already in Russia. For details, the reader is referred to Dr Angermüller's interesting articles.[1]

On 5 April Beethoven, who had meanwhile been engaged by Schikaneder to be a kind of 'house composer' in the new Theater an der Wien and was also provided with living quarters there, took advantage of his new position to hold a benefit concert in the Theatre. Among other things, attention was concentrated on Beethoven's first effort to place himself in direct confrontation with Haydn, namely with an Oratorio. In the announcement of the concert in the *Wiener Zeitung*, the new Oratorio, *Christus am Ölberg*, is singled out as the only work to be specifically named in the rich and varied programme. The whole concert was a shambles from beginning to end, mainly because of Beethoven's total lack of organization. At five o'clock in the morning Ries arrived to find the master

> . . . writing on *separate* sheets of paper. To my question as to what it was he answered, '*Trombones*'. The trombones also played from *these* sheets at the

1 *Haydn-Studien* III, Heft 1 (1973), p. 39, and III, Heft 2 (1974), pp. 151ff.

performance . . . The rehearsal began at eight o'clock in the morning . . . It was a terrible rehearsal, and at half past two everybody was exhausted and more or less dissatisfied. Prince Karl Lichnowsky, who attended the rehearsal from the beginning, had sent for bread and butter, cold meat and wine, in large baskets. He pleasantly asked all to help themselves, and this was done with both hands, the result being that good nature was restored again. Then the Prince requested that the Oratorio be rehearsed once more from the beginning, so that it might go well in the evening and Beethoven's first work in this genre be worthily presented. And so the rehearsal began again. The concert began at six o'clock, but was so long that a few pieces were not performed.[1]

According to the *AMZ*, Beethoven raised the prices, no doubt in direct emulation of Haydn's double prices for his Oratorio performances at the Burgtheater for the Tonkünstler-Societät. The price of first chairs was doubled, that of the reserved seats [*Sperrsitze*] was tripled, and for a box he asked twelve ducats instead of four florins (approximately a six-fold increase):

> . . . no one could understand [these prices]. Still, one must not forget that this was Herr Beethoven's first attempt of this kind. I sincerely wish that the box-office receipts will be as successful the second time; as far as the composition [*Christus am Ölberg*] is concerned, it needs more characterization and a better thought-out plan.
> [*AMZ* V, 25 May 1803, p. 590]

Beethoven was furious at this criticism and wrote later to Breitkopf & Härtel concerning the '*downright lying about the prices* I charged and in which I am so infamously treated' (Thayer-Forbes I, 329). But the prices were certainly raised, because Beethoven took in the very considerable sum of 1,800 gulden.

The composer Seyfried turned pages and, as Mozart had done on several occasions, Beethoven had only sketched the piano part of the Third Concerto (composed in 1800, revised after the arrival in Vienna of the Erard piano 'with the extended keys'). 'He gave me a secret glance whenever he was at the end of one invisible passage.' Apart from the Concerto, the First and Second Symphonies were performed.

August von Kotzebue wrote about the concert in his periodical *Der Freymüthige*:

> Even the valiant Beethofen [*sic*] . . . was not quite happy and was not able, despite the efforts of his numerous admirers, to obtain much applause. Both the symphonies and parts of the Oratorio were received with approval but the whole was too drawn out, too contrived in construction and lacking in expressive relevance, especially in the vocal writing. The text, by F. X. Huber, seemed as casually thrown together as the music. Yet the performance brought Beethofen 1,800 gulden, and he has, together with the celebrated Abbé Vogler, obtained an engagement in that theatre. He will compose one opera while Vogler will write three. For this they receive free lodgings as well as ten percent of the receipts for the first ten performances.
> [Landon, *Beethoven*, 147]

The *Zeitung für die elegante Welt* (16 April 1803) thought that

the First Symphony is better than the later one because it is developed with a lightness and is less forced, while in the Second the striving for the new and surprising is already more apparent. However, it is obvious that both are not lacking in surprising and brilliant passages of beauty. Less successful was the

---

1 Wegeler-Ries, *Notizen*, 75f.; English translation from Thayer-Forbes I, 328f.

following Concerto in C minor which Hr. v. B., who is otherwise known as an excellent pianist, performed also not completely to the public's satisfaction.

[Thayer–Forbes I, 330]

Another writer for the *AMZ* was also at the concert:[1]

> Vienna, 6th April. In new works of musical interest there is (apart from an oratorio by Paer, which did not very much please) only the Oratorio by Beethoven, *Christus am Oelberg*, which was performed yesterday and received extraordinary approbation. It confirms my long-held opinion that Beethoven can in time effect just such a revolution in music as did Mozart. He hastens to his goal with great strides. [*AMZ* V, 13 April 1803, p. 489]

A few months later an anonymous correspondent from Vienna, perhaps the one whose faintly negative criticism we have already quoted, replied to the favourable criticism. 'In the interests of truth I must contradict a report in the musical journal, to wit: Beethoven's Cantata did not please' (V, 734). In fact Beethoven later admitted to Schindler that it had been a mistake to treat the part of Christ in the modern vocal manner (Thayer–Forbes I, 330f.).

Christ on the Mount of Olives is not one of Beethoven's more popular works, and perhaps it was a grave mistake on the part of his friends to have persuaded him to enter into opposition with Haydn on the level of *The Creation* and *The Seasons*. This work of Beethoven's has some magnificent moments, especially the Soldiers' Chorus, so prophetic of *Fidelio*, and the dazzling burst of choral and orchestral sound in the final number. As to the failure of the concert, Beethoven had been up since well before five o'clock and had rehearsed the whole day: small wonder that his piano playing was not the greatest. But Beethoven would have blamed the whole failure on quite another source. Rosenbaum's Diary tells us:

> Tuesday 5th [April]: ... I went ... to Fuchs's; we talked about the performance today of Bethowen's [*sic*] cantata *Christus am Ölberg*. It is bound not to be a satisfactory one because [Baron] Braun is using both orchestras [Italian and German opera] at the B[urg] Th[eater] for *The Creation*, in a benefit performance for the poor of the theatres. Wednesday, 6th: . . . At the Lusthaus [in the Prater], I talked with [Max] Willmann about Bethowen's academy; he spoke highly of it, although I heard just the opposite from everyone else. – [Anton] Eberl told me that Bethowen did not measure up to the public's legitimate expectations at his academy yesterday; nothing was entirely worthy of a great master.
> [Radant, *Rosenbaum*, 106f.]

Baron Braun, then, had hired away Vienna's best instrumentalists and chorus members for *The Creation* performance, leaving Beethoven with the second-rate remainders; and, typically, Beethoven held Haydn to account for his concert's, and the Oratorio's, failure. His 'great pride' towards Haydn, of which we will soon be hearing from Haydn himself (see letter of 4 January 1804 from Griesinger to Breitkopf & Härtel), will have hardly been assuaged by the following concluding note from the review in the *Zeitung für die elegante Welt* – where, by the way, we also read clearly that Beethoven 'went so far [*sic*] as to raise the price of the tickets to his Cantata' – : 'In the closing chorus, several of the audience claimed to recognize ideas from Haydn's *The Creation*.' This was adding insult to injury!

---

1 The writer was none other than Andreas Streicher, the well-known piano builder and friend of Beethoven; see W. Lütge, 'Andreas und Nanette Streicher', in *Der Bär* (1927), p. 58.

An interesting comment comes from Paul Struck, Haydn's pupil, in writing to Silverstolpe. Struck could not go to the Beethoven Oratorio because of a toothache, but he had this to say:

> Of course Beethoven has many enemies, but now no one speaks about the academy, and the Oratorio will not be performed any more. Beethoven himself excused it by saying it was too quickly composed. . . .

Many years later, in a letter written to the Gesellschaft der Musikfreunde on 23 January 1824, Beethoven actually said '*Christus am Ölberg* was written by me and the poet in a period of 14 days, but the poet was musical and had already written many things for music. I was able to consult him at any moment.' In another, earlier (1804) letter to Breitkopf & Härtel, he speaks of 'a few weeks' (Thayer-Forbes I, 328). If there is a single monument to Beethoven's angry pride towards Haydn, *Christus am Ölberg* is certainly one of the most dumbfounding candidates.

Meanwhile Johann Michael Haydn in Salzburg had received another commission from the Empress, to which the following unpublished letter of 5 April 1803 refers:[1]

Salzburg, 5th April 1803

Well born, gracious Sir,

I received your most pleasant letter today and hasten to answer it. The desire of Her Majesty the Empress is the highest command for me, and to obey the same a most exceptional delight and pleasure. I will follow most exactly everything that is requested in order (as far as my small talents are able) to deliver something respectable.

I would only like to have clear information about one point. You write: <u>The Offertorium[2] will be a 4-part Canon.</u> Should it then be composed like my 4-part songs? Or should it be interpreted as a most strict canon, in which one voice after the other begins, and sings in a circle that which the other has sung? – I would ask you please, when the occasion offers, to let me know. As a result of all this I have received much grace; to which, as to further examples, I commit myself respectfully and with true esteem I remain,

Your Grace's

most obedient servant
Joh: Michael Haydn mpr.

N: S: Here everything is in a state of expectancy about the arrival of our new *Landesherr*, H. R. H. Archduke Ferdinand.[3]

1 Autograph in the Pierpont Morgan Library, New York, which institution kindly sent a photograph to us.
2 The Offertorium was part of a series of new works for the Empress: a mass, which should be the approximate length of the 'Theresa Mass' but with no solo [i.e. instrumental] parts. The Et incarnatus est is to be for solo vocal quartet, with only violoncello and basso continuo accompaniment; while the Benedictus is to be a duetto for soprano and bass with choral ending. The Offertorium was to be a four-part canon – Marie Therese obviously meant a strict canon – and in the Mass there should be two fugues. Apart from the Mass, which turned out to be the *Missa sub titulo S. Francesci Seraphici*, was completed on 16 August 1803. The Empress further requested a Graduale and a Te Deum, the latter being completed on 20 September. The Graduale was entitled 'Cantate', the Offertorium 'Domine Deus', and both were completed between those dates. The first performance of them all was at the Hofburgkapelle in Vienna on 4 October 1803. See Jancik, *Michael Haydn*, op. cit., 257.
3 The French had, of course, captured and occupied Salzburg in December 1800, and Michael had been robbed of his money and his belongings. In the peace treaty of Lunéville, Land Salzburg was given to the Tuscan line of the Habsburgs in exchange for the Grand Duchy of Tuscany, which went to the Napoleonic creation, the Kingdom of Etruria.

On 9 April 1803 Haydn's protégée, the great soprano Anna Milder, who had been given to Neukomm for training, made her hugely successful début as Juno in Süssmayer's Opera *Der Spiegel von Arkadien*. Later in the season, on 22 September, we shall find her singing Haydn in the last Augarten concert (*infra*).[1]

In May Haydn received yet another mark of honour and affection from the Vienna city authorities:

[To Haydn from Vienna City Magistracy. *German*]
Well born,
Most highly respected Sir!
    In view of the many demonstrations of philanthropy by which you, Sir, have contributed to alleviate the pitiable condition of old and impoverished citizens of St. Marx, male and female, the Economic Committee of the Citizens' Hospital, established by the highest command [the Emperor], has felt obliged to inform us here of your high-minded actions, and has suggested to us that this act of charity should not go unnoticed.
    You, most esteemed Doctor of Music, undertook to conduct personally those Cantatas [*sic*], the justly admired masterpieces of your genius, and you conducted them many times without payment; as a result of this, many hearts were inspired to generosity, and the poor citizens of St. Marx received substantial sums. The Magistracy of this Imperial and Royal capital city, Vienna, has long waited for an opportunity to show in some manner its esteem for a man whose talents have made him immortal, and whom every educated nation has already showered with honours, and who brilliantly combines the advantages of the artist with the virtues of the citizen; it therefore takes advantage of the present occasion.
    In order to offer at least a modest tribute to you for this enduring act of merit, the Magistracy has unanimously voted to confer on you the present twelve-fold golden citizens' medal, as a small token of the gratitude felt by the poor male and female citizens of St. Marx whose spirits you have thus revived, and in whose name we venture to address you.[2]
    May it shine on your breast fully as long as these thankful hearts continue to pour forth their gratitude for your noble gesture! May you give us the opportunity whereby we may show you the esteem in which we hold you! In which hope we remain, Sir,

Your willing
Joseph Georg Hörl, Councillor to the Imperial and
Royal Lower Austrian Government, and Lord Mayor.

Stephan Edler von Wohlleben, Imperial and Royal
Councillor and Chancellor of the Exchequer.

Joh. Bapt. Franz, President of the Economic
Committee of the Citizens' Hospital

Vienna, 10th May 1803   [CCLN, 216f.]

---

1 Pohl III, 156; *Wiener Fremdenblatt* (signed 'E.P.') 19 March 1872.
2 The so-called 'Salvator Medal' (from its title 'Salvator mundi'). The 'Cantatas' to which reference is made are, of course, the three oratorios, *The Seven Words*, *The Creation* and *The Seasons*, performances of which Haydn had conducted for charity for several years past. Haydn was very much touched by the medal, and was more proud of it than of any of the other honours he had received. He said to Griesinger: 'I thought to myself: *vox populi, vox Dei*.' (Griesinger, p. 44).

[To the Vienna City Magistracy. *German*]

[Vienna, *c.* 15 May 1803]

Most Worthy Magistracy,
Nobly born, most highly honoured Gentlemen,

When I endeavoured to help in the support of old and impoverished citizens, by placing at their disposal my knowledge of the art of music, I esteemed myself very fortunate in having thus fulfilled one of my most agreeable duties, and could not flatter myself that the worthy Magistracy of the Imperial and Royal capital city would deign to bestow on me so distinguished a mark of their consideration, in return for my modest exertions.

It is not the noble gift alone, most highly respected gentlemen, much as I shall prize it as a mark of your favour during all the remaining days that Providence has seen fit to allot to me; but even more your kind letter, which so clearly bears the imprint of your noble convictions. My heart, deeply moved, is uncertain whether it should wonder more at your magnanimous conduct towards myself, or at the benevolent care you bestow on your citizens.

I wish here to express my profound gratitude for both; and allow me, esteemed gentlemen, to conclude by the fervent wish that, for the sake of this Imperial city, Providence may long preserve so humane a Magistracy.

I remain most highly esteemed gentlemen, with profound respect,

Your obedient servant,
Joseph Haydn [m.p] ria.
[CCLN, 217]

Later the official announcement was published in the *Wiener Zeitung*. It read as follows:

The local Doctor of Music, Joseph Haydn, generally known by his music works, has several times conducted *gratis* performances of his masterpiece, *The Creation*, as a result of which he has been responsible that an impressive sum of money was able to be raised ... Considering this ... humane [*menschenfreundlichen*] use the present city magistracy wrote to the Doctor of Music, Joseph Haydn, under date 10 May *ult.*, a sincere letter of thanks, to which as a sign of their gratitude was included the twelve-fold golden citizens' medal. Both were accepted by the artist, as famous as he is patriotic, with modest expressions of sentiment and with the promise to participate in future manifestations of this charitable kind, insofar as his powers allow of it.

[*Wiener Zeitung* No. 44, 1 June 1803]

On 13 May Rosenbaum was invited to a private performance of *The Seasons* at the Schmierer family (Johanna had made her début at the Leopoldstädter Theater in October 1801, while her brother Carl was also an actor). Joseph Lipavsky, whose dance music was successful, 'conducted very well from the pianoforte. There were violins (doubled), violoncello and violone. Including the boys, there were about 16 in the chorus . . . – The performance was a success . . .' (109).

On the 16th Cherubini's *Lodoiska* was given at the Theater an der Wien – Cherubini was at the moment extremely popular in Vienna, and it is well known that Beethoven considered Cherubini the greatest living composer 'apart from yourself'

---

1 This letter was drafted by one of Haydn's friends, the *Abbé* Felix Franz Hofstätter (librarian, 1741–1814) (Pohl III, 217).

(i.e. Beethoven); this was in answer to a question by Cipriani Potter to the composer in 1817 (Thayer-Forbes II, 682). At any rate, who should Rosenbaum meet at *Lodoiska* but the erstwhile child prodigy Bridgetower, 'first violin to the Prince of Walles [*sic*] and the son of August the Moor who had been in the service of Prince Niklas [Nicolaus I Esterházy] as valet. I asked him to come to lunch tomorrow' (Rosenbaum, 109). Bridgetower was also taken up by Beethoven, who wrote for him the famous 'Mulattick Sonata. Composed for the mulatto Brischdauer, great lunatick and mulattick composer',[1] later known – after Bridgetower and Beethoven had broken up because of a 'silly quarrel about a girl' – as the 'Kreutzer' Sonata. Rosenbaum (109) went to hear the performance of the Sonata Op. 47 at a noon concert in the Augarten on Tuesday, 24 May: Beethoven accompanied, and Rosenbaum noted (109): 'It was not too crowded; a select company. . . .' Of course Bridgetower must have looked up Haydn, with whom he had given concerts in London; the result was an invitation to go to Eisenstadt during the second part of July, for we read in Rosenbaum's Diary under date 22 July: '. . . At mid-day the actor [Ignaz] Schuster, his wife and [Joseph Friedrich] Korntheuer lunched with us. Bridgetower came later. He has spent 8 days in Eisenstadt' (111).

Two letters concerned with Haydn's position in the Esterházy administration speak for themselves:

[To Johann Nepomuk Fuchs,[2] Eisenstadt. *German, 'Du' form*]

Vienna, 18th May 1803

Dearest Fuchs!
Herr Diezl[3] has applied to me for permission to remain in Vienna for a few more days, in order to finish some important business; he will certainly return to Eisenstadt before Whitsun. So please give him your kind blessing. Otherwise, I am told that you are exceptionally diligent, for which I heartily embrace your beautiful wife, and remain,

Your old, but unfortunately useless friend,
Joseph Haydn.
[CCLN, 217f.]

[To Joseph Elssler Jr.,[4] Eisenstadt. *German, 'Du' form*]

Vienna, 5th June 1803

Dearest Elsler [*sic*]!
    Please be good enough to send up to me, at the very first opportunity, the old Symphony (entitled *die Zerstreute*),[5] for Her Majesty the Empress expressed a desire to hear the old pancake. Thus I ask Herr Messner[6] to lend it to me for a few days: I won't damage it in any way. Otherwise, I should be happy to hear that

---

1 'Sonata mulattica. Composta per il Mulatto Brischdauer gran pazzo e compositore mulattico'. See also Landon, *Beethoven*, 148ff.
2 See *supra*, p. 229.
3 Johann Die(t)zl: see *infra*, p. 273.
4 Joseph was Johann's brother, and oboist in the *Feldharmonie*.
5 Symphony No. 60 (incidental music to *Der [recte] Zerstreute*). The original copy, and the one Haydn made in 1803 (copied by Johann Elssler) are both preserved in the Esterházy Archives. A page of the 1803 copy is reproduced in Landon *SYM*, p. 33 (facing).
6 In charge of the music archives.

everyone else is in good health; my compliments to all of them, especially my brother, Luigi, Fex, and his better half,[1] &c.

Jos. Haydn m.p.

[Address:]

Haydn asks that this letter be expedited as soon as possible.

An Herrn Elsler, Oboist bey Sr. Durchl. Fürst Esterhazy,

in

Eisenstadt. [CCLN, 218]

We now return to Griesinger's correspondence with Breitkopf & Härtel. It will be remembered that Haydn had looked out three pieces of music and offered them for twenty-five ducats, which Griesinger thought too expensive. Haydn now added an old organ Concerto (XVIII: 1) to the three pieces.

6 June 1803

. . . There are people who save a penny to lose a pound. 'Haydn must be senile [*kindisch*]', said someone to me, 'because he sells three of his compositions for 25 fl.' [= gulden; but Haydn had said ducats]. Apart from these three pieces you will also receive a Haydn organ concerto – with the purchase. It is from the year 1756, perhaps thus above the epoch of the present taste, but of its kind certainly of interest to the collector of Haydn's music. It is the same one that I once wrote you about. *Send back the original* when it has been copied. . . .

[Olleson, *Griesinger*, 42]

The Concerto appears again in the correspondence and was not sent until after January 1804; in the event Breitkopf & Härtel forgot to return the original and did not publish it until 1953 (edited by Michael Schneider); the work has since become famous and has the distinction, with the other organ concertos, of being among the most played and certainly the most recorded work of its kind in Haydn's *œuvre*. Haydn remembered writing it to celebrate the taking of the vows by his first love, Therese Keller, in 1756; but the date was added by Haydn to the autograph of the Concerto much later, perhaps as late as 1803.

Breitkopf & Härtel were still searching for appropriate texts for Haydn to set to music. They now sent to Griesinger the text of a trio from a cantata after Dryden by Christian Schreiber entitled *Polyhymnia, oder die Macht der Töne* (Polyhymnia, or the Power of Music). Griesinger reported:

18 June 1803

. . . Haydn has the firmest intentions to compose the Cantata of which the subject is the Praise of Music. Handel too composed a similar subject. The Trio, which is really very well done, pleased him and I had to leave it with him. But before he undertakes the least responsibility, he wishes to see the whole poem. He gives his word of honour that no wrong use of it will occur. This poem should not be all too long and the performance should last an hour at the most. Send the text, my most worthy friend, as soon as possible. During Esterhazy's absence and the friendly season of the year H. has his head and hands free; later that might no longer be the case. . . .

. . . You can imagine that all these marks of honour put the Papa in a good mood. For some months he was entirely idle and not capable of anything; now he

---

1 Haydn's brother Johann (tenor); Luigi Tomasini; 'Fex' (an Austrian expression which, in modern slang, might be translated as 'nut') and 'his better half' are Luigi's son (Anton) and his wife Thekla, who were married on 30 April.

is strengthened by the good time of year and the baths, and he can, as he told me, 'once again improvise a little' [Viennese dialect: 'doch wieder a bisserl phantasieren']. . . .   [Olleson, *Griesinger*, 42]

Three letters to Thomson now follow:

[To George Thomson, Edinburgh. *Italian*]

Vienna, 30th June 1803

Dearest Friend!

I send you herewith the remaining ariettas, and hope that you and all other lovers of music will be satisfied by this music. I only regret that in this world I am obliged to serve any gallant gentleman who pays me; and moreover, Mr. Whyte gives me two guineas for every single arietta,[1] that is to say, twice as much. My dearest Friend, I hope to be able to serve you on another occasion. Meanwhile I am, with the greatest esteem,
Your most sincere friend and servant,

Giuseppe Haydn [m.p] ria.

[Thomson's clerk notes: '30 June 1803/Haydn/ Vienna/ with a number/ of Airs harmo-/nized by him/ for me/ And that Mr White pays him 2 guineas/ for each air he has/ harmonized'.]   [CCLN, 218f.]

[To George Thomson, Edinburgh. *Italian*]
Most esteemed Sir!

I send you herewith forty new Scottish ariettas, and the rest will be finished shortly. I am most grateful to you for the payment of 120 gold ducats which I received not long ago[2] from Messrs. Fries & Co., and I embrace you, dear Friend, for the handkerchiefs, which are very beautiful, especially those intended for my poor wife. She lies buried these past three years, and so I have given them to a married lady who is most accomplished in the field of music. I hope you will agree with what I did. I am, with every respect, your most sincere friend, Giuseppe Haydn.
Vienna, 1st July 1803.
[Thomson's clerk notes: 'Haydn / Vienna 1 July 1803 / W^t 40 Airs harmon-/ized p^e by him – /thanks for the money/ paid him & for In-/dia handkerchiefs.']

[CCLN, 219]

[To George Thomson, Edinburgh. *French*. Only the signature autograph]
Mon très chère Amis!

I have received the money you sent me through the bankers Frise [Fries]: don't be angry at me for having to wait so long for the 25 songs, but they have been ready to be sent to you for 5 months. The Secretary of the Embassy, Sir Seward [Charles Stuart] has not known, or rather he hasn't told me, when he was

---

1 Haydn had undertaken to do some symphonies and accompaniments to Scottish airs published by William Whyte of Edinburgh; an autograph receipt to this effect is reproduced in CCLN, facing p. 106. Naturally, Thomson was rather aghast at this new development, and wrote to his go-between, Charles Stuart, at the British Legation in Vienna, to find out what had happened. In August 1803 Stuart writes that he has broached Haydn with regard to the Whyte arrangements 'in as delicate terms as possible for fear he might take offence. Haydn admitted that he had done the accompaniments for Whyte, but said the airs were quite different from those he had done for Thomson.

[After] a long conversation, he informed me that being now 74 [*sic*] years of age and extremely infirm he found himself wholly incapable of further application to study; that he must therefore beg leave to decline all offers whether on your part or from any other person whatsoever. He even declared that notwithstanding the repeated requests of Prince Esterhazy, he felt himself utterly incapable of finishing several pieces of music which he had undertaken, and being possessed of a competency he desired nothing so much as to pass the short time he has yet to live in repose and quiet.
[Hadden, *Thomson*, 306]

2 The receipt (only signature is autograph) is dated 8 June: British Museum, Add. 35263, fol. 168.

to leave; till now I have not found an opportunity to send these and 14 more songs to you. I shall choose a safe way by which to send you the other 11 which I have yet to compose. I am much indebted to you for your gifts: I am having the handkerchiefs hemstitched.

The copy you sent me[1] is unparalleled, not only for its engraving but also for the beauty of the paper. I beg you to send me the 1st and 2nd volumes together with the 4th, for I admire this distinguished collection and the musicians who have worked on it. I shall be glad to pay for all of them, and am, with profound esteem, your most devoted servant,

Joseph Haydn [m.p] ria

Vienna, 6th July 1803.
[Thomson notes: 'Haydn, Vienna 6 July 1803 acknowledging to have rec^d pay^t from Frise [*sic*] & Co. of the price of the Ritornelles & Accomp^{ts} soon to be sent me (120 ducats, or £59.13.5) acking also to have rec^d. the presents I sent him and expressing his admiration of the manner in which the 3^d volume is printed – & requesting the other volumes. . . .']   [CCLN, 219f.]

We now arrive at a rather complicated but interesting contretemps between Haydn and the Viennese copyist and publisher Johann Traeg. We owe our information on the entire episode to the Griesinger correspondence, of which a part is paraphrased in Pohl (III, 214). It seems that in 1788 Traeg had bought some Haydn operas from the legacy of Count Ladislaus von Erdödy (1746–86), who was related to the Count Johann Nepomuk von Erdödy who had been instrumental in establishing the theatre at Pressburg which had performed so many of Haydn's operas in the 1780s. When these operas were no longer needed at Eszterháza, they were sent to Pressburg, translated from Italian to German, and given in the Erdödy Court Theatre. Ladislaus acquired works quite distinct from those given at Pressburg – not only Italian operas but also German marionette operas. Traeg now owned the autographs of *Il mondo della luna, L'isola disabitata, Philemon und Baucis* and a comic opera (*Die Feuersbrunst* or *Das abgebrannte Haus*). In his Catalogue of 1799, Traeg offered MS. scores of these works as well as the first part of *Philemon und Baucis*, a *Vorspiel* entitled *Der Götterrath*, and *La vera constanza*. Traeg copies of all these works except, alas, *Der Götterrath* have been located.[2] Haydn heard that Traeg owned the autograph of *L'isola disabitata* and, when preparing the new edition for Breitkopf & Härtel – of which we have spoken (see *supra*, p. 218) – arranged for Traeg to send over the manuscript.

After a certain time [continued Griesinger] Traeg asked to have it sent back or that he be given 12 ducats instead. Haydn, enraged by this demand, sent for Traeg and, in the presence of other persons, thoroughly dressed him down. To avoid further complications, however, he finally handed over the Sonata *quaestionis* [the Trio in E flat No. 41, XV: 31, published by Traeg and dedicated to Madame Moreau, *vide infra*, p. 269] which he had composed in London [in 1795]. . . .

. . . During my last visit something occurred which I want to bring to your attention. It is a large Oratorio by Handel (Haydn says it is the only one he composed to a *German* text), entitled: 'Der für die Sünden der Welt gemarterte und sterbende Jesus'. The Queen of England gave it with her own hands to Haydn

---

1 The Third Volume of Scottish Songs (see Thomson's notes).
2 See Landon, 'Haydn's Marionette Operas and the Repertoire of the Marionette Theatre at Esterház Castle', in *Haydn Yearbook* I (1962), 133f. It seems that *La vera costanza* was not part of the estate of Count Ladislaus von Erdödy.

as a present. Swieten who has, if I am not mistaken, 24 Handel Oratorios does not have this one and Haydn doubts altogether if it exists in Germany. It is supposed to be excellently composed. The manuscript is bound in red morocco with gold lettering, but the copyist made mistakes which Haydn has to correct. What do you think about it? Shall I try to get hold of it and how much should I offer for it? Tell me approximately so that I can settle the affair at once if H. doesn't string the bow too tightly. You must know best how much such works are worth and if anything can be done about it. Could I drop a word about 20 and if that doesn't work 30 ducats (in paper)? . . .   [Olleson, *Griesinger*, 42f.]

The Handel Oratorio was the so-called *Brockes-Passion*, and some years ago Frederick Hudson managed to find Haydn's copy: it is in the Österreichische Nationalbibliothek in Vienna.[1] Griesinger's next letter is still concerned with the Handel work.

30 July 1803

. . . I put out feelers to Haydn about the Handel Oratorio. The manuscript has 400 pages & 10 lines on each page. Haydn considers it a great rarity; the Queen of England told him that no one owned it and he thinks that after his death the Empress [Marie Therese] will try to get hold of the work. It ends with a chorale; H. would like to compose a concluding chorus for it (but he has no text). The price? 200 fl! because he has to go through it carefully because of copyist's errors. I was so thoroughly convinced that H. would not let it out of his hands as not even to broach the question. The excuse, that it isn't fully corrected, was also too convenient. The most he would do is to allow a selection of themes [*incipits*] and text which I perhaps could do in his room . . . As to the question if he really had no manuscripts of piano compositions, he answered that he would have to look; he doesn't really know because he is gradually putting his manuscripts in order. Recently he found a concerto for the organ and one violin[2] which he wrote 50 years ago for his sister-in-law when she took the veil. If you want to have the Handel Oratorio he will include this Concerto with the purchase; but I should tell you what an old beard it has. . . .   [Olleson, *Griesinger*, 43]

Breitkopf & Härtel were apparently not very enthusiastic about either the Oratorio or the old Concerto, but they must have been very pleased about another item of news in the letter of 30 July, namely that Haydn – now that Swieten was dead and could no longer object – agreed to the transfer of the engraving plates of *The Creation*: '. . . Well, it's Härtel and I'm fond of him; let the 100 ducats price remain. . . .'

Meanwhile great preparations were being made to welcome back Prince Esterházy. As early as March, *Vice-Kapellmeister* Fuchs had gone to Rosenbaum and asked the latter to write the text of a cantata. On 22 March Rosenbaum had finished the text and read it to Fuchs, who then went to Princess Marie Hermenegild; she agreed to defray all the expenses and suggested having Therese Rosenbaum come to Eisenstadt to sing the soprano part. On 7 August the Rosenbaums went to Eisenstadt and then to Eszterháza; two days later they were at the Esterházy fortress in Forchtenstein, 'went down to the dusty cellar where we drank some of Luther's 1526 *Donnerskirchner* . . .' (Radant, *Rosenbaum*, 106, 111f.). Haydn must have arrived at Eisenstadt sometime in

1 See *Musica*, July–August 1952, p. 404. We are much indebted to the late O. E. Deutsch for drawing this fact to our attention.
2 Possibly the Double Concerto in F (XVIII: 6). At other times Haydn thought he had written the Organ Concerto XVIII: 1 for his sister-in-law; see *supra*, 6 June.

August, but a great deal of the conducting seems to have been done by Fuchs. Rosenbaum (112) writes under date 15 August: 'In Eisenstadt. Ascension of the Virgin . . . only Masses by Fuchs were done.'

Tuesday 23rd [August] . . . The Prince had arrived safe and sound at about 7:30; he brought golden repeating watches for Prince Paul and Karner, with his coat-of-arms on the case. He will travel to Eisenstadt on Saturday, and so our cantata [will be performed] on Saturday. – Th.— is not well; she has a headache and toothache and I am really anxious about her. Wednesday, 24th: Overcast, cold . . . She took to her bed immediately and had a terrible temperature during the night . . . Thursday 24th: Cold, at times overcast. Th— is feeling very bad . . . Together with [Joseph] Ruttrich, the administrator, I went to the Engl [sic] inn to negotiate with the inn-keeper about the board for the chorus from Vienna. We made out a price of 3 gulden 30 kreuzer per head, without wine. – Friday, 26th: In the morning Th— was no better. I visited Haydn and invited him to lunch at the Engl. To Fuch's at about 12 o'clock . . . then the dress rehearsal of the cantata [*Der Unterthanen Jubel über Ihres Fürsten Ankunft*] began. Korner sang Th—'s part. It was done in the large room at the Engel in the presence of well-disposed listeners and was a complete success. Off home after the rehearsal. – Th— is still in bed and has no hope of singing tomorrow.

Saturday, 27th August 1803: In Eisenstadt. The Prince's arrival. I spoke to Haydn about beginning the cantata earlier. Th— was somewhat better, giving me new hope for the performance of the cantata. – The Prince's reception was impressive. At the Trauben Inn the citizens of the town received him with trumpets and drums. The Jews stood in ranks along the street and had decorated the walls with embroidered hangings, the princely coat-of-arms and a verse. On the left-hand side of the square the citizen-guards of Oberberg stood at attention, to the right the company of grenadiers was drawn up. At the steps he was received by the officials, led by Szint Galy [Johann von Szentgály, director of the princely estates], and in the small hall by the musicians, led by Haydn in uniform. – The Prince arrived at about 11:30, was most gracious and courteous to everyone. Haydn and Fuchs told him of the performance of the cantata today, adding at the same time that Th— was here, but that she was ill and therefore asks his indulgence. They gave him text-books in atlas folio, and I gave 2 to Kárner and Szént Galy [sic] . . . Th— is feeling somewhat better and is getting ready to sing. – I fetched Haydn from the castle and we went to join the large company at the Engel for lunch; I also invited Jean Haydn and Tomasini *père* today . . . In the hall, the Prince went up to Th— and was most charming. Haydn joined them and told the Prince, in the presence of several listeners, many good things about the music and poetry, repeating what he had told me yesterday at lunch, that my poetry is good, has a lot of variety, gives the composer excellent material for setting to music, that he would be happy to set my texts himself, and so on. – The sinfonia began. Everyone sat in tense expectation, their text-books in hand. Th— sang the first duet with [Jakob Joseph] Richter [the tenor] excellently; her weakness was not in the least noticeable. Richter made a mistake in the second duet, and only Th—'s fine musicianship was able to smooth it over. The Turkish music at the end was extremely effective. The cantata was a success and created quite a furore. . . .

Sunday, 28th: . . . At about 10 o'clock I went . . . to the Berg Kirche, in front of which the grenadiers stood church parade. A Mass by Haydn was sung. During the [Haydn?] Te Deum the grenadiers fired 3 times, and 4 times during the Mass . . . Monday, 28th: . . . At mid-day we lunched with my mother. – I did some writing afterwards . . . in the meantime Haydn, Elsler [sic] and [the actor Johann?]

Mayer came. . . . Wednesday, 31st August: Quartets by the Parisian [Rodolphe] Kreutzer were played at the castle. After supper the two Prinsters played Waldhorn duets! – They also gave Th— the pleasure of hearing them, surprising her in a very enjoyable way by playing them under her window . . . Thursday 1st [September]: Cold and rain. Our journey to Vienna . . . I said farewell to Haydn too; he kissed me several times and assured Th— and me of his close friendship. He thinks the cantata, which the Prince and she [the Princess] liked so much, will be performed again on Annunciation Day. [Radant, *Rosenbaum*, 113f.]

On 3 September Rosenbaum, back in Vienna, informs us that at the Kärntnerthortheater he 'saw the newly-engaged soprano, Bianchi, whose father [Benedetto Bianchi] was a fine buffo at Esterhás'. Meanwhile Griesinger was in constant communication with Leipzig. On 20 August we learn that:

[Haydn] offers you a Stabat Mater, which has been already engraved in England, but to which he has added several wind instruments some weeks ago, so as to be able to perform it upon his Prince's return (he is expected daily).

The 1803 copy of the *Stabat Mater* parts, largely prepared by Johann Elssler (and his assistants), has survived and is in the Esterházy Archives, Budapest.[1] Haydn asked no fee for the work beyond the copying charges.

7 September 1803
. . . I wrote you recently about Haydn's *Stabat Mater*; but a little while ago I read in the *Allgem. Zeitung* that you have already printed it during the Easter Fair. So you won't need it any longer. The Haydn receipt has arrived safely? . . .

17 September 1803
. . . Day before yesterday I received from Träg [Traeg] two copies of the *Stabat Mater* for Haydn; I will send them to Eisenstadt today and at the same time ask him if it is the same *Stabat Mater* as the one of which he spoke to me; I almost think it must be, because Hn. talked to me of it as being a work already engraved in England but for which he quite recently added some wind instruments. At the same time I will find out about the Mass and let you know as soon as I have an answer. . . . [Olleson, *Griesinger*, 43f.]

We have no accurate information about the precise date when this new version of the *Stabat Mater* was performed at Eisenstadt, but it must have been after Rosenbaum left. Before then, the musicians were busy rehearsing the Cantata. We suspect that the 'new' *Stabat Mater* was Haydn's name-day offering for Princess Esterházy in 1803; too weak to compose a new Mass, he presented the *Stabat Mater* instead. The added wind instruments were in fact done by Neukomm (see latter of 2 November, *infra*).

On 17 September, Franz Xaver Süssmayer died of consumption, in Vienna. On Thursday, 22 September, Rosenbaum (114) tells us of 'The final concert at the Augarten. Milder sang an aria by Haydn, Stummer played a pianoforte concerto by Mozart.' The *Zeitung für die elegante Welt* reviewed the concert and enables us to identify the Haydn work as the *Scena di Berenice*, composed for Banti in London in 1795: '. . . An aria by Metastasio, set to music by Haydn, was excellently sung by Mlle Milder, whose voice is extremely lovely; the aria is distinguished by its boldly impetuous spirit and high pathos.' The success of the Scena, as sung by the woman

---

1 For further details, the reader is referred to the new critical edition of the *Stabat Mater*, edited by the present writer, for Faber Music.

who would soon be Beethoven's Leonore, seems to have inspired Tranquillo Mollo to publish the piano score about this time: it was in fact the first edition.[1]

Haydn may have managed to escape some of the conducting duties at Eisenstadt, but the following document shows that Prince Esterházy still considered him responsible for the administrative affairs of the musicians.

[To Haydn from Prince Nicolaus II Esterhazy. *German*]
To *Kapellmeister* Haydn!
　　The distribution of uniforms, concerning which the wind band players and the tenor have petitioned in the enclosed *Suppliquen*, cannot be systematized into any CATEGORY, and moreover was not included in the duly appointed salaries of these above-mentioned members of the band[2] – neither in form of a uniform each year, or much less in form of a cash substitute; proof of this is seen in the fact that when one or the other of these members of the band leaves, some other member must take over his uniform; and when the wind band was formed, there was no uniform at all. Thus it is quite obvious that the suppliants are neither entitled to any compensation, nor is it intended that in their new contracts they should receive 400 Fl. instead of 300 Fl. annually.
　　To which end you will instruct the members of the band who petitioned, explaining fully all the circumstances enumerated above pertaining to the petition submitted.[3]
Eisenstadt, 13th October 1803.　　　　　　　　　　　　Exp. Esterhazy
[CCLN, 220]

At the end of October Haydn returned to Vienna and one of his first tasks was to write a letter to Madame Moreau, as follows:

[To Madame Moreau.[4] *French*. Only signature autograph]
　　　　　　　　　　　　　　　　　　　　　　　　Vienna, 1st November 1803
Madame,
　　Prince Esterhazy did me the honour of informing me that you wish to have a Sonata of my composition. Nothing more than the ardent desire to please you would be necessary to incite me to begin this work; my age and my sicknesses have prevented me from accomplishing anything during the past two years, and I tremble that you may not perceive this fact: but indulgence is always the handmaiden of charm and talent, and I am sure that I may count on yours. My doctors lead me to hope for a mitigation of my ills; and I wish for nothing more, *Madame*, than to repair the weakness of my composition – a new work which I offer to you in reverence. I hope that it will be worthy of you and *M. le général*

1　The newspaper does not mention a Miss (or Mrs) Stummer but on the contrary says that Frl. Hohenadl performed Eberl's piano Concerto in C major.
2　'Musik Individuen'.
3　It is interesting to compare this rather grim document with a similar petition submitted to Nicolaus I: see letter written at the beginning of October 1789 (CCLN 88f.).
4　The beautiful and talented creole wife of Jean Victor Moreau, the famous French general who refused to marry Caroline Bonaparte and thus earned Napoleon's undying hatred. Madame Moreau has been described as 'Femme de grande distinction, parlant plusieurs langues, bonne musicienne, peintre de talent, elle exerçait une vivre séduction sur tous ceux qui l'approchaient' (J. Dontenville, *Le général Moreau* [*1763–1813*]. Paris, 1899, p. 142). Prince Esterházy seems to have thought it politic to have Haydn write her a new Sonata. Haydn, of course, did not dream of composing a new Sonata for her or anyone else, and gave her a copy of the pianoforte Trio No. 41 in E flat minor (1795), without the 'cello part. See Hoboken, p. 716, Pohl III, 213ff., etc.

Moreau; I beg him not to judge me too sternly, and to remember that it was only Timotheus who had the privilege of singing in front of Alexander!

I have the honour to be, *Madame*, most respectfully,

Your most humble and most obedient servant,

Joseph Haydn [m.p] ria.

[CCLN, 221]

The following day Griesinger could report to Leipzig of a meeting with Haydn:

2 November 1803

. . . Haydn did not answer the letter which I sent to Eisenstadt; but now he has come back and I heard from his own lips that the Mass [*Schöpfungsmesse*] of which you sent me the theme is really his penultimate. He presumes that you received it from the Beck brothers in Munich, who pressed him hard for it and supported their request with a light tabatière in gold and for that reason got the Mass. The *Stabat Mater* which you printed is the one which Haydn offered to you and for which one his pupils, Neukomm, wrote new and fuller woodwind parts under his [Haydn's] supervision. If you are still interested to receive these additions, I hope to agree with Hn. to have them for the copying costs.

[Olleson, *Griesinger*, 44]

The Beck brothers, listed in *AMZ*'s article about the Munich orchestra ('Über den Zustand der Musik in München', V, 275ff.), are reported as of that date – January 1803 – to be 'with the permission of the Bavarian Elector on a trip to St Petersburg'. We wonder if it is possible that Haydn can have composed his lost Concerto for two horns, of which we have only the *incipit* in the Elssler Catalogue of 1805, for the Beck brothers.

In the middle of November we have more evidence of Haydn's wearisome administrative duties:

[To Prince Nicolaus II Esterházy. *German*]
[Text by Johann Elssler, the numbers filled in by Haydn and the signature also autograph]

[Beginning of November 1803][1]

In my humble but well considered opinion, all four suppliants deserve to have their requests granted, Barbara Philhofin [*recte*: Pilhofer[2]], discant, with an additional yearly allowance of 50 Fl., the other three with 25 each.

Haydn [m.p.] ria.
Kapellmeister

[CCLN, 221]

In the middle of December Griesinger had more news to report:

14 December 1803

. . . I am to receive the missing parts for the *Stabat Mater*; he also promised me his last Mass [*Harmoniemesse*] and the Ten Commandments, an earlier work in four-part canons that no one owns; the text is from the old catechism, but it would be easy to put better chosen expressions underneath the music. I voiced the wish to take it all with me on the spot, but then it was said he wanted to look for it all and make up a parcel for you towards the end of the year and give it to me. . . .

1 Esterházy's answer is dated 18th November 1803 and names the other three suppliants: Johann Bader, bass; and Magdalena and Josepha Schöringer. Haydn's financial suggestions were accepted. (Esterházy Archives, Acta Musicalia Fasc. XXVII, 1988).
2 Barbara Pilhofer had been engaged as soprano in 1782; she was affectionately known as 'Babette' – see also Haydn's will.

. . . Haydn was in such a good mood that I could not omit discussing the question of the Polymnie [*Polyhymnia*]. 'For that composition,' he said, 'one needs continuing good health and the *paga Pantalon*.' 'Oh,' said I, 'if you are only worried about that, I'm half sure of my side of the bargain; if you establish an inexpensive fee, H. Härtel will either pay you a sum in advance or give you assurance of future payment.' He answered that he wouldn't take anything in advance; he must, however, read through the poem several times before he can make up his mind. That meant that the matter was again postponed; so I told him that Beethoven was looking for good poems and that he might be pleased to be able to compose the Polymnia [*sic*]. This piece of information made so much impression on him that the Papa asked me (without, however, mentioning his name) to show the poem to Beethoven and to ascertain from him whether he thinks it suitable for setting to music and if he thinks one could gain honour with it. This condescension on the part of Papa will astound you no less than it did me; but that is what happened! I ran, as you can easily imagine, with the Polymnia to Beethoven, who promised to let me have his impressions of it within a period of 8 days. Haydn will presumably decide on the basis of Beethoven's statement. His opinion is certainly more competent than Swieten's, to whom Haydn used to apply for advice in such cases. As far as I know Haydn, the poem is perhaps too high for him, for he is more used to 'süße Liebe, reine Triebe' [from *The Seasons*] &c . . . Beethoven told me that a poem 'Die Feyer der Töne', if I am not mistaken, also by Schreiber, has been offered to him. . . .   [Olleson, *Griesinger*, 44f.]

On 17 December the *Wiener Zeitung* (No. 101) announced a performance of *The Seven Words* for the benefit of the Bürgerspital (citizens' hospital) for 26 December, to be conducted by Haydn himself. On 18 December Haydn wrote his Scottish publisher Thomson:

[To George Thomson, Edinburgh. *Italian*]

Vienna, 18th December 1803

My most esteemed Friend!

At last I can send you the thirteen songs you asked for, and hope that they will give equal pleasure to you and your dear – dearest – daughter, whose hands your good old Haydn kisses. – Some of these songs, contrary to my intention, turned out to be rather difficult, but when they have been more frequently played, they will be seen to have the same value as the others. – Many thanks for the 50 ducats which I received from Messrs. Fries et Comp.

Concerning that which you wrote me in your last letter – 'in about a fortnight I shall write you about a composition of an entirely different sort' – I have not as yet heard anything further.

Since I have done so many Scottish songs for you, I am willing, if you so wish, to do another twenty-five more, and if your beautiful daughter wants some little English songs by me, with pianoforte accompaniment, I shall send them at once. It is enough if she will send me a little catalogue of those which she has already received from London. For the rest, I am as always, with the greatest esteem,

Your most sincere friend and servant,
Giuseppe Haydn [m.p] ria.

P.S.: Milord Minto will have seen my portrait *en buste*,[1] and not the medallion made by the famous Grassi in Vienna in a certain process rather like *terra cotta*

---

1 Probably the lead bust, also by Grassi (or Thaller); see pl. 1.

porcelain;[1] the latter is very like me, and if the war does not prevent it, I shall try to send you one.

[Thomson notes: '18 Dec 1803 / Haydn/ with 13 Airs,/ chiefly Welsh,/ & Receipt for the/piece declaring these/to be my property &/ He agrees to do/more if wanted, &/ offers some Airs of his / comp^n to my dau^r.']

[Separate receipt:]

[English]

I acknowledge to have received of Mr Georg Thomson Esq: of the City of Edinburgh in Scotland by the hands of Messrs Fries et Comp: per order of Mess^ers Thos Coutts et Comp: of London Fifty ducats for composing Ritornelles et Accompaniments for the Piano Forte etc: to twelve Welsh et Scottish Airs, and I declare these, in addition to the 158 which I before composed for the Said G: Thomson to be his sole property. –

Given under my hand at Vienna, the 18th of December 1803.

Dr Haydn [m.p] ria.

[Address in Elssler's hand, with postal stamp of foreign office indicating date of arrival: 'JA[N] 11 1804'.] [CCLN, 222f.]

Almost simultaneously Thomson sat down to write to Haydn:

[To Haydn from George Thomson, Edinburgh. *English*: from Thomson's copy-book]

T.O. Edinburgh 20 Dec 1803.

To D^r. Haydn
    Vienna
  (translated into Italian &
sent to M Coutts Trotter to
be transmitted through
Fries & C°.)

My dear Sir

[Copyist's hand:] Altho' I do not wish to harass you with more business than may be agreeable to you, I must beg leave to send you [number added later:] 24 more Airs, WHICH WILL MOST CERTAINLY BE THE LAST. Your Ritornelles & Accompaniments delight me so much, that I realy [*sic*] cannot bear the idea of seeking an inferior Composer to finish a work already so nearly finished by you. I do flatter myself therefore that you will not give me the pain & mortification of a refusal. I ask it as a most particular favour, & I am willing to pay you [number added later:] 4 ducats for each Air, & as the Airs are in general very short, they will not ocupy [*sic*] much of your time. Let me beg you then that you will be so good as to do them in your usual charming manner, as soon as you can, & if you please to send me the one half without waiting till the other half is finished, I shall be very glad to receive them. Messrs. Fries & Co: will pay the price of whatever number you deliver to them on my account. I am expecting every day to receive the Airs which I sent you on the 6th September last for the payment of which a draft of 50 ducats was inclosed. I hope these airs are on the road to me.

Allow me to mention, that if you find any of the Airs fit for an accomp^t similar to that in your 1st Canzonet in C, published by Corri & Dussek,[2] I am particularly fond of that kind of easy motion in accomp^t.

---

1 The splendid *terracotta* bust, the original of which is reproduced in the *Musical Quarterly* Vol. XVIII/2 (April 1932), facing p. 191.
2 'The Mermaid's Song' (Anne Hunter), the first of the 'VI Original Canzonettas'.

I remain with Affectionate regard & the higest [*sic*] respect Dear Sir Yours faithfully

P.S. remember to send me your portrait [:] the one which Lord Minto saw in Vienna which he told me is very like you.[1]   [CCLN, 223]

By now Haydn was a real Viennese celebrity, of course, and it must have occurred to many that they might be seeing the frail old man conduct for the last time on 26 December. And so it was. This charitable perforance of *The Seven Words* was Haydn's last appearance as a conductor. Rosenbaum (117) was there and wrote: '. . . to the Redouten Saal shortly after 11 o'clock. There was a concerto by young [Joseph] Mayseder, then *The Seven Words* by Haydn, which he himself conducted. Soloists were [Amalie] Schmalz, [Antonie] Flamm, [Carl] Weinmüller and [a singer from the Leopoldstädter Theater] Bondra; it was a benefit performance for the poor townspeople of St. Marx. It was very crowded. The Emperor gave 1,000 gulden . . .'.[2] The total income was 3,900 fl., with lighting expenses of 250 fl.[3]

Our Chronicle for 1803 closes with the following undated document from the Esterházy Archives:

[To Prince Nicolaus II Esterházy. *German*]

My humble opinion would be to grant Madame Siess[4] an additional allowance of 50 Fl. per year, because of her especial diligence and good conduct; and that you graciously heed the request of Jean Dörzel,[5] who is the only good double-bass player in Vienna and the whole of the Kingdom of Hungary.

Jos: Haydn [m.p] ria.

[On the cover of the file is the following pencilled note: '*Quoad* RUMFELD none, Haidn should propose DÜZEL's additional allowance.']   [CCLN, 224]

At this point in our Chronicle two little-known portraits of Haydn may be introduced to the reader. The first is a good wax medallion by Sebastian Irrwoch (also spelled 'Ihrwach', etc.) which used to exist in several versions. One, signed 'Irwach sc. 1803 / Vienna', was taken to Sweden by Silverstolpe and is still preserved at Näs Castle (reproduced on p. 266 of Mörner, also in Somfai, No. 19 on p. 217). The Irrwoch portrait was also engraved in 1810 by David Weiss and used as the frontispiece for the Dies biography (see pl. 3).

---

1 See also previous letter: Thomson had obviously asked Haydn about the portrait in an earlier letter.
2 The *Wiener Zeitung* No. 2 (7 January 1804) reports that the Court and the cream of Viennese society were present. 'J. Haydn, who despite his great age and weak health took it upon himself to conduct the whole music, gave through this kindness new evidence that he is as great a friend of man as he is an artist, and the administration of the People's Hospital proffers him and the excellent singers . . . public thanks for their unselfish willingness to lend their art to such a purpose.' Pohl III, 221f.
3 Hanns Jäger-Sunstenau, op. cit., 134.
4 Madame Siess was Anna *née* Rumfeld (Rhumfeld).
5 Jean Dörzel (or Düzel) is apparently Johann Dietzl. Pohl and others have confused the four Dietzls, who were: (1) Joseph, schoolmaster and tenor, who died in 1777. See letter of 22 Dec. 1768. (2) Joseph Wolfgang, son of the above, who was a horn player. He was engaged in the Esterházy band in 1776, and died at Eisenstadt in 1795. (3) Johann, the double bass player, who died at Eisenstadt in 1806 at the age of 52, and who was also a son of the first. (4) Joseph, violinist, probably a son of Joseph Wolfgang. He died in 1801. (Pohl I, 261, corrected by André Csatkai, 'Die Beziehungen Gregor Josef Werners, Joseph Haydns und der fürstlichen Musiker zur Eisenstädter Pfarrkirche', *Burgenländische Heimatblätter* I/1 [1932], p. 16.)

The second portrait is much more mysterious. It is a miniature signed by Christian Horneman, an artist who has quite recently been described[1] as one whose 'use of soft colouring mixed with brilliant draughtsmanship makes him one of the most skilled miniaturists of the Swedish school'. His beautiful miniature of Beethoven was dated 1803 and was made in Vienna (colour reproduction *inter alia* in Landon, *Beethoven*), and his signed but apparently undated portrait of Haydn was probably executed during the same period. Alas, the Haydn portrait, first reproduced in Geiringer 1932, p. 37, has disappeared. Professor Geiringer lists the source as the National Museum in Budapest; but the Museum authorities state that the caption is in error, for they have never owned the miniature. Professor Geiringer kindly informed us that this particular illustration was furnished by the publisher, and the publishing house (Akademische Verlagsgesellschaft Athenaion, Potsdam) no longer exists. Horneman's miniature of Haydn, as far as the black-and-white illustration reveals (see pl. 4), is somewhat idealized and not up to the fine standards of his Beethoven portrait. Whether the original is better than the photograph must remain an unanswered question until the rediscovery of the Horneman portrait.

1 Sotheby & Co., Catalogue 18 December 1972, lot 93.

CHAPTER SIX

Works of 1803

The Unfinished String Quartet in D Minor
('Opus 103', III:83, composed in 1803)

IN THE HOBOKEN CATALOGUE (I, 439), the description of the autograph is fragmentary; using Otto Albrecht's *Census of Autograph Music Manuscripts of European Composers in American Libraries*, Philadelphia 1953, we may see that in 1953 the autograph (item 927) was owned by Broude Brothers in New York; they subsequently sold it to Mr Otto Kallir, whose important Haydn collection has never been made available to scholars. The manuscript, once owned by Breitkopf & Härtel (who issued the first edition), is signed and dated 'di me giuseppe Haydn mpria $\overline{803}$'. It consists of the two middle movements, the B flat *Andante grazioso* and the D minor *Menuetto ma non troppo – Presto*. Obviously the Quartet was to be in D minor, but we cannot say if Haydn intended the two middle movements to remain in the order in which they now stand.

Critical edition: Doblinger (edited by the present writer, 1973).

Some years ago Dr Georg Feder of the Haydn Institut kindly made available to us a hitherto unknown sketch of the Minuet in full score. The MS. is entitled 'Scherzo' but in an unknown hand, and there is no tempo. Interested readers may consult the Doblinger score for the textual details, but here we would point out only one very interesting and characteristic change. Originally bar 36 (the bar of rest) was lacking; Haydn added it afterwards.

The single most striking characteristic of Haydn's late string quartets is surely their harmonic breadth. The relationship of the two extant movements of this work is flattened submediant to tonic (a more obvious choice would have been F major, or possibly D major). The Andante grazioso has an air of lonely resignation about it; we are not burdened with hindsight, because the curiously melancholic middle parts (especially the viola) of such a passage tells us more than any autograph letter (see musical example overleaf).

New as this harmonic language is, the form is equally fresh. The first section is a miniature a–b–a, which we will call 'A'. 'B' introduces not only new thematic material but is in the extraordinary key of G flat major. Here is another series of flattened submediants (and, characteristically, downwards): D minor (the opening movement or the Minuet, whichever would have preceded this movement in the final scheme) to B flat to G flat and then, in the 'C' section to C sharp minor. 'C' uses the thematic material of 'B', i.e. the

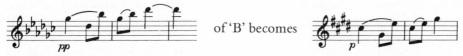

of 'B' becomes

in 'C'. At the end we have 'A' again with a coda. This brief description can, of course,

['Op. 103': Andante grazioso]

give merely a suggestion of the tonal freedom and modulatory depth of this beautiful movement. In the coda there is an almost heartbreaking moment when Haydn seems to bid farewell to music itself. This 'dying fall' is as poignant as anything Mozart ever wrote:

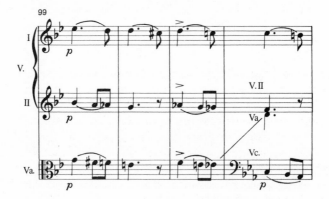

The ending is a sudden *f* outburst. Matching this sense of sorrow is, in fact, an equally arresting sense of uneasiness. The Minuet is restless to the point of edginess, especially the big build-up before the grand pause (that Haydn added later in the sketch): bars 33–35. The Trio, in D major, has something of that yearning quality that we associate with Beethoven's music of this period. But behind even this movement is a profound sense of sadness that Haydn makes no attempt to conceal. The whole beautiful torso is a rather forlorn ending to a genre which had always been Haydn's particular favourite. In the 1750s, before there was a single symphony in Haydn's catalogue, there were string quartets; now, over half-a-century later, we close Haydn's artistic life with this quartet fragment.

Preoccupations with harmonic problems came, as we have seen throughout this biography, to occupy an ever more central position in Haydn's musical thought, and it is characteristic that Op. 103 should contain one of these 'enharmonic deceptions' of which Professor Somfai has spoken so authoritatively. After pointing out that 'Haydn commits his small acts of enharmonic deception almost always with the simple trials of [minus] four fifths (third relation) to [minus] three fifths (*maggiore-minore*) in order to stay within keys which are comparatively easy to play', Somfai goes on to discuss Op. 103:

> The purest, simplest realization of this modulatory model is to be found in the *Andante grazioso* in B flat major of the Quartet opus 103:

After the B flat major cadence of the first section (bar 28) the basic key of the trio section is the third related G flat major (−4). After the D major harmony,* so widely used in the Trio's conclusion, the recapitulation (bar 71) begins in B flat major, again a third relation (−4). The enharmonic 'deception' occurs in the middle of the Trio section. After the cadence in D flat major (bar 48) constituting a *maggiore*, we hear a *minore* (−3) of D flat minor, although Haydn actually wrote C sharp minor. (The continuation in C sharp minor is logical: modulation through E major and A minor to G major). Haydn takes care of the pure intonation by having the D flat major chords followed by *melodic* C sharp minor broken chords, instead of C sharp minor chords. Under the leadership of the first violin, the different instruments appear in succession and thus have sufficient time to 'rectify' their intonation.

---

* [Original footnote: 'As a matter of fact a dominant half cadence in G major: ♯ IV♭⅜ − V.'] László Somfai: 'A Bold Enharmonic Modulatory Model in Joseph Haydn's String Quartets' in *Studies in Eighteenth-Century Music* (Geiringer *Festschrift*), London 1970, pp. 372f.

When Breitkopf & Härtel printed the work, they added the *incipit* of Haydn's Part Song 'Hin ist alle meine Kraft, alt und schwach bin ich' – 'Gone is all my strength, old and weak am I'. Haydn had these words printed as a visiting card to explain, if words and music could, why such a mighty source had, at last, dried up. And it was his idea to include this message at the end of the unfinished D minor Quartet.

CHAPTER SEVEN

Chronicle 1804

Now that Haydn had retired from public life, the nature of this Chronicle must undergo a considerable change. The public concerts and opera performances in Vienna went on, of course, at an undiminished rate but Haydn hardly ever participated or indeed even attended them. Occasionally we shall have the opportunity of noting an event of particular interest even if Haydn did not attend personally, but on the whole our Chronicle now shows Haydn living in quiet retirement in his house in the Kleine Steingasse in Gumpendorf, writing an occasional letter and – the most important activity in his life during the years 1804–5 – preparing, with the aid of Johann Elssler, the various catalogues of his library and his works which we shall examine in detail at the end of the Chronicle for 1805.

It must have been at about this period – the end of 1803 or the beginning of 1804 – that Carl Maria von Weber and his father came to see Haydn, in the hope of placing Weber as one of the old man's composition pupils. The talented young composer had been studying with Johann Michael Haydn in Salzburg ('a serious man', wrote Weber in his autobiographical sketch; 'I learned little from him and at great effort').[1] But Michael Haydn had high words of praise for Weber, and it is possible that the future composer of *Der Freischütz* arrived in Vienna with a letter of recommendation from brother to brother. 'I felt impelled to go to the musical world of Vienna,' wrote Weber in his autobiographical sketch. 'Here [in Vienna] I came to know, apart from a circle of the most important artists, the unforgettable Father Haydn, &c., then Abbé Georg Joseph Vogler, who with the love that is characteristic of every really great mind . . . unlocked . . . the treasures of his knowledge for me.' In 1804, Weber wrote the following notes about his visits to Haydn:

> I was at Haydn's several times. Except for the weaknesses of old age, he is still cheerful and in a good humour [*aufgeräumt*], speaks very gladly about his affairs and is especially pleased to talk to pleasant young artists: the real stamp of a great man, and all that is true of Vogler, too; only with the difference that his literary wit is much sharper than the natural kind of Haydn's. It is touching to see grown-up men coming to him, and how they call him Papa and kiss his hand.

Our actual Chronicle for the year 1804 begins on Sunday, 1 January, with a concert at the Court. Although we have no idea if Haydn attended – probably he did not – the concert is interesting to us for quite another reason. Rosenbaum (117) tells us: 'At about 11 o'clock Th— . . . and I drove to Court . . . An illustrious, glamorous circle was assembled. – . . . The concert began with a symphony, continued with arias by Cimarosa and Mayer [Giovanni Simone Mayr], sung by [Joseph] Simoni and

---

1 *Karl Maria von Weber. Seine Persönlichkeit in seinen Briefen und Tagebüchern und in Aufzeichnungen seiner Zeitgenossen*, herausgegeben von Otto Hellinghaus, Freiburg [1924], pp. 6, 10. Pohl III, 221.

Th—, the trumpet concerto written for Weidinger by Hummel, and a duet by Mayer. It closed with a symphony.' The revealing item about this programme was the presence of Hummel's attractive Concerto for organized trumpet and orchestra in E major,[1] the autograph manuscript of which is entitled 'Concerto a Tromba principale / Composto dal Sig^re. Giov. Nep. Hummel di Vienna, Maestro di Concerto di S. Altezza il principe regnante / di Esterhazy etc. etc.' Judging from the autograph's date, this Court performance, by Haydn's old friend Weidinger, was probably the first; and this leads us to wonder if Haydn's Trumpet Concerto of 1796 was first performed, several years earlier than the first public performance (March, 1800), at a similar Court function.

What also gives credence to this supposition is the fact that Hummel already signs himself *Maestro di Concerto* (i.e. *Konzertmeister*) to Prince Nicolaus. Exactly when this event was made official cannot now be established, but Hummel had obviously received the information from Esterházy during December 1803. In the Hummel literature, it is always said that he received the appointment at Haydn's instigation.[2] In

---

1 Dieter Zimmerschied (hereinafter abbreviated: 'Zimmerschied'): *Thematisches Verzeichnis der Werke von Johann Nepomuk Hummel*, Hofheim am Taunus 1971, pp. 197f. The first edition of this Concerto, edited by the late Fritz Stein (Hofmeister 1957), was transposed to E flat. The original work, in E major, edited from the autograph manuscript in the British Museum (dated 8 December 1803), is published by Universal Edition.

2 The autobiographical sketch which Hummel made (Weimar, 22 May 1826) twenty years after the event is unreliable as to chronology but clear as to Haydn's participation. '. . . J. Haydn suggested me for the post of Ducal Music Director at Württemberg in 1806 [*sic*]; but since the Duke later changed his mind (for a reason known only to a few persons) and wished to have no more *Kapellmeisters* from Vienna, Haydn then recommended me to the reigning Prince Esterházy, his patron, as *Concertmeister*, to assist him [Haydn], as he became increasingly weak in his old age, in his duties. . . .' In this same document, Hummel sets the size of the Esterházy establishment ('considering orchestra, singers male and female') at nearly 100 persons. Pohl III, 229.

Hummel was dismissed by Esterházy in 1811 – hardly surprising after his description of the Prince quoted in *Haydn: the Years of 'The Creation' 1796–1800*, p. 48n. In an autograph document from the Hummel Archives in Florence (Vienna, end of 1811) Hummel lists the following works as having been composed for the Prince between 1804 and 1811: five Masses, 1 Litany, 1 Te Deum, 1 Tantum ergo, 4 Offertories, 1 Graduale, 3 Operas (*Die vereitelten Ränke, Das Haus ist zu verkaufen, Mathilde von Guise*).

The contract between Hummel and Prince Nicolaus II took effect on 1 April 1804. Hummel was engaged as *Concertmeister* and composer at 1,200 fl. *per annum* and free lodgings in Eisenstadt. In 1805, Hummel also received forage for his horse (letter signed by Nicolaus II on 2 August 1805, now in the Hummel Archives) while at Eisenstadt.

The Prince also asked Hummel to put the music archives at Eszterháza in order, to dispose of worthless material and transport the rest to Eisenstadt. Hummel in this fashion found some Haydn autographs and started a small collection, obviously without Haydn's knowledge. For this aspect of Hummel's activity at Eisenstadt, see also Larsen, *HÜB* 40, esp. footnote 39. A large part of Hummel's Haydn MSS. ended up in the British Museum.

Hummel did things on a grand scale. In 1804, we find a document in the Esterházy Archives (Pohl III, 230) instructing the disbursar to pay Hummel 108 fl. 3 kr. for 'entertaining the tenor Treitler, actor Jendl, lady-singer Lauscher. . . . But in the future *Concertmeister* Hummel should make previous arrangements with the restaurant-keeper on an approximate basis'.

As a token of appreciation for the old master, Hummel dedicated his piano Sonata Op. 15 to Haydn in the year 1805. We shall see that *Kapellmeister* Johann Fuchs, and later Beethoven, found Hummel less easy to deal with (though for different reasons). The history of Hummel's dealings with his fellow-musicians in Eisenstadt is not a happy one. In 1807, Haydn's pupil Antonio Polzelli was asked, during Hummel's absence, to lead the orchestra. Hummel heard of this and wrote a furious letter to Polzelli, suspending him from service and ending: 'No longer consider that you have my confidence, of which I deem you unworthy.' Esterházy reinstated Polzelli and cancelled Hummel's order of suspension, which 'was not submitted through proper channels'(!). Later the female singer Josepha Schull complained that she was being 'persecuted' by Hummel. The *Concertmeister* seems to have been casual about rehearsals but renowned for his unpleasant words. A document in the Esterházy Archives warns him 'to conduct the music productions more precisely and attentively, to discipline seriously every careless member but not to castigate them unjustly.' Moreover, we read: 'since every member of the chorus and chamber music,

any case, it is clear from the letter of 28 September 1804 (*vide infra*) that Haydn was on good terms with Hummel, and it appears that the old man helped the younger with his first efforts in church music. Until recently, it was not clear which Masses Hummel composed for Esterházy, and in which order; but we now know that the Mass in E flat (Op. 80) was actually composed, as the dated autograph in the British Museum informs us, in 1804 (Zimmerschied, 121); while the Mass in B flat (Op. 77, Zimmerschied 117), though published earlier, may have been chronologically the second work to be completed. Both show the strongest influence of Haydn, but particularly that in E flat. The choice of E flat may have been dictated by the fact that Haydn had not composed any Mass in that key since the *Missa in honorem B.V.M.* of *c.* 1769. When Vincent Novello was in Vienna talking to Streicher, he heard an 'anecdote of Hummel showing one of his early Masses to Haydn who was obliged to alter so much of it that at last there was nothing left. Hummel evidently formed his style of sacred music upon that of Haydn – see his No. 1 in B [flat] and No. 2 in E flat.' Mary Novello, who kept a parallel diary, notes 'Haydn, he [Streicher] thinks, did much for Hummel especially at first correcting his attempts at writing Masses.'[1] From the further anecdotes about Hummel, one gathers that Streicher received the information from Hummel himself. Hummel also began an impressive Mass in D minor, patently modelled on the 'Nelson' Mass, in August 1805 (autograph draft in the Hummel Archives, Florence); a year later he composed a *Missa solemnis* in C major. Authentic MS. parts, by Elssler and his assistants, of all these early Masses are in the Esterházy Archives in Eisenstadt; unfortunately, they were not used in Zimmerschied's *Verzeichnis* of 1971.

Hearing the solemn splendour of the Hummel Mass in E flat, Prince Nicolaus and his consort must have been pleased at the unbroken Haydnesque tradition of church music at Eisenstadt – a tradition which was to be rudely, if briefly, interrupted by the arrival of Beethoven with his Mass in C major in the year 1807.

The reader will remember the curious episode (*supra*, p. 271) in which Griesinger was asked by Haydn to take the textbook of *Polyhymnia* to Beethoven for his opinion (without informing the latter on whose behalf the opinion was being sought). Here is Griesinger's report to Breitkopf & Härtel of 4 January 1804:

> . . . The 8 days, during which Beethoven wanted to examine that poetry, have grown into 3 weeks . . . His opinion about the Polymnia [*sic*] is the following: the poetry is well written, but there is not enough action in it; the beginning reminds one completely of *The Creation* by Swieten, it is too rich in paintings [*Mahlereyen*] and thus too monotonous. In the art of teaching-poems [*Lehrgedichten*], Haydn established masterpieces in *The Creation* and *The Seasons*, and he knows no more fortunate composer in this genre than Haydn. To him, the Oratorios which Handel composed are more suitable for musical composition; at least he thinks he would succeed better in them. I want to leave Polymnia with him for a while;

[p. 280, note 2, *cont.*]
beginning with *Herr Kapellmeister* Haydn, appears in the regular uniform, His Serene Highness wishes to see *H[err] Concertmeister* Hummel wearing the regular uniform in the future.' Hummel was summarily dismissed, after a chaotic performance, on Christmas Day, 1808. After repeated requests, the Prince took him back again and in October 1810 we read that he and Fuchs received 500 fl. each 'as a reward for their diligent services' (Pohl III, 232; Valkó II, 630).

1 *A Mozart Pilgrimage*, p. 197.

after repeated readings he will perhaps not be able to resist setting it to music. Now I brought my report, leaving out the last bit, to H[aydn]. But he lamented bitterly about the influence of the wet weather on his health; if he works for only half-an-hour he gets dizzy; he must take care of himself, otherwise he will have a stroke at the piano, &c. He was very pleased that Beethoven judges him so favourably, for he accused the former of showing great arrogance towards him [*eines großen Stolzes gegen ihn*]. . . .   [Olleson, *Griesinger*, 45]

It appeared to him curious that Beethoven wanted more action in the poem, for after all it's only supposed to be an oratorio, and not a drama. . . .
[Hitzig, op. cit., p. 30]

I reminded him of the music that he had promised you. He hasn't forgotten, for several days ago he ordered a lot of it to be collected. But then he found that a Salve Regina [in E] and an Organ Concerto [in C], two of his earliest and not yet published works which he had intended for you, had disappeared. He immediately arranged to write to Eisenstadt, if they might be among his papers there and he is now awaiting an answer. The 10 Commandments are also arranged by him for piano; you have his last Mass already, it's the one of which you sent me the theme [*Schöpfungsmesse?*]. At present he is working during good moments on quartets. 'Write to *H[err]* Härtel,' he said as I was leaving, 'that he will probably get my last composition'.   [Olleson, *Griesinger*, 45]

Both the Haydn autographs mentioned in this letter eventually found their way to the Breitkopf & Härtel archives. It is curious that there is no mention, either by Haydn or Beethoven, of a setting of *Polyhymnia* by Peter von Winter, performed at the Tonkünstler-Societät in 1796 and 1797 and obviously known to both men. Perhaps, in the event, it was the Winter setting that discouraged Beethoven from setting it to music.

The remark about Beethoven and the 'great arrogance towards' Haydn represents the nadir in relations between the two great men. But when it became clear to Beethoven that Haydn would compose no more – and no doubt Griesinger told Beethoven all the latest news from Gumpendorf – it is as if Beethoven were liberated from a great weight. Before 1804, Beethoven had hardly composed a single work which, as it were, obliterated Haydn's (or Mozart's) fame; but in 1804 we have a work of Michelangelo-like proportions, the *Sinfonia Eroica*, which in power, size and concept was as towering, and as final (in the sense of overall stylistic considerations) as the ceiling of the Sistine Chapel – both creations written, it would seem, by the hands of a 'giant on the walls of some primeval temple'. With the *Eroica*, Beethoven began a new era which would lead him to the *Missa solemnis*, the Ninth Symphony and the late quartets; and he could not, it seems, begin on this long road until his only serious rival and former teacher was out of the way. Not only is the *Eroica* a work which looms mightily on the symphonic horizon, it is also the work to rival, in a way that the unfortunate *Christus am Ölberg* could never do, *The Creation* and *The Seasons*. Our Chronicle of Beethoven's relationship to Haydn now changes. We shall pick up the strands once more, in 1808, when Beethoven made a kind of public homage (and private apology?) to Haydn when he appeared for the last time in public. At that time we shall also consider Beethoven's words about Haydn in 1827.

And what did Haydn think about this mammoth fresco? Did he see a score? The only answer we can provide is that the first three Beethoven Symphonies were owned by the Esterházy Archives and are listed in the Hummel Catalogue of 1806. Perhaps Haydn heard Hummel (or Beethoven himself) conduct a performance of the *Eroica* in the Esterházy Palace in the Wallnerstraße. History does not tell us.

On 25 January 1804 Griesinger again provides a long report about Haydn:

. . . An educated and cultivated music lover, Mad. Sara Levi geb. Itzig[1] from Berlin, whom I introduced to Haydn some years ago, has asked the latter to compose some fugues for the singing school [*Singschule*] of He[rr] Zelter, without any instrumental accompaniment. Zelter offers for each 10 Friedr. d'or & freedom to deal with the manuscript as he sees fit. I brought this letter yesterday to Hn. [Haydn], but he excused himself, saying that because of his uncertain and weakened health he must turn down all such offers. I asked Papa if he still remembered his promise to deliver a parcel of music for you. He said that he had found the Organ Concerto and a Regina coeli [*recte*: Salve Regina] in four parts; he is finished with the Allegro, an Andante and variations, and the Minuet & Trio of his Quartet ['Op. 103'];[2] only another Allegro is wanting. The 10 Commandments (as canons) he wishes to be published only after his death. 'You could at the same time make available the 40 or 50 canons that hang in your bedroom' [suggested Griesinger]. This idea seemed to earn his approbation; he considered the matter for a while and finally he said that he wants to make you a rather odd proposal. I include them number by number:

1. You give him, for a period of two years, 150 fl. annually at any intervals or payable in one sum.

2. For this sum you receive *at once* his Organ Concerto, the Regina coeli [*sc.* Salve Regina] and the Handel Oratorio which he received from the Queen of England; further, the assurance that his newest Quartet, on which he is working, shall appear in your publishing house (under conditions to be agreed upon). If Haydn dies within these two years, you shall receive according to the terms of his last will the 10 Commandments and the Canons in his room as your exclusive property.

3. If Hn. survives the two years, the music listed first remains as before, but in regard to the 10 Commandments and the Canons a new contract will be drawn up & Hn. will attempt to add other, as yet unprinted works.

The idea of having some works appear after his death is firmly entrenched with Hn., and he has spoken to me several times on the subject; he himself admits it to be a caprice, about which the non omnis moriar[3] is partly responsible. Now what do you say to Hn's proposition? Whether it will be profitable for you depends on the grave digger's beckoning, which you won't want to occur, because of all this, a minute before it is fated to happen to the 72-year-old man. If you find the matter acceptable, I would ask you to send the above contract with your signature; I will copy it and have it signed by Hn. I would very much have liked to know how high a price Hn. intends to set on his Quartet; he never likes to make up his mind before it is quite finished, 'because [I] never know if the work will turn out well.'   [Olleson, *Griesinger*, 46f.]

Breitkopf & Härtel promptly turned down this very eccentric proposal, and Haydn himself reflected (Olleson, *Griesinger*, 47) that 'it could be disadvantageous for him if the world would one day discover that he had been paid while still alive for works that were to come out after his death'.

---

1 Mendelssohn's great-aunt, to whom Haydn gave the autograph of the *Missa Sancti Bernardi de Offica*. Possibly the draft of 25 February 1804 (*infra*) which begins 'Most esteemed Lady' was intended for Frau Levi. See Brand *Messen*, 261f. [H.C.R.L.]
2 If Haydn actually finished such an Allegro to 'Op. 103', it has not survived; possibly advanced sketches existed at that time such as the sketch to the Minuet, which happens to have survived. See p. 275.
3 The quotation from Horace was a favourite of Haydn's and was particularly well-known in Masonic circles. It was used by Neukomm on Haydn's gravestone in the Eisenstadt Bergkirche.

It is perhaps worth noting that all these negotiations between Haydn and Breitkopf & Härtel took place without the knowledge of Prince Nicolaus II Esterházy, who would certainly not have approved of the various transactions. He considered this unpublished Haydn music as princely property, and one of his many accusations against Hummel, after the *Concertmeister* had left the princely service, was that he had made illegal use of the Haydn canons and had been involved in their publication (which was not true, as we have seen), 'to the detriment of His Serene Highness' (Pohl III, 233). But the rumours were no doubt true that Hummel had illegally 'requisitioned' some Haydn autographs and copies at Eszterháza, though he cannot be held responsible in any way for the posthumous publication of the Ten Commandments and Canons through Breitkopf & Härtel in Leipzig.

Haydn now took the trouble to answer Zelter:

[Draft of a letter to Karl Friedrich Zelter,[1] Berlin. *German*]

[Vienna, 25th February 1804]

Most esteemed Friend!

My extreme weakness does not permit me to write you more than a few words, but they are words from my heart. You are one of the few people who are thankful – you have shown this by the beautiful biography of your teacher Fasch.[2] You are a man with a profound knowledge of the science of music: this is evident from your faithful analysis of my 'Chaos', which you could have composed fully as well as Haydn did. I thank you for your interest, but posterity will thank you even more for your attempts again to resuscitate the half-forgotten art of singing by means of your concerts.[3] May God preserve you for many years to come! Meanwhile I am, most respectfully,

Your indebted servant,

P. S. I am most grateful to you for the portraits you sent me, but there is a little mistake: 1733 should read 1732. It is [originally: 'quite'] very like me. N.B. I was born in 1732, that means I am a year older.[4]

One thing more: I wish that my dear Zelter would go to the trouble of taking Gellert's *Abend Lied*, 'Herr, der Du mir das Leben &c.',[5] from my score, and arrange it for his whole choir, alternating 4 soloists with the semi-chorus and full chorus. N.B. It is absolutely necessary, however, that the pianoforte accompaniment be included, JUST as it stands.

Address:[6]   A Monsieur
Monsieur Zelter Maitre de la Musique
tres Célebre

a

Berlin.   [CCLN, 224f.]

---

1 This letter to Zelter (1758–1832), conductor of the famous Berlin *Singakademie* and friend of Goethe, is included in a series of drafts. The page begins as follows: 'Wienn, den 25^m Februar 804 / Hochzu-Verehrende Frau! / Es gab eine Zeit' ('Most esteemed Lady. There was a time . . .'). The draft of the present letter begins just underneath. Obviously the date belongs to the letter written to the lady, but this letter was also drafted the very same day, as Zelter's answer shows.
2 K. F. C. Fasch (1736–1800), composer, harpsichord player and Zelter's predecessor as director of the *Singakademie* in Berlin.
3 The *Singakademie*.
4 The portrait (copy in the present author's collection) is at best quite (not 'very'!) like Haydn, and is obviously based on the famous Hardy engraving (London 1792). It is marked 'A Chaponnier del. Laurens sculp 1803' and, as Haydn points out, gives 1733 as the year of his birth.
5 From Haydn's *Mehrstimmige Gesänge* which Breitkopf & Härtel published. See *Haydn: the Years of 'The Creation'*, p. 191.
6 This draft of Zelter's address is preserved at the top of another set of drafts.

[To Haydn from Karl Friedrich Zelter, Berlin. *German*]

Berlin, 16th March 1804

I have not words, revered Master, to express the joy I felt on receiving your friendly letter of 25th February, which I shall bequeath as a relic, as a noble letter, to my eleven children. I know that I must ascribe such praise rather to your own kindness and goodness than to my merits; but praise from you is so precious that I shall in all seriousness strive earnestly to deserve it.

As I see, you are aware that I wrote the criticism of your masterpiece, and that long before this I fervently admired you; but to have written the work as you have done, great master, that I could not have done, and will never be able to. Your spirit has penetrated the sanctuary of heavenly wisdom: you have brought down fire from heaven, to warm and to illuminate our earthly hearts, and to lead them to a sense of the Infinite. The best which we others can do is simply this: to give thanks and praise to God, who sent you to us so that we may discern the miracles which He has revealed in this art through you.

What I wanted to have from you, my dear Friend, for my *Singakademie* (which now consists of two hundred voices, of which 160 may be regarded as energetic and useful) is one of your sacred compositions, and this I have wanted for a very long time; but it took 15 years before the funds of our institution were sufficient to afford the expense of such a masterpiece. I feel only too well how small is the fee we can offer you for a work of yours, which indeed no gold in the world can repay; and as a matter of fact I relied more on your love of art and the glory of God, than on our paltry money. I beg you then, if your physical strength permits, to undertake this work, so that your great name may resound in our circle to the glory of God and the honour of art; our circle has only one purpose, to preserve and revive CHURCH and SACRED MUSIC, HITHERTO SO SHAMEFULLY NEGLECTED.

In order to have at least something of yours, I took the liberty of arranging the two Gellert songs, 'Herr, der Du mir das Leben' and 'Du bist's, dem Ruhm und Ehre gebühret' for our choir. Thus your wish was fulfilled more than seven months ago; you will be able to judge from the accompanying whether I have done them properly, and I sincerely beg you to let me know any improvements you may suggest.

I do wish I could give you the pleasure of hearing your choruses sung here, and find edification in the peace, piety, purity and reverence with which they sing your beautiful chorus, 'Du bist's dem &c.'. The best and finest youths of Berlin assemble here with their fathers and mothers, like a heaven filled with angels, praising in joy and honour the glory of Almighty God, and practising the works of the greatest master the world has yet seen. Oh! come to us! Come! You will be received like a god among mortals; we will sing a *gloria* in your praise, so that your venerable grey hair will be transformed into a crown of laurel, for our teacher Fasch has taught us how to honour great men.

Farewell, dear and beloved master! May God long, long preserve you! You have not written a single work in which one notices your advanced age. Your *Seasons* is a work of youthful energy and venerable mastery. I commend you to God!

Your
Zelter.

[CCLN, 225f.]

On 25 and 26 March the Tonkünstler-Societät put on *The Creation* (soloists: Therese Saal, Matthias Rathmayer, Ignaz Saal), probably with Paul Wranizky as director; Wranizky had fulfilled this function in December 1800 when Haydn had returned exhausted from Eisenstadt.

The following letters deal with business matters for the Esterházy administration:

[Draft of a letter to Prince Nicolaus II Esterházy. *German*]

[Spring 1804][1]

The suppliant Joseph Richter,[2] tenor in the Princely choir, is a quiet and reserved man but also one of the most diligent in fulfilling his duties. Apart from this, he knows all the church ceremonies that occur throughout the year, understands and speaks Latin, and took the trouble to teach the proper pronunciation, especially in Graduals and Offertories, to all the other singers, male and female. He also understands the Gregorian chant and its declamation, and is eminently fitted to teach all 4 choir boys. Therefore I am so bold as to suggest that my gracious Prince help him by supporting his petition for a small bonus.

[CCLN, 226f.]

[To Prince Nicolaus II Esterházy. *German*]

[Spring 1804][3]

Inasmuch as in these mournful times His Serene Highness has favoured almost all the individuals in His Highness' service in various ways; and since the suppliant Johann Fuchs[4] distinguished himself in various new compositions on the occasion of Your Serene Highness' happy return last year, my duty demands that I earnestly recommend him to Your Serene Highness.

Joseph Haydn,
Kapellmeister. [CCLN, 227]

For his charitable services Haydn was now made an honorary citizen of the city of Vienna.

[To Haydn from Vienna City Magistracy. *German*]

Know all men by these presents that we, Lord Mayor and Councillor of the Imperial and Royal capital city of Vienna, inform the citizens as follows: The nobly born Herr Joseph Haydn, Doctor of Music, *Kapellmeister* to His Serene Highness Prince Esterhazy, member of the French National Institute of Science and the Arts, of the Royal Swedish Academy, and of the Musical Academy here, upon request of the Economic Committee of the Citizens' Hospital, assisted the impoverished citizens, male and female, of St. Marx by holding public performances of Cantatas [*recte*: Oratorios] the proceeds of which were given to them; not only did he show great generosity in agreeing three different times to undertake to conduct the performance of his own justly celebrated musical compositions; for as a result of his presence, the number of persons attending the concerts was increased, and the proceeds for charity were thus greater; but he also showed himself at all times ready to give of his services freely and without remuneration, although these performances were a great strain to him.

By this remarkable and noble act of generosity, the citizens at the hospital, crippled by age, poverty and broken health, enjoyed for a considerable length of time comfort and relief from their fate. Through his exceptional talent, too, he has done much to raise the aesthetic taste of a large part of the community here. He has already received from abroad well-deserved marks of esteem and gratitude, in the form of honourable distinctions. In view of all these services, we have wished to

---

1 Written on the same sheet as the letter to Zelter, but apparently a little later.
2 Jacob Joseph Richter, who was probably the solo tenor in many of Haydn's late Masses. See Brand, pp. 460f.
3 Final version of letter in the 1804 files of the Esterházy Archives: the draft, however, is written on the sheet containing the draft of Zelter's address (25 February).
4 Johann Nepomuk Fuchs, the Assistant *Kapellmeister*. For a description of the 'various new compositions', see the contemporary report quoted in Pohl III, 220.

show our gratitude in some form, also to posterity, and thus we, Lord Mayor and Councillor, have unanimously and with one mind voted that said Herr Joseph Haydn, Doctor of Music &c., should herewith receive, at the instigation of the Economic Committee of the Citizens' Hospital here, the honorary freedom of this Imperial and Royal capital city; he is thus invested with the rights of a citizen of the city of Vienna, and his name shall be incorporated in the citizens' land-registry office.

In witness and in affirmation whereof we have prepared this diploma, given under our hands and privy seals this First Day of April, 1804

Joseph Georg Hörl
Imperial & Royal Court Councillor and Lord Mayor.
Stephan Edler von Wohlleben,
Imperial & Royal, and Magisterial Councillor; and
Chancellor of the Exchequer.

[CCLN, 227f.]

[Haydn's answer to this document has not been preserved. That given erroneously in Pohl III, 225, is the answer to the letter conferring the Salvator Medal: see *supra*, p. 260].

Haydn now sent off a further collection of Scottish Songs to Edinburgh:

[To George Thomson, Edinburgh. *Italian*]

[Vienna] 6th April 1804.

Most esteemed Sir,

I have the honour of sending you twelve songs, and also the other two which I received a little while ago, with the one hope that they shall give the same pleasure as the others; in a little while you shall also receive the remainder.

Meanwhile I commend myself to your friendship, and kiss the hands of your dear and gracious daughter for her charming letter. I am, with every esteem and veneration,

Your most sincere and most humble servant
Giuseppe Haydn [m.p] ria.

I shall make every effort to procure
that little portrait of myself.
[Thomson notes: 'Haydn Vienna 6 Ap[1]. 1804/ With 14 Welsh airs/ more harmonized / by him.']
[Address no longer extant]   [CCLN, 228f.]

We now learn of a novel way of sending music to Leipzig. Griesinger writes on 2 May 1804: 'I hope you will have found the newly added parts [by Neukomm] to the Stabat Mater packed in one of the f[orte]pianos by Streicher. Haydn asked nothing for it and I have not been able to give a token to his servant [Johann Elssler], who organized the copying, because I have not seen him for some time.' Breitkopf & Härtel did not print the Neukomm additions but circulated them in manuscript (Olleson, *Griesinger*, 47).

On 10 May another shipment of Scottish songs was announced:

[To George Thomson, Edinburgh. *German*]

Vienna, 10th May 1804.

Most esteemed Sir!

At last I send you all the remaining Scottish Songs, the composition of which has cost me great effort, for I have been very ill for some time now; but nevertheless I hope that all of them will give at least some pleasure, though it's difficult for a man of seventy-three to be able to satisfy the world. Well, be that as it may, I have done my very best not to disappoint my dear friend. In a little while I shall send my portrait in two different forms, both simple, to your dear and beautiful daughter, whose hands I kiss. God preserve every one of you, I love and esteem you all, though I have not had the honour of your acquaintance. Farewell. I am, and will always be,

dearest Friend,

Your most humble, most sincere friend and servant,

Giuseppe Haydn [m.p] ria.

[Thomson notes: 'Haydn/ Vienna 10 May 1804/ With 11 other Welsh / airs harmonized / by him –'.]   [CCLN, 229]

In May, the money from the English subscriptions to copies of *The Creation* was finally announced, by Hammersley & Co., as being ready for delivery to Vienna:

[Draft of a letter to the bankers Hammersley & Co., London. *German*]

[Vienna, May 1804[1]]

Monsieur!

     Yesterday I received a letter, dated 12th April 1804, from my friend Salomon in London, with the pleasant news that you have received on my behalf seventy-two pounds Sterling, eleven shillings and sixpence from Doctor Burney. Thus I would ask you to have this money transferred to me at your earliest convenience through a safe banker; I should prefer it to go through the bankers Fries & Compag. If you should be a lover of music, I shall be happy to send you something brand new, either by a courier or with the mail-coach. Meanwhile I am

[CCLN, 229]

Dr Charles Burney, Haydn's English friend who had 'procured him more subscribers to that sublime effort of genius – *The Creation*, than all his other friends, whether at home or abroad, put together', was obviously rather hurt that when the copies of *The Creation* arrived in England, the 'bale of books' contained 'no letter, or particular book for my own use . . . directed to me by Dr. Haydn'.[2] But now Haydn sat down to thank Dr Burney in a letter of which we possess not only the draft

[To Charles Burney, Chelsea. *German*]

[Vienna, May 1804]

[Contents][3] A thousand thanks, my dearest Friend, for having taken the trouble to collect on my behalf seventy-two pounds Sterling 11 sh. and sixpence, and for having given this sum to the bankers Hammersley, through whom I shall receive it quite safely. God preserve you and your good family many years – I had just written them a word of greeting myself. I am and will ever remain your admirer and sincere friend

D^r. H

[CCLN, 230]

but also the finished letter which, not having been available for CCLN, we now publish for the first time.[4]

---

1 Haydn would have received the letter of 12 April about four weeks later, if not a little sooner. The draft of the letter to Burney shows us to whom the present letter was addressed.
2 Lonsdale, 401.
3 Haydn translated the letter into French.
4 Our thanks must go to Professor J. M. Osborn, from whose vast Burney collection at the Yale University Library this letter comes; Professor Osborn kindly sent us a photograph of the letter.

[To Charles Burney, Chelsea. *French.* Only signature autograph]

Vienne le 19 May 1804

Très cher et très avoué Ami!

J'ai reçu hier une lettre de monsieur Salomon établie à London, par la quelle j'étois pleinement convincu de vôtre ençienne Amitié; je m'estime que trop hereux d'avoir un homme de vôtre Probité, qu'il s'intèresse pour moi et qu'il me fait faire part d'un compte de 72. livres Sterlings, 11 Escallings et 6 Pinçes, acceptable par monsieur le Banquier Hamersley, maison par la quelle je serois certainement satisfait et dont je lui en ai fait part aujourd'hui. Dieu veuille vous accorder une santé parfaite, et vous et vôtre très aimable famille complait[1] [?] de tous viens possible étant

Vôtre tres affectione

Ami

Dr Haydn mpria

The following correspondence is self-explanatory:

[To Haydn from János Karner,[2] *German*]

To *Herr Kapellmeister* Haydn:

Well born, most esteemed Herr Doctor of Music and *Kapellmeister*!

I had sincerely entertained the hope that you, as director of, and presiding official over your people, would, in profound gratitude and thankfulness over the success of the musicians' petitions, personally proffer your note of thanks, as is meet and proper in such cases. But since, however, such a tone has been wanting in your previous correspondence with me, you will please have the goodness to instruct the subordinate personnel accordingly; I myself shall not fail in the future to bring to your attention such official lapses of conduct among the members of the band, and I shall send you from here the necessary copies of such correspondence for your information.

In this connection, I have had prepared a new list of the salaries and number of persons in the choir and band [*Kammermusik*], because there have been various increases in salary and changes during recent times; I have enclosed this document for your information and use. Taking it as a basis, you are kindly requested to submit a report to His Highness not only concerning the petition – returned again – of Anton Tomasini, but also concerning the two petitions, herewith enclosed, of the leader Louigi [*sic*] Tomasini and the trumpeter Sebastian Binder, which His Highness ordered me to forward to you. Meanwhile I have the honour, Sir, of remaining, with every respect and veneration,

Your most obedient servant,

Exp. Karner.

1804 [date on the file], probably May.[3]   [CCLN, 230]

[To Prince Nicolaus II Esterházy. *German*]

[Vienna, May 1804][4]

My humble recommendation for the leader Luigi Tomasini will certainly not meet with my magnanimous Prince's disapproval, if, in view of his merits in so

---

1 The word 'complait' added as an insertion and difficult to decipher, but Haydn obviously means a derivative of the verb 'complaire' (to delight in).

2 Karner was Prince Esterházy's Economic Administrator, a position similar to that of Rahier (see the letters of 1765 *et seq.*, CCLN, 3ff.).

3 See next letter.

4 The draft of this letter, in the Burgenländisches Landesmuseum (*ex coll.* Sándor Wolf) at Eisenstadt, is on the same page as that to the bankers Hammersley & Co. (see *supra*), and thus Karner's letter to Haydn, and Haydn's answer, may be dated with some certainty in the month of May 1804.

many and varied fields, I personally ask Your Serene Highness to support his request in some manner.

My recommendation for his son Anton Tomasini, however, who only five months ago received an additional yearly allowance of 40 Fl. and lodging money, depends entirely on Your Highness' generosity.

I suggest that in your graciousness you grant to the trumpeter Sebastian Binder, and to the trumpeter Michael Altmann, the modest extra allowances [*Deputat*] they ask for.

Joseph Haydn [m.p] ria,
Kapellmeister.   [CCLN, 230f.]

[To the father of one of Haydn's pupils. *German*]

[Vienna, (?) Spring or Summer 1804[1]]

Sir,

I am very sorry that in this short time I have not been able to give more than 30 lessons to your son, whom people here have robbed of the hope that he might ever learn how to compose. He is a good boy, I love him, and he has enough talent to prove to those gentlemen that they are wrong, and to show the world quite the contrary. His conduct, as far as I have observed it, is exemplary, but I, too, wish that he would better study, first, thorough bass; 2ndly, the art of singing; and lastly the pianoforte; for I assure you, dearest Friend, that by application and effort he can become a distinguished man yet.[2]   [CCLN, 231]

[To Prince Nicolaus II Esterházy(?)[3]. *German*. Only the signature autograph]
Your Serene & Princely Highness!

I must recommend the bearer of this letter, Herr Thieriot from Leipzig, to Your Serene Highness as a most talented man, and one who could perform with success at the greatest courts. His especially beautiful execution, the full tone of his violin playing, his beautiful *cantabile* and his great technical prowess have delighted as much as they satisfied me.

He was in Paris for a time, where he studied, and at present he wishes a satisfactory position. Since his personal character is particularly exemplary, I have taken the liberty of recommending this young man to Your Serene Highness' grace and favour.

In boundless admiration and indebted esteem,

Your Serene Highness'
humble
Joseph Haydn [m.p] ria.

Vienna, 21st June 1804.   [CCLN, 232]

1 There is no date on this draft, which is written on a smallish octavo sheet. The handwriting is similar to that of the drafts of May 1804, and we think it possible that someone (Johann Elssler?) happened to save all of them at once from the waste-paper basket. The dating of 'Spring or Summer 1804' is therefore entirely conjectural, but the handwriting is certainly that of this late period.
2 At the top of the letter 'mit Fleiss und Mühe' (by application and effort). In the bottom left-hand corner the words 'Emanuel Bach', underlined and then crossed out (possibly an indication that the young man should study Bach's *Versuch über die wahre Art das Clavier zu spielen*). In the bottom righthand corner the word 'Wienn' (Vienna), preceded by a wobbly letter 'W'.
3 There is no address, and it is just possible that the letter is addressed to another prince. Paul Emil Thieriot (Leipzig, 1780 – Wiesbaden, 1831) was not engaged in the Esterházy orchestra.

[To Prince Nicolaus II Esterházy. *German.* Letter in Johann Elssler's hand, only signature autograph]

Inasmuch as the Colonel's wife, Frau Spiellmann,[1] has had the kindness to recommend to His Serene Highness that the suppliant Anton Tomasini[2] receive an additional allowance, I, too, dare to add my humble petition for him.

Vienna, 6th July 1804.   Joseph Haydn [m.p] ria.

[Remarks on the outside of the file:] '2nd Aug. 1804' and 'Since, by decree of 16th July 1804, the suppliant is to receive immediately an annual supplementary fee of 150 fl. for [teaching] 3 boy chorister apprentices, this petition is at present placed *ad acta.*]   [CCLN, 232]

[To Haydn from William Gardiner,[3] Leicester. *English*]
To Joseph Haydn, Esq., Vienna.

Sir, – For the many hours of delight which your musical compositions have afforded me, I am emboldened (although a stranger) to beg your acceptance of the enclosed small present, wrought in my factory at Leicester. It is no more than six pairs of cotton stockings, in which is worked that immortal air 'God preserve the Emperor Francis', with a few other quotations from your great and original productions. Let not the sense I have of your genius be measured by the insignificance of the gift; but please to consider it as a mark of the great esteem I bear to him who has imparted so much pleasure and delight to the musical world.

I am, dear Sir, with profound respect, your most humble servant,
William Gardiner.

Leicester, Aug. 10, 1804.   [CCLN, 233]

Although Haydn's 'resignation' as acting director of all the musical activities was undoubtedly informal and given to the Prince orally, in dutiful submission, nevertheless Haydn must have been very firm about it, and Esterházy was civilized and gracious enough to allow Haydn to retire to Gumpendorf. Of course, Haydn's absence required many adjustments in the Eisenstadt *Capelle*, and that Esterházy was aware of these adjustments, and aware, too, of Haydn's previous role as a supreme diplomat – almost a courtier – is made eminently clear from the following document in the Esterházy Archives:

Resolution for my *Kapelle*.
Pursuant to my order of 14 August 1802 No. 2341 and with reference to the reminders for the choir music personnel contained therein, the implementation of said order is entrusted to *Vice Kapellmeister* Fuchs and also to *Concertmeister* Hummel, in such a manner that in the absence of *Herr Capellmeister* Haydn the

1 'Frau Obristin' ('Obrist' = obs. for 'Oberst', or 'Colonel'); apparently the Colonel was in one of the Prince's regiments.
2 Luigi's son: see *supra*, p. 225.
3 William Gardiner, who printed this letter in his *Music and Friends*, adds: 'The war was raging at this time, and as Mr. Salomon had no reply, we concluded that it never arrived at its place of destination. . . .'. In a footnote Gardiner says: 'The subjects quoted and wrought on the stockings were the following:- 'My mother bids me bind my hair' [English canzonetta]; the bass solo of "The Leviathan" [from *The Creation*]; the andante of the surprise sinfonia [No. 94]; his sonata "Consumatum est" [from *The Seven Words*]; and "God preserve the Emperor".' Gardiner owned the Salomon-Monzani & Cimador edition of the London Symphonies (Hoboken Coll.), and also annotated the English edition of Stendhal's piracy of Carpani's Haydn biography; the English edition was published in London in 1817 '. . . With notes by the author of the Sacred Melodies' (i.e., Gardiner).

direction of the choir and church services is to be given to *Vicecapellmeister* Fuchs, further the direction of the chamber music to *Concertmeister* Louigi [*sic*] Tomasini the Elder, and likewise, in the continued absence of *Herr Kapellmeister* Haydn the *Concertmeister* Hummel is to have the direction of cantatas, oratorios and such music pieces as do not fall under the genre of church music, and altogether in rehearsals and productions of his own works.

In cases where I order a rehearsal or production in the choral or church music genre not to be conducted by the Vice *Kapellmeister* but by *Concertmeister* Hummel, or in case the latter finds it necessary to conduct such rehearsals and productions, this may be arranged by the *Concertmeister* Hummel but in such a fashion that the V. *Kapellmeister* is informed thereof by the *Concertmeister*, so that the V. *Kapellmeister* may convocate the music personnel to appear for service through the Music Announcer.

Therefore there should exist the necessary understanding, for all matters which may occur in the implementation of their duties, between the Vice *Kapellmeister* and the *Concertmeister* (without the one being subordinate to the other), nor should matters be arranged only by one party but rather by reciprocal arrangement to further the service and for serene princely enjoyment, and not by disagreement (which will produce our disapproval) or unpleasant and bothersome actions which proper *artists* know how to avoid by good behaviour, but in such a way as to encourage our approval. The entire chapel, with male and female singers, will according to the order which already exists, hold a weekly rehearsal every Thursday and are to appear, every individual without exception in *uniform*, in service at the Castle at 10:30 o'clock before my presence or that of my wife and children, with the further addition that no one except those in pursuance of their duties is to be admitted to the choir.

The musical *catalogue* is to be continued diligently and kept up to date.

All newly appointed individual members of the band, or those that may in the future be appointed, are to report properly to the *Vicekapellmeister* and to the two *Concertmeister* Hummel and Tomasini, the Music Announcer, however, will when the court is in residence at Eisenstadt present himself every day between 9:00 and 10 o'clock in the morning, and also at the same time on Thursdays, at the *Concertmeister* Hummel's in order to arrange the necessary matters between him and the *Vicekapellmeister*.

If the one or the other circumstance, proposal or disciplinary affair should occur among members of the music personnel, they are to be reported in proper form at my C[entral] D[irection] or in case they are absent to the oldest Secretary who will make note of the case in question and according to the circumstances take the appropriate action. Moreover, this my present resolution is to be made public by the head of my C[entral] Chancery Office in front of the assembled *Kapelle* and then put into effect.   Nicolaus Prince Esterhazy.
Eisenstadt, 23rd June 1804.   [Valkó II, 628]

Readers of the Chronicle will soon observe that a certain friction between Hummel and Fuchs developed – partly due to a wide difference in temperaments, no doubt. Fuchs was primarily responsible for the administration and tried to do his best. In 1804, we see that the spirit of Haydn was still omnipresent, and his name appears in sundry documents as the old *spiritus rector*. On 27 October, we have a typical letter from Fuchs to the Esterházy administration.

. . . Since the time when the suppliant Johann Wolf was called by *H. Kapellmeister* Haydn to be the flute player, he was always so diligent that I really must admit that he has very much improved, also he has had entirely to give up his work for dance music, firstly so that he can be at home to be on princely call for service and secondly to lose no time in order to practise the flute diligently, and thus I recommend him to the post of second flute with a salary of 100 gulden and a uniform. . . .

Johann Fuchs V. *Capellmeister.*

Eisenstadt, 27th October 1804.

[Valkó II, 629]

For the first time, Haydn did not go to Eisenstadt during 1804, and the various musical events were either conducted by Hummel or Fuchs. On 10 August, Mozart's *Die Zauberflöte* was performed, with Hummel conducting, at the *Engel* Inn; Therese Gassmann-Rosenbaum sang the Queen of the Night and her husband defrayed the costs of the lighting, wine, bread, orchestra attendants, etc. (Radant, *Rosenbaum*, 120). On Saturday, 8 September (Birth of the Blessed Virgin), 'A Mass by Haydn was performed at the castle' (ibid., 120), and on Sunday, 9 September (Name-Day of St. Mary) we read in Rosenbaum (120) 'Following the Mass [by Fuchs] came the [Haydn?] Te Deum, during which cannon were fired. The princely entourage drove to church in 10 coaches. . . .' In the following letter we have a remarkable account of the difficulties that Hummel seemed to bring with him to Eisenstadt.

[Johann Fuchs to the Esterházy Administration. *German*]
  While still in August Hummel asked Haydn for his last Mass [*Harmoniemesse*] but did not receive it because Herr Haydn was having some duplicate vocal parts copied. During this time, however, *Konzertmeister* Hummel went to Vienna, took the Mass with him and did not give it to me. On the 25th. ult. His Highness specifically ordered me to do the last Mass by Haydn, and therefore I went to Herr Hummel and requested the Mass, because I imagined he had it, but Herr Hummel denied it. . . . Finally, yesterday the 11th inst. he appeared with this Mass and rehearsed it, without informing me whatever; also I know that some *Musici* amused themselves at my expense during the rehearsal, because a Mass was rehearsed without me, for everyone knows that His Highness has appointed me the director of church music affairs. Through this business, Hummel gives the *Musici* an excuse not to fulfil their duties for me. . . .
  I ask you, Highly Born Sir, to procure me peace from this person, for I am fed up with this teasing. . . . His unnecessary teasings are really quite impossible for me.

Johann Fuchs
Eisenstadt, 12 Oct. 804.   Kapellmeister.

[On the outside of the letter is the note: 'Arranged by His Highness personally on 13 Oct. and the *Concertmeister* Hummel reprimanded.']
[Pohl III, 230f.; Valkó II, 629]

Since Haydn's retirement, we can see a change came over the members of the Eisenstadt establishment; no doubt Haydn was far from 'ruling like a severe regiment' (Pohl III, 233), but he obviously kept a highly disciplined musical group – something which neither the pedantic Fuchs nor the rather wild Hummel was able to do.
  Returning to Vienna, we find Griesinger writing to Breitkopf & Härtel on 22 August that

. . . Haydn has stopped all work because of his health, and a quartet of which he has finished two movements is the child [*Schooßkind*] whom he now cares for and to whom he sometimes devotes a quarter of an hour. Otherwise he is now occupied with the complete catalogue of his works, which he will send you when it is finished. He is finding a lot of things which are not in your Cahiers [*Oeuvres Complettes*]; but unfortunately he has only the theme of many such works, i.e. the first few bars. Hn. himself is astonished at the fruitfulness of his mind. In looking through his manuscripts he hopes to find some things which could be of use to you; he showed me a German aria that he has already put aside.

He cannot yet decide to let his canons go; a piano accompaniment belongs to them, which he showed to me. . . . [Olleson, *Griesinger*, 47f.]

This is the first official reference to the great thematic catalogue of 1805 (terminal date), known variously as the 'Elssler Catalogue' and the 'Haydn-Verzeichnis' (hereafter referred to as *HV*). Its final title was 'Catalogue of all those compositions that I remember approximately to have composed between my 18th and 73rd years.' A full discussion of the Catalogue's importance may be found in Larsen (*HÜB*, 53–119), who also published it, except for the Scottish songs, in facsimile in 1941. Two copies were known to have been made, one for Breitkopf & Härtel which was destroyed during the Second World War and one, Haydn's own copy, which later went to the Esterházy Archives in Budapest – it was this copy that was used for the facsimile – and which disappeared in 1945. Breitkopf & Härtel took the lion's share of the credit for this Catalogue, when they published Griesinger's *Biographische Notizen*, first in the *AMZ* (XI, 641 *et seq.*) – without Härtel's notes – and then in book form (1810). It is true that the thematic catalogue Härtel had sent Haydn in 1799 may have been the incentive for *HV*. Haydn's memory was failing, and there are not only many omissions in *HV* – all the dance music, for example – but occasionally a 'changeling' crept in; of the latter, the worst offenders were the Op. 3 Quartets, now known to have been composed by Roman Hoffstetter. Elssler, it would seem, simply incorporated Pleyel's new edition, complete as it was, into *HV* as the authentic list of string quartets, and Haydn had not examined the list thoroughly enough to spot the spurious Op. 3. This is not the place to enter into a full discussion of *HV*, but the reader may be interested to learn the principal sources which Haydn used in compiling it:

(1) The *Entwurf-Katalog* (*EK*), a running draft catalogue of *incipits* begun by Joseph Elssler and Haydn about 1765 and continued until after 1800. This is the principal source for many catagories of *HV*; it includes many lost works known in each case only by the *incipit*. State Library, Berlin.

(2) The *Quartbuch*, a thematic catalogue of music, possibly drawn up in Melk Abbey about 1780, which came into Haydn's hands. He crossed out many spurious works wrongly attributed to him in the *Quartbuch*. Esterházy Archives, Budapest (disappeared 1945).

(3) The Kees Catalogue. A thematic catalogue of Haydn's symphonies, drawn up with his collaboration about 1790, with the addition of the two London Symphonies (Nos. 96, 95) in 1791. The complete Catalogue is in the Thurn und Taxis Archives, Regensburg; Haydn owned a duplicate copy to which he added personally, but only fragments have survived (State Library, Berlin).

(4) Works in Haydn's own library, especially printed editions of the quartets (Pleyel), songs (Artaria, Napier, Thomson, Corri & Dussek, etc.) and *Oeuvres Complettes* (Breitkopf & Härtel), which formed the basis for their respective genres. But Haydn also had other sources which have since disappeared, e.g. for the lost Concerto in E flat for two horns (see *Haydn: the Years of 'The Creation' 1796–1800*, p. 226).

Larsen's fine summing-up of *HV*'s importance (*HÜB*, 321f.) may be paraphrased here. Apart from Haydn's early works (to *c.* 1765) and *pièces d'occasion*, *HV* may, especially for the 'central group of works composed in his maturity', be considered a 'firm foundation for research'. Considering that Haydn was not a scholar, and that he lacked his brother Michael's learned side to his nature, the compilation of *HV* is an astounding feat, especially if we consider Haydn's weak health and failing memory in 1804–5.

A useful side-effect of *HV* was that Haydn was forced to put his rather large music library in order; before this was done, he could hardly work seriously on the Catalogue. Three unpublished catalogues owe their existence to *HV*, and we propose to include them as an Appendix to the Chronicle of 1804: (1) Elssler's Catalogue of Haydn's Music Library; (2) Haydn's Catalogue of his Libretto Collection; (3) A Summary Catalogue (several versions exist, partly in Haydn's hand, partly in Elssler's hand). All these catalogues bear eloquent witness to Haydn's and Elssler's industry during a period when the composer was unable to write music but was still possessed of sufficient energy not to wish to spend his days sitting stiffly in his chair, with his gloves and walking-stick on the nearby table, dressed as if ready to go out.

A performance of *The Creation* was planned at Eisenstadt, and Hummel asked its composer to come to Hungary to conduct it personally. Haydn politely refused in these terms:

[To Johann Nepomuk Hummel, Eisenstadt. *German*]

Vienna, 28th September 1804

Dearest Hummel,

I terribly regret that I cannot have the pleasure of conducting my little work for the last time, but on the other hand I am convinced that everyone (WITHOUT EXCEPTION) will do everything in their power to support their old Papa, especially since the worthy Hummel will be their guide.

Your most sincere
Joseph Haydn [m.p] ria.

P. S. My compliments to everyone.

[Address, in Elssler's hand:] A Monsieur
Monsieur Jean Nep: Hummel
Maitre de la Musique tres Celebre.
au Service de S: Alt: Monseigneur
le Prince d'Esterhazi

a
EISENSTADT.

Jos. Haydn.
[Haydn's seal 'JH']   [CCLN, 233f.]

The performance took place at Eisenstadt on 30 September (the libretto was 'Gedruckt von J. L. Stotz, hochfürstl. Buchdrucker') under Hummel's direction. A few days afterwards, Haydn received the following note from his *Concertmeister*:

[To Haydn from J. N. Hummel, Eisenstadt. *German*]

Eisenstadt, 8th October 1804

Most beloved Papa!

Since, like an obedient son, I count on the kindly indulgence of the great musical father, I have dared to dedicate the enclosed little piece[1] to you. I was not

---

1 *Sonata pour le Pianoforte*, Op. 13, in E flat (Tobias Haslinger, Vienna): Hummel's first published piano Sonata.

moved to do so by any desire to shine; but rather the strong feeling of gratitude, of respect and of sincere love which I bear for you – these were the moving factors. If you continue to honour me with your kindly trust and benevolence, then I shall feel entirely happy as

Your devoted son,
Joh. Nep. Hummel, m.p.
[CCLN, 234]

The following two letters to Thomson in Edinburgh mark the end of Haydn's correspondence with his Scottish publisher and are also the last two known letters of any length that Haydn wrote in his own hand; from 1805, letters were written by a secretary (such as Elssler) and only signed by Haydn. Some idea of the rapid deterioration of Haydn's mental faculties between 1804 and 1805 may be seen by comparing the facsimiles in CCLN of the period, and in particular the neat, clear handwriting of the letter to Hummel of September 1804 (facsimile XXV) compared to the shaky, senile lines written to Artaria in August 1805 (facsimile XXVI).

[To George Thomson, Edinburgh. *Italian*]

Vienna, 17th October 1804

Most esteemed Sir,

In your last letter of July, you paid me many compliments about my *Creation of the World*. I esteem myself most fortunate that God gave me these little talents wherewith I can give satisfaction to the amateurs of music, the more so, because – as a result of that Divine grace – I can benefit my neighbour and the poor: now I should like to know whether they have given my *Creation* in London for the benefit of the poor, or for the benefit of the Professional Concerts, and how much money they made. With those two pieces of music, i.e. *The Creation* and *The Four Seasons*, I have made, here in Vienna over a period of three years, forty-thousand florins for our poor widows of musicians. I would be most grateful if you could let me have an answer on this point sometime.

I now send you these thirteen songs with the same hope that they will give pleasure; I should like before I die to finish twenty-five, or at any rate a dozen of these songs, but only for you, dear friend, for I can no longer take on anything larger than this – my old age makes me steadily weaker.

In the hope of receiving a short reply, I am, with every esteem,

Your humble servant,
Joseph Haydn.

I kiss the hand of your dear daughter.

[Thomson notes: 'Vienne 17th Oct. 1804 / Dr. Haydn / With more 13 Airs to which he composed Symph^s and / Accomp^{ts} and Enquiring whether the Creation has been / perf^d in London for the benefit of the poor – and that / he will yet do some more airs for me and only for me!'] [CCLN, 234f.]

Vienna, 30th October 1804

Most esteemed Sir,

I now send you the piece you wanted, which I received three days ago. On this occasion I must thank you cordially for the payment, *viz.* fifty gold ducats,[1] which I received from Messrs. Fries. I want to see whether I am capable of satisfying your dear daughter, and should like her to choose two or three of the last Scottish canzonets, according to her taste, and then to send me a few bars of the vocal parts,

---

1 Haydn sent a receipt, written in English (only the signature, place and date are autograph), and signed 'Vienna the 11th of June . . . 1804 Doctor Haydn'. British Museum, Add. 35263, fol. 238.

so that I can make variations or rondos from them. For the rest, I am, and will always be, Sir,

Your most devoted servant, Giu. Haydn.

Today I feel very weak, but I hope that God will give me more strength. I kiss the hands of your dear daughter.

When the fourth volume is finished, I beg you to send me a copy; I shall very happily bear the expenses. *Addio.*

[Address, in Elssler's hand:]
      Mr George Thomson Esqr
        Trustees Office
            Edinburgh,
             IN SCOTLAND.

WIEN   [Postal stamps, indicating
                  date of arrival in England:
                  'Foreign Office No[v] 19 1804'
JOSEPH HAYDN   and 'AO N[ov] 19 804']
Gumpendorf Kleine-
Steingasse N° 73.   [Haydn's seal 'JH']
                  [Thomson notes: '30th Oct 1804/
                  Dr Haydn/ With a single Air,/
                  w^t an easier Accomp^t/ thanks
                  for the last/ 50 ducats paid to/
                  him for 13 add^l Airs.']

[CCLN, 235]

On 10 November Griesinger reports his promotion from tutor to Secretary of Legation to the Saxonian Embassy in Vienna at a handsome salary of 1,000 *Reichsthaler*; Griesinger confessed to Härtel that the promotion had occurred six weeks earlier: '. . . that long ago . . . Who could be more genuinely pleased for me than you?' (Olleson, *Griesinger*, 48).

That same day the *Wiener Zeitung* announced a remarkable publication – Joseph Haydn's edition of Six Fugues composed by his predecessor, Gregor Werner. Readers of CCLN will remember the angry words that the dying Werner had for Haydn in 1765 (CCLN, 6), and the general contempt that the older compcser had for the younger ('*G'sanglmacher*', a 'cheap tunester'). No doubt Haydn had suffered a great deal in those early Eisenstadt years, and this extraordinary publication, the title page of which read

> VI Fugues in quartets for two violins, viola and violoncello by G. J. Werner, formerly *Kapellmeister* to His Highness N. Esterhazy &c &c. Now published out of special regard for this celebrated master by his successor, J. Haydn. Most respectfully dedicated to His Highness the reigning Prince N. Esterházy, Captain of the Royal Hungarian Noble Bodyguard &c., by his most obedient servants Artaria et Comp. To be had in Vienna from Artaria & Comp. 2 fl.[1]

[Hoboken I, 462]

was his way of setting his mind at peace. 'A public act of apology' is perhaps the gesture of an old man; though Werner probably had more on his conscience than Haydn had on his. It is extraordinarily similar to the kind of private-public act of apology that Beethoven uttered on his death–bed concerning Haydn and the humble

---

1 1 fl. 45 xr. in some copies.

cottage at Rohrau where Haydn was born (*vide infra*, p. 359). Some years ago, the great Hungarian scholar László Somfai published an article in which he was able to demonstrate from which various Werner Oratorios Haydn took these introductions and fugues: *Esther, Absolon, Holoferne, Der verlorene Sohn, Adam* and *Job*. Somfai was able to disprove the old theory, promulgated *inter alia* in Eitner's *Quellenlexikon*, that Haydn himself wrote the introductions; in fact they, too, are all by Werner. A new edition was prepared in 1960 by the late Ernst Fritz Schmid.[1] Of course, we know only the angry letter from Werner to Prince Esterházy of 1765 and the 'G'sanglmacher' remarks from Pohl's biography. But perhaps there was, after all, some truth in Neukomm's assertion (made in a biographical sketch of Haydn in 1809) that 'Bientôt après [1761], Werner, maître de chapelle du Prince Esterhazy et artiste très versé dans l'art du contrepoint, le [Haydn] prit en affection. Haydn le révérait à juste titre et il aimait à répéter qu'il devait tout ce qu'il savait à ce respectable vieillard.'

It is unlikely that Haydn attended the Christmas concerts of the Tonkünstler-Societät, which took place on 22 and 23 December. *The Seasons* were given (soloists: Saal, Rathmayer, Saal), probably with Paul Wranizky conducting. We have a sad description of Haydn from his pupil Paul Struck, in a letter to Silverstolpe of 22 December 1804. He says that Haydn was very weak, 'he is preparing himself for death'.

> He cannot work at all. Recently I had to play something to him. At the beginning he sat next to the fortepiano, but then took his chair to the end of the room because the fortepiano was much too loud for him; there, however, he sat a long time and said it pleased him to listen. [Mörner, 399f.]

We may close the Chronicle for the year 1804 with a note from Cherubini to an unnamed correspondent in Vienna.[2] (Cherubini had not yet made Haydn's personal acquaintance, which was to occur shortly.)

> . . . Nous nous flattions tous ici du bonheur inexprimable de voir à Paris le grand Haydn; d'après vôtre lettre cependant je vois que toutes nos espérances sont deçues. Voulés-vous bien le saluer de ma part, et lui témoigner toute l'admiration dont je suis pénétré à son égard. Vous lui dirés qu'il est pour moi le seul compositeur que j'admire, et qu'avant que la nature ne produise un autre comme lui, il se passera bien des siècles, et peut-être sera-t-il le dernier.[3]

---

1 L. Somfai, 'Haydns Tribut an seinen Vorgänger Werner', in *Haydn Yearbook* II (1963/4), pp. 75ff. E. F. Schmid's editions published by Archiv für Hausmusik, Verlag Heinrich Hohler, Augsburg. Neukomm document: *Haydn Yearbook* II, 83.
2 Quoted in 'Nekrolog. Joseph Haydn' *Vaterländische Blätter*, January 1810, XXX–XXXVII, pp. 203 ff. The article is signed 'M'.
3 The reader has followed the many attempts on the part of the French to lure Haydn to Paris. The composer refused in the first place during the war, but afterwards because of failing health. In his biographical sketch of Haydn (1809), Neukomm gives a slightly different reason for Haydn's refusal to visit Paris.

> Je le priai de céder aux instances de ses admirateurs qui eurent l'attention de l'inviter à se rendre à Paris et de lui assigner même une somme pour son voyage. Touché de ces procédés délicats, il était sur le point de l'effectuer lorsque certains individus, jaloux de voir un artiste aller au devant de distinctions qui, pour l'ordinaire, ne son réservées qu'à des êtres placés par l'aveugle hasard dans un rang plus élevé, parvinrent à le détourner de ce projet. Sa caducité et les évènements politiques qui survinrent dans la suite, s'opposerent à ce voyage, et il regretta plus d'une fois de ne pas avoir profité du moment favorable pour voir la France.

CATALOGUES PREPARED *c.* 1804–1805

(1) *Elssler's Catalogue of Haydn's Music Library.*

A tall folio manuscript (*c.* 31 × 21·5 cm), 72 pages, British Museum, Add. 32070. Facsimiles in photostatic copies were sold by William Reeves, one of which is owned by the present writer.

Principal title: 'J. Haydn's / Verzeichniß musicalischer Werke / theils eigner, theils fremder / Composition.' The following is the first publication. We have followed Elssler's orthography, retaining his headings (e.g. 'Authoren', 'Nro' 'Gestochene Musicalien', etc.). The list was patently used and 'controlled' by several hands, and we have omitted these little checks, crosses, etc. as well as mechanical underlinings, all of which are of no interest even to scholars. A few points of textual interest follow: there is usually a dot over the figure '1' (1762) – here omitted; double 'm' is usually written m̄ (with a line over it); the old sign /::/ (still used by Hungarian scholars) is synonymous with our parentheses (). The identification of the Haydn works (and a few others of particular importance) follows the actual catalogue.

J. Haydn's
Verzeichniss musicalischer Werke
theils eigner, theils fremder
Comp[o]sition.

[Neue Seite] [New page]

J. Haydn's
Verzeichniss gestochener
musicalien.

Authoren	N.º	Gestochene Musicalien.*
Jos: Haydn.	1.	Collection complete de Quatuors à Paris. 4 Bände groß folio gebunden, worin 80 Quartetten sind.
	2.	Die Jahrszeiten in Partitur. Leipzig 2 Bände groß fol: gebunden mit deutsch und französischen Text.
	3.	Die Worte des Erlösers am Kreuze Clavierauszug Leipzig. 1 Band quer fol: gebunden deutsch und italienischer Text.
	4.	Die Jahrszeiten in Clavier auszug von von Neukomm[1] übersetzt 4 Bände quer fol: gebunden.
	5.	Cahier N.º 1. Contenant 8 Sonates pour le Piano=forte sans l'accomp: Leipzig. quer fol: gebunden.
	6.	Cahier. N.º 2. Contenant 11. Piéces pour le Piano=forte, Leipzig quer fol: gebunden.
	7.	Cahier N.º 3. Contenant 3 Sonates pour le Piano=forte avec l'accomp: d'un Violon et Violoncelle. Leipzig. quer fol: gebunden.

* For explanatory notes and identification of works listed, see pp. 318–20.

Authoren	№	Gestochene Musicalien.
	8.	Cahier № 4. Contenant 8 Piéces pour le Pianoforte. 6. Sonates et 1. Air variée pour le Pianoforte seul, 1 Trio pour le Pianoforte avec l'accomp: d'un Flute et Violoncelle. Leipzig quer fol: gebunden.
	9.	Cahier № 5. Contenant 5 Sonates pour le Pianoforte avec l'accomp: d'un Violon et Violoncelle Leipzig quer fol: gebunden.
	10.	Cahier № 6. Contenant 5 Sonates pour le Pianoforte avec l'accomp: d'un Violon et Violoncelle Leipzig quer fol: gebunden.
	11.	Cahier № 7. Contenant 6 Sonates pour le Piano forte avec l'accomp: d'un Violon et Violoncelle Leipzig quer fol: gebunden.
	12.	Cahier № 8. 15 Airs et Chansons, et Arianne à Naxos, Scéne avec l'accomp: du Pianoforte Leipzig quer fol: gebunden.
	13.	Cahier № 9. Contenant 33. Airs et Chansons avec l'accomp: du Pianoforte Leipzig quer fol: gebunden.
	14.	Drey- und vierstimmige Gesänge mit Begleitung des Pianoforte 1. Band ethält 13. Stück Leipzig quer fol: gebunden.
	15.	Messe № 1. en Partition. Leipzig 2 Exempl: quer fol: gebunden.
	16.	Messe № 2. en Partition Leipzig 2 Exempl: quer fol: gebunden.
	17.	Deux Quatuors pour Deux Violons, alto, et Violoncelle. Composés et dediés a Son altesse Mons: le Prince Reg: de Lobkowitz. groß fol: gebunden. artaria.
	18.	Die Jahrszeiten als Quartetten bearbeitet von Neukomm.[2] Mollo e Comp: groß fol: gebunden.
	19.	Select Collection of Original Scottish Airs for the Voice. With Introductory & Concluding Symphonies & accomp: for the Pianoforte Violin & Violoncello. Edinburgh Thomson. groß fol: gebunden.
	20.	A Selection of Original Scots Songs London Willm Napier. groß fol: gebunden.
	21.	Te Deum in der Partitur mit unterlegten lateinischen und deutschen Texte Leipzig, groß fol: gebunden.
	22.	Die Jahrszeiten im Clavier Auszug mit unterlegten deutschen und französichen Texte Leipzig 3 fach, zweÿ sind in Kupferstich gleich, und ein Exempl: ist mit einen andern Kupferstich versehen quer fol: gebunden.
	23.	Die Schöpfung in der Partitur mit unterlegten deutschen und englischen Texte 2 Band groß fol: gebunden. Wien.
	24.	Bibliotheque musicale, en Partition Quatuors à Paris chez Pleyel. 1 Band worin 3 Quartetten sind, in Taschenformat gebunden.
	25.	Bibliotheque musicale, en Partition Quatuors à Paris chez Pleyel. 1 Band worin 3 Quartetten sind, in Taschenformat gebunden.
	26.	Bibliotheque musicale, en Partition Quatuors à Paris chez Pleyel. 1 Band worin 3 Quartetten sind, in Taschenformat gebunden.
	27.	Bibliotheque musicale, en Partition Quatuors à Paris chez Pleyel. 1. Band worin 3 Quartetten sind, in Taschenformat gebunden.
	28.	Bibliotheque musicale, en Partition Quatuors à Paris chez Pleyel. 1 Band worin 3 Quartetten sind, in Taschenformat gebunden.
	29.	Bibliotheque musicale, en Partition Quatuors à Paris chez Pleyel. 1. Band worin 3 Quartetten sind, in Taschenformat gebunden.
	30.	Bibliotheque musicale, en Partition Quatuors à Paris chez Pleyel. 1. Band worin 3 Quartetten sind, in Taschenformat gebunden.
	31.	Bibliotheque musicale, en Partition Quatuors à Paris chez Pleyel. 1. Band worin 3 Quartetten sind, in Taschenformat gebunden.

Authoren	N<u>o</u>	Gestochene Musicalien.
	32.	Bibliotheque musicale, en Partition Quatuors à Paris chez Pleyel. 1. Band worin 3 Quartetten sind, in Taschenformat gebunden.
	33.	Bibliotheque musicale, en Partition Quatuors à Paris chez Pleyel. 1. Band worin 3 Quartetten sind, in Taschenformat gebunden.
	34.	Bibliotheque musicale, en Partition Quatuors à Paris chez Pleyel. 1. Band worin 3 Quartetten sind, in Taschenformat gebunden.
	35.	Bibliotheque musicale, en Partition Simphonies à Paris chez Pleyel, 2 Exempl: worin in jeden Band 1 Sÿmphonie ist, in Taschenformat gebunden.
	36.	Bibliotheque musicale, en Partition Simphonies à Paris chez Pleyel, 1. Band worin eine Sÿmphonie ist, in Taschenformat gebunden.
	37.	Bibliotheque musicale, en Partition Simphonies à Paris chez Pleyel, 1. Band worin eine Sÿmphonie ist, in Taschenformat gebunden.
	38.	Bibliotheque musicale, en Partition Simphonies à Paris chez Pleyel, 1. Band worin eine Sÿmphonie ist, in Taschenformat gebunden.
	39.	Stabat Mater. in der Partitur mit unterlegten deutschen und lateinischen Texte, 2 Exempl: Leipzig. groß fol: gebunden.
	40.	Die Worte des Erlösers am Kreuze in der Partitur mit unterlegten deutschen und Italienischen Texte Leipzig, quer fol: gebunden.
	41.	Die Jahrszeiten in Clavier auszug mit unterlegten deutschen und englischen Texte 2 Exemple: Leipzig. quer fol: gebunden.
	42.	La Création traduit de l'Allemand et mis en vers français par Desriaux, et en Italiens, avec l'accomp: du Pianoforte à Paris chez Pleyel, quer fol: gebunden.
	43.	Trois Sonates pour le Pianoforte avec l'accomp: d'un Violon et Violoncelle. Composées et dediees à Son altesse Madame La Princesse d'Esterhazj née Hohenfeldt. London groß fol: gebunden.
	44.	Dreÿstimmige Gesänge, mit Begleitung des Pianoforte 3 Exempl:, jedes in 4 Liedern bestehend. artaria. quer fol: gebunden.
	45.	Vierstimmige Gesänge mit Begleitung des Pianoforte 3 Exempl:, jedes in 9 Liedern bestehend, artaria. quer fol: gebunden.
	46.	Symphony. Composed for & Performed at M<u>r</u> Salomons Concert, Hanover Square Adapted, for the Pianoforte, with an Accomp: for a Violin & Violoncello, London, groß fol:
	47.	Overture. Composed for & performed at M<u>r</u> Salomons Concert Hanover Square. Adapted for the Piano forte, with an accomp: for a Violin & Violoncello London, groß fol:
	48.	Overture. Composed for & performed at M<u>r</u> Salomons Concert Hanover Square Adapted for the Piano forte, with an accomp: for a Violin & Violoncello London. groß fol:
	49.	Duetto. /: Quel cuor Umano e tenero :/ Sung by Sig<u>r</u> Morelli, & Sig<u>ra</u> Morichelli, at the King's Theatre, Haymarket; In the Opera of Il Burbero di Buon cuore. at Partition & with an accomp: for the Piano forte, the Words by Sig<u>r</u> Da Ponte. London groß fol: gebunden.
	50.	Trois Quatuors pour deux Violons Alto, et Violoncello Composés et dediés a Son Excel: Mons: le Comte Joseph Erdödy de Monyorökerék. Artaria et Comp: groß fol: gebunden N<u>m</u> 1. 2. 3.
	51.	Chor der Sturm. in Partitur mit beÿgefügten Clavierauszug, Leipzig 2 Exempl: mit unterlegten deutschen und italienischen Texte groß fol: gebunden.
	52.	6 Original Canzonettas for the Voice with an Accomp: for the

Authoren	N⁰	Gestochene Musicalien.
		Pianoforte Dedicated to M⁹ John Hunter. London. groß fol: gebunden.
	53.	Trois Sonates pour le Pianoforte avec l'accomp: de Violon & Violoncelle, Composées et Dediées à Son altesse Madame la Princesse Dovariere Esterhazj née Hohenfeldt. London groß fol: gebunden.
an Herrn von Ham [Stam?] verschenkt.	54.	6 Symphonies Composed for and performed at M⁹ Salomon's and the Opera Concerts adapted for the Pianoforte, with an Accomp: for a Violin & Violoncello London groß fol: gebunden.
	55.	Sonates pour le Pianoforte. München groß fol:
	56.	12. Menuetten. für das Clavier übersetzt, welche in dem Kaÿs: Königl: Redouten Sale in Wien aufgeführt worden. Artaria & Comp: quer fol:
	57.	12. Deutsche Tänze, für das Clavier übersetzt welche in dem Kaÿsl: Königl: Redouten Sale in Wien aufgeführt worden. Artaria & Comp: quer fol:
	58.	6 Lieder zum Singen beym Clavier offenbach. groß fol:
	59.	La Creation en Partition, traduit de l'allemand et mis en vers français par Desriaux et en Italiens, a Paris chez Pleyel groß fol:
	60.	La Creation en Partition, traduit de l'allemand et mis en vers français par Desriaux et en Italiens, à Paris chez Pleyel, groß fol:
	61.	12 Lieder für das Clavier gewidmet dem Fräulein Francisca Liebe. Edle von Kreutznern. Artaria & Comp: quer fol: 2ᵗᵉʳ Theil.
	62.	Trois Sonates pour le Pianoforte avec l'accomp: de Violon & Violoncelle, Composeés et dediées à Son Altesse Madame la Princesse Marie Esterhazj. Née Princesse de Lichtenstein. London. groß fol: gebunden.
	63.	Grande Sonate pour le Clavecin ou Pianoforte Composée et dediée à Mademoiselle Madelaine de Kurzbek. Artaria et Comp: quer fol: 2 Exempl:
	64.	Trois Quatuors. pour deux Violons, Alto, et Violoncelle Composés et dedié a Monsʳ Le Comte Antoine d'Appony. Artaria et Comp: groß fol:
	65.	Variations pour le Clavecin ou Pianoforte Sur le Thème /: Gott erhalte Franz den Kaÿser :/ artaria et Comp: quer fol:
	66.	Musica Instrumentale Sopra le sette ultime Parole del nostro Redentore in Croce, o sieno sette Sonate Con un' Introduzione ed al Fine un Teremoto. groß fol:
	67.	Twelve Sentimental Catches and Glees, for Three Voices, Melodized by the Right Honᵇˡᵉ The Earl of Abingdon, The Accomp: for the Harp or Pianoforte, London. quer fol: gebunden 3 Exempl:
	68.	Stabat Mater in Partition as Performed at the Nobility's Concert, London. groß fol: gebunden.
	69.	Messe. N⁰ 3. en Partition. Leipzig. quer fol: gebunden 2 Exempl:
	70.	Ein Gesang. Der Schlaue und dienstfertige Pudel, mit Begleitung des Forte Piano, Wien. quer fol: 4 Exempl:
	71.	6. Lieder beÿm Clavier zu singen. Die Worte von dem beliebtesten Dichtern 1ᵗᵉ Theil Artaria et Comp: quer fol:
	72.	6. Lieder beÿm Clavier zu singen. Die Worte von den beliebtesten Dichtern 2ᵗᵉ Theil Artaria et Comp: quer fol:
	73.	6. Lieder beÿm Clavier zu singen. Die Worte von den beliebtesten Dichtern 3ᵗᵉ Theil Artaria et Comp: quer fol:
	74.	6. Lieder beÿm Clavier zu singen. Die Worte von den beliebtesten Dichtern 4ᵗᵉ Theil Artaria et Comp: quer fol:
	75.	La Creation, traduit de l'Allemande et mis en vers Français par Desriaux et en Italiens avec Accomp: de Pianoforte, à Paris chez Pleyel quer fol:
	76.	Sonate pour le Pianoforte avec Accomp: de Violon &

Authoren	N°	Gestochene Musicalien.
	77.	Violoncelle, Composée & dediée à Mademoiselle Madelain de Kurzbek, Wien chez Jéan Traeg. quer fol: gebunden. A Selection, of Original Scots Songs, in Three Parts. dedicated by Permission to her Majestÿ. Vol III. London Willm Napier. groß fol: gebunden.
	78.	Trois Quatuors, pour deux Violon, Alto, et Violoncelle, Composés et dediés a Son Excel: Mons: le Comte Joseph Erdödÿ de Monyorokerék. artaria et Comp: N° 4.5.6. groß fol: gebunden.
	79.	Variations pour le Clavecin, ou Pianoforte Composés et dediées a Madame la Baronne Josephe de Braun. Artaria et Comp: quer fol: 2 Exempl:
	80.	Sonata for the Pianoforte with Accomp: for a Violin et Violoncelle, London. Preston groß fol:
	81.	Ariana a Naxos Cantata a Voce Sola Accomp: col Clavicembalo o forte Piano, London. quer fol: gebunden.
	82.	Die Schöpfung. übersetzt für das Clavier von Sigmund Neukomm, Artaria et Comp: quer fol: gebunden.
	83.	Gott, erhalte Franz den Kaÿser. Die Worte von Lorenz Leopold Haschka, zum ersten mahle abgesungen den 12ten Februarÿ 1797. 7 Exempl:
	84.	Gott! gieb unsern Waffen Siege, Friede dann dem Vaterland! Ein Kriegslied nach beÿgedruckter Melodie: Gott erhalte Franz den Kaÿser! Verfasset und mit Anmerkungen erläutert von Leopold Föderl. ehedem Professor der Poetik am akademischen Gÿmnasium zu Wien, jezt Stadtpfarrer zu Weitra.
	85.	6. Lieder beim Clavier zu singen, die Worte von den beliebtesten Dichtern. 3 Theil Artaria et Comp: quer fol:
	86.	Menuetto Con Trio in Canone per il Forte Piano. Artaria et Comp: 2 Exempl: quer fol:
	87.	Ländler für 2 Violinen und Basso aus den Jahrszeiten, Artaria et Comp: groß fol:
	88.	Aria /: Or vicina a te mio Cuore :/ in der Partitur, artaria et Comp: quer fol:
	89.	Ländler fürs Clavier aus den Jahrszeiten artaria et Comp: quer fol:
	90.	Die Singpart von die Jahrszeiten für den französichen Texte, Leipzig quer fol:
	91.	6 Sinfonie a Grand Orgestra, artaria et Comp: groß fol:
	92.	Passionsmusik, oder Stabat Mater. für das Clavier und singstimme in deutschen Texte, quer fol:
	93.	Quartetto. op. 72. as performed at Mr Salomon's Concert, arranged as a Sonata for the Pianoforte, with accomp: for à Violin et Basso, dedicated to her Royal Highness the Princess of Wales, London. 2 Exempl: groß fol: gebunden.
	94.	Le tout Ensemble pour le Pianoforte ou Clavecin, avec Accomp: London. groß fol:
	95.	Two Favorite Overtures, adapted for the Pianoforte, by T: Haigh London. groß fol:

Gestochene musicalien
von Verschiedenen Authoren.

Authoren.	N°	Gestochene Musicalien.
Mozart.	1.	Messe de Requiem N° 1. en Partition. Leipzig. in lateinischen und deutschen Texte quer fol: Sehr schön gebunden.
	2.	Don Jean, oder der steinerne Gast komische Oper in zweÿ Aufzügen in Partitur, mit unterlegten Italienisch und deutschen Texte. Leipzig 2 Band quer fol: gebunden.
	3.	Cahier N° 1. Contenant 6 Sonates pour le Pianoforte, Leipzig. quer fol: gebunden.
	4.	Cahier N° 2. Contenant douze Thémes variés pour le Pianoforte, Leipzig. quer fol: gebunden.

Authoren	№	Gestochene Musicalien.
	5.	Cahier № 4. Contenant 6 Sonates pour le Pianoforte avec l'accomp: d'un Violon, Leipzig. quer fol: gebunden.
	6.	Cahier № 6. Contenant 14 différentes Piéces pour le Pianoforte. Leipzig. quer fol: gebunden.
	7.	Cahier № 7. Contenant 6. Sonates pour le Pianoforte, à quatre mains, Leipzig. quer fol: gebunden.
	8.	Cahier № 8. Contenant 6. piéces pour le Pianoforte à deux et à quatre mains Leipzig. quer fol: gebunden.
	9.	Cahier № 9. Contenant 5 Sonates pour le Pianoforte avec l'Accomp: d'un Violon Leipzig. quer fol: gebunden.
	10.[3]	Sei Quartetti per due Violini, Viola, et Violoncello composti e dedicati al Sig.r Giuseppe Haydn, Artaria & Comp: groß fol: gebunden.
J: G: Graeff.	11.	Three Quartetts. for a Flute, Violin, Tenor, and Violoncello, composed & dedicated to D.r Haydn, London. groß fol: gebunden.
Miss Barthelemon.	12.	Sonata for the Pianoforte or Harpsichord, composed & dedicated to Jos: Haydn, London. groß fol:
Struk.	13.	Trois Sonates pour le Clavecin ou Pianoforte avec Accomp: de Violon et Violoncelle composées et dédiées à M.r Jos: Haydn, Offenbach. quer fol:
Woelfl.	14.	Trois Trios. pour le Piano-forte, Violin & Violoncelle composés & dediés à M.r Jos: Haydn. Augsbourg. groß fol: gebunden.
Haigh.	15.	Three Sonates. for the Piano-forte, composed & humbly dedicated to D.r Haydn, London. quer fol: gebunden.
Bertini.	16.	Three Grand Sonates for the Piano-forte, (:with or without additional Keys:) with an Accomp: for a Violin, composed & dedicated to D.r Haydn. London. groß fol: gebunden.
Beethoven.	17.	Trois Sonates pour le Clavecin ou Piano-forte composés et dediées à M.r Jos: Haydn. artaria quer fol:
Schultesius.	18.	Ricociliazione Fra due Amici, Tema originale con delle Variazioni analoghe al Soggetto; Saggio de composizione patetico = caratteristica per il Forte Piano. In Segno di vera stima ed amicizia Dedicato al celeberrimo compositore, e Dottore di Musica il Sig:re Giuseppe Haydn. Augsburg. 3 Exempl: quer fol:
Wikmanson.	19.	Tre Quartetter för Två Violiner, Alt och Violoncelle Tillägnade Joseph Haydn. Stockholm. groß fol:
Gallus.	20.	Trois Quatuors. ou Fantaisies pour deux Violons, alto, et Violoncelle, composés et dediés a M.r Jos: Haydn. à Vienne chez Traeg. groß fol: gebunden.
Latrobe.	21.	Tree [sic] Sonatas for the Piano-forte composed & dedicated by Permission to M.r Haydn. London. groß fol: gebunden.
Romberg.	22.	Trois Quatuors pour deux Violons, Alto, & Basse obligée composés et dediés à Jos: Haydn. à Paris, groß fol: gebunden.
Eberl.	23.	Grande Sonate caractéristique pour le Pianoforte, composée et dediée à Mons: Jos: Haydn. D.r en Musique, à Vienne chez Mollo et comp: quer fol:
Lessel.	24.	Trois Sonates pour le Piano-forte, composées et dediées à M.r= Joseph Haydn, à Vienne chez Veigl. quer fol:
Barth.	25.	Schlesische musicalische Blumenlese. S.r Wohlgebohrnen den Herrn Joseph Haÿdn zu geeignet. Beslau, 2 Exempl: 2.tes Heft quer fol: gebunden.
Zulehner.	26.	Andante et Rondeau pour le Piano-forte a quatre mains composées et dediées a Mons.r Joseph Haydn. à Mayence. quer fol: gebunden.
Campbell.	27.	Twelve Songs. from the Mountains of Scotland. the Author of this little work presents it with his best Wishes to Signor Giuseppe Haydn, of Vienna. Edinburgh. groß fol: gebunden.
Hummel.	28.	Sonate pour le Piano-forte, composée et dediée à Mons.r Joseph Haydn. á Vienne au Bureau d'arts et d'Industrie, quer fol: gebunden.
Weber.	29.	Trois Quatuors pour deux Violons, Alto, & Violoncelle,

Authoren	Nº	Gestochene Musicalien.
		composés et dediés a Son Grand maitre. Mʳ Joseph Haydn, Augsburg. groß fol: gebunden.
Edelmann.	30.	Chaconne de l'union de l'amour et des Arts arangés pour le Clavecin forte Piano ou Harpe et un Violon ad libitum. à Paris, quer fol:
Albrechtsberger.	31.	Sei Quartetti con Fughe per diversi Stromenti cioe il 1ᵐᵒ e il 2ᵈᵒ con due Violini, Viola, e Basso, il 3ᵗⁱᵒ e il 4ᵗᵒ con un Violino, due Viole, e Basso, e il 5ᵗᵒ e 6ᵗᵒ con un Violino, e Viola, Violoncello et Basso. Artaria et Comp: groß fol:
Leidesdorf.	32.	Grand Trio pour Pianoforte Flute, et Alto, Composé et dédié à Mʳ Joseph Haydn. à Vienne au Bureau des Arts et d'industrie. quer fol:
Ritter v Gluck.	32. [sic]	Oesterreichs Fama eine Kantate fürs Klavier. Vienn. quer fol: gebunden.
Bachmann.	33.	Gesänge aus dem Singspiel Der Todt des Orpheus v Jacobi. Braunschweig. quer fol:
Baron de Bagge.	34.	3 Sinfonie. Executées au Concert Spirituel. à Paris groß fol:
Sixt.	35.	12. Lieder beÿ den Clavier zu singen, Basel. quer fol: 2 Exempl:
v K⁺⁺⁺	36.	Sammlung von Liedern aus den beßten deutschen Dichtern, zum singen und spielen am Clavier, Vienn. quer fol: gebunden.
von verschiedenen berühmten Tonkünstlern.	37.	Allgemeine musikalische Bibliothek für das Clavier und die Singkunst. Enthält Arien und Lieder aus den beßten Dichtern Deutschlands zum singen und spielen am Clavier. Vienn. quer fol: gebunden.
Bengraf.	38.	Sinngedicht auf Joseph und Friedrich. zu singen beÿm Clavier. Pest. groß fol:
Abt Vogler.	39.	Clavierauszug aus Hermann von Unna einem Schauspiele in 5 Acten mit Chören und Tänzen. Kopenhagen. quer fol: begunden.
Callcott Stevens & Webbe.	40.	The Professional Collection of Glees for three four and five Voices. composed by the following Authors, London. quer fol: gebunden.
Schulz.	41.	Johann Peter Unzens lyrische Gedichte religiösen Inhalts mit Melodien zum singen beÿ dem Clavier. Hammburg. quer fol: gebunden.
Dupuis Dʳ	42.	Pieces for the Organ or Harpsichord. Principally intended for the use of Young Organists, London. quer fol: gebunden.
Destouches.	43.	Trois Sonates pour le Clavecin ou forte-Piano. Offenbach. groß fol: gebunden.
Chrinazzi.	44.	Sei Treni osia Cantate lugubri in Morte Di Maria Theresa Imperatrice Opera terza Artaria et Comp: quer fol: gebunden.
Cramer.	45.	Marcia per il Clavicembalo, Artaria. quer fol:
Hoffmeister.	46.	Quatuor à deux Violons, Alto, et Violoncelle, à Vienn. groß fol:
Albrechtsberger	47.	Sei Fughe per l'Organo o Clavicembalo à Vienna Artaria et Comp: quer fol:
Händel.	48.	Te Deum laudamus, zur Utrechter Friedensfeÿer in Partitur. ehemals in Englischer Sprache Componirt, und nun mit dem bekannten lateinischen Texte herausgegeben von Johann Adam Hiller, Leipzig quer fol:
J: S: Bach.	49.	Musicalische Kunstwerke im strengen Style, Zürch. Das wohltemperirte Clavier, oder Präludien und Fugen durch alle Töne. quer fol: gebunden.
Kranz.	50.	Romanze aus der Oper= Theatralische Abentheuer: an den Schönsten Frühlingsmorgen Veimar, groß fol:
Naumann.	51.	Cora. Eine Oper in Clavier auszug, mit deutschen Texte Leipzig. quer fol: gebunden.
Eberlin.	52.	9. Toccate e Fughe per l'Organo, Augsburg. quer fol: gebunden.
Schmidt.	53.	Hymne. Beÿ Gelegenheit der Huldigungsfeÿerlichkeit zu Königsberg in Preußen als Serenade den 8ᵗᵉⁿ Junj 1798. aufgeführt. Clavierauszug Berlin. quer fol: gebunden.
Förster	54.	Kantate auf die Huldigungs= Feÿer Sʳ Königlichen Apostoli-

Authoren	N°	Gestochene Musicalien.
		schen Majestät Franz als Erzherzog von Oesterreich am 25ten april 1792. Clavierauszug, Vien. quer fol: gebunden.
Lubi.	55.	12. Deutsche Lieder fürs Clavier, Vienn quer fol: gebunden.
Struk.	56.	Menuetto pour le Clavecin ou Pianoforte à quatre mains Vien. quer fol: gebunden.
Klein.	57.	Fantasia per il Forte Piano, Presburg. quer fol:
Duny.	58.	Lisle des Toux, Parodie de l'arcifanfano de goldoni en Partition. à Paris. groß fol:
Händel.	59.	Aria dell'opera di Rinaldo, London. Italienisch. Äuserst empfohlen von Herrn Kapellmeister Joseph Haÿdn, enthält 6 Opern. groß fol: gebunden.
Bach.	60.	Sturms, geistliche Gesänge mit Melodien beÿ dem Clavier zu singen, zweÿte Samlung Hamburg. quer fol: gebunden.
Lampugnani.	61.	The favorite Song in the Opera Call.'d Siroe. by Sig:^{re} Lampugnani London. groß fol: gebunden.
antient and Modern	62.	A Collection of Catches Canons Glees Duetts. Selected from the Works of the most Eminent Composers. Vol. 2. Edinburgh quer fol: gebunden.
	63.	A Collection of Catches Canons Glees Duetts. Selected from the Works of the most Eminent Composers. Vol. 3. Edinburgh quer fol: gebunden.
	64.	A Collection of Catches Canons Glees Duetts. Selected from the Works of the most Eminent Composers. Vol. 4. Edinburgh quer fol: begunden.
Grünwald.	65.	Erste Samlung zwölf Deutsche Lieder für das Clavier oder forte Piano. quer fol: gebunden Vienn.
Dr Benjamin Cooke.	66.	Nine Glees and Two Duets. London. quer fol: gebunden.
Lickl.	67.	Six Variations sur L'air /: Gott erhalte Franz den Kaÿser :/ pour le Clavecin ou Pianoforte. à Vienne, quer fol:
Chretien Bach	68.	Six Sonates pour le Clavecin ou forte Piano avec l'accomp: d'un Violon, à Vienne quer fol: gebunden.
Emanuel Bach.	69.	Clavier Sonaten nebst einigen Rondos fürs forte Piano. für Kenner und Liebhaber, Leipzig. quer fol:
Baron de Bagge.	70.	Air de Malbrough Variée pour le Clavecin ou Pianoforte, avec l'accomp: d'un Violon. à Paris, groß fol:
Brandes.	71.	Musikalischer Nachlaß fürs Clavier mit Liedern und einer Aria mit dem Orchester, Hamburg, quer fol: gebunden.
Br. B——j unbrauchbar	72.	Lieder zum gebrauch der Loge zur wahren Eintracht, fürs Clavier, Wien. quer fol:
Sterkel.	73.	Trois Sonates pour le Pianoforte avec l'accomp: d'un Violon Obl: Mayence, quer fol:
Häsler.	74.	Clavier= und singstücke verschiedener Art. Erfurt, erste Sammlung, quer fol:
Mr Harrison.	75.	Never till Now a Favorit Glee for four Voices as sung with the greatest applause at Harrison & Knyvelt's Vocal Concerts Willis's Rooms, London. quer fol:
Händel.	76.	jephtha an Oratorio in Score. Englisch, London, groß fol: gebunden.
Webbe.	77.	Address to the Thames, with song and forte Piano London. groß fol:
Callcott.	78.	Explanation. of the Notes, Marks, Words, &c. used in Music, Organist of St Pauls. London, quer fol:
Sidler.	79.	Phantasia per il Cembalo. Tugii, quer fol:
Wanhall.	80.	Caprice pour le Clavecin ou Pianoforte à Vienne, quer fol:
Telemann.	81.	6. Ouverturen. nebst zween folgesätzen beÿ jedweden, französich, Polnisch, oder sonst Tändelnd, und Welsch, fürs Clavier, Nürnberg. groß fol:
Dretzel.	82.	Harmonische Ergözung, bestehend in einem Conzert auf das Clavier. Nürnberg. groß fol:
Kunzen.	83.	Hÿmne auf Gott. von C. F. Schmidt. Phiseldeck.[?]. Zürch, quer fol: gebunden.
Webbe.	84.	The favorite Glees of Hence all ye Vain Delights. London, quer fol:

Authoren	N.º	Gestochene Musicalien.
Schroeter.	85.	Six Sonatas for the Pianoforte, or harpsichord, with an Accomp: for a Violin and Bass, London. groß fol:
	86.	Six Sonatas for the Pianoforte or harpsichord, with an Accomp: for the German Flute or Violin, London. groß fol:
	87.	Three Sonatas for the Pianoforte or harpsichord with an Accomp: for a Violin and Violoncello, London. groß fol:
	88.	Six Concertos for the Harpsichord or Pianoforte with an Accomp: for Two Violins, a Tenor and Bass, London. groß fol: gebunden.
	89.	Six Concertos for the Harpsichord or Pianoforte with an Accomp: for Two Violins and Bass, London. groß fol:
	90.	Three Quintettos for the Harpsichord or Pianoforte, Flute Violin, Tenor and Violoncello, London. groß fol:
Diettenhoffer.	91.	The Celebrated Canon. Non nobis Domine adapted as a Fugue for the Organ, London. groß fol:
Hoffmeister.	92.	Terzetto Scolastico. per due Violini et Violoncello, Vienn. groß fol:
Pasterwiz.	93.	8. Fughe secondo l'A.B.C. di musica per l'organo o Clavicembalo, a Vienne. quer fol:
Eminent Composers.	94.	The Ladies Collection of Catches, Glees, Canons, Canzonets, Madrigals etc: London. groß fol:
	95.	The Ladies Collection of Catches, Glees, Canons, Canzonets, Madrigals etc: London. groß fol:
	96.	The Ladies Collection of Catches, Glees, Canons, Canzonets, Madrigals etc: London. groß fol:
Webbe.	97.	Ode, on S.ᵗ Cecilia, for Six Voices, London. groß fol:
Trnka.	98.	12. Canoni. a tre Voci, Pest. quer fol:
Kozeluch.	99.	Tre Sonate per Clavicembalo, o Piano forte accomp: d'un Violino et Violoncello, artaria et Comp: quer fol:
Lessel.	100.	Trois Duos pour deux Flutes, artaria et Comp: groß fol:
Schulz.	101.	Religiöse Oden und Lieder aus den besten deutschen Dichtern mit Melodien zum singen beÿ dem Clavier, Hamburg. quer fol:
Emanuel Bach.	102.	Heilig mit zweÿ Chören und einer Ariette zu Einleitung, Hamburg groß fol:
Piticchio.	103.	12. Canzonette italiane con Accomp: di Pianoforte, Vienna. 2 Exempl: quer fol:
Kein Author.	104.	Air qui fut chantée à Paris à l'occasion d'un concert donné à la Princesse de France dans une maison prés du temple, Vienne. quer fol:
Haensel.	105.	Trois Quatuors à deux Violons, Alto, et Violoncelle. Offenbach, groß fol: gebunden.
Kreusser.	106.	Der Tod Jesu eine Kantate in der Partitur, Maynz. quer fol:
Webbe.	107.	Six French Ariettes. newly arranged for the Voice and Pianoforte, London. quer fol: gebunden.
Attwood.	108.	The Adopted child a Musical Drama in Two Acts for the Voice and Piano-forte. London. quer fol: gebunden.
Webbe.	109.	A Collection of Vocal music, in two Three, four, and five parts London. quer fol: gebunden.
Barthelemon.	110.	Three Hymns and three Anthems for the Voice and Pianoforte, London. groß fol: gebunden.
Jenkins.	111.	New Scotch music, Consisting of Slow Airs, Strathspeys, Quik, Rells, Country Dances, and a Medley on a New Plan, with a Bass for a Violoncello or harpsichord. London. groß fol: gebunden.
Beethoven.	112.	Variazioni, Sopra il Thema /: Quant' è più bello l'amor Contadino :/ Nell'opera la Molinara. per il Pianoforte. Vienna. quer fol:
Struk.	113.	Die Geburts-Feÿer einer Mutter. Kantate für zweÿ Singstimmen mit Begleitung des Claviers. Wien quer fol:
Tomich.	114.	Three Sonatas for the Piano-forte or harpsichord with an Accomp: for a Violin or Flute, London. groß fol:
	115.	a Sonata for the Piano-forte with an Accomp: for a Violin and Violoncello, London. groß fol:
Nugent.	116.	Six French Romances and one Italian arietta for the harpsichord

Authoren	N.º	Gestochene Musicalien.
		or Pianoforte with an Accomp: for the Violin to the Italian arietta, London. 2. Exempl: groß fol:
Emanuel Bach.	117.	Clavier Sonaten und Freye Fantasien nebst einigen Rondos fürs Piano forte, für Kenner und Liebhaber. fünfte Sammlung, Leipzig. quer fol: gebunden.
Struk.	118.	Quatuor. pour deux Violons, Alto, et Violoncelle, Offenbach. groß fol:
Kein Author.	119.	Madrigale Primo Tom 1mo à due Voci. Canto, e Alto, groß fol:
Miss Barthelemon.	120.	Three Sonates for the Pianoforte or harpsichord the Second with an Accomp: for the Violin, London. groß fol:
Clementi.	121.	Three Sonatas for the Pianoforte or harpsichord with an Accomp: for a Violin and Violoncello, London. groß fol: gebunden.
Kein Author.	122.	Schlesische musikalische Blumenlese fürs Clavier und gesang 1tes Heft, Breslau. quer fol: gebunden.
	123.	Monats-Früchte, fürs Clavier und gesang den Freunden des Schönen und Edlen gewidmet, Oranienburg. 1tes Heft, quer fol: gebunden.
	124.	Monats Früchte, fürs Clavier und gesang den Freunden des Schönen und Edlen gewidmet, Oranienburg. 2tes Heft, quer fol: gebunden.
	125.	Monats Früchte, fürs Clavier und gesang den Freunden des Schönen und Edlen gewidmet, Oranienburg. 3tes Heft, quer fol: gebunden.
	126.	Monats Früchte, fürs Clavier und gesang den Freunden des Schönen und Edlen gewidmet, Oranienburg. 4tes Heft, quer fol: gebunden.
Barthelemon.	127.	Glee. for the anniversary of the Philanthroppic [*sic*] Society, London. quer fol:
Sebastian Bach.	128.	Motetten in Partitur, mit deutschen Texte Leipzig. groß fol:
Sebas. Bach.	129.	Motetten in Partitur mit deutschen Texte Leipzig, groß fol:
Polzelli.	130.	Serénade en Trio Concertant pour Flute, Violon, et Alto, Vienne. groß fol. gebunden.
Clementi.	131.	Fuga. Ricavata dal famoso Requiem di Mozart messa per il Piano-forte a Vienna artaria et Comp: quer fol:
Kanne.	132.	Der stille geist. Gedicht von Böhlendorf. fürs Clavier und gesang, Leipzig, quer fol:
	133.	La Tempesta Cantata di Metastasia. [*sic*] Composta per Voce Sola coll Accomp: di Pianoforte. Leipzig. quer fol:
Reichardt.	134.	Douze Elegies et Romances avec Accomp: de Pianoforte ou Harpe. Oranienburg. groß fol:
Himmel.	135.	Gesänge aus Tiedge's Urania. Oranienburg. quer fol: gebunden.
Pleyel.	136.	Trois Quatuors, Concetans, pour deux Violons, alto, et Basso, composées et dediés a son ami Louis Bocherini, 9e œuvre de quatuors. à Strasbourg, groß fol: gebunden.
Burney.	137.	12. Canzonette a due Voci in Canone Poesia dell Abate Metastasio, London. quer fol: gebunden.
Reicha.	138.	Trente six Fugues pour le Piano forte Composées d'aprés un nouveau systéme à Vienne. quer fol: gebunden.
Earl of Abington.	139.	A Representation of the Execution of Maria queen of Scot's in Seven Views, London. quer fol: gebunden.
Eminent Composers.	140.	The Ladies Collection, of Catches, Glees, Canons, Canzonets, Madricals, etc: London. groß fol: gebunden.
Eminent Composers.	141.	Volume 3^{d} Consisting of National Airs Notturni, Duetts, Terzetts, Canzonets, Rondo's, Catches and Glees, in the Italien, French, English Scotch and Irish languages. London. groß fol: gebunden.
Eminent Composers.	142.	A Selection of the most favourite Scots Songs chiefly Pastoral, adapted for the harpsichord with an Accomp: for a Violin. London. groß fol: gebunden. 2 Exempl:
Dr Arnold.	143.	The Psalms of David for the use of Parish churches. the words Selected by the Rev: Sir Adam Gordon Bar.^{t} M.A. London, groß fol: gebunden.

Authoren	№	Gestochene Musicalien.
Favart.	144.	Acajou Opéra Comique en trois Actes les Accomp: des Vaudeviles sont de M͟r Moulinghen. a Paris, groß fol: gebunden.
Gretri.	145.	Les deux Avares Opéra Boufon, en deux actes en Parttion a Paris, groß fol: gebunden.
par M͟r + + +	146.	Aline. Reine de Golconde, Ballet-héroique en trois Actes, Grande Partition. a Paris, groß fol: gebunden.
Phelidor.	147.	Les Femmes vengées Opera Comique en Partition, en un Acte, a Paris. groß fol: gebunden.
par M.D.Z.	148.	Julie. Comédie en Partition en trois actes, à Paris. groß fol: gebunden.
Gretri.	149.	Lucile. Comédie en un Acte en Partition, a Paris groß fol: gebunden.
Monsigny.	150.	Le Deserteur. Drame en trois Actes, en Partition, a Paris groß fol: gebunden.
M.D.Z.	151.	L'erreur. D'un moment ou le Suite de Julie, Comédie en un acte en Partition, à Paris, groß fol: gebunden.
par M͟r + + +	152.	L'Isle Sonate, Opera Comique, en trois actes en Partition, a Paris. groß fol: gebunden.
Kein Author.	153.	The Edinburgh musical miscelleny: a Collection of the most approved Scotch, English, and Irish songs. set to music. in Taschenformat gebunden.
Borde.	154.	Choix de chansons. mit schönen Kupfern versehen, und in Taschenformat gebunden.
Tattersall.	155.	Improved psalmody in Three parts, printed separately for each Voice. in Taschenformat gebunden.
Radicati.	156.	Quatuor pour deux Violons, Alto et Violoncelle Composé et Dedié a son Ami Pierre Haensel. groß fol: nicht gebunden.
	157.	Trois Quatuors pour deux Violons, Alto et Violoncelle, Composés et Dediés à M͟r J. B. Viotti. groß fol: nicht gebunden.
	158.	Quatuor pour deux Violons, alto, et Violoncelle Composé et Dedié à Mad͟lle Louise Gerbini. groß fol: nicht gebunden.
Neukomm.	159.	Gebet beÿ der Abreise S͟r Majestät unseres allergnädigsten Kaÿsers zur Armee, den 16͟ten März 807. Ver faßt von G. P. Derschawin. in Musik gesätzt von Sigmund Neukomm. quer fol: blausteif gebunden.
Felix Radicati	160.	Trois Quatuors pour deux Violons, Alto et Violoncelle Composés et dediés A Mons: Joseph Haydn Docteur en Musique:

[Neue Titelseite] [New title]
J. Haydn's
Verzeichniss geschriebener
musicalien.

Authoren	№	Geschriebene Musicalien.
Jos: Haydn	1.	Eine Copierte Partitur von der Opera Orfeo. welche in England componirt worde [*sic*]. auf kleinen Postpapier geschrieben.
	3.	Concerto per la Lira Organizata in der Partitur.
	4.	Divertimento per il Pianoforte, Violino et Violoncello.
	9.	Die 3. und 4. stimmigen Gesänge 10 N͟ro.
	10.	Missa Brevis in F. in der Partitur.
	12.	Miserere, aus die 7 Worte von einen englischen Organisten fürs Pianoforte und einer Singstim übersetzt.
	13.	Capricio per il Clavi=Cembalo à Violino con Basso.
	14.	Sinfonia. in D minor in der Partitur, eine von die 12 Englischen.
	15.	Sinfonia in G. in der Partitur, eine von die 12 Englischen.

Authoren	Nº	Geschriebene Musicalien.
	16.	Sinfonia in Emol. in der Partitur, eine von die 12. Englischen.
	17.	Sinfonia in Bfâ. in der Partitur.
	18.	Sinfonia in F. in der Partitur.
	28.	Ein englisches Lied. Shakespear 2 Exempl: mit Begleitung des forte Piano. /: She never told her Love :/
	29.	Ein englisches Lied. mit Begleitung des Forte Piano. /: In Thee I bear so Dear a part :/
	30.	Ein englisches Lied. mit Begleitung des Forte Piano. /: High on the giddy bending Mast :/
	31.	Ein Adagio fürs Pianoforte.
	32.	Cavatina in the Opera of Orfeo. in der Partitur. /: del mio core il voto estremo :/
	33.	Ein deutsches Lied, mit Begleitung des Pianoforte. /: Dir nah ich mich nah mich dem Thore :/
	34.	Ein deutsches Lied, mit Begleitung des Pianoforte. /: Hier sein Grab, beÿ diesen stillen Hügeln :/
	38.	Ein deutsches Lied, mit Begleitung des Piano forte. /: Von allen Sterblichen auf Erden :/
	40.	Jacobs Dream. Ein Allegro fürs Piano forte.
Mris Hodges.	41.	Original. dieses Lied ist von der Mris Hodges. das schönste Weib, so ich zeit lebens gesehen, eine große Clavierspiellerin [*sic*] Text und Musik von Ihrer Composition. /: when from thy Sight I waste :/
Werner.	42.	Ein Oratorium. Debora. in der Partitur deutschen Texte. 2 theil manuscript $\overline{760}$.
	43.	Oratorium. Daniel, in der Partitur deutschen Texte 2. theile. $\overline{752}$.
	44.	Oratorium. Der gute Hiert, in der Partitur deutschen Texte 2 theile $\overline{757}$.
Werner.	45.	Oratorium. Judas Machabaeus, in der Partitur, deutschen Texte 2 theile $\overline{757}$.
	46.	Oratorium. Die allgemeine Auferstehung deren Todten mit darauf erfolgenden lezten Gericht, in der Partitur, deutschen Texte. 2 theile. $\overline{745}$.
	47.	Oratorium, Adam in der Partitur, deutschen Texte 2 theile. $\overline{749}$.
	48.	Oratorium, Job. in der Partitur, deutschen Texte 2 theil. $\overline{748}$.
	49.	Oratorium, Der Verlohrne Sohn, in der Partitur, deutschen Texte 2 theile $\overline{747}$.
	50.	Oratorium, David. in der Partitur, deutschen Texte 2 theile. $\overline{743}$.
	51.	Oratorium, Holoferne. in der Partitur. deutschen Texte 2 theile $\overline{747}$.
	52.	Oratorium, Esther. in der Partitur. deutschen Texte 2 theile $\overline{746}$.
	53.	Oratorium, König Saul. in der Partitur. deutschen Texte 2 theile. $\overline{750}$.
Kranz.	54.	Ein Lied aus Piccolomini. von Schiller, in der Partitur manuscript. /: Der Eichwald braußet, die Wolken ziehn :/
	55.	Cantatina, in der Partitur manuscript. /: Seÿ du auf's neu, uns heut willkommen :/
Jos: Haydn.	60.	Sinfonia in D. in der Partitur, eine von die 12 Englischen.
	61.	Sinfonia in G. in der Partitur.
	70.	6. Sinfonien, zusam geschrieben auf kleinen Postpapier.
	71.	Sinfonia in Es. auf kleinen Postpapier geschrieben.
	72.	Sinfonia in C. auf kleinen Postpapier geschrieben.
	73.	Quartetto in C. à due Violini, Viola, et Violoncello, auf kleinen Postpapier geschrieben.
	74.	Quartetto in Es. à due Violini, Viola, et Violoncello, auf kleinen Postpapier geschrieben.
	75.	Quartetto in B. à due Violini, Viola, et Violoncello, auf kleinen Postpapier geschrieben.
	76.	Quartetto in Fis minor. à due Violini, Viola, et Violoncello, auf kleinen Postpapier geschrieben.
	77.	Quartetto in D. à due Violini, Viola, et Violoncello, auf kleinen Postpapier geschrieben.

Authoren	N°	Geschriebene Musicalien.
	78.	Quartetto in F. à due Violini, Viola, et Violoncello auf kleinen Postpapier geschrieben.
	79.	Quartetto in Es. in der Partitur à due Violini, Viola, et Violoncello.
	80.	Quartetto in Dminore in der Partitur.
	81.	Quartetto in Bfà. in der Partitur.
	84.	Der Sturm, in der Partitur, mit dem deutschen Texte. /: Hört die winde furchtbar heulen :/
	85.	Der Sturm, in der Partitur, zum Clavier mit dem deutschen Texte. /: Hört die winde furchtbar heulen :/
	86.	Concerto per la Lira Organizata in der Partitur.
	87.	Concerto per la Lira Organizata ausgeschrieben. $\overline{786}$.
	88.	Concerto per la Lire Organizata ausgeschrieben.
	89.	Notturno in C. per due Lire Organizate con due Clarinetti, due Viole, due Corni, et Violoncello, in der Partitur.
	90.	Notturno in C. per due Lire Organizate con due Clarinetti, due Viole, due Corni, et Violoncello in der Partitur.
	91.	Concerto in C. per due Lire Organizate con due Violini, due Viole, due Corni, et Violoncello, ausgeschrieben.
	92.	Notturno in F. à due Violini, Flauto, Oboe, due Corni, due Viole, et Violoncello, ausgeschrieben.
	93.	Notturno in C. à Flauto, Oboe, due Violini ò Clarinetti due Corni, due Viole et Violoncello, ausgeschrieben.
	94.	Notturno in C. à Flauto, Oboe, due Violini, due Viole, due Corni, et Violoncello, ausgeschrieben.
	96.	Notturno in F. per due Lire Organizate con due Clarinetti, due Viole, due Corni, et Violoncello, in der Partitur.
	97.	Divertimento per il Pariton, Viola, et Violoncello, ausgeschrieben.
	98.	Divertimento per il Pariton con Basso. ausgeschrieben.
	99.	Duetto per il Pariton 1mo et 2do ausgeschrieben.
	100.	Divertimento per il Pariton, Viola et Violoncello, ausgeschrieben.
	101.	Divertimento per il Pariton, Viola et Violoncello ausgeschrieben.
	102.	Divertimento per il Pariton, Viola, et Violoncello ausgeschrieben.
	103.	Divertimento per il Pariton, Viola, et Violoncello, ausgeschrieben.
	104.	Divertimento per il Pariton, Viola, et Violoncello, ausgeschrieben.
	105.	Divertimento per il Pariton, Viola et Violoncello, ausgeschrieben.
	106.	Divertimento per il Pariton, Viola et Violoncello, ausgeschrieben.
	107.	Divertimento per il Pariton, Viola et Violoncello, ausgeschrieben.
	108.	Divertimento per il Pariton, Viola et Violoncello, ausgeschrieben.
	109.	Divertimento per il Pariton, Viola, et Violoncello, ausgeschrieben.
	110.	Divertimento in F. per il Clavicembalo, con due Violini et Violoncello, ausgeschrieben.
	111.	Divertimento in C. per il Clavicembalo, con due Violini, et Violoncello, ausgeschrieben.
	112.	Divertimento in C. per il Clavicembalo, con due Violini, et Violoncello, ausgeschrieben.
	113.	Divertimento, in F. per il Clavicembalo, con due Violini, et Violoncello, ausgeschrieben.
	114.	Quartetto dall'Isola disabitata, in der Partitur gebunden. /: Sono contento appieno appresso al caro :/
	115.	Aria. la Scuola de Gelosi, in der Partitur. /: Dice benissimo chi si marito :/

Authoren	Nọ	Geschriebene Musicalien.
	116.	Aria. in der Partitur. /: Signor voi Sapete :/
	118.	Aria. in der Partitur. /: la moglie quando è buona :/
	127.	Sonata fürs Piano forte, mit Begleitung einer Violin und Violoncello.
	128.	Lines from the Battle of the Nile by M^{ris} Knight. and sat [*sic*] in Musik by Dr Haydn. bey den Piano forte zu singen.
	129.	Gott! erhalte Franz den Kaiser, in der Partitur mit dem Orgesta.
	130.	Sonata fürs Piano forte mit begleitung einer Violin.
	131.	Duetto in der Partitur. Armida & Rinaldo/: Cara sarà fedele :/
	137.	Sinfonia in F. ausgeschrieben in Dupl:.
	138.	Sinfonia in Es. ausgeschrieben. in Dupl:
	139.	Sinfonia in D. ausgeschrieben in Dupl:
	140.	Sinfonia in Dis. ausgeschrieben in Dupl:
	141.	Sinfonia in C. Le Midi ausgeschrieben in Dupl:
	142.	Concertino in B. ausgeschrieben in Dupl:
	143.	Sinfonia in H maggiore ausgeschrieben in Dupl:
	144.	Sinfonia in G minore ausgeschrieben in Dupl:
	145.	Sinfonia in Bfà ausgeschrieben in Dupl:
	146.	Sinfonia in G. ausgeschrieben.
	147.	Sinfonia in C. ausgeschrieben in Dupl:
	148.	Sinfonia in D # ausgeschrieben in Dupl:
	149.	Sinfonia in C. ausgeschrieben.
	150.	Sinfonia in Es. ausgeschrieben in Dupl:
	151.	Sinfonia in bfà. ausgeschrieben.
	152.	Sinfonia in Emol. ausgeschrieben in Dupl:
	153.	Notturno per due Lire Organizate, due Clarinetti, due Viole, due Corni, et Violoncello, in der Partitur.
	154.	Quartetto in D major à due Violini, Viola et Violoncello, ausgeschrieben.
	155.	Quartetto in G. à due Violini, Viola, et Violoncello, ausgeschrieben.
	156.	Quartetto in Es. à due Violini, Viola, et Violoncello, ausgeschrieben.
	157.	Quartetto in D minore à due Violini, Viola et Violoncello, ausgeschrieben.
	158.	Quartetto in bfà. à due Violini, Viola et Violoncello, ausgeschrieben.
	159.	Quartetto in C. à due Violini, Viola, et Violoncello, ausgeschrieben.
	160.	Quartetto in B. à due Violini, Viola, et Violoncello, ausgeschrieben.
	161.	Quartetto in D. à due Violini, Viola, et Violoncello, ausgeschrieben.
	162.	Quartetto in Es. à due Violini, Viola, et Violoncello, ausgeschrieben.
	163.	Quartetto in C. à due Violini, Viola, et Violoncello, ausgeschrieben.
	164.	Quartetto in Fis. à due Violini, Viola, et Violoncello, ausgeschrieben.
	165.	Quartetto in C. à due Violini, Viola, et Violoncello, ausgeschrieben.
	166.	Sinfonia. in F. ausgeschrieben in Dupl:
	167.	Sinfonia. in bfà. ausgeschrieben in Dupl:
	168.	Sinfonia in D. ausgeschrieben.
	169.	Sinfonia in bfà. ausgeschrieben.
Maschek.	170.	Sinfonia, Das allgemeine Wiener aufgeboth, ausgeschrieben in Dupl:
	171.	Sei Partitte, à due Fagotti, due Oboe, due Clarinetti, due Corni, ausgeschrieben.
Ant: Wranitzkj.	172.	Quintetto in D. Nọ 5. à due Violini, due Viole, et Violoncello, ausgeschrieben.
	173.	Quintetto in C. Nọ 4. a due Violini, due Viole et Violoncello, ausgeschrieben.

Authoren	N°	Geschriebene Musicalien.
Werner.	174.	Lamentationes, 3. In Sabato Sancto. cum Sequentibus Responsorÿs, a 4ᵗʳᵒ Voci et Diversis Instromentis con Cembalo et Violone ausgeschrieben.
	175.	Lamentiones 3. In Coena Domini, cum Sequentibus Responsorÿs alla Capella à 4ᵗʳᵒ Voci con Cembalo accompagnante Moderno Stillo alaborate, ausgeschrieben.
	176.	Lamentationes, 3. In Parasceve à 4ᵗʳᵒ Voci con Cembalo, Viola, et Violone, ausgeschrieben.
Emanuel Bach.	177.	Concerto fürs Pianoforte in der Partitur.
	178.	Quartetto fürs Clavier Flöte, und Bratsche in der Partitur.
	179.	Quartetto fürs Clavier Flöte, und Bratsche in der Partitur.
	180.	Trio à Cembalo et Violino in der Partitur.
	181.	Freÿe Fantasie fürs Clavier.
Ant: Wranizky:	182.	Quintetto in D minore N° 2. à due Violini, due Viole, et Violoncello ausgeschrieben.
Georgio Reutter.	183.	Offertorium. à 4ᵗʳᵒ Voci con Organo in der Partitur.
Stanislao Matrÿ.	184.	In manus tuas à Canto Solo due Violini, Viola con Organo, in der Partitur.
Antonio Brunetti	185.	Scenè loghubre, nel Finale del Rè Teodoro in der Partitur.
Martini.	186.	Duetto, Una cosa rara, in der Partitur /: Pace caro mio sposo :/
Rameau.	187.	Nouvelle Suite de pieces de Clavecin.
Jos: Fux.	188.	Messa Canonica a Capella tutta in Canone con qualche diversita particolare in der Partitur.
Gayer.	189.	Sinfonia in Es. in der Partitur manuscript.
	190.	Sinfonia in D. in der Partitur manuscript.
	191.	Sinfonia in A. in der Partitur manuscript.
Carl Ockl.	192.	Deutsches Amt, mit 4 Singstimmen und ganzen Orgesta in der Partitur. manuscript.
Joh: Sebastian Bach.	193.	Missa. à 5 Voci, erster und zweÿter Theil in der Partitur.
Fran: Reichardt.	194.	Carmen funebre a due Cori in der Partitur, gebunden.
Jos: Kraus.	195.	Musik zur Beÿsetzung Königs Gustaf des Dritten in der Partitur gebunden.
Jos: Eybler.	196.	Opfer tiefster Verehrung auf 4 Singstimmen in der Partitur, gebunden.
Fran: Lessel.	197.	6. Variazionen für das Pianoforte, dem Herrn Joseph Haydn, an seinen Namenstage aus wahrer Liebe und Dankbarkeit unterthänigst gewidmet, gebunden.
+ + +	198.	Ein Te Deum in der Partitur.
+ + +	199.	Ein auszug von einen Compositions=Buch.
+ + +	200.	Invocation of Neptun, and his attendant Nereids, to Britania.
Jos: Haydn.	201.	Ein Terzet übersetzt fürs Piano forte.
+ + +	202.	Ein lied in der Partitur mit dem Orgesta. /: An den schönsten Frühlings Morgen :/
+ + +	203.	Ein Allegro fürs Pianoforte.
Neukomm.	204.	Ein Lied in 4 Singstimmen gesetzt manuscript. /: Töne Lied . . . auf sanften Schwingen hebe dich :/
+ + +	205.	3. Ungarische tänze fürs Pianoforte.
+ + +	206.	Cabala per Comporre Menuetti fürs Pianoforte.
+ + +	207.	Ein Violoncello Concert auf kleinen Postpapier geschrieben.
Werner.	208.	Fugen, aus Messen herausgezogen.
von Pater Clementi Wohanska.	209.	Capricen für Pianoforte manuscript. nicht ausgemacht.
Graf Zizini.	210.	Zigeinerische fürs Pianoforte manuscript.
Jos: Haydn.	211.	4. Lieder fürs Pianoforte. weggegeben. Die Landlust. / Der Feldzug. / Das strikende Mädchen. / An Iris. /
Jos: Haydn.	212.	12 Lieder fürs Pianoforte deutsch und französisch.
		1. Das strikende Mädchen franz.
		2. Kupido, französisch.
		3. Der erste Kuß, französisch.
		4. Ein [*sic*] sehr gewöhnliche Geschichte französisch.
		5. Die Verlassene.
		6. Der Weichsinn. [=Gleichsinn]
		7. Trost unglücklicher Liebe.

Authoren	№	Geschriebene Musicalien.
		8. An Iris, französisch.
		9. An Thÿrsis, französisch.
		10. Die Landlust, französisch.
		11. Liebes Lied.
		12. Die zuspäte ankunft der Mutter.
Caldara	213.	2. Messen in der Partitur manuscript gebunden.
Muffat.	214.	Missa in Labore Requies in der Partitur, gebunden.
Ordonez.	215.	Alceste. Eine Marionetten Opera in der Partitur gebunden.
Johann Sebas: Bach.	216.	24. Preludi Fughe ovvero. Das wohl Temperirte Clavier 2ter theil gebunden.
Cimarosa.	217.	L'Infedeltà fedele, eine italienische opera in 3 acten, gebunden.
Jos: Haydn.	218.	Der Ritter Roland Eine heroisch = komische Opera in 3 aufzügen.
	219.	Die Schöpfung ausgeschrieben samt der Partitur nach dem Original.
	220.	Die 7 Worte ausgeschrieben, samt der Partitur zum Clavier.
	221.	item die 7 Worte auf ein Kleines Orgesta ausgeschrieben.
	222.	Stabat Mater, ausgeschrieben.
	223.	Die Partitur von die Jahrszeiten nach dem Original copirt.
	224.	Coro, der Sturm, ausgeschrieben.
	235.	24. Divertimenti per il Pariton, Viola, et Basso, ausgeschrieben, gebunden, und in einen Futteral.
Händel.	225.	Oratorium. Der für die Sünden der Welt gemarterten und sterbenden Jesus, in gebundener Rede vorgestellet, sehr schön gebunden. Regalirt von der Königin-aus Engeland.
Albrechtsberger.	236.	Cannone perpetuo a 4. Voci. Dedicirt von Georgius Albrechtsberger.
Stadler.	237.	An Herrn Kapellmeister Joseph Haydn. von seinem jnnigsten Verehrer Maximilian Stadler Pfarrer in Altlerchenfeld.

[Neue Seite] [New page]
Compositions = Bücher

Authoren	№	Compositions = Bücher
Jos: Riepel.	1.	Grundregeln zur Tonordnung insgemein.
Herbst und Werner.	2.	Musica Poetica: daß ist kurze andeitung und unterweisung, wie man eine schöne Harmoniam oder Lieblichen Gesang nach gewissen praeceptis und Regulis Componieren und machen soll.
Fux.	3.	Gradus ad Parnassum Sive Manuductio ad Compositionem Musica Regularem. Methodo novà, ac certà, nondum antè tam exacto ordine in lucem edita:
Kircheri.	4.	Neue Hall = und Tonkunst, oder Mechanische Geheim = Verbindung der Kunst und Natur, durch Stimme und Hallwissenschaft gestifftet.
Mattheson.	5.	Der Vollkommene Kapellmeister, das ist Gründliche Anzeige aller derjenigen Sachen, die einer wissen, können und vollkommen inne haben muß, der einer Kapelle mit Ehren und Nutzen vorstehen will:
Marpurg.	6.	Handbuch beÿ dem Generalbasse und der Composition mit zweÿ = dreÿ = vier = fünf = sechs = sieben = acht und mehrere Stimmen. Nebst einem vorläufigen kurzen Begriff der Lehre von Generalbasse für Anfänger.
Brossard.	7.	Dictionaire de Musique, contenant une explication des Termes, greco, latins, Italiens, & François les plus usitez dans la musique.
Heinichen.	8.	Der Generalbaß in der Composition. oder Neue und gründliche Anweisung, wie Ein Musik- Liebender mit besonderm Vortheil durch die Principia der Composition, nicht allein den Generalbaß ein Kirchen = Cammer = und Theatralischen stÿlò vollkommen, & in altiori Cradu erlernen; sondern auch zu

Authoren	N°	Compositions = Bücher
		gleicher Zeit in der Composition selbst, wichtige Profectus machen könne. 2 Band.
Mattheson.	9.	Grosse Generalhaß = Schule, oder der exemplarischen Organisten = Probe zweite, verbesserte und vermehrte Auflage.
Mancini.	10.	Pensieri, e Riflessioni pratiche Sopra il Canto Figurato.
Grossi.	11.	La cetra D'Apollo.
Marpurg.	12.	Kritische Einleitung in die Geschichte und Lehrsätze der alten und neuen Musik.
Marpurg.	13.	Anleitung zum Clavierspielen der schönen Ausübung der heutigen zeit gemäß. 2 Exempl:
Kellner.	14.	Treulicher Unterricht im Generalbaß, worinnen alle Weitläufigkeit vermieden, und. dennoch gantz deutlich und umständlich vielerleÿ neuerfundene Vortheile an die Hand gegeben werden, vermöge welcher einer in kurtzer zeit alles, was zu dieser Wissenschaft gehöret sattsam begreifen kann.
Gugl.	15.	Fundamenta partiturae in Compendiodata. Das ist: kurtzer und gründlicher Unterricht, den Generalbaß oder partitur nach denen Regola recht und wohl schlagen zu lernen.
Marpurg.	16.	Anfangsgründe der Theoretischen Musik.
Daube.	17.	General = Baß in dreÿ Accorden, gegründet in den Regula der Alt = und neuen Authoren, nebst einen hierauf gebauten unterricht: wie man aus einer jeden aufgegebenen Tonart, nur mit zweÿ Mittelsaccorden, in eine von den dreÿ und zwanzig Tonarten die man begehrt, gelangen kann, und der hierauf gegründeten Kunst zu präludiren, wie auch zu jeder Melodie einen Baß zu setzen.
Hinrichs.	18.	Entstehung fortgang und jetzige Beschaffenheit der Russischen Jagdmusik.
Adlungs.	19.	Anleitung zu der musikalischen Gelahrtheit theils vor alle Gelehrte, so das Land aller Wissenschaften einsehen; theils vor die Liebhaber der Edlen Tonkunst.
Schwannenberg.	20.	Gründliche Abhandlung über die unnütz = und Unschicklichkeit des H im musikalischen Alphabete; nebst einer Anmerkung, der künstlichen Töne betreffend.
Beerens.	21.	Musicalische Discurse durch die Principia der Philosophie deducirt, und in gewisse Capitel eingetheilt, deren Innhalt nach der Vorrede zu finden. Nebst einen Anhang von eben diesen Authore, genannt der Musikalische Krieg zwischen der Composition und der Harmonie.
Kalkbrenner.	22.	Histoire de la musique.
Dalberg.	23.	Über die Musik der Indien. Eine Abhandlung des Sir William Jones aus dem Englischen übersetzt, mit erläuternden Anmerkungen und zusätzen begleitet 2 Band. Herrn Joseph Haÿdn, Als ein Denkmal Seiner Hochachtung und innigster Verehrung gewidmet von Übersetzer.
Dᴿ Burney.	24.	A General History of Music. from the Earliest Ages to the present period. sind 4 Bände mit schönen Kupfern versehen und schön gebunden.
	25.	La Musica poema por D. Tomas de Yriarte con superior permiso: en Madrid.
Carissimi	26.	leichte Grund = Regeln zur Sing = Kunst, nach welcher alles was zu den Gregorianischen Choral-Gesang erfordert wird, erlernet werden kann. Samt einer nöthigen Anweisung die Orgel recht zu schlagen, besonders was den General = Baß betrift.
Mattheson.	27.	Lere Melodischer Wissenschaft bestehend in den auserlesensten Haupt- und Grund = Lehren der musikalischen Satz = Kunst oder Komposition, als ein Vorläuffer des Vollkommenen Kapellmeisters ausgearbeitet von Mattheson.
Münster.	28.	Scala Jacob, ascendendo, & Descendendò. Daß ist: Kürtzlich, doch wohlgegründete Anleitung, und vollkommener Unterricht, die Edle Choral-Music denen Regeln gemäß recht aus dem fundament zu erlernen.

Evlero.	29.	Tentamen novae theoriae Musicae ex certissimis Harmoniae principiis Dilucide expositae.
Böhm.	30.	Auszug der gründlichen Musikschule, zum Gebrauch der Musikschüler, erster Theil.
Emanuel Bach.	31.	Zweÿ Litaneÿen aus dem Schleswig = Holsteinischen Gesangbuche nach ihrer gewöhnlichen Melodie für acht Singstimmen in zweÿ Chören und den dazu gehörigen Fundamente.
Röllig.	32.	Orphica. Ein musikalisches Instrument mit Kupfern. 275 Verschiedene Opern, Oratorien, Marionetten, und Cantatten Büchel.
	33.	Verses on the Arrival in England of the Great Musician Haydn. January 1791. London. from the Author Dr Burney.

[Neue Seite] [New page]

J. Haydn's
Verzeichniss eigner
manuscripten.

N^o	Manuscript Partituren.
2.	Coro 2do aus dem Oratorium il Ritorno di Tobia. 1784. /: Svanisce in un momento :/
5.	Missa in B. 1802. Neukomm geschenkt den 16^t Feb: 809.
6.	Missa in C. 1796.
7.	Missa in D minor 1798.
8.	2 Quartetten 1799.
11.	Die 7 Worte.
19.	Sinfonia in D. 1771.
20.	Sinfonia in G. 1774.
21.	Sinfonia in Emol 1764.
22.	Sinfonia in Bfà 1767.
23.	Sinfonia in Fis minor. 1772. NB: wo einer nach dem andern abgehet.
24.	Sinfonia in G. 1772.
25.	Sinfonia in H maggiore 1772.
26.	Sinfonia in D. 1776.
57.	Sinfonia in A. 1764.
59.	Sinfonia in D. 1765.
62.	Sinfonia in D. 1774.
63.	Sinfonia in C. 1761. Le Midi.
64.	Sinfonia in G. 1764.
65.	Sinfonia in C. 1765.
66.	Sinfonia in E ♯ 1765.
67.	Sinfonia in D. 1764.
68.	Sinfonia in E♯ 1763.
69.	Sinfonia in D. 1763.
58.	Sinfonia in G. 1794. eine von die [*sic*] 12 Englischen.
82.	Madrigal in Englischen Texte / 1792. /: Hark the wild Uproar of the Winds. :/
83.	Der Sturm in deutschen Texte / /: Hört die winde furchtbar heulen :/
35.	Chor der Dännen. /: Triumph :/
56.	Divertimento. für ein Pariton, 2 Violin, 2 Corni, 1 Viola, Violoncello, et Violone.
95.	Notturno in G. à Flauto, Oboe, 2 Violini, 2 Viole 2 Corni, et Violoncello.
117.	Aria. /: d'una Sposa meschinella :/
119.	Aria. /: chi vive, amante :/ 1787. Nach Modena abgeschickt worden durch die Mademoiselle Sessi.
120.	Duetto mit Begleitung des Pianoforte / /: Senti qui che il Sentirai. :/
121.	Aria. /: la beltà che m'innamora dolce :/ 1762.
122.	Aria. /: ah tu n'Senti amico :/ 1786. [the letter n = non]
123.	Aria. /: da che penso a maritarmi :/ 1790.
135.	Aria. /: Se men genti le [*sic*] l'aspetto ostento. :/

N<u>o</u>	Manuscript Partituren.
134.	Divertimento, à 2 Violini, 2 Corni Inglaise, 2 Fagotti, 2 Corni, 1760.
124.	Divertimento, per il Clavi = cembalo solo 1766.
125.	Divertimento per il Pariton, Viola et Violoncello 1767.
132.	2. Sonaten fürs Pianoforte mit Begleitung einer Viola blos Violinstimme; also unbrauchbar.
36.	Ein deutsches Lied mit Begleitung des Piano forte / /: auch die Sprödeste der schönen :/
37.	Ein deutsches Lied mit Begleitung des Pianoforte / /: Beÿm schmerz der dieses Herz :/
39.	Hungarischer National Marsch. 1802.
126.	der Mademoiselle de Kurzbek gegeben. Ein Lied beym Clavier zu Singen /: /: Ein kleines Haus von Nußgesträuch umgeben :/
133.	12 Menuetten übersetzt fürs Pianoforte.
136.	Ein Marsch 1795.
226.	Opera. L'Incontro Improviso. 1777. in 3 acten. NB: Von diesen angezeigten Opern sind die gedruckten Büchel vorhanden, wie auch die Personen angemerkt, welche es abgesungen haben.
227.	Opera. L'Infedeltà Delusa. in 2 Acten.
228.	Opera. La Canterina. 1766.
229.	Opera. Le Pescatrici. 1769. in 3 acten.
230.	Opera. Lo Speziale in 3 Acten.
231.	Opera. Il Mondo della Luna. in 3 Acten.
232.	Opera. Orlando Paladino. 1782. in 3 acten.
233.	Opera. La Fedeltà Premiata. 1780. in 3 acten.
234.	Arien. per la Comedia Marchese 1763.
235.	Quartetto aus der Opera Acide et Gelatea. /: ah vedrai :/
236.	Aria. /: Caro volpino amabile. :/
237.	Aria. /: Tergi i vozzosi rai il tuo Martir. :/
238.	Aria. /: Perchè Stupisci tanto :/
239.	Aria. /: un cor Si tenero in petto :/ Bass:
240.	Aria. /: Voglio amar e vuo Scherzare :/ Sop:
241.	Aria. /: infelice sventurata sono oppressa. :/ 1789.
242.	Aria. /: Se tu mi Sprezzi ingrata. :/ 1788.

[marginal note beside Nos. 229–233:] nicht ganz. können aber ganz gemacht werden.

Vierzig Sinngedichte als

Canon's Bearbeithet.
Der Verlust.
Der Fuchs und der Adler.
Die Hofstellungen.
Die Flinte und der Hase.
Die Schalks Narren.
Der Fuchs und der Marder.
Die Weld.
Der Wunsch.
Der Kobold.
Vixi.
Die Tulipane.
Vergebliches Glück.
Der Esel und die Dohle.
Zweÿerleÿ Feinde.
Die Mutter an ihr Kind in der Wiege.
Abschied.
Hilar an Narciss.
Auf einen Adelichen Dumkopf.
Der Furchtsamme.
Das Sprichwort.
Der Spiess.
Phoebus und sein Sohn.
Aus Nichts wird Nichts.
An einen Geizigen.
Der Nachbar.

Der Bäcker und die Maus.
Aspettare e non Venire etc:
Die Gewißheit.
Der Freÿgeist.
An Dorilis.
Das Reitpferd.
Grabschrift.
Das böse Weib.
Tod und Schlaf.
An den Marull.
Cacatum non est pictum.
Der Gänsewitz zu seinen Kam̅erdiener.
Überschrift eines Weinhauses.
Liebe zur Kunst.
Das größte Gut.

item Die zehn gebothe Gottes.
den H: Legations Rath v Griesinger geschenckt.

NOTES AND IDENTIFICATION OF WORKS LISTED
(see pp. 299–317)

1, 2 Elssler writes what appears to be 'Neukamm'.

3 A new page begins with No. 10 at the top of which is the following: 'Gestochene Musicalien. Dedicirte. bis 29'. This new designation, which refers to music dedicated to Haydn, continues up to and including No. 29. Later Elssler added No. 32 (Leidesdorf), another dedication to Haydn, at the bottom of a page. That he added the Leidesdorf later can be seen by the fact that there was already a No. 32 (Gluck) at the top of the next page.

GESTOCHENE MUSICALIEN
(numbers refer to list of works; Hoboken numbers in parenthesis)

1. Pleyel's complete edition of the Haydn Quartets.
5–13. The 'Oeuvres Complettes' of Breitkopf & Härtel.
15–16. The *Missa Sancti Bernardi de Offida* and the *Missa in tempore belli* in the Breitkopf edition.
17. Op. 77.
24–38. Pleyel's edition of Haydn works in pocket score.
46–48. Salomon Symphonies in the arrangement for piano trio: Nos. 93–8.
49. The Duet from *Orlando Paladino* with da Ponte's new words.
50. Op. 76.
53. Piano Trios Nos. 32–4 (XV: 18–20).
54. Symphonies Nos. 99–104.
55. Perhaps Trio No. 43 (XV: 27) or No. 32 (XV: 18), issued by Falter in Munich as Sonate pour le Piano Forte avec Violon et Violoncelle Nos. I and II.
56. } Redoutensaal Dances IX: 11 and 12.
57. }
58. The First English Canzonettas XXVIa: 25–30 (Hoboken II, 255).
61. *Lieder* XXVIa: 1–12 (Hoboken II, 245).
62. Piano Trios Nos. 35–7 (XV: 21–3).
63. Piano Sonata No. 62 (XVI: 52).
64. Op. 71 or 74.
71–4. *Lieder* XXVIa: 1–24 (Hoboken II, 245).
76. Piano Trio No. 41 (XV: 31).
78. Op. 76, Nos. 4–6.
79. The so-called *Andante con variazioni* (XVII: 6).
80. Piano Trio No. 31 (XV: 32).
85. *Lieder* (Hoboken II, 245).
86. Symphony No. 44/II (Hoboken I, 52).
88. Rezia's Aria in Act II of *L'incontro improvviso* (Hoboken II, 365).
91. Six Overtures (Hoboken I, 289).
93. Quartet Op. 71, No. 1 (Hoboken I, 427).
94. Bland's edition of one of the piano Trios (Nos. 27–31; XV: 14, 16, 15, 17, 32).
95. Symphony No. 70 and *Armida* Overture (Hoboken I, 104).

GESTOCHENE MUSICALIEN VON VERSCHIEDENEN AUTHOREN

3–9. The Mozart 'Oeuvres Complettes' in the Breitkopf & Härtel edition.
10. The six Quartets dedicated to Haydn (K. 387 etc.).
17. Op. 2, dedicated to Haydn

GESCHRIEBENE MUSICALIEN

3. Concerto VIIh: 3 or 5.
4. We cannot identify this copy.
10. *Missa brevis* in F (XXII: 1).
13. Piano Trio No. 10 (XV: 35).
14. Symphony No. 101.
15. Symphony No. 94.
16. Symphony No. 99.
17. Cannot be identified.
18. Symphony No. 89.
31. Second movement of Piano Trio No. 36 (XV: 22) in an authentic version for piano solo.
32. Euridice's death aria (with recitative acc.) from Act II of *L'anima del filosofo*, 'Dov'è'.
40. The work is now lost.
60. Symphony No. 93.
61. Symphony No. 92.
70. The Six Overtures published by Artaria (Hoboken I, 289).
71. Probably a lost copy of Symphony No. 91 (Hoboken I, 169).

72. Symphony No. 82.
73.
78. } Quartets Op. 50, Nos. 1–6 (in different order).
79–81. Quartets Op. 76, Nos. 6, 2, 4.
86. VIIh:3 or 5.
87. VIIh:4.
88. VIIh:2.
89. II:25 or 31.
90. II:25 or 31.
91. VIIh:1.
92. II:28.
93. II:29?
94. II:29?
96. II:26.
97. XI:117.
98. XII:19?
99. XII:4.
100. XI:101.
101. XI:73.
102. XI:111.
103. XI:120.
104. XI:113.
105. XI:107.
106. XI:106.
107. XI:114.
108. XI:D2.
109. XI:97.
110. XIV:2 or 9.
111. XIV:7 or 8.
112. XIV:7 or 8.
113. XIV:2 or 9.
114. Finale from *L'isola disabitata*, 'Sono contento appieno'.
115. Aria 'Dice benissimo' (XXIVb:5).
116. Aria "Signor, voi sapete' (XXIVb:7).
118. Aria 'La moglie quando è buona' (XXIVb:18).
127. Piano Trio No. 42 (XV:30).
130. Cannot be identified.
131. Finale of Act I in *Armida*.
137. Possibly Symphony No. 89, or No. 79.
138. Cannot be identified.
139. Cannot be identified.
140. Cannot be identified.
141. Symphony No. 7.
142. *Sinfonia concertante* (I:105).
143. Symphony No. 46.
144. Symphony No. 39 (or 83?).
145. Cannot be identified.
146–152. Cannot be identified.
153. II:30?
154–165. Cannot be identified, though No. 157 is probably Op. 76, No. 2, and No. 164 Op. 50, No. 4.
166–168. Cannot be identified.
235. XI:73–96.

HAYDN's MANUSCRIPT PARTITUREN

5. 'Harmoniemesse'.
6. *Missa in tempore belli*.
7. *Missa in angustiis*.
8. Op. 77, Nos. 1–2.
11. The score of the vocal version by Elssler with additions by Haydn.
19. Symphony No. 42.
20. Symphony No. 54.
21. Symphony No. 22.
22. Symphony No. 35.
23. Symphony No. 45.

24. Symphony No. 47.
25. Symphony No. 46.
26. Symphony No. 61.
57. Symphony No. 21.
59. Symphony No. 31.
62. Symphony No. 57.
63. Symphony No. 7.
64. Symphony No. 23.
65. Symphony No. 30.
66. Symphony No. 29.
67. Symphony No. 24.
68. Symphony No. 12.
69. Symphony No. 13.
58. Symphony No. 100.
35. Chor der Dänen from *Alfred* (1796).
56. X:5?
95. II:27.
117. XXIVb:2.
119. XXIVb:13.
120. XXVa:1.
121. *Acide* (Aria by Acide).
122. XXIVb:10.
123. XXIVb:16.
135. Aria (*recte:*) 'Se men gentile l'aspetto ostento' by Polyfemo in *Acide*.
134. II:16.
124. Piano Sonata No. 29 (XVI:45).
125. XI:53.
132. Actually the violin part of the Duets VI:1–2 (see Hoboken I, 512).
133. IX:12 (or IX:3?).
136. VIII:1.
236. Aria from *Le pescatrici*.
237. Aria from the second (1773) version of *Acide. Recte:* 'Tergi i vezzosi . . .'.
238. Aria of Glauce from *Acide*.
239. XXIVb:11.
240. Aria from *Le pescatrici*.
241. XXIVb:15.
242. XXIVb:14.

(2) *Haydn's Catalogue of his Libretto Collection.*

In the previous Catalogue, there is an item just before the end of the section on theoretical treatises: under item 32 is the note '275 Verschiedene Opern, Oratorien, Marionetten, und Cantatten Büchel'. At the end of the present Catalogue, Haydn notes: 'in allem 207 Büchel / davon sind 62 duplirt' (in all 207 libretti / of which 62 are duplicates). The discrepancy suggests that Elssler's Catalogue was made later than Haydn's, and that a number of libretti had been added in the interim period; either that, or Haydn may have had a separate collection among his papers in Eisenstadt which was subsequently reunited to the '207 Büchel'.

Haydn's Libretto Catalogue is in small 'pocket' format and is now owned by the Museum der Stadt Wien; it is at present on exhibition in Haydn's house in Gumpendorf. It was never published. The Catalogue is interesting from several standpoints. It shows that Haydn carefully collected a large number of libretti, either works he performed at Eszterháza or works for study. Not all his own operas are included; some never had textbooks (i.e. 'La Marchesa Nespola'), and of others (e.g. *Hexen-Schabbas*) he no longer owned the textbook. The libretto of *Die bestrafte Rachgier (Rachbegierde)* was printed, but apparently Haydn did not own a copy, for the entry was added later and in another hand.[1] The fact that *Genovevens Vierter Theil* is included twice, once as item two under letter "G" with no composer (Bauersbach is the author Pauersbach, the Director of the Eszterháza marionette theatre), and once under the German operas as 'by various masters' is strong proof that Haydn's role, if any, was a very minor one as far as the music is concerned. The problem is discussed at length in the *Haydn Yearbook I*, 183ff.

It is impossible to deduce exactly when Haydn wrote this Catalogue; but the handwriting suggests that it was made sometime between *c.* 1799 and *c.* 1804. The sentence at the beginning 'Die hier' etc. appears to have been added later; possibly also the slightly shaky 'v[on] Jos: Haydn' after the title of *Philemon und Baucis*. We have published the list with all Haydn's annotations[2] and occasionally odd spellings ('Eibler' for Eybler, 'Burcksteiner' for 'Purksteiner') and have only added '[*sic*]' for the very oddest ('Locroscino').

Die hier auf der 1ten Seite angemerkten *Opern Büchel* sind alle in Music gesezt v Haydn[mpr]ia

Philemon und Baucis. ein Singspiel iii v. Jos: Haydn
Dido, eine parodirte Marionetten opera ii . . . .
       Opere Italiane.

+ la Canterina. ii . . . .
+ lo Speziale . . . . ii . . . .
+ la fedeltà premiata . . . .
   gli Amori di Cefalo. 668 [crossed out] . . . .
+ Acide et Galatea die aller Erste opera ii 763
+ il Mondo della Luna. iii . . . .
+ la vera costanza. iii . . . .
*il Mondo della Luna. iii . . . .
   L'infedeltà delusa iiii . . . .
+ Armida . . . . i . . . .
   L'incontro improviso . . . . i ['La fedeltà premiata' entry crossed out] . . . .
+ le Pescatrici . . . . i . . . .
+ l'Isola disabitata . . . . ii . . . .
+ Orlando Palatino . . . .
+ Orfeo et Euridice . . . .
   il ritorno di Tobia. oratorio iii . . . .
   die Schöpfung . . . .
   die Jahreszeiten . . . .
   die worte des Heylands . . . .
   Stabat Mater – auch mit deutschen Text . . . .
   der Krume Teufel eine deutsche opera . . . .
   die Bestrafte Rachgier. Die wort v Raufer [?][3]
   Musick von Haydn . . . .

                          A.
L'Arbore di Diana. v ii . . . . Martini
Arcifanfano. v . . . . iiiii . . . . Ditters
Aci e Galatea nella lingua italiano and English v Bianchi . . . . London 795.
l'amore Artigiano . . . . iii . . . . Gasman

1 In *Haydn Yearbook I*, 141, we wrote that the words after the title read 'die – 2 text v[on] draußen'. The words are very difficult to read but they are apparently 'Die Wort [Austrian dialect for "Worte"] v[on] Raufer [Rauster?]'.
2 The little crosses in front of the Italian Operas are probably Haydn's method of 'checking them off', perhaps when preparing the Elssler Catalogue of 1805. The *Entwurf-Katalog* has many such crosses. It is less clear what 'i', 'ii' etc. mean – possibly the available number of copies of the libretto in question.
3 Entry in an unknown hand; the libretto was in fact by Bader.

l'Amore Soldato. v .... Sacchini
e del Alessandro Felici
Allessandro nell'India. v .... Bianchi
Alcide al Bivio .... Hasse
l'Austria consolata. 702 .... Ziani
Amor prigionero ....
l'amante di tutte .... Galuppi
l'Assedio di Gibilterra. ii ....
l'Amore innocente .... Salieri
Adamo componimento Sacro .... Galuppi
l'Amante che spende .... Guglielmi
l'Amor costante . . iiii ....
Armida .... Nauman
l'Avaro .... Anfossi
gl Amori di Cefalo. 668 .... Draghi
l'Artaserse .... Scarlatti
l'Amore industrioso .... Ruttini
Amor lunatico .... Galuppi
le Astuzie amorose .... Paisiello
li tre amanti ridicoli .... Galuppi
l'Americana in olanda .... Anfossi
Alcina e Ruggero .... Allessandri
l'Amor contrastato .... Paisiello
Amor n vuol rispetto[1]
l'Astrologo Ignorante in 2 Atti .... Galuppi
Alsinda .... Zingarelli
Amor contadino .... Lampugnani
l'amore senza malizia .... ottani

B.

il Barone della Rocca .... iiii .... Ditters
la Betulia liberata Azione Sacra .... Holzbauer
piu Bricconi piu fortuna .... Guglielmi
Bacco vincitore ....
il Barone di terra asciuta .... Marescalchi
la Ballerina .... Cimarosa

C.

la Circe. v .... Cimarosa
la Contessina. v .... Gasman
il Convito v ii .... Cimarosa
il Cavaliere Errante v .... ii .... Trajetta
la Contadina ingentilita .... Sacchini
la chimera .... Draghi
i contratempi v ii .... Sarti
le contadine Furlane v .... Boroni
il calandrano .... Gazaniga
le due contesse .... iii .... Paisiello
la Circe ed ulisse .... Astaritta
il Re alla Caccia .... Michl
il Paese della Cuccagna ....
il finto Cavalier .... Monza
il convitato di Pietra .... Righini
il Conte Baggiano ....
il curioso indiscreto .... Anfossi
i constalliani [*sic*] burlati .... ii .... Valentini
chilonida. 676 .... Draghi
il ciarlone ....
il carnovale .... Borroni
la campagna ....
la conversazione .... Scolari
Castor e Polluce .... Bianchi
la Circe. 665 .... Ziani

1 The letter 'n' means 'non'.

D.

il Disprezzo v . . . . ii . . . . Anfossi
le Donne letterate . . . . Salieri
la Dea Riconciliata . . originale . . . . Badia
il Disertore . . . . Bianchi
Diana et Endimione. iii . . . . Weigl

E.

l'Eroe Cinese . . . . Bono

F.

il Falegname . . . . v . . . . . . due Exempl. i . . . . Cimarosa
la buona Figliuola. v . . . . ii . . . . Piccini
il Fiore de l'Eroine . . . . Bononcini
la Frascatana. iii . . . . Paisiello
la Fiera di Venezia . . . . Salieri
la Fama . . . . Draghi
il Francese bizzaro iii . . . . Astarita
il Filosofo inamorato . . . .
la forza delle Donne . . . . Anfossi
il Favore degli Dei . . . . Sabadini
La famiglia del Antiquario . . . .
il Filosofo di Campagna . . . . Galuppi

G.

le gelosie Villane. v iiii . . . . Sarti
Genovefens 4ter Theil ein Marionetten Opera v . . . . Bauersbach
Giuseppe riconosciuto. Azione Sacra . . . . Porsila
Gioas Re di Giuda . . . . Wagenseil
Giulio Sabino . . . . Sarti
Giannina e Bernadone . . . . Cimarosa
Giunio Bruto . . . . Cimarosa
le gelosie fortunate . . . . Anfossi
la gelosia . . . . Locroscino [*sic*]
il geloso in Cimento . . . .
il geloso Sincesato . . . . Monti
la galatea . . . . Kozeluch

H.

Das Fest des Dankes und der Freude Musik von Hummel. . . . .
Habsburg von Geramb. Musik von Salieri. [Complete entry in a different hand] . . . .

J.

L'Isola disabitata. v . . . . Bianchi
l'Isola del piacere . . . . Martini
Idalie. originale . . . .
l'Italiana in Londra . . . . Cimarosa
l'Incognita persequitata . . . . Piccini
l'Isola disabitata . . . . ii . . . . Scarlatti
l'Imbroglio delle tre Spose . . ii . . . . Anfossi
l'Ipermestra . . . . Caffaro
l'Impressario . . . . Cimarosa

L.

Fra i due litiganti. v . . ii . . . . Sarti
la Locanda . . . . iii . . . . Gazaniga

M.

la Merenda . . . .
il Marito geloso . . . . Caruso
il Matrimonio per inganno . . . .
il Marchese Villano. iii . . . . da diversi Maestri
il Marchese Carbonaro . . . . Salari
Mitridate Re di Ponto. 771 . . . . Wolfgango Mozart
la Moda . . . . Boroni
Merope . . . . Perez
il Mercato di Malmantile . . . . Fischietti

N.

le Nozze in Campagna. v .... Sciroli
Numa al Trono .... Hasse
le Nozze in Contrasto .... Valentini
le Nozze di Figaro .... Mozart

O.

la orfana Svizzera .... Boroni
Orfeo ed Euridice .... Bertoni

P.

i Fratelli Papamosca .... Guglielmi
i Presagi gloriosi di Scipione 704 .... Ariosti
Pirro Re di Epiro .... Paisiello
il Pazzo per forza .... Weigl Jos
il Pittore Parigino ii .... Cimarosa
Pizzaro nell'Indie .... Giordani [*sic*]
la Principessa di Malfi [*sic*] .... Weigl
Pirro ...... An: 675 .... Draghi
il Protettore alla moda ....
Protesilao. 1mo Atto dal Reichardt. il 2do dal .... Nauman
la Pupilla.. Garzia
la Pazzia d'Orlando .... Guglielmi
i Pazzi per disimpegno .... Andreozzi
la Pace universale 751 in Roma..

R.

Romolo et Ersilia. v .... Hasse
il Roveto di Mose .... Wagenseil
la nuova regia sull'aqua.................................... nel Bucintoro mit einen Kupferstich
il Re Pastore .... Gluck

S.

la Sposa in contrasto .... Astarita
la Sposa fedele. iii ....
Siroe Rè di Persia. and English..
Sesostri .... Cocchi
la Sposa Persiana .... Felice

la Serva astuta .... Piccini
lo Sposalizio per dispetto. ii .... Monti
Selene al Calvario. del Metastast: .... Caldara
il Sogno di Scipione ....
il Socrate immaginario. ii .... Rust
il Silenzio di Harpocrate 677 .... Draghi
i Solitari .... weigl
la Serva rivali.. Traetta
il Sogno d'olimpia.. Majo
NB: quest'opera fu eseguita dai primi virtuosi del mondo Cioè. Madame Tesi. Sig: Caffarelli;
Egiziello. Manzuoli. Babbi. Sig^{ra} Conti.

T.

il Tutore e la Pupilla .... Ditters
Tito Manlio .... Abbos [*sic*]
il Re Teodoro .... Paisiello
la Tati piu gloriosa. Scherzo Musicale

U.

la Figlia Ubbidiente .. v .... Carlo Bosi
i Viaggiatori felici. ii .... Anfossi
la Villanella astuta. intermezzo .. ii ....
il villano gelòso .... Galuppi
chi dell'altrui Si veste presto Si Spoglia.. Cimarosa
Venere ed Adone .... Weigl
la vedova Scaltra .. ii .... Righini
la vendetta di Nino .... Prati
il viaggiator ridicolo .... Gasman
la Vendemia .... Gazzaniga

Z.

Zemir et Azor v. auch Englisch .... Gretry
la Zenobia 6̄6̄2̄ ....

Verschiedene deutsche in Music gesezte Bücheln

Die Zauberflöte von .... Mozart
Die Wahl des Hercoles v .... Händel
Der Retter in gefahr .... Süssmayer
zweÿ Lytaneyen .... Em: Bach
Acis und galatea.. Händel
Daß zauberschwerdt .... Eibler
Die Erlösung .... Jos. Haydn
Genovefens 4ᵗᵉʳ Theil ii......................... von verschiedenen Meistern
Judas Machabäus .... Händel
Ovids Verwandlungen v .... Dittersdorf
Daß Irrlicht .... Umlauf
Der Kampf für den Frieden .... Süssmayer
Teutsches Monument v der Freyle ii .... Paradies
Daß ländliche Hochzeitsfest .... v .... Burcksteiner
Alexanders Fest.   v .... Händel
Auf das erste Ballfest der bildenden Küste:
Der Apoteker v .... umlauf
Faust. ein Singspiel in 3 Aufzüge. geschrieben original

in allen 207 Büchel
davon sind 62 duplirt.

Das Fest des Dankes und der Freude [the last word 'Freude' was written incorrectly and repeated again] Freude

von Hummel

Habsburg. [the word 'opera' cancelled] von Geramb. Musik v Salieri.

(3) *Summary Catalogues*
(a) Haydn's Own Summary Catalogue

This document was owned by Anthony van Hokoben who subsequently gave it to the National Széchényi Library in Budapest; it is reproduced in facsimile, complete, as the frontispiece to Hoboken's *Verzeichnis*, Volume I. On the basis of the handwriting, we would be inclined to date this Catalogue in the later part of 1804 or the year 1805.[1] Presumably it cannot have been completed until the *HV* was ready. What is rather baffling about this Summary Catalogue is that it contains several works not found in *HV*, e.g. the mysterious Bassoon Concerto discussed elsewhere[2] and lyra works for the King of Naples. Perhaps it was prepared on the basis of EK, the Kees Catalogue and the Quartbuch; notice that the number of symphonies was changed from 120 to 121. It is this kind of list that Haydn must have given, for example, to Carl Bertuch who visited Haydn in 1805 (the visit will be mentioned in the Chronicle, *infra*). But in Bertuch's summary we find an item of information not in *HV* or either of the two summary catalogues now under consideration; namely that Haydn wrote '400 Menuetten und Teutsche'; this information is also repeated in a *Nekrolog* that appeared in the Austrian

1 A hint as to the Catalogue's dating is the note about the Masses, 'In allen 14 und die kurze aller Erste'' (in all 14 and the short very first one), i.e. the *Missa brevis* in F. This work was 'rediscovered' in the Viennese Servite Monastery sometime about October 1805 (Griesinger reports its existence on 26 October). This sentence in the Catalogue, moreover, does not appear to be a later addition.
2 See *Haydn: the Years of 'The Creation' 1796–1800*, p. 226.

journal, *Vaterländische Blätter* (Jänner XXX–XXXVII 1810, pp. 203ff.), where we read '400 Menuetten und deutsche Tänze'. This information was provided by Haydn himself in a summary catalogue dated December 1805. Certainly a vast number of such dances from Haydn's earlier years has disappeared, probably forever.

We reproduce the document *in extenso*, indicating the changes by means of brackets. The interested reader may consult the facsimile to see how we have attempted to transcribe Haydn's abbreviations (which of course can only be approximately rendered in type). As far as we can tell, this is the Catalogue's first publication.

<table>
<tr><td>475</td><td></td><td>12 Fl 30</td></tr>
<tr><td>25</td><td></td><td>12   30</td></tr>
<tr><td>500</td><td></td><td>24</td></tr>
</table>

item für den Bariton 3 quinteten
concerto per 2 Bariton N^{ro} 1   ⎫
concerto per il Bar N^{ro} 2   ⎬   3 Concerten
item N^{ro} 3   ⎭

Duetten für den Bariton 16.
1 Divertiment für 2 Bariton
Sinfonien 121. [at first 120?]
Bariton Trio 124
12 Cassations Stück
quartetten 80.
3 und 4 Stimige gesäng. 13
erstens die Violin Solo mit begleitung einer Viola 6 2^{ens} die Trio 21 in allen
3^{ens} die quartetten 80 Stück [entry crossed out]
alsdan 5^{et} 6^{tetten} und so weiter 16 Stück
noch 5 B lieder 300 schottische [5B = 5 Bücher]
Teutsche 30 als einst mit schönheit [*sc*: 'Als einst mit Weibes Schönheit' XXVIa:44] graf [word cancelled] hat graf Brown. item der schutzgeist.

Englische 11		gott erhalt.	
Concerten für die Violin	3	orgl Concert	1
für den Contra Bass	1	Cembalo	3
Violoncello	3	Vier leyern Concert. 4	
Waldhorn	2	ein Notturno für die leyer.	
Flauten	1		
Fagott	1		

Grosse Italienische Chör 3.
Märsche Stücke Salve Regina 2.   [entry crossed out]
Messen 14.   [entry crossed out]
4 Marsch für Feld Music
Sonates pour le pianoforte 1te Cahier 8te ohne begleitung
                  in 2te 11. ohne begleitung
Sonates pour le P:f: avec l'Accomp: in 3te Six Sonates avec l'accomp: d'un Violon et Violoncelle
                                      in 4te
                                      in 5te Sonaten avec l'Accomp:
                                      in 6te Sonaten avec Accomp:
                                      in 7te Sonates avec Accomp:
                                      in 8te Airs et chansons
                                        9te Airs et chansons

34. Divertiment per il Cembalo Solo.
     mit Accompagn:
indess 21. es gehn noch zwey Cahiers ab.
Messen. in Tempore belli in C,⎫
— St^j Bernardi in bfa. ⎬ in allen 14 und die kurze aller Erste.
         Salve Regina 2 ⎭
Italienische Opern.   14
Teutsche   ,,   3

(b) Elssler's Summary Catalogue

has never been published. It consists of two tall folio pages, of which the first bears only the title. The manuscript is owned by the Internationale Stiftung Mozarteum in Salzburg, from which institution we received a photograph; we have to thank Dr Geza Rech and the Mozarteum for many kindnesses over the past twenty-five years, and also for permission to publish this Elssler Catalogue.

The list contains more information than Haydn's: we find certain works also missing in *HV* – the *Scena di Berenice* and the 'Nelson' Cantata ('Lines from the "Battle of the Nile" '), the former identified by Elssler as 'Cantatta für die Madame Banti' and the latter as 'Sonata Pianoforte für den Nelson' respectively. We find the Bassoon Concerto, known to us, otherwise, only from Haydn's Summary Catalogue, also in this Elssler list. It will be seen, morever, that the totals do not always agree with Haydn's Summary Catalogue, and that Elssler's are those of *HV*. Therefore we may presume (1) that Elssler's Summary Catalogue is later than Haydn's; (2) that Elssler's was compiled after *HV* was completed; (3) that Elssler used not only *HV* but also other sources to complete it, very likely manuscripts in Haydn's possession: the *Scena di Berenice* was owned by Neukomm who obviously received it from Haydn (and the composer certainly had a complete source of the work, because we know that Elssler copied it for Mrs Peploe in 1797 and in Vienna), and a copy of the Cantata 'Lines from the "Battle of the Nile" ' passed from Haydn's library to the Esterházy Archives.

We cannot explain the '7' at the top of the title on page one.

7.
Haydn's
Vollendete Compositions Werke.

[Neue Seite; new page]

[Haydn's Vollendete Compositionen	Stück]
Für den Bariton Quintetten	3
Concerten	3
Duetten	16
Divertimenten für 2 Bariton	2
Trio	124
Sinfonien	121
Cassations Stücke	12
Quartetten	83
3 und 4 Stimmige Gesänge	13
Cañons	52
Violin Solo mit Begleitung einer Viola	6
Trio für die Violin	21
Quintetten und Sextetten	16
Schottische Lieder	300
Deutsche Lieder	36
Englische Lieder	11
Concerten für die Violin	3
Concert für die Violone	1
Violoncello Concerten	3
Waldhorn Concerten in Duett	2
Flauten Concert	1
Fagott Concert	1
Clarin Concert	1
Leyer Concerten für den König von Neapel	4
Notturni für die Leyer	1
Cembalo Concerten	3
Organo Concert	1
Große Italienische Chöre	3
Englischer Chor	1

[*Haydn's Vollendete Compositionen*	Stück]
Te Deum	I
Salve Regina..	2
Ave Maria	I
Messen	14
Divertimenti per Cembalo	
Sonaten pour le Pianoforte avec	
Accompagnement	34
Gott erhalte den Kayser	
Volks Lied	I
Italienische Opern	14
Deutsche Opern	3
Cantatta für die Madame Banti	I
in England Componirt	
die Schöpfung	
die Jahreszeiten	
die 7 Worte	
Stabat Mater	
Il Ritorno di Tobia	
Marsch	4
Sonata Pianoforte für den Nelson	
Summa	925

CHAPTER EIGHT

Chronicle 1805

IN 1805 THE EMPRESS MARIE THERESE was still attempting to commission music from both the Haydn brothers. Early in the year she ordered a *Requiem* and a *Libera me* from Michael who felt, like Mozart writing his *Requiem* in 1791, that he would not live to finish it; and in fact only the Introitus and Kyrie were completed. The Emperor, visiting Salzburg in October 1807 after both Michael and the Empress were dead, gave Michael's widow 600 gulden for the unfinished work. Meanwhile Joseph Haydn fobbed off an old work on the Empress. He had Elssler make a copy of the Ninth Dance from the Twelve German Dances for the Redoutensaal (1793) and sent it to the Empress with the following dedication: 'Ein/Deutscher Tanz./von/Joseph Haydn./Im 74. Jahr seines Lebens. Jänner 1805' and before that: 'Für Se. Mayestätt/Die Kayserin'.[1]

A rumour had spread round Europe that Haydn had died. Cherubini, who worshipped Haydn's music, wrote a Funeral Cantata which was to be performed at the Concert dans le Théâtre Olimpique (formerly Concert de la rue Clery). At the last minute news arrived in Paris that Haydn was still alive; most of the concert's programme had to be changed, but Kreutzer played a concerto based on Haydn's themes, which the reviewer of the *Berlinische Musikalische Zeitung* (No. 29, 1805, 116) thought was 'too motley [*bunte*] in form and more a medley', though excellently performed by the great virtuoso. Haydn is supposed to have heard about the Parisian concert and said, 'The good gentlemen! I am really much indebted to them for this unexpected honour. If I had known of the ceremony I would have gone there myself to conduct the [Requiem] Mass in person' (Pohl III, 236). In England, the *Gentleman's Magazine* put Haydn in its obituary list for January: 'At Vienna in his 97th [*sic*] year the celebrated musical composer Haydn.' In their February issue, however, we read: 'The celebrated musician Haydn (says a letter from Vienna dated Jan. 26) for whom a funeral service has been performed in France is still living, and as hearty and well as a man of 75 [*sic*] can be expected to be.' Thomson read the news of Haydn's death in Edinburgh and wrote a letter of condolence to Fries & Co., the Viennese bankers who arranged the financial transactions between Thomson and Haydn. On 6 February 1805, Fries & Co. wrote back to Scotland and told Thomson, 'We have received your Favour of the 7th January and as the celebrated Haydn is not dead as it was generally reported, but only in a weak state of health, we communicated your letter to him and send you enclosed the answer he has dictated to your inquiries'. The French answer (CCLN, xxv) reads:

> Kindly say to Mr Thomson that Haydn is very sensible of the distress that the news of his alleged death has caused him, and that this sign of affection has added, if

1 Jancik, *Michael Haydn*, 269. The (now lost) Elssler copy of the Dance (IX: 12), No. 9 in B flat was photographed before the Second World War for the Hoboken *Photogrammarchiv* (Austrian National Library, Music Division) and a copy made of this photograph for the Haydn Society in 1950.

that be possible, to the esteem and friendship he will always entertain for Mr Thomson. . . . You will notice that he has put his name and the date on the sheet of music to give better proof that he is still in this base world. At the same time he begs to have the letter of condolence copied and the copy sent to him . . .

Thomson immediately sent out a new collection of airs for Haydn to harmonize – one batch in April and another in August (*infra*, 5 September). On 26 January 1805 Griesinger hastened to write to Leipzig about the false news:

> . . . Perhaps you too have heard the rumour which went the rounds even in Vienna for several days, that Haydn had a stroke and suddenly died. I hereby proclaim to you that this news is totally wrong . . . Now he [Haydn] only occupies himself from time to time with Scottish songs. . . .
>
> [Olleson *Griesinger*, 48]

Haydn had sent his part-songs to the Empress Dowager of Russia *via* his pupil Neukomm, who had left Vienna to seek his fortune in St Petersburg as an opera conductor. The Empress remembered, as Griesinger reminds us in his biography (42f.), taking 'several hours of instruction' from Haydn when she visited Vienna in 1781 as a grand duchess.

[To Haydn from Maria Feodorovna,[1] Empress Dowager of Russia, St Petersburg. *German*]
Herr Kapellmeister HAYDN:

> The letter and composition which your pupil Neukomm brought me gave me much pleasure, and I remembered with joy that I had met you personally in Vienna. This, and the flattering description of me you gave to the bearer, moved me to have him play it for me at once; and I did not fail to recognize his teacher in him. I do thank you so much for the beautiful songs that you sent me, and I hope with my whole heart that you will continue to enjoy good health, and that, for many years to come, you will earn the admiration of all music lovers through your exceptional talent and your masterpieces – an admiration which you so richly deserve. I hope that the musical public will be able to enjoy one of your beautiful works soon again, and I beg you to regard the enclosed remembrance as a token of my sincere good wishes, with which I am, as always,
>
> Your ever well-disposed[2]
> Maria.

St Petersburg,
15th February 1805. [CCLN, 236]

Having allowed Haydn's seventieth birthday to pass almost unnoticed in 1802, the Viennese decided to create a special celebration to mark his seventy-third birthday in 1805. The young Wolfgang Mozart was to be presented to the public for the first time, playing works by his father but also as the young (thirteen-year-old) composer of a birthday cantata of which Griesinger wrote most of the text. Originally planned for 31 March, the concert was then postponed to 8 April. We learn about the details from Griesinger:

16 March 1805
> . . . On 8th April the young Mozart will appear at a public concert for the first time. He composed a cantata for J. Haydn's birthday of which (between ourselves) [the text is], except for the first chorus, by me. Streicher assured me that an aria in it would not be unworthy, even of his father [W. A. Mozart]. Haydn was touched

---

1 See also *supra*, p. 86. The present letter was accompanied by a beautiful ring.
2 'Wohl affektionierte.'

to tears when we told him of the plan. To make the youngster's entrance more solemn, his uncle, the actor Lang [Joseph Lange], will hold a small speech in front of the public, and according to our plans, Haydn should have then taken him [Wolfgang Jr.] by the hand to the public. The enthusiasm about such a scene would have been indescribable; unfortunately one won't be able to execute it because it is to be feared that Haydn would be all too shaken by it. . . .

[Olleson, *Griesinger*, 49]

The concert took place in the Theater an der Wien, and in the event Constanze Mozart led her son in front of the public. The second part of the concert was devoted to excerpts from *Idomeneo*, and Rosenbaum (122) was 'bored by the second part but enjoyed the cantata [for Haydn's birthday] and the concerto [Mozart, K. 503] played by the charming and lively boy.' Haydn was too weak to attend.

One of Haydn's faithful Viennese patrons, Count von Fries, actually offered Haydn the stupendous honorarium of 300 or 400 ducats for a new symphony. Griesinger, writing on 3 April to Breitkopf & Härtel, suggests that

. . . such an offer might well be capable of awakening his old mind; but as long as he still feels so weak he can promise nothing. He wants to wait if the favourable weather and the use of the baths will inspire him. . . .

A few days later, the Spring concerts of the Tonkünstler-Societät took place: *The Creation*, given on 7 and 8 April with new soloists: Antonie Laucher, Abbé Bevilaqua and Carl Weinmüller (Pohl, *Denkschrift*, 67).

On 15 April, a visit of considerable consequence took place in the house in the Kleine Steingasse in Gumpendorf: the painter A. C. Dies paid his first visit to Haydn. A contemporary, Carl Bertuch,[1] writes about artists living in Vienna and has this to say about Dies:

Dies (A.C.), long known as a landscape painter, was formerly in Rome, where he, together with Reinhart and Mechau, issued a large collection of Italian places on engraved sheets. For the last eight years he has been living in Vienna with his wife, a Roman lady. . . . Perhaps we will have to thank Herr Dies in the future also for an interesting life of Joseph Haydn. [Footnote: Nothing has yet been published of it. But *Leg. Rath* Griesinger has given us a very interesting outline of Haydn's life in the [*Allgemeine*] *Musikalische Zeitung*. – It was from him that I also received the information about Haydn which are contained in my *Bemerkungen* on p. 181, which I can now say since Herr Griesinger himself has shed his incognito. Later note.] Dies is one of the few, apart from our friend the Saxonian *Legations-Rath* Griesinger who, from time to time, sees the worthy old man. During these visits, Haydn little by little told him of all the remarkable events in his so active life, in uninterrupted chronological order, and Dies wrote it all done accurately after each visit. Since these conversations have already progressed to Haydn's visit to England, it is to be hoped that the whole thing will at least be preserved in the interviewer's *portefeuille*.

Dies himself, writing of the first visit, tells us that

Grassi [the sculptor] brought me to Haydn. It seemed to me that I did not displease him, for he came towards me, although sick for a long time and with both legs swollen, gave me both his hands, and received me with a cheerfulness that spread over his whole features and with such a penetrating [*geistigem*] look that I was

1 *Bemerkungen auf einer Reise aus Thüringen nach Wien im Winter 1805 bis 1806.* Weimar im Verlage des Landes-Industrie-Comptoirs, Zweiter Heft, pp. 52ff.

surprised. This lively expression, the brownish (tinged with reddish) facial colour, the exceptionally neat clothing – Haydn was fully dressed –, his powdered wig and, the swelling notwithstanding, the boots he was wearing and the gloves; all this made one forget any trace of illness and gave the old man of seventy-three the healthy look of a fifty-year-old, which was supported by his medium height and the fact that he was not at all heavy. 'You seem,' he said to me, 'to be surprised about my being fully dressed, though I'm still sick and weak, can't go out and breathe nothing but indoor air. My parents accustomed me from my earliest youth with discipline [*Strenge*] concerning cleanliness and order, and these two things have become second nature to me.' He also thanked his parents for encouraging him in fear of God and, because they were poor, they were obliged to be thrifty and hard-working. All things that one encounters very rarely in our young geniuses.

. . . I feared that Haydn's weak state of health might prevent him from further conversation. I told him to look after himself, and my friend [Grassi] and I left him, because it was in any case time for his afternoon nap. They told me that for this nap Haydn undressed completely, put on a night dress and dressing gown and then went to bed. He was severely punctual and winter or summer he kept to the period from half-past four to five o'clock; thus he slept no more than half-an-hour. After his rest was over he dressed completely, climbed down the stairs with great difficulty and went to the housekeeper's room. There he had some of the neighbour's children come and their cheerful play delighted Haydn; their jokes made him forget his sad condition . . . He admits that his spirit is weak. He cannot think, cannot feel, cannot write, cannot hear music . . .   [Dies, 15f., 21f.]

Being a painter, Dies's visual description of the old Haydn is one of the most accurate we have. His biography of Haydn, the information for which he collected in a long series of interviews, is often tiresomely garrulous and, its subject being old and with a failing memory, full of inconsistencies and mistakes. Yet it is an important and authentic account. It lacks two advantages that Griesinger had: the *Legationssekretär's* greater accuracy and the fact he had known Haydn since 1799, when he was at the summit of his intellectual powers. The Haydn of 1805 was merely a shell of his former self; on 5 May, when Dies went to visit Haydn for the third time, Haydn asked to be excused. The housekeeper said, 'He is always depressed when the weather is cold, or windy, or rainy.' Our 'official' biographies of Haydn, whether by Griesinger, Dies or the hopelessly inaccurate Carpani, are vignettes of an old, depressed man; the ruin of a giant intellect whose old wit and penetrating glance could only occasionally be called from its now perpetual slumber.

Haydn's depression was to be increased by a series of deaths. On 8 May Dr Peter Edler von Genzinger died; he had been Esterházy's physician and the husband of Marianne, Haydn's intimate friend. A few days later Dies went to visit Haydn, on 11 May, and was told that Princess Esterházy and her daughter had been announced; Dies did not learn the reason for their visit until later, but in fact it was to tell Haydn of the death of his brother Johann (also known as Jean or Hansl), the tenor, in Eisenstadt, the quietest and obviously least gifted of the three Haydn brothers. He had died on 10 May 1805. Probably Johann had been engaged as a tenor in the Esterházy band as a kindness to Joseph, for his voice seems not to have been first-rate. Rosenbaum (119) says, in March 1804, 'Frl. Dichtler came after lunch, and Salieri later. She tested her voice. Salieri finds that she sings without any method whatever, and through her nose like Hanßl Haydn.' Yet the quiet, unassuming Johann had friends, because shortly after he died, Rosenbaum (122) wrote (13 May) that Madame Csekovics 'came before lunch (I did not see her) and brought elegies on the death of Johann Haydn.' Joseph, as Dies tells us (Sixth Visit, 17 May), was given the news as gently as possible by Princess Marie Hermenegild, but he was nevertheless 'painfully moved'. At the end of the month a dear friend, Anton Stoll of Baden, also died. On 28 May the impoverished Luigi Boccherini died in Madrid, his music already half-forgotten. Haydn was now often alone with his memories, relieved from time to time by an occasional visit.

Some of these visitors left a record for posterity; others talked of themselves. Late in 1804 the composer Friedrich August Kanne from Delitzsch (Saxony) was taken to Haydn by Griesinger, who reported that Kanne 'seems to have no small opinion of himself and entertains no doubt that he will make his fortune here.' In a letter to Leipzig of 13 February 1805 we have a typical example of Griesinger's poised judgement, not only about Beethoven's *Eroica* but also about Kanne.

> . . . This much I can, however, assure you; that the [*Eroica*] Symphony has been heard at Academies at Prince Lobkowitz's and at an active music-lover named Wirth, with unusual applause. That it is a work of genius, I hear from both admirers and detractors of Beethoven. Some people say that there is more in it than in Haydn and Mozart, that the Symphony-Poem has been brought to new heights! Those who are against it find that the whole lacks rounding out; they disapprove of the piling up of colossal ideas. . . . Eight days later a new Symphony by Eberl was given at Wirth's and fourteen days later one by Kanne. . . . Kanne himself attended the burial of his symphony.
>
> [Pohl III, 234f.; Landon, *Beethoven*, 159]

In the Spring of 1805, the French violin virtuoso Pierre Baillot was taken to see Haydn by the composer Anton Reicha, who also happened to be in Vienna at the time. Baillot was so touched when he saw Haydn that he wanted to kiss his hand, but Haydn opened his arms into which the visitor jumped with such force that Haydn almost lost his few remaining teeth. When Baillot paid his respects a second time, alone, the two men talked in Italian, and at one point Haydn pointed to a picture of his wife and said, 'That's my wife; she often made me furious' (Pohl III, 239).

Ignaz Pleyel finally made his long-expected visit to Vienna, and on 27 Prairal XIII (16 June 1805) he wrote to his family in Paris about Haydn, whom he found old and weak, 'a man in his seventies who looks as if he were more than eighty, continually praying with a rosary'. Pleyel found the house very attractive and nicely furnished but he had the impression that Haydn received very few callers (Pohl III, 240).

A more interesting visit was that of Luigi Cherubini, who had accepted an invitation by Baron von Braun to come to Vienna to conduct at the Opera. Cherubini brought with him the membership diploma of the Paris Conservatoire de Musique, and the membership medal, to Haydn; it is also likely that Cherubini brought a slightly earlier letter, from the Institut National. Here are both letters, with Haydn's response to the Conservatoire:

[To Haydn from L'Institut National, Paris. *French*]

Institut   National
Classe des Beaux arts.   [Letter-head]

Paris, le 1. Messidor an 13 de la République française [20th June 1805]
The permanent Secretary of the section [letter-head] to Mr. Haydn, composer, associated member of the *Institut National*.
Monsieur,
L'Institut National de France elected you associated member; from the moment of its formation, it has considered this a tribute which it was pleased to have

rendered to your deserved celebrity. The changes which have since taken place within the Institute are such as to increase substantially your ties with it; a musical section has been created, and it consists of dignified gentlemen who are the appreciators of your genius.

As a non-resident member, you have, in the capacity of a consultant, a voice in the Institute, the right to attend its assemblies, to wear its uniform – in short, you are part of it. In this capacity, then, I send you the medal which constitutes your right to the title, and the book containing our by-laws and likewise the names of our members. You will find yours in the article dealing with the section on the fine-arts.

I would wish, *Monsieur*, that you would show sufficient interest in the fine-arts section of the *Institut de France* for it to benefit from your wise observations on the art which is your profession, and with which you have gained such glory in Europe. I can assure you that it would receive this mark of your confidence with profound esteem. As for my own person, I regard as one of the most precious advantages of the duties with which I am honoured, that of corresponding with you, and of being able frequently to assure you of my profound respect.

I have the honour to greet you,

> Joachim Le Breton.
> Perpetual Secretary of the fine-arts section of the *Institut national de France*, member of the *Classe d'histoire*, the *Littérature Ancienne*, and *Légion d'honneur*.

[CCLN, 236f.]

[To Haydn from the Conservatoire de Musique, Paris. *French*]
[Letter-head:] *Paris, le* [*ink:* '7. *messidor*'] *an* [*ink:* '13']
de la République française
26th June 1805.

Le Conservatoire de France to Haydn:

The members of the *Conservatoire de France*, filled with the most profound sentiments of esteem and veneration for the immortal talent of Haydn, have the most fervent desire to inscribe the name of this celebrated artist in the annals of this institution.

The expression of this wish, carried to the celebrated Haydn by Chérubini, could not but be received kindly; the members of the *Conservatoire*, thus filled with confidence, have charged their colleague to deliver to this great man, whom they consider to be one of their fathers in the art of music, the plans of the monument which the *Conservatoire* hopes to see erected in its midst, and of which the model has been chosen to celebrate the happy date of the foundation of this establishment.

Should this legitimate tribute of admiration to one of the greatest geniuses which has illuminated the republic of the arts be accepted by Haydn, it would represent to the *Conservatoire de France* a trophy which it would honour forever.

In the name of the members of the
Conservatoire de France

Méhul   Gossec   Cherubini   Sarrette.[1]   [CCLN, 237]

---

1 The leading French composers ÉTIENNE NICOLAS MÉHUL (1763–1817), FRANÇOIS JOSEPH GOSSEC (1734–1829), and BERNHARD SARRETTE (1765–1858), founder and director of the Paris *Conservatoire*.

[To the Paris *Conservatoire. French*]
[Written by Luigi Cherubini and signed by Haydn]

Vienna, 6th March 1806.

Gentlemen,

M. Cherubini, in delivering to me the medal which you sent me, was a witness to the vivid satisfaction with which I received it. The letter which accompanied it, informing me, with expressions flattering to myself, that the members of the *Conservatoire de France* will hereafter regard me as their colleague, have raised my satisfaction to the highest pitch.

I beg you, gentlemen, to accept my thanks, and to convey them to the members of the *Conservatoire*, in whose name you had the kindness to write; add that, as long as Haydn lives, he will carry in his heart the memory of the interest and consideration which they have shown him . . .

I have the honour to subscribe myself, gentlemen. . . .

[not in CCLN; *Mercure de France* for April 1806, discovered by François Lesure and published during the Haydn Congress at Budapest in 1959; Bartha 458f. Mr Richard Macnutt has recently (1977) rediscovered the Cherubini-Haydn autograph and kindly communicated a description of it to us.]

Cherubini arrived with his wife and youngest daughter in Vienna towards the end of July 1805. Rosenbaum (125) reports on the 31st that

since Cherubini was conducting the *Deux Journée[s]* for the 2nd time at the B[urg]th[eater], I went along to see it. The theatre was not full, and except for a change of tempo in the overture and romanza there was nothing to make his presence known. . . . Ch— was welcomed with an ovation and most of the numbers were applauded; he came out on stage at the end.

In Bellasis' book[1] we learn that Cherubini took the overture more slowly than usual, whereby (a contemporary reports) 'this difficult music gained in clarity'.

Cherubini at once addressed Haydn as 'Father', whereupon the latter answered, 'Yes, as far as age is concerned, but not as far as music goes.' He said to Griesinger about the Italian, 'He's an attractive little man, with charming manners' ('er ist ein hübsches Mandl, voll Art'; Pohl III, 244). Cherubini spent the whole of 1805 and the first few months of 1806 in Vienna, later conducting the première of his new opera, *Faniska* (25 February 1806 with Anna Milder). It is reported that it 'excited the admiration of all competent judges: Beethoven and, it is asserted, Haydn perfectly agreeing with the opinion of the public'. Bellasis sensibly doubts 'whether Haydn, at his advanced age, still visited the theatre; but, according to the general account, both he and Beethoven were present at the first performance; Cherubini, on his part, going to hear *Fidelio* twice' (op. cit.).

We shall follow Cherubini's fortunes when Napoleon was at Schönbrunn Castle later in the year, and in 1806 when, on 24 February – the day before the first performance of *Faniska* – he went to visit Haydn.

On 17 August we have a short letter from Haydn to Artaria in which the shaky handwriting betrays the disease which was now reducing Haydn to a dotard: arterio-sclerosis.[2]

---

1 Edward Bellasis: *Cherubini: Memoirs illustrative of his life*, London 1874, pp. 149ff.
2 We are indebted to our old friend, Dr William B. Ober of Beth Israel Hospital in New York, for an analysis of Haydn's terminal sickness. Apparently the symptoms – swollen legs, etc. – are quite unmistakable.

[To Artaria & Co., Vienna. *Italian*]
Most esteemed *Signor* Artaria,
 I hope that for these twelve pieces of music[1] the old Haydn shall have merited a small reward. Your sincere friend and servant,

D[r] Haydn [m.p] ria.
[Vienna] 17th August 1805[2]

[Address in Elssler's hand:]
 [Haydn's seal 'JH']

A
Monsieur
Monsieur d Artaria
& Comp:

[CCLN, 238]

Haydn's letter of 17 August 1805 to Artaria & Co., Vienna (see above), from a photograph of 1909. Up to the Second World War the original was owned by Artaria's successors in Vienna, Messrs Freytag & Bernt, but it has since disappeared.

A few days later, Griesinger reports to Leipzig:

21 August 1805.

. . . But I won't forgo my visits to Father Haydn. His shell, alas, continues to get more fragile and every little raw breeze annoys him. He has given up hope of being able to complete the Quartet ['Op. 103'] he has begun. But he is now finished with the Catalogue of everything which he recalls having composed from his 18th to his 73rd years. Just the *incipits* alone make a volume of 60 sheets. If you are interested in owning this document, which is certainly interesting of its kind, write me a couple of lines; Haydn promised me yesterday that he would have it copied for you. Among his musical effects there are certainly things that are not printed; I asked him urgently to find something for you, but it takes quite a decision to get the good old dear out of his room, down the stairs and into the somewhat cooler temperature of a little room where he can fuss about in his papers. I must try to get his servant [Elssler] to do it instead. . . .

[Olleson, *Griesinger*, 49]

The great Catalogue (*HV*), then, was copied by Elssler by the middle of August 1805, and on 21 September Griesinger could report to Breitkopf & Härtel that the Catalogue 'was sent off yesterday by the wheeled post' (ibid).
 Now that Neukomm was no longer in Vienna, Haydn seems to have had no pupil capable of editing the Scottish songs for Thomson, and on 5 September the Edinburgh publisher enlisted the help of C. R. Broughton, in the Secretary of State's Office,

---

1 It is hard to imagine what these 'twelve pieces of music' were: the most likely explanation is that they were autographs, for Artaria later owned many Haydn autographs of pieces which the firm had never published.
2 The date added by another (Elssler's?) hand.

asking him to induce Mr Jenkinson, the successor of Charles Stuart in the Vienna Legation, to

> . . . call upon the great Haydn, and represent to him as emphatically as possible my [Thomson's] earnest desire, that he would compose Ritornelles and Accompaniments without delay to the 20 Airs which I sent him . . . Mr J. may be so good as to ask the Doctor whether the India Handkerchiefs I sent him be worn out, and if he would wish to have a few more. . . .[1]

But Haydn had neither the students nor his own strength to continue this lucrative assignment and in 1806 he asked Fries & Co. to inform Thomson that the work must stop. Thomson then got Haydn to sign a formal cession of rights for all the arrangements which comprised 170 Scottish and Irish and 62 Welsh songs, for which Haydn received £291 18s 1d – a very substantial sum in those days – to which may be added the 130 guineas he had received from Whyte for the twenty-five songs in his edition.

European history had allowed Austria a few years of peace. In 1803 England was again at war with France but Austria remained neutral. In 1804 Napoleon had – to Beethoven's fury – crowned himself Emperor of France, while in 1805 there followed a third coalition against France, this time consisting of England, Austria, Russia, and Sweden, with Naples later joining and Prussia remaining neutral. After Napoleon's planned invasion of England proved to be impossible, the huge army, some 200,000 men, was put in readiness for the war against Austria. In September the Austrians moved into Bavaria and Napoleon crossed the Rhine. One disaster for the Austrians was followed by another, and Nelson's stunning victory at Trafalgar had no effect on the land war, which soon ended with Napoleon entering Vienna and establishing himself at Schönbrunn Castle in November. There was, in the meantime, steady monetary inflation in Austria, and in July there had been a riot which had started when a baker's shop was plundered. The grenadiers had opened fire on the mob, and Rosenbaum, who was an eye-witness to many of the scenes, graphically describes this small but bloody revolution. Incredibly, Prince Nicolaus II Esterházy ordered the name-day festivities to proceed as usual at Eisenstadt, though of course without Haydn, and we read that for the first time, the princely opera troupe (not strolling players) began to operate in full force as in the old times of Nicolaus 'The Magnificent'. We read of a season, during the autumn of 1805 but especially between 13 September and 12 October, which included Mozart's *Die Entführung aus dem Serail*, three operas by Schenk and a piece by the new theatrical director at Eisenstadt, Heinrich Schmidt, *Der Junker in der Mühle*, with music by Antonio Polzelli, performed on Princess Marie Hermenegild's name-day. Heinrich Schmidt, in his memoirs, gives us a last vignette of life at Eisenstadt as the Napoleonic armies swept through Germany on their way towards the Austrian capital.

> So now I have become the leader of Prince Esterházy's theatre at Eisenstadt and, in my capacity as a secretary of all matters concerning art, I am responsible also for the Prince's musical and art collections. The theatre in which nothing but operas were performed was far from being a simple and common one. Joseph Haydn, Hummel, Fuchs and – later – Henneberg were the conductors of a

---

1 Karl Geiringer in the *Musical Quarterly* XXXV, No. 2 (April 1949), pp. 190f.

prominent orchestra whose manager was Tommasini [*sic*], the reputed violinist. ... Performances were always held in September, October, November and December, together with splendid hunting parties and other celebrations, the costs of which truly expressed the splendour of the princely house. The guests belonged to the highest élite, and usually almost the entire aristocracy and the *corps diplomatique* of Vienna were present. The singers and, in bad weather, the greater part of the audience were brought in closed carriages to the theatre which was situated in a huge hall of the palace. The charging of entrance fees was unknown: on the contrary, refreshments of all kinds were offered *gratis* to singers and audience alike.   [Horanyi, 179f.]

Landrath Carl Bertuch, in the above-quoted memoirs of his trip to Vienna, went to see Haydn and left an interesting description which is especially valuable for the one hint it gives concerning the frequency of Haydn's and Mozart's visits to one another (recently there have been some extremely odd attempts to suggest that they in fact hardly ever saw each other in Vienna)[1] in the years before Haydn left for England:

I was several times at the worthy Joseph Haydn's – it is to the good *Leg[ations]r[ath]* Griesinger, who is a friend of Haydn's, that I owe the first introduction which is difficult for a stranger to receive because Father Haydn very much feels the weight of his 73 years and is very frail. The 13th of Oct. is unforgettable, when together with Griesinger and *Medizinalrat* Longermann from Bayreuth we went the first time to Haydn. The thirteen-year-old Wolfgang Mozart was with us. The visit of the young Mozart, whom he had not seen for some time, gave much pleasure to the worthy old man. With the gentleness of a musical friend he spoke to Wolfgang about his musical education and praised the memory of his great father whom he, whenever he was in Vienna, saw almost daily and with whom he always lived in the most complete harmony. We broke off the conversation, sorry as we were to do so, quickly, at the end of half-an-hour, for Haydn was tiring. He bade us farewell in a very friendly way and gave me the pleasant permission to continue visiting him, which I also did several times, but always for only a short time. The last time, on 20th December, I found Haydn exceptionally cheerful. By a chance he had found one of his earliest works, a small Mass [*Missa brevis* in F], just for vocal parts,[2] which as a choir-boy at St Stephen's he had composed in 1742. This composition pleased him anew, and now he is adding parts to it, in order that this earliest and perhaps last product of his genius could be presented to Prince Esterházy as a sign of grateful recognition.
                                                        [Pohl III, 242f.]

Actually Haydn had already told Griesinger about the 'lost' Mass much earlier:

26 October 1805.
... Father Haydn intends 12 compositions for you which he finally produced after much encouragement: 1) an inserted opera aria with the text 'Sono le donne

---

1 The oddest being J. P. Larsen's article 'Haydn und Mozart', in the *Österreichische Musikzeitung* 1959, pp. 216ff. An equally strange picture of the Haydn–Mozart relationship is to be found in Bartha–Somfai.
2 Bertuch has confused Haydn's words. The original (not written as early as 1742, surely) was scored for two soprano soloists, mixed choir and an orchestra of two violins, *basso continuo* and organ. Haydn intended to add a larger orchestra in order to bring the work up to date, but of course he was too weak to do so, and it appears that the new orchestration, with an additional flute, two clarinets, two bassoons, two trumpets, timpani with divided violoncello and organo-basso, was probably given to Joseph Heidenreich. The score of the work in Eisenstadt has winds which are said to have been added by Antonio Polzelli. See Hoboken II, 70f. Haydn's Summary Catalogue of 1805, given to Bertuch, is given overleaf on p. 341.

capricciose' [Aria 'Dice benissimo', XXIVb: 5]; 2) a Salve Regina [XXIIIb: 1]; 3) a Mass that he composed in his 24th year and which turned up in the local Servite Monastery; 4) nine grand scenes from an Opera, *Orpheo e Euridice*. The text is by Battini [C. F. Badini], and Haydn composed this opera in England for 3,000 fl. for the impresario Gallini. The famous singer Davide should have sung Orpheo in it; the roles were already studied when Gallini was forbidden by the London Magistracy, under heavy penalty, to open a theatre which he had constructed without any permission. Therefore Haydn was robbed of the joy of hearing his opera.

. . . Haydn wants 100 ducats in paper money for all 12 pieces. If everything goes properly with this purchase, he wants to look through another 'Pakerl' in which he hopes to find sundry things. . . .   [Olleson, *Griesinger*, 50]

Breitkopf & Härtel, as we shall see, made a counter-offer and eventually they received all the music, of which however they only published the Aria and the extracts from *L'anima del filosofo* in 1806 and 1807.

On 4 November, Rosenbaum (125) noted that the Court was leaving. It was 'taking everything, even the warming pans and boot trees. It seems as though it never intends to return to Vienna.' Life was hideously expensive and the city was in a state of turmoil, but the next day, 5 November, the Tonkünstler-Societät issued an open letter for the violinist Joseph Mayseder (1789–1863) which was signed by 'Joseph Haydn/D^r der Tonkunst', Antonio Salieri, Leopold Koželuch, Joseph Weigl, Georg Albrechtsberger, and Joseph Eybler. Mayseder was described as possessing talents 'really in advance of his age . . . so that he must be considered in the class of the first virtuosi'.[1] It is typical that as the French were galloping towards Vienna, Haydn and his colleagues should find the time to assist young musical talent.

On 6 November Griesinger replied to a letter from Leipzig. '. . . Father Haydn is glad if you want to publish the catalogue of his compositions. . . . To the 9 scenes from the Opera, *Orpheo e Euridice* about which I wrote to you, two are to be added, without raising the price' (Olleson, *Griesinger*, 50). In the 'Pakerl' Haydn obviously found another two scenes from his English Opera.

As we have said, Rosenbaum's Diary is an authentic source for the war in Vienna, and on 13 November he noted (127): 'At about 11:30 o'clock, a crowd of people streamed in at the Burg Thor, all shouting "The French are coming!" . . . Cavalry, some of the riders with beards like Jews, opened the procession . . . At their centre rode Prince Murat surrounded by generals. . . .' On the 16th another diarist, Count Zinzendorf, noted 'A 2^h Bonaparte a passé la ville en deux voitures a 8 chevaux . . .' (MS. Diary). 'Several distinguished French officers,' writes Griesinger in his biography (57), 'along with Maret and Soult [Soulte]' went to visit Haydn during these days of the French occupation and wrote their names in Haydn's visitors' book. Dies, who went to see him on 21 November, found him much better than he had seen him for a long time; even the swelling in his legs had disappeared. Dies thought this turn of Haydn's health for the better was the result of the newly rediscovered *Missa brevis*; the composer had even begun to work again, adding the wind instruments (perhaps as a model for Heidenreich? or Polzelli?): 'What I find especially nice about this little work,' said Haydn to Dies (75), 'is the melody and a certain youthful fire, and that moves me to write down several bars every day, so that the voices can be accompanied

---

1 Sold at J. A. Stargardt's auction (Marburg/Lahn) in 1972, in the catalogue of which it is reproduced in facsimile (p. 163).

with wind instruments.' His eyes sparkled as he said this. But his renewed good health was not to last.

The night before, Beethoven's *Fidelio* had had its première, given at the Theater an der Wien. 'It had no success and the theatre was empty,' wrote Rosenbaum (129); probably the absence of most of the aristocracy, Beethoven's principal patrons, and the presence of members of the French army, who went to the theatre but can have understood nothing of the spoken German dialogue, contributed to the initial failure.

On the 26th the news of Trafalgar reached Vienna. Zinzendorf writes 'La flotte . . . a eté battue à Cadiz. L'amiral Nelson mort des blessures . . .' (MS. Diary). Nelson's death will have brought back old memories to Haydn, of Aboukir and the *Missa in angustiis*, and of the Admiral himself. But the ogre, Napoleon, was now ensconced in Schönbrunn Castle, and Rosenbaum repeats Schindlöcker's fascinating description of Cherubini conducting a concert there for the French Emperor.

> . . . Napoleon appeared at approximately 7:30, in a uniform with small embroidery and with the star of the Legion of Honour, and wearing boots. He is of small and somewhat heavy build, his face black-brown-yellow shadowed; a pair of brilliant eyes penetrate the inmost recesses of everyone he sees; his head is covered by unruly black hair. He was followed by Murat and surrounded by roughly 300 generals, ministers, adjutants and chamberlains in gold-embroidered scarlet uniforms and powdered wigs, all in gala dress . . . Throughout the performance – it lasted not quite one hour – he sat virtually motionless, with an earnest, sombre (one is tempted to say sullen) air. He spoke only once with Murat, who stood two paces behind him to the right, and did not express the least satisfaction or dissatisfaction during the concert. – His retinue stood behind him in a semicircle, as silent as the train of an oriental despot; not one of them spoke so much as a syllable to another. When the music was over, he went off at the double, paying no heed to anything whatever. . . .   [Radant, *Rosenbaum*, 132]

From Rosenbaum we also learn that on 24 December

> Braun is giving *The Creation* at the Redoutensaal. The soloists are Neumann, Lauchter [Laucher] and Weinmüller; the prices are 2 gulden 40 kreuzer, 2 gulden and 1 gulden . . . Today there is a concert for Napoleon. Wednesday, 25th, Christmas Day: Very muddy. Today is the performance of *The Seasons* at the Redoutensall [*sic*].[1] The soloists are the same as yesterday . . . Salieri . . . told me about the concert yesterday at Schönbrunn; Napoleon did not like it, was very sullen and did not even wait for it to finish.   [ibid.]

Napoleon, who thought Cherubini's accompaniments heavy, ignored Haydn's presence, and of course Haydn's music, while he presided at Schönbrunn.

Politically, Napoleon had every reason to be satisfied: after the battle of Austerlitz, in which 15,000 allied troops were killed or wounded, the Russians withdrew and the Austrians had to sue for peace. On 26 December the Peace of Pressburg was signed, as a result of which Austria lost Vorderösterreich, the Tyrol and the Venetian lands. Naples was given to Joseph Bonaparte and the other conquered lands divided up among Napoleon's family. The war indemnity was 40,000,000 francs. It was one of the most stupidly planned wars in the Emperor Franz's disastrous reign. Men were

---

[1] This performance of *The Seasons* was attended by an English physician, Dr Henry Reeve, then visiting Vienna. For his reporting of this and other events, including a visit to Haydn himself, see Addenda to this volume.

appalled about the war, about Napoleon, about the whole situation; but thankful, at least, for peace. Rosenbaum (132f.) went out to buy Therese '3 pairs of white silk stockings as a small memento of the Peace. . . .' Zinzendorf, writing a few days later on 31 December, asked that

> Le grand moderateur de l'univers permet que les Humains présomtueux au milieu de leur faiblesse et de leur inconséquence ne fassent point le meilleur usage de leur raison pour conferer le bonheur des actions et des individues . . . La manie de s'aggrandir par les conquéres enleve aux chefs des grand etats jusqu'a la volunté de rendre leurs peuples heureux . . .' (MS. Diary).

And Haydn, hearing of all these momentous events second-hand, felt more and more useless. Griesinger (52) quotes what may have been Father Haydn's thoughts as the long year 1805 came to a close: 'I am of no more use to the world. I have to be nursed and cared for as if I were a child: it is time that God called me to Himself!'

HAYDN'S SUMMARY CATALOGUE FOR BERTUCH (1805)

'Verzeichniß aller derjenigen Compositionen, welche ich mich beyläufig erinnere, von meinem 18. bis in das 73. Jahr verfertigt zu haben. Wien, im Dec. 1805. Joseph Haydn' [Compare title of *HV*]

I. *Für die Kirche*, 32 Stücke, als 2 Te Deum laudamus. 15 Messen. 4 Oratorien. 1 Salve Regina, à 4 Voci. 1 Salve, Organo solo. 1 Cantilena pro Adventu. 4 Responsoria de Venerabile. 1 Stabat Mater. Die sieben Worte am Kreuze. 3 Chöre.

II. *Fürs Theater*, 14 italienische und 5 deutsche Opern, wovon die gedruckten Bücher noch vorhanden sind, als 1) *La Canterina.* 2) *L'incontro improviso.* 3) *Lo speziale.* 4) *La pescatrice.* 5) *Il Mondo della Luna.* 6) *L'Isola disabitata.* 7) *L'infedeltà fedele* [*La fedeltà premiata*]. 8) *La fedeltà premiata.* 9) *La vera Costanza.* 10) *Orlando Paladino.* 11) *Armida.* 12) *Acide e Galatea, à 4 Voci.* 13) *L'infedeltà delusa.* 14) *Orfeo.* Deutsche Marionetten-Opern: 1) Genovefens 4ter Theil. 2) Philemon und Baucis. 3) Dido. 4) Die bestrafte Rachgier, oder das abgebrannte Haus [in reality two different operas, 'Das abgebrannte Haus' also known as 'Die Feuersbrunst']. 5) Der krumme Teufel.

III. *Oratorien.* 1) *Il Ritorno di Tobia.* 2) Die Schöpfung. 3) Die Jahreszeiten.

IV. *Mehrstimmige Gesänge und Lieder.* 13 drey- und vierstimmige Gesänge. 40 Canons. 42 deutsche und englische Lieder, auch ital. Duetten. 366 *A Selection of Original Scots Songs, the Harmony by Dr. Haydn.*

V. *Für Instrumente.* 118 Sinfonien. 83 Violinquartetten. 15 Concerte, als 3 für V[ioline], 3 fürs Vc. 1 für den C[ontra] B[ass], 2 fürs Horn, 1 für die Trompete, 1 für die Fl. 1 für die Orgel und 3 für den Flügel. 20 *Divertimenti* für verschiedene Instrumente, à 5, 6, 7 und 9. 21 *Trii p. 2 V. e Basso.* 3 *Trii p. 2 Fl. e Vc.* 6 Violinsolo's, mit Begl. einer Viola. 66 Sonaten für das Pianoforte, mit und ohne Begl. 163 Baryton-Stücke. Als 8 Konzerte, 17 *Cassationi*, 125 *Divertim. p. il Baritono, Viola e Vllo*, 6 *Duetti*, 12 *Sonate p. il Barit. col Vllo*, 3 Märsche. 400 Menuetten und Deutsche.

[Gerber *NTL* I, 593f.]

CHAPTER NINE

Chronicle 1806

GRIESINGER'S LETTER OF 26 OCTOBER 1805 to Breitkopf & Härtel in Leipzig concerning Haydn's twelve compositions – for which the composer had wanted to be paid 100 ducats – resulted in the publisher offering less than half this sum, as is shown in a letter written by Griesinger on 15 February 1806:

> . . . I came out with the offer of 200 fl. and it was accepted: 'I want to show H. Hartel, he Haydn added, 'that I am not unappreciative; he shall receive everything I intended for him, and at that price.' Just now I received a Mass (the first, which Hn. wrote in his 18th year), 11 Arias and Duets from the Opera *Orpheus & Euridice*, an inserted Opera-Aria of 1780 ['Dice benissimo'] and a Salve Regina of 1756. The last two are holograph manuscripts and Haydn asks you to return them at your convenience.[1] The 200 fl. I organized and paid to him at once. Everything is to be sent next Tuesday by the mail coach.
>
> I told H. Hn. your remark that his Catalogue [*HV*] was not complete. He freely admitted that some things could be omitted, and he hopes you are fortunate enough to complete it. . . .
>
> [Olleson, *Griesinger*, 50]

In this same letter, apparently, Griesinger also related that Haydn had now given up all hope of completing his last Quartet ('Op. 103'). Two Russian officers came to see him and asked for one of his latest compositions. Haydn offered them the Quartet for fifty ducats, whereupon the officers asked for eight weeks' time [*Bedenkzeit*], for they wanted to dedicate the work to their Emperor (Pohl III, 246). Haydn was anxious to sell his 'children' for as much as possible, and on 19 February we find Griesinger writing to Breitkopf & Härtel that:

> I am forced, my most excellent friend, with an unpleasant *postscriptum*. Father Hn. sent and told me yesterday that he had forgotten to tell me that the cost of copying the Mass and the 11 opera scenes was 17 fl. 40 X. That shouldn't actually be charged to the publisher, but I answered that I would inform you about it. Yesterday the parcel was sent to you by the mail coach . . .
>
> [Olleson, *Griesinger*, 51]

Haydn was now so weak and distracted that he actually forgot Zelter's name and sent to Dies to ask him 'the name of his most esteemed and scholarly friend from Berlin'. The servant, probably Elssler, who came to Dies reported that Haydn was 'extremely weak' and had been searching the whole forenoon for a letter from 'the Kapellmeister' and could not find it. Dies himself came on the 19th and Haydn said:

---

1 These MSS. were not returned.

. . . I need an occupation. Usually musical ideas pursue me to the point of torture, I can't get rid of them, they are in front of me like walls. If it's an Allegro that haunts me, then my pulse beats more quickly and I can't sleep. If it is an Adagio, then I note that my pulse beats more slowly. My imagination [*Phantasie*] plays on me as if I were a piano.' Haydn laughed and, blushing, he said: 'I'm really a living piano. For the last few days it has been playing within me an old song that I often played in my youth, in E minor, *O Herr! wie lieb' ich dich von Herzen*. Whether I'm walking or sitting, everywhere I hear it. – But it's curious, when I am inwardly persecuted and nothing will help to rid me of the persecution, and my song occures to me *Gott erhalte Franz den Kaiser*, then it's easier; that helps.

'That doesn't surprise me,' I [Dies] said, 'for without flattery I hold that song to be a masterpiece.'

'I almost do so myself, though I shouldn't really say so.'

The day before Cherubini conducted the first performance of his new Opera *Faniska*, he went to visit Haydn, who gave him a very valuable present, the autograph of one of the most popular Salomon Symphonies – No. 103 ('Drum Roll'). In a shaky, spidery hand he dedicated it to his young friend 'Padre del celebre Cherubini/ai 24:ᵗʳᵒ di Febr: 806' under the still vigorous original signature of London, 1795 (facsimile of this page *inter alia* in R. Hughes *Haydn*, facing p. 178). Shortly after the successful première of *Faniska* Cherubini left Vienna; it is said that he did so mainly because his wife, a Parisian, did not find the Viennese climate congenial. Possibly the visit of the 24th to Haydn, recorded above, was Cherubini's last. Griesinger in his biography has left us two authentic and interesting statements. 'I was never a swift writer and always composed with deliberation and industry. But such works are intended to last, and a connoisseur can see this at once by looking at the score. When Cherubini looked through some of my manuscripts he always found the places that merited attention.' When giving Cherubini the 'Drum Roll' Symphony, Haydn knew that it was especially popular in Paris and said to Cherubini, 'Let me call myself your musical father, and you my son.' Cherubini melted into tears of sadness.[1] Possibly Cherubini himself delivered Haydn's answer – dated 6 March 1806 – to the Paris Conservatoire de Musique, which we have quoted above (p. 335); this circumstance would also explain the tardy response.

In a now lost letter of 12 March 1806, Griesinger wrote to Leipzig that in the previous parcel of Haydn's works was the *Lied* 'Der schlaue Pudel' [XXVIa: 38] which, according to the composer, had been written twenty-four years earlier, in 1782. On 15 March Dies visited Haydn, who 'could not speak without effort'. Various visitors had come and gone and now Haydn's lawyer, perhaps Sarchi, was announced. Dies asked if Haydn had a lawsuit. 'Not that, but now and then a few codicils are added to my will. . . . I am ready for death at any moment.' Then Haydn rose with difficulty from his chair, went to his desk, and pulled out the famous visiting card with the Gleim text that Haydn had set to music some years before, 'Hin ist alle meine Kraft, alt und schwach bin ich' (*vide supra*, p. 278). Dies was so moved that he had to leave 'to hide my feelings'.[2]

It was in answer to this visiting card that Albrechtsberger sent Haydn the following canon – perhaps for Haydn's birthday on 31 March.

1 Pohl III, 245; Griesinger, 56, 61.
2 Olleson, *Griesinger*, 51; Dies 114f.

[To Haydn from Johann Georg Albrechtsberger, Vienna. *Latin, 'Tu' form*]

[Sometime during March 1806]

Pieridum Frater! qui dudum noster Apollo diceris: hunc Canonem fecit, dedicatique Tibi vetus et sincerus Amicus Georg Albrechtsberger.

Josepho Haydn   1806

Canone perpetuo a 4 Voci in hypodiapente, et hypodiapson L'istesso Canone in hypodiatesseron ed hypodiapson.

So - la - ti - um mi - se - ris so - ci -
-os ha - bu - is - se do - lo - rum, do - lo - rum.

[CCLN, 242]

On 1 April *The Seven Words* was performed at the Burgtheater for the benefit of the poor people from the theatre, with Antonie Flamm, Therese Gassmann-Rosenbaum, Wilhelm Ehlers and Ignaz Saal as soloists; this year the winter concerts of the Tonkünstler-Societät had featured a vocal and instrumental concert (30, 31 March; Pohl, *Denkschrift*, 67) with a symphony by Kanne and a piano concerto by Mozart. The Haydn Oratorios had been overplayed in Vienna, and the Tonkünstler-Societät gave none in 1803, none in 1806 and none in the March concerts of 1807.

On 2 April Griesinger could report to Breitkopf & Härtel that despite attractive offers by Russian officers, he had been able to secure Haydn's last Quartets for the Leipzig publishers.

> . . . Here, my friend, is Haydn's swan-song, his 83rd Quartet in the original [manuscript]. . . . As an excuse that the Quartet is not complete, Haydn sends you his characteristic visiting card; the words are by Gellert. Haydn doesn't give up the hope that in a fortunate moment he might be capable of adding a small rondo. We hope it will happen, but there is not much chance that what Haydn could not finish since 1803 could be added now. But wouldn't it be fitting to print the visiting card instead of the missing rondo? [Count Moritz von] Fries is entirely in agreement; wherever this Quartet sounds, one will see immediately, from these few words, why it is not complete, and one will thus be filled with sad emotions.
>
> . . . [Haydn at this point said to Griesinger that] his field is boundless; that which could take place in music is far greater than that which has already occurred. Ideas float before him by means of which his Art could be brought much further, but his physical condition no longer permits him their execution. . . . [When Haydn handed over the work, he said: 'It's my last child but it still looks like me']
>
> [Olleson, *Griesinger*, 47, 51]

Abbé Maximilian Stadler promptly answered Haydn's visiting card with a composition using the music but enlarging it to new words, 'Doch, was sie erschuf, bleibt stets – Ewig lebt dein Ruhm' ('but what [that spirit] created remains forever – ever may thy fame live'); this response so charmed Haydn that he urged its compiler to have it printed, and this was brought about by the publisher Johann Cappi in Vienna.

When Count von Fries heard that Breitkopf & Härtel had secured the publication rights for the Haydn Quartet for fifty ducats, he hastened to Griesinger and offered the firm the fifty ducats with interest if they would let him have the work. Fries seems to have had some rights, at least moral, for it might be considered either that Op. 103 was to be the third of Op. 77 (as Griesinger sometimes imagined), which was of course for Prince Lobkowitz; or on the other hand it might have been thought the first of six quartets which Haydn intended to write for Fries for the fee of 300 ducats. It would seem that Griesinger would not consider any such offer and the best that Fries could achieve was the request that the edition would be handsomely printed, that he would be sent a dozen copies as soon as it left the presses, and that on the title page there would be the note, 'dédié au Comte Maurice de Fries' with the further information '83me et dernier Quatuor' and 'Schwanengesang' (if the title page happened to be in German) – all details to which Breitkopf & Härtel were glad to agree. The visiting card, with the words and music, were included, too, at the end of the quartet.[1]

Even letter-writing was becoming a drudgery for Haydn, who now used a secretary for all his correspondence, including the following two letters which were dictated at this time:

[To Bonifazio Asioli,[2] Milan. *Italian*]
My dear Colleague,
I should like Carlo Mozart to have the honour of being numbered among your pupils. I should congratulate him on having such a teacher as you, whose works and talents I very much admire.

Permit me to recommend this young man to you, as the son of my late friend, and as the heir to a name precious to all connoisseurs and friends of the art. I am sure that Carlo Mozart will prove himself worthy of all the goodness and trouble with which you will favour him, in order to make of him a person who will be a credit to his teacher and to his father. I pray you to forgive me if I, burdened as I am with the infirmities of old age, limit myself here to expressing the honour of subscribing myself, with every esteem and consideration,

Signore,
Your most humble and obedient servant,
Giuseppe Haydn [m.p] ria.

Vienna, 23rd April 1806.   [CCLN, 238f.]

[To Prince Nicolaus II Esterhazy. *German*]
[Letter in Johann Elssler's hand, only signature and title autograph]
Your Highness,
My experience of Your Highness has been not only that of the kindest of princes, but you have also earned respect as a most energetic patron of all that is beautiful and useful; and thus I humbly support the suppliant Herr Rupp's[3] request that, in your graciousness, his son be allowed to join the boys' choir. I can recommend this the more easily since the father has served many years, with every

---

1 Stadler's MS. autobiography (Gesellschaft der Musikfreunde, Vienna); see Pohl III, 248. The Fries information from a now lost letter from Griesinger to Breitkopf & Härtel, paraphrased in Pohl III, 247. For a description of Stadler's prints see Hoboken I, 441; also *AMZ* IX, 594 (where Haydn's card and Stadler's first version are printed) and 654ff. (where a complicated canon by Stadler on the theme is printed).
2 Asioli (1769–1832), a well-known composer, was professor of counterpoint at the Milan Conservatorio. Karl Mozart, Wolfgang's elder son (born in 1784), went to study with Asioli and took this letter of recommendation with him. See also Walter Hummel, *W. A. Mozarts Söhne,* Kassel 1956, p. 37.
3 J. Martin Rupp had been engaged as a horn player in 1777.

mark of distinction, as a horn player in Your Highness' band. Therefore I have considered it my duty to add my most humble plea to his, in the confident hope of your granting a request from which he would derive such advantages.

Your Highness'
most humble
Joseph Haydn [m.p] ria,
Kapell Meister.

Vienna, 3rd May 1806.

[On the outside of the file is the following pencilled note: '1° to Hummel for his information. 2° to Haydn, that at present no vacancy, however the matter will be noted'. See next letter.]

[CCLN, 239]

[To Haydn from Prince Nicolaus II Esterhazy. *German*]
To *Kapellmeister* von Haydn:

As pleasant as it would be, in view of your written application, to appoint the son of J. Martin Rupp, court chamber-musician and horn player, to the boys' choir, yet I must inform you that this cannot be, for there is no vacancy there at present; but I shall take note of the matter and, when the time comes, give it favourable consideration.

This is to inform you how matters stand. I am, with all esteem,

Your most willing,
Exp: Esterházy.

Vienna, 5th May 1806.

[CCLN, 240]

The warm weather had a highly beneficial effect on Haydn's health. On 18 June Dies went to visit the house in the Kleine Steingasse and heard that

[the previous day some friends] had invited him to go in their company to a famous instrument-maker's, there to inspect a new musical instrument with [built-in mechanical] organ pipes. Haydn was easily persuaded even though the artist's quarters were far from Gumpendorf. When the carriage stopped, the young men sprang out, eased Haydn's descent and then carried him up a few flights to the artist's apartment. The [mechanical] organ pipes also played a Haydn composition. Haydn listened with pleasure, and this pleasure imparted new strength to his spirit.

Haydn may have visited his old friend Pater P. Niemecz, or Mälzel's mechanical instrument, the 'Panharmonicon', one of the barrels of which contained Haydn's 'Military Movement' (from Symphony No. 100),[1] and which is known to have existed as early as 1805. Haydn had always had a special affection for these mechanical instruments with their built-in *Orgelwerk*, and this was his farewell to a miniature art for which he had composed more pieces than any other great master.

On 10 August 1806 Johann Michael Haydn died at Salzburg of consumption ('an der Auszehrung' is the official medical explanation given in the Salzburg death register). Joseph knew that his brother had been ill, and had sent gifts of money from time to time; but apparently no one in Salzburg thought to inform Joseph of his brother's death, and in Johann Michael's 'official' biography[2] we read that one of the anonymous authors, J. G. Schinn, was obliged to write on the Feast of the Guardian Angels (2 October!):

1 Dies 133; Hoboken I, 827f.; for Mälzel see Frimmel's *Beethoven-Handbuch* I, 378ff.
2 *Biographische Skizze von Michael Haydn. Von des verklärten Tonkünstlers Freunden entworfen und zum Besten seiner Witwe herausgegeben*, Salzburg 1808, p. 43.

Joseph Haydn sent another 50 fl. to his sick brother and wrote at that time: he had to hear from third parties that his brother had died, and please inform him at once about it because in that case he would have to change his last will and testament in which he had named him [Michael] residuary legatee. . . .

Schinn then goes on to explain in this letter that 'Joseph therefore must not have received two letters, one after another'. It was not until 25 November 1806, in any case, that Joseph had to explain officially the family situation to the Vienna City Magistracy:

[To the Vienna City Magistracy. *German*; Archive Copy]

Vienna, 25th November 1806

Worthy Magistracy!

The undersigned has the honour to make the following statement regarding my late brother Michael Haydn of Salzburg: he raises no objection to the widow being deemed without further ado the principal recipient of the testator's estate; and also that he and his brother had but 2 sisters, both of whom are deceased, and who left the following children: from the deceased sister, Anna Rafler – Anna Maria Moser, seamstress at Esterhasz in Hungary; Elisabeth Böheim, seamstress at Rohrau in Lower Austria; Theresia Hamer, cobbler-mistress at Gerrhaus in Hungary; Mathias Fröhlich, farrier in Fischament; and Anna Loder, cobbler-mistress in Vienna. Further: from the deceased sister Franziska, there is only one daughter, by the name of Anna Wimmer, restaurant-keeper at Nikola in Hungary.

Joseph Haydn,
Kapellmeister to Prince Esterházy
and Dr. of Music.

[CCLN, 240]

In fact Michael was not exactly a 'residuary legatee', either in the first will, quoted above *in extenso* (*supra*, pp. 50ff.) or in the second (*infra*, pp. 379ff.), but perhaps there was another will made in between which was superseded by the final version.

Johann Michael lived all his life – at least from the early 1760s – in the shadow of his brother's fame. Retiring and extraordinary diffident about the dissemination and publication of his music, Michael Haydn's work was only very fragmentarily known until quite recently. Though his church music was widely circulated throughout the Austrian Monarchy in manuscript copies, his instrumental music, even the late symphonies, remained hardly known outside Salzburg. It is typical that a local Salzburg cleric, Abbot Dominikus, should write in his Diary after Michael's death:

. . . a worthy brother of the Esterhazi Kapelmeister [*sic*] Joseph Haiden. He was 43 years in local service and was especially esteemed by the church since he composed astonishingly much in the real church-music style . . . Haiden was, apart from his music, a scholarly, pleasant and quiet man.[1]

Dies imagined that it was the news – or at least rumours – of Michael's death that had reduced Haydn to a sorry state on 17 August 1806, when Dies came to call. He persuaded Haydn to sit down at the piano.

He started to improvise, struck some wrong notes as if he were a student, looked at me, corrected the wrong notes and in the corrections always made new mistakes. 'Ah', he said after a minute (the playing lasted no longer), 'You hear for yourself, I can't do it any longer! Eight years ago it was different, but *The Seasons* has

1 Jancik, op. cit., 276.

brought me this ill; I never should have written it! I overworked myself when composing it.' Haydn stood up and paced slowly up and down the room. Profound depression had once again settled on his brow; no more cheerful glance could penetrate this dark gloom. 'You see', he said, 'I live out my remaining days in this fashion.'

[Dies, 137]

In October Breitkopf & Härtel sent Haydn the piano score of *L'anima del filosofo*, or as they called it, *Orfeo ed Euridice*, and the parts of the last quartet. Haydn was much pleased about the handsome publications but pointed out two inaccuracies: the Quartet was not his 82nd but his 83rd (Haydn was using the Pleyel Catalogue of his Quartets for this numbering) and (Griesinger to Leipzig on 29 October), 'The Song, *Hin ist alle meine Kraft*, is no canon . . .' (it had been listed as such in the *AMZ*, which Haydn apparently still read with interest).[1]

Dies was accidentally a witness to a rather touching scene. He went to Haydn's house on 9 June 1806, and the composer was showing his future biographer a portfolio of engravings, some of which Haydn had purchased in London, some of which were gifts. Then Prince Paul, son of Nicolaus II Esterházy, was announced. He covered Haydn with kisses and embraced him: 'Mein bester Haydn, Gott erhalte Sie noch viele Jahre!' (Dies, 131f.)

Towards the end of the year, Dies found Haydn in great good humour – 'I'm not doing so badly for this time of year, am I?' said Haydn, who explained that it was all the Esterházy family's doing.

A short time ago Princess Maria honoured me with a visit. Every visit is another proof of her charity, and she knows how to steer the conversation towards another opportunity for her to show her generosity.[2]

During our conversation the Princess managed to extract the information from me that, on account of my great age and the frequent indispositions that accompany such a state, I require more attention. I could not ignore in silence the increasing inflation and remarked that I had numerous relations who had to be remembered after my death; but I would certainly not be able to do so if I should continue to live for long, because for some years I have had to dip into capital to the extent of 2,000 fl.

The Princess interrupted me and asked how much I thought I might need in order to satisfy all my wishes. I mentioned the sum and she said to me, 'Leave it to me.'

The very next day the Princess herself brought a personal note from her husband, the reigning Prince.   [Dies, 144f.]

The correspondence in this connection reads as follows:

[To Haydn from Prince Nicolaus II Esterházy. *German*]
Dear *Kapellmeister* Haydn!

My dear wife, the Princess Maria, told me of your wish to receive from me six-hundred gulden annually, in addition to your regular emoluments; she added that the realization of this would be a great source of comfort and consolation to you. It is with great pleasure that I hasten to use this opportunity to show my esteem and friendship for you, and inform you herewith of my guarantee that you

---

1 Olleson, *Griesinger*, 51.
2 Haydn was also allowed wine from the princely cellars, and in particular Tokay and Malaga, which Haydn's doctors had ordered him to take so as to strengthen his heart. Moreover, the princely carriages (*Equipage*) were at Haydn's disposal. Pohl III, 253. See also *supra*, p. 231.

shall receive the sum of three-hundred gulden semi-annually from my Court Treasury Office, whom I shall inform of this under separate cover.[1]

I hope that you continue to enjoy good health, and am your most willing

Fürst Esterhazy.

Vienna, 26th November 1806. [CCLN, 240f.]

[To Prince Nicolaus II Esterházy. *German*]

[Beginning of December 1806]

Most Serene Prince
and Gracious Lord!

I cannot find the words to express how touched and pleased I was to receive from Your Highness the most gracious note [*Hand billet*] addressed to me, for it went to my heart; and I am equally unable to describe my most heartfelt thanks for this most gracious of acts, extended to an old and enfeebled servant. Your Highness has thereby given me once again the proof that Your Highness is accustomed to reward an artist generously even when, because of his advanced age and weakness, he is no longer able to fulfil his duties.

May the Almighty grant me just enough strength, before my end, to enable me to express in music the emotions which this undeserved act of special grace has awakened in me.

I remain ever your most devoted, submissive and most obedient servant,

Joseph Haydn,
Kapellmeister to Prince Esterházy.

[CCLN, 241]

Musical history had come a long way in Haydn's hands from the *Vice-Capellmeister* kissing the hem of Prince Paul Anton Esterházy's garment, in 1761, to Prince Paul Esterházy embracing his father's retired *Capellmeister* and covering him with kisses. It is a social transformation that Paul Anton would simply have not believed possible, and there is no doubt that it was principally Haydn himself, with his modest firmness, his generosity and his world fame, that made this fantastic change not only possible but desirable.

We may close this year's Chronicle with a letter from Haydn to his Swedish friend, Silverstolpe:

[To F. S. Silverstolpe,[2] St Petersburg. *French*. Entire letter and signature in dictation]

Vienna, 30 December 1806.

Monsieur,

You will forgive an old man of nearly 75 if he makes use of a hand other than his own to thank you, *Monsieur*, for your kind remembrance of me, and for the good tea which you were good enough to send me. I never forget my friends, and I remembered you, *Monsieur*, as soon as I had opened your letter. Since the time

---

1 The order to the Treasury Office is preserved in Budapest (Esterházy Archives, Acta Musicalia XXX, 2226), and reads as follows:

Since I have decided to grant an additional yearly salary of six hundred gulden to my worthy *Kapellmeister* and Doctor of Art [*sic*] Joseph Haydn, my Court Treasury Office is herewith notified to tender this sum in semi-annual instalments as of the 27th of the previous month, November. Eisenstadt, 1st December 1806. Exp. Esterházy.

2 Silverstolpe had become *chargé d'affaires* at the Swedish Embassy in St. Petersburg. He noted the expenses for '2 canisters of caravan-borne tea, a present for Haydn in Vienna, 10 roubles' (see Mörner, op. cit., p. 406, n. 3). Haydn included his famous visiting card, with the *incipit* 'Hin ist alle meine Kraft, alt und schwach bin ich,' in the above letter.

when we first met, my life has become more monotonous: I struggle against the infirmities of old age, and I dare not occupy myself with my art any longer, for fear of injuring my health. Thus there is nothing that gives me more pleasure than to retrace past times, and to hear, from time to time, that there are people in this world still interested in me.

Please be good enough, *Monsieur*, to give my kind regards to our good Neukomm; I most sincerely wish him all the success which his talent and his character deserve. The caravan-borne tea which you were good enough to send me is the kind I prefer to all others. You have guessed my taste exactly, and I promise you that I shall never drink a cup without gratefully recalling the source from which I received it.

I remain, *Monsieur*, &c.,
Joseph Haydn.
[CCLN, 241f.]

A single portrait of Haydn survives from this period: a large painting in oils showing the composer holding sheets of *The Creation* in his left hand and seated at his writing desk (see pl. I). The artist, Isidor Neugass, received 500 fl. from Prince Nicolaus II Esterházy for the painting, (which still hangs in the Esterházy Castle at Eisenstadt) and a monthly stipendium of 50 fl. for further study. The painting is a rather good likeness of Haydn's features; it is signed 'peint par J. Neugaß 1805' but the request for Esterházy to accept the finished picture was not made until 7 December 1806, and it is therefore probable that Neugass began the portrait in 1805 and finished it the following year. After having disappeared for many years, the 'Brunsvik' Beethoven portrait by Neugass – one of two Beethoven portraits that Neugass executed in 1806(?) – was rediscovered (see pl. II).

One of Haydn's colleagues in the Esterházy administration was the Librarian and Curator of the princely collections, Georg von Gáal, a poet and scholar. In 1806 Gáal printed a poem in Haydn's honour on the subject of the *The Creation*, inspired, possibly, by one of the Viennese performances – or indeed, perhaps even that which took place under Hummel's direction in Eisenstadt in the autumn of 1804. A copy of the poem was owned by Haydn and passed to the National Széchényi Library (Ha. I. 13), through the courtesy of which we reproduce it herewith:

Dem
unsterblichen Sänger der Schöpfung
Herrn Herrn
Joseph Haydn,
Doctor der Tonkunst, der königl. Schwedischen Academie der Musik Mitgliede, Ehren Mitgliede der Academie der Künste und Wissenschaften, imgleichen des Conservatoriums zu Paris, und Kapellmeister in wirklichen Diensten Seiner Durchlaucht des regierenden Fürsten Nikolaus Esterhazy von Galantha.

———————

Unterthänigst dargebracht
von
Georg von Gaal.

———————

1806

---

1 Pohl III, 251. The other Beethoven portrait by Neugass, done for the Lichnowsky family and formerly in Grätz Castle, is signed and dated 'peint par Neugass Wienne 1806'; presumably the 'Brunsvik' version is from the same year. See Landon, *Beethoven* 10, 11, 235.

[New Page]

Werde! rief der Schöpfer, und es fuhren
Aufgejagt die Trümmer der Naturen
Aus des Chaos alter Nacht.
Angezündet von des Vaters Glanze
Strahlten diese Sonnen, und das Ganze
Trug das Urbild seiner Macht.
Schimmernd, doch nur stumm pries seinen Meister
Dieses All, darum erschuf er Geister
Höh're Bilder seiner Herrlichkeit,
Darum schuf er diese sel'gen Kinder,
Seiner Allmacht würdige Verkünder,
Spiegel seiner Göttlichkeit.
Muthig an des Bildnergeistes Zügel
Drangen sie dem lichten Sonnenhügel
Der Vollkommenheit hinzu;
Aber schon sechs tausend Jahre sanken,
Stand je Einer ihren hohen Schranken
Haydn! noch so nah,' wie Du?
Götter, heilig ihrem Heidenthume,
Prangten pompend mit der Schöpfung Ruhme –
Steine horchten ihrem Lied:
Wie versteinert sah'n Dich Nationen,
Bothen liefen aus entfernten Zonen
Sich zu Dir die Füsse müd.
Furien, bey Orpheus Leyertönen
Schwammen einst in eignen Schmerzensthränen,
Und ihr Herz schlug ungestüm:
Fama folgte Deinem Adlergange,
Engel horchten, – Deinem Hochgesange
Jubelten die Serafim.
Banne Philadelphia, deine Puppen!
Rufe deiner Geister Zaubergruppen
Aus des Grabes Nacht hervor!
Nimmer schaffen diese Gaukelscenen
Wie der große Hayden nur aus Tönen
Ganze Welten uns vor's Ohr!
Weltsystheme maaßen die Newtone,
Zu den Sternen klommen Robertsone
Mit dem Aetherflug Genie,
Näher schon dem Riesen – Orionen,
Schifften sie durch's Strahlenmeer der Sonnen –
Hörten ihren Schimmer nie.
Hörten selbst im Flammenraum der Blitze
Von des Aares hohem Wolkensitze
Nie des Mondes stillen Gang:
Sonnenscheine, Lichtesströme drangen
Zu des Horchers Ohren, Strahlen klangen
Wo dein Schöpfergeist sie sang.
Und das Herz, wie vom Gestirn gezogen;
Wechselnd oft der Meere Fluten wogen –
Wogt es Deiner Allgewalt:
Wirbelnd aus der Körperwelt Gewühle

Schwindeln höher'n Schwunges die Gefühle
Wo Dein heil'ger Zauber wallt.
Sendet durch das Meer der Geistersterne,
Astronomen! durch die Flammenferne
Sendet euren Falkenblick!
Glänzt vom Raume ihres Strahlenreiches
Dem Gestirne Hayden noch Ein Gleiches
Euer'm Seherohr zurück? –

It cannot be within the scope of this volume to take detailed notice of what might be called 'secondary' publications of Haydn, i.e. of new publications of his symphonies, etc. Yet one enterprise must be mentioned because it had enormous influence on the German-speaking musical world: the Breitkopf & Härtel publication of a series of scores not only of Haydn but also Mozart symphonies. No doubt inspired by the good reception of the Pleyel editions of Haydn's music in score, the Leipzig publishers began their new series with Haydn's Symphony No. 103, which they called No. 1; No. 2 was No. 104; and so on; these numbers were used to identify Haydn's symphonies until 1907. An enthusiastic review of the new undertaking appeared in the *AMZ* VIII (June 1806), pp. 619ff. As a next number, a Mozart symphony was announced. 'Quod Deus bene vertat!' closed the reviewer hopefully. These Breitkopf & Härtel scores gradually broke the pernicious habit of issuing symphonies in parts only, and moreover the new series tried to 'edit' the works sensibly for performance, adjusting contradictory phrasing marks, and so on. Only someone who has worked critically with the hopelessly inaccurate eighteenth-century editions of Haydn's symphonies in parts can realize what an event the Breitkopf scores were. Soon, the Leipzig house began to issue matching scores and parts, and with that process we finally reach a modern standard of printing-orchestral-conducting practice without which serious and properly rehearsed performances of such complicated works as Beethoven's symphonies were simply not possible. We must not forget the credit due to Breitkopf & Härtel for making the great classical literature – Haydn, Mozart, Beethoven – available in cheap and (for their time and circumstances) accurate editions; really *Volksausgaben* in the true sense of that much misused word.

CHAPTER TEN

Chronicle 1807

IN ITS ISSUE DATED 31 JANUARY 1807, the *Journal des Luxus und der Moden* printed a report from Vienna. We read:

> Our veteran *Haydn* leads his quiet, patriarchal life, not without troubles which come from a body weakened by years and work. Even his piano [*Clavier*] has now been removed from his room – a piano that was the witness of many a beautiful fruit of his creative spirit – because at almost every attempt to pursue his favourite occupation he becomes dizzy. He puts up with all this, however, in an air of submission and resignation, and even in hours when he suffers, his good humour seldom deserts him.

When Dies came to see Haydn on 23 February, he found that the composer had just recovered from another illness. Haydn was now up and dressed, ready to joke about the fact that he had escaped death once again. Dies quoted: 'Die Dichter irrten nicht, die Dich unsterblich machen' (the poets did not err, who thee immortal called). Haydn delicately took this to refer to his physical condition and parried, 'My aching bones remind me only too often that I am still alive' (Dies, 148f.).

Griesinger tells us in his biography (53) that as early as 1807

> Haydn arranged, on good terms,[1] that his books, music, manuscripts and medals were to go after his death to the princely house of Esterházy. There are only very few unprinted (and complete) works among the manuscripts, except for some church pieces. The most interesting are forty-six canons, mostly on German texts, which hung in glass frames in Haydn's bedroom. 'I wasn't rich enough,' he said, 'to buy beautiful paintings, so I made myself a wallpaper that not everyone can have.'

---

1   There is something odd about this statement from an unimpeachable source like Griesinger. No such document, agreeing to purchase the music and medals from Haydn, exists during 1807, and indeed Esterházy had to purchase all the music and medals – except the medals left to him in Haydn's will – from the estate. Franz Ferdinand Klemp, in the name of Mathias Fröhlich [*sic*], agrees, in a document dated Vienna, 29 March 1810, to sell to Prince Nicolaus II Esterházy, for the sum of 4,500 gulden, the musical works in the catalogue of Haydn's legacy (*infra*), Nos. 81–608; these items were not auctioned. On 3 May, a similar document is extant concerning the medals which Esterházy wanted to purchase from the Haydn estate and one of which, the 1802 gold medal from St Petersburg, the Prince had to purchase from a goldsmith, one Hauptmann, for 800 gulden. It was Hummel himself (bill to Esterházy of 15 May 1810) who 'on the orders of His Highness concerning the Haydn legacy went twice to Gumpendorf and twice back and then with an extra carriage to bring the music into town, and also for string . . . 20 Fl.' Hummel also went to the auction to purchase some Haydn medals, and reported to Esterházy on 13 April 1810 that he had actually bought the gold medal of the Société d'Appollon (*infra*) for 155 fl., the silver one from the Institut National for 70 fl. 30 xr., and another silver one, from the Conservatoire, for 27 fl. 59 xr. Valkó II, 637f. It was possibly at this time that Hummel helped himself to the music which he is known to have taken from the Haydn legacy. Unless some verbal agreement was made between Haydn and the Prince regarding this material, it is difficult to see what Griesinger meant. Perhaps Esterházy simply promised Haydn he would buy the music and the medals from his heirs after his death.

Posterity can be very grateful both to Haydn and Prince Nicolaus II for this arrangement: if this vast amount of music had come under the hammer after Haydn's death, it is certain that a large part of it would have disappeared into private possession, perhaps including the (not so small) collection of unpublished Haydn operas such as *Lo speziale*, *L'infedeltà delusa*, and so on. The precise list of what was left among these musical manuscripts and engravings, etc., after Haydn's death will be printed *in extenso* at the end of the Chronicle for 1809.

On 13 April 1807, the Empress Marie Therese died following a dangerous confinement, and her new-born infant lived for only a few days. In her, the Emperor Franz lost a good-hearted, warm wife and mother, and Haydn lost a patron of taste and sympathy.

On 3/17 April Neukomm wrote from Russia; Dies (151) was present some time after Haydn received this letter and witnessed the 'extraordinary pleasure' it gave the composer. 'Haydn asked me to publish the letter in my account. I promised, and hope that since Herr Neukomm is one of my most honoured friends that I will receive his pardon for doing so':

[To Haydn from Sigismund Neukomm, St Petersburg. *German*]

St Petersburg, $\frac{3}{17}$ April 1807.

My dear Papa!

Yesterday I gave a concert here, the *affiche* of which I include. Your excellent choruses from *Tobia* were received with the great enthusiasm which I have always noticed, with deep satisfaction, is accorded to your unrivaled masterpieces whenever they are performed here. As No. 2 I chose the chorus, 'Ah gran Dio! sol tu sei &c.', as No. 4 'Odi le nostri voci &c.' and as No. 6, 'Svanisce in un momento' where, even at the end of the first part, they began to applaud with the utmost vigour. I conducted, and the excellent Court Chorus, combined with a selected band of large size, played with such affection that you certainly would have been completely satisfied with the performance, should we have had the good fortune to have had you with us.

I spared no costs to have my concert well cast, and thus I had expenses of more than 1,100 roubles, but despite that, I made over 1,200 roubles clear profit after deducting all expenses; and what increased my joy no end was that everyone went away from the hall satisfied.

I am writing you all this because I cannot show you my gratitude in any other way than to assure you that every stroke of good luck which will ever happen to me is only YOUR doing. – You are my father and the creator of my luck.

How I envy Vienna for having the good fortune to have you within its walls! How often, dear Papa, I long to see you, even for an hour! Shouldn't this bliss soon be mine?

Let me know from time to time how you are, and no one will be happier than

Your grateful pupil,
Neukomm.
[CCLN, 243]

[Haydn to Neukomm, St Petersburg. *German*]

[? June] 1807.

[*Contents:*] Haydn congratulates Neukomm and encourages him in his work on the oratorio, *Tobia* [Neukomm was reorchestrating it, to bring it in line with 'modern times']. He relies on his pupil.

[Charavay's Catalogue of the Kafka Collection, Paris 1881 No. 32.]
[CCLN, 243]

Being a true son of the Church, Haydn thought that perhaps the spirit might help to cure the flesh, and on 27 April, the Feast of Peregrino Laziosi, he had himself carried to the Servite Monastery – the same institution in which the *Missa brevis* in F had been discovered (in 1805) – where, in the chapel dedicated to that Saint, he hoped to find relief for his swollen legs. The same procedure was repeated in 1808.[1]

Haydn's doctors had removed the 'little piano' from his sitting-room in the summer of 1806, on the grounds that it would prove a temptation to improvise.

Haydn himself realized how necessary it was for the preservation of his health to follow this advice, because when, from time to time, he sat down at his English pianoforte [Longman & Broderip] to improvise, he was overcome with dizziness after a few minutes. 'I would never have believed,' he said on 3 September 1807, 'that a man could fall to pieces as thoroughly as I feel has happened to me. My memory is gone. Sometimes I still have good ideas at the pianoforte, but I would like to weep at my inability even to repeat them and to write them down.'
[Griesinger, 48]

Griesinger goes on to tell us that Haydn did not go from one room to the other for months on end; he spent his time praying, remembering the past (and especially his stay in England), reading the newspapers and looking through his household accounts.

In the long winter evenings he discussed the daily news with the neighbours and his servants, and occasionally he played cards with them and was amused at the pleasure they took in winning a few pennies [*Kreuzer*] from him. (ibid., 48.)

On 9 September Griesinger wrote to Leipzig about a new project:

. . . Haydn has had his beloved pupil Neukomm in St Petersburg arrange his [Haydn's] first Oratorio, *Il ritorno di Tobia*, in full score according to today's taste; it is intended for the annual concert of the widows and orphans of musicians [Tonkünstler-Societät]. Haydn is not entirely satisfied with Neukomm's work, because he omitted several good passages, and he doesn't want it published in this arrangement as a complete score. But he thinks that the arrangement might be a success if published as a piano score. [Olleson, *Griesinger*, 52]

As early as 4 June of this year, Haydn's thoughts were on his first Oratorio and he said to Dies (154) that Neukomm would probably have to adapt the choruses – probably Haydn meant, or said, the arias –, which were far too long, to the present taste and shorten them, saying:

When I wrote the Oratorio, long notes were still worth something, but now everything swarms with hemidemisemiquavers. It's just like money: formerly only heavy gold and silver were in circulation; now you see only copper pennies [*Kreuzer*] and farthings [*Pfennige*].

In the middle of September, the new Mass in C (Op. 86) which Prince Nicolaus II Esterházy had commissioned from Beethoven, was first performed under the composer's direction in Eisenstadt. Beethoven intended to give, moreover, another concert at Eisenstadt, but there was trouble with the Mass. The rehearsals went badly, and on 12 September a furious Esterházy inquired of Johann Fuchs why 'only one of the five contraltos was present'. The performance itself was a resounding failure. The

1 Griesinger, 54. The date, 27 April, for the feast of St Peregrine Laziosi, from *Diario ossia Giornale per l'anno 1801*, Padua, 'Si vende sul Ponte di S. Lorenzo', p. 97. Other sources have 1 May. St Peregrine (1260–1345) was a Servite monk who suffered from a foot cancer and yet is said not to have seated himself for thirty years.

Prince wrote shortly afterwards to Countess Henriette von Zielinska, 'Beethoven's Mass is unbearably ridiculous and detestable, and I am not convinced that it can ever be performed properly. I am angry and mortified. *Gulistan* [an opera by Dalayrac] was well played. This is our news.' It must have seemed to the half-deaf and suspicious Beethoven that Haydn's weak and sick presence had somehow contrived to poison the new Mass in C. It is in fact typical of the ill-luck that bedevilled their relationship.[1]

In November Haydn received a visit from a German composer, Gottlob Benedict Bierey, who had subscribed to *The Creation*. Bierey was a successful opera composer who had been called to Vienna to conduct his new stage work, the historical opera in three acts, *Wladimir, Fürst von Nowgorod* (libretto by Stegmayer).[2] Bierey wrote to Härtel as follows:

> On 2nd November, today, I had the happiest day of my life. Secretary Griesinger came to me, fetched me, and took me to Father Haydn. I cannot possibly describe to you my emotions upon seeing this remarkable man. Despite his age (in April[3] he will be 77 years old) and his bodily weakness, there is still fire in his eyes, coupled with a charming joviality that must delight everyone. He told me, among other things, how he missed meeting Naumann in Dresden. I gave your message to him; he would like to meet you personally, and asked me if at least your engraved portrait existed. He sends his best regards to you. Haydn will have seen how moved I was when I took my leave; I could hardly speak. He gave me his hand, squeezed it, looked me in the eye and said, 'Give me a kiss' (*Geben Sie mir ein Bussel*). I would not exchange this remarkable moment for great treasures and I thank you from my heart that you helped me to achieve it, through H. Griesinger.
>
> [Pohl III, 254]

The annual Christmas concerts of the Tonkünstler-Societät, which Haydn of course no longer attended, took place on 22 and 23 December and consisted of *The Creation* (soloists: Antonie Laucher, Joseph Gottdank, Carl Weinmüller).

A few days later the French once more honoured Haydn in a particularly warm-hearted letter from an amateur society:

[To Haydn from the Société académique des enfans d'Appollon, Paris. *French*]

Paris, 30th December 1807.

Monsieur!

The French honour the immortal productions of your genius, because there are several things which you have composed for them. A grand concert in Paris does not seem to be complete unless one hears one or two of your symphonies. Moreover, one may say, in all truth, that artists consider it a sacred duty to pay the utmost attention to their [the symphonies'] performance, fully assured of the taste and sensibility of the listeners, who always share their just enthusiasm.

Our Society has, among its members, your most zealous admirers. It enjoys a certain esteem. But it believes that this esteem would be better deserved, and the cult of Apollo more appropriately served, if it could be enriched by your companionship, and if it could inscribe your name in the list of its members.

Condescend, *Monsieur*, to accept this tribute! It would fain have the glory and the good fortune of your assent.

Please also accept with indulgence the attached copy of our statutes and by-laws, followed by a description of the Society, and likewise a gold medal, struck

---

1 Landon, *Beethoven*, 218f.

2 Bierey was, according to this source, then *Kapellmeister* of the Breslau Opera. *Pressburger Zeitung* No. 96, 8 December 1807; *Haydn Yearbook* VIII, 225.

3 Haydn's official birthday was on 31 March but he himself thought he had been born on 1 April.

in the fashion of a voucher for attendance, which every member receives as a token of his right to attend each one of the sessions.

We have the honour to be, *Monsieur*, with every esteem, &c.

[For Haydn's answer, see 7 April, 1808]
[CCLN, 243f.]

That same day, the organist and composer Johann Baptist Gänsbacher, in the service of Count Firmian, went to visit Haydn.

. . . Before I went with the house of Firmian to Prague in 1804, I often visited the widow Mozart; there I met the old Bar. van Swieten, who much occupied himself with her son, Wolfgang. He played the piano excellently even then, and among other things he could transpose Bach fugues at sight in another key; Neukom [*sic*] was then his teacher. I was often asked for my opinion about his piano pieces, which I frankly told him. On the eve of the year 1808 I paid a visit with Mozart's widow and another artist to Jos. Haydn in his lodgings in Gumpendorf. We found him very neatly dressed with a freshly dressed wig, sitting at a table on which his three-cornered hat and walking-stick lay, as if he were just about to go out. In the entire room there were little pictures in black frames. When Haydn saw that we had noticed them and wanted to look at them more closely, he assured us that they were not engravings; on the contrary, they were all handwritten canons and other songs of his compositions. He regretted painfully that he was too weak to compose even though he was not lacking in ideas. He spoke of Mozart with the greatest respect. He was especially pleased with the news that our companion brought, that all his quartets had just appeared in a Parisian edition in which you did not need to turn the page. I had already made Haydn's acquaintance some years before through my friend Neukom[m], his pupil; the latter took me to the first rehearsal of Haydn's vocal quartets and terzets [*Mehrstimmige Gesänge*], not yet published, in which I had to sing second tenor in the terzets and learned many a useful thing from Haydn's lips. During the quartets Saal's daughter [Therese] sang the soprano, Simioni the tenor and [father Ignaz] Saal the bass, I can't remember the name of the alto.

It was during this visit that Haydn broke into tears when Mozart's name was mentioned and said, 'Excuse me, I must always weep when the name Mozart falls.' Word of this quotation reached the Viennese newspapers and in the *Zeitung für Theater, Musik und Poesie* (No. 28, Wednesday 13 April 1808) we read the following curious comment:

How does Haydn hear and speak the name of Mozart?

Curious question! Like anyone else who has physiologically normal organs of hearing and speech (sad answer!). Or does he get up from his chair, take off his hat and make a bow? – God forbid! Here you may read and feel powerfully these words of an immortal man,[1] accompanied by an *outburst* of tears: '*Excuse me – I must – always weep – at the name of my Mozart*'.

Review of this section . . .: The reviewer thinks Haydn weeps like every old man, and wishes Herr —— would take a physiologically, psychologically *normal* attitude towards Mozart. . . .[2]

On 31 December the sculptor Anton Grassi died; Haydn had loved him and 'took his death hard' (Griesinger 52). His world now consisted mainly of memories.

1 [Original footnote:] Spoken to some musical friends on 30 December, at which time they went to congratulate him on the New Year; and the conversation turned to Mozart.
2 The 'review' is much longer and, to sum up its message briefly, objects to the growing Mozart cult. August Schmidt, *Denksteine*, Vienna 1848, pp. 124f; Deutsch, *Mozart, Dokumente*, 473; Pohl III, 255f.

CHAPTER ELEVEN

Chronicle 1808

ON THE FEAST OF ST JOSEPH, Haydn's name-day, Antonio Polzelli congratulated his *Kapellmeister* on behalf of the orchestra; it is not quite clear, from Haydn's answer, whether Polzelli and a few members of the band came to visit Haydn, or whether they wrote.

[To Antonio Polzelli on behalf of the Esterházy band, Eisenstadt. *German, 'Du' form*. Only the signature autograph]

Vienna, 20th March 1808

My dear Son!
    Your truly heart-warming remarks and those of all the members of the Princely Esterházy band, on the occasion of my name-day, moved me to tears. I thank you and all the others from the bottom of my heart, and ask you to tell all the members in my name that I regard them all as my dear children, and beg them to have patience and forbearance with their old, weak father; tell them that I am attached to them with a truly fatherly love, and that there is nothing I wish more than to have just sufficient strength so that I could enjoy once more the harmony of being at the side of these worthy men, who made the fulfilment of my duties so pleasant. Tell them that my heart will never forget them, and that it is the greatest honour for me, through the grace of my ILLUSTRIOUS PRINCE, to be placed at the head, not only of great artists, but of NOBLE AND THANKFUL HUMAN BEINGS.

Joseph Haydn [m.p.] ria.
[CCLN, 244]

Musical Vienna decided to honour Haydn's seventy-sixth birthday with a gala performance of *The Creation*. The Liebhaber-Konzerte (Amateur Concerts), under the sponsorship of Prince von Trauttmannsdorf, put on the Oratorio in their regular hall, the Aula of the University – the hall still exists – with Antonio Salieri as conductor, Conradin Kreutzer at the piano (he would later become a well known operatic composer) and the soloists Therese Fischer, Carl Weinmüller and Julius Radicchi. The Oratorio was sung in Carpani's Italian translation, and the date was set for 27 March 1808. Griesinger relates:

I was surprised that he could make up his mind, considering his failing health, to attend the . . . [concert] . . . on 27 March. . . . He [Haydn] answered: 'Consideration for my health could not stop me. It's not the first time that I have been honoured, and I wanted to show that I'm still capable of receiving it.'

Dies tells us that Prince Esterházy 'was at court that day' but sent a carriage to Gumpendorf in which 'Haydn drove slowly' to the city. The crowd at the University Hall was so large that police were required to keep order. On his arrival Haydn was greeted *inter alia* by Prince Lobkowitz, Princess Esterházy, his two pupils Baroness von Spielmann and Magdalena von Kurzbeck (Kurzböck), the poet Heinrich von Collin and Beethoven. After years of misunderstandings and suspicions, Beethoven made his peace with Haydn, and publicly at that; it was a gracious thing to do. Altogether from this moment, students of Beethoven will observe a profound change in his attitude towards Haydn. Together with Mozart, Beethoven clearly now regarded his illustrious predecessors as the founders of the great school of which he was the giant conclusion. This is the place to complete our short and of necessity modest psychological study of the complicated relationship, which we will do by citing just two of the many documents at our disposal. In 1825 a Viennese copyist named Ferdinand Wolanek, with whom Beethoven had a series of troubles, wrote him a letter in which we read:

> I remain gratefully obliged for the honour rendered by your employment of me; as for [your] discordant behaviour towards me, I can only regard it smilingly as a good-natured outburst to be accepted. In the ideal world of tones there are so many dissonances, shouldn't they exist also in the real world? My one comfort is the first conviction that had Mozart and Haydn, those celebrated artists, been hired as your copyists they would have shared a fate similar to mine.

To this, alas, typically arrogant manifestation of lower-class Viennese ignorance, Beethoven responded by crossing out the letter and himself scrawling in letters two inches high the words 'Dummer, Eingebildeter, Eselhafter Kerl' ('Stupid, conceited, asinine Idiot').

> Dirty Scribbler! Stupid dolt! Correct the blunders which you have made in your ignorance, insolence, conceit and stupidity; this would be more to the purpose than to teach me, which is as if a *Sow* were to try to give lessons to Minerva. Beethoven.
> *I pray you to do* Mozart and Haydn *the honour* of not mentioning *their names*.

But perhaps the most revealing of all the Haydn stories in Beethoven's later life is the extraordinary one told to us in the book *Aus dem Schwarzspanierhause* by Gerhard von Breuning, son of Beethoven's friend Stephan von Breuning. Diabelli gave the composer a lithograph of Haydn's birthplace, and Breuning decided to have it framed. Gerhard's piano teacher, Heller, wrote underneath the engraving: 'Jos. Hayden's Geburtshaus in Rohrau'.

> Pleased as Beethoven at first was over the picture, which by the way was so prettily executed, suddenly he was just as angry. His face grew red with rage, and he loudly asked me: 'Who wrote that?' – 'My piano teacher'. – 'What is the name of that idiot? Such an ignoramus wants to be a piano teacher and doesn't even know how to write correctly the name of a master like Haydn. He should correct it at once; that's a scandal,' &c., &c. [The mistake was corrected and the picture was again brought to Beethoven] who kept on growling about the mistake and would not accept the excuses I several times offered on behalf of my piano teacher and answered: 'He may be sufficient as a teacher, but he is just the same a superficial person, who like most of them has learned nothing more than that which is absolutely necessary.' [Earlier he had said about the picture:] 'Look, I got this today. See this little house, and in it so great a man was born!'

All his life Beethoven had himself wilfully misspelt Haydn's name as 'Haidn' – 'Haidn 8 groschen', '22 x[Kreuzer], chocolate for Haidn and me', 'Coffee, 6 x for Haidn and me' (October 1792) – or even 'Heiden'[1] (November 1793). Beethoven's castigation of young Breuning's piano teacher on this very point is, of course, the final step in a series of private and public apologies which began magnificently with the public gesture in the University Hall on 27 March 1808.

To return to that stimulating event, having been greeted, Haydn was seated in an armchair and borne into the hall, to the tumultuous applause of the assembled public, who cried 'Vivat!' and 'Long live Haydn!' to the accompaniment of fanfares from the trumpets and timpani. He was placed next to Princess Esterházy, and on the other side was Fräulein von Kurzbeck. The nobility crowded round him. People were afraid he might catch cold, and he was obliged to keep his hat on his head.

The French Ambassador, Count Andreossy, noticed that Haydn was wearing on a ribbon in his buttonhole the gold medal which the Concert des Amateurs had presented to him. Andreossy said, 'You ought to have not only this medal but all the medals awarded in the whole of France.'

Haydn thought he felt a draught, and Ritter Cappellini, a leading physician ('medico di prima sfera,' says Carpani) also considered that Haydn's legs were not sufficiently covered. Princess Esterházy at once put her shawl on him, and her example was followed by many aristocratic ladies, 'their *schals*,' says Carpani (adding a new English word on the subject) 'departing from those delicate bosoms to find a place round the feet of the beloved old man.' The occasion was celebrated by Collin in German and Carpani in Italian verse, presented to Haydn by Baroness von Spielmann and Fräulein von Kurzbeck.

An Joseph Haydn bey Aufführung der Schöpfung
im Universitäts-Saale zu Wien, den 27ten März 1808

Du hast die Welt in deiner Brust getragen
der Hölle düstre Pforten stark bezwingen,
den freyen Flug in Himmelsräume wagen
hört man dich auf der Töne kräftgen Schwingen.
Drum sollst du, theurer Greis, nicht trauernd klagen,
daß mit dem Alter deine Kräfte ringen:
zwar weicht der Leib den düstern Zeitgewalten;
was du gewirkt, wird ewig nie veralten.

---

1 Also 'Haiden' in a letter to Prince Nicolaus II Esterházy of 26 July 1807. One of the most revealing pieces of evidence about Beethoven's attitude towards Haydn after the latter's death appears in the Conversation Books of 1814–5. Here there are not only conversations with visitors but also diary-like jottings. We read:

[Beethoven's hand:] A little court – a little orchestra, its song written there by me, performed to the honour of the Almighty, the Eternal, the Unending. So may the last days flow by. . . . The portraits of Handel, Bach, Gluck, Mozart, Haiden in my room – they might help me to lay claim to submission. [R. H. Schauffler, *Beethoven*, New York 1927, p. 349]

Here is a genuine, private confession of Beethoven's evaluation of Haydn – *viz.*, one of the five musicians he most respected and admired. But even at this late date, flashes of the old jealousy and depreciation appear. At the beginning of February 1824, Schindler was certainly repeating an old Party-line thought when he wrote, in one of the Conversation Books, 'Haydn didn't even have to have lived, and you & Mozart would still have become what you are' (*Haydn hätte nicht leben dürfen, so wären Mozart u. Sie eben das geworden, was Sie sind*) – a statement that must automatically be placed in the category of famous last words. Karl-Heinz Köhler, 'Die Konversationshefte Ludwig van Beethovens als retrospektive Quelle der Mozartforschung', in *Mozart-Jahrbuch* 1971/72, p. 135.

Wie nun in dieses Musentempels Hallen
erwartungsvoll sich frohe Schaaren drängen;
so sieht man einst die späten Enkel wallen
zu deiner Schöpfung hohen Himmelsklängen;
so hört man noch der Enkel Jubel hallen
bey deiner Engel Hallelujahsängen.
Was rein der Mensch aus reiner Brust gesungen,
ist wohl nie leicht in Menschenbrust verklungen.

O lausche lang' entzückt den eignen Tönen,
in deiner Freude dicht gedrängtem Kreise,
so wirst du sanft der Erde dich entwöhnen,
so froh dich rüsten zu der großen Reise.
Die Erde mit dem Himmel zu versöhnen
war deiner Kunst erhabne Lebensweise.
Noch schallt dir Dank tief von der Erde Klüften,
empfängt dich Hallelujah in den Lüften.

H. v. Collin.

Sonetto.
Di Giuseppe de Carpani.

A un muover sol di sue possenti ciglia
    Trar dal nulla i viventi e l'Universo,
    E spinger soli per cammin diverso,
    E imensa attorno a lor d'astri famiglia;
Tal natura formar che di sè figlia,★
    Si rinnovi ogni istante, e il dente avverso
    Le avventi invan lo struggitor perverso,
    Se Dio lo volle, e il fé', qual meraviglia?

Ma ch'uom l'opra di Dio stupenda e rara
    Pareggiar★★ tenti con pittrici note
    E la renda al pensier presente, e chiara,

Non possibil cimento a ognun parea.
    Haydn, tu il festi! In te, chi tutto puote,
    Tanto verso di sua divina idea!★★★

Haydn burst into tears when he was presented with these poems and had to take a glass of wine before he could go on. Salieri came down from the orchestra, through the crowds of standing, cheering people, and went to Haydn. 'The two celebrated composers embraced tenderly,' says Carpani, who adds, 'I had my seat just behind *Haydn*'s. *Salieri* wrung *Haydn*'s hand and flew to the orchestra. A general enthusiasm possessed the players, the singers, the audience.' At the words, 'And there was light', thunderous applause interrupted the performance and Haydn, 'the tears streaming down his pallid cheeks and as if overcome by the most violent emotions, raised his

★ Or: 'E natura sì ordir, che, di sè figlia',
★★ Or: 'Eguagliar'
★★★ [Original footnote in Carpani, 246:] NB. This sonnet was set to music by *Salieri* in the praiseworthy intention of having it played the following year, should, as one hoped, this academic solemnity be repeated. [Salieri's copy of the sonnet is in the Vienna City Library (I.N. 1317).]

trembling arms to Heaven, as if in prayer to the Father of Harmony . . .' (*AMZ*). It was feared that the whole event might be too much for him, and Haydn himself thought it would be better to leave after the first part, 'also so as not to depart from his accustomed régime' (Carpani). 'Asked how he found his *Creation*' – probably Carpani meant the performance – 'he answered, smilingly: "It's been four years since I heard it last and it's not bad".'

> Two robust athletes [continues Carpani] picked up the armchair in which he was seated, and amidst the greetings, the applause and the acclamations of the whole room, the harmonious man of triumph approached the stairs; but having arrived at the doors, he made a sign to stop. The porters obeyed and turned him round to the public; he thanked them with the usual gestures of acceptance, then, looking at the orchestra with the most intense expression, he raised his eyes and his hands to heaven, and with tears in his eyes he blessed his children.

The company, intensely moved, realized that they were seeing Haydn for the last time in public. Prince Esterházy, as soon as he could, sent a messenger to ascertain whether it were not too late for him to come; but it was too late; Haydn had already left.

The fine miniaturist, Balthasar Wigand, whose vignettes of Vienna have always been the delight of connoisseurs, was commissioned by Princess Esterházy to record the scene of Haydn, sitting in the middle of the room, surrounded by his friends, admirers, patrons and former pupils. Wigand did this beautifully in a miniature painting on the cover of a box intended for Haydn; when the box was sold in the auction of Haydn's effects, Princess Esterházy repurchased it for 400 fl. and later gave it to Franz Liszt. It finally found its way to the Museum der Stadt Wien from which it was stolen in 1945. Fortunately the city of Vienna had organized a fine colour reproduction of this box-top in the year 1909, which in some way recompenses us for the loss of the original. The Wigand picture is reproduced here in colour plate IV.

The poet Collin, with whom Beethoven was on friendly terms, also recorded his impressions of the scene:

Haydn's Jubelfeyer
Aus: Gedichte von J. H. v. Collin. Wien 1812 gedruckt
und im Verlage bei Anton Strauss.

Es war ein Tag, an dem Wiens Musenhalle,
Du herrliche, der froh ich Bildung danke,
Ertönte von der Schöpfung Feyerschalle,
Und ob ich gleich, ein Mann, nicht leichtlich wanke,
Befiel mich plötzlich doch ein starkes Bangen,
Denn mich durchfuhr mit Schauer der Gedanke:
'Wird Alter mich entnervend auch umfangen?'
Als sie den Meister hin zum Sitze trugen,
Den auf die Kraft zum Ziel einst hieß gelangen.
Doch, ob die Jahr' ihn grausam niederschlugen,
Noch sah man Geist ihm aus den Augen blitzen;
So kam's, daß leichter wir den Anblick trugen.
Emporgerichtet, auf der Füsse Spitzen
Stand jeder, in die Hände freudig schlagend,
Bis man den Alten sah im Kreise sitzen.
Doch er, des Jubels Brausen nicht ertragend,
Der Pauken Wirbel, der Trompeten Dröhnen,

Verhüllte sich die Augen, gleichsam sagend:
'Nicht kann ich solcher Ehren werth mich wähnen'!
Schnell wird die Menge tieferseufzend stille,
Gewährt ihm Zeit, des Orts sich zu gewöhnen.
O Frauen = Zartheit, holde Mitleids = Fülle!
Sie sah man nun des Greises Bein umwinden
Mit ihres Nackens ätherleichter Hülle,
Und Mäntel, köstliche, zum Schemel ründen,
Der weich und warm des Greises Füße bette,
Und Stärkungsdüfte für den Schwachen finden.
Wie drängte sich so jung, als alt, zur Wette,
So Fürst als Künstler an des Meisters Seite,
Als ob er Heil von seinem Blicke hätte.
Auch Salieri kam mit im Geleite;
Wohl ist der Greis ihm lange her gewogen,
Weil er sich seiner gar so herzlich freute.
Mich hat mein spähend Auge nicht betrogen,
Kein Ende nahm der Greis ihn liebzukosen,
Und als er nun leiten ging des Tonmeers Wogen.
Schon hörte man der Kräfte dumpfes Tosen,
Wie Elemente feindlich sich verwirren,
Nach Formen ringend in dem Formenlosen.
Doch leise lispelt aus des Chaos Irren
Ein sanfter Geist empor, wie Hauch der Liebe,
Die wild verschlungnen freundlich zu entwirren.
Und mählich schweigen die empörten Triebe
Und nur noch hört man auf den Wassern schweben
Wie Frühlingsluft, dahin, den Hauch der Liebe.
'Licht werd' es', scholl's! Licht werd's! dem Rufe beben
Die dunklen Schatten, reißen, schwinden, fliehen! –
Ein Jubelruf: 'Hoch soll der Meister leben!'
Da weint der Greis, und seine Wangen glühen;
Begeistert streckt zum Himmel er die Hände:
'Nicht ist es Frucht von menschlichem Bemühen,
'Gott gab mir's ein, daß ich es recht vollende!'
Das sagt der Blick, die Hand, des Kopfes sinken.
Doch Frauenengel eilten stets behende,
– Ihm saß zur Rechten einer, zwey zur Linken –
Ihn aufzuheitern, freundlich, mit Gespräche,
Sobald ihm Thränen in den Augen blinken,
Daß nicht das Herz ihm noch vor Wonne breche,
Daß nicht der Wehmuth Gluten in verzehren,
Daß Tod sich nicht am Neuverjüngten räche. –
Nun hörten wir die Welt sich neu gebähren,
Wild braust der Sturm, der Blitz entfährt den Lüften,
Und Donner soll uns Gottes Allmacht lehren.
Auf ihren Wink versinkt in tiefen Grüften
Der Ozean, muß so dem Lande weichen,
Und Ströme rauschen her aus Bergesklüften.
Gott läßt den Bach durch Thale rieselnd schleichen,
Beblümtes Grün sich über Matten breiten,
Der Cedern Pracht bis an die Wolken reichen.
Jetzt steigt herauf in unermeßnen Weiten

Die Sonn' im hellen Glanze goldner Strahlen,
Den Lauf der Jahre froh und stolz zu leiten.
Leis athmend schaut Gewölke magisch mahlen
Die stille Nacht den Mond mit Silberscheine; –
Und Sterne funkeln – Ha! wer zählt die Zahlen?
Der Engelchöre leuchtende Gemeine
Grüßt jeden Schöpfungstag mit Lobgesange: –
Wer ist so hart, daß er vor Lust nicht weine?
Der Greis erliegt so vieler Wonnen Drange.
Drum zart besorgt beschließen klug die Frauen:
Genug hab er gehorcht dem Zauberklange.
O hätt' ich tausend Augen nun zu schauen!
Seht, winkend will der Vater Küsse spenden
Den Künstlern, die er läßt in finstern Auen,
Indeß er bald sich wird zum Lichte wenden,
Doch diese, von des Tongerüstes Höhen,
Sieht weinend man ihm Gegenküsse senden:
Beethoven's Kraft denkt liebend zu vergehen,
So Haupt als Hand küßt glühend er dem Greise: –
Da wogte sich mein Herz vor Lust und Wehen.
So fühlten Tausend auf die gleiche Weise,
Als sie den Meister mit dem Sitze hoben,
Und weg ihn trugen aus der Freunde Kreise.
Laut hörte man des Lebewohles Toben,
Geklatsch' und Mitleidsruf zum Himel dringen.
Er aber wandte seinen Blick nach oben,
Und dachte so sein volles Herz zu zwingen;
Doch aufgeregt will sich der Sturm nicht legen,
Und reißt ihn fort. Umsonst ist all sein Ringen.
Rasch sieht man vorwärts sich den Greis bewegen;
Und als er nun der Pforte nah gekomen: –
Aus streckt er seine Hand zum Vatersegen!
Und alles weint! — — Wohl wird er nie mehr komen.[1]

On 5 April, Dies went to see Haydn and found that:

it was as if an electric current were flowing in Haydn's veins . . . He urged me once
again . . . to convey his warmest thanks to all the musicians who had taken part in
the performance of *The Creation*. In praising Demoiselle Fischer, he said: 'She sang
her part with the greatest delicacy and so accurately that she did not permit herself

---

1 Sources for this episode: Griesinger, 48; Dies, 163ff.; Carpani, 242ff.; *AMZ* X (20 April 1808), 479f.
(written by Griesinger?); *Wiener Zeitung* No. 26, 30 March 1808; *Vaterländische Blätter* No. VI (27 May
1808), pp. 40ff.; *Zeitung für die elegante Welt* (15 April 1808); Pohl III, 256–8, 395ff. (poems). We can find
only Collin's poem of 1812 to confirm that, as Haydn left, 'Beethoven, forgetting incidents of early days,
bent down and fevently kissed his [Haydn's] hand and forehead' (Hadden, *Haydn*, 153), but the story is
clearly true. Also: Thayer-Forbes I, 138, 145; II, 937, 1037. Kerst *Die Erinnerungen an Beethoven* II, 174.
Anderson and Tyson (*Letters* and *Selected Letters of Beethoven*) have always corrected Beethoven's spellings
to 'Haydn'.
  In the account of the concert in *Prometheus* (quoted *in extenso* in Thayer III, 60f.), however, we read:
'The enthusiastic friend of Art, Prince Lobkowitz, like Salieri and like Beethoven, weeping, kissed the
hand of their master.' Musicians present included Salieri, Beethoven, Hummel, Gyrowetz, Giuliani,
Conradin Kreutzer, and Franz Clement.

the least unsuitable addition', by which Haydn means cadenzas, ornaments, *Eingänge*, and so on. 'I survived the day of *The Creation* well,' said he; 'I doubted if I should be able to summon so much strength.' [Dies, 167]

Two days later Haydn answered the letter from the 'Children of Apollo' in Paris who had written to him on 30 December 1807:

[To the Société académique des enfans d'Appollon, Paris. *French*. Only the signature autograph]

Vienna, 7th April 1808.

Messieurs,

The wish of the *Société académique des enfans d'Appollon* to inscribe my name on the list of its members is highly flattering to me, and I am most sensible of this honour. I assure them, through you, that they could not have thus honoured anyone more capable of appreciating their esteem, or of feeling the value of the honour conferred on me. I pray you, *Messieurs*, to allow my emotions to echo yours, and at the same time be the interpreters of my gratitude for the marks of distinction which you sent me – the copy of the statutes and by-laws, accompanied by a gold medal.

You, *Messieurs*, have strewn flowers on the path of life that yet remains for me to traverse. I am profoundly touched, and I feel keenly that though old age indeed numbs the faculties, it does not diminish my sensibility; for it is that which causes me to regret that my advanced age does not permit me to entertain the hope of ever being in your midst, of sharing in your labours, of cooperating in the cultivation of an art which constitutes the charm of society, or of participating in the celebrity which, because of its cherished and precious qualifications, the academy enjoys.

My infirmities force me to do without this comfort, and my regret is as lively as my gratitude is profound; pray receive this assurance, which is accompanied by the expression of my most sincere esteem. I have the honour to be, *Messieurs*, with profound respect,

Your most humble and most obedient servant,
Joseph Haydn [m.p.] ria.
[CCLN, 244f.]

On 10 and 11 April the Tonkünstler-Societät gave *The Seasons* with the usual new group of soloists (see 22–23 December 1807: Laucher, Gottdank, Weinmüller). A few days later, on 16 April, the *Wiener Zeitung* announced a kind of *Gesamtgastspiel* of *The Creation* in the forces used for Haydn's birthday celebration, to be given on Easter Sunday for the benefit of the charitable organizations. 'With Italian text. Dlle. Fischer, Herr Weinmüller, Herr Radicchi. Direktion des Orchesters Herr Wranitzky, jene am Klavier Kapellmeister Umlauf. Leitung des Ganzen Salieri.' It was the last time that Haydn's faithful Paul Wranizky would conduct the Oratorio; on 26 September, aged only fifty-two, he was dead. The link with the future was Michael Umlauf, who would be the principal *Kapellmeister* at the historic concert in May 1824 in which the Beethoven Ninth Symphony and parts of the *Missa solemnis* were first performed.

On 26 April Luigi Cherubini wrote from Paris:

[To Haydn from Luigi Cherubini, Paris. *Italian*]
Dearest and most esteemed Father. Forgive me for bothering you with my letter, but I have a favour to ask of you.

A merchant and music publisher in Paris has asked me to do a new edition of all your divine Quartets. Since the only way he can do this publication is by taking those [Quartets] found in various old editions, which are very incorrect, he has marked for me all the doubtful things which he thinks are incorrect in a little music copy-book, which please find enclosed. Now celebrated, and dear Father Haydn, please have the kindness to cast your eye over these fragments, in order to see if they are correct and conform to the originals, and if they are not, to correct the mistakes where you find it necessary to do so.

I do ask you to forgive me for taking this liberty, and for putting you to this trouble, and I beg you to consider the matter as soon as you can.

Now that I have got over the more disagreeable part of this letter, dear Father, I can add that I am unchanged, and still sick as a result of nervous attacks; and this has prevented me from working, and from trying to emulate you, OH! DEAR MASTER OF US ALL.

Here in Paris we heard with indescribable delight of the honours which were offered to you by the University of Vienna, on the day when they performed your immortal *Creation*. I wept for joy at this news, and so much wanted to be there, in order to offer up my portion of incense, too.

Farewell, dearest Father, my wife embraces you tenderly. I do the same, and am, with respect and admiration,

Your affectionate son,
L. Cherubini.

Paris, 26th April 1808.

[Address:] Au très célébre [*sic*]
     Joseph Haydn.
      Die Kleine Steingasse
       À VIENNE.   [CCLN, 245f.]

On 22 May 1808, the entire Esterházy forces gave a guest appearance in Vienna: sixty-three persons in ten waggons, each with four horses, went from Eisenstadt to Vienna, where they gave a Mass by Hummel and a vesper by Fuchs in the Chapel of the Ursuline Sisters in the Johannesgasse. The performance was repeated on 29 May. The members of the *Kapelle* came in small groups to pay their respects to Father Haydn, Hummel with the choirboys and male choristers in their new uniforms (green coats with black facings, gold lacing and gold buttons; the waistcoats, breeches and stockings white; each wore a hat with a feather). Haydn received them, dressed in black, sitting at a table, with his wig on his head and beautiful cuffs on his sleeves; on the table lay his gloves and a walking-stick with a gold top. 'Well, dear Hummel,' said Haydn, 'I've already heard that you've written such a beautiful Mass and was pleased about it. I often said to you that you would be somebody. Continue like this and consider that everything beautiful and good comes from above.' (Pohl III, 259)

In the Summer of 1808, Joseph Preindl, Cathedral Chapel Master of St Stephen's and an old colleague of Haydn's, brought a young musician, Johann Wenzel Tomaschek, to see Father Haydn. Tomaschek, later a composer of some local renown, wrote down his recollections in 1846:

Haydn was sitting in an easy-chair [*Sorgenstuhl*], very neat. A powdered wig with side-curls; a white collar-piece with golden buckle; a white, richly embroidered waistcoat of heavy silk; between which a massive jabot jutted forth; a dress jacket of coffee-brown material and with embroidered cuffs; black silk breeches; white silk stockings; shoes with large silver buckles curved across the instep; and on the table at his side a hat and a pair of white leather gloves. . . . Haydn complained in a tearful tone about his disappearing memory, on account of which he has had to give up composing entirely; he can't keep an idea in his head long enough to write it down. Preindl told me that he [Haydn] and Salieri have been proposed for the [newly created] Leopold's Order, about which he [Haydn] was quite delighted. Alas, the idea was never realized. Haydn asked to come with him to the next room, to look at all the presents for *The Creation*, from all the music societies and crowned heads, mostly in the form of gold medals. A bust in plaster of Paris, which impressed me, was at the beginning of the room and I asked Haydn, whom it represented. The poor thing broke into tears and whimpered rather then spoke: 'My best friend, the sculptor [Johann Martin] Fischer [Grassi?]. O! Why don't You call me to Yourself.'   [Pohl III, 260]

Haydn told Griesinger about the proposed Order of Leopold. 'Then there would be a Chevalier Haydn just as there had been a Chevalier Gluck! Only it's a pity that I have no children to whom it might prove useful' – the order conferring perpetual nobility (Griesinger, 57). Haydn had prepared a little speech for the Emperor, who would confer the medal, in which he would have said that of all the songs he had written, he preferred 'Gott erhalte' the most.

Although the following correspondence is of different dates, much of it arrived late (because of the great distance from Russia to Vienna) and we have preferred to keep it all together:

[To Haydn from Philharmonic Society of St Petersburg. *German*]
Well born Sir,
Most esteemed *Herr Kapellmeister*,
        The directors of the Philharmonic Society here hasten to fulfil a commission which they consider one of the most pleasant and most honourable of their lives. They are to deliver to the immortal composer of the most sublime music a token of the boundless admiration which inspires them, and every lover of music, upon the mention of the name Haydn; but this token is also one of gratitude, seldom better deserved and never proffered with more sincerity and emotion.
        The Philharmonic Society owes its existence to the philanthropic zeal of a few admirers of music; they were fortunate enough to see even their most audacious hopes fulfilled more quickly and more beautifully than they could have dared hope. Thus an association came into being which has already been able to ensure an old age free of care to a by no means inconsiderable number of widows; and which, magnanimously supported by a philanthropically minded Imperial House and by a generous public, entertains the most optimistic hopes for the future.
        And this wonderful success we owe to a masterpiece which is everywhere extolled; we owe it to – YOUR *Creation*! Please therefore, most honoured man, accept the enclosed medal of this Society as a token of our sincere and boundless gratitude. Receive it with the kindness which is characteristic of you, and of all great men, and bestow your good will and sympathy on an organization which you may regard as your own work; its beneficial effects will also call forth blessings on you in the serene evening of your life, devoted – as it was – to the joy of mankind. We sign, Sir, in the most heartfelt admiration,
                                        Your most devoted servants,
Georg Johann Berwald. Epmatz. H. Czervenka. Dan. Gottlob Bachmann. Johann Gottfried Hartman.

St. Petersburg, 29th May 1808.[1]   [CCLN, 246]

---

1 This letter was delivered by the Russian Ambassador in Vienna: see letter of 25 July 1808.

[To Haydn from Sigismund Neukomm, St Petersburg. *German*]

St Petersburg, 4 June 1808.
16

My dear Papa!

This is the last letter which I shall be writing to you from here; I leave the day after tomorrow, and hope to arrive in Vienna in September. I am making a very large detour, and will travel through a large part of Germany in a northerly – westerly – easterly direction. My trip to Germany will be of interest to me only because I shall be so delighted to see you again.

The Philharmonic Society in St Petersburg has struck a medal in your honour, and sent it to you through the Russian Ambassador in Vienna. The directors of the Society wanted me to take it, but I refused, because I won't arrive in Vienna for three months, and because it is more dignified for you if it is presented by the Ambassador. The directors also asked me to tell you that the year 1802[1] is the year in which the Society was founded, and since your masterpiece, *The Creation*, which is admired by all, was the corner-stone of their building, the Society thought that this particular year, of such importance to them, could be thus best preserved for posterity. The medal weighs $42\frac{1}{2}$ ducats.

Your diploma as honorary member of the Society has not yet been prepared.[2] Soon I shall be fortunate enough to see you again. Meanwhile farewell, my dear Papa, preserve your affection for me, which is the only thing which renders my lot an enviable one, and makes me one of the happiest inhabitants on this earth.

Always, Your thankful son,

Neukomm.

[CCLN, 247]

[To Haydn from Prince Kurakin, Russian Ambassador at Vienna. *German*]

Vienna, 25th July 1808.

The Philharmonic Society of St Petersburg wishes to deliver the enclosed medal to the immortal Haydn, Doctor of Music, and Father of Harmony. It was with the greatest pleasure that I undertook to fulfil this task, which provided me with a happy opportunity to indicate my profound admiration and my boundless respect for the composer of *The Creation*, *The Seasons*, and so many other great works.

A. *Fürst* Kurakin.

[CCLN, 247]

[To the Philharmonic Society, St Petersburg. *German*. Only the signature autograph]

Well born Gentlemen!

Most esteemed Directors of the Philharmonic Society!

It will be difficult for me to find words to express the profound gratitude which your esteemed letter of 29th May, and the medal sent with it, caused me to feel. Be assured that I am proud to know that my works have been received with approbation also by the inhabitants of your great and famous Imperial City, and that I attach appropriate value to the testimonial with which your Society has honoured me: a Society of connoisseurs and amateurs of the art to which I have devoted my life. You have thus rejuvenated my waning powers; and the realization that I have assisted – even if remotely – in your efforts to comfort the unhappy and to dry the tears of the widows and orphans, has provided me with many a happy hour in my old age.

---

1 Engraved on the medal (it is reproduced in Griesinger, Appendix).
2 Neukomm was not aware of the letter which the Society had already written.

May an institution formed for such a worthy purpose continue in ever increasing prosperity! May it succeed in developing talent, in furthering the cultivation of musical art, and in encouraging men of good will to further acts of charity!

With these sincere wishes, which I would ask you to communicate to all the members of the Philharmonic Society, I remain, worthy Gentlemen and Patrons,

Your grateful admirer,

Jos. Haydn.

Vienna, 28th July 1808.   [CCLN, 247f.]

One of the best descriptions of the old Haydn comes from the pen of an actor and theatrical writer, August Wilhelm Iffland. When Prince Esterházy, together with other Austro-Hungarian aristocrats, was called to manage the Viennese theatres, he took with him, in an advisory capacity, his theatrical director, Heinrich Schmidt, whose activities at Eisenstadt have been noticed above. Schmidt was sent to Berlin and Weimar to engage actors and actresses for the Vienna theatres, and among them he persuaded Iffland to visit the Imperial City. Iffland arrived on 13 August 1808 and on 8 September he was taken by Schmidt to see Father Haydn. Two versions of Iffland's account have survived; they differ from each other only in small details and are compared in a scholarly article by Max Unger.[1]

[*Almanach für Theater und Theaterfreunde 1811* edited by August Wilhelm Iffland, Berlin 1811, E. Salfeld.]

When the editor was in Vienna for the first time, ten years ago [June 1800] he felt an inner need to see in closer proximity the great man to whom he owed so many happy hours in life.

[Iffland was shy about going.] In this embarrassment the first weeks passed and when he finally overcame it, he learned that Haydn was in the country and occupied with completing a large work [*The Seasons*]; he would not be pleased to be interrupted, especially by people who were complete strangers to him.

He [Iffland] realized that he must give up his wish, but he did so very unwillingly. . . . He was now the more determined, when he was in Vienna two years ago, not to leave the city without having seen the dear poet [Haydn].

Upon enquiring casually among his acquaintances, the answer came back that although he was not actually sick, his weakened condition required postponing the visit. Meanwhile he prepared himself for the profound delight of making the acquaintance of those two distinguished artists, the painter [Hubert] Mauer and the sculptor [Johann Martin] Fischer. [Iffland then heard that Haydn was somewhat stronger, that one was not previously announced or an appointment made, and that such a visit was best made in the morning.]

Herr [Heinrich] Schmid[t], director of Prince Esterhazi's [*sic*] theatre in Eisenstadt, and personally known to Haydn, promised to make the introduction. Both rejoiced from the bottom of their hearts at the moment when they would see (and meet, respectively) the dear man. Wednesday morning, 7th September, was selected for the visit.

It was St Mary's Day [Thursday, 8th September], good weather, and the good, faithful, happy people streamed in numbers from the churches and went home. Other crowds were just leaving for the temples, from the open doors of which poured masses of people, heart-lifting song and incense, uplifting the happy and pious heart.

1 *Die Musik* VIII (1908–9), 232ff.; Pohl III, 261ff. The date of Iffland's visit is in some doubt: 8 September 1808 was a Thursday, but it was in fact St Mary's Day. Iffland writes 'Wednesday, 7 September'.

We gradually left these thick crowds of solemnly inclined people and came to quieter parts of the city, and finally to the still street in which Haydn lived. When we reached the house door, we had a careful look at the surroundings of the place where Haydn had chosen to rest after the rigorous and heat of the day. Peace – quiet – stillness! Otherwise the usual surroundings of working people. Probably he chose this place, which is otherwise undistinguished, because it is comfortably situated for those who love him and are loved by him. Perhaps his friends persuaded him to choose this place because he found stillness here and can find help quickly if needed.

We enter the bright, cheerful house; we are greeted trustingly.

'The gentleman is at home,' said the maid. We should take our places upstairs for a moment; he is returning with his servant from the garden. As soon as he has come upstairs, she will announce us. He walks rather slowly; we should be patient. We are led to a room next to which is an alcove [*Kabinett*] with small pieces of music in his handwriting and of his composition, each framed with a garland of flowers round it. A valuable wall and one – we said sadly to ourselves – that will one day have an even higher price. In the room next door was a painting that showed him as he once was: a penetrating expression, very far-looking. After a while the maid entered and said in a very friendly way: the gentleman is now upstairs and expects us.

We entered a room. – Haydn sat, his face turned to the window, fully dressed, hat in his hand, a walking-stick and a bunch of flowers in the other. His servant [Johann Elssler] stood behind his chair, in front of which chairs were waiting for us. He wore a brown coat, a grey overcoat and a carefully dressed wig. . . .

He made a motion to get up. The servant helped him and he came towards us a few short steps, his hand in front of his eyes; his legs, though he wished them to move quickly, dragged along the ground rather slowly, one after the other. He gave Herr Schmid[t] his hand and nodded with a friendly expression towards the editor [Iffland], whom he led to a chair. We all sat down. He breathed with difficulty, therefore we sought to converse on subjects of no import so that he would not have to answer, thus giving him time to collect himself. He often looked at the flowers in his hand and took obvious pleasure from their scent.

'I said my prayers in the open today,' he said. 'I can't do otherwise.' His eyes crinkled in tears. 'It's also best that way,' he said, glancing up towards Heaven. Our answers are of no importance. At this point we spoke of how lovingly and marvellously he had described nature, how truly he must have studied her. *The Seasons*.

'Yes, *The Seasons*,' he interrupted with some energy; '*The Seasons* finished me off. Yet I wanted, I wanted' – here he sought for expressions and moved energetically back and forth – 'But words are far too insufficient! No, really too insufficient. I had to torment myself whole days over one passage, and then, then – no, you won't believe what martyrdom I went through.' Here he struck the floor with his cane. – The servant looked at him, searchingly and in a friendly way.

'Hm, it's true,' he said; 'you're quite right; it's all done and finished with.' – Whereupon he again sat down in his previous quiet position.

'Yes, yes, it's finished, as you see, and *The Seasons* is the reason for it. – Altogether I've had to work much and hard in my life.'

A while later: 'I didn't work easily; no, not easily. My youth was very difficult.' He related how in his early years he had lived very high up in a house on the Michaelerplatz and had to go up and down a great number of steps – he said how many – every day. He pointed to his chest: 'You see, that now comes and strikes me down! But it's a defeat with honour – it was a hard piece of work, only God helped.'

He came to speak of the theatre and how it pained him not to hear anything new. But – he doesn't go out any more at all.

At this point he said something complimentary about how he had seen the editor eight years ago – a word about his work – he looked at him for a little while and nodded at him several times in a most friendly way. [Iffland] asked him if he could place that dear hand, which the revered old man was even then stretching towards him, on his heart. – Quickly [Haydn] reached over with both arms, kissed him, and wept from the heart.

'I'm all right,' he said, 'quite all right. But I cannot act differently nowadays; if something pleases me, I have to cry. I don't want to, but I can't prevent it.'

'Before it was different. Before.' He looked as if at a great distance towards the window and sighed.

Gradually we came to speak of an excellent Mass by Haydn which had been excellently performed a few days ago at Eisenstadt by the princely Esterhazi *Kapelle*. Particularly the Credo of this Mass impressed the editor. Haydn spoke with great liveliness about his church music altogether to Herr Schmied [*sic*], who answered him with knowledge, emotion and love.

The excellent artist had without noticing become so vivacious that without realizing it he had put aside hat and cane and was speaking with such swift gestures that one could believe one saw him again at the head of his orchestra. His eye shone with pleasure – but gradually his weakness returned again, warning him – he looked unhappily at his servant, nodded to him, took back hat and stick in his hands, let us continue to talk for a while, seeking to collect himself and looking quietly at the floor.

He came to speak of the Esterhazi *Kapelle* – asked questions about them, about his acquaintances, about the newest music that was given at Eisenstadt, and heard the answers with particular sympathy. He spoke of the reigning Prince, of the kindness with which he treated [Haydn], of the services which the house of Esterhazi has rendered the arts. That which he said on the subject had the expression of innermost recollection and love.

The performance of *The Creation* in Vienna at which he himself was present not so long ago excited this good, enthusiastic people – so thankful to its great artists, in particular – to the most heartfelt delight. At that time everyone still spoke with real joy of that unforgettable evening. [Here follows a description of Haydn's being covered with shawls, etc.]

We did not want to remind him of that evening and to arouse his emotions, but since we were speaking of *The Creation* altogether, he added: 'On the evening when I was last present, I heard the best performance of it!' He folded his hands together in happy recollection, and since he saw proof of our feelings in our eyes which we could not conceal, he continued: 'Too much was done for me! Too much, too much! But what a good, good people!' This he pronounced with a tone of enthusiasm, with chest thrust out and almost with a loud voice.

The editor told him of the joy with which the work was received also in Berlin, and how there had once been a performance for a religious organization which brought in over two thousand thaler.

He looked upwards and repeated slowly and with a beaming countenance. 'Over two thousand Thaler – for the poor! Over two thousand Thaler? Do you hear that?' – here he turned to his servant – 'my *Creation* in Berlin brought in two thousand Thaler for the poor.' Then he leaned far back in his chair and let his tears run freely. – 'For the poor! My work gave the poor a good day. That's wonderful, that's comforting.'

After a while he raised himself and said rather sadly – 'That's now finished. I have no more effect. But' – he looked at those present in a friendly way – 'it went well, didn't it? – How much did *The Creation* earn for the poor? Remember it; I shall often delight in it.'

For a while he was now quite genuinely happy and said: 'You would probably like to see my things of honour? – Bring them in!'

The servant brought in the medals which were struck for him in Paris, Petersburg and London. He showed us each one and then put it down beside him.

'I was greatly pleased to have received these signs of good will, and I still find pleasure in looking at them with friends. – You'll say that they are an old man's playthings, but for me they are more than that – I count my life backwards and for a few moments I'm young again. All these things should remain in faithful hands after my death.'

We assured him of our deep feelings for him and tried to conceal them as best we could. After a while he continued: 'I ought to play something for you. Do you want to hear something of mine?' It was our innermost desire but we had not dared to express it.

He looked at the instrument: 'Of course I can't do much any longer. – You shall hear my last composition. I wrote it just when the French army was pressing towards Vienna three [*sic*] years ago.'

He stood up, gave his arm to his servant. We all took him in our arms and accompanied him to the pianoforte. He sat down and said: 'The Song is called "Gott erhalte Franz, den Kaiser." ' He played the melody all the way through with indescribable expression, with deep feeling – which his glistening eyes reflected. After the Song was ended he remained in front of the instrument for a while, placed both hands on it and said in the tone of a worthy patriarch: 'I play this song every morning, and often I have gained comfort and strength from it, in days of unrest. I can't do differently; I must play it every day. I feel very well indeed when I'm playing it, and for a while afterwards, too.'

He indicated that he wanted to return to his seat at the window. We wanted to accompany him there, but with a certain energy he himself closed the instrument and it was clear that he did not want any help in the process. Quietly and with a somewhat hanging head, our arms round him, he went back to his seat. On his features one could read much emotion which he sought to control.

We moved back a pace. He looked at us and said: 'God be with you. I'm not of much more use today. Be well! Adieu!' He stood up. We embraced him and said few words. He sat down and reached for the bunch of flowers that lay on the chair before him.

The editor asked for a flower as a keepsake. Haydn looked at him benevolently, sunk his face in the bunch and with both hands offered it to the traveller and hugged him firmly in his arms.

'Adieu!' he cried with a gentle, broken voice, turned, sat and we left him with emotions that each of us felt without communicating them. We could not free ourselves of the strong feelings that we had when looking at this setting sun; nor did we wish to. . . .   [Pohl III, 262ff.]

Two days later Iffland wrote: 'I still see the transfigured face of Haydn before me, and his features told me things – about artistic and wordly life that up to now have deeply moved my soul.'

In the Autumn of 1808, Neukomm returned from Russia. He wrote on 15 November to the Leipzig publisher A. Kühnel:

He [Haydn] is very weak and has to be led in order to go up and down the room slowly; despite this, he plays three or four times daily his ever-beautiful song, 'Gott erhalte den Kaiser', sometimes he succeeds in discovering a new bass to it, but sometimes the old man can't rightly proceed, and then he becomes impatient and says: he well realizes that it doesn't go any more.

[Grasberger, *Hymnen*, 35]

Neukomm wrote in his notes for the Dies biography that after he had returned from Russia.

I spent the whole winter in Vienna in order to see my dear Father Haydn every day; for my visits I chose the later afternoon hours after he had risen somewhat strengthened from his afternoon nap and, as Dies relates, was dressed again. One day I appeared rather later than usual. H. came to greet me and was quite cheerful, saying with a triumphant expression: 'Do you know that today I played my prayer (that was they way he used to call his Song "Gott erhalte den Kaiser" in this final period) quite *nicely*, really quite nicely?' I could not hold back the tears over this outburst of self-satisfaction on the part of the sublime creator of so many hundred masterpieces, who barely ten years earlier would not allow me to express my admiration about passages in his *Creation* and *Seasons*; for example in my enthusiasm over the Chorus 'Der Herr ist groß in seiner Macht' I allowed the following to slip out – 'Papa, you wrote that above yourself', whereupon he answered me rather seriously but with his usual goodness, 'Don't say that! You are flattering me – You know I can't stand that.' [Neukomm, 30]

Now Haydn received another distinguished visitor, the German composer and critic Johann Friedrich Reichardt, who wrote down his experiences in Vienna in an interesting book entitled *Vertrauten Briefen geschrieben auf eine Reise nach Wien und den Österreichischen Staaten zu Ende des Jahres 1808 und zu Anfang 1809.*[1]

Vienna 30 November 1808
. . . I have been eagerly waiting for a quiet free moment to describe faithfully a touching scene I had with the old Haydn. Fräulein von Kurzbeck [Kurzböck], whom he loves like a father, and Frau von Pereira – full of enthusiasm as they are for him and everything great and beautiful – took me out . . .
    To arrive at one of the remotest suburbs we had to drive almost an hour through back streets and corners. There we found the marvellous old man in a small but really quite nice garden-house, which he owns, on the second floor in a small room, sitting at a table covered with a green cloth, fully dressed with white buttons and a delicately prepared and powdered wig with curls. There he sat, very stiff and almost rigid, close by the table, both hands on the table, not unlike a living wax-figure. Fräulein von Kurzbeck first explained to him that she would very much like to introduce me; I was almost afraid he wouldn't know my name or in his state of apathy not remember it, and was really touched and I must really say ashamed, as the old hero opened his still very lively, sparkling eyes wider and said: 'Reichardt? A — — man! Where is he?' I had just entered and he called to me across the table with outstretched arms: 'Best Reichardt, come here! I must press you to my heart!' And now he kissed me and gave me a strong, spasmodic handshake. Then he passed his thin hand across both my cheeks and said to the others: 'That which pleases me is that the — — artist also has an honest, good face.' I sat down next to him and held his hand in mine. He looked at me a while, touched, and then said: 'Still so young! Ah, I have strained my spirit too much; I'm already just a child', and wept bitter tears. The ladies wanted to leave in order to protect him. 'No, it's all right, children,' called the dear old man, 'that does me

1 Superb modern edition in two volumes, edited by Gustav Gugitz, the great Austrian historian, Georg Müller Verlag, Munich, 1915. I, 120ff.

good and they are really tears of joy about that man, who will have a better fate.' I could scarcely bring forth a heartfelt, thankful word and could only kiss his hand in heartfelt fashion.

Frau von Pereira, whom with his weak memory he didn't at first recognize, reminded him in a child-like, playful tone of all sorts of jokes and soon he joined her in this tone which he is said always to have very much liked. Now the ladies thought that we should leave the weak old man; it is too much of a strain for him in the end, and we made our farewells. Hardly had we reached the door, however, when he called us back and said: 'I must also show Reichardt my treasures.' Then a maid brought in all sorts of beautiful, and in part expensive, things. The most interesting was a rather large, flat box which the Princess Esterházy . . . had ordered to be constructed after her own careful plans. [There follows a description of the box and Wigand's miniature of *The Creation* performance of March 1808.] In the box lay a large commonplace book, also black with gold, with the Princess' signature and inside the heartfelt signatures of the whole princely family. I must be the first artist to sign it, said the dear old man; he will send it to me. [There follows further descriptions of the writing instruments in the box, etc.]

Then he showed me a whole series of medals from the Petersburg Musical Society, from the Paris *Concert* for which he especially composed several symphonies, and from many others; also a quite marvellous ring from the Russian Emperor; diplomas from the Parisian National Institute, the Vienna Right of Citizenship and many other similar objects. The good old man seemed quite happy to live these experiences again.

As we finally took our leave after a good hour, he held me back alone, holding my hand firmly and said, between many kisses, I must come and visit him once a week so long as I stay here. I don't want to soil this episode with small, fearful signs of avarice in the midst of his riches which he could not even use any more; but they went to my very soul.

I have also sought out and visited the good Beethoven. People pay so little attention to him here that no one could tell me where he lives, and it entailed quite a lot of trouble on my part to locate him. [For the rest of the description, see Landon, *Beethoven*, pp. 221f.]

When contemporaries had a chance to compare Iffland's and Reichardt's visits to Haydn, many people took exception to Reichardt's tone, and we find some rather sharp criticisms in the *Zeitung für die elegante Welt* (6 February 1810) and the Berlin journal, *Der Freimüthige* (22 December 1810), where we read *inter alia*: '. . . and that is all that one can learn from a Reichardt about a Haydn, though the visit lasted "a good hour"!' But probably it was the last sentence about Haydn's avarice that annoyed people.

A final witness of Father Haydn this year was the horn-player and composer Johann Risle, who published his 'Erinnerungen aus Wien, Ungarn, Sizilien und Italien', in the *Berliner Allgemeine Musikalische Zeitung* of 1829 (Pohl III, 268):

Here, my dear friend, I would have wished you to be an eye and ear witness. The good-natured, cheerful expression with which Papa Haydn related even doleful pictures of earlier times – the pious, modest tone of his voice – the way in which he sees in all his works only the Grace of God – even his childlike, joyful recollection of honours received and also presents – it was a wonderful morning. His whole being seemed to be in most beautiful harmony with his works. That is the way it really was, as he related to me scenes from his life: I seemed to hear his music underneath – here a comfortable Andante from his symphonies, there one of his merry rondos or joking minuets & trios; or when his beautiful religious feelings predominated, some extract from his excellent Masses or his *Seven Words of the Saviour.*

He specially liked to dwell on his youthful years and to tell me what difficulties he had to combat; how he had to worry and often to eke out a wretched existence. His good housekeeper, who this time cleaned the coloured cups and finely cut glass [parts] of the shining furniture rather more than was necessary, was on pins and needles when the great master made himself so humble in front of a stranger; she allowed her busy hand to stop several times and burst out with the words, 'But now' —— (think of an expression, the importance of which is supposed to assist Haydn's childlike unembarrassment, and think of the 'now' at least as a crotchet in common time). 'Well then', interrupted Haydn, speaking easily, 'now, with God's help, I have my livelihood.' Well, I thought, good man, may you enjoy it for a very long time! Among his misfortunes he also counted the fact that reviewers were frequently hard on him and that it was altogether impossible to please everyone. 'But,' he added quietly, 'later I calmed myself with the thought – you must write that which your heart dictates; and I felt well doing so.' With such a talent and pure sense for the beautiful, certainly the best way. After many remarks which were altogether most interesting to me, also concerning my own attempts [at composition?], Haydn closed the last conversation with the words: 'Yes, my young friend, I've managed to arrive at this point, and now' (but no; dear friend, I cannot relate everything. What is missing will perhaps come later). No father could have bade a more heartfelt farewell than Haydn vouchsafed me. But it seemed to me that I noticed a certain reservation during his friendly farewell; his hand, which grasped mine with youthful warmth, moved, as the conversation became somewhat reserved, steadily, timidly, upwards – I had not the faintest idea what he wanted – but finally, taking a breath, he woke me, distracted as I was, out of the dream: 'Well, you really could kiss the hand of an old man like me!' 'Best Father Haydn, with what joy!' I squeezed the hand, through which the restless activity of a beautiful spirit had produced so much of greatness, to my lips – then he fell on my neck and kissed me. – Well, you'll say, didn't you really know that all young composers call him Father Haydn and kiss his hand?

We now come to the last surviving letter of Haydn; fittingly, it is addressed to his now much mellowed and indeed almost sympathetic Prince:

[To Prince Nicolaus II Esterházy. *German.* Only the signature autograph]
Most Serene Highness,
Gracious Prince and Lord!

I humbly place myself at Your Serene Highness' feet for the gracious approval of my request, whereby with the utmost kindness you take over my yearly expenditures for the doctor and apothecary. By this new act of generosity. Your Serene Highness has freed me from a most pressing anxiety, and thus enabled me to await the end of my earthly existence in peace and serenity. May Heaven grant my zealous wish that Your Serene Highness live in everlasting well-being and Your Gracious Highness' illustrious family in ever increasing prosperity! I remain ever your most devoted and

Your Serene Highness'
humble servant,
Joseph Haydn [m.p.] ria.

Vienna, 22nd December 1808.

[CCLN, 248]

The request made in this letter to Haydn's princely patron, namely to pay all his *Kapellmeister*'s doctor's and apothecary bills, did indeed require a gracious act on the latter's part. Possibly once again, Princess Marie had been the go-between, but the outcome is clearly established in the following letter from Prince Esterházy to his House Inspector:

> To my House Inspector Giay!
> Since I intend in the future to pay to the *Kapellmeister* Joseph Haydn according to his enclosed memorial the annual expenses he incurs for doctors and apothecaries, my House Inspector is to go to him and inquire what his medicines cost during the past year. Whom did he have for a doctor? And what honorarium does he generally pay to him each year? Which is to be reported to me.
> Vienna, 15th December 1808.
> Vidit Karner.   exp. Esterházy.
>   [Valkó II, 632]

In due course, on 6 January 1809, Joseph Giay submitted a bill for the huge sum of 1,017 gulden, which represented Haydn's expenses for his doctor and apothecary for the year 1808. It was no wonder, then, that Haydn was genuinely alarmed about this large expenditure, which was the equal of the pension awarded to him by Prince Nicolaus I 'The Magnificent'. Esterházy ordered this sum to be paid, in a document dated 7 January 1809, but suggested to Giay that it would be better to organize future bills every month, a procedure which was followed. If we may break the Chronicle for a moment, the situation with regard to these bills suggested to Joseph Giay, in a letter to the princely House Inspector of 25 April 1809, that the Prince's new idea to pay Haydn's doctor, Franz Edler von Hohenholz, an annual salary instead of per visit, would require no less than five hundred gulden per annum 'for the reason that *Herr Kapellmeister* is not satisfied with the two visits that also have to be made even if the patient feels better but very often, at any hour of the day or night, calls him again' (Valkó II, 634f.). On 6 June 1809, Esterházy and also *Hofrat* Karner were in Budapest and unaware that Haydn was dead. Karner agreed to the proposal about Dr Hohenholz, and Prince Esterházy ordered the following bill to be paid:

> Enclosed are the bills for *Kapellmeister* Haydn from the Apothecary at the Golden Cross in [the suburb of] Mariahilf for medicines during the month of March this year, amounting to   45 f. 45
>   Then the following visits of Herr Doctor Franz Edler v. Hohenholz from 1 Jan. to middle March . . . .   189 f.
>   Total   234 f. 45 x.

herewith humbly submitted for princely approval & payment
                                                         Vienna the 8th April 80 g.

Passed for payment
     Pest 6th June 809.   F[ürst] Esterházy mp.
                                                                              [Pohl III, 273]

We have seen that Sigismund Neukomm had made a new arrangement of Haydn's old Oratorio, *Il ritorno di Tobia*. It was now decided to produce the work at the Christmas concerts of the Tonkünstler-Societät and, because of its length, to do the first part on 22 December and the second half on the day following. The soloists were Marianna Marconi, Therese Fischer, Antonia Campi, Julius Radicchi and Ignaz Saal.

On 22 December the concert opened with a 'Phantasie for the whole orchestra, composed and dedicated to Joseph Haydn by his pupil Sigmund [*sic*] Neukomm', who conducted both evenings. Haydn was not present. It was, incidentally, the last time that the Society ever gave an Oratorio in Italian; Haydn's German Oratorios had dug an early grave for Italian-language productions.

Il ritorno di Tobia was not a success. Rosenbaum (145) wrote in his Diary, 'Cold . . . Mayer went to the concert at the B. Th.: *Rückkehr des Tobias*, by Haydn, an antiquated pot-boiler; it was not well received. . . .' Reichardt (op. cit., 214f.) wrote on Christmas Day:

> In the Burgtheater a very old Oratorio by Haydn, *Tobia*, was given, one of his earliest[!] works which one probably only brought forth to honour also his very old age with it. At least I had here the opportunity of getting to know the excellent contralto voice of Demoiselle Marconi, one of the finest voices of her kind that I ever heard. She was entirely trained, moreover, in the fine Mannheim school; she is from Mannhein and sang with large, quiet expression; particularly fine were the recitatives that she 'recited' and declaimed . . . As far as she was concerned I was sorry to have to leave the music before the end, but at Prince Lobkowitz's there was also a concert planned for that evening, where two beautiful female singers were to be heard. . . .

Actually Reichardt was present at the second evening (23 December). On the 22nd, Beethoven had the misfortune to have organized a very large-scale concert (*Akademie*) for his benefit at the Theater an der Wien. It was the second time – the first had been in 1803 with *Christus am Ölberg* – that circumstances had forced Beethoven to give an important benefit concert the same evening that a Haydn Oratorio was produced. Not only was much of the *haut monde* at the Tonkünstler-Societät, but Beethoven was forced to take the left-over musicians, all the best that Vienna had to offer having been engaged in the huge band (as usual, 180 strong) that played Haydn's music. As might be expected, everything went wrong at the Theater an der Wien, not only in rehearsal but also in concert. The gargantuan programme included the Fifth and Sixth Symphonies, the Choral Fantasy, Op. 80, parts of the Mass in C for Prince Esterházy – who donated 100 gulden to Beethoven in support of his 'musical Akademie' – and the Fourth Piano Concerto. At one point the whole performance broke down and Beethoven had to start the piece – it was the Choral Fantasy – again. The theatre was not even properly heated, and Beethoven's admirers shivered in icy boxes.

As if to add insult to injury, works by Haydn not only ruined what was potentially the greatest orchestral-choral concert in Vienna's history after *The Creation* and *The Seasons*, but it also seemed to disturb another attempt on Beethoven's part to enter the glittering world of the Tonkünstler-Societät. We have seen that on 22 December, the concert began with Neukomm's new 'Phantasie'. It was planned to give the new Beethoven Fourth Piano Concerto at the concert on 23 December. From the Wegeler-Ries *Notizen* we learn that Ries was chosen to perform the G major Concerto but was given only five days to learn it. Ries thought this impossible and asked to play the Third Concerto in C minor instead. Beethoven went in one of his usual rages to another pianist, the young Carl Friedrich Stein, and offered the performance of the Fourth Concerto to him. Stein accepted but he, too, failed to learn it in time and also asked to do the Third Concerto instead. Beethoven had to acquiesce. Ries tells us that whether the fault was the theatre's, the orchestra's, or Herr Stein's, the Concerto made no impact. Beethoven was very angry. Once again, a work of his had failed in connection with a Haydn concert – first *Christ on the Mount of Olives*, then the *Akademie* of 22 December, now the Third Concerto on 23 December. It is, alas, a typical state of affairs and it is here that we leave relations between the two men, albeit at second-hand, in this Chronicle.[1]

It was about this time that Haydn's old colleague Muzio Clementi arrived in Vienna; no doubt he went to visit Haydn, with whom he had been on business terms for some time, but now it was Beethoven with whom Clementi was intent on doing business. A letter from Clementi to his partner in London under date 28 December 1808 has survived; possibly he was present at the aforementioned concerts; in any event he had acquired six new works from Beethoven in 1807, including the Fourth Piano Concerto.

Did faint echoes of these mighty new works reach the Kleine Steingasse in Gumpendorf?

1 Pohl, *Denkschrift*, 68; Thayer-Forbes, *Beethoven* I, 446–51 for contemporary comments on the Beethoven concert; Wegeler-Ries, *Notizen*, 114f. See also Landon, *Beethoven*, 223ff., where on pp. 232f. the original, uncut version of the Trio of the Fifth Symphony was reproduced for the first time from the original performance material (Beethoven later shortened the Trio by about half). Clementi: Thayer-Forbes I, 450. 417ff.

CHAPTER TWELVE

Chronicle 1809

HAYDN HAD MADE HIS First Will in 1801 (*supra*, pp. 50ff.), but since then many of the legatees named therein had died, including his brothers Johann and Michael, who were to have received 4,000 gulden each. Haydn obviously thought it was time to draw up a new and, presumably, final Will, which he had his lawyer prepare and which is dated 7 February 1809.[1] (For explanatory notes see p. 382.)

[Haydn's Final Will]

[note by the Vienna City Magistracy:] ps. 2 Juny 809.

LAST WILL

In the name of the most holy Trinity, God the Father, Son and the Holy Ghost, Amen.

As the time and hour of death is [*sic*] most uncertain, and since death often surprises us at an hour when we do not at all expect it, I, being of a fully sound mind, do order that the following instructions with regard to my estate be followed precisely after my death.

1stly: I recommend my soul to the boundless mercy and goodness of God.

2ndly: My body shall be laid to earth according to Christian and Catholic rites of the first class.

3rdly: At my death the attending clergyman [*Seelsorger*] shall receive *ten gulden*.

4thly: I bequeath *twelve gulden* for Holy Masses, which shall be read for the comfort of my soul in the Parish Church where I die.

5thly: I bequeath *five gulden* for this particular purpose to the Parish Priest of the Royal Hungarian Free City of Eisenstadt, *two gulden* to each of the two vicars there, and *two gulden* to the beneficiary there.

6thly: For the same purpose I leave *two Gulden* for Holy Masses each to the Priest at Möllendorf and at St. Georg in Hungary, likewise

7thly: *twelve gulden* to the Priest of my birthplace, Rohrau.

8thly: For the primary school fund [*Normalschulfonde*] here [in Vienna] *five gulden*.

9thly: I leave *one thousand gulden* to the poor citizens, male and female, of [the district of] St Marx, which shall be distributed in cash by my residuary legatee.

10thly: To the Brothers of Mercy [*Barmherzige Brüder*] at Eisenstadt I bequeath *fifty gulden*, and *fifty gulden* to the Franciscan monks of that town.

11thly: I leave *one hundred gulden* to Herr Mathias Stöfinger, R. I. Court War Councillor's *Hofkonzipist*.

12thly: I leave *five hundred gulden* to the 4 children of my late sister who was married to Rafler, to wit the married woman Anna Maria Moser, seamstress at

---

1 Published by Robert Franz from the original document in the Archives of the City of Vienna: *Die Musik* XXIV/6 (March 1932), pp. 440ff.

Esterházy [Eszterháza] in Hungary; *five hundred gulden* to Elisabeth, married to Böhm, seamstress in Rohrau; *five hundred gulden* to Theresia, married to Hammer, cobbler-mistress at Gerhaus in Hungary; and to Anna, married to Loder, cobbler-mistress in Vienna, a life-long income of *thirty kreutzer per diem*; but for each of her three children a capital of *five hundred gulden*, a total therefore of *one thousand five hundred Gulden*; should one of these three children die before coming of age its part shall fall to the other two. Moreover, Ernestine Loder who, of these children, is living with me, is to have the bed on which she lies, together with four sheets, a small bureau drawer with top section [*Aufsatzkasten*], a mirror, the relic of the True Cross and other small items of furniture for a room, and apart from the 500 f. already bequeathed to her she is to receive another *five hundred gulden*, thus a total of *one thousand gulden*. Moreover, I order that the legacy of 3,000 f., which I formerly assured in writing to Anna Loder and her previous husband Joseph Lugmayer, be declared invalid since in this Will I have cared for their livelihood in a fatherly fashion, and also I paid more than 5,000 f. of debts incurred by her previous husband Joseph Lugmayer.

13thly: I leave to the daughter of my deceased sister Franziska, Anna, married to Wimmer, restaurant-keeper at Nikola in Hungary, and her husband, together *one thousand gulden.*

14thly: I leave *one hundred gulden* to the above-mentioned Anna Wimmer's daughter, who is married to a surgeon at Koposvar [Kapuvár] in Hungary.

15thly: I leave to my niece [*Muhme*], *née* Koller, the saddler's wife [or tanner-mistress] in Eisenstadt and her stepdaughter, together *three hundred gulden.*

16thly: I leave *three hundred gulden* to her blood-brother Koller.

17thly: I leave to Rosalia Weber; who was formerly in my service, the sum of *three hundred gulden* which was promised her in writing.

18thly: I leave *twenty-five gulden* together to the widow of the late gardener Michael and her children.

19thly: I leave a year's salary of *thirty-six gulden* to my kitchen maid, Theresia Schaller.

20thly: I leave *one hundred gulden* as a remembrance to Roschnitz, the princely Esterhazi wine steward's assistant.

21stly: To Antonia Wierländer I bequeath the sum of one year's salary, *thirty gulden.*

22ndly: I leave *fifty gulden* to the church singer Babette of the princely Esterhazi Parish in Eisenstadt.

23rdly: I leave *fifty gulden* each to the unmarried woman Anna and her sister Josepha Till, butcher's daughters in Eisenstadt.

24thly: I leave *two hundred gulden* together to the four sisters Sommerfeld, wig-maker's daughters and relatives of my late wife.

25thly: I leave *fifty gulden* to the hospital fund for the poor in the Royal Free City of Eisenstadt.

26thly: I leave *twenty-four gulden* to the poor blind man in Eisenstadt known as Adam.

27thly: I leave *six gulden* for the school-children there.

28thly: I leave *one hundred gulden* to Herr Wammerl, formerly *valet-de-chambre* at Herr Count v. Harrach's.

29thly: I leave *fifty gulden* to the Herr Cashier of Herr Count v. Harrach.

30thly: I leave *one hundred gulden* together for Philipp Schimpel, choirmaster at Haimburg [Hainburg] and his wife, also the portrait of her father on the ground-floor of my house, by the name of Frank, who was my first master in music.

31stly: I leave *one hundred gulden* together to Theresia Eder and her daughter Aloysia, lace-maker in the neuen Wieden.

32ndly: I leave *one hundred gulden* to the unmarried woman Anna Buchholz, living in the Wieden.

33rdly: I leave to Madame Aloisia Polzelli, formerly singer at His Highness the Prince of Esterházy's, a life-long income of *one hundred and fifty gulden* annually, for which purpose 3,000 f. from my financial estate is to be invested in five-per cent state bonds at the Probate Court in order to assure Madame Polzelli of that life-long income which she has been willed;

but after her death I wish

34thly: that half of these 150 f., to wit *seventy-five gulden*, is to be made available in perpetuity for the two poorest orphans of my birthplace Rohrau, and for their education until they come of age, whereupon this sum shall pass on to two other of the poorest orphans in Rohrau. As for the other half, to wit *seventy-five gulden*, it should

(35thly:) pass to the Lords of Rohrau for the purpose of keeping in good condition the monument to me which they have erected, and also the statue which my late father arranged to be erected next to the sacristy of the church there. However, I order in respect of §33 of this Will that should Madame Polzelli attempt to extract from my legacy the contents of a document prepared by me some 18 years ago [*recte*: 23 May 1800], the terms of §33 of this Will, containing her legacy, are to be declared null and void, and the terms set forth in §34 and §35 of this Will are to take effect immediately.

36thly: I leave *one hundred gulden* together for Antonia and Susanna Fischer, daughters of the First Lieutenant.

37thly: I leave *fifty gulden* to Josepha Haugwitzl.

38thly: I leave *one thousand gulden* to my sister-in-law Frau Magdalena Haydn in Salzburg.

39thly: I leave *one hundred gulden* to Theresia Höller [Köller?], ex-nun of Eisenstadt and organist.

40thly: I leave *one hundred gulden* to Herr Franz Kugler, solicitor.

41stly: I bequeath *six hundred gulden* to my faithful and honest cook, Anna Kremnitzer, and also the bed to be found in her room and on which she lies, then two sheets, 4 chairs, a hard-wood table, then a bureau drawers of hard wood, a repeating clock, the mirror, the picture of the Holy Virgin, the relic of the True Cross, the iron, the earthenware kitchen crockery together with other small articles of kitchen utensils; apart from that, I bequeath to her those *two hundred gulden* which she lent to me in cash.

42ndly: I leave *six thousand gulden* to my true and faithful servant Johann Elßler; then a plain [i.e. not embroidered] coat and waistcoat, one pair of knee breeches, an overcoat, a hat; and I order that my residuary legatee shall pay all the necessary expenses such as death duties, inheritance taxes, etc. so that none of this will be deducted from the legacies as ordered in §41 and §42.

43rdly: I leave a year's salary of *twenty gulden* to Theresia Mayer, the house-porter of my house.

44thly: I set aside *fifty gulden* for each of the two witnesses who will be asked to sign this Will.

45thly: I leave *one hundred gulden* to Demetrio Lichtenthal, son of the married woman Frau Oberauer in Eisenstadt.

46thly: I leave *three hundred gulden* to the daughter of the innkeeper Lugmayer in Vienna.

47thly: I name Herr Franz Klemp, registered justice and register of landed property of the Monastery Estate of Dornbach to be the executor of this Will, *viz.* to see that its contents are carried out as best as possible, and trusting in his honesty I bequeath him *one thousand gulden*, of which 500 f. is to be used for those purposes known to him, according to his conscience and without his having to show evidence therefor.

48thly: I leave the large golden commemorative medal from Paris together with the attached letter from the musicians there to His Highness the Prince von Esterházy and ask him to allow this keepsake to have a place in the treasure chamber at Forchtenau [*recte*: Forchtenstein].

49thly: I leave to the Count von Harrach, Lord of the Manor of Rohrau, the small gold medal from Paris with the attached letter from the Amateurs of Music, and further the large bust [of Haydn] *à l'antique*.

50thly: Since the pillars and foundation of every Will consist in naming a residuary legatee, I hereby name Mathias Frölich, son of my late sister Anna Maria Rafler, farrier in Fischament, as the true and sole residuary legatee of everything that should remain after subtracting the above bequests. Should, however, he die before me, I name as further residuary legatee Anna Maria Moser, daughter of my late sister Anna Maria Rafler, seamstress at Esterházy [Eszterháza] in Hungary.

Finally, I ask the worthy Probate Court to treat this document as my last Will in every respect, and if not as a last Will at least as a codicil or whatever be required to render it legally binding.

To which I add my signature and seal and those of two witnesses whom I have requested to do so (but who are both unprejudiced) [i.e. not beneficiaries].

Vienna, 7th February 809.

Joseph H Haj mpria

[seal]

Haydn[1] mpria

Kilian Ast des auß rath [Member of the Outer Council] as requested witness

    [seal]

Anton Meilinger as requested witness

    [seal]

NOTES TO HAYDN'S LAST WILL
(listed by clause numbers; for First Will see pp. 50ff.)

12: see First Will, 10, 11, 12*bis*, 13.
13: see First Will, 15.
14: see First Will, 17.
15, 16: see First Will, 22, 40.
17: see First Will, 26.
18: see First Will, 26.
20: Probably the man who delivered to Haydn the Tokay and Malaga wines from the Esterházy cellars.
21: Another of Haydn's servants.
22: see First Will, 39.
23: see First Will, 41 (there 'Dill').

24: see First Will, 43.
31: see First Will, 53.
32: see First Will, 58.
33: see First Will, 51.
35: ditto.
36, 37: unidentified.
39: Probably Haydn's first love, Theresia Keller, his wife's sister, who had taken the veil in 1755 and was now, apparently, living in Eisenstadt.
40: Probably relatives of the infamous Luegmayer family – see First Will, 12*bis*.

---

1 Haydn's hand was so weak that he required several attempts before he could sign the document properly. See the facsimile in *inter alia* Somfai, 200.

From Dies (194) we learn that

About six weeks before Haydn's death, he had his will read to his servants in the presence of witnesses and then asked them if they were satisfied with the provisions or not. The good people were surprised at the goodness of their master; they saw their future assured and thanked him for that with tears in their eyes.

It is also from Dies (196) that we learn something of Mathias Frölich. When Haydn's sister died, he took Mathias to live with him; the boy was then eleven years old and Haydn allowed him to pursue the profession he wished to learn, to wit that of blacksmith. 'The present war caused him such a great misfortune that he would have lost everything and fallen into great need, had not the inheritance saved him.'

Haydn's Last Will disposed of some 24,000 gulden, but it turned out that his estate brought a very large amount of money. At the auction of his effects, which was crowded with people, rich and poor, who wished to have some keepsake from the great man's possessions – Hummel, for example, bought Haydn's signet-ring and walking-stick – 23,163 gulden 24 x. was raised.[1] Haydn left 14,800 gulden in bonds, and 650 gulden in money lent privately. Finally the house was sold to an art-dealer named Ludwig Maisch and his wife for 17,100 gulden. It is, as Pohl (III, 279) points out, curious to find that at Haydn's death jewellery pawned for 1,092 gulden was held by the official state pawn-organization, a sum which the heirs had to repay, with interest.

Luigia Polzelli, true to her character, did try to present her claim dating from the year 1800 and thus forfeited all the rights to the income Haydn agreed to leave her. On 9 January 1816 she was given a small sum of money and had to sign a statement that she thereby waived any rights to Haydn's legacy. On 30 January 1816 the Vienna Court considered Haydn's legacy legally 'closed'. The son of the Rohrau wheelwright had left behind a fortune of 55,713 gulden (equivalent to £5,571 sterling at the rate of that period) – a very considerable sum in those days. It is also worth mentioning that Haydn's clothes were costly and plentiful: fifteen various coats, most of them with matching breeches, one of them 'violet-blue, closely fitted, with gold embroidery'; there were coats of brown velvet embroidered with silk, metal-green (*stahlgrün*), blue, of fawn-coloured wool, gunmetal-grey (*stahlgrau*), a 'green tail-coat' (*grüner Klappenfrack*), four other tail-coats, various great-coats, twenty-nine different waistcoats, one of them 'richly embroidered with gold and silver', eleven pairs of breeches, thirty shirts, many lace ruffles, etc.

In the *Nachlaßverzeichnis* ('List and Valuation of the works of art left behind by . . . Herr Joseph Haydn') there are also two pianos – Haydn had sold his Schanz piano on 1 April 1809 – listed:

'79. A French pianoforte in mahogany wood embellished with metal inlay from low F to high C. $5\frac{1}{2}$ octaves with the usual pedals by Erard et Frères Comp.' Valued at 200 gulden. Later note: 'Withdrawn by the res. legatee'. Mathias Frölich took the instrument to Rohrau.

'80. Ditto in massive mahogany wood, same range as above, by Longman et Broderip in London.' Valued at 300 gulden, it fetched 700 gulden and was later owned by Abbé Stadler.

---

1 Prince Johann von Liechtenstein paid over 1,400 fl. for a talking parrot (Griesinger, 53).

On 7 March 1809, Haydn's old friend Albrechtsberger died in Vienna. Better known as a contrapuntal teacher and theorist, Albrechtsberger was also a respectable composer; and we must not forget that he was one of Beethoven's best teachers.

On 26 and 27 March, the Tonkünstler-Societät gave *The Creation* (Fischer, Radicchi, Weinmüller). A few days later Haydn sold his piano by Wenzel Schanz. By an accident, one page of Haydn's account book, for which he used the so-called 'Krakau Calendar' that year, has survived (Österreichische Nationalbibliothek), and we may read, in Haydn's own trembling hand, the following note: 'Today the 1st of April [1809] I sold my beautiful fortepiano for 200 ♯ [ducats]. Jos. Haydn in his 78th year.' It is not known to whom Haydn sold his Schanz instrument, which has completely disappeared; indeed, no grand pianos by Wenzel Schanz seem to have survived at all.

For Austria the terms of the Peace of Pressburg were too hard. While Napoleon was occupied with the situation in Spain, the Austrian war-party under Stadion, a Rhinelander who had lost all his possessions to France, gained ground. Archduke Carl had undertaken widespread reforms in the army during 1806 and 1807; twenty-five generals had been dismissed and the whole structure improved. Archduke Johann was meanwhile organizing the militia. But these reforms were still being carried through and were by no means completed, and Carl doubted that they were ready for a new war. Apart from that, the country's finances were in a very bad state – inflation was rampant. England had decided to provide the Austrians with money and to invade Holland, if Emperor Franz could see his way to starting another war. Stadion's party won the day and on 9 April, Austria declared war again. It was an act of such folly that the historian can scarcely believe it possible. Archduke Carl crossed the Inn, Archduke Johann invaded Italy, while a third army attacked Tyrol, where Andreas Hofer had mobilized the peasants to revolt. But Germany and Russia did not participate – despite the hopes and encouragements given by the war party in the Hofburg – and Napoleon promptly defeated the Austrians at Regensburg and once more attacked Vienna and set up headquarters there on 13 May. It cannot be the purpose of this book to consider the Napoleonic Wars in any further detail;[1] suffice it to say that Napoleon lost a nearly decisive battle at Aspern but then won at Wagram. When peace was finally re-established, Austria lost Tyrol, Salzburg, Western Galicia, a part of Eastern Galicia, the Hungarian part of Dalmatia and part of Croatia, apart from a war 'contribution' of 85,000,000 gulden. Stadion was dismissed and the great era of Metternich began.

In our Chronicle for these post-London years, we began the great Napoleonic offensive in Italy with his famous rabble-rousing speech to his hungry, ill-equipped soldiers (see *Haydn: the Years of 'The Creation'*, p. 109). At the eve of the battle of Wagram, he issued a similar kind of proclamation, with which we shall close this very brief excursion into the war.[2]

> Soldats,
> Le territoire de la Confederation a été violé. Le Général Autrichien veut que nous fuyons à l'aspect des ses armes et que nous lui abandonnions nos alliés. J'arrive avec la rapidité de l'aigle. Soldats, j'étais entouré de vous, lorsque le souverain

---

1 See among other items of literature already cited, C. A. Macartney, *The Habsburg Empire 1790–1918*, London 1968, pp. 187ff. for a lucid account of these days.
2 A manuscript, signed by Napoleon and dated 'Donauwerth [*sic*], le 17 avril, 1809', containing this proclamation was sold at Sotheby's on 25 May 1976 (Catalogue, item 277), from which our text is taken.

d'Autriche vint à mon bivouac de Moravie. Vous l'avez entendu implorer ma
clémence et me jurer une amitié eternelle. Vainquers dans trois guerres, l'Autriche
a dû tout à notre générosite, trois fois elle a été parjuré! ! ! nos succès passés nous
sont un sûr garant de la victoire qui nous attend. Marchons donc, et qu'à notre
aspect, l'ennemi reconaisse ses vainqueurs.

It was the kind of dynamic leadership which the Allies, for the most part, had so
signally lacked on the field of battle (if not on the waters) until the Peninsular
Campaign.

Haydn was heartbroken at this new outbreak of the war. Griesinger was called
away to Störmthal and paid a final visit to Haydn on 3 May. 'This unhappy war pushes
me right to the floor', said Haydn with tears in his eyes. Later, Griesinger wrote from
Störmthal that he was convinced that Haydn's death was hastened by the 'latest events
in Vienna' (letter to Härtel of 18 June 1809).[1]

Haydn's last days have been described by many people, but upon investigation
they are all based upon a few eye-witnesses accounts. At the risk of slightly disturbing
the chronology of these May days, we have preferred to allow these authentic sources
to speak for themselves. No modern historian, however skilled, could recapture the
atmosphere conjured up by these contemporaries in their devotion to the subject.

We have seen that Griesinger was away from Vienna when Haydn died. Perhaps
he arranged with Elssler beforehand for a faithful account, should Haydn not survive.
In any case Haydn's death is here described by his copyist and valet, Johann Elssler, in a
letter to Griesinger: Vienna, 30th June 1809

> Most nobly born
>   Highly respected Herr v. Griesinger!
>   It has long been my intention, Sir, to give you news of the death of our
> beloved benefactor and father. Right after his death I went to [your] H[err] Porter
> and asked whether I could not send a letter to you, Sir. H[err] Porter said to me,
> however, that there is no possibility yet because it is not known which roads are
> open. Now I ask you, Sir, for your pardon and kind patience if I come so late with
> your request for I know that you, Sir, are always anxious to know how our good
> and kind Papa Haydn fares. But the confusion at that moment was too great.
>   With tears in my eyes I report to you, Sir, of our dear Father's death. The day
> that you, Sir, said good-bye to our good Papa and said, we won't see each other for
> a long time or perhaps we will see each other soon, just after Your Grace left the
> room, our good Papa said, we really won't see each other for a long time, he
> started to weep and said, my dear Johann, I won't be seeing Herr v. Griesinger any
> more, the war business depresses me right down to the ground. We had a lot of
> trouble (I and [cook] Nannerl) to get these thoughts out of our good Papa's mind
> and to quiet him down, but our good Papa was too weak and altogether couldn't
> quite pull himself together and was always anxious about how the war was going
> to continue.
>   When the Imp. French army moved into the *Maria Hülfer Lienie* [the outer
> walls of Vienna] on 10th May in the morning at a quarter of seven o'clock, our
> good Papa was still lying in bed. I and Nannerl were just busy getting Papa out of
> bed. – For the noise and confusion on the street were too great at this particular
> moment and we didn't have any people at our side who could comfort our good
> Papa; anyway as we were still busy getting the Papa out of bed, four canister-shots
> exploded by the *Lienie*, one after the other, and really, we kept a ball that fell in the

1 Griesinger, 50; Olleson *Griesinger*, 52.

courtyard as a souvenir, because of these explosions the door to the bedroom blew wide open and all the windows rattled, our good Papa was shocked and cried in a loud voice, 'Children, don't be afraid, for where Haydn is, nothing can happen' and trembled violently all over his body. But the whole day they were shooting from the fortress [in town], and our good Papa composed himself a bit though it was very hard for him, his nerves were hit too hard, and well! His whole body sank, but he still enjoyed his food and drink but as for walking I couldn't get our good Papa on his feet all by myself and the strongest medicines didn't help any longer. The *Kayser Lied* was still played three times a day, though, but on May 26th at half-past mid-day the Song was played for the last time and that 3 times over, with such expression and taste, well! that our good Papa was astonished about it himself and said he hadn't played the Song like that for a long time and was very pleased about it and felt well altogether till evening at 5 o'clock then our good Papa began to lament that he didn't feel well, but he still stayed up another half-an-hour but at 5:30, Well! Our good Papa asked to be taken right to bed and then he began to shiver a little and had a headache. All sorts of things were given him, and our good Papa felt so much better on that same evening and had quite a good night's sleep and was so well when he got up and the other things were all right too, so that of a dying moment nothing was felt. Saturday the 27th of May our good Papa asked about 8:30 o'clock to get up as usual and get dressed, but his bodily strength wouldn't allow it, and so our good Papa didn't leave his bed any more. The numbing got much worse, but so quietly and willing in everything that we were all astonished, our good Papa didn't complain of any pains, and when we asked him how he felt, we always received the reply, 'Children, be of good cheer, I'm well.'

The 29th of May we asked for a *Consillium* to be held with the permission of H[err] v. Hohenholz. The medicus Doctor Böhm was asked to come, for our good Papa needed it and he [Böhm] is also a very clever man, so the *Consillium* was held on the 30th in the morning, but despite all kinds of medicines administered, it was all of no use, and our good Papa got steadily weaker and quieter, 4 hours before his death our good Papa still spoke but then we didn't hear another sound, our good Papa had reactions and knew us 10 minutes before the end, for our good Papa squeezed Nannerl's hand, and the 31st of May in the early morning five minutes before a quarter to one o'clock our good Papa went quietly and peacefully to sleep, at his death there was no one there but me, the servants and a neighbour who also signed the will as a witness [Anton Meilinger, of 74 Kleine Steingasse]. Our good Papa is buried in God's field [cemetery] in front of the *Hundsturmer Lienie*, in his own grave.

The 31st March 1732 our good Papa was born, and 1809 the 31st of May was for us all the saddest day of death for ever. Our good Papa was 77 years and 61 full days old.

Otherwise everything is in the best order and everything remains until the whole business [of the legacy proceedings] starts, the Nannerl and the niece [*Mum*] of the late Papa and also the maid are still in the house, I'm with my wife and children at home and carry on as best I can in these trying times. May God help us out of our sad position, I eagerly hope to see Your Grace, God keep Your Grace in the best of health and we all kiss your hands

> Your thankful
> Johann Elssler m.p.
> Copyist and Servant of the
> late Herr v. Haydn.

N.B. I have taken my good Papa in plaster [death-mask; see pls. 5, 6].

[Pohl III, 385ff.]

Another letter about Haydn's final days survives; it is from the piano-maker Andreas Streicher – also Beethoven's friend – and is addressed to Griesinger:

> Vienna, 2nd July 1809
> Landstrasse Unger [*sic*] Gasse No 334
>
> You know, most worthy friend, that before you left I asked Fräul[ein]. Kurzbeck to let me know at once when Haydn might be reaching his end, but she did not hear of it until it was already too late, namely on the day of the funeral.[1] I myself did not hear until five days after that, and then Fräul. Kurzbeck told me. I asked her to send Johann [Elssler] to me; she promised but he didn't come. Twice I sent out to [Haydn's] house for him. He had left and finally my hall porter [*Haus Knecht*] succeeded in finding his new address in town. I asked him to come to me and he has just left after giving me the enclosed letter for you. Since he gave it to me sealed, I can't copy it in order to safeguard it from loss. But he said to me that he still has the letter's draft and he will keep that. Therefore if you do not receive this letter by the end of the month, or by the middle, I suppose you will write again and the draft will be sent to you at once. Johann assured me that he wrote you everything he told me, except for the following, which in any case is something worth preserving.
>
> Three days before Haydn's death, on the 24th[2] of May in the afternoon after 2 o'clock, just as Haydn was having his afternoon nap, a French officer of the Hussars came to make his acquaintance. Haydn received him, spoke to him about music and especially about *The Creation* and was so lively that the officer sang to him the Aria, 'Mit Würde [*sic*] und Hoheit angethan', with the Italian text. The officer sang in such a manly way, with such sublimity, and with such truth of expression and genuine feeling for music that Haydn could not hold back tears of joy and not only told the singer but afterwards other people that he could altogether recall no voice and no song that had given him so much and such real pleasure. After half-an-hour the officer got on his horse and – rode off to fight the enemy. He left his address which (as far as one can tell) reads: 'Sulimy, Capitain des Hussards'. Let us hope this noble gentleman learns that it was he to whom Haydn owed his last musical pleasure, for after that he did not hear a single note. . . . [Pohl III, 388f.]

Rosenbaum heard of Haydn's death immediately. On Wednesday, 31 May, he wrote:

> Warm, choking dust. – At 12:15 [*sic*] at night the great Haydn Joseph died of debility at his home in the Kleine Steingasse No. 73; he will be buried tomorrow. He was 77 years and 61 days old . . . I pondered Haydn's destiny and wished to

---

1 Fräulein von Kurzbeck wanted Haydn to move to her lodgings in the inner city (now First District), but the plucky old man refused. Pohl III, 275.

2 Griesinger in his biography (50) has a different date and adds some details which he presumably later heard from Elssler; the different dates may be due to the fact that Streicher had the information wrong and Haydn's visitors book, which Griesinger later consulted, has the right one. Griesinger writes: 'Haydn received his last visit on 17 May. It was from a French army captain who was Italian by birth; he wanted to speak to him. The servant [Elssler] said that his master was lying in bed, but the captain begged that he might at least be allowed to see through the keyhole the man he admired so much. Haydn was informed about all this and had the officer come in. The Officer described with enthusiasm the emotions that Haydn's proximity gave him, and the great delight that he found in studying his works. At Haydn's request he sang at the piano, in the next room, 'Mit Würd' and Hoheit angethan' from *The Creation*, performed with great perfection. Haydn was much moved, the officer not less; they embraced and parted with the hottest tears shed on both sides. With a trembling and quite illegible hand the captain wrote down his name. If I have deciphered it correctly, it was Clement Sulemy. From Haydn's room duty called him straight to the Lobau, and from there to the battle chaos of Aspern, where he was probably killed. . . .' Dies (192) also describes the visitor as a captain of the Hussars 'named Sulemi' and gives the date as 26 May. Dies's report is otherwise substantially that of Griesinger.

read his biography, for which I could supply several items of information. He was the son of a penniless cartwright in Rohrau on the Hungarian frontier, came to St Stephen's as a choirboy and remained there until the age of 16. Later years brought him to Eszterháza in the princely Eszterházy [*sic*] service. After the death of Prince Nicolas, he made two journeys to London which truly laid the foundations of his great fame and modest fortune . . .   [Radant, *Rosenbaum*, 148f.]

While Rosenbaum was writing this modest epitaph about his friend, he was planning one of the most horrendous and audacious thefts in Vienna's history: no less than having Haydn's head cut off for purposes of phrenological study. The story, in all its gruesome details, cannot concern us here; those who have a taste for such matters may consult the whole episode in Rosenbaum's Diary. We include here only the actual theft itself, in so far as it concerns our Chronicle up to the Memorial Service in the Scottish Church on 15 June.[1]

> Corpus Christi, 1st [June 1809]: A hot day . . . At 5 o'clock in the afternoon the funeral of the great and immortal singer of *The Creation* and *The Seasons*, Joseph Haydn . . . With Mme Rodler to Haydn's funeral at about 4 o'clock. He lay in his large room dressed in black, not at all disfigured, at his feet the seven medals of honour from Paris, Russia, Sweden and the citizen's medal from Vienna. [Franz] Klemp, the administrator of the Registry Office for real estate in Dornbach, is the executor; his sister's son, [Mathias] Fröhlich [Frölich], a smith in Schwechat, is his sole heir. Johann Elsler [*sic*] inherited 6,000 gulden and his older clothes and linen. Shortly after 5 o'clock Haydn was brought to the Gumpendorf Church in an oaken coffin, carried around it three times, blessed, and taken to the churchyard just inside the Hundsthurmer Linie. Not one Viennese *Kapellmeister* was in the funeral cortège. The Prince [Esterházy] was represented by [the singers] Grell and Möglich, [chief gardener] Pölt, Mme Stocklaß [perhaps the wife of the cook], Dewirth and [book-keeper Joseph] Kerner. – Joseph Haydn was born on March 31st of the year 1732 . . . The hour of his birth was 4 o'clock in the afternoon. . . . – He is buried at [engraver Johann] Löschenkohl's[2] right, on whose left is [the actress] Roose's grave. – After the grave was covered over, I spoke to our worthy [grave-digger and Rosenbaum's accomplice] Jakob Demuth (who has been completely plundered by the French), an Austrian and a rather plump, tall jovial man, about the removal of what is in every respect a venerable head. I arranged everything in detail, appointed tomorrow evening for removing the head and early Sunday morning for delivering it. – Completely exhausted . . . from the dust . . . I dragged myself along the bastions to [Rosenbaum's old friend, Johann Nepomuk] Peter's [another accomplice] and told all the details to that cold man. . . .

---

1 Radant, *Rosenbaum*, 99ff. In February 1802 we find Rosenbaum saying, 'We talked a great deal about Schall's theory of phrenology'. By 'Schall' Rosenbaum meant Dr Franz Joseph Gall (1758–1828), according to whose theory one 'could determine, from the skull, the degree and extent of the mental powers' (Griesinger: see Olleson, *Griesinger*, letter of 26 April 1800). The theft of Haydn's skull was to further the Gallian study, conducted by Rosenbaum and his friends. About Haydn's skull, which (since 1954) has now been reunited with the body in Eisenstadt (whither Prince Esterházy had arranged to have Haydn's remains brought in November 1820), see Julius Tandler *Über den Schädl Haydns* (*Separatum* from a lecture held at the Anthropologische Gesellschaft in Vienna on 24 March 1909; *Mitteilungen der anthropologischen Gesellschaft in Wien*, Jahrgang 39); Ämilian Kloiber, *Franz Joseph und Johann Michael Haydn: Eine familienanthropologische Studie* (*Separatum* from *Burgenländische Heimatblätter*, 21. Jg. Heft 2), Eisenstadt 1959, pp. 113ff. We would suggest that the pastel picture supposedly representing Joseph Haydn (reproduced there on p. 130, also in Somfai, p. 193), from the Esterházy Castle at Eisenstadt, may in fact represent Johann Haydn, the tenor.

2 He had published Haydn's silhouette in 1786. Rosenbaum had already arranged that Betty Roose's head be cut off: see Radant, 143ff.

Friday, 2nd June 1809 : . . . at about 9 : 30 o'clock with Th— and Kerner to Jos. Haydn's Requiem in the Gumpendorf Church. A Requiem [for Archbishop Schrattenbach, 1771 ?] by Mich. Haydn was performed abominably. Except for Th—, not a single Viennese artist sang . . . Not one *Kapellmeister* from the whole of Vienna appeared . . . Saw Eckhardt [another accomplice] in the evening, went with him to find the grave-diggers in the dead house . . . We spoke with them about the removal of Haydn's head and arranged to come at 9 o'clock tomorrow. – From there I drove to Gumpendorf . . . then to the church-yard which I found quite empty; and I waited in vain . . .

Saturday, 3rd: . . . To the Hundsthurmer Linie with Peter at about 8 o'clock. We waited for Jakob Demuth to bring the head. He did not appear, because he had been given a beating [by French soldiers] during the night . . . From there to the hospital to inform the corpse-bearers that we will bring the head tomorrow . . . [Eckhardt worked at the Allgemeines Krankenhaus – general hospital – in Vienna].

Sunday, 4th: [Löschenkohl's former mistress] Mme Geissler, Peter and [valuer in the city tax office Michael] Jungmann arrived at about 8 o'clock. We drove to the Hundsthurmer Linie, I got out and received, from Jakob Demuth, the most valuable relic of Joseph Haydn. – It smelled fearfully. When I climbed into the carriage with the bundle I had to vomit – the stench had overcome me. We drove to the general hospital. I remained during the dissection. The head was already quite green, but still completely recognizable. The sight made a life-long impression on me. The dissection lasted for one hour; the brain, which was of large proportions, stank the most terribly of all. I endured it to the end. We then drove to the corpse-bearer's dwelling. Peter bought a bleached head . . . With a thousand reminders of the diligence and precision with which this head is to be macerated and bleached (I handed it over to him only on Eckhardt's guarantee), we drove into town.

Thursday, 15th [June 1809] . . . at about 10 o'clock I went with Th—, Goldmann and Maffacioli to the Schotten Church. A. W. [*sic*] Mozart's Requiem for Haydn, who died on May 31st, performed by the Tonkünstler and the Friends of Music with a double orchestra of excellent players. In front of the church door and in the church itself civil grenadiers of the 2nd Regiment stood watch together with the French. The church, the pews and altar were draped in black and . . . adorned . . . with lamps. In the middle, a Castrum doloris was erected, on which the 7 medals of honour [lay]. – The prelate of the Schotten Monastery sang the Requiem himself, the soloists were Campi, Marconi (now Schönberger), Frühwald and Pfeiffer [conducted by Joseph Eybler] . . . They were not a good choice, the blend was not good; Campi has no more middle-voice. – The instrumentalists were good; they had needed only one rehearsal. – Secretary of State Maret, several generals, staff officers and senior officers, and many other French were present. – The whole of Viennese society appeared, for the most part in mourning. – The whole was most solemn and worthy of Haydn.

[Radant, *Rosenbaum*, 149–51]

One of the members of the French contingent was Stendhal, later to plagiarize Carpani's biography of Haydn. In a letter to his sister Pauline dated 25 July 1809,[1] Stendhal writes:

. . . Haydn s'est éteint ici il y a un mois environ; c'était le fils d'un simple paysan, qui s'était élevé à l'immensité créatrice par une âme sensible et des études qui lui

---

1 *Aux âmes sensibles* (lettres choisies et présentées par E. Rondot-Lemotte), Paris 1942, p. 100. We are indebted to our old friend, M. Marc Vignal, for bringing this letter to our attention.

donnèrent le moyen de transmettre aux autres les sensations qu'il éprouvait. Huit jours [*sic*] après sa mort, tous les musiciens de la ville se réunirent à Schotten-Kirche pour exécuter en son honneur le Requiem de Mozart. J'y étais, et en uniforme, au deuxième banc; le premier était rempli de la famille du grand homme: trois ou quatre pauvres petites femmes en noir et à figures mesquines. Le Requiem me parut trop bruyant et ne m'intéressa pas; mais je commence à comprendre Don Juan, qu'on donne en allemande presque toutes les semaines au Théâtre de Wieden. . . .

How typical of Haydn's career that even in death he should be reunited for the last time with Mozart and be the (as yet unsuspected) link to the magical world of Stendhal's fantasy – like the Haydn of real life, one part of his being was firmly rooted in the past, but the other peered far forward into the future.

From all these sordid days of grave robbery, armies of occupation and forgetful Viennese *Kapellmeister*, one great reminder of Haydn's physical presence remains to us: the death-mask that Johann Elssler took (pls. 5, 6). It shows us a face of great peace and spirituality – indeed, the features of a man who had died in a state of grace.

Some Documents for 1809–1810

In the chaos of the war, news of Haydn's death took rather longer than usual to reach, for example, the French capital. On 14 June 1809, Luigi Cherubini wrote to Haydn and by some accident, the letter has survived and is at present in the Gesellschaft der Musikfreunde.[1]

[To Haydn from Luigi Cherubini, Paris. *Italian*]

Paris, 14 June 1809.

Dearest Father,

Signor Vienney, who is going to Vienna and who wishes to have the honour of being acquainted with and admiring in person the illustrious and beloved Haydn, is the bearer of this letter. I take the opportunity of this occasion not only to have the advantage of commending myself to my dear Father but also to ask you to receive graciously my friend De Vienney, who is an admirer of the celebrated Haydn, patriarch of music. He will give me your news, which I hope will be such as I wish to hear. Meanwhile I embrace my dear Father tenderly and with respect I am with unchanged admiration,

Your aff^te child
L. Cherubini.

[Address:]   Al celebre
        Giuseppe Haydn.

The second document that must claim our attention is the 'Catalog der hinterbliebenen Joseph Haydnischen Kunstsachen . . .' (Catalogue of the late Joseph Haydn's artistic effects . . .) which – continues the title – 'are to be sold by auction'. This is a MS. in 4° format of which there are two versions: (1) the official document prepared for the Vienna City Magistracy, now in the Archives of the City of Vienna, under the catalogue reference: 'Persönlichkeiten 4/2 der Verlassenschaftsabhandlung'; and (2) a copy prepared for the Court by Ignaz Sauer, the music publishers, with comments by Court *Kapellmeister* Joseph von Eybler, who functioned in two capacities, both as Court Chapel Master and privately, in selecting desirable items

1 To the best of our knowledge this letter was first published in Franco Schlitzer, 'Lettere inedite de Luigi Cherubini', in *La Rassegna Musicale* 1960, Vol. II, 116, in the original Italian.

from the list; this copy is now in the Österreichische Nationalbibliothek, Musiksammlung, cat. S. M. 4843. At the time this catalogue was prepared, it would seem that the Magistracy was in ignorance of the private agreement of 1807 between Haydn and Prince Esterházy, whereby the latter had promised to purchase all the composer's musical effects; thus Eybler and the Court never had a chance to bid for musical items at all. As we have noted earlier, Prince Nicolaus II received Haydn's music and it now forms the core of the Haydn collection in the Esterházy Archives (now National Széchényi Library, Budapest). Professor Larsen (*HÜB*, 28ff.) has worked out in tabular form a concordance between the Elssler Catalogue of Haydn's Library – reproduced *in extenso*, *supra*, pp. 299 ff. –, the present Catalogue, and the whereabouts of the MSS. in question. In a very few cases, the MS. works did not end in the Esterházy Archives; some of them were given away by Haydn himself and some seem to have been permanently 'borrowed' from the Esterházy Archives by Hummel and later found their way to the British Museum (Larsen, *HÜB*, 40); thus these particular MSS. had been, in fact, part of the material that Prince Nicolaus II had promised to purchase from his *Kapellmeister* in 1807. (Hummel was something of a collector, and we were privileged to see the extant Hummel collection of autograph scores so long as it was still housed in the family house at Florence.) Why these Haydn MSS., and many other works by Hummel himself (including the autograph of his Trumpet Concerto of 1803), were detached from the Hummel collection and sold, *via* a Leipzig antiquarian, List & Franke, to the British Museum in 1883, cannot be explained by the present owner of the Hummel estate, Frau Maria Hummel; she believes, however, that the family may have needed money at that time and sold that valuable collection of no less than seventy-one volumes of music to the antiquarian bookseller. The interested reader is referred to Professor Larsen's researches on this subject which, although made prior to 1939, require no emendations whatever.

A second list, showing the contents of Haydn's library (other than music, books on music, and engravings), is also preserved in the same file in the Archives of the City of Vienna as version (1) of the Catalogue of Haydn's artistic effects (see above); we have been obliged, for reasons of space, to omit it here. In version (2), reproduced below, we have, as previously, kept our commentary to the minimum. Since the Catalogue has never been printed, we have listed it in German, as it stands, translating the most important longer items, e.g. the comments at the end by Eybler but not Haydn's titles at the beginning. We have also not considered it necessary to identify in great detail the engravings ('Kupferstiche im Portfeuille') and have limited our commentary; thus we give the dates of the Neidl engraving of Lord Nelson (item 8) and of the Battle of Aboukir (item 29), because they are of interest to students of Haydn, but not the dates of Bartolozzi, etc. prints, which are of only peripheral interest to readers of this book. For explanatory notes see p. 404.

Pour
Mons: Ignaze
Sauer ——
Auf dem St: Stephansplatz
neben dem deutschen
Haus in den Sauer'schen
Kunst und Musickalien-
Handlungsgewölb.

CATALOG
der hinterbliebenen
Joseph Haydnischen
Kunstsachen
welche lizitando verkauft werden.
wird nicht gedruckt.

CATALOG

der hinterlassenen Kunstsachen des am 31. May 809. zu Guntendorf in der kleinen Steingasse in seinem eigenen Hause No. 73. verstorbenen Herrn Joseph Haydn Doktors der Tonkunst, des franz. Nationalinstitutes der Wissenschaften und Künste, wie auch der Königl. Schwedischen und der Wiener musikal. Gesellschaft Mitgliede und Kapellmeisters in wirklichen Diensten des regierenden Herrn Fürsten von Esterhazy, dann Ehrenbürgers der k.k. Haupt- und Residenzstadt Wien, welche am 26. März 810. und die folgenden Tage lizitando verkaufet werden.

No.	KUPFERSTICHE IM PORTEFEUILLE
1.	4. Visitbillets und 4. Ansichten von Rohrau.
2.	6. Portraits verschiedener Tonkünstler.
3.	2. gezeichnete Köpfe.
4.	1. Monument und 1. anderes.
5.	Lady Elizabeth Lambert von Guttenbrunn.
6.	Misstresse Gautherot von Bartolozzi.
7.	Mar. Antoine Königin von Frankreich von Dies.
8.	Admiral Nelson von Neidl und
9.	detto andres.
10.	Peter Hænsel von Pfeiffer.
11.	The persian Sybille nach Guercino und
12.	die Herodias nach Guido Reni, beide von Facius.
13.	The Nun nach Westall von Chesmann.
14.	a Smoking Club.
15.	Cupido nach Correg[g]io von Pichler.
16.	J. L. Dussek.
17.	Pleyel von Nutter
18.	Cramer.
19.	Salomon.
20.	Ein anderes Portrait von der Schrift.
21.	4. ovale Unterhaltungsstücke.
22.	Age and Infancy nach Opie von Smith.
23.	29. Blatt Abbildung der neuen Adjustierung der k.k. Armee nach Kininger von Mannsfeld auf Velin
24.	4. Thierstücke nach Morland von Smith.
25.	The Judgment of Britan[n]ia von Bartolozzi.
26.	6. Unterhaltungen nach Morland von Smith.
27.	2. Blatt: Albina und Eloisa von dto.
28.	Ladana nach Cosway von Bartolozzi.
29.	Plan der Schlacht bei Abbukir, englisch.
30.	12. Blatt: die 12. Monate, ovale Unterhaltungen nach Hamilton von Bartolozzi und andere.
31.	2. Blatt: Doctor primrose und Thornhill, oval nach Ramberg von Bartolozzi.
32.	The Nymph of immortality nach Cipriani von dto.
33.	Diva Magdalena nach Correg[g]io von dto.
34.	John Earl of Chatham nach de Koster von Keating.
35.	2. Blatt: Sabrina regleasing [*sic*] the Lady from the Enchanted Maaid [*sic*], und the Brothers driving off Comus and his Spirits nach Stotthard von Scott.
36.	Eine Loge die heilige Familie vorstellend nach del Sarto von Bartolozzi.
37.	The Boxing Match nach Einsle von Grozer.
38.	2. Unterhaltungen nach Westall von Hogg.

39.	The Woodmann nach Parker von Bartolozzi.
40.	The Mouse-trap nach Huck von Park.
41.	Cupid sleeping nach Westall von Nutter.
42.	The Weird Sisters nach Fuseli von Smith.
43.	1. Blatt mit den berühmtesten Compositeurs von verchiedenen Meistern.
44.	The Resurrection of a pious Family nach Peters von Bartolozzi.
45.	Eine bei einem Sterbbette trauernde Familie nach Peters von dto, von der Schrift.
46.	2. Blatt: Rosalie et Lubin, dann Lubin et Rosalie nach Beechey und Paye von Park.
47.	2. Blatt The Mouse's petition und Marian nach Bunburg von Bartolozzi und Tomkins.
48.	The Death of Œdipus nach Fuseli von Ward.
49.	2. Blatt: Education dann Natura nach Singleton von Bond und Godby.
50.	Bartolozzi nach Violet von Bouilliard.
51.	Apollo and the Muses nach Guttenbrunn von Facius.
52.	Antioppe nach Van Dyk und
53.	Castor and Pollux nach Rubens, beide von Green.
54.	1. Unterhaltung von Grozer.
	Nota. Nach diesen wird der Nachtrag bei No. 610 anfangend, ausgerufen.

KUPFERSTICH UNTER GLAS UND RAHME, DANN ANDERE SACHEN.

55.	3. Stück: Patience in a punt, dann Bethnal Green und ein anderes nach Drawing von Bunburg.
56.	2. Stück: Pretty Dick und Jump Pussey nach Metz von Scott.
57.	2. Unterhaltungen nach Ciprian[i] von Bartolozzi.
58.	2. Stück: Prince and Princess of Walles von Orme.
59.	2. ovale Kindergruppen von Bartolozzi.
60.	2. Stück: Comic readings, dann Tragic readings nach Boyne von Knight.
61.	Cherubini in Handzeichnung.
62.	Gyrowetz in dto oval.
63.	Kaiser Franz und Gemahlin M. Teresia in Medaillons, dann
64.	Lignovsky detto, alle 3. Gypsabdrücke.
65.	Mozart dto in Gyps und
66.	Bach, dann eine Virtuosin aus Scottland in Silhouette [Sophia Corri?].
67.	Michael Haydn poußirt und
68.	ein mythologischer Gypsabdruck.
69.	Joseph Haydn in Porzelainerde.
70.	detto in Wachs poußirt von Irwach.
71.	detto als Wachsbüste unter Glassturz von Thaler.
72.	Monument: Rohrau gab ihm das Leben.
73.	Gestickter Lichtschirm.
74.	Ein Apollo aus Allabaster von Sack unter Glassturz.
75.	1. Perspektiv mit 4 Zügen, wobey jedoch das Objektivglas abgehet.
76.	Joseph Haydn's Büste aus Porzelainerde von Grassy, legirt dem Herrn Grafen v. Harrach.
77.	detto aus Bley auf Postament.
78.	Die Pero ernähret ihren Vater, Conon im Gefängniß durch ihre Brust. Ganze Figuren in Wachs poußirt unter Glassturz.

MUSICALISCHE INSTRUMENTE.

79.	Ein mit Mahagonyholz ausgelegtes mit Metalleisten verziertes franz. Pianoforte von tief F bis hoch C. $5\frac{1}{2}$ Octav mit den gewöhnlichen Veränderungen von Erard et Freres Compagnie.
80.	Ein detto aus massiven Mahagonyholz, die Klaviatur so wie oben von Longman and Broderip in London.

JOSEPH HAYDN'S GESTOCHENE COMPOSITIONEN.

×	81.	Der Sturm. Chor mit Orchester deutsch und italienisch. Leipziger Auflage. 2. Exemplarien.
	82.	Die Jahreszeiten in Partitur. Leipziger Auflage. 2. Bände groß Fol gebunden, deutsch und ital., zugleich mit den besondern Singspart.
	83.	Dieselben im Klavierauszuge übersezt von Neukomm. 4. Bände.
	84.⎫ 85.⎬ 86.⎭	Ebendieselben für dto, Leipz. Auflage deutsch und französisch. 3. Exempl.

87. 88. }	detto für detto deutsch und englisch. 2 Ex.
89.	detto in Quartetten übersezt von Neukomm. 4. Bände.
90.	Die Worte des Erlösers am Kreuze in Partitur, deutsch und ital. Leipz. Auflage. 1. Band.
91.	detto in Instrumentalmusick bei Artaria.
92.	detto in Klavierauszug deutsch und ital. Leipzig 1. Band.
93.	Die Schöpfung in Partitur englisch und deutsch, eigenen Auflage in 2. Bänden.
94.	Dieselbe in Partitur ital. und franz. pariser Aufl.
95.	detto gebunden.
96.	Dieselbe im Klavierauszug, eben auch pariser Auflage.
97.	detto.
98.	Dieselbe in detto, übersetzt von Neukomm, deutsch.
99.	Stabat Mater in Part. engl. Aufl. mit lat. Text.
100.	detto leipziger Aufl mit lat. und deutschen Text.
101.	detto.
102.	detto im Klavierauszug mit deutschen Text.
103.	Missa in B. No. 1. in Part. leipz. Aufl.
104.	detto.
105.	Missa in C. No. 2. detto. detto.
106.	detto.
107.	Missa in D. mol No. 3. detto. detto.
108.	detto.
109.	Te Deum Laudamus in Partitur, leipz. Auflage mit lat. und deutschen Text.
110.	Oeuvres d'Haydn en Partition, à Paris chez Pleyel: Simphonie in Dis, Taschenformat.
111.	detto.
112.	detto „ D mol.
113.	detto „ B.
114.	detto „ Dis.
115.	6. Sinfonie a grand Orchestre Oeuv. 35. presso Artaria.
116.	Oeuvres d'Haydn en Partition à Paris chez Pleyel: 3. Quatuors No. 1.
117.	detti „ „ 2.
118. 119. }	detti „ „ 3. 2. Ex.
120.	detti „ „ 4.
121.	detti „ „ 5.
122.	detti „ „ 6.
123.	detti „ „ 7.
124.	detti „ „ 8.
125.	detti „ „ 9.
126.	detti „ „ 10.
127.	Collection complette de Quatuors, à Paris chez Pleyel, enthält 80. Quartetten, 4. Bände groß Fol.
128.	3. Quat. für den Grafen Appony. Oeuv. 74.
129.	3. detti „ —— Erdödy. „ 75. No. 1.2.3.
130.	3. detti „ —— —— „ 76. „ 4.5.6.
131.	2. detti „ den Fürsten Lobkowitz. „ 77.
× 132.	82.<u>me</u> Dernier Quatuor für Comte de Fries. Das letzte ist ein nur bis zum Men. und Trio ausgeschriebenes Werk, denn den Schluß Canon hat Breitkopf aus den Haydnischen 3. und 4. stimmigen Gesängen entlehnt. 2. Ex.
133.	Oeuvres d'Haydn contenant 5. Son. p. Clav. avec Violon et Vlle, Leipziger Auflage, Cahier 3.
134.	detti „ „ „ 4.
× 135.	detti „ „ „ 5.
× 136.	detti „ „ „ 6.
× 137.	detti „ „ „ 7.
× 138.	detti p. Clav. seul ∮.1.
× 139.	detti „ „ „ ∮.2.
140.	3. Son: p. Clav. avec Violon et Vlle, Oeuv. 70. engl. Auflage.
141.	3. detti.
142.	Son p. Clav. London.
143.	Grand Son. p. Clav. Oeuv. 82.
144.	detto.
145.	Son. p. Clav. „ 87.

146.	3. Son. p. Clav. avec Violon et Vlle. Oeuv. 70. engl. Aufl.
147.	Son. p. Clav. No. 213. bei Traeg.
148.	Two favorite Overtures p. Clav.
149.	Trio p. Clav. avec Violon et Vlle engl. No. 14.
150.	Overture adapted for the Harpsichord with an Accomp. Violin and Violoncello. No. 2.
151.	detto „ „ 3.
152.	detto „ „ 5.
153.	Quartetto Op. 72: arranged for the Clav. with Violin and Vllo.
154.	detto.
155.	Symphonies No. 7. 8. 9. 10. 11. and 12. adapted for the Piano Forte with Violin and Violoncello.
156.	Variations p. Clav. Oeuv. 83.
157.	Variations p. detto.
× 158.	Var. p. detto über Gott erhalte den Kaiser.
159.	12. Men. p. Clav. und
160.	12. deutsche p. detto dann.
161.	Landler für detto.
162.	Diese Landler dreystimmig.
163.	Men. con Trio in Canone p. Clav.
164.	detto.
165.	Oeuvres d'Haydn. 15. Airs et Chanons avec Clav. mit deutsch und franz. Text. Cah. 8.
166.	detti. „ „ „ 9.
167.	Dreystimmige Gesänge am Klavier, bei Artaria.
168.	detti noch 2. Ex.
169.	Vierstimmige detti.
170.	detti noch 2. Ex.
× 171.	3. und 4. stimmige beisammen, leipz. Aufl.
172.	Duetto with Clav. mit ital. Text.
173.	12. Lieder am Klavier 2ter Theil bei Artaria.
174.	Aria: Or vicina a te mio Cuore in Part bei detto.
× 175.	Ariana à Naxos with Clav. mit ital Text.
176.	detto.
177.	6. Lieder am Klavier 1ter Theil bei Artaria.
178.	6. detti 2ter ——
179. 180.	6. Lieder am Klavier 3ter Theil bei Artaria. 2 Ex.
181.	6. detti 4ter ——
182.	6. Lieder am Klav: 76.st Werk bei Andrè [*sic*].
183. 184. 185. 186.	Der schlaue und dienstfertige Pudel, Gesang am Klav. 4. Ex.
187.	6. engl. Lieder am Klavier.
× 188.	Orfeo e Euridice, Drama im Klavierauszug mit ital: und deutschen Text.
189. 190.	detto 2. Ex.
191.	12. Catches and Glees with Clav.
192. 193.	detti.
194.	Selection of Original Scots Songs with Clav. Vol. 2.
195.	detti „ „ „ „ 3.
196.	Fifty scottish songs with Clav. Violin and Vllo. 3ter Theil.

GESTOCHENE MUSICALIEN VON VERSCHIEDENEN MEISTERN.

197.	Mozart. Messe de Requiem in Part mit deutsch und lat. Text steif in Seide gebunden mit Goldschnitt.
198.	—— Don Juan in Part. mit ital und deutschen Text. 2. B. und 1. Heft Worte allein.
199.	—— 6. Quat. p. 2. Vlini, Viola è Vllo. Op. 10. bei Artaria.
× 200.	—— 6. Son. p. Clav. leipz. Aufl. Cah. 1.
× 201.	—— 12. erley Var. p. detto „ 2.

×	202.	——	6. Son. p. clav. avec Violon	„ 4.
×	203.	——	14. Differ. Pieces p. Clav.	„ 6.
×	204.	Mozart	6. Son. a 4. Mains	„ 7.
×	205.	——	6. Pieces, worunter 2. a 4. mains	„ 8.
×	206.	——	5. Son. p. Clav. avec Violon	„ 9.
	207.	Gräff.	Three Quartetts for a Flute, Violin, Tenor and Vlle. Op. 8.	
	208.	Barthelemon. Glee for the anniversary of the philantropic [sic] Society.		
	209.	Barthelemon. Miss. Three Hymnes. Op. 3.		
	210.	—— —— 3. Son. for the Pianoforte Op. 1.		
	211.	—— Son. for detto „ 3.		
	212.	Struck. Kantate: Die Geburtsfeyer einer Mutter und		
	213.	—— Menuetto a 4. m.		
	214.	—— 3. Son. p. Clav. Violon et Vlle: Offenbach Oeuv. 1.		
	215.	—— Quatuor p. 2. Vlons, Alto et Vlle. „ „ 2.		
	216.	Wölfl. 3. Trios p. Clav. Oeuv. 5.		
	217.	Haigh. 3. Son. p. Clav. „ 8.		
	218.	Bertini. 3. grand Sonatas for the Clav. with Violin. Op. 1.		
	219.	Beethoven. 3. Son. p. Clav. Oeuv. 2. bei Artaria.		
	220.	— Var. p. Clav. Op. 2. bei Træg.		
	221.⎫			
	222.⎬	Schulthesius. Riconciliazione fra due Amici p. Clav. Op. 12. 3. Ex.		
	223.⎭			
	224.	Wikmanson. tre Quartetter för tva Violoner, Alt och Violoncelle. OP. 1. Stockholm.		
	225.	Gallus. 3. Quat. p. 2. Vlons, Alte et Vlle. Oeuv. 6. bei Træg.		
	226.	Latrobe. 3. Sonatas for the Clav. Op. 3.		
×	227.	Romberg. 3. Quat. p. 2: Vlons, Alto et Basso. Oeuv. 1. Liv. 1.		
	228.	Eberl. Grand Son. p. Clav. Oeuv. 12.		
	229.	Lessel. 3. Duos p. 2: Flutes.		
	230.	—— 3. Son. p. Clav. Oeuv: 2.		
	231.	Barth Schlesische musikalische Blumenlese 1. und 2tes Heft.		
	232.	—— detto.		
	233.	Zulehner: Andante et Rondeau p. Clav. Oeuv. 5.		
	234.	Campbell. Twelve Songs.		
	235.	Hummel. Son. p. Clav. Op. 13.		
	236.	Weber. 3. Quat. p. 2. Vlons, Alto et Vlle. Oeuv. 8.		
	237.	Edelmann. Chaconne p. Clav. et Violon.		
	238.	Albrechtsberger. 6. – Fughe p. Organo. Op. 7.		
	239.	—— 6. Quat. p. 2. Violoni, Viola e Basso. Op. 20.		
	240.	Leidesdorf. Grand Trio p. Clav. Flute et Alto. Op. 14.		
	241.	Lubi Mariane. Oestreichs Fama, eine Kantate, dann noch andre 12. deutsche Lieder am Klavier.		
	242.	—— Leonardo und Blandine.		
	243.	—— detto.		
	244.	Bachmann. Gesänge aus dem Orpheus am Klavier.		
	245.	Bage le Baron. Air de Malbrough, Var. p. Clav.		
	246.	—— 3. Sinf. a grand Orchestre.		
	247.⎫			
	248.⎭	Sixt. 12. Lieder am Klavier. 2. Ex.		
	249.	Sammlung von Liedern aus den beßten deutschen Dichtern. Gesänge am Klavier, 1tes Heft und Allgemeine musikalische Bibliothek 4tes Heft, dann Bengraf Sinngedicht, alle 3. zusammen.		
×	250.	Vogler. Hermann von Unna, Klavierauszug.		
	251.	Callcott, Cooke, Damby, Hindle, Stevens pp Professional Collection of Glees für 3. bis 5. Stimmen.		
	252.	Schulz. Uzens lyrische Gedichte religiösen Inhaltes, Gesänge am Klavier.		
	253.	—— Religiöse Oden und Lieder am Klavier.		
	254.	Dupuis. Pieces for the Organ or Clav. Op. 8.		
	255.	Destouches. 3. Son. p. Clav. Oeuv. 1.		
	256.	Crinazzi. 6 Treni o sia Cantate lugubri in Morte di Maria Teresa. Op. 3.		
	257.	Kromer. Marcia p. Clav.		
	258.	Hoffmeister. Quat. p. 2. Vlons, Alto et Vlle, dann		
		—— Terzetto primo p. 2 Violini è Vlle.		
×	259.	Händel. Te Deum Laudamus mit lat. Text.		
×	260.	—— Jephtha an Oratorio.		
×	261.	—— Aria dell'Opera di Rinaldo mit ital. Text. London.		

	262.	Bach Chretien. 6. Son. p. Clav. avec Violon.
×	263.	Bach Emanuel. Klaviersonaten und Rondos. 3te Sammlung.
×	264.	—— —— detti und freye Fantasien 5te ——
×	265.	—— —— Heilig in Partitur.
	266.	—— —— geistliche Gesänge 2te Sammlung.
×	266. [*sic*]	Bach Sebastian. Motetten in Part. 1te und 2te Heft.
×	267.	—— —— Præludien und Fugen durch alle Töne. zürch. Aufl.
	268.	Kranz. Romanze aus dem theatralischen Abentheuer.
×	269.	Naumann. Cora eine Oper mit deutschen Text.
	270.	Eberlin. 9. Toccate et Fughe per l'Organo.
	271.	Schmidt. Hymne zur Königl. preuß. Huldigungsfeyer in Königsberg a 798. dann.
	272.	Förster. Kantate zur Huldigungsfeyer in Wien a 792.
	273.	Klein. Fantasia p. Clav. Op. 2.
	274.	Duny. Lisle des Foux in Part. mit franz. Text.
	275.	Lampugnani. The Favourite Songs in the Opera call'd Siroe in Part. mit ital Text.
	276.	a Collection of Catches, Canons, Glees, Duetts pp von verschiedenen Meistern. Vol. 2.3.4. 3.B. mit engl Text.
	277.	Collection of Catches, Glees, Canons, Canzonetts, Madrigals pp in engl. Sprache von verschied. Meistern. 3. Hefte und 1. Band.
	278.	Tomo terzo. Ariette nazionali, Noturni mit Slavischen, inländischen, franz. und ital Text. 1. Band.
	279.	a Selection of the most favourite Scots Songs by eminent Masters mit 1. Titelblatt von Bartolozzi.
	280.	detto.
	281.	Arnold. The Psalms of David mit engl Text und einem Titelkupfer von Medland.
	282.	Cooke. Nine Glees and two Duets.
	283.	Grünwald. 12. deutsche Lieder am Klavier.
	284.	Brandes. Musikalischer Nachlaß. 1. Band.
	285.	Sterkel. 3. Son. p. Clav. avec 1 Violon, dann
	286.	Lickl. 6. Var. p. Clav.
	287.	Haesler. Klavier- und Singstücke 1te Sammlung.
	288.	Webbe. Ode on St. Cecilia dann Address to the Thames. 2. Hefte mit engl. Text und Favorite Glees. 2. Ex.
	289.	—— 6. French Ariettes for the Voice and Clav.
	290.	—— Vocal Music in two, three, four and five Parts, ninth Book.
	291.	Harrison. a Favorite Glee : never till now, dann
	292.	Sidler. Phantasia p. Clav.
	293.	Callcott. Explanation of the Notes, Marks, Words pp in Music.
	294.	Wanhal. Caprice p. Clav.
	295.	Teleman. 6. Ouverturen p. Clav. dann
	296.	Dretzel. Harmonische Ergötzung am Klavier.
	297.	Kunzen. Hymne auf Gott, Gesang am Klavier.
	298.	Schröter. Three Quintettos for the Clav. Flute, Violin, Tenor and Violoncello.
	299.	—— 6. Sonatas for the Pianoforte. Op. 2.
	300.	—— 6. Conc. for detto „ 3.
	301.	—— 6. Son. for detto „ 4.
	302.	—— 6. Conc. for detto „ 5.
	303.	—— 3. Son. for detto „ 6.
	304.	Diettenhofer. The Celebrated Canon : non nobis Domine, adapted as a Fugue for the Organ.
	305.	Pasterwitz. 8. Fugues p. l'Organo. Op. 2.
	306.	Trnka. 10. Canoni a tre Voci.
	307.	Kozeluch. 3. Son. p. Clav. Violino e Vllo.
	308.	Piticchio. 12. Canzonette italiane con Clav. 2. Ex. dann
	309.	Air qui fut chante à Paris. bei Träg.
	310.	Hänsel. 3. Quat. a 2. Vlons, Alto et Vlle. Oeuv. 1.
	311.	Kreusser. Der Tod Jesu, eine Kantate in Partitur.
	312.	Attwood. the adopted Child mit engl. Text.
	313.	Jenkins. new Scotch Music with a Harpsichord.
	314.	Tomich. a Sonata for the Clav.
	315.	—— 3. Son. for detto, Op. 3.
	316.	Nugent. 6. french Romances and one italian Arietta for the Clav. 2. Ex.
	317.	Madrigale primo. Tom. 1. mit ital. Text ohne Author.
	318.	Clementi. Fuga p. Clav.
	319.	—— 3. Son. for the Clav. with Violin and Vllo. Op. 28.

320.	Monatsfrüchte für Klavier und Gesang, 1tes bis 4tes Heft.
321.	Polzelli. Serenade en Trio p. Flute, Violon et Alto. Oeuv. 1.
322.	Kanne. Der stille Geist, gedicht von Böhlendorf.
323.	—— La Tempesta. Op. 17. deutsch und ital.
324.	Reichard. 12. Elegies et Romances p. Clav. mit franz. Text.
325.	Himmel. Gesänge aus Tiedges Urania. Op. 18.
326.	Pleyel. 3. Quat. conc. p. 2. Vlons, Alte et Basse. 9$^{\underline{e}}$ Oeuvre de Quatuors. Straßburger Aufl.
327.	Burney. 12. Canzonetti a due Voci in Canone mit ital Text.
328.	Reicha. 36. Fugues p. Clav.
329.	Earl of Abingdon. a Representation of the Execution of Mary Queen of Scots, dann Selection twelve Psalms and Hymns mit 8. feinen Kupfern. 1. Band.
330.	Favart. Acajou, Opera comique mit franz. Text.
331.	Gretri. Lucile, Comèdie mit franz. Text in Part. Oeuv. 2.
✕ 332.	—— Les deux Avares, Opera boufon franz. Part. „ 5.
333.	par M^{r}. L'Isle sonante, Opera comique. dto.
334.	—— Aline, Ballet heroique detto.
335.	Philidor. Les Femmes vengees, Op. comique detto.
336.	M.D.Z. L'Erreur d'un moment, Comèdie detto.
337.	—— Julie, Comèdie detto.
338.	Monsigny. Le Deserteur, Drama detto.
339.	The Edinburg musical. Miscellany.
340.	Borde. Choix de Chansons mit in Kupfer gestochenen Noten und 26. bildlichen Vorstellungen von Moreau. 1. Band.
341.	Tattersall. Improved Psalmody für 3. Singstimmen 3. Heft.
342.	Radicati. Quat. p. 2. Vlons, Alte et Vlle. Oeuv. 8.
343.	—— detto. „ 11.
344.	—— 3. Quat. p. detti „ 14.
345.	—— 3. detti „ 16.
✕ 346.	Neukomm. Musikalisches Gebet für den rußischen Kaiser 4. stimmig beim Klavier in rußischer und deutscher Sprache.

Geschriebene Musicalien von Jos. Haydns Composition.

347.	Orpheo. Eine in England komponirte ital. Oper in Partitur, jedoch nicht ganz.
348.	Die Jahreszeiten in Partitur. 4. Hefte.
349.	Die Schöpfung in Part. mit engl. und deutschen Text. 3. Bände.
350.	detto ausgeschrieben mit doppelten Stimmen für ein stark besetztes Orchester.
351.	Die sieben Worte für ein kleines Orchester ausgeschrieben, die Singstimmen sind von Fribert.
352.	detto für ein großes Orchester 3. fach ausgeschrieben mit der Klavierspart. Die Singstimmen sind von Haydn selbst.
✕ 353.	Stabat Mater. 2. fach für ein großes Orchester ausgeschrieben mit lat. Text.
✕ 354.	Chor: Der Sturm, detto mit deutschen Text.
355.	detto.
356.	Missa brevis in F. in Partitur. Diese war die erste Messe, welche Herr Haydn noch als Student komponirte.
✕ 357.	Missa ex C. in tempore belli, geschrieben in Eisenstadt a 796. eigenhändige Partitur.
358.	Nelson. Missa in D. minor, geschrieben in Eisenstadt a 798. eigenhändige Partitur.
359.	Die sieben Worte, eigenhändige Partitur.
360.	Coro aus dem Oratorio Tobias, eigenhändige Partitur.
✕ 361.	Triumph Chor der Dänen, eigenhändige Partitur, welche Komposition Niemand hat.
362.	Sinfonie in D. eigenhändige Partitur a 776.
363.	—— „ A. detto „ 772.
364.	—— „ G. detto mit Men. und Trio al reverso „ 772.
✕ 365.	Sinfonie in Fis minor mit einem scherzhaften Finale, während welchem sich von der Schlußzeit nach und nach alle Instrumentisten bis auf 2. Violinspieler vom Orchester verlieren. Eigenhändige Partitur. a 1772.
366.	—— in B. eigenhändige Partitur „ 1767.
367.	—— in Dis detto „ 1764.
368.	—— le midi in C, durchaus mit Violino conc. eigenhändige Partitur a 761.
369.	—— in D. eigenhändige Partitur. „ 774.
370.	—— „ G. detto „ 764.
371.	—— „ C. detto „ 765.
372.	—— „ E. detto „ 765.

373.	——	,, D. detto	,, 764.
374.	——	,, E. detto	,, 763.
375.	——	,, D. detto	,, 763.
376.	——	,, G. detto	

376. ist eine von den 12. englischen, wovon jedoch das Adagio fehlet.

377.	——	in A. eigenhändige Partitur	a 764.
378.	——	,, D. detto	,, 766.
379.	——	,, D. detto	,, 771.
380.	——	,, G. detto	,, 774.

381. Coro Der Sturm. Partitur mit deutschem Text.

382. detto.

383. detto in Partitur, worein Herr Haydn die Instrumentierung eigenhändig geschrieben hat, mit deutschem Text.

384. detto eigenhändige Partitur mit engl. Text a 792.

385. 2. Quart. in G. und F. p. 2. Violini, Viola e Vllo. dem Herrn Fürsten von Lobkowitz zugeeignet. eigenh. Part. a 799.

386. 3. Quart. in F.B. und Dis für ebendenselben in Partitur.

387. Divertimento in G. für den Pariton, 2. Violini, 2. Corni, 1. Viola Violoncello è Violone eigenhändige Partitur a 775.

388. —— in F. p. 2. Violini, 2. Corni inglaise, 2. Fagotti, 2. Corni eigenhändige Partitur a 760.

389. —— in G. p. Pariton, Viola è Vlle eigenhänd. Part. a 766.

390. Notturno in G. p. Flauto, Oboe, 2. Violini, 2. Viole, 2. Corni und Vlle. eigenhändige Partitur.

391. —— in F. p. 2. Lire, 2. Clarinetti, 2. Viole, 2. Corni, 1. Vlle. Der erste Ternion ist eigenhändige Partitur.

392. Opera. Le Pescatrici in 3. Akten, eigenhändige nicht ganze Partitur, welche jedoch durch den Kunsthändler Træg ergänzet werden kann. mit Büchel a 769.

393. —— lo speziale in 3. Akten. Anmerkung wie oben.

394. —— il Mondo della Luna in 3. Akten. detto.

395. —— la fedelta premiata in 3. Akten. detto.

396. —— Orlando Paladino in 3. Akten. detto.

397. —— die nämliche ganz kopirt in Part. mit deutschem Text.

398. Opernarien. eigenhändige jedoch nicht ganze Partituren.

399. Opera. L'Incontro improviso in 3. Akten a 777.
Eigenhändige ganze Partitur mit Büchel.

400. —— L'Infedelta delusa in 3. Akten, eigenhändige Partitur mit Büchel.

401. —— la Canterina a 766. eigenhändige Partitur mit Büchel.

402. —— Von Armida den 3ten Akt kopirt in Partitur mit Büchel.

403. —— Quartetto. ah vedrai aus Acide et Galatea, eigenhändige Partitur.

404.	Aria.	Caro volpino amabile.	detto.
405.	——	Tergi in vozzosi.	detto.
406.	——	Per che stupisci tanto.	detto.
407.	——	un Cor si tenero in petto.	detto.
408.	——	Voglio amar e vuo scherzare.	detto.
409.	——	in Felice sventurata a 1789.	detto.
410.	——	se tu mi sprezzi ingrata 1788.	detto
411.	——	se men gentile l'aspetto ostento.	detto
412.	——	la beltà che m'innamora dolce a 762.	detto
413.	——	ah tu n'senti amico a 1786.	detto
414.	——	da che penso a maritarmi a 790.	detto.
415.	——	d'una sposa mechinella mit Oboe Solo.	detto.
416.	Duetto.	Senti qui che il sentirai am Klavier.	detto.
417.	2. Deutsche Lieder am Klavier.		detto.

418. 12. Menuetten eigenhändig übersezt aufs Klavier.

× 419. Hungarischer Nationalmarsch für eine große Harmonie, eigenhändige Partitur.

× 420. Englischer Marsch für detto in detto.

× 421. Concerto in G. per la Lira organizata in Partitur. Wurde mit den folgenden für den König von Neapel komponirt.

422. —— in F. detto.

423. —— in F. ein anderes, ausgeschrieben für detto.

424. —— in G. detto.

425. —— in C. detto.

426. Notturno in C. per la Lira in Partitur für ebendenselben.

427. —— in C. detto detto.

	428.	——	in G. detto detto.
	429.	——	in C. a Flauto, Oboe, 2. Violini o Clarinetti, 2. Viole e Vlle in Stimmen ausgeschrieben.
	430.	——	in C. a 2. Violini, Flauto è Oboe, 2. Corni, 2. Viole et Vlle. in detti.
	431.	——	in F. für detto in detti.
	432.	Sinfonie in D. in Partitur, eine von den englischen.	
	433.	——	„ Dis. detto, detto.
	434.	——	„ D mol. detto, detto.
	435.	——	„ D. detto, detto mit dem Paukenschlag.
	436.	——	„ G. in Partitur.
	437.	——	„ F. detto.
×	438.	——	„ Dis auf blaues Postpapier ausgeschrieben.
×	439.	——	„ C. detto.
×	440.	——	6. beisammen detto.
×	441.	——	in F. auf Orchesterpapier ausgeschrieben.
×	442.	——	„ Dis. detto.
×	443.	——	„ D. detto.
×	444.	——	„ Dis. detto.
×	445.	——	„ H. detto.
×	446.	——	„ B. detto.
×	447.	——	„ B. detto.
×	448.	——	„ C. detto.
×	449.	——	„ D. detto.
×	450.	Sinfonie in C. mol ausgeschrieben.	
×	451.	——	„ B. detto.
×	452.	——	„ Dis detto.
×	453.	——	„ C. detto.
×	454.	——	„ G. detto mit abgängiger Baßstimme.
×	455.	——	le midi ausgeschrieben.
×	456.	——	concertante in B. detto.
×	457.	——	in F. ausgeschrieben.
×	458.	——	„ B. detto.
×	459.	——	„ B. detto.
×	460.	——	„ D. detto.

461.	Quartetto in C.	⎫	
462.	——	„ Dis	
463.	——	„ B.	a 2. Violoni, Alto è Violoncello auf klein Postpapier. Sind die 6.
464.	——	„ Fis mol	preußischen, und können auch auf einmal verkaufet werden.
465.	——	„ D.	
466.	——	„ F.	⎭
467.	——	in D.	⎫
468.	——	„ G.	
469.	——	„ Dis.	für die nämlichen Instrumente auf Kirchenpapier für Erdödy
470.	——	„ D. mol.	ausgeschrieben.
471.	——	„ B.	
472.	——	„ C.	⎭
473.	——	in B.	⎫
474.	——	„ D.	detti für Apony ausgeschrieben.
475.	——	„ Dis.	⎭
476.	Quartetto in C.	⎫	
477.	——	„ Fismol.	p. detti für ebendenselben ausgeschrieben.
478.	——	„ C.	⎭
479.	Divertimento ex F.	⎫	
480.	——	„ C.	
481.	——	„ D.	
482.	——	„ D.	
483.	——	„ G.	
484.	——	„ D.	× per il Pariton, Viola e Violoncello.
485.	——	„ G.	[later addition:] nb wenn sie nicht hoch lauffen
486.	——	„ D.	
487.	——	„ D.	
488.	——	„ D.	
489.	——	„ D.	
490.	——	„ A.	
491.	Duetto	in G.	⎭

×	492.	24. Divertimenti p. detti 2ter Theil gebunden in Schuber.
	493.	Duetto in B. aus Armida in Partitur.
	494.	Aria „ Dis: la moglie quando e buona in detto.
	495.	Aria „ Dis: dice benissimo aus la Scuola de Gelosi in detto.
	496.	—— „ B: Signor voi sapete aus la vera Costanza in detto.
	497.	10. drey- und vierstimmige deutsche Gesänge am Klavier.
	498.	Miserere mit lat. Text einstimmig am Klavier, aus den sieben Worten von einem englischen Komponisten.
	499.	Quartetto: dall'Isola disabitata in Partitur. Die Oper ist mit dem Esterhazyschen Theater verbrannt.
	500.	Cavatina in the Opera of Orfeo in Partitur.
	501.	Ein englisches Lied Shakespear am Klav. 2. Ex. dann noch zwey andere engl. Lieder.
	502.	3. Deutsche Lieder am Klavier.
×	503.	Gott erhalte Franz den Kaiser; Partitur fürs große Orchester.
×	504.	Lines from the Battle of the Nile by M^ris Knight, and set in Music by Dr Haydn, am Klavier zu singen. Ein Blatt darin ist eigenhändig, und das Ganze hier noch unbekannt.
×	505.	Divertimento p. Clav. eigenhändig.
×	506.	—— in D. p. Clav. Violino e Vlle.
× ⌈	507.	—— in F. ⌉
{	508.	—— „ C. } p. Clav. 2. Violini e Violoncello. ×
	509.	—— „ F.	
⌊	510.	—— „ C. ⌋
×	511.	Sonata in G. p. Clav. con Violino.
×	512.	—— in Dis p. Clav. con Violino e Vlle.
×	513.	Capricio in A. p. detti.
× ⌈	514.	Jacobs Dream Son. p. Clav. dann
⌊	515.	Adagio p. detto.
	516.	Sonata p. Clav. ist aus einem Haydnischen Terzett übersezt von seinem Schüler Polceli.
	517.	16. franz. und deutsche Lieder am Klavier.
♯	518.	40. Canons mit deutschen, ital und lat. Text, welche in Herrn Haydns Studirkabinett als Bilder hingen und in 6. abgetheilten Parten hergegeben werden.

Geschriebene Musicalien von verschiedenen Componisten.

×	519.	Werner/: Fürst Esterhazyscher Kapellmeister und Vorfahrer des Herrn Haydn, ein gründlicher Compositeur:/ Debora ein Oratorium, eigenhändige Partitur in deutscher Sprache von a 1760.
×	520.	—— Daniel ein Oratorium aufgeführt in Esterhazy a 1752. Partitur in deutscher Sprache.
×	521.	—— Der gute Hirt detto a 757.
×	522.	—— Der jüngste Tag detto „ 745.
×	523.	—— Adam detto „ 749.
×	524.	—— Job detto „ 748.
×	525.	—— Der verlorne Sohn detto „ 747.
×	526.	—— Judas Machabæus detto „ 757.
×	527.	—— Der vom Saul verfolgte David. detto „ 750.
×	528.	—— Esther. detto „ 746.
×	529.	—— Judith. detto „ 747.
×	530.	—— Der treulose Absolon. detto „ 743.
×	531.	—— 3. Lamentationes in lat. Sprache für ein Orchester ausgeschrieben.
×	532.	—— 3. detti andere.
×	533.	—— 3. detti noch andere.
×	534.	—— 6. aus seinen Messen gezohene Fugen für die 4. Singstimmen mit der Orgel für Komponisten.
	535.	Kranz/: Schüler des Herrn Haydn:/Aria aus Piccolomini in Partitur, deutsch, dann
	536.	—— Cantatina in Partitur, deutsch.
	537.	Hodges Misstriss. Ein englisches Lied am Klavier, eigenhändig u. die Poesie auch von ihr. Herrn Haydns eigenhändige Aufschrift saget, sie sey das schönste von ihm gesehene Weib und eine große Klavierspielerin gewesen.
	538.	Maschek. Sinfonia betittelt: Das allgemeine Aufgeboth, für ein Orchester ausgeschrieben.
	539.	—— 6. Harmonieparthien ausgeschrieben.
	540.	Wranizky A. 3. Quint. p. 2. Violini, 2. Viole e Vlle.
×	541.	Bach Emanuel. Freye Fantasie p. Clav.
×	542.	—— —— Trio p. Clav. e Violino.
×	543.	—— —— 2. Quat. p. Clav. Flute e Viola.

× 544. —— —— Conc. für 2. Pianofortes mit dem Orchester in Partitur.

× 545. Bach Sebastian. 24. Prælude è Fughe, ovvero das wohl temperirte Klavier. 2ter Theil gebunden.

× 546. —— —— Missa a 5. Voci, 2. Soprani, Alto, Tenore, Basso, 3. Trombe, Tamburi, 2. Traversi, 2. Oboe, 2. Violini, 1. Viola è Continuo in Partitur sehr nett geschrieben und gut erhalten. Ein höchst schätzbares Exemplar.

× 547. Muffat. Missa in labore Requies für 2. Wechselchöre in Partitur, gebunden. Eben auch schäzbar.

× 548. Fux. Messa canonica a Capella tutta in canone con qualche diversita particolare. rar!

× 549. Caldara. 2. Messen in noch eigenhändiger Partitur. Die Nachschriften sagen, daß die erste am 14. Juny 1717. und die zweyte am 5ten Juny 1718 in Wien geschrieben worden sey. Auch Seltenheiten.

550. Ockl/: Lebte in Plan:/Deutsches Hochamt für ein gutbesetztes Chor, eigenhändige Partitur von a 1801.

551. Reutter. Offertorium in G. mol, p. 2. Soprani, Alto, Tenore, Basso con Organo.

552. Matej. Sopran Solo mit 2. Violini, Viola è Organo.

× 553. Eybler, Albrechtsberger, Stadler, Neukomm, Lessel pp verschiedene musikalische Geschenke, dem Herrn Haydn zum Andenken.

554. Kraus/: Königl. Schwed. Kapellmeister:/Musick zur Beisetzung Königs Gustafs des dritten, ohne Singstimmen für ein Orchester in Partitur. Ich kenne diesen soliden Mann auch aus persönlichen Umgang.

555. Reichard. Carmen funebre a 786. in Part. für 9. lat. Singstimmen und das große Orchester.

556. Clausum Invocation of Neptune mit 4. engl. Singstimmen und dem Orchester in Partitur.

557. Ordonez. Alceste eine deutsche Marionettenoper in Partitur.

558. Te Deum Laudamus für ein wohlbesetztes Kirchenchor in lat. Sprache, Partitur.

559. Brunetti. Scene loghubre nel Finale del Rè Teodoro in ital Sprache, Partitur.

560. Martini. Duetto aus una Cosa rara mit ital Text, dann eine andere deutsche Aria, beide in Partitur.

562. Cimarosa. L'Infedeltà fedele, ital Oper in 3. Akten in Partitur 3. Bände.

563. Neukomm. Fantasie à grand Orchestre, ausgeschrieben mit der Zueignungsschrift von a 808.

♯ 564. Händel. Oratorium: Der für die Sünde der Welt gemarterte und sterbende Jesus, deutsch in Partitur. Das Original wird an der Universität zu Oxford verwahrt. 1. schöner Band, regalirt von der Königin aus England. Eine große Seltenheit.

565. Concerto p. Violoncello in Part. auf klein Postpapier.

566. Gayer. 3. Sinfonien in Partitur.

× 567. Cabala, woraus Jedermann der auch nicht komponiren kann, durch Hilfe der Würfel, Menuetten zu verfertigen, im Stand gesezet wird.

× 568. Ungarische Nationaltänze.

569. Verschiedene musikalische Bruchstücke.

× 570. Thematischer Katalog verschiedener Kompositionen von verschiedenen Meistern. 2. Bände.

♯ 571. Thematischer Katalog aller Kompositionen, welche sich Herr Haydn beiläufig erinnert hat, von seinen 18ten bis in das 73te Jahr, geschrieben zu haben. Von ihm selbst veranlaßt. Ein höchst interessanter Band zu seiner Lebensgeschichte.

Geschriebene und gedruckte Methoden.

× 572. Eulero. Tentamen novæ theoriæ Musicæ.

573. Burney. a General History of Music mit schönen Kupfern meißt von Bartolozzi und vielen Noten in 4. sauberen Bänden. London 1776.

× 574. Dalberg. Uiber die Musick der Indier aus dem englischen des Sir William Jones ins deutsche mit Noten. 2. Bände.

575. Yriarte. La Musica poema in ital Sprache mit vielen Kupfern. 1. Band.

576. Marpurg. Anfangsgründe der theoretischen Musick. 1. Band.

577. —— Anleitung zum Klavierspielen mit Noten. 1. Band. 2. Ex.

× 578. —— Kritische Einleitung in die Geschichte und Lehrsätze der alten und neuen Musick mit Noten und Kupfern. 1. Band.

× 579. —— Handbuch vom Generalbaß und der Komposition mit 8. Kupfern. 1. Band.

580. Schwanenberg. Uiber die Unschicklichkeit des H. in der Tonleiter. 1. Band.

581. Münster. Die Leiter Jakobs über der Choralmusik, 2te Aufl.

582. Grossi. La Cetra d'Apollo. Venezia 1673. 1. Band.

× 583. Matheson. Kern melodischer Wissenschaft. 1. Band.

× 584. —— Große Generalbaßschule. 1. Band.

× 585. —— Der vollkommene Kapellmeister. 1. Band.

586. Gugl. Fundamenta partitura, deutsch 1. Band.

587.	Mancini. Pensieri e riflessioni pratiche sopra il Canto figurato ital. 1. Band.
588.	Beerens. Musikalische Discourse. 1. Band. und.
589.	Kalkbrenner. Histoire de la Musique. 1. Band.
590.	Kellner. Unterricht im Generalbaß. 1. Band.
591.	Carissimi. Grundregeln zur Singkunst. 1. Band.
592.	1. Faszikel Opernbüchel und andere musikal. Kleinigkeiten.
593.	Brossard. Dictionaire de Musique. 1. Band mit Noten.
594.	Daube. Generalbaß. 1. Band.
595.	Herbst. Musica poetica geschrieben. 1. Band.
596.	Anleitung zum Komponiren, geschrieben.
597.	Kircher. Neue Hall- und Tonkunst. 1. Band.
598.	Geschriebene Worte zur Schöpfung, mit eigenhändigen Anmerkungen des Freyherrn van Swieten, auf welche Art er Haydns Musick hierüber eingerichtet zu haben wünschte.

× 599. Scheiger. Poesie zum Oratorio das jüngste Gericht, welches Herr Haydn als Gegenstück zur Schöpfung in Musick setzen sollte. Manuskript.

600. Baumberg Gabriele von. Gedicht an den großen unsterblichen Haydn, mehrere Exemplarien, dann 2. kleine engl. Piecen.

× 601. Elementarbuch der verschiedenen Gattungen des Contrapunktes, aus den größeren Werken des Kapellmeisters Fux von Jos. Haydn selbst zusammengetragen. Manuskript.

602. Allerley vorräthig geschriebene Oden und Lieder zu Kompositionen.

603. Hinrichs. Entstehung, Fortgang und itzige Beschaffenheit der rußischen Jagdmusik. Petersburg 796. ein nettes Heft.

× 604. Forkel. Uiber Seb. Bachs Leben, Kunst und Kunstwerke. 1. Heft.

605. Zelter. Karl Friedrich Christian Fasch. 1. Heft.

606. Fux. Gradus ad Parnassus sive Manuductio ad Compositionem Musicæ. 1. Band.

607. Riepel. Grundregeln zur Tonordnung. 1. Band.

608. Henichen. Der Generalbaß in der Composition. 1. Band.

NACHTRAG VON KUPFERSTICHEN

welche erst beim Schluß des Inventarii vorgefunden wurden. Sind nach No. 54. auszurufen.

609. 26. Stück gestochene Theaterszenen.

610. Verschiedene Landkarten.

611. 50. verschiedene Portraits.

612. 2. Kupferplatten mit 2. Portraits, nämlich: Joannes und Sigismundus Theopholus Staden.

613. 2. alte mit gemahlten Umfaßungen geschriebene Gebetbücher.

EIN LEBENDER PAPAGEY

614. aus dem Geschlechte der gelehrigen Jako's in Taubengröße grau mit rothen Schweif. Da die Pagagey's nach allen Naturhistorikern ein hohes Alter bei 100. Jahren erleben so ist dieser noch jung. Herr Haydn kaufte denselben vor 19. Jahren noch nicht völlig erwachsen, in London um einen hohen Preis, und unterrichtete ihn selbst. Wohnt, wie gewöhnlich, in einen blechenen Hause.

Wien 26. Dez. 809   Ignaz Sauer
beeideter Inventurs- und Schätzungskommissair
in Kunstsachen bei den adelichen, kaufmannschaftl
und bürgl Justizbehörden.

Die mit × bezeichneten Stücke/: wenn selbe nicht zu übermässig hoch lauffen:/ sind zu nehmen.

Die mit ♯ bezeichneten wünschte ich vorzüglich zu besitzen.

Von den 4^{tetten} ist meines Wissens ohnedieß die ganze Sam̅lung da; dahero sind selbe nicht bezeichnet.

Von den Synfonien haben wir vorzüglich die herausgeschriebenen nöthig, sollten sich dahero ausser den × bezeichneten welche vorfinden, so sind sie auch zu nehmen.

Eybler

NOTES
(numbers refer to catalogue entries)

6. Louise Gautherot, violinist, who participated in the first Haydn-Salomon concert, on 11 March 1791.
7. Marie Antoinette, from a design by A. C. Dies, Haydn's biographer.
8. Issued in 1798, the year of the Battle of Aboukir.
29. Issued in 1799; perhaps given to Haydn by Nelson or Lady Hamilton in 1800.
54. End: '*Nota.* After this, the addition at No. 610 will be auctioned.'
64. Lignovsky = Prince Lichnowsky.
65. Probably one of the Mozart portraits by Posch.
67. 'paußirt' = a silhouette.
69. A Grassi bust (probably the lost one).
70. The Irrwoch (Irwach) wax profile.
71. The Thaller bust under a glass 'dome'.
72. An engraving or drawing of the Haydn monument in Rohrau.
76. For some reason, Harrach inherited not No. 76 but No. 77; No. 76 is probably the later (1802) bust by Grassi.

79–80: *vide supra*, p. 55f.
241. This work is listed in Elssler's Catalogue (*supra*, p. 305) under Gluck.
252. Listed in Elssler's Catalogue (*supra*, p. 305) as 'Unzen'.
356. 'This was the first Mass that Herr Haydn wrote, while still a student.'
361. It was thought worthwhile to stress that this item was 'an autograph score of a composition no one has'; the Chorus from *Alfred* of 1796, later issued by Breitkopf & Härtel.
392. 'Autograph, not the whole score which, however, can be completed through the art-dealer Traeg, with libretto 1769.' Traeg owned several Haydn operas in original scores or copies, but not this one, nor *Lo speziale.*
479–91. [Eybler's later addition:] 'NB if they don't fetch too much'.
545. J. S. Bach: Mass in B minor, the score 'very nicely written out and well preserved. A most valuable copy'. It went to the Esterházy Archives at Eisenstadt and during World War II it, the Haydn *Missa brevis* in F and the parts of the *Missa in tempore belli* were stuffed up an unused chimney for safe-keeping and were recovered some years ago.
548. 'new!' sounds strangely like a modern antiquarian's description.
549. Autographs, described as 'also rarities'.
554. The last sentence appears to be a copy of Haydn's own autograph addition to the score: 'I knew this solid man also personally.'
563. The work performed at the Christmas concerts of the Tonkünstler-Societät in 1808, 'with the dedication of [1]808'.
564. The much-discussed *Brockes-Passion.* 'The original is owned by Oxford University, given by the Queen of England. A great rarity'. Now in the Österreichische Nationalbibliothek, Vienna.
570. The so-called 'Quartbuch'.
571. The so-called '*HV*' (*Haydn-Verzeichnis*), the Elssler Catalogue of 1805.
592. Probably Haydn's Catalogue of Libretti, quoted above *in extenso.*
598. Swieten's autograph of *The Creation*; that of *The Seasons* was already missing.
599. The Oratorio, *Das jüngste Gericht*, 'which Herr Haydn should have composed as a *pendant* to *The Creation.* Manuscript.'
614. A live parrot. From the lineage of the teachable Jako's, the size of a pigeon, grey with a red tail. Since according to the natural historians, parrots reach an old age at 100 years, this one is still young. Herr Haydn bought it 19 years ago [1791], not fully grown, in London, for a high price, and taught it himself. Lives as is customary in a metal cage.

[Eybler's postcript]
The pieces marked × (if they are not simply too expensive) are to be taken.
The pieces marked ♯ I would very much like to own. Of the 4tets the whole collection is already there [in the Imperial Library], as far as I know; therefore they are not marked.
Of the symphonies we need primarily those in parts; therefore if there are any, apart from those marked ×, they are also to be taken.

Appendix

HAYDN AND POSTERITY:
A STUDY IN CHANGING VALUES[1]

At the end of the eighteenth century, shortly before Haydn's seventieth birthday in March 1802, it must have seemed to Europe's music-loving public that never had any composer been so completely popular among all levels of society, so thoroughly understood by his contemporaries and so certain of a place in the history of music. If they could have seen Haydn's position a hundred years later, they simply would have refused to believe their eyes and ears. The spectacular rise in Haydn's popularity was only matched by his equally spectacular eclipse. It is the purpose of this concluding section to trace this eclipse by means of documents. Naturally, an entire book could be written on this complicated subject, and this chapter cannot be more than a general survey.

To begin this survey, we must go back to the year 1800, when Haydn's music was at the height of its international popularity. Yet even then, there were dissenting voices, as the following letter from Berlin, printed in the *AMZ*, shows:

[Berlin, 25 October 1800.]
Yesterday Herr Schuhmacher, supposedly from Hamburg, gave a concert in the Freemasons' Hall 'Royal York'. First there was a Haydn Symphony in G major. I had not heard a Haydn symphony for a long time and felt the old impression again that the wonderful pieces by this master always made on me. I cannot begin to tell you what feelings of pure cosiness [*Behaglichkeit*] and well-being I have when listening to Haydn's music. It is about the same feeling I have when I read Yorick's writings, after which I always have the urge to do something good. The cheerful, teasing, good-natured, witty mood, linked with a highly spirited imagination, with strength and learnedness and richness – in short, this intoxication [*Schwelgen*] in a spring-time of notes and lovely modulations can make life pleasant. That very evening I argued with W––; he found the Symphony only droll [*schnurrig*], trifling [*tändelnd*] and irritating [*reizend*]; but you know his seriousness. He requires everything to be according to his kind and mentality. He cannot be satisfied with that which an artist has to give; he always wants passion and seriousness, and thereby he misses many a gush of pleasure [*Erguß*]. He has attached himself too much to Mozart's genius, as many another Christian soul who forgets the Father for the Son and do not themselves know how it is with their belief. It's true that on the whole one might easily find more

---

1 This essay utilizes parts of the present author's article, 'Box-Office Failure', in *The Listener*, 22 August 1968. The literature on this aspect of Haydn is scanty: see Geiringer 1947, 323ff.; Friedrich Blume, 'Gibt es ein neues Haydn-Bild', in *Neue Zürcher Zeitung*, 1 December 1968; Clemens Höslinger, 'Der überwundene Standpunkt: Joseph Haydn in der Wiener Musikkritik des 19. Jahrhunderts', in *Beiträge zur Musikgeschichte des 18. Jahrhunderts – Publikationen des Instituts für Österreichische Kulturgeschichte* 1/2, 1971, 116ff.; Karl Geiringer, 'Haydns Werk im Lauf der Jahrhunderte', in *Neue Zürcher Zeitung*, 23 July 1972. The present writer held a lecture series on this subject in various American universities in the Spring of 1969, *inter alia* at the University of Rochester, N.Y., and the University of Pennsylvania.

passion in Mozart; but must and should every salvation [*Heil*] come only from the explosions of a strong violence? Should there not also be an art which works peacefully and refreshingly on the imagination and nevertheless manifests a sharp mind? Naturally I don't want to dance every day and also I don't want to hear Haydn symphonies every day either; but who would want to perform them every day, anyway?

[*AMZ* III, November 1800, 130f.; letterspaced words ignored]

There are two features about this review, or rather about Herr W's opinion, which were soon to become typical of the anti-Haydn movement. One is that the language in which Haydn wrote was about to become obsolete to the point where nineteenth-century listeners could no longer hear the emotions with which Haydn was obviously filled when writing even such a movement as the *Largo cantabile e mesto* from the Quartet Op. 76, No. 5; we shall soon cite an interesting instance in connection with this work. The other might be summed up in Zoé Oldenbourg's words, 'The world is not enough'. For many people, once they had assimilated Mozart and Beethoven, Haydn was not enough.

It might have been expected that Berlin – the city whose inhabitants had resisted Haydn for many years, finding his music frivolous – would be one of the first to return to her early judgement of Haydn in the 1760s: too Austrian, too humorous, etc., etc. It is perhaps more surprising to find that even in Haydn's lifetime the Viennese audiences were becoming tired of his symphonies. In a letter from Vienna, printed in the *AMZ*, we read:

Vienna, 26th January [1807].

The Amateur Concerts in the University Hall continue encouragingly. We heard there the beautiful Haydn Symphony in D performed with a delicacy and expression with which – we must confess – we seldom hear them [Haydn's symphonies] performed nowadays. It is, moreover, one of the characteristics of our age, and depends upon many other factors, that the Haydn symphonies are not longer quite respected according to their value,[1] even though the cheerful, entirely uncomplicated sense of poetry that so brilliantly streams from them will perhaps never be equalled. . . . [The reviewer then mentions, as 'a beautiful contrast', Mozart's Symphony in G minor (K. 550) and Beethoven's *Eroica*, a work of which he does not entirely approve and which, he suggests, would benefit from a revision.]

This review, too, is highly prophetic. While the Oratorios, and especially *The Creation*, continued to be the adored favourites of the Viennese and were performed all through the nineteenth century, year in and year out, Haydn's symphonies gradually began to disappear from the repertoire in Vienna. In the 1950s, when the present writer was a witness of the Viennese musical scene, many late-period Haydn symphonies were as good as unknown in Vienna; Symphony No. 99, for example, had never been on a programme of the Vienna Philharmonic Orchestra. In contrast to the sparsity of Haydn's symphonies, not only the Oratorios but also the Masses were regularly performed; one could hear about ten Haydn Masses on Easter Sunday in Vienna during the years 1947 *et seq*.

Another prophetic review of the relationship between Haydn, Mozart and Beethoven appeared in Johann Friedrich Reichardt's *Vertraute Briefe*, written at Vienna

1 [*AMZ* footnote:] The writer must be speaking only of Vienna? At least we Leipzigers protest against being included in this judgement, and we ground our protest on frequent and very careful performances of these symphonies, and on the always equal success that they enjoy with the mixed public.

while Haydn was still alive. Here we find the Victorian concept of progress, that history consists of 'improvement'; we shall soon find this theory generally applied to the Viennese classical school, and also to musical history altogether.

On Thursday [15 December 1808] I again heard the beautiful quartet. They played three quartets, one by Haydn, then one by Mozart and finally one by Beethoven, the latter quite exceptionally well given. It was very interesting for me to follow the way in which these three real humorists widened the genre, each according to his individual nature. Haydn created it from the pure, clean source of his charming and original nature. For naïvety and cheerful humour he therefore remains still unique. Mozart's stronger nature and richer imagination grasped further and in many a movement he expressed the highest and deepest of his nature; he was also more a performing artist himself and entrusted far more to the players; he also set more store by artistically developed work and in this way he built a palace upon the lovely and fantastic garden-house that was Haydn's. Beethoven had at an early age made himself at home in this palace and it only remained to him, if he were to express his own nature also in his own forms, to erect his daring, stubborn tower, on the top of which no one could easily build anything without breaking his neck. Several times there occurred to me Michelangelo's proud, impudent idea of putting the marvellous Pantheon as a cupola on his St Peter's Church.

[Gugitz edition, 1915, I, 185]

When Haydn died, there were, as might have been expected, a spate of obituaries, some excellent and some trivial. One of the most interesting occurred in the *Gentleman's Magazine* (July 1809, p. 678), that famous arbiter of British taste, wherein we read of quite another aspect of Haydn's impression on his contemporaries, *viz.* the overwhelming effect of the Haydn *scuola* that even threatened to supplant the original in the minds of less perspicacious listeners.

31 [May]. In Guppendorff [*sic*], aged 76 [*sic*], Joseph Haydn, the celebrated composer. He was born at Rhorau [*sic*], in Lower Austria, in 1733 [*sic*]; and was justly considered as the Father of Musick in our day; for although in his youth he diligently studied the works of every great master, antient and modern, his transcendant genius soaring above them all, soon called the attention of the whole Musical World upon himself; all admiring him, first for the beauty, boldness, and originality of his works, and afterwards regarding him as the best model for study and imitation. Far from being actuated by the impulse of envy, he was never heard to speak of his numerous imitators, whose airy productions, more suited to the indolence of some, and the weak musical capacity of others, seemed to supplant the original in the public esteem, without allowing them all the merit they possessed. To enter into a description of his works, both as one of the greatest masters of his art and as a private character, would exceed our limits.

We have noted that *The Seasons* did not become known in England until its publication by Clementi in that composer's adaptation, issued in 1813. It received quite a friendly review, for example, in the *Gentleman's Magazine*, where we read:

To relish all the excellencies of the present work, requires not only nerves delicately strung, but a complete acquaintance with the mysteries of musical composition. To the pianoforte player who is neither singer nor composer it cannot afford much pleasure, without the assistance of three pretty good vocal performers. . . . It commences with an Overture in G minor . . . [which] is so full of uncommon harmony and abrupt modulation, that the numerous persons who are partial to musick of a gay character, who consider pandéan airs as the most agreeable sort of musick, would find it less to their liking than the 'daddy-mammy' of a squad of drummers. Lively musick is what delights the multitude. . . . We have mentioned only the overture: – the rest of the present number [Spring] consists of recitatives, airs, and choruses, with accompaniments the most ingenious, in which musical imitation and expression are carried to the highest pitch of excellence. – Summer, the second number of the work, is just published. . . .

[1813, p. 563]

Other British reviewers continued to be fascinated by Haydn's late Oratorios. William Gardiner, the English translator and editor of the Stendhal Haydn plagiarism – it came out in London in 1817 – thought 'Chaos' a magnificent piece of music when he reviewed it in the *Monthly Magazine* for March 1811; he describes it as:

a treasure of sublimity, [in which] we find every voice and instrument conspiring to raise the mind of man to contemplate the wonderful work of God. . . . Were it necessary to bring further illustrations of the superior powers of the new music, compared with that of the antients, we might attempt a description of the *Chaos*, which opened the work we have been quoting. – It commences with all the known instruments, displayed in twenty-three distinct parts. After these are amalgamated in one tremendous note, a slight motion is made perceptible in the lower parts of the band, to represent the rude masses of nature in a state of chaos. Amidst this turbid modulation, the bassoon is the first that makes an effort to rise, and extricate itself from the cumbrous mass. The sort of motion with which it ascends, communicates a like disposition to the surrounding materials, but which is stifled by the falling of the double basses, and the *contra fagotto*. – In this mingled confusion, the clarionet struggles with more success, and the ethereal flutes escape into air. A disposition verging to order is seen and felt, and every resolution would imitate shape, and adjustment, but not a concord ensues! After the volcanic eruptions of the *clarini* and *tromboni*, some arrangement is promised; a precipitation follows of the discordant sounds, and leaves a misty effect that happily expresses the 'spirit of God moving upon the face of the waters'. At the fiat, 'Let there by light!' the instruments are unmuted, and the audience is lost in the refulgence of the harmony.

But a 'Musical Student', writing in the *Quarterly Musical Magazine* nine years later (III, 13), found that:

The *Creation* does not add essentially to the fame of Haydn. – We discover great invention and variety, joined to a consummate knowledge of the orchestra, and of the powers and peculiar properties of every instrument which it contains. The best parts are the choruses, which seem to be written on the Handelian model. – The *Chaos* seems only calculated to excite gaping astonishment in the hearers. Some, indeed, may think that there is absurdity in the attempt to paint disorder and confusion by means of modulated sounds. And it may be observed that Haydn, with all his pains, has not made his chaos sufficiently chaotic; for there are certain places where the parts imitate each other in a manner which shews too much art and contrivance.

Parts of *The Creation* were performed at the York Festival in 1823, and in the excellent *Account* by John Crosse there is long section dealing with the Oratorio and its critics, from which we have quoted two passages *supra*. Here is what he has to say, and to quote, on the most famous Chorus in the work.

The merits of this chorus [The Heavens are telling] have been a subject of widely conflicting opinions, which we shall endeavour briefly to lay before the reader both for his amusement and decision. 'Concerning the popularity of "*The heavens are telling*",' says the author of the *Musical Student* (see above), 'I can only account for it on the ground of its being the longest, and the loudest in the whole work. "It begins," says a friend of mine, "at Vauxhall and ends at the Opera-House." Indeed, considering the magnitude of the composition, and hand from which it comes, we cannot fail in being struck at the woeful common-place of its commencement and termination, which is not redeemed by the pleasing trio in the middle.' [*Quarterly Musical Magazine*, vol. iii, p. 13]. On the other hand, Mr. Gardiner declares, that 'the concluding movement of "*The Heavens are telling*", is penned with a majesty of thought, that transcends the powers of musical expression. . . .' [He quotes *Account of the First Edinburgh Musical Festival*, 1816, p. 42, by George Farquhar Graham] 'At the 153rd bar, the first part of the second period of the *motivo* appears in the bass with much effect; and again at the 174th bar, whence the chorus rises rapidly to a climax of astonishing power and grandeur. Here, indeed, every thing conspires to "*tell the glory of God*" in a language of sublimity which shakes the frame, and makes every soul tremble.'
. . . It will scarcely be expected that we shall presume to undertake the task of sitting in judgment upon these contending criticisms, by which we are strongly reminded of the need of requesting the reader's candid indulgence for those that have been advanced in these pages, on points which manifestly involve principles of taste as yet undetermined, and opinions embracing every possible shade of variety that can exist. The air, indeed [of The Heavens are telling], is too easy and familiar to have much claim to originality; Mr. Hook's song of '*Richmond Hill*' [Vauxhall, *c*. 1790], and several other popular melodies, greatly resemble it; and Haydn himself had previously [*sc*. later] made use of it in the '*Gloria*' of his third Mass, where its lightness deserves to meet with even less excuse. Yet. if success be the test of merit, and permanent success assuredly is so, this chorus must be allowed to take the highest rank among sublime compositions. . . . Here, then, we take our leave of this immortal work, which genius dared to plan and persevered to execute, but of the dramatic unity of which, the present partial selection prevents our taking any general and connected view. If Haydn be inferior to his great predecessor [Handel] in simplicity and solemnity, it must be granted that he at least fully equals him in beauty, tenderness, and grace, and far surpasses him in the knowledge and employment of instrumental effect, notwithstanding the anathemas poured forth against 'trombones, and such like stuff' [which were, however, brilliantly used in *Israel in Egypt* by Handel], by those who can perceive no merit but in one class of compositions, and who refuse to consider the vast additions to the power of orchestral expression, derived from the improvements of wind instruments in modern times.   [pp. 335–7]

If the older generation of British critics followed Dr Burney in admiring *The Creation*, the younger men had entirely different ideas. Two influential British critics may be cited here. The first is Thomas Busby, whose *General History of Music* was widely read; it was published in two volumes in 1819. Perhaps no more scathing opinion of Haydn's Oratorios appeared before Runciman's at the end of the century.

At the age of sixty-three, he commenced what he evidently intended to be his greatest work. At the end of 1795 he began his Oratorio of *The Creation*, and at the beginning of 1798 completed the undertaking, saying, 'I have spent much time over the piece, because I intended it should last.' In the succeeding Lent it was performed, for the first time, at Schwartzenberg [!] Palace, at the request and expense of the Dilettanti Society. It was received, says a writer, who tells us he was present, with the most rapturous applause; and I can easily believe him; because the audience were unacquainted with the sublime loftiness, and profound contrivance of Handel, and went to the Schwartzenberg Palace with ears and minds prepared to be enchanted. But what are the real and prominent features of this composition? A series of attempted imitations of many things inimitable by music, the sudden creation of light happily expressed by an unexpected burst of sound, airs not abundantly beautiful or original, smothered with ingenious accompaniments, and choruses in which the composer toils under his incumbent weight, labours in fugue, copies with faint pencil the clear lustre of a glorious prototype, and supplies the absence of a true taste and dignity, with the congregated powers of a complicated band.★ My respect for the great talents of Haydn obliges me to be sorry that his judgment did not forbid his compromising himself in oratorial composition. In his operas and cantatas, his failure was only partial; in his Oratorios almost total. But it should be the first policy of so great an artist, *never* to be seen failing; never to let it appear that he can fail.†

About two years after the production of his *Creation*, Haydn composed his *Seasons*. In this piece he was more successful, because he was less out of his natural tract. Not including the complicated grandeur of numerous voices and instruments, that ponderous combination and multiplied intertexture and evolution, manageable only by such powers as those of the composer of *Samson*, the *Messiah*, and *Israel in Egypt*, – *The Seasons*, lay within the compass of his strength, and only betrayed his *awkwardness*. It is not a little curious, that a master, whose whole *distinguishing* greatness lay in the instrumental province of his art, should conclude his career with a vocal composition. *The Seasons* was his last production.‡   [vol. II, pp. 399–401]

The other influential writer on music was William Crotch who in 1831 published a book entitled *Substance of several courses of lectures on music, read in the University of Oxford, and in the Metropolis*, in which we find the following passage about Haydn's style:

Haydn, whom we have already mentioned, formed another school of instrumental music, which continues to the present day. Of his vocal sacred productions his Stabat Mater is the best. The first chorus is learned, ingenious, and dignified; the songs for a bass voice are extremely fine, and the accompaniments throughout the piece delicate and fanciful, particularly that to the chorus 'Quis est homo'. The extraneous modulations, and passages in counterpoint are, in all his works, admirable: his fugues are, on simple subjects, not treated with much skill, the interest often declining instead of increasing, and the terminations being abrupt, or in a modern style. His Oratorio of the Creation contains the same merits and the same defects. The Chaos is awful, but contains passages that want dignity.

★ [Original footnote] If in any one of the melodies of *The Creation*, I could discover the celestial grace of Sacchini, in the recitatives the profound science of Sebastian Bach, or in the choruses, a single sample of that transcendent force of imagination, profound adjustment of parts, or sublimity of aggregate effect, so uniformly conspicuous in Handel, I would allow Haydn to be an oratorio composer.
† [Original footnote] Haydn (a Catholic) really was, or really thought himself, very religious. At his first sitting down to the composition of his *Creation*, he prayed the *Virgin* to enable him to praise God worthily. The *Queen of Heaven*, sensible of his circumscribed powers, or of her own, or of both, does not appear even to have made the attempt.
‡ [Original footnote] After this piece, he did not, strictly speaking, *compose* anything. The quartets he attempted were never finished; and the few publications he subsequently sent to the press, consisted only of old Scotch tunes, to which he condescended to subscribe new basses.

The recitatives are in common style. The principal excellence lies in the accompaniments; but the use of the full orchestra, including trumpets and drums for five or six movements in succession, is fatiguing to the ear, and diminishes their effect. The opening of the third act, 'In rosy mantle', with the duet and chorus which follow, 'By thee with bliss', is however a happy mixture of all styles in their due place and proportion; a most masterly production, and worthy of study. His Oratorio of the Seasons, and his choral Masses, have generally the same characteristics as above. Compared with the productions of the former half of the eighteenth century, they are deficient in sublimity and science. His opera of Orfèo contains some fine airs; and indeed the style of his vocal music seems much more adapted for the opera than the Oratorio. His detached songs are admirable. His cantatas, 'Ah, come il core', with orchestral accompaniments, and 'Arianna in Naxos', with only the piano-forte, have great merit, particularly the first set. But it is chiefly as an instrumental composer that we acknowledge the unrivalled powers of Haydn. His sonatas for the piano-forte, like Handel's Suite de Pièces pour le Clavecin, seem to have been written, not to display the powers of the instrument, or the execution of the performer, but to gratify the ear and the mind of the hearer; and if studied with this object kept in view, they will appear preeminent and perfect. His quartetts are allowed to be unrivalled. And the number of sonatas and quartetts he produced is astonishing. His Passione Stromentale is not in the church style. The addition of voice parts to it by Michael Haydn was no improvement; but in its original state, considered as an instrumental piece, it is full of science, pathos, and gravity. The finale, intend to depict an earthquake, is deficient in dignity of style. Haydn's sinfonias, for number, variety, novelty, brilliancy, and gaiety of style, surpass all others. It was this gaiety which was objected to when his compositions first appeared. But it is this alone which renders them more pleasing and amusing than the equally scientific productions of his pupils Mozart and Beethoven, both for the piano-forte and the orchestra. Pleyel and Kozeluch were also pupils of Haydn. The quartetts of the former and the piano-forte sonatas of the latter were once much used. Pleyel's music was light and pretty; Kozeluch's full of propriety, taste, and elegance; but both were inferior to Haydn, Mozart, and Beethoven, in originality, genius, and science. Upon the whole we must consider Haydn as the greatest of all instrumental composers. [pp. 140–4]

The last sentence would soon be considered highly eccentric, of course, but the rest of the article represents what would become the standard British opinion, namely, that Haydn was primarily an instrumental and not a vocal composer.

We have noted the 'progress' theory with regard to Haydn, Mozart and Beethoven. It was not exclusively limited to the Continent, for we read a similar idea in *Macculloch's Letters to Sir Walter Scott, on the Highlands and Western Isles of Scotland,* published in 1824. 'Laws,' he writes, 'inviolable laws for the regulation of harmony have been made and violated.

The rules for the preparation and resolution of chords are only now obeyed, when it is not found preferable to disobey them. A Haydn trembles at his own boldness; his hands recoil even at the sounds himself has made; but still he goes on: more fearless, steps in a Mozart; and, at length, a Beethoven plunges into a congregation of sounds, that might raise from the very grave the spirits of his early predecessors. The audience keeps pace, but it is a lagging one, with these innovations; first wondering what they mean, and lastly wondering at their former insensibility. Such is the progress of human ears; and of human improvement too, in many other matters. . . . Many of us remember when Beethoven was Greek and

Hebrew to our ears; – we have lived to see, that scarcely another could command the attention of the audience. Nay, there are some of us who can recollect when Haydn, and even Boccherini, was as Beethoven; when the shorter step from Haydn to Mozart was a serious effort; and when the prudent kept silence, and pretended to believe, in hopes, that the day of admiration would come at last.

[II, 385–416]

We must not forget, however, that although Haydn's Oratorios were now coming in for some very severe criticism in England, his symphonies were the regular fare of the Philharmonic concerts in London and throughout the provinces. It is usually the late symphonies that we find on the programmes, and they were played with distressing frequency. Part of the trouble with Haydn's music, at least in England, was that his most popular symphonies were overplayed. When they were withdrawn and brought forward after an interval, they achieved a signal success. This 'come-back' quality in Haydn's music has in fact been its principal *raison d'être* for some two hundred years; despite all the tomes of adverse criticism which have been levelled against it, the music manages to 'come back' in a way which, as we shall see, surprised even the Viennese during their most anti-Haydn period.

At a Philharmonic Concert on 26 April 1824, Haydn's Symphony No. 94 ('Surprise') opened the programme. The *Harmonicon* had this to say:

> Haydn's 3rd Grand Symphony, known by the name of *The Surprise*, was now performed at these concerts for the first time. Like all very beautiful music, it had, for a long series of years, been so continually before the public, that, in spite of its great merit and originality, the ear had become thoroughly satiated with it, and good policy therefore dictated that it should, for a time, be withdrawn. This prudence in the managers was rewarded by the delight and applause with which it was received on the present occasion: never before has it been so executed in England, and never did it afford more satisfaction, for each movement was followed by the strongest testimonies of approbation, and the Andante was unanimously encored. [II, 121f.]

In 1822, a Colonel John Macdonald published *A Treatise on the Harmonic System*, the preface of which (p. xiii) contains the following statement:

> Haydn's style is beautiful; but with some sameness and occasional brilliancy, it probably resembles a picture of *still life*; And certainly it does not possess the power and exhilarating effect of the music of Mozart, Beethoven, and Cherubini. Be this as it may, Haydn, after a long reign, seems, with no sufficient reason, to be proceeding slowly to the undisturbed repose of the shelf.

There were still many lovers of Haydn, including the critic of the *Harmonicon*, for whom Macdonald's remarks rankled. After a Philharmonic Concert on 21 February 1825, conducted by Sir George Smart, which contained Beethoven's Fourth Symphony and Haydn's 'Military', the critic wrote:

> The two simphonies performed in this concert' are less known than most of the other orchestral compositions of the same authors. That by Beethoven has few traits that strike generally, and at once, but possesses much to please the true connoisseur; it is written carefully, and betrays none of those eccentricities that are often at variance with established rules. The other, which is the eleventh of those composed for Salomon's Concerts, is much more airy and popular in its style; the Andante of this, in G, is one of the most elegant of Haydn's productions; how beautifully the first violins *sing* the melody – how ingenious and effective the

accompaniments of the other instruments, – and how masterly the climax. Haydn, says a modern writer on music, begins to be laid on the shelf; an assertion in which we cannot acquiesce. Grant it, however, to be true, he is only where Milton has long been placed, by a majority of those who are denominated well-educated persons. But do the real admirers and judges of poetry and music consign either of these great geniuses to darkness and dust? Certainly not, for true taste recognizes a standard, and is never swayed by fashion. We admit that in the indulgence of a sense, satiety may be produced, and indiscreet zeal is too apt to force a composer before the public so often, as to excite an ennui that is frequently mistaken for a change in opinion. [III, 48]

Nissen's biography of Mozart had meanwhile appeared, and from it the musical world learned of his incredible output. They also learned that Mozart had written his greatest symphonies before Haydn's 'Salomon' Symphonies; thus Haydn was, as it were, robbed even of his supposed title as Father of the Symphony. The *Foreign Quarterly Review* of 1829 carried a long review of Nissen's book, and this review was quoted not only in *The Scotsman* but also in the *Harmonicon*. We read:

When Mozart is arbiter, there can be no appeal from the decision. The revelations of the biography before us throw a new light on the subject of Mozart's invention, of his rank with respect to other composers, and of the real services which he rendered to music: and truly in the contemplation of the sublime attributes of his genius, and the imagination and feeling which he displayed from childhood to manhood, there is enough to gratify his warmest admirers, and to elevate and ennoble humanity. Of his six-and-thirty sinfonias for the full orchestra, it appears that the half-dozen masterly compositions with which we are familiar in England, were written considerably before Haydn's journey to this country, to complete his engagement with Salomon; so that Mozart had reached perfection in the Sinfonia style, and won the race, long before the man who had made the first strides in it, and who had the start of him in years and experience. Respecting the operas of Mozart, ★★★★★★ *Idomeneo* occupied him but six weeks, – *La Clemenza di Tito* but eighteen days. These, be it remembered, are works which defy the most scrutinizing and rigorous examination, exhibit melodies which never tire, and unequalled management of the orchestra. For the production of these models of the dramatic style, Mozart required no longer time than a common-place Italian composer takes for the concoction of his ephemeral novelties; and it is not unreasonable to conclude, that had his dramatic genius been properly appreciated and encouraged, instead of being opposed, we might have enjoyed at least five-and-twenty operas from his pen. When we bring into one view all the qualifications of Mozart as a composer and practical musician, the result is astounding. The same man, under the age of thirty-six, is at the head of dramatic sinfonia, and piano-forte music – is eminent in the church style – and equally at his ease in every variety, from the concerto to the country dance or baby-song: he puts forth about eight hundred compositions, including Masses, motets, operas, and fragments of various kinds; at the same time supporting himself by teaching and giving public performances, at which he executes concertos on the piano-forte, the violin, or the organ, or plays extempore. But when we learn that the infant Mozart, at four years of age, began to compose, and by an instinctive perception of beauty to make correct bases to melodies; and also that he became a great performer on two instruments without the usual labour of practise, we cease to be surprised at the mechanical dexterity of his fingers in after-life, when composition and other pursuits had engrossed the time usually employed in preserving the power of execution.

The critic of the *Harmonicon* sought to defend Haydn, but historically his facts were as wrong as the article he was discussing; Mozart, of course, really did write at least thirty-six symphonies, and of the earlier works in the form by Haydn which are mentioned – they might be No. 53 for the work in D and Nos. 84 or 91 for one in E flat – only No. 44 in E minor was actually composed before Mozart's great symphonies.

> Of the six-and-thirty symphonies here mentioned, nearly half, I suspect, never advanced beyond the mere *brouillon* – never were fairly copied out, much less performed. And with regard to what is said of Haydn, it should have been recollected, that though his twelve symphonies written for Salomon are, and deserve to be, considered as his best works in this class, yet he had composed that beautiful one in D, with the exquisite and unsurpassed andante in A – the fine work in C, with the *danse des Ours* – that in E♭, with the lovely andante in B♭ – and the E minor, all long before Mozart had composed a single one of those now in use, and so unaffectedly admired. Haydn is unquestionably the father of symphony; and with all my enthusiasm for the symphonies of Mozart, and my wonder at Beethoven's, there still are for me more charms in some few of those composed by the parent of this species of composition, than in any by the other two, beautiful and wonderful as they are. It is worthy, too, of consideration, that the latter are by comparison more new to us, less hackneyed, therefore more pleasing to many on account of their greater novelty. For Haydn's *twelve*, though produced subsequently to Mozart's, were all performed and thoroughly known in this country, before any one by the latter been heard, or at least fairly heard, in England.   [VII, 254f.]

The *Harmonicon*'s critic was, however, already in the minority. On 14 June 1830, a Philharmonic Concert began the second half with Haydn's Symphony No. 99. One of the critics in a daily newspaper suggested that the work should be banned. Our defender in the *Harmonicon* retorted that

> Haydn's symphony, though the allegro movements were played rather too quick, especially the last, was executed with the greatest spirit and feeling. A critic in a weekly paper, wishing no doubt to signalize himself, speaks slightingly of this great work of the great master, and even goes so far as to recommend that Haydn's compositions be withdrawn, hinting that they are worn out and wearisome! We regret not being able to quote the exact words – they would amuse our readers, and at the same time show to what excess enthusiasm in favour of any one style, or thirst after novelty, sometimes leads those who ought to be most free from everything bordering on prejudice. The writer would, no doubt, long ago, have banished Shakespeare from the stage, and have tolerated only the performance of the few last dramas, had he possessed the power to exclude and appoint.
>
>   [VIII, 304]

Yet when, a year later, John Cramer opened the second part of a Philharmonic Concert with Symphony No. 88 (21 February 1831), the *Harmonicon* found it too much to stomach. 'With all our respect for Haydn – and it is hardly possible for any one to entertain more – we must say that his Symphony in G [footnote identifying it as Letter V] wants seasoning to render it agreeable to the taste which prevails among true connoisseurs at the present moment. It was not chosen with judgment. . . .'

                                                                          [IX, 70f.]

In German-speaking countries, it was still the late Oratorios – taking Haydn's *œuvre* as a whole – which continued to make the greatest impression – in stark contrast to the

situation in England. If we examine the famous correspondence between Zelter –
Haydn's old defender in the *AMZ* – and Goethe,[1] we find many references to the
Oratorios and hardly any to the instrumental music. Some extracts will, of course,
reveal the personality of the writer but they also reflect to some extent the general
opinion held in Berlin by thinking musicians of the slightly older school.

[9 March 1814]

. . . I remember very clearly that the music of the Leipzig [J. S.] Bach and his son,
the Hamburg [C.P.E.] Bach, both new and original, was almost incomprehensible to me then, although a dark feeling of reality drew them to me. Then
came Haydn, whose style [*Art*] was criticized because it immediately made a
burlesque of the deadly seriousness of his predecessors, as a result of which they
again enjoyed a high opinion. Finally Mozart arrived, through whom all three
could be explained, and out of whom he developed. . . .

[30 July 1819]

. . . Beethoven is raised to heaven because he really lets his temper fly and because
he is living; but the man who carries to them the national humour like a pure
stream that accepts no other current, that is Haydn, who lives in them because he
comes from them. They seem to forget him every day, and daily he continues to
revive them. . . .

[28 April 1830]

Haydn's *The Creation* was once again performed and not yet exhausted
[*erschöpft*]. Everyone who calls himself a music director, according to name, rank
and position, gathered together under Spontini's direction to honour the work. It
seemed that I could only really enjoy the work nowadays, since thirty years ago I
publicly defended it against the accusation of forbidden descriptions [*Ausmahlun-
gen*] of exotic things. What my predecessors overlooked was the simple fact that
the text was precisely made to describe the exterior circumstances of creation, and
what we must ask ourselves is: how is the task accomplished? Afterwards, to get
rid of the words as superfluous scaffolding and to have an architectonic musical
work in front of one that one listens to as if it were a significant symphony or
sonata won't do because it isn't, inasmuch as it proceeds from an unthinkable
negative to over-thinkable, tangible mass effects. Nothing, emptiness, a desert, the
depths, darkness are given; chaos – God rules it! – there should be light; sun, moon
and stars; the children of light should be witnesses of something that does not yet
exist and out of which chaos will come. Now the music: beginning, *initium* a
monstrous unison, between discernible height and depth; the space between the
poles – 'the world in lowest depths' – hard and broad, not major and not minor –
'without longing, without sound'. In tone and yet none, heavy, thick, a mass of
fog. With electrical force we hear 'a painful sigh' [etc., etc., in the vein of Zelter's
famous criticism of 'Chaos' in the *AMZ*]. . . . At the end the poet cannot find an
end and chatters; there has to be a third part. Man appears, a Philistine; hardly is
the word spoken, 'be fruitful and multiply' but we have flirting and marrying;
with your ears you can see the old Haydn himself, as he lives, courting and
waltzing with his Marzebille [girl] so that your mouth waters:

These dogs of poets,
They do ruin nature!

---

1 *Briefwechsel zwischen Goethe und Zelter in den Jahren 1796 bis 1832*, edited by Friedrich Wilhelm Riemer,
Berlin 1834, letters 205, 329, 728 and 761.

[17 December 1830]

. . . I told you that we performed Haydn's *The Seasons* with Thomson's text. A piece of music which ought to belong to the lost treasures because it sings of country people, wine-growing and agriculture, in a true country-like and sensitive fashion, so persuasive to the ear that I am always put into an innocent frame of mind, into a perfect equilibrium of the soul. There developed two groups during the rehearsals. The gentle company did not want to join the *Heida! Hopsa! Juche!* of the good country-people and I – thinking of the time involved – allowed myself to be persuaded to omit these pieces since if given without pleasure they will transmit no pleasure. . . . The performance was splendidly received and now they want to repeat the whole thing, but I shall let myself be courted. . . .

Zelter's star pupil was Felix Mendelssohn-Bartholdy, and he grew up with profound respect for Haydn and his music. Felix's father had also pondered the question of Haydn's Oratorios and expressed himself on the subject to his son in a letter of 10 March 1835.[1]

The heights of religious feeling on which Bach, Handel, and their contemporaries stood, were such that they required no large orchestras for their Oratorios; and I well remember from my earliest years that the 'Messiah', 'Judas' and 'Alexander's Feast', were given exactly as Handel wrote them, without even an organ, and yet to the delight and edification of everyone.

But how is this matter to be stopped nowadays, when vacuity of thought and noise in music are gradually being developed in inverse ratio to each other? The orchestra is now established and is likely to maintain its present form without any essential modification, for a long time to come. Wealth is a fault only when we do not know how to use it. How, then, is the wealth of the orchestra to be applied? What guidance can the poet give for this and in what regions? Or is music to be entirely severed from poetry, and work its own independent way? I do not believe it can accomplish the latter; at least, only to a very limited extent, and – in general – not authentically. To effect the former, an object must be found for music – just as for painting – which by its fervour, its universal sufficiency and perspicuity may take the place of the pious emotions of former days. It seems to me that also from this point of view both the Oratorios of Haydn are very remarkable phenomena. The poems of both, as poems, are weak, but they have happily substituted the old positive and almost metaphysical religious impulses with those which nature, as a visible emanation of the Godhead, in her universality and her thousandfold individualities, instils in every susceptible heart. Hence the profound depth, but also the cheerful efficiency, and certainly genuine religious influence of these two works, which hitherto stand by themselves. Hence the combined effect of the playful and detached passages with the most noble and sincere feelings of gratitude produced by the whole; hence it is, also, that I, individually, would like as little to be deprived – in *The Creation* and in *The Seasons* – of the crowing of the cock, the singing of the lark, the lowing of the cattle, and the rustic glee of the peasants, as in nature herself. In other words, *The Creation* and *The Seasons* are founded on nature and on the visible service of God; and are no new materials for music to be found there?

But even among such highly cultivated musical families, some aspects of Haydn's style now presented insuperable obstacles. In a letter from Fanny Hensel, Felix's sister, to

---

1 *Felix Mendelssohn, Letters*, edited by G. Selden-Goth, New York 1945, pp. 241ff.

Moscheles we read the following significant passage about the slow movement of the Quartet Op. 76, No. 5:

> . . . Do you still remember, dear Herr Moscheles, that one evening during the autumn that he spent with us Felix played the wonderful Adagio in F sharp major from a Haydn Quartet? Father loved Haydn especially, every piece was new for him and moved him strangely. He wept when he heard it and said afterwards that he found it so profoundly sad. This description astonished Felix greatly, because *Mesto* [sadly] was in the tempo and all the rest of us in fact found that it rather made an impression of cheerfulness on us. . . . [Pohl III, 313]

Here, surely, is the crux of the matter: it is not the first time, nor will it be the last, that we observe the language of a composer gradually ceasing to carry its message to the audiences. That which was obviously profoundly sad to Haydn and his contemporary audiences was no longer sad but on the contrary jolly (*heiter*) to the young Mendelssohns, and probably to most young people. Of course this mental block about the eighteenth century was not limited to Haydn but also extended to Mozart, and in some respects the many nineteenth-century and even twentieth-century misunderstandings of such works as *Così fan tutte* are more incomprehensible than the general lack of respect for Haydn. When Cobbett's *Cyclopaedia of Chamber Music* appeared with an article on Mozart by Abert, the editor felt constrained – and this was the 1920s! – to warn his readers that Abert's concept of Mozart, with its demonic side, would be very new and strange to most Anglo-Saxon lovers of that composer. The above extract from an account of a soirée at the Mendelssohns' house in Berlin is prophetic of what was to come and shows in a dramatic fashion the 'generation gap' in an appreciation of Haydn's music.

Mendelssohn himself often visited France. There, too, Haydn was becoming unfashionable. Before we proceed to Felix's comments on the subject, we might preface the whole with the following extract from the Paris correspondent of the *Harmonicon* in 1823.

> This reflection occurred whilst listening to the first piece of the concert, which is the subject of this article, an admirable, a most extraordinary, and astonishing symphony by Beethoven. No person can admire more than the author of these remarks does, the richness, purity, and variety of Haydn's genius, – the classic of symphony; – but all the form of his musical language are now known to us – his style is familiar to us – his passages and his movements are fully impressed on our memories, not only by frequent repetition, but because they have, in an imperfect disguise, been so often produced by others. The ear fatigues with reiterated excellence; it requires novelty. Beethoven affords the mind those strong and sudden emotions, those delightful surprises, which are absolutely necessary to rouse it from the dullness it acquires amongst its old enjoyments. What an original and brilliant style! What an extraordinary freedom, yet at the same time, so conformable to the rules of the art! What unexpected transitions, and absolutely created! What lively and animated melodies! What a profound knowledge of all the resources of harmony! You, who love novelty, come and hear Beethoven, you will be completely satisfied. He is something wild, it has been said, but what does that matter? Admirers of Mozart, enthusiasts of Rossini, you will unite your admiration and your enthusiasm in Beethoven, for in him you may find both Mozart and Rossini. [I, 94f.]

In 1832, when Mendelssohn was in Paris for one of his regular visits, the anti-Haydn and anti-Mozart sentiments had grown considerably. On 15 February Felix writes to his old teacher Zelter as follows:[1]

> The musicians themselves [in Paris] really enjoy the great Beethoven symphonies, they are thoroughly familiar with them and take pleasure in having mastered them. Some people, for instance Habeneck himself, are certainly sincere in their love of Beethoven. But of the others, and especially the greatest shouters and enthusiasts, I do not believe one word; for now they make a point of disdaining the other masters; they speak of Haydn as of an old wig and of Mozart as of a good fellow, and such narrow-minded ecstasy cannot possibly be genuine. If they really appreciate what Beethoven had in mind, they must also know what Haydn was and feel very small. But they do not, and go briskly ahead with their judgements. The public at these concerts also loves Beethoven devotedly because it believes one has to be a connoisseur in order to love him; but only the fewest can take genuine pleasure in him, and I simply cannot bear to listen to people depreciating Haydn and Mozart; it makes me wild. The Beethoven symphonies to them are a kind of exotic plant, people sniff at their perfume but look upon them as curiosities, and if anybody goes far enough to count the stamens, and finds that they really belong to a familiar species, he is satisfied and lets the matter drop. . . .

A few years later Robert Schumann began to publish music criticism, and although he wrote very little about Haydn – a composer who if anything irritated him – that which he did publish is typical of the young musician. Reviewing Haydn's 'Military' Symphony at a Leipzig subscription concert in 1840,[2] Schumann found that:

> The Symphony has, more than others by Haydn, something pigtail-like about it; the Turkish music [*Janitscharenmusik*] therein even has about it something childish and tasteless which, with all love for the master (and that remains everywhere), we should no longer deny. The scherzo, in our opinion the movement that is closest to our age, was curiously enough not applauded; all the others were.

Reviewing an all-Haydn concert on 28 January 1841, Schumann says:

> Varied as the programme was, many will have been tired by the evening, and naturally: for Haydn's music has been always frequently played here; one can learn nothing more from him; he is like a regular house-friend, who is always gladly and respectfully received; but he has no deeper interest any longer for our age.   [III, 87]

A few years earlier, in 1836, however, Schumann had found warm words of praise for an unidentified B flat symphony by Haydn:

> . . . this sunny clarity! – Heavenly well-being is in these sounds that allow us no glimpse of satiety of life and give us nothing but happiness, the pleasure of being alive, childish joy over everything and – what a service has he thus performed for the present age, this sickly epoch in music when one is so seldom satisfied in one's *innermost*.   [II, 232]

---

1 *Letters* (Selden-Goth), 192.
2 *Gesammelte Schriften über Musik und Musiker*, Leipzig (Reclam) 1888, edited by Heinrich Simon, Vol. III, 78.

Curious indeed that one and the same intelligent man could vacillate so much about Haydn, and yet this particular quality will be found throughout nineteenth-century criticism of our composer.

In Austria, Haydn's Oratorios continued to be the main staples of that genre. Critical disapproval seemed to make no difference in the public's esteem of *The Creation* and *The Seasons*. As early as 1813, we find a broad attack on the latter in the *Allgemeine Wiener musikalische Zeitung*,[1] objecting as usual to the work's *Thonmahlerey*. 'But the whole is tasteless,' concludes the writer, to no avail whatever, as a glance at contemporary concert programmes shows.

Church music had undergone a profound transformation since Haydn's day. There was a distinct 'back to Palestrina' movement which when later consolidated became known as the 'Caecilians' (from St Cecilia, patroness of music) and which concentrated their attacks on the extremely popular Masses by Haydn and Mozart – again largely to no avail, because the public adored the martial sounds of the 'Coronation' or 'Nelson' Masses in church. When Neukomm produced his Mass for double choir in D, the *Allgemeine Wiener Musikzeitung* of 1845 wrote that 'here and there (e.g. in the Dona) a somewhat trivial figuration reminded one of some blunders in the great hero of tones Haydn (his teacher)'. By this time Haydn's Masses had not only many enemies in England – where almost all *settecento* Catholic church music caused Anglican critics to wince – but even in Vienna. In 1844, a critic in an Austrian paper found the 'Nelson' Mass

> . . . formidable, excellent and a work of genius in *musical* aspects, but from the *churchly* standpoint hardly to be tolerated. . . . I must openly confess that after hearing *this* Mass, I well understand the old Werner's objection, for Jos. Haydn took the worldly (operatic) music of his period, put it in the church and made almost a concert hall out of the house of God.[2]

Even in the *Allgemeine Wiener Musikzeitung* of the same year we find someone commenting on the Agnus Dei in Haydn's Masses that:

> . . . he loves soli all too much, and they have no place here. But his 'Dona nobis', except for those Masses in which he uses the melody of the 'Kyrie' to these words and with fortunate effect [*Missa brevis* in F; *Missa Sancti Nicolai*; *Missa brevis S. Joannis de Deo*], are in the highest degree unchurchly. They are pure effect-pieces, and are only there to provide a brilliant ending. Also the fugues that Haydn often uses – e.g. in the 'Mariazellermesse', 'Cecilia' Mass, and so on – seem to me to be thoroughly out of place.

One of the few pieces of Haydn's religious music to survive the Victorian disapproval was, interestingly enough, *The Seven Words*, Queen Victoria herself, an ardent musician, wrote (with characteristic distaste) of the previous century[3] – 'I can't understand their not admiring Meyerbeer, and Mendelssohn and Weber; Mozart I am not always quite so fond of, as I think the instrumentation so poor (it was so in those days)' – but later in the same year (1860) we find her saying that 'This evening [Windsor Castle, 7 April 1860] Haydn's Passion or *The Seven Words* are to be given,

---

1 In following the course of Haydn in nineteenth-century Austria we are much indebted to the afore-mentioned article by Clemens Höslinger; see pp. 127ff.
2 Höslinger, 130f.
3 *Dearest Child, Letters between Queen Victoria and the Princess Royal 1858–1861*, edited by Roger Fulford, New York 1965, pp. 231, 245, 246.

which are so beautiful . . .'; and a few days later she relates (11 April) '. . . and in the evening had Haydn's Passion – very beautiful, though all Oratorios even the very finest – (and I am particularly fond of them) affect my nerves if they last above three quarters of an hour and make me sleepy (I think from the slow time and the attention one naturally pays) and it was extremely well done. . . .' Mozart, then, was considered a primitive orchestrator but Haydn's *The Seven Words*, being a piece calculated to uplift the soul and improve the morals, was admired. We mention this episode to show that there is no hard and fast rule by which the nineteenth century judged Haydn; the general trend is clear but there are some odd detours.

Returning to Vienna, we encounter once more the person of W. J. Tomaschek, whose slightly supercilious description of the ageing Haydn has been quoted in our Chronicle for 1808. In his autobiography (1846) he speaks of the 'low level' of Haydn's aesthetic character, and this description was of profound influence, not least on Vienna's most celebrated music critic, Eduard Hanslick, whom Wagner immortalized in *Die Meistersinger* as Beckmesser. Hanslick was not interested in Haydn and was particularly annoyed with the Viennese entrepreneurs and public for being content, year after year, with *The Creation* and *The Seasons* at the expense of Bach's Passions and Handel's masterpieces.

It was not only Schumann who found Haydn symphonies irritating; the Viennese found them not only irritating but rather foolish. A critic of the *Allgemeine Wiener Musikzeitung* in 1844 found when, one heard the symphony, that:

> . . . it is as if the old Father Haydn himself entered the hall; full of a burgomaster's dignity; but soon cheered up, we see him tripping about valiantly as if he wanted to dance; stamps several times quite energetically on the floor as if annoyed; – not at all! he laughs heartily, he trills quite a nice tune, in a comfortable fashion, walks round the hall several times in a quite fresh and youthful manner but with bent knees and leaves the hall with a friendly bow.   [Höslinger, 134]

Of course the Viennese were subject to the 'progress theory' with regard to Haydn, Mozart and Beethoven; the old poet Castelli was quoted approvingly when he said that Haydn 'had built a country house, another [Mozart] had added a storey and finally a third [Beethoven] put a great tower on it' (1845; Höslinger, 134). Beethoven had come to dominate musical thinking everywhere. Talking of string quartets, Hanslick in 1856 found an anonymous quality in Haydn's works of that genre:

> . . . a Haydn quartet, we say, very typically, whereas one certainly speaks, and always, of the one or the other *specific* quartet by Beethoven. The listener is very much interested in knowing *which* of the row of Beethoven quartets he will hear; different with Haydn . . . Since Beethoven wrote ten times less music [than Haydn] he could impress it with ten times as much.   [Höslinger, 135]

Yet the come-back tendency of Haydn's music made itself felt also in Vienna. Writing in 1860, Hanslick was forced to admit that:

> In the third of the society concerts, Haydn's Symphony in C [No. 97?] made the freshest impression. The repetition, stormily demanded, of two movements must be counted as one of the late triumphs of the old gentleman. Yes, the quiet, nice grand-daddy, so sweet that you want to kiss him, is enjoying great popularity with us . . .   [Höslinger, 138]

This subtle piece of sarcasm soon gave way to Hanslick's more normal prose in dealing with the kissable grand-daddy. Reviewing *The Storm* in 1891, he writes:

. . . during these 99 years [since it was supposedly written] we have had quite different 'storms' in music, in poetry, in world history, in our own souls. When Haydn after a short storm repeats the prayer 'Komm doch wieder, sanfte Ruh'' in endless and long-drawn repetitions, then quite gently [*ganz sanft*] the 'gentle quiet' [*sanfte Ruh'*] begins to drip into gentle boredom [*sanfte Langeweile*]. . . .

[Höslinger, 140]

This was the time when Haydn's D major Concerto for 'Cello and Orchestra (VIIb: 2), in the monstrous edition by Gevaert (Breitkopf & Härtel, 1890), was being relaunched. Despite such scathing attacks on it as Hanslick's (1895), it soon turned into one of Haydn's most popular works – indeed it was often the only work by Haydn in an average concert season of, say, the Boston Symphony Orchestra in the 1920s or 1930s.

. . . With such an old-fashioned, insipid, occasional or courtesy piece it will be hard for the best violoncellists to create an effect. There we have series of thoughts and non-thoughts, used by Papa Haydn a hundred times and since then passed through thousands of hands. No brilliant orchestral ritornello awakens us from the light slumber of this violoncello solo, no energetically contrasting atmosphere differentiates one movement from another. Surely the most thankful admirers of Haydn's quartets will have to admit that we have grown out of this Violoncello Concerto, which neither piety nor virtuosity can awake to new life . . .

[Höslinger, 140]

It is indeed a quirk of fate that this much maligned Concerto soon became part of the standard repertoire.

Hugo Wolf, like Schumann a discerning critic, once described a Haydn symphony as the typical fare of the Philistine *rentier* who objects to every locomotive whistle, every new coffee-machine, Schopenhauer's philosophy, Liebig's meat extract, Wagner's musical drama, etc. 'They like to talk about the good old wonderful times. Their favourite composer is Haydn' (Höslinger, 140).

From the available, and vast, literature by and about Wagner, it was always assumed that Beethoven was the Wagnerian hero; and so he was, but the Bayreuth master is now, in the fascinating Cosima Wagner Diaries which appeared just before this volume went to press,[1] revealed to have had a profoundly sympathetic and understanding attitude towards Haydn. It was a very rare attitude in those days. Some extracts will illustrate:

28 May 1869 . . . After lunch played [four hands] with R. [Richard], a Haydn symphony. . . . [99].

2 August 1869 . . . Afternoon R. played Faust Overture and two Haydn symphonies, during which we noted that in formal construction H. is a greater master than Mozart. . . . 3 August . . . In the evening a Haydn symphony four hands with R. 5 August . . . After lunch a Haydn symphony four hands with R. . . . In the evening a Haydn symphony; great joy about its mastery, 'you can see clearly in him', said R., 'how a people's genius [*Volksgenie*] helps himself. The form is more compact than in Mozart, who is always after the *Canto*; except for the four great symphonies he simply didn't take the time. That is why these Haydn symphonies are much more interesting.' [136f.]

6 August . . . In the evening we again played two Haydn symphonies four hands . . . [138]

---

1 Cosima Wagner, *Die Tagebücher 1 (1869–1877)*, edited and with commentary by Martin Gregor-Dellin and Dietrich Mack, Munich 1976; an English translation is in preparation.

25 February 1871. Yesterday I woke up, singing the Minuet & Trio from Haydn's D major Symphony, which much pleased R. . . . [362]

18 June 1873 . . . [Richard talks] about the Slavic people, their service to music through the dance, Haydn's service to have discovered these tunes, which Beethoven presented in such an ideal form. We Germans don't know much about our dance melodies. . . . [696]

19 October 1873 . . . at the end of the evening R. played for me the Andante from the Symphony in D (London Symphony) [No. 104]; endless joy over this masterly Art; Haydn, inspired after the death of Mozart by the latter's genius, becomes the real predecessor of Beethoven; rich and yet so finely worked orchestration, everything 'speaks', everything is inspiration; 'nowadays people's daring ideas all say nothing to me, they are not inventions but collections'. . . . [742].

20 October 1873 . . . No reading [aloud] in the evening but a Haydn symphony (in D) four hands with R., much joy with it.

3 February 1874 . . . In the evening R. plays the D major Symphony by Haydn with them [Richter and Lalas], then he plays the Andante (G minor) [Symphony No. 83, slow movement?] of another Symphony, explaining to them the beauties, especially the concision, everything has meaning, the two themes circle round each other like sun and moon. . . . [789].

13 May 1874 . . . At the end of the evening I say to R. that I would like to live with you on a lonely island, 'we do just that', said R., 'I am living now as if after my death, you have to reach that point; it happened to the good Haydn, who was actually dead after Mozart's appearance and after Mozart's death he wrote and enjoyed his best . . .' [818].

27 October 1875 . . . R. plays quartets by Haydn, finds them marvellous. . . . [945].

9 November 1877 . . . Beforehand a Haydn quartet, masterly and highly intelligent, then a Mozart, alas very banal. Only in the Adagio is a page which sounds to me like the consolation of an angel . . . In the evening once again [Beethoven's Quartet] Opus 135 with the tempi given by R. . . .; at the end the wonderful Adagio by Haydn from the Quartet [left blank], R's great favourite. R. had much pleasure from the beautiful evening. 'I much prefer to have to do with *Musikanten*, they are so capable.' . . . [1084f.].

To Richard Wagner Haydn was definitely a musician's musician.

As the nineteenth century became the twentieth, irritation with Haydn grew to a point where even a man like Theodor Billroth could ask the rhetorical question if 'it is not impossible that in not too far a time in the future, *every* piece of music written before Beethoven will be put aside as not interesting enough' (1898; Höslinger, 141).

The brilliant young conductor, Felix von Weingartner, continued this thought to its logical conclusion when, in 1907,[1] he wrote about Beethoven:

Much of Haydn, Mozart and Schubert, most of Weber, enjoy an artistic existence only in the light of the imperishable works of this master, but already belong to past history; not true of Beethoven, if we perhaps except some youthful works and *pièces d'occasion*.

It is characteristically ironic that, as Weingartner was writing these lines, he was seeing through the press his critical edition of the first forty Haydn symphonies in the new

1 Preface to the *Beethoven-Jahrbuch* edited by Theodor Frimmel.

Breitkopf & Härtel *Gesamtausgabe* which was being planned to celebrate the centenary of Haydn's death in 1909. We shall return to this project shortly, but before doing so, we must introduce something of a landmark in Haydn criticism.

The last year of the nineteenth century saw the publication, in London, of a book by one I. F. Runciman entitled *Old Scores and New Reading*. On page 92, we find the following summing-up of *The Creation*, to which the author devotes an article. 'After considering the songs, the recitatives, and the choruses in detail it really seems to contain very little. Perhaps it may be described as a third-rate Oratorio, whose interest is largely historic and literary.'

In 1902, J. Cuthbert Hadden published a biography of Haydn in which (p. 142) he found Runciman's article 'an admirably just and concise appreciation[!]'. Following Runciman's justice and conciseness, Hadden contributes a book which easily represents the nadir of Haydn's biographical existence. A few extracts will give something of the book's inimitable flavour.

[On Haydn quartets (p. 174)] It would be too much to say that even Haydn fully realised the capacities of each of his four instruments. Indeed, his quartet writing is often bald and uninteresting. But at least he did write in four-part harmony. . . .
[On Haydn's symphonies for Morzin (p. 175:] The circumstances were not such as to encourage him to 'rise to any pitch of real greatness or depth of meaning'; and although he was able to build on a somewhat grander scale when he went to Eisenstadt, it was still a little comfortable *coterie* that he understood himself to be writing for rather than for the musical world at large. [About the pre-Salomon symphonies (p. 176):] The other, and especially the earlier works are of practically no account. . . . Regarded in themselves, as absolute and individual entities, they are not for a moment to be placed by the side of the later compositions.

[About Haydn and the pianoforte (p. 179):] . . . we may doubt whether [his genius] was multiplex enough or intellectual enough to satisfy the deeper needs of our time. [Of Haydn's Masses (p. 180):] . . . the progress of the art would not have been materially affected if it had never come into existence. [Of Haydn's stage works (p. 181):] Haydn lacked the true dramatic instinct. His placid, easy-going, contented nature could never have allowed him to rise to great heights of dramatic force. He was not built on a heroic mould; the meaning of tragedy was unknown to him. [On Haydn's music in general (p. 183):] That he was not deep, that he does not speak a message of the inner life to the latter-day individual, who, in the Ossianic phrase, likes to indulge in 'the luxury of grief', must, of course, be admitted.

And Hadden was only expressing, if anything in a rather milder form, the prevailing sentiment at that time. Ernest Newman, writing in 1895,[1] suggests that:

When we examine the character of the pacific and timorous Haydn and reflect how much of this was due to long-continued subserviance to the wishes and habits of his patrons, it is impossible to avoid the conclusion that much of the out-of-the-word repose that pervades his music is the expression of a spirit almost emasculated by undue seclusion from the active life of men – a spirit of weak complaisance and unambitious compromise, turned away from the outer world to the inner, rarely returning to touch upon a phase of life of which, indeed, it was almost wholly ignorant.

---

1 *Gluck and the opera*, London 1895, p. 49.

In conversation, Newman went even further: he used to propose, in the same way that others have done when suggesting that Vivaldi wrote the same concerto six hundred times, that one could at random interchange any first, second, third or fourth movement of a Haydn symphony with any other comparable movement, without anyone noticing any difference whatever.[1]

Given informed critical judgements of this kind, it is hardly to be expected that the centenary celebrations of 1909 produced much more than a vast musicological congress at Vienna (at which Wanda Landowska played the harpsichord) and a few articles in scientific journals. The new *Gesamtausgabe* had managed, as we have pointed out, to present three volumes of symphonies (Nos. 1–40) to the musical world, but it was not until after the First World War that any further volumes were forthcoming. The complete piano sonatas, edited by Karl Päsler, required three volumes, and were followed, in the 1920s, by *The Creation*, *The Seasons* and *The Seven Words* (the plates of the latter engraved but the score never issued in the *Gesamtausgabe*). By this time the world was ready to celebrate the bicentenary of Haydn's birth in 1932, and Breitkopf & Härtel managed by a vast exertion of its publishing skills to produce two more volumes of its Haydn edition, the *Lieder* and a fourth volume of symphonies (Nos. 1–49); after which the *Gesamtausgabe* quietly, and apparently to no one's regret, ceased to publish.

It cannot be said that Haydn's position had improved very strikingly between the two celebrations of 1909 and 1932. In judging his position we ought not to overlook the mammoth celebrations that marked the centenary of Beethoven's death in 1927, a position which may perhaps be clarified by glancing briefly at an enormously popular Beethoven biography which appeared in New York two years later. Entitled, characteristically, *The Man who freed Music*, its author, Robert Haven Schauffler, has preserved for us the typical American attitude not only towards Beethoven, but also towards Haydn and Mozart, with which the present author grew up. In the 1930s, Mozart was hardly performed at symphony concerts, apart from the occasional overture, one or two concertos and perhaps the G minor or 'Jupiter' Symphonies. Haydn fared even worse in American concert programmes. The explanation may be found in Schauffler's incredible book, which is interesting in that Mozart and Haydn are now lumped together as typical of the enslaved servant-musician from whose scullery-mentality Beethoven was to free music:

> [On the Op. 1 Piano Trios (p. 36):] 'These compositions instantly overshadowed all that Haydn and Mozart had ever composed in that form.'
> [On the Op. 2 Piano Sonatas (p. 40):] 'The next two sonatas [from Op. 2] bear the unmistakable stamp of Vienna. They were chiefly intended for the display of their composer's virtuosity as pianist. This they accomplished in a fashion that took the wind out of Haydn's and Mozart's sails and established a new standard of sonata techni[que].'
> [About the First Symphony (pp. 63f.):] 'In it Beethoven leaned heavily on the more rococo qualities of Haydn and Mozart. . . . But the fact remains that this work, tentative though it is, surpassed all other existing symphonies except a handful of Mozart's and Haydn's.'
> [About the Op. 18 Quartets (p. 69):] '[In No. 4] a new note had been struck. A deeper level of the psyche, heretofore voiceless, had been reached and set free for musical expression.'

1 Repeated to us by Mr Walter Legge, a long-time friend of Newman.

[About the piano Sonatas Opp. 26 and 27:] 'Not that the slow beginnings of these sonatas were any more of an absolute innovation than his term *scherzo*, or his substitution in the C minor quartet of a slowed-down *scherzo* for the usual *adagio*. The rococo masters had made tentative beginnings along this line. Mozart had commenced his A major piano sonata with a slow theme and variations. And Haydn, in his C major quartet [Op. 64 No. 1] had substituted an *Allegretto scherzando* for a slow movement. . . . The Mozart and Haydn movements had the gay, sportive, often trifling tone of the old-fashioned rococo culture. Even their pathos went scarcely more than skin deep.'

[On classicism and romanticism (p. 118):] '. . . the Nineteenth Century should perhaps be called, not romanticism, but Beethovenism. In the rococo age form was all in all – beautiful, smoothly rounded, superficial form, which covered with fashionable éclat no little poverty of content and of emotion; graceful form which harmonized with the frivolous elegance of gentry, blind and insensible to the misery of the masses.'

[On Beethoven and Jesus Christ (p. 145):] 'In the authoritative accents of this new lawgiver there is an echo of the way in which Jesus sometimes talked to his disciples.'

[On the origins of *Fidelio* (p. 162):] 'Having surpassed Mozart in the symphonic and chamber music fields Beethoven was tempted to triumph over his illustrious predecessor in opera as well. He began casting about for a suitable libretto.'

[On the opening of the Fourth Symphony compared to 'Chaos' from *The Creation*:] '. . . the introduction's gropings and stumblings in a twilit diminished-seventh chaos [footnote:] This opening of the Fourth Symphony may have been inspired by Haydn's *Creation*, produced in 1798, only eight years before. But what an improvement!'

[On the Mass in C (Op. 86) (p. 209):] '. . . Beethoven realized quite well that his own work surpassed all previous Masses with which he was familiar. . . . He must have realized also that its dignity and devotional spirit made it a poineer in emancipating church music from the profane and theatrical tone which had, since Bach, invaded it, and which showed plainly in the Masses of even Mozart and Haydn.'

Naturally, faced with a whole generation who thought as Schauffler did, it was difficult for the movers of the Haydn festivals in 1932 to accomplish much. But compared to the relatively barren products of 1909, the bicentenary celebrations produced a number of excellent things, among them a refreshingly vigorous biography by Karl Geiringer and a great deal of useful specialized literature. Perhaps the most significant by-product of this festival was the foundation, by Mr Walter Legge, of the Haydn Quartet Society for the Gramophone Company in England. Beginning in 1932, this Society issued a large album of Haydn string quartets every year until the outbreak of the Second World War – eight volumes in all; for many people, these gramophone records were their first introduction to Haydn's quartets. From this point, the gramophone record was to become a decisive factor in the so-called Haydn Renaissance.

Altogether, a certain shift in interest from Central Europe to England can now be observed. Sir Donald Francis Tovey had written his brilliant and authoritative article on Haydn's quartets for the Cobbett *Cyclopaedia*, and in the 1930s Oxford University Press began to publish his famous 'Essays on Musical Analysis', which included penetrating analyses of the two late Oratorios and a series of symphonies. It would be difficult to overestimate the influence that these articles (books) enjoyed: they formed the basis for countless programme notes and indeed their spirit extends directly to Charles Rosen's recent (1971) book, *The Classical Style*.

The bicentenary publications also brought forth some extraordinary dross, foremost among which must be classed an article published by Paul Henry Lang in the *Musical Quarterly* for April 1932, entitled 'Haydn and the Opera' which has the dubious eminence of having been written by someone who had hardly seen the scores of more than two or three Haydn operas (and probably bowdlerized versions of *Lo speziale* or *Il mondo della luna* at that), and who filled out the required space with statements such as this one:

> The most fervent admirers of Haydn have to admit that his Masses correspond neither to the liturgy, nor to the ideas, exigencies or artistic traditions of the Catholic church. His naïve devotion could not rise to that region, just as his jovial nature could not interpret, in the opera, tumultuous passions. There are deeply felt vocal passages, yet the instrumental accompaniment with its witty figures scoffs at the well invented parts for the singers.

The scholarly world of Haydn research hardly existed at all in the 1930s – Haydn scholars could have been numbered on the fingers of one hand. In 1939, Professor Jens Peter Larsen published *Die Haydn-Überlieferung*, an important book which set out to establish the basis for authenticity in Haydn's *œuvre*. This was especially needed because shortly before that date, a German musicologist, Adolf Sandberger, had suggested that Haydn had composed not only the 104 known symphonies but seventy-eight in addition. Now that the acrimonious musicological battle between Larsen and Sandberger, which took place in *Acta Musicologica* and in the *Zeitschrift für Musik* from 1935 to 1937 (and led to the publication of Larsen's monumental *Die Haydn-Überlieferung*), has died down, it may be said with confidence that all the symphonies supposedly resurrected by Sandberger are spurious; we now know the genuine composers of most of them. Using the authentic catalogues, the autographs, and examining the watermarks of those autographs for chronology, Larsen's book for the first time put Haydn scholarship on a systematic basis. Pohl's work had appeared during the 1870s and 1880s but had remained unfinished; the third and final volume, completed by Hugo Botstiber, appeared in 1927. It was hardly noticed by the musical world and never translated into any foreign language, as the standard Bach biography by Spitta and Jahn's *Life of Mozart* had been.

But important though Larsen's book was, its diffusion was radically hindered by historical circumstances: the Second World War had already broken out and it was not until after the war that international scholarship began to take cognizance of the importance of Larsen's publication which, moreover, was completed by the appearance at Copenhagen, in 1941, of his facsimile edition of *Drei Haydn-Kataloge* (*EK*, *HV* and the so-called Kees Catalogue). In 1949, the Haydn Society (Boston, Massachusetts) asked Professor Larsen to be the general editor of a new Haydn Complete Edition; he agreed and four volumes were issued by 1951, when the Society had to disband. It also undertook to publish recordings of unknown Haydn music, but the public's support did not match the critical approval. The same fate befell the first attempt to record all Haydn's symphonies in 1960, conducted by Max Goberman and issued first by the Library of Recorded Masterpieces and later by Columbia Records. Goberman died shortly after starting the project, and Columbia was sufficiently disenchanted by the sales of the first twenty-two symphonies that they forthwith discontinued the series thereafter. By this time, not only gramophone records but also the wireless – and especially the British Broadcasting Corporation – were slowly changing the public's knowledge of Haydn; in 1958, the BBC put on an elaborate Haydn series, prepared by the present writer, which gave the first performances in modern times of several works by Haydn. The literature on Haydn had also grown and by the next festival, the sesquicentenary of his death in 1959, there existed monographs on the symphonies, the Masses, the quartets, the operas, and so on. Following the collapse of the Haydn Society, a German Haydn Institut was formed in Cologne, directed first by Professor Larsen and later by the brilliant scholar, Dr Georg Feder; since the mid-1950s, the Haydn Institut has been slowly issuing a new and, one may hope, definitive Collected Edition of Haydn's music (*Joseph Haydn Werke*) which is a model of scrupulous editing and beautiful printing. Apart from that monumental edition, which will probably be completed about the year 2000, there are now practical and scholarly editions of all the symphonies, quartets, piano sonatas, piano trios, most of the operas and a huge quantity of other music, mostly issued by Universal Edition (Vienna), Verlag Doblinger (Vienna), Eulenburg (London), Schott (Mainz and London), Faber Music (London), Schirmer (New York), and so on.

Most of Haydn's music has by now either been recorded or will shortly be available on records. Decca (London) planned in 1969 to record all the symphonies, with the Philharmonica Hungarica conducted by Antal Dorati (that undertaking was completed in the autumn of 1972); another complete edition of Haydn's symphonies was issued by the Musical Heritage Society of New York (a Vienna orchestra was conducted by Ernst Märzendorfer), which firm has also issued all the piano works by Haydn. Several complete editions of all the string quartets have been, or are in the process of being, recorded, and the same is true of the piano trios. At the present time of writing (1973), the Philips Company has proposed to record all the Haydn operas,[1] conducted by Antal Dorati. This enormous amount of recorded Haydn has, in its way, enacted just as profound an effect for the dissemination of Haydn as the complete printed editions had done (for the latter were necessary before the former could be made). It is hard to know whether this activity constitutes a real Haydn Renaissance, as has been occasionally suggested, or if the public will actually respond to all these projects *à la longue*; but from the latest sales figures which Decca (London) have made public, it appears that before the present symphony series has even been issued complete, a million records of it will have been sold.[2]

And yet, this music is still not everywhere accepted. Reviewing a French recording (Orchestre de la Fondation Haydn, conducted by Antonio de Almeida) of Symphonies Nos. 62, 66, 67 and 69 – this was the proposed beginning of another complete series of the symphonies – in the journal *Harmonie* (No. 55, March 1970), Antoine Goléa, a well-known French critic, has this to say about the music:

> Les 'intégrales', c'est la grande maladie du disque; je les qualifie de maladies, lorsqu'il ne vaut pas la peine de les faire, sinon dans un but strictement scientifique et musicologique; j'y ai trouvé trois minutes de musique intéressante, c'est le trio du Minuetto de la Symphonie No. 67. C'est peu, pour deux faces de 33 centimètres en longue durée.

The world, it would seem, is still not enough, and it appears that the Haydn Renaissance is still not a crusade for many educated and thinking people.

1 Meanwhile (1976) they have issued one, *La fedeltà premiata*, and two others have been recorded: *Orlando Paladino* and *La vera costanza*; a further two, *L'isola disabitata* and *Il mondo della luna* are in production.
2 By the end of 1976, two million copies had been sold.

It would be wrong, however, to overlook a very real and spontaneous public affection for Haydn which continues to exist, as it always has, regardless of the critics. During the 1930s, one of Haydn's most persuasive champions was Sir Thomas Beecham and the present writer was a witness to the storm of applause that greeted Sir Thomas's Haydn symphonies in Carnegie Hall in New York or in the Royal Albert Hall in London. After Sir Thomas's death, the late Sir John Barbirolli continued to conduct many highly successful performances of Haydn's symphonies, some in Berlin and some elsewhere. On 9 February 1962 he wrote:[1]

> . . . They [the Los Angeles Philharmonic] have played superbly for me, almost sounding like my own Hallé [Orchestra] at times . . . A real triumph for our delicious and wonderful old friend Haydn. You remember how we sat and looked at his entrancing, enigmatic and surely mischievous smile from all angles in that statuette presented to me in Budapest [which depicted Haydn without his wig], well, we opened with the [Symphony No.] 98 in B flat last night and this afternoon (the one with the slow movt. that begins with the National Anthem) and the audience cheered and clapped as if it was the end of a concert. I confess it gave me the greatest pleasure.

Haydn ended his life as the public's composer *par excellence*; for many years thereafter he became, at best, a musician's musician; it now remains to be seen whether, after all, he will not once again become the public's composer. Only the passing of time will be able to determine that.

[Completed at Buggiano Castello, Italy,
24 August 1973. *Laus Deo.*]

---

1 Michael Kennedy, *Barbirolli, Conductor Laureate*, London 1971, p. 271.

Bibliography

IN THIS BIBLIOGRAPHY we have attempted to list all the critical editions of Haydn's *oeuvre* and all the major publications relating to the composer. As for the vast literature concerning the European cultural, political and economic background, we have – for obvious reasons – limited ourselves to works dealing primarily with Austrian and English life, and even here we have been forced to be selective and have thus included those books and articles from which we derived useful background material and which may be recommended to any student of the second half of the eighteenth century.

The subdivisions within the Bibliography are as follows: (1) critical editions of Haydn's music; (2) eighteenth-century periodicals and journals; (3) eighteenth-century music publishers' catalogues; (4) MS. catalogues; (5) eighteenth- and nineteenth-century topographical studies; (6) general bibliography of books and articles.

Critical Editions of Haydn's Music

This is a selected list of critical editions of Haydn's music. It does not include many worthwhile editions of the nineteenth century – such as Pohl's edition of the Overture in D (Ia:4) – which is now available in a new critical edition (Doblinger). It also does not include Eulenburg editions which have been supplanted by newer critical editions, such as Symphonies 92, 98 and 100. It also does not list in detail the numerous reprints of Haydn's works published recently and clearly based on available critical editions, e.g. the Schirmer edition of the *Missa in tempore belli*, which is reprinted, with small changes, from the edition of the Haydn-Institut.

Apart from the obvious intrinsic value of the scores, the prefaces and critical notes form a vital part of the critical apparatus needed to establish an *Urtext*. It has not been thought necessary to list these forewords and notes (*Revisionsberichte*) in detail.

GESAMTAUSGABEN

Joseph Haydns Werke (Breitkopf & Härtel, 1907 *et seq.*; ceased publication during World War II)

The Complete Works (Haydn Society, Boston-Vienna, 1949–51)

Werke (Joseph-Haydn-Institut, Cologne, and G. Henle Verlag, Munich–Duisburg, 1953 *et seq.*)

BÄRENREITER

Divertimenti, Op. 31 (X:1, 5) (E. F. Schmid)

Notturni (II:31, 32) (ed. E. F. Schmid; formerly Musikwissenschaftlicher Verlag)

L'isola disabitata (Landon)

Il mondo della luna (Landon)

Philemon und Baucis (Landon)

Concerto for Organ (XVIII:3) (Nagels Musik Archiv – Heussner)

Reprints (small scores) from Haydn *Werke* (including Masses, symphonies, quartets etc.)

BREITKOPF & HÄRTEL

The Seven Words, vocal version (Mandyczewski)

The Creation (Mandyczewski)

The Seasons (Mandyczewski)

Concerto for Organ (XVIII:1) (Schneider)

BROUDE BROTHERS

Six English Psalms (Hoboken, vol. II, p. 181) (Landon)

Dr Harington's Compliment (XXVIb:3) (Landon)

DOBLINGER

SECULAR VOCAL MUSIC

Cantata: *Applausus* (XXIVa:6) (Landon)

Cantata: 'Qual dubbio' (XXIVa:4) (Landon)

Madrigal: 'The Storm' (XXIVa:8) (Burkhart)

Trio: 'Pietà di me, benigni Dei' (XXVb:5) (Landon)

Cantata: 'Miseri noi, misera patria' (XXIVa:7) (Landon)

Scena di Berenice (XXIVa:10) (Landon)

Aria di Lindora (XXXII:1) (Landon)

Two Italian Duets (XXVa:1,2) (Landon)

ORATORIO

Mare Clausum (XXIV:9) (Landon)

CHURCH MUSIC

Missa brevis in F (Moder)

Missa in honorem B.V.M. in E flat ('Grosse Orgelmesse') (Strassl)

Te Deum (1764) (XXIIIc:2) (Landon)

Te Deum (1799) (XXIIIc:1) (Landon)

433

Litaniae de B.V.M. in C (XXIIIc:C2) (Landon) [= J. Hayda; see *Haydn at Eszterháza (1766–1790)*]

Salve Regina in G minor (XXIIIb:2) (Landon)

SYMPHONIES

Complete Edition. Large scores Doblinger and Universal Edition; small scores Philharmonia (Füssl, Landon, Schultz)

CONCERTI

Violin Concerto in G (VIIa:4) (Landon)

Cembalo Concerto in D (XVIII:2) (Landon)

Organ Concerto in C (XVIII:8) (Landon)

5 concerti for 2 lyre (VIIh:1–5) (Landon)

DANCES AND MARCHES

Menuetti Ballabili (IX:7) (Landon)

Six Allemandes (IX:9) (Landon)

24 Minuets for Orchestra (IX:16) (Landon)

March for the Royal Society of Musicians (VIII:3 *bis*) (Landon)

Complete marches for wind band (VIII:1, 2, 3, 4, 6, 7; also *Marche Regimento de Marshall*, Hoboken *deest*) (Landon)

OVERTURES

'Acide e Galatea' (Landon)

'Lo speziale' (Landon)

'L'incontro improvviso' (Landon)

'La vera costanza' (Landon)

Sinfonia (Overture) in D (Ia:7) (Landon)

Ouverture in D (Ia:4) (Landon)

'La fedeltà premiata' (Landon)

'Orlando Paladino' (Landon)

DIVERTIMENTI, ETC.

Divertimento in C (II:11) (Landon)

Cassatio in F (II:20) (Landon)

Divertimento in C (II:17) (Steppan)

Cassatio in G (II:G1) (Landon)

Cassatio in D (Hoboken *deest*) (Landon)

8 Notturni (II:25–32) (Landon)

Six 'Scherzandi' (II:33–38) (Landon)

Leopold Mozart: Cassatio ex G (including the three movements of the so-called 'Toy Symphony' [II:47]) (Landon)

CHAMBER MUSIC FOR WIND INSTRUMENTS

Divertimenti Nos. 1–8 (II:15; II:23; II:7; II:14; II:D18; II:3; *deest*; *deest*) (Landon)

Divertimento a tre in E flat (IV:5) (Landon)

Seven Marches for Wind Instruments (*deest*; VIII:1–4, 6, 7) (Landon)

CHAMBER MUSIC FOR STRINGS

String Quartets, complete critical edition (Barrett-Ayres, Landon)

String Quintet in G (II:2) (Landon)

String Quintet in A (II:A1) (Landon)

Six Sonatas for Violin and Viola (VI:1–6) (Zatschek)

Complete String Trios (V) (Landon)

SMALL PIANO CONCERTINOS

Concertino in C (XIV:11) (Landon)

Divertimento in C (XIV:8) (Landon)

Divertimento in F (XIV:9) (Landon)

PIANO TRIOS

Complete critical edition (Landon)

434

PIANO SONATA
Sonata No. 52 in E flat (XVI:52) (Badura-Skoda)

EDITION EULENBURG

Missa in angustiis ('Nelson' Mass) (Landon)
The Creation (reprint of Breikopf & Härtel *Gesamtausgabe* volume, *vide supra*)
The Seasons (reprint of Philharmonia edition, *vide* Universal Edition), etc.
Concertos for Violin: – in C (VIIa:4) and – in G (VIIa:4) (both Landon)
Concerto No. 1 for Horn (VIId:3) (Landon)
Concerto in E flat for Trumpet (VIIe:1) (Redlich)
Overture to *Die Feuersbrunst* (*Das abgebrannte Haus*) (Landon)
Overtures, symphonies, concertos, complete quartets (a non–critical edition)[1]

FABER MUSIC

Missa Sancti Nicolai (Landon)
Stabat Mater (Landon)

HENLE VERLAG

Many reprints of critical editions from *Werke* (*vide supra: Gesamtausgaben*), e.g. Piano Sonatas (Feder), church music (Becker-Glauch), including *4 Responsoria de Venerabili*

KISTNER & SIEGEL

Redoutensaal Dances (IX:11, 12) (Deutsch; E. F. Schmid)

MUSIKWISSENSCHAFTLICHER VERLAG

Double Concerto (XVIII:6) (Schultz)
L'incontro improvviso (Schultz; now Bärenreiter)

NAGELS MUSIK ARCHIV (now Bärenreiter Verlag)

Complete pieces for musical clock (E. F. Schmid)

EDITION PETERS

'London' Trios (IV:1–3) (Köhler)
Piano Concerto (XVIII:11) (Soldan)
Violoncello Concerto (VIIb:2) (Soldan)
Divertimenti (Lassen, etc.)

G. SCHIRMER

Masses – complete edition in preparation (in 1974 there were lacking only the early *Missae breves* in F and G, the *Missa Cellensis in honorem B.V.M.* (1766) and the *Missa in honorem B.V.M.* (c. 1769; Grosse Orgelmesse) (Hermann, Landon etc.)
The Seasons – orchestral overture and interludes in the uncut versions (Landon)
Symphony in D ('The Lost'; I:106) (Landon)

SCHOTT

Missa in angustiis ('Nelson' Mass) (Landon)
Das abgebrannte Haus (*Die Feuersbrunst*) (Landon)

SHV (Artia, Prague)

Violoncello Concerto (VIIb:1) (Pulkert)

UNIVERSAL EDITION
(Haydn-Mozart Presse; Philharmonia)

OPERAS
Lo speziale (Landon)
Le pescatrici (Landon)
L'infedeltà delusa (Landon); also miniature score (Philharmonia)

---

1 Eulenburg will issue miniature scores of the new Doblinger edition (*vide supra*)

La vera costanza (Landon)
La fedeltà premiata (Landon)
L'anima del filosofo (Landon)

ORATORIO

The Seasons (Philharmonia; reprint of Breitkopf & Härtel volume in *Werke – vide supra, Gesamtausgaben*)

SECULAR VOCAL MUSIC

Aria di Dorina (XXIVb:1) (Landon)
Aria di Donna Stella (XXIVb:2) (Landon)
Aria di Nannina (XXIVb:3) (Landon)
Aria di Agatina (XXXIc:5) (Landon)
Aria di Rosina (XXIVb:7) (Landon)
Cavatina di Alcina (XXIVb:9) (Landon)
Aria di Cardellina (XXIVb:12) (Landon)
Aria di Errisena (XXIVb:13) (Landon)
Aria di Beatrice (XXIVb:15) (Landon)
Aria di Merlina (XXIVb:17) (Landon)
Aria di Giannina (XXIVb:18) (Landon)
Arie des Schutzgeistes (XXX:5b) (Landon)
Aria da 'Il Canzoniere' (XXIVb:20) (Landon)
Aria di Oreste (XXIVb:10) (Landon)
Aria di Ernesto (XXVIII:7/6) (Landon) (*Il mondo della luna*: variant version)
Aria del Cavaliere (XXIVb:14) (Landon)
Aria di Titta (XXIVb:16) (Landon)
Aria di Nettuno (XXVIII: 1/K) (Landon) (*Acide e Galatea*: later addition)
Aria di Lumaca (XXIVb:5) (Landon)
Aria di Corrodino (XXIVb:11) (Landon)
Cantata: Arianna a Naxos (XXVIb:2) (Flothuis)

CHURCH MUSIC

Missa brevis alla capella 'Rorate coeli desuper' (Landon)
Missa Cellensis in honorem B.V.M. (1766 – formerly known as the *Missa Sanctae Caeciliae*) (Landon)
Missa ('Theresienmesse'; miniature score, Philharmonia) (Schnerich)
Libera (XXIIb:1) (Landon)
Cantilena pro Adventu (XXIIId:1) (Landon)

SYMPHONIES

See under Doblinger

CONCERTO

Violin Concerto in A (VIIa:3) (Heiller, Landon)

OVERTURE

'Overture to an English Opera' (Ia:3) (Landon)

CHAMBER MUSIC

Three Duets for two Violins, Op. 99 (VI, p. 521)

PIANO SONATAS

Complete Piano Sonatas (XVI:1–52) (C. Landon)
Complete Piano Sonatas (XVI:1–52), LEA Pocket Scores (Päsler)

Eighteenth-century Periodicals and Journals

ENGLISH

(a) Magazines

The Gentleman's Magazine; and Historical Chronicle, London 1731 *et seq.*
The European Magazine, and London Review, London 1782 *et seq.*
The Ladies' Magazine, London 1791 *et seq.*
The Monthly Review, or Literary Journal, London 1786 *et seq.*
The Sporting Magazine, London 1791 *et seq.*

(b) London Newspapers

The Argus, 1791–95
The Craftsman; or Say's Weekly Journal, 1791–95
The Daily Advertiser, 1791–95
The Diary; or Woodfall's Register, 1791–95
The Evening Mail, London 1791–95
The Gazetteer, and New Daily Advertiser, 1791–95
The General Evening Post, 1791–95
Johnson's British Gazette and Sunday Monitor, 1791–95
The London Chronicle, 1791–95
The London Recorder, or Sunday Gazette, 1791–95
The Morning Advertiser, 8 Feb., 1794 *et seq.*
The Morning Chronicle, 1791–95, also 1796 *et seq.*
The Morning Herald, 1791–95, also 1796 *et seq.*
The Morning Post, 1791–95, also 1796 *et seq.*
The Observer, 1791–95
The Oracle, Bell's World (after March 1, 1794: *The Oracle, and Public Advertiser*), 1791–95, also
    1796 *et seq.*
The Public Advertiser (merged with *The Oracle* on March 1, 1794), 1791–95
The St. James Chronicle or, British Evening Post, 1791–95.
The Star, 1791–95
The Sun, 1791–95, also 1796 *et seq.*
The Times, 1791–95, also 1796 *et seq.*
The True Briton, 1791–95
The Whitehall Evening Post, 1791–95

FRENCH

Affiches, Annonces et Avis Divers, Paris
Almanach Musical, Paris
L'Avant-coureur, Paris
Gazette de France, Paris
Mercure de France, Paris

GERMAN

Allgemeine Deutsche Bibliothek (ed. by C. F. Nicolai), Berlin–Stettin, 1766–96
Allgemeine Musikalische Zeitung, Leipzig, Breitkopf und Härtel, 1798 *et seq.* (ed. by J. F.
    Rochlitz)
Allgemeiner Theater Almanach von Jahr 1782, Vienna
Almanach der k.k. National-Schaubühne in Wien auf das Jahr 1788 (F. C. Kurz)
Berlinische Musikalische Zeitung, Berlin 1792 *et seq.* (ed. J. F. Reichardt)
Geschichte des neunzehnten Jahrhunderts, Vienna 1805 *et seq.*
Gothaer Theaterkalendar, Gotha, 1776–1800
Grazer literarisch-ökonomisches Wochenblatt, Graz 1787
Historisch-kritische Theaterchronik . . . von Wien, Vienna 1774

Bibliography (periodicals and journals)

Jahrbuch der Tonkunst in Wien und Prag, 1796
Journal des Luxus und der Moden, Weimar
London und Paris (ed. C. Bertuch), Weimar 1798 *et seq.*
Magazin der Musik, Hamburg, 1782 *et seq.* (ed. C. F. Cramer)
Die Meinungen der Babet, eine Wochenschrift, Vienna 1774–5
Musik, Copenhagen 1789 (ed. C. F. Cramer)
Musikalische Korrespondenz (ed. H. P. Bossler), Speyer, 1790–92
Musikalische Realzeitung & Bibliothek der Grazien (Bossler), Speyer 1789
Musikalischer Almanach (ed. J. F. Reichardt) Berlin 1796
Musikalischer Almanach (Musikalischer und Künstler-Almanach), 'Alethinopel' and 'Kosmopolis'
    (read Freiburg), 1782 *et seq.* (ed. C. L. Junker)
Musikalischer Almanach für Deutschland, Leipzig 1782, 83, 84, 89 (ed. J. N. Forkel)
Der Musikalische Dillettante: cf. Daube in General Bibliography
Musikalisches Wochenblatt, Berlin 1792 *et seq.*
Pressburger Zeitung (newspaper), Pressburg 1761 *et seq.*
*Nützliches Auskunftsbuch oder Kommerzialschema für Handelsleute, Fabrikanten, Künstler,
    Professionisten und die Jenigen, welche in der k. k. Haupt- und Residenz-Stadt Wien
    Handlungsgeschäfte oder andere Verrichtungen zu schlichten haben*, Vienna 1797
Realzeitung der Wissenschaften, Künste und der Commerzien, Vienna 1770–86
Taschenbuch des Wiener Theaters, Vienna 1777
Taschenbuch zum geselligen Vergnügen für 1791 [*et seq.*: 1792ff.], Leipzig
Theater-Kalender auf das Jahr 1775 [*et seq.*], Gotha [the so-called 'Gotha Theater-Kalender']
Theaterkalender von Wien, Vienna 1772–73
Wiener Blättchen & Neues Wiener Blättchen (newspapers)
Wiener Diarium (newspaper)
Wienerisches Musenalmanach, Vienna 1777–98
Wienerisches Kommerzialscheme oder Bürger-Almanach [etc.], Vienna 1789
Wiener Priviligierte Real-Zeitung (newspaper)
Wiener Theater Almanach für das Jahr 1794 [1795], Vienna
Wiener Zeitung (newspaper)
Wöchentliche Nachrichten und Anmerkungen, die Musik betreffend, Leipzig 1766 *et seq.* (ed. J. A.
    Hiller)

ITALIAN

Gazzetta Toscana (newspaper)
Gazzetta Universale (newspaper)

Eighteenth- and Nineteenth-century Topographical Studies

Topographisches Post-Lexikon aller Ortschaften der k.k. Erbländer, ed. Christian Crusius, 4 vols.,
    Vienna 1801
*Neueste Geschichten und Beschreibungen der merkwürdigsten Gotteshäuser, Stifte und Kloster,
    Wallfahrtskirchen, Gnadenörter, Calvarienberge, Grabmähler und Gottesäcker in der
    österreichischen Monarchie*, Vienna 1821
Reise von Venedig über Triest, Krain, Kärnten, Steiermark, und Salzburg, Frankfurt and Leipzig
    1793

Eighteenth-century Music Publishers' Catalogues

André (Offenbach/Main); Artaria (Vienna); Mad. Berault (Paris); Betz (London); Birchall (London); Bland (London); Blundell (London); Bossler (Speyer and Darmstadt); Bouin (Paris); Breitkopf & Härtel (Leipzig; see under General Bibliography); Bremner (London); Chevardière (Paris); Corri, Dussek and Co. (London); Forster (London: William Forster, London, issued a thematic catalogue of the Haydn symphonies and other works published by Forster. British Museum, London); Guera (Lyon); Huberty (Paris); Hummel (Hague, Amsterdam and Berlin: see under General Bibliography, Johannson); Imbault (Paris), Longman & Broderip (London); Nadermann (Paris); Pleyel (Paris); Preston (London); Ringmacher ('Catalogo de' Soli, Duetti, Trii, Quadri, Quintetti, Partite, de Concerti e delle Sinfonie. . . . che si trovano in Manoscritto nella Officina musica di Christiano Ulrico Ringmacher Libraio in Berolino MDCCLXXIII); Schmitt (Amsterdam); Sieber (Paris: Jean-Georges Sieber issued a thematic catalogue of the Haydn symphonies published by Sieber. Copies: Paris, Bibliothèque Nationale; author); Traeg ('Verzeichniss / alter und neuer / sowohl geschriebener als gestochener / Musikalien, / welche in der / Kunst- und / Musikalienhandlung / des / Johann Traeg, / zu Wien, in der Singerstrasse Nr. 957, / zu haben sind. / Kostet 30 Kr. / Wien, 1799 / Gedruckt, mit. c. Ghelenschen Schriften'.);[1] Venier (Paris); Westphal ('Verzeichniss / derer / Musicalien, / welche / in der Niederlage auf den grossen Bleichen / bey / Johann Christoph Westphal und Comp. / in Hamburg / in Commission zu haben sind / 1782 / . . . . / Hamburg / Gedruckt bey Joh. Philipp Christian Reuss.' (with various supplements).

1 Reproduced in facsimile in (ed. A. Weinmann) 'Beiträge zur Geschichte des Alt-Wiener Musikverlages', Reihe 2, Folge 17, Band I, Universal Edition, Vienna 1973, under the title 'Johann Traeg: Die Musikverzeichnisse von 1799 und 1804'.

Ms. Catalogues

The catalogues are listed according to the name of the compiler or former owner, place of origin or familiar or distinctive titles.

British Museum: see Dunwalt, Elssler, d'Ogny.

Chotek (Kacĭna Castle; now Prague, National Museum): various thematic catalogues.

Clam-Gallas: (1) 'Catalogo / Delle Carte di Musica / appartenenti alla / Sig / Contessa Carolina Clam = / Gallas' (arias; thematic); (2) 'Catalogo / Delle Carte di appartenenti / al Sig Conte Cristiano / Clam e Gallas / da me per conservare / Speer / Maest[ro] di Musica' (instrumental music; thematic).

Donaueschingen: thematic catalogue of 1804; also a non-thematic catalogue, 'Copia / Catalog / über / Vorhandene Clavier = und Sing = Musik / Sr Hochfürstlichen Durchlaucht / Carl Joachim / Regierenden Fürsten / zu / Fürstenberg / &c &c / [later:] 1803–1804'.

Dunwalt: music in the collection of Gottfried Dunwalt, Cologne 1770, 'Franz Commer / Catalogus / Musicalium / Godfridi Dun = / = walt / Canonici Collegiatae / Eccle = / siae B. Mariae V. ad Gradus / Coloniae'; under title is an illegible erased word, then '1770'; also a few later additions in the same(?) hand but in different ink.

Ehreshofen, Schloss (Germany): thematic catalogue (microfilm in *Neue Mozart Ausgabe*, Augsburg).

Eisenstadt: (1) thematic catalogue of Esterházy Archives, 1759, see J. Harich in *Haydn Yearbook* IX (1975); (2) 'CATALOGUE / raisonné des / Vêpres, des Litanies, des Te Deum des / Hymnes des Miserere / qui se trouvent / dans les archives de musique / d'église / de Son Altesse Serenissime / le prince regnant / Nicolas Esterházy', a beautifully bound MS. formerly in the princely music archives, then Sándor Wolf (Eisenstadt), now Burgenländisches Landesmuseum, Eisenstadt; this thematic catalogue must have been drawn up *c.* 1802.

Elssler: 'J. Haydns Verzeichnis musikalischer Werke, theils eigener, theils fremder Composition', non-thematic catalogue compiled by Johann Elssler; British Museum (Add. 32070); see also Haydn Verzeichnis.

Entwurf Katalog: thematic catalogue begun *c.* 1765 by Joseph Elssler and continued by Haydn, with interruptions, until *c.* 1800; Berlin, Staatsbibliothek (Mus. ms. Kat. 607) – facsimile in Larsen, *Drei Haydn-Kataloge* (see General Bibliography).

Esterházy: see under Eisenstadt, Hummel, Quartbuch.

Freising: catalogue of Fürstbischöfliches Archiv (now in Kreisarchiv, Munich), 'Themata / Von Jenen Musicalien, welche vom Jahre 1789. Bis / 1796. inclusive Theils Neu angekauft, Theils darzu [*sic*] / hergeschenkt, auch einige wenige ohne Nro. schon vor- / handen gewesene die dem Cathologo Einverleibt worden, / und Ebenfals [*sic*] im Musicalien Kasten auf dem Dom / Chor, kundig sind'; the catalogue is thematic, but does not give orchestration.

Freudenthal: 'Catalogue / des / Diverses Musiques', thematic; now in the Zentral-Archiv of the Deutsche Ritterorden in Vienna (Freudenthal is in Austrian Silesia, near Troppau).

Fürstenberg: see Donaueschingen, above.

Göttweig (Benedictine monastery in Lower Austria): catalogue in two volumes, the first entitled 'KATALOGUS / OPERUM MUSICALIUM / in / Choro musicali / MONASTERII / O.S.P.B. GOTTWICENSIS / R.R.D.D. / ALTMANNO / ABBATE per R. D. / Henricum / Wondratsch / p.t. chori regentem, conscriptus. / Anno MDCCCXXX Tom I'; the catalogue consists, with a few exceptions, of a list of all the *MSS.* then in the music archives, and includes the title, orchestration, the name of the copyist and date, in so far as these were known. Since most of the actual *MSS.* have long since disappeared, the catalogue is of unique documentary value.

Herzogenburg: thematic catalogue, listing music then in the Augustinian monastery of Herzogenburg, Lower Austria, 'Conscript / Ludovicuo Kintschner / Regenschori an 1846'. None of the entries is dated, and the catalogue is primarily of interest because it lists a number of sources no longer in the monastery. The orchestration, however, is included: There is also a small thematic catalogue of Masses, in oblong format.

Hummel: non-thematic catalogue, prepared by J. N. Hummel in 1806, of the music in the Esterházy Archives, Eisenstadt; Hummel Archives, Florence–Düsseldorf; a facsimile publication is in preparation, edited by Else Radant. Title: 'Inventarium der Hoch fürstlich Esterhazyschen Kammer & Theater Musik 1806'.

HV (Haydn Verzeichnis): thematic catalogue written in 1805 by Johann Elssler, under Haydn's supervision, 'Verzeichniss aller derjenigen Compositionen welche ich mich beyläufig erinnere von meinem 18ten bis in das 73ste Jahr verfertiget zu haben'. Esterházy Archives (copy by Elssler in Breitkopf & Härtel archives); the Esterházy copy disappeared in 1945. Facsimile in Larsen, *Drei Haydn-Kataloge* (see General Bibliography).

Kees: thematic catalogue of Haydn's symphonies, prepared for Franz Bernhard, Ritter von Kees, 'Catalogo Del Sinfonien Del Sig: Giuseppe Haydn'. Regensburg, cat. J. Haydn 85. Facsimile in Larsen, *Drei Haydn-Kataloge* (see General Bibliography).

Lambach: thematic catalogue, Benedictine monastery of Lambach, Upper Austria, 'Catalogus / Musicalium et Instrumentorum / ad Chorum Lambacensem pertinentium conscriptge [= conscript*um*] MDCCLXIIX [*sic*] / 1768'.

Lang, J. S. & Rettensteiner, Pater Werigand: thematic catalogue of Johann Michael Haydn's music; Bayerische Staatsbibliothek, Munich.

d'Ogny: thematic 'Catalogue de la Musique de Monsieur Le Comte d'Ogny', *c.* 1785(?); British Museum (Hirsch IV, 1085).

Quartbuch: thematic catalogue by Johann Nep. Weigl, *c.* 1775; in two volumes; Haydn seems to have acquired this catalogue and glanced through it, making a few corrections. Title: '2 Thematischer Cathalog verschiedener Compositionen von verschiedenen Meistern 2 Bände'. Esterházy Archives, Budapest (disappeared 1945); copy in Vienna Nationalbibliothek (s.m. 9040).

Raghrad (Raigern): thematic catalogue; now Brno (microfilm in *Neue Mozart Ausgabe*, Augsburg).

Sarasin: thematic 'Catalog der Luc. Sarasinschen Musik-Sammlung'; Universitätsbibliothek Basel (Sign Handbibl. Kunst d.III.9).

Sigmaringen: thematic catalogue, begun in 1766, in two volumes; a list of music once at the Hohenzollern castle of Sigmaringen, Germany; none of the sources has survived. Title: 'CATALOGUS / Über die / Sämtliche Musikalische Werck, / und derselben Authora, nach Al- / phabetischer Ordnung; welche von Ihro Hochfürst: Durchlaucht / dem Durchlauchtigsten Fürsten und Herrn Carl Friedrich Erbprinzen / zu Hohenzollern [etc.] consignitt von mir dem / Expeditions Rath, und / Music: Directore / Schindele / aº: 1766. The main section of the catalogue was made in 1766, but several groups of themes were added later, probably *c.* 1768, 1769 and *c.* 1770.

Zeil, Schloß: catalogues (microfilms in *Neue Mozart Ausgabe*, Augsburg); Fürstliches Archiv (ZAZ 4709): (1) 'Register / de anno 1767' (thematic catalogue); (2) 'Katalog / der / Sinfonien' (thematic, 18th century); (3) [Katalog ohne Jahresangabe] (chamber music, 18th century).

General Bibliography

Books and articles, listed chronologically under individual authors

ABERT, H., *Niccolò Jommelli als Opernkomponist*, Halle 1908

——, 'Joseph Haydns Klavierwerke', in *Zeitschrift für Musikwissenschaft* II, 1919/20

ABERT, H., and JAHN, O., *Mozart*, Berlin 1923/24

ADAM, A., 'Haydns Jugendjahre' in *Hamburgische literarische und kritische Blätter*, 1848

ADLER, G., 'Wiener Instrumentalmusik vor und um 1750' (Foreword to *Denkmäler der Tonkunst in Österreich*, XV. Jahrgang, vol. 2 [1908])

——, 'Ein Beitrag zur Haydn-Literatur', in *Neue Freie Presse* (Vienna), January 1909

——, *Joseph Haydn, Festrede*, Vienna 1909

——, 'Die Wiener klassische Schule', in *Handbuch der Musikgeschichte*, Leipzig 1920

——, 'Haydn and the Viennese Classical School', in *Musical Quarterly* XVIII (1932)

AITKEN, J. (ed.), *English Letters of the Eighteenth Century*, London 1946

ALALEONA, D., *Studi su la storia dell'oratorio musicale in Italia*, Turin 1908

ALBRECHT, O. E., *A Census of Autograph Music Manuscripts of European Composers in American Libraries*, Philadelphia 1953

ALLORTO, R., *Le Sonate per pianoforte di Muzio Clementi: Studio critico e catalogo tematico*, Florence 1959

ALTENBURG, W., *Versuch einer Einleitung zur heroisch-musikalischen Trompeter- und Pauken-kunst*, Leipzig 1795

ALTMANN, W., 'Die beiden kürzlich erstmalig veröff. Violinkonzerte Joseph Haydns', in *Die Musik* VIII, 1908/9

ANDERSON, E. (ed.), *The Letters of Beethoven*, London 1961

——, *The Letters of Mozart and his Family*, London 1966

ANDERSON, W. R., *Haydn*, London 1938/39

ANGERMÜLLER, R., 'Antonio Salieri': Teil I ('Werk- und Quellenverzeichnis') and Teil III ('Dokumente'), in *Schriften zur Musik*, Bände 16, 19, Munich 1971 and 1973

——, 'Sigismund Ritter von Neukomm (1778–1858) und seiner Lehrer Michael und Joseph Haydn. Eine Dokumentation', in *Haydn-Studien* III/1 (1973)

——, 'Neukomms schottische Liedbearbeitungen für Joseph Haydn', in *Haydn-Studien* III/2 (1974)

ANGERMÜLLER, R., and OFNER, R., 'Aspekte Salierischer Kirchenmusik', in *Mitteilungen der Internationalen Stiftung Mozarteum*, 21. Jg., Heft I/2 (February 1973)

ANONYMOUS, *Weisen zu den Liedern der Kirche, aus den römischen Tagzeiten und Messbuche übersetzt*, Vienna 1773

——, *Relation des fêtes données à sa majesté l'impératrice par S.A. Mgr. le Prince d'Esterhazy Dans son Château d'Esterhaz. Le 1ʳ & 2ᵉ 7bre 1773*, Vienna [1773]

——, *Das gelehrte Österreich. Ein Versuch*, Vienna 1778 (Haydn's autobiographical sketch)

——, *Wahrheiten die Musik betreffend gerade heraus-gesagt von einem teutschen Biedermann EDE*, Frankfurt/Main 1779

——, *A B C Dario Musico*, Bath 1780

——, *Sichtbare und unsichtbare Sonnen- und Mondfin-sternisse ... im musikalischen Handbuch oder Musenalmanach fürs Jahr 1782*, Alethinopel (pseudonym; possibly Freiburg?), n.d.

——, *Beschreibung des hochfürstlichen Schlosses Esterhaz im Königreiche Ungern* [*sic*], Pressburg 1784

——, *Excursion à Esterhaz en Hongrie en Mai 1784*, Vienna 1784 (by A. H. Traunpaur, Chevalier d'Ophanie)

——, 'An Account of Joseph Haydn, a celebrated composer of music', in *European Magazine,* London 1784 (8 October)

——, *Portefeuille für Musikliebhaber*, Leipzig, Ostermesse 1792 (reprint of Junker, C. L., q.v., 1776)

——, *Biographische Skizze von Michael Haydn* (by G. Schinn and F. J. Otter, possibly with assistance of W. Rettensteiner), Salzburg 1808

——, *Essai historique sur la vie de Joseph Haydn ...* [etc.], Strasbourg 1812

——, *Denkschrift zur 25jährigen Jubelfeier der Gesellschaft der Musikfreunde des österreichischen Kaiserstaates durch Aufführung der Schöpfung ... Von einem Kunstfreund*, Vienna 1840

——, 'Unsere Brüder im 18. Jahrhundert', in *Fünf Jahre Libertas*, published by the Grossloge in Wien, Vienna 1965

——, 'Haydn as a Freemason', *Journal für Frey-maurer* (Festschrift der Grossloge von Österreich zum 250. Jahrestag der englischen Grossloge), Vienna 1967

ANREP-NORDIŃ, B., 'Studier över Josef Martin Kraus', in *Svensk tidskrift för musikforskning* V [1923] and VI [1924]

ARBLAY, MADAME d', *Diary and Letters of Madame d'Arblay (1778–1840)*, 6 vols., ed. C. Barrett, London 1905 (foreword and notes by Austin Dobson); see also Burney, F.

ARNDT, E. M., *Reisen durch einen Theil Teutsch-lands, Ungarns, Italiens und Frankreichs in den Jahren 1798 und 1799*, 4 vols., Leipzig, 2nd ed. 1804 [Haydn pp. 231–5]

ARNOLD, D., 'Haydn's Counterpoint and Fux's "Gradus"', in *Monthly Musical Record* 87, March–April 1957, pp. 52ff.

ARNOLD, I. F., *Joseph Haydn, seine kurze Biographie und ästhetische Darstellung seiner Werke*, Erfurt 1810 (2/1825)

——, *W. A. Mozart and Joseph Haydn. Nachträge zu den Biogr. und aesth. Darstellungen ihrer Werke*, Erfurt 1810

ARTARIA, F., [*Verzeichnis der musikalischen Auto-graphe von Joseph Haydn*], Vienna 1893

ARTARIA, F., and BOTSTIBER, H., *Joseph Haydn und das Verlaghaus Artaria*, Vienna 1909

ASOW, E. H. M. VON, 'Joseph Haydns Tod in zeitgenössischen Berichten', in *Musikerziehung* XII/3 1959

AYLING, S., *George the Third*, London 1972

AZEVED, L. H. C. DE, 'Sigismund Neukomm, An Austrian Composer in the New World', *Musical Quarterly* XLV/4 (Oct. 1959)

BACH, C. P. E., *Versuch über die wahre Art das Clavier zu spielen*. Part I, Berlin, 1753; 1759. Part II, Berlin, 1762. English translation (ed. W. J. Mitchell), London 1949

BÄDER, M. E., *Studien zu den Streichquartetten Op. 1–33 von Joseph Haydn*, Göttingen 1945 (1946) (Dissertation)

BADURA-SKODA, E., '"Teutsche Comoedie-Arien" und Joseph Haydn', in *Der junge Haydn: Kongressbericht Graz 1970*, Graz 1972

——, 'Reflections on Haydn Opera Problems', in *Haydnfest*, Washington, D.C., 1975

BARBAUD, P., *Haydn*, Paris 1957

BARBEDETTE, H., 'Haydn, sa vie et ses oeuvres', in *Le Ménestrel* XXXVI, 1870/72

BARESEL, A., *Joseph Haydn, Leben und Werk*, Leipzig 1938

BARRETT-AYRES, R., *Haydn and the String Quartet*, London 1974

BARTHA, D., 'Zur Abstammung Joseph Haydns', in *Acta Musicologica* VII, Fasc. IV, 1935

——, 'The unknown Haydn – Haydn as an opera conductor at Esterháza', in *New Hungarian Quarterly*, I/1 (Sept. 1960), pp. 139ff.

——, 'Haydn als Opernkapellmeister', in *Bericht über die Internationale Konferenz zum Andenken Joseph Haydns, Budapest 1959*, Budapest 1961

——, 'A "Sieben Worte" Változatainak Keletkezése az Esterhazy-Gyüjtemény Kéziratainak Tükrében', in *Zenetudományi Tanulmányok* VIII (1960), pp. 107ff.

BARTHA, D., and SOMFAI, L., *Haydn als Opernkapellmeister*, Budapest 1960

BAUDOT, DOM., *Dictionnaire d'Hagiographie mis à jour à l'aide des travaux les plus récents par Dom. Baudot O.S.B.*, Paris 1925

BAUER, W. M., 'Der Roman der josephinischen Aufklärung. Strukturen und literaturhistorische Bedeutung, gezeigt an Johann Pezzels "Faustin"', in 'Joseph Haydn und seine Zeit', *Jahrbuch für Österreichische Kulturgeschichte* II, Eisenstadt 1972

BAUMGÄRTNER, P., *Gottfried van Swieten als Textdichter von Haydns Oratorien*, Vienna 1930 (Dissertation)

BAWEL, F. H., *A Study of Developmental Techniques in Selected Haydn Symphonies*, Ohio State University 1973 (Dissertation)

BAYER, F., 'Über den Gebrauch der Instrumente in den Kirchen- und Instrumentalwerken von W. A. Mozart', in *Festschrift, Beethoven-Zentenarfeier* (*Denkmäler der Tonkunst in Österreich*, 1927)

BAYNE-POWELL, R., *Travellers in Eighteenth Century England*, London 1951

BECK, F. M., 'Joseph Haydn', in *Greg. Rundschau* (Graz), VI, 1907

BECKER, C. F., *Joseph Haydn*, Leipzig 1832

BECKER-GLAUCH, I., 'Neue Forschungen zu Haydns Kirchenmusik', in *Musikforschung* XVII/4 (1964)

——, 'Haydns Cantilena pro adventu in D', in *Haydn-Studien* I/4 (1967)

——, 'Joseph Haydns Te Deum für die Kaiserin', in *Colloquium Amicorum* (Schmidt-Görg Festschrift), Bonn 1967

——, 'Neue Forschungen zu Haydns Kirchenmusik', in *Haydn-Studien* I/4 (1967)

——, 'Joseph Haydns "Ave Regina" in A', in *Studies in Eighteenth Century Music: A Tribute to Karl Geiringer on his Seventieth Birthday* (ed. H. C. R. Landon and R. E. Chapman), London 1970

——, 'Die Kirchenmusik des jungen Haydn', in *Der junge Haydn: Kongressbericht Graz 1970*, Graz 1972

——, 'Die Haydniana der Lannoy-Sammlung. Eine archivalische Studie', in *Haydn-Studien* III/1 (1973)

——, 'The Masses of Joseph Haydn', in *Haydnfest*, Washington, D.C., 1975

BECKING, G., *Studien zu Beethovens Personalstil*, Leipzig 1921

BEDBUR, M., *Die Entwicklung des Finales in den Symphonien von Haydn, Mozart und Beethoven*, Cologne 1953 (Dissertation)

BEETHOVEN, L. v., *Werke*, Leipzig 1862–65

BELL, A. C., 'An Introduction to Haydn's Piano Trios', in *Music Review* XVI/3 (1955), pp. 191ff.

BELLER, M., *Philemon und Baucis in der europäischen Literatur. Stoffgeschichte und Analyse*, Mainz 1965 (Dissertation)

BENKÖ, A., 'Haydn-Bemutató Kolozsváron', in *Zenetudományi Tanulmányok* VIII (1960), pp. 675ff.

BENNINGER, E., 'Joseph Haydns Bedeutung für den Klavierstil', in *Musikpädagogische Zeitschrift*, 1927

BENYOVSKY, K., *Das alte Theater-Kulturgeschichtliche Studie aus Pressburgs Vergangenheit*, Bratislava-Pressburg 1926

BERETHS, G., *Die Musikpflege am kurtrierischen Hofe zu Koblenz-Ehrenbreitstein*, Mainz 1964

BERNET-KEMPERS, K. P., 'Haydn en het strijkkwartet', in *De Muziek* (Amsterdam) VI, 1931/32

BERNHARDT, R., 'Aus der Umwelt der Wiener Klassiker, Freiherr Gottfried van Swieten (1734–1803)', in *Jahrbuch der Bär* VI, 1929/30, Leipzig 1930

——, '"Der für die Sünden der Welt gemarterte Jesus." Eine Händel-Partitur aus Joseph Haydns Besitz', in *Die Musik* XXI/4 (1929)

BERNLEITHNER, E., 'Sind Haydns Violonzellkonzerte echt?' [cf. H. Volkmann], in *Österreichische Musikzeitschrift*, 1948

BERTHA, A. DE., 'Joseph Haydn', in *Bulletin Sammelbände der Internationalen Musikgesellschaft* V, 1909, Heft 5

BERTUCH, C., 'Haydns Lebensabriss', in *Journal des Luxus und der Moden*, Weimar 1805

——, *Bemerkungen auf einer Reise aus Thüringen nach Wien*, Weimar 1808–10

——, see also *supra* under Periodicals: *London und Paris*

BESSELER, H., 'Einflüsse der Contratanzmusik auf Joseph Haydn', in *Bericht über die Internationale Konferenz zum Andenken Joseph Haydns, Budapest, 1959*, Budapest 1961

BEYLE, H. (pseud., Stendhal), [*Vie de Haydn*], Paris 1814

——, *Vie de Haydn, de Mozart et de Métastase*, Paris 1817; also English translation, London 1817

BEYSCHLAG, A., *Die Ornamentik der Musik*, Leipzig 1908

BIBA, O., 'Die Pflege der Kirchmusik in der Piaristenkirche', in *250 Jahr Piaristenpfarre Maria Treu*, Vienna 1969

——, 'Die Wiener Kirchenmusik um 1783', in *Beiträge zur Musikgeschichte des 18. Jahrhunderts* I/2, Eisenstadt 1971

BIHL, V., *Erzherzog Karl*, Vienna–Leipzig 1942

Biographical Dictionary of Musicians, New York 1940

BIRNBAUMER, U., *Das Werk des Joseph Felix von Kurz-Bernadon und seine Szenische Realisierung*, 2 vols., Vienna 1971

BLANNING, T. C. W., *Joseph II and Enlightened Despotism*, London 1970

BISCHOFF, S., 'Haydn in Graz', in *Grazer Tagespost*, 12 March 1909

BLUME, F., 'Joseph Haydns künstlerische Persönlichkeit in seinen Streichquartetten', in *Jahrbuch der Musikbibliothek Peters*, 1931; see also *Musik in Geschichte und Gegenwart*

——, 'Gibt es ein neues Haydn-Bild?', in *Musica* XXIII/4 (1969)

BOBILLIER (see under pseudonym: Brenet)

BODENSTEIN, C., *Hundert Jahre Kunstgeschichte Wiens, 1788–1888. Eine Festgabe anlässlich der Säcular-Feier der Pensions Gesellschaft Bildender Künstler Wiens*, Vienna 1888

BOGATI, A., 'Gregor Joseph Werner. Biographisches über den Vorgänger Haydns in Kapellmeister-Amt zu Eisenstadt', in *Burgenländische Heimat-Blätter* (Eisenstadt) V, 1936

BOGDÁN, I., 'A Lékai (Hámori) Papírmalom a XVIII. Században', in *Különlenyomat a Történelmi Szemle* 1960/1, Számábol, pp. 46ff.

BÖKLIN, F. F. S. A. VON, *Beyträge zur Geschichte der Musik*, Freiburg i.B., 1790

BONAVENTURA, A., *Boccherini*, Milan and Rome 1931

BONAVIA, F., 'The Essential Haydn', in *Monthly Musical Record* LXII, 1932, No. 736

BOSWELL, J., *Boswell on the Grand Tour: Germany and Switzerland 1764* (ed. F. A. Pottle), Yale University, New Haven, Conn., 1928, 1953

BOTSTIBER, H., 'Zur Entstehung der Schottischen Lieder von Joseph Haydn', in *Der Merkur*, 1910

——, 'Die Instrumentation bei Joseph Haydn', in *Das Orchester*, 1928

——, *Geschichte der Ouvertüre*, Leipzig 1913; (see also under Artaria and Pohl)

——, 'War Antonio Polzelli Haydns Sohn?', in *Österreichische Kunst*, Jg. III, Heft 3/4 [1932]; translation in *Musical Quarterly* 1932 (April)

BRAND, C. M., *Die Messen von Joseph Haydn*, Würzburg 1941

BRANSCOMBE, P., 'Music in the Viennese Popular Theatre of the Eighteenth and Nineteenth Centuries', in *Proceedings of the Royal Musical Association*, vol. 98 (1971–2)

BRAUBACH, M., *Maria Theresias jüngster Sohn Max Franz*, Vienna–Munich 1961

BRAUNSTEIN, J., 'Über Haydns Skizzenbuch', in *Festschrift für G. Alder*, 1925

BREITKOPF, J. G. I., 'Nacherinnerung', in *Catalogo delle Sinfonie che si trovano in manuscritto nella officina musica di Giovanno Gottlob Immanuel Breitkopf, in Lipsia*, Parte Ima 1762. Cat. reprinted, ed. N. Brook, New York 1968

BRENET, M., 'La mélodie chez Haydn', in *Le courrier musical*, 1908

——, 'La librairie musicale en France de 1653 à 1790, d'après les Registres de privilèges', in *Sammelbände der Internationalen Musik-Gesellschaft* VIII [1906/07]

——, *Joseph Haydn*, Paris 1909 (English translation, London 1926)

——, 'Stendhal, Carpani et la vie de Haydn', in *Bulletin Sammelbände der Internationalen Musikgesellschaft* V, 1909

——, 'A propos du Centenaire de Haydn', in *Le courrier musical*, Paris 1909, No. 12

BRIDI, G., *Brevi Notizie intorno ad alcuni più celebri compositori di musica*, Rovereto 1827

BRION, M., *Daily Life in the Vienna of Mozart and Schubert*, London 1959

BROOK, B. S., *La Symphonie Française dans la seconde moitié du XVIIIe siècle*, 3 vols., Paris 1962; from dissertation, 1959

——, 'The Symphonie Concertante', in *Musical Quarterly* XLVII (1961)

——, 'Sturm und Drang and the Romantic Period in Music', in *Studies in Romanticism* IX/4 (1970)

BROWN, A. P., 'Problems of Authenticity in Two Haydn Keyboard Works (Hob. XIV:7 and XVI:47)', in *Journal of the American Musicological Society* XXV/1 (1972)

——, 'A Re-Introduction to Joseph Haydn's Keyboard Works', in *Piano Quarterly* XXI/79 (1972)

——, 'The Earliest English Biography of Haydn', in *Musical Quarterly* LIX/3 (1973)

——, 'The Chamber Music with Strings of Carlos d'Ordoñez. A Bibliographic and Stylistic Study', in *Acta Musicologica* XXVI/II (1974)

——, 'The Structure of the Exposition in Joseph Haydn's Keyboard Sonatas', in *Music Review* XXXVI/2 (1975)

——, 'An Addendum to Weinmann's "Eine Variante zu einem Porträt Haydns"', in *Haydn Yearbook* IX (1975)

——, 'Critical Years for Haydn's Instrumental Music: 1787–90', in *Musical Quarterly* LXII/3 (July 1976)

BROWN, A. P., and BERKENSTOCK, J. T., 'Joseph Haydn in Literature: A Bibliography', in *Haydn-Studien* III/3, 4 (1974)

BROWN, M. J. E., 'Haydn, Mozart and Schubert in English Musicology', in *Österreich und die angelsächsische Welt: Kulturbegegnungen und Vergleiche*, Band II, Vienna 1968

BRUCE, I. M., 'An Act of Homage', in *Music Review* XI/4 (1950)

BRUCKNER, M., 'Eine unbekannte Haydn-Sinfonie [No. 27 in G]', in *Mitteilungen aus dem Baron Brukenthalischen Museum, Hermannstadt* XI (1946), pp. 8ff.

BRUNNER, S., *Das Benediktinerbuch*, Würzburg 1880

BRUNSVIK, T., *Beethoven und die Brunsviks, nach Familienpapieren aus Therese Brunsviks Nachlass* (ed. La Mara), Leipzig 1920

BRYAN, P., 'Haydn's Hornists', in *Haydn-Studien* III/1 (1973)

——, 'The horn in the works of Mozart and Haydn: some observations and comparisons', in *Haydn Yearbook* IX (1975)

BRYANT, A., *The Years of Endurance 1793–1802*, London 1942

BRZEZOWSKY, G., and HERGET, A., *Joseph Haydn (Leben in Bildern)*, Leipzig 1917

BÜCKEN, E., *Die Musik des Rokokos und der Klassik*, Potsdam 1928

BURGH, A., *Anecdotes of Music*, London 1814

BURKAT, L., 'Haydn's Symphonies, a collation', in *Notes* 1942

BURKHARDT, M., 'Haydn und Beethoven', in *Musikalisches Wochenblatt* (Leipzig) XL, 1909, No. 9

BÜRKLI, J. G., *Biographie von Joseph Haydn*, Zürich 1830/31

BURNEY, C., *The Present State of Music in France and Italy*, London 1771

——, *The Present State of Music in Germany, the Netherlands and United Provinces* (2 vols.), London 1773 and 1775

——, *A General History of Music* (4 vols.) London 1776 *et seq.* (new edition, London 1935)

——, 'Pleyel', in Rees's *Cyclopaedia* (39 vols.), London 1819–20 (also in *Musical Times*, May 1909)

BURNEY, F., *Journals and Letters* (2 vols., ed. J. Hemlow and A. Douglas), Oxford 1972; (see also under Madame d'Arblay)

BUSBY, T., *A Dictionary of Music*, London 1786

——, 'Biographical Memoir of Joseph Haydn from Authentic Sources', in *English Musical Gazette* (1819)

——, *Concert Room and Orchestra Anecdotes* (3 vols.), London 1825

BUSCHING, A. F., *Erdbeschreibung*, Hamburg 1788

CALLCOTT, J. W., *Musical Grammar*, London 1806

CARPANI, G., *Le Haydine, ovvero lettere su la vita e le opere del celebre maestro Giuseppe Haydn*, Milan 1812 (2/1823)

CARSE, A., *The History of Orchestration*, London 1925

——, *The Orchestra in the XVIIIth Century*, London 1940 (2/1950)

CASES, COMTE DE LA, *Mémorial de Sainte-Hélène*, Paris 1842

CASTELLI, J. F., *Memoiren meines Lebens. Gefundenes und Empfundenes*, Vienna 1861

CASTIGLIONI, N., 'Antologia degli Scritti di Haydn', in *L'Approdo Musicale* No. 11 (1960)

CATALOGUES: *Check List of Thematic Catalogues*, Music Library Association 1954; Queens College Supplement, Flushing, New York, 1966

CHAILLEY, J., 'Joseph Haydn and the Freemasons', in *Studies in Eighteenth-Century Music: A Tribute to Karl Geiringer on his Seventieth Birthday* (ed. H. C. R. Landon and R. E. Chapman), London 1970

CHERBULIEZ, A. E., *Joseph Haydn*, Zürich 1932

CHEW, G., 'The Night-Watchman's Song Quoted by Haydn and its Implications', in *Haydn-Studien* III/2 (1974)

CHOISY, F., 'Joseph Haydn et l'influence française', in *Le Ménestrel* (Paris), XCIV/15 (1932)

CHOP, M., *Haydns Schöpfung*, Leipzig 1912

——, *Joseph Haydn und die 'Jahreszeiten'*, Leipzig 1916

CHUSID, M., 'Some observations on liturgy, text and structure in Haydn's late Masses', in *Studies in Eighteenth Century Music: A Tribute to Karl Geiringer on his Seventieth Birthday* (ed. H. C. R. Landon and R. E. Chapman), London 1970

CIMAROSA, D., *Katalog der Ausstellung anlässlich der Centenarfeier Domenico Cimarosas*, Vienna 1901 (A. v. Eisner-Eisenhof)

CLERCX, S., *Le Baroque et la Musique: Essai d'esthétique musicale*, Brussels 1948

——, *Pierre van Maldere* (Académie royale de Belgique, Classe des Beaux-Arts, Mémoires, Tome V), Brussels 1948

CLEWING, C., *Musik und Jägerei*, Kassel 1937

CLOUGH, F. F., and CUMING, C. J., *The World's Encyclopaedia of Recorded Music*, London 1952

COBBETT, W. W., *Cobbett's Cyclopedic Survey of Chamber Music* (2nd ed.), London 1963

COHEN, R., *The Art of Discrimination: Thomson's 'The Seasons' and the Language of Criticism*, Baltimore, Md, 1964

——, *The Unfolding of 'The Seasons': A Study of Thomson's Poem*, Baltimore, Md, 1970

COLE, M. S., 'The Rondo Finale: Evidence for the Mozart-Haydn Exchange', in *Mozart-Jahrbuch* 1968/70

——, 'Momigny's Analysis of Haydn's Symphony No. 103', in *Music Review* XXX/4 (1969)

CONRAT, H., 'Joseph Haydn und das kroatische Volkslied', in *Die Musik*, 1904–5

COOKE, J. F., *Franz Joseph Haydn. A Short Biography*, Philadelphia 1928

COOPER, G., and MEYER, L. B., *The Rhythmic Structure of Music*, Chicago and London 1960

COWEN, SIR F., *Haydn*, New York 1912

CRAIG, D. M., 'When Haydn met Nelson', in *Musical Times* LXXX, 1939

CRANKSHAW, G., 'Haydn's Masses', in *Monthly Musical Record* 1950

CRASS, E., and PETZOLDT, R., *Joseph Haydn – Sein Leben in Bildern*, Leipzig 1959

CROCE DI DOJOLA, LUIGI DELLA, *Le 107 sinfonie di Haydn*, Turin 1975

CROLL, G., 'Mitteilungen über die "Schöpfung" und die "Jahreszeiten" aus dem Schwarzenberg-Archiv', in *Haydn-Studien* III/2 (1974)

CROSSE, J., *An Account of the Grand Musical Festival, held in September 1823, in the Cathedral Church of York . . .*, York 1825

CSATKAI, A., 'Beziehungen Werners, Haydns und der fürstl. Musiker zur Eisenstädter Pfarrkirche', in *Burgenländische Heimatblätter*, Haydn-Gedenkheft, 1932

——, 'Aus dem Haydnzimmer der Wolfsammlung' (*ibid.*)

——, 'Die fürstlich Esterházischen Druckereien in Eisenstadt' (*ibid.*, 1936)

——, 'Goethes Schüler [Heinrich Schmidt] als Theaterdirektor in Eisenstadt', in *Neue Heimatblätter* [Budapest] 1935

——, 'Haydnra és zenekarára Vonatkozó a Datok a Süttöri Anayakönyvekböl', in *Zenetudományi Tanulmányok* VIII (1960), pp. 669ff.

CSUKA, B., 'Haydn és a Baryton', in *Zenetudományi Tanulmányok* VI (1957), pp. 669ff.

CUCUEL, G., 'Quelques documents sur la librairie musicale au XVIIIᵉ siècle', in *Bulletin Sammelbände der Internationalen Musikgesellschaft* XIII [1911/12]

——, 'La question des clarinettes dans l'instrumentation du XVIII siècle', in *Zeitschrift der internationalen Musikgesellschaft* vol. XII [1910–11]

——, *Études sur un Orchestre au XVIIIme siècle*, Paris 1913

——, *La Pouplinière, et la musique de chambre au XVIIIe siècle*, Paris 1913

CUMING, G., 'Haydn: where to begin', in *Music and Letters*, 1949

CUSHMAN, D. S., *Joseph Haydn's Melodic Materials . . .*, Boston, Mass., 1973 (Dissertation)

CUYLER, L., 'Tonal Exploitation in the Later Quartets of Haydn', in *Studies in Eighteenth-Century Music: A Tribute to Karl Geiringer on his Seventieth Birthday* (ed. H. C. R. Landon and R. E. Chapman), London 1970

DACK, J., 'The Church Music of Karl Schiringer', in *Haydn Yearbook* IX (1975)

DAFFNER, H., *Die Entwicklung des Klavierkonzertes bis Mozart*, Leipzig 1906

——, 'Über die Instrumentalpraxis des 18. Jahrhunderts', in *Neue Zeitschrift für Musik*, 1907

DALE, K., 'Schubert's Indebtedness to Haydn', in *Music and Letters*, 1940

DANNREUTHER, E., *Musical Ornamentation*, London [n.d.]

DA PONTE, L., *Memoirs of Lorenzo da Ponte*, trans. from the Italian by Elizabeth Abbott; edited and annotated by Arthur Livingston; new edition, New York 1967; German translation (and with notes by Gustav Gugitz), 3 volumes, Dresden 1924

DAUBE, J. F., *Der Musikalische Dilettante, eine Wochenschrift*, Vienna 1770 *et seq.*

——, *Anleitung zum Selbstunterricht in der Musikalischen Komposition*, Vienna 1798

DAWES, F., '"William": Or the Adventures of a Sonata', in *Musical Times*, 1965

DAWSON, R. V., 'Haydn and Mozart', in *Musical Quarterly* XVI/4 (1930)

DELDEVEZ, E.-M.-E., *Curiosités Musicales*, Paris 1873

DELLA CORTE, A., *L'Opera Comica Italiana nel '700* (2 vols.), Bari 1923

DEMAREE, R. W., *The Structural Proportions of the Haydn Quartets*, Bloomington, Ind., 1973 (Dissertation)

DENISON, W. J., *Address to the People of Great Britain*, London 1803

Denkmäler der Tonkunst in Österreich:

——, XV. Jg./II (Vol. 31) *Wiener Instrumentalmusik im 18. Jahrhundert* I (ed. Horwitz and Riedel), Vienna 1908;

——, XIX Jg./II (Vol. 39) *Wiener Instrumentalmusik im 18. Jahrhundert* II (ed. Fischer), Vienna 1912;

——, XXII Jg./(Vol. 45) *Johann Michael Haydn Messen* (ed. Klafsky), Vienna 1915;

——, XXXII Jg./(Vol. 62) *Johann Michael Haydn Kirchenwerke* (ed. Klafsky), Vienna 1925;

——, XXXIII Jg./I (Vol. 64) *Deutsche Komödienarien 1754–58* (ed. Haas), Vienna 1926;

——, Vol. 88 *Georg Reutter Jr., Kirchenwerke* (ed. Hofer), Vienna 1952;

——, Vol. 124 *Fürstlich Esterházysche Hofkapelle – Luigi Tomasini* (ed. Schenk), Vienna 1972

Denkmäler Deutscher Tonkunst: Zweite Folge – Denkmäler der Tonkunst in Bayern:

——, III Jg./I *Sinfonien der Pfalzbayerischen Schule I* (ed. Riemann), Leipzig 1902;

——, VII. Jg. *Mannheim II* (ed. Riemann), Leipzig 1906;

——, VIII. Jg. *Mannheim III* (ed. Riemann), Leipzig 1907;

——, IX. Jg./II *Leopold Mozart: Ausgewählte Werke* (ed. Seiffert), Leipzig 1908

DENNERLEIN, H., *Der unbekannte Mozart, Die Welt seiner Klavierwerke*, Leipzig 1951

DENT, E. J., 'Haydn's Pianoforte Works', in *Monthly Musical Record* LXII, 1932

DEUTSCH, O. E., 'Joseph Haydn und Kaiser Joseph II', in *Musikbuch aus Österreich*, 1910

——, 'Zwei Scherzkanons von Mozart und Haydn', in *Die Musik* XXIV, 1931/32

——, 'Haydn und Nelson', in *Die Musik* XXIV, 1931/32

——, *Mozart und die Wiener Logen*, Vienna 1932

——, 'Haydns Kanons', in *Zeitschrift für Musikwissenschaft* XV [1932]

——, 'Der "Lehrling" Haydn' [H. as Freemason], *Neue Freie Presse*, 14 March 1933 (reprinted in *Musica*, 1959)

——, *Das Freihaustheater auf der Wieden 1787–1801*, Vienna–Leipzig 1937

——, 'Haydn in Cambridge', in *Cambridge Review* LXII/1522, 1941

——, 'Haydn's Hymn and Burney's Translation', in *Music Review* VIII (1943)

——, *Music Publisher's Numbers*, Association of Special Libraries and Information Bureaux, London 1946

——, 'Theme and variations with bibliographical notes on Pleyel's Haydn editions', in *Music Review* 1951

——, *Handel, A Documentary Biography*, London 1955

——, *Mozart, Die Dokumente seines Lebens*, Kassel 1961

DIEMAND, A., 'Joseph Haydn und der Oettingen-Wallersteinsche Hof', in *Zeitschrift des historischen Vereins für Schwaben und Neuburg*, vol. 45, Augsburg 1920/22

DIES, A. C., *Biographische Nachrichten von Joseph Haydn*, Vienna 1810; new edition by Horst Seeger, Berlin [1959]; see also Griesinger

DITTERSDORF, K. D. VON, *Lebensbeschreibung, seinem Sohn in die Feder diktiert, 1801*; new edition by Miller, Munich 1967; English translation, London 1896

DLABACZ, G. L., *Allgemeines historisches Künstler-Lexikon für Böhmen*, Prague 1815

DOBSON, A., *Eighteenth Century Vignettes* (second series), London 1894

DOLMETSCH, A., *The Interpretation of the Music of the XVII and XVIII Centuries*, London 1916 (2/1946)

DONATH, G. (with additions by HAAS, R.), 'Florian Leopold Gassmann als Opern-Komponist', in *Studien zur Musikwissenschaft*, 1914

DREO, H., 'Die fürstlich Esterházysche Musikkapelle von ihren Anfängen bis zum Jahre 1766', in *Beiträge zur Musikgeschichte des 18. Jahrhunderts* I/2, Eisenstadt 1971

DUNHILL, T. F., 'Franz Joseph Haydn', in *The Heritage of Music* I, Oxford 1927 (1948)

DUNNING, A., *Joseph Schmitt*, Amsterdam 1962

DWORSCHAK, F., *Joseph Haydn und Karl Joseph Weber von Fürnberg*, Sonderdruck from *Unsere Heimat, Monatsblatt des Vereines für Landeskunde und Heimatschutz von Niederösterreich und Wien*, 1932

EBERS, G., *Das Lied bei Haydn*, Innsbruck 1943 (Dissertation)

EBERT, J., *Joseph Haydn, der Mann und das Werk*, Mainz 1939

ECCARIUS-SIEBER, A., 'Haydn als Vater des Streichquartettes', in *Neue Musikzeitung* XXIX/3 (1907)

EDWALL, H. R., 'Ferdinand IV and Haydn's Concertos for the *Lira organizzata*', in *Musical Quarterly* XLVIII/2 (April 1962)

EIBNER, F., 'Joseph Haydns musikalische Sendung. Die Bedeutung der österreichischen Volksmusik für die musikalische Klassik', in *Österreichische Musikzeitschrift* 22 (1967)/9, pp. 540ff.

——, 'Die authentische Klavierfassung von Haydns Variationen über "Gott erhalte"', in *Haydn Yearbook* VII (1970)

EINEDER, G., *The Ancient Paper-Mills of the former Austro-Hungarian Empire and their Watermarks*, Hilversum 1960

EINSTEIN, A., 'Haydns Sinfonie', in *Zeitschrift für Musikwissenschaft* LXXXXI, 1924, No. 4

——, 'Opus I', in *Musical Quarterly* XX/4 (1934)

——, *Gluck*, London 1936

——, *Mozart, his Character, his Work*, New York 1945

——, see also under Riemann

EISENMANN, A., 'Haydn's Sonaten und Konzerte für Violine', in *Neue Musikzeitung* (Stg.) XXX, 1909, No. 17

ELVERS, R., 'Ein nicht abgesandter Brief Zelters an Haydn', in *Musik und Verlag* [Vötterle Festschrift], Kassel 1968

ENCYCLOPAEDIAS:

——, *Enciclopedia della Musica*, Milan 1972 *et seq.*

——, *Enciclopedia dello Spettacolo*, Rome 1954–68

——, *Encyclopaedia Britannica*, 1967 edition

ENGEL, H., *Die Entwicklung des deutschen Klavierkonzertes von Mozart bis Liszt*, Leipzig 1927

——, 'Über Mozarts Jugendsinfonien', in *Mozart-Jahrbuch*, 1951

——, 'Haydn, Mozart und die Klassik', in *Mozart-Jahrbuch*, 1959

ENGL, J. E., *Haydns handschriftliches Tagebuch aus der Zeit seines zweiten Aufenthaltes in London*, Leipzig 1909

ERPF, H., 'Die Lehre von den Instrumenten und der Instrumentation', in *Hohe Schule der Musik*, vol. 2, 1935

ESSNER, W., *Die Thematik der Menuette in den Streichquartetten Joseph Haydns*, Erlangen 1923 (Dissertation)

ESZTERHÁZY, J., *Az Esterházy Család és Oldalágainak Leirása*, Budapest 1901

EWEN, D., *Haydn, a Good Life*, New York 1946

FÁBO, B., *Haydn in Ungarn*, Budapest 1909

FALK, M., *W. Fr. Bach*, Leipzig 1913

FÄRBER, S., *Das Regensburger Fürstlich Thurn und Taxissche Hoftheater und seine Oper 1760–1786*. Verhandlungen des historischen Vereins von Oberpfalz und Regensburg, vol. 86 (1936)

FARINGTON: *The Farington Diary* (ed. James Greig), 6 vols., London and New York 1923

FEDER, G., 'Zur Datierung Haydnscher Werke', in *Anthony van Hoboken, Festschrift zum 75. Geburtstag* (ed. J. Schmidt-Görg), Mainz 1962

——, 'Zwei Haydn zugeschriebene Klaviersonaten', in *Kongressbericht . . .*, Kassel 1962

——, 'Die Überlieferung und Verbreitung der handschriftlichen Quellen zu Haydns Werken (Erste Folge)', in *Haydn-Studien* I (1965)/1

——, 'Zu Haydn Schottischen Liedern', in *Haydn-Studien* I (1965)/1

——, 'Ein vergessener Haydn-Brief', in *Haydn-Studien* I (1966)/2

——, 'Aus Roman Hoffstetters Briefen', in *Haydn-Studien* I (1966)/3

——, 'Gedanken über den kritischen Apparat aus der Sicht der Haydn-Gesamtausgabe', in *Colloquium Amicorum*, Bonn 1967

——, 'Manuscript sources of Haydn's works and their distribution', in *Haydn Yearbook* IV (1968)

——, 'Lo stato attuale degli studi su Haydn', in *Rivista Musicale Italiana* II, No. 4 (1968)

——, 'Typisches bei Haydn', in *Österreichische Musikzeitschrift* 24 (1969)

——, 'Einige Thesen zu dem Thema: Haydn als Dramatiker', in *Haydn-Studien* II (1969)/2

——, 'Ein Kolloquium über Haydns Opern', in *Haydn-Studien* II (1969)/2

——, 'Similarities in the works of Haydn', in *Studies in Eighteenth Century Music: A Tribute to Karl Geiringer on his Seventieth Birthday* (ed. H. C. R. Landon and R. E. Chapman), London 1970

——, 'Wieviel Orgelkonzerte hat Haydn geschrieben?', in *Die Musik-Forschung*, XXIII. Jahrgang (1970), Heft 4, pp. 440ff.

——, 'Haydns frühe Klaviertrios', in *Haydn-Studien* II (1970)/4

——, 'Haydn und Eisenstadt', in *Österreichische Musikzeitschrift* 25 (1970)/4, pp. 213ff.

——, 'Stilelemente Haydns in Beethovens Werken', in *Bericht über den internationalen musikwissenschaftlichen Kongress Bonn 1970*, Kassel 1971

——, 'Die beiden Pole im Instrumentalschaffen des jungen Haydn', in *Der junge Haydn: Kongressbericht Graz 1970*, Graz 1972

——, 'Joseph Haydn als Mensch und Musiker', in 'Joseph Haydn und seine Zeit,' *Jahrbuch für Österreichische Kulturgeschichte* II, Eisenstadt 1972

——, 'Eine Haydn-Skizze in Ostiglia', in *Analecta Musicologica* XII (1973)

——, 'Apokryphe "Haydn"-Streichquartette', in *Haydn-Studien* III/2 (1974)

——, 'Haydn's Piano Trios and Piano Sonatas', in *Haydnfest*, Washington, D.C., 1975

——, 'Zwei unbekannte Haydn-Briefe', in *Haydn-Studien* IV/1 (1976)

——, 'Ein Kanon-Autograph von J. Haydn in Leningrad', in *Haydn-Studien* IV/1 (1976)

FEDER, G., and GERLACH, S., 'Haydn-Dokumente aus dem Esterházy-Archiv in Forchtenstein', in *Haydn-Studien* III/2 (1974)

FEDERHOFER-KÖNIGS, R., 'Neues zur Lebensgeschichte von Johann Spech', in *Die Musikforschung* XVIII (1965)

FEKETE DE GALANTHA, GRAF J., *Wien im Jahre 1787*; new edition, Vienna 1921

FELLERER, K. G., *Beiträge zur Musikgeschichte Freisings. . .*, Freising 1926

——, 'Zum Joseph-Haydn-Bild im frühen 19. Jahrhundert', in *Anthony van Hoboken, Festschrift zum 75. Geburtstag* (ed. J. Schmidt-Görg), Mainz 1962

——. 'Joseph Haydns Messen', in *Bericht über die Konferenz zum Andenken Joseph Haydns, Budapest 1959*, Budapest 1961

——, 'Klavierbearbeitungen Haydnscher Werke im frühen 19. Jahrhundert', in *Festskrift Jens Peter Larsen*, Copenhagen 1972

FERRARI, G. G., *Aneddoti piaceroli e interessanti, Occorsi nella vita di* [etc.], 2 vols., London 1830

FÉTIS, F. J., *Biographie universelle des musiciens*, Brussels 1837–44

FEUCHTMÜLLER, R., 'Farbe und Raum in Spätbarock', in 'Joseph Haydn und seine Zeit,' *Jahrbuch für Österreichische Kulturgeschichte* II, Eisenstadt 1972

FINSCHER, L., 'Joseph Haydn und das italienische Streichquartett', *Analecta Musicologica* 4 (1967)

——, *Studien zur Geschichte des Streichquartetts. I. Die Entstehung des klassischen Streichquartetts. Von den Vorformen zur Grundlegung durch Joseph Haydn*, Kassel 1974

FISCHER, W., 'Zur Entwicklungsgeschichte des Wiener klassischen Stils', in *Studien zur Musikwissenschaft*, 1915

——, Foreword to *Denkmäler der Tonkunst in Österreich*, 22. Jg., vol III (1915)

——, 'Stilkritischer Anhang', in Schnerich, A., *Joseph Haydn und seine Sendung*, 2/1926

——, 'Instrumentalmusik von 1750–1828', in *Adlers Handbuch der Musikgeschichte* [1929]

FISKE, R., *English Theatre Music in the Eighteenth Century*, London 1973

FITZPATRICK, H., *The Horn and Horn-playing, and the Austro-Bohemian Tradition 1680–1830*, London 1970

——, 'Waldhorntechnik um die Jahrhundertmitte', in *Der junge Haydn: Kongressbericht Graz 1970*, Graz 1972

FLAMM, C., 'Ein Verlegerbriefwechsel zur Beethovenzeit', in *Beethoven-Studien* (ed. E. Schenk), Vienna 1970

FLUELER, M., *Die norddeutsche Symphonie zur Zeit Friedrichs des Grossen und die Werke Philipp Emanuel Bachs*, Berlin 1908

FORKEL, J. N., *Musikalisch-kritische Bibliothek*, Gotha 1778 (cf. 'Periodicals')

FÖRSTENMANN, E., *Die Gräflich Stolbergsche Bibliothek zu Wernigerode*, Nordhausen 1866

FOSTER, J., 'The Tempora Mutantur Symphony of Joseph Haydn', in *Haydn Yearbook* IX (1975)

FOTHERGILL, B., *Sir William Hamilton*, London 1969

FOX, D. G. A., *Joseph Haydn*, London 1929

FRAMERY, N., *Notice sur Joseph Haydn*, Paris 1810

FRANCOEUR, L. J., *Traité général des voix et des instruments d'orchestre*, Paris 1772

FRIEDLAND, B., *Haydn's Sturm und Drang Period: A Problem of Esthetics* (Thesis), Queens College, New York 1968

FRIEDLÄNDER, M., *Das deutsche Lied im 18. Jahrhundert*, Stuttgart–Berlin 1902

——, 'Van Swieten und das Textbuch zu Haydns "Jahreszeiten"', in *Jahrbuch der Musikbibliothek Peters*, 1909, pp. 47ff.

——, Foreword to Series XX, vol. I of the Breitkopf und Härtel Haydn *Gesamtausgabe* (1932)

FRIMMEL, T., *Beethoven-Handbuch*, Leipzig 1926

FRÖHLICH, J., 'Joseph Haydn', in Ersch, J. S., and Gruber, J. G., *Allgemeine Encyclopädie* [1828]; new edition by A. Sandberger, Regensburg 1936

FUCHS, A., *Thematisches Verzeichnis der sämtlichen Kompositionen von Joseph Haydn*, 1839; facsimile reproduction (R. Schaal), Wilhelmshaven 1968

GAMBERRA, C. A., *Haydn coronato in Elicona*, Brescia 1819

GARCIA, E. Jr., *Traité complet du chant*, Paris 1847 (numerous translations into German, English, Italian, etc.)

GARDINER, W. (trans.), *The Life of Haydn, in a Series of Letters written at Vienna, followed by The Life of Mozart with observations on Metastasio and on the present state of Music in France and Italy translated from the French by L. A. C. Bombet*, London 1817

——, *Music and Friends* ..., 3 vols., London 1838–53

GÁRDONYI, Z., 'Haydn Oratórium-Formálása', in *Zenetudományi Tanulmányok* VIII (1960), pp. 95ff.

GARROS, L., *Quel roman de ma vie. Itinéraire de Napoléon Bonaparte 1769–1821*, Paris 1947

GÄSSLER, W., *Die Sinfonien von Franz Xaver Richter und ihre Stellung in der vorklassischen Sinfonik*, Munich 1941 (Dissertation)

GAUTIER, A., 'A propos des quatuors de Haydn', in *Schweizerische Musikzeitung* LXXII, 1932, Heft 8

GEIRINGER, K., *Joseph Haydn*, Potsdam 1932

——, 'Haydn's sketches for "The Creation"', in *Musical Quarterly*, 1932

——, 'Das Haydn-Bild im Wandel der Zeiten', in *Die Musik*, 1932

——, 'Haydn und die Oper', in *Zeitschrift für Musik* IC, 1932, Heft 4

——, 'Haydn as an opera composer', in *Proceedings of the Royal Musical Association*, 1939/40

——, 'The operas of Haydn', in *Musical America*, 1940

——, *Haydn, A Creative Life in Music*, New York 1946; 2nd ed., 1963; 3rd ed., 1968

——, 'Haydn and the folksong of the British Isles', in *Musical Quarterly* XXV (1949)/2

——, *Analytical Notes to the complete string quartets of Joseph Haydn* (with M. Scott), Boston, Mass., 1953 *et seq.*

——, 'The small sacred works by Haydn in the Esterházy Archives at Eisenstadt', in *Musical Quarterly* XLV (1959)

——, *Joseph Haydn*, Mainz 1959

——, 'Sidelights on Haydn's activities in the field of sacred music', in *Bericht über die Internationale Konferenz zum Andenken Joseph Haydns, Budapest 1959*, Budapest 1961

——, 'Eigenhändige Bemerkungen Haydns in seinen Musikhandschriften', in *Anthony van Hoboken, Festschrift zum 75. Geburtstag* (ed. J. Schmidt-Görg), Mainz 1962

——, *Studies in Eighteenth Century Music: A Tribute to Karl Geiringer on his Seventieth Birthday* (ed. H. C. Robbins Landon and R. E. Chapman), London 1970 (see also individual articles under names of contributors)

GEORGE III, *The Later Correspondence of George III* (ed. A. Aspinall), 5 vols., Cambridge 1962–70

GEORGIADES, T., 'Zur Musiksprache der Wiener Klassiker', in *Mozart-Jahrbuch* 1951

GÉRARD, Y., *Catalogue of the Works of Luigi Boccherini*, London 1969

GERBER, E. L., *Historisch-biographisches Lexikon der Tonkünstler* (2 vols.), Leipzig 1790–92

——, *Neues historisch-biographisches Lexikon der Tonkünstler* (4 vols.), Leipzig 1812–14; new edition (ed. O. Wessely) in facsimile, Graz 1966

GERBER, R., 'Haydn und Mozart', in *Die Musik* XXIX, 1936/37

——, *Christoph Willibald Ritter von Gluck*, Potsdam, 1941 (2/1952)

GERICKE, H., *Der Wiener Musikhandel von 1700 bis 1778*, Vienna 1960

GERLACH, S., 'Die chronologische Ordnung von Haydns Sinfonien zwischen 1774 und 1782', in *Haydn-Studien* II (1969)/1

——, 'Ein Fund zu Haydns verschollener Sinfonie', in *Haydn-Studien* III/I (1973)

GERMANN, J., *Die Entwicklung der Exposition in Joseph Haydns Streichquartetten*, Berne 1964 (Dissertation), printed at Teufen

GERSTENBERG, W., *Musikerhandschriften von Palestrina bis Beethoven*, Zurich 1960

GERSTINGEN, H., *Ludwig van Beethovens Stammbuch* (facsimile edition with comments), Bielefeld-Leipzig 1927

GHISI, G. C., *Elogio Storico del Maestro Francesco Gius. Haydn*, Florence 1839

GHISLANZONI, A., *Giovanni Paisiello: Valutazioni, critiche, rettificate*, Rome 1969

GIAZOTTO, R., *Giovan Battista Viotti*, Milan 1956

GIBBON, E., *The Miscellaneous Works of Edward Gibbon, Esq., with Memoirs of his Life and Writings, composed by Himself* (ed. John, Lord Sheffield), London 1837

GIBBS, T. J., *A Study of Form in the Late Masses of Joseph Haydn*, University of Texas 1973 (Dissertation)

GIRDLESTONE, C. M., *Mozart's Piano Concertos*, London 1948

GLEICHEN-RUSSWURM, A. VON, *Das Galante Europa 1600–1789*, Stuttgart 1911

GLUCK, C. W., *The Collected Correspondence and Papers of Christoph Willibald Gluck* (ed. H. and E. H. Mueller von Asow), London 1962

——, *Sämtliche Werke*, Kassel, etc., 1951 *et seq.*

GOETHE, J. W. VON, *Briefwechsel zwischen Goethe und Zelter* (4 vols., ed. M. Hecker), Leipzig 1913

GÖLLNER, K., 'Authentisch oder nicht?', in *Burgenländische Heimatblätter* XXI/2 (1959)

GÖRNER, K. VON, *Der Hans Wurst-Streit in Wien und Joseph von Sonnerfels*, Vienna 1884

GOTWALS, V., 'Haydn in London again', in *Music Review* 22, No. 3 (1961)

——, 'Joseph Haydn's Last Will and Testament'. in *Musical Quarterly* XLVII/3 (July 1961)

——, see also under Dies and Griesinger

GRADENWITZ, P., *Johann Stamitz* (Veröffentlichung des Musikwissenschaftlichen Institutes der Deutschen Universität, Prag), 1936

——, 'The Symphonies of Johann Stamitz', in *Music Review*, 1940

GRANDSARD, A., *La jeunesse de Haydn; suivie d'une notice sur Auguste Pajou*, Lille 1864

GRASBERGER, F., 'Form und Ekstase. Über eine Beziehung Haydn-Schubert-Bruckner in der Symphonie', in *Anthony van Hoboken, Festschrift zum 75, Geburtstag* (ed. J. Schmidt-Görg), Mainz 1962

——, *Die Hymnen Österreichs*, Tutzing 1968

GRAY, C., *Analytical Notes for the Haydn String Quartet Society*, London 1932–39

——, *A limited Edition of Haydn's Trios*, London 1940

——, 'Joseph Haydn', in *The Symphony* (ed. Ralph Hill), London 1949

GRIESINGER, G. A. VON, *Biographische Notizen über Joseph Haydn*, Leipzig 1810; new edition (ed. F. Grasberger), Vienna 1954

——, *Denkwürdigkeiten aus der Geschichte der österreichischen Monarchie. Auf jeden Tag des Jahres gesammelt*, Vienna 1804

GRIESINGER, G. A. VON, and DIES, A. C., *Biographische Nachrichten von Joseph Haydn*, trans. Vernon Gotwals as *Joseph Haydn: Eighteenth Century Gentleman and Genius*, Wisconsin 1963

GROSSER, J. E., *Biographische Notizen über Joseph Haydn*, Hirschberg 1826

GROSSMANN-VENDREY, S., *Felix Mendelssohn-Bartholdy und die Musik der Vergangenheit*, Regensburg 1969

GROVE, SIR G., *Dictionary of Music and Musicians* (1st ed. London 1879–89; 5th ed., London 1954)

GRÜBER, G., 'Haydns Marionetten-Opern in ihren kulturgeschichtlichen Zusammenhängen', in *Haydn-Studien* II (1969)/2

——, 'Musikalische Rhetorik und barocke Bildlichkeit in Kompositionen des jungen Haydn', in *Der junge Haydn: Kongressbericht Graz 1970*, Graz 1972

GRUNDMANN, H., 'Per il Clavicembalo o Piano-Forte', in *Colloquium Amicorum*, Bonn 1967

GRÜNINGER, F., *Die Himmel erzählen. Ein Joseph-Haydn-Buch*, Freiburg 1951 (2nd ed. 1954)

GRUNSKY, K., 'Haydn und die deutsche Musik', in *Bayreuther Blätter* LV, 1932/2

——, 'Haydn und das Streichquartett', in *Die Musik* XXIV (1932)/6, pp. 412ff.

GUGITZ, G., *Die Ehetragödie Ferdinand Raimunds, nach den unveröffentlichen Akten des Wiener Stadtgerichtes im Archiv der Stadt Wien*, Wiener Bibliophilen-Gesellschaft, Vienna 1956

GUGLIA, E., *Maria Theresia: Ihr Leben und ihre Regierung*, 2 vols., Munich–Berlin 1917

GUIDE: *Guide to the Loan Collection and List of Instruments, Manuscripts, Books, Paintings and Engravings, exhibited in the Gallery and Lower Rooms of the Albert Hall*, London 1885

GÜNTHER, U., '. . . über alles in der Welt? Studien zur Geschichte und Didaktik der deutschen National-hymne*, Neuwied/Rhein 1966

GUTKAS, K., 'Österreich und Europa zur Zeit Joseph Haydns', in 'Joseph Haydn und seine Zeit', *Jahrbuch für Österreichische Kulturgeschichte* II, Eisenstadt 1972

GÜTTLER, H., *Königsbergs Musikkultur im 18. Jahrhundert*, Kassel 1925

GYROWETZ, A., *[Selbst]-Biographie des Adalbert Gyrowetz*, Vienna 1848; new edition (ed. A. Einstein), Leipzig 1915

HAAS, K., 'Haydn's English Military Marches', in *The Score*, January 1950

HAAS, R., 'Zur Frage der Orchesterbesetzungen in der 2. Hälfte des 18. Jahrhunderts', in *Haydn-Jubiläumsfeier, Kongressbericht*, 1909

——, 'Die Musik in der Wiener Stegreifkomödie', in *Studien zur Musikwissenschaft*, 1925

——, *Die Musik des Barocks*, Potsdam 1928

——, 'Von dem Wienerischen Geschmack in der Musik', in *Biehle-Festschrift*, Leipzig 1930

——, *Aufführungspraxis der Musik*, Potsdam 1931

——, *Wolfgang Amadeus Mozart*, Potsdam 1933 (2/1950)

HADDEN, J. C., *George Thomson, the Friend of Burns: His Life and Correspondence*, London 1898

——, *Haydn*, London 1902 (2/1934)

——, 'George Thomson and Haydn', in *Monthly Musical Record*, 1910

HADOW, SIR W. H., *A Croatian Composer, Notes towards the study of Joseph Haydn*, London 1897 (reprinted in W. H. H.'s 'Collected Essays', London 1928)

——, 'The Viennese Period', in *Oxford History of Music*, Vol. 5, 2/1931 and 1939

——, 'Haydn', in *Musical Times* LXXIII, 1932, No. 1069

HAERING, H., 'August von Griesinger', in *Schwäbische Lebensbilder*, V, Stuttgart 1950

HAILPARN, L., 'Haydn: The Seven Words: A new look at an old masterpiece', in *Music Review* XXIV/1 (1973), pp. 1ff.

HALBREICH, H., *Joseph Haydn, Les Seize Derniers Trios*, Paris 1971

HALM, H., 'Eine unbekannte Handschrift der "Kinder-Symphonie"', in *Anthony van Hoboken, Festschrift zum 75. Geburtstag* (ed. J. Schmidt-Görg), Mainz 1962

HAMMELMANN, H. A., 'The Poet's Seasons Delineated', in *Country Life Annual*, 1970

HANSLICK, E., *Geschichte des Concertwesens in Wien*, Vienna 1869; 2nd ed., 1897

HARASZTI, E., 'Les Eszterhàzy [sic], d'après des documents inédits de l'époque', in *La Revue Musicale* XIII (1932), pp. 85ff.

HARICH, J., 'Az Esterházy-Zenekar elsö karmestere', in *Muzsika* (Budapest) I/4 (1929)

——, 'Werner Gergely József (Haydn József elöde az Esterházyudrarban)', in *Muzsika* (Budapest) II, 1930, Nos. 4 and 5

——, 'Beethoven in Eisenstadt', special supplement in *Burgenländische Heimatblätter*, Eisenstadt 1959, 21. Jg., No. 2

——, *Esterházy-Musikgeschichte im Spiegel der zeitgenössischen Textbücher*, special number of *Burgenländische Forschungen*, Heft 39, Eisenstadt 1959

——, 'Das Repertoire des Opernkapellmeisters Joseph Haydn in Eszterháza (1780–1790)', in *Haydn Yearbook* I (1962)

——, 'Haydn Documenta (I)', in *Haydn Yearbook* II (1963/64)

——, 'Haydn Documenta (II)', in *Haydn Yearbook* III (1965)

——, 'Das fürstlich Esterhazy'sche Fideikommis', in *Haydn Yearbook* IV (1968)

——, 'Haydn Documenta (III)', in *Haydn Yearbook* IV (1968)

——, 'Das Opernensemble zu Esterháza im Jahr 1780', in *Haydn Yearbook* VII (1970)

——, 'Haydn Documenta (IV)', in *Haydn Yearbook* VII (1970)

——, 'Das Haydn-Orchester im Jahre 1780', in *Haydn Yearbook* VIII (1971)

——, 'Haydn Documenta (V)', in *Haydn Yearbook* VIII (1971)

——, 'Inventare der Esterházy-Hofmusikkapelle in Eisenstadt', in *Haydn Yearbook* IX (1975)

HARRISON, B., 'Some Notes on Haydn', in *Monthly Musical Record* XXXVIII, June 1908

HARTOG, J., *Joseph Haydn, zijn broeder Michael en hunne werken, benevens de thematische ontwikkeling van zeven der meest-bekende symph.*, Amsterdam 1905

HASE, H. VON, *Joseph Haydn und Breitkopf und Härtel*, Leipzig 1909

HASTINGS, B., 'Vergleich der konzertanten Techniken in den Sinfonien Mozarts und Haydns', in *Mitteilungen der Internationalen Stiftung Mozarteum Salzburg* XVI/3–4 (1968)

HATTING, C. E., 'Obligater Satz versus Generalbaß-Satz ...', in *Festskrift Jens Peter Lansen*, Copenhagen 1972

——, 'Haydn oder Kayser? – Eine Echtheitsfrage', in *Die Musikforschung*, XXV. Jahrgang (1972), Heft 2.

HAUSSWALD, G., *Mozarts Serenaden, ein Beitrag zur Stilkritik des 18. Jahrhunderts*, Leipzig 1951 (see also: H. Engel's criticism in *Die Musikforschung*, 1952)

——, 'Der Divertimento-Begriff bei Georg Christoph Wagenseil', in *Archiv für Musikwissenschaft* IX (1952)

HAWKINS, J., *A General History of the Science and Practice of Music*, London 1776

HAYDN, F. J., *J. Haydn's Verzeichnis musikalischer Werke, theils eigener, theils fremder Composition* (MS. catalogue by Johann Elssler), British Museum (Add. 32070)

——, *Haydns Taschen buch i[m] Jahr [1]791, in London* (his own title), MS. notebook for years 1791–92, Vienna, Österreichische Nationalbibliothek (Codex 1539)

——, *[Haydns Zweites Taschenbuch]*, London 1791–92, Vienna, Österreichische Nationalbibliothek (Codex 15391)

——, *[Haydns Drittes Taschenbuch]*, London 1794–5, Mozarteum, Salzburg

——, Letters to (and partly from) Marianna von Genzinger, 1789–92, Vienna, Österreichische Nationalbibliothek (Codex 14300)

——, 'Autobiographische Skizze', in *Wiener Diarium* 1776, No. 84; also in Luca, J. de, *Das gelehrte Österreich, Ein Versuch* (2 parts), Vienna 1776–78

——, *Expositia: Joseph Haydn (1732–1809): Cluj 23–30 Mai 1959*

——, *Haydn Compositions in the Music Collection of the National Széchényi Library, Budapest*, Budapest 1960

——, *Zeitgenössische Drucke und Handschriften der Werke Joseph Haydns in der Musikbibliothek der Stadt Leipzig*, Leipzig 1962

——, facsimile editions of autograph scores of works by Haydn:
Symphony No. 7 (National Széchényi Library, Budapest), ed. L. Somfai, Budapest 1972;
String Quartets, Op. 77, Nos. 1 and 2 (National Széchényi Library, Budapest), Budapest 1972;
Symphony No. 45 (National Széchényi Library, Budapest), ed. L. Somfai, Budapest 1959;

Schöpfungsmesse, ed. Wilhelm Virneisel, Munich–Duisburg 1959;
Piano Sonata No. 41 (XVI:26), ed. G. Feder, Munich–Duisburg 1959;
see also Landon; Engl; and Manuscript Catalogues, *supra*

HAYDN-JUBILÄUMSFEIER. *Kongressbericht*, Vienna 1909

HAYDN SOCIETY:
——, First Musicological Report, Vienna 1950
——, Second Musicological Report, Vienna 1950

HAYDN-ZENTENARFEIER: *Programmbuch*, Vienna 1909

HAZARD, P., *European Thought in the Eighteenth Century*, London 1954

HAZLITT, W., *Memoires of the late Thomas Holcroft* (ed. and completed by Hazlitt), 3 vols., London 1816

HEAWOOD, E., *Some watermarks, mainly of the 17th and 18th centuries*, Hilversum 1950

HECKSCHER, W. S., 'Sturm und Drang: Conjectures on the Origin of a Phrase', in *Simiolus* I (1966–67)/2, pp. 1ff.

HEINICHEN, J. D., *Der General-Bass in der Composition*, Dresden, 2/1728

HEINZEN, C., '"L'Incontro improviso", eine ausgegrabene Oper Haydns', in *Die Musik* XXIV/6 (1932), pp. 424ff.

HELFERT, V., 'Zur Geschichte der Wiener Singspiele', in *Zeitschrift für Musikwissenschaft*, 1922/23

HELL, H., *Die Neapolitanische Opernsinfonie in der ersten Hälfte des 18. Jahrhunderts*, Tutzing 1971

HELLER, F., 'Haydns "Londoner" Symphonie, D-dur: Eine Analyse', in *Beiträge zur Musikgeschichte des 18. Jahrhunderts*, 1 and 2, Eisenstadt 1971

HELLWIG, F., 'Der Wandel des Streichinstrumentariums zwischen Barock und Klassik', in *Der junge Haydn: Kongressberichte Graz 1970*, Graz 1972

HELLYER, R., 'Mozart's "Harmoniemusik" with bibliographical notes on Haydn and Pleyel', in *Haydn Yearbook* IX (1975)

HELM, S. H., *Carl Friedrich Abel, Symphonist: A Biographical, Stylistic and Bibliographical Study*, University of Michigan, 1953 (Dissertation)

HENNERBERG, C. F., 'Schwedische Haydn-Handschriften', in *Haydn-Jubiläumsfeier, Kongressbericht* 1909

HERING, H., 'Das Klavier in der Kammermusik des 18. Jahrhunderts', in *Die Musikforschung* XXIII (1970), Heft I

HERTZMANN, E., 'The Newly Discovered Autograph of Beethoven's *Rondo à Capriccio*, Op. 129', in *Musical Quarterly*, vol. 32 (1946)

HESS, R., *Serenade, Cassation, Notturne und Divertimento bei Michael Haydn*, Mainz 1963

HETSCH, G., *Joseph Haydn*, Copenhagen 1901

HEUSS, A., 'Der Humor im letzten Satz von Haydns Oxford-Symphonie', in *Die Musik*, 45, 1912

——, 'Haydns Kaiserhymne', in *Zeitschrift für Musik* I/1 (1918); (cf. O. E. Deutsch's reply in I/5 [1919])

451

——, 'Über die Dynamik der Mannheimer Schule', in *Zeitschrift für Musikwissenschaft*, 1919/20

——, 'Joseph Haydns Londoner Sinfonie in c-moll eine Charakter-Sinfonie?', in *Zeitschift für Musik* XCIX/4 (1932)

HEUSSNER, H., 'Zwei neue Haydn Funde', in *Musikforschung* XIII/4 (1960)

——, 'Joseph Haydns Konzert (XVIII:5) . . .', in *Musikforschung* XXII/4 (1969)

HIBBERT, C., *George IV*, London 1976

HILGER, W., '"Kammermaler" der österreichischen Spätbarocks', in 'Joseph Haydn und seine Zeit', *Jahrbuch für Österreichische Kulturgeschichte* II, Eisenstadt 1972

HILLER, J. A., *Anweisung zum Musikalischen richtigen Gesang*, Leipzig 1774 (see also 'Periodicals')

HINDENBERGER, A., *Die Motivik in Haydns Streichquartetten*, Turbenthal 1935

HIRSCH, F., *Zeitgenössische Drucke und Handschriften der Werke Joseph Haydns in der Musikbibliothek der Stadt Leipzig*, Leipzig 1962

HIS, M. E., 'Zu Haydns "Ein Mächen, das auf Ehre hielt"', in *Zeitschrift der Internationalen Musikgesellschaft*, 1911

HITZIG, W., 'Aus den Briefen Griesingers an Breitkopf & Härtel entnommene Notizen über Beethoven', in *Der Bär* 1927

HOBOKEN, A. VAN, *Joseph Haydn: Thematisch-bibliographisches Werkverzeichnis*, vol. I (1957), vol. II (1971), Mainz

——, *Anthony van Hoboken, Festschrift zum 75. Geburtstag* (ed. J. Schmidt-Görg), Mainz 1962 (see also individual articles)

——, 'A rare contemporary edition of Haydn's "Hymn for the Emperor"', in *Studies in Eighteenth Century Music: A Tribute to Karl Geiringer on his Seventieth Birthday* (ed. H. C. R. Landon and R. E. Chapman), London 1970

——, 'Joseph Haydns Schwager', in *Festschrift Josef Stummvoll*, Vienna 1970

——, 'Nunziato Porta und der Text von Joseph Haydns Oper "Orlando Paladino"', in *Symbolae Historiae Musicae* [Federhofer Festschrift], Mainz 1971

HODGSON, A., 'Joseph Haydn – The Pre-London Symphonies. A critical Assessment of the Microgroove Recordings (with supplementary discography of 78 rpm recordings)', in *Haydn Yearbook* VII (1970)

——, 'Joseph Haydn – The London Symphonies. A Critical Assessment of The Microgroove Recordings', in *Haydn Yearbook* IX (1975)

HOFER, H., *Christian Cannabich*, Munich 1921 (Dissertation)

HOFER, N., *Die beiden Reutter als Kirchenkomponisten*, Vienna 1915 (unprinted dissertation)

HOFFMANN, F., *Haydns Jugendjahre*, Leipzig 1899

HOFFMANN, H., 'Über die Mozartschen Serenaden und Divertimenti', in *Mozart-Jahrbuch*, 1929

HOHENEMSER, R., 'Joseph Haydn als Instrumentalkomponist', in *Die Musik*, 1909

Hohe Schule der Musik, ed. Müller-Blattau, J. (4 vols.), Potsdam 1935/39

HOPKINSON, C., *A Dictionary of Parisian Music Publishers*, 1700–1950, London 1954

HOPKINSON, C., and OLDMAN, C. B., 'Thomson's Collections of National Song, with special reference to the compositions of Haydn and Beethoven', in *Transactions of the Edinburgh Bibliographical Society*, 1940

——, 'Haydn's Settings of Scottish Songs in the Collections of Napier and Whyte' (*ibid.*, 1954)

HORÁNYI, M., 'Az Esterházy-Opera', in *Zenetudományi Tanulmányok* VI (1957), pp. 729ff.

——, *The Magnificence of Eszterháza*, London 1962 (original: Hungarian, Budapest 1959; also German, Budapest, 1959)

HOŘEJŠ, A., 'Haydn mit heutigen Augen gesehen', in *Bericht über die Internationale Konferenz zum Andenken Joseph Haydns, Budapest 1959*, Budapest 1961

HORN, H.-J., 'FIAT LUX. Zum kunsttheoretischen Hintergrund der "Erschaffung" des Lichtes in Haydns Schöpfung', in *Haydn-Studien* III/2 (1974)

HORSETZKY, A. VON, *Kriegsgeschichtliche Übersicht der wichtigsten Feldzüge seit 1792*, 7th ed., Vienna 1913

HORWARTHNER, M., 'Joseph Haydns Bibliothek – Versuch einer literar-historischen Rekonstruktion', in *Joseph Haydn und die Literatur seiner Zeit* (ed. H. Zeman), Eisenstadt 1976

HORWITZ, K., *Georg Christoph Wagenseil als Symphoniker*, Vienna, n.d. (unpublished dissertation) [*c.* 1907?]

HÖSLINGER, C., 'Der überwundene Standpunkt: Joseph Haydn in der Wiener Musikkritik des 19. Jahrhunderts', in *Beiträge zur Musikgeschichte des 18. Jahrhunderts*, Eisenstadt 1970

HRABUSSAY, Z., 'Joseph Haydn und Bratislava', lecture at the Haydn-Kongress, Bratislava, Sept. 1959

HUEMER, G., *Die Pflege der Musik im Stifte Kremsmünster*, Wels 1877

HUGHES-HUGHES, A., *Catalogue of Manuscript Music in the British Museum* (3 volumes), London 1906/09

HUGHES, R. S. M., 'Haydn at Oxford', in *Music and Letters*, 1939

——, 'Dr Burney's Championship of Haydn', in *Musical Quarterly*, 1941

——, *Haydn*, London 1950 (and later revised editions)

——, 'Haydn and Folksong', in *Music and Letters* XXXI, 1950

——, 'Two Haydn Masses', in *Musical Times*, 1950

——, [Haydn] in *Chamber Music* (ed. A. Robertson), London 1957

——, 'The Haydn-Orchestra', in *Musical Times* 93, 1952

——, *Haydn's String Quartets*, London 1966 (BBC Music Publication)

HUMMEL, J. J., see Johannson, C.

HUMMEL, J. N., *Johann Nepomuk Hummel – Komponist der Goethe-Zeit und sein Sohn Carl – Landschaftsmaler des späten Weimar*, catalogue of an exhibition at the Goethe-Museum, Düsseldorf, August–October 1971

HUMPHRIES, C., and SMITH, W. C., *Music Publishing in the British Isles*, London 1954

HUNTER, A., *Poems*, London 1802

HUSCHKE, K., 'Beethoven und Haydn', in *Neue Musikzeitschrift* IV/12 (1950)

HUTCHINGS, A., *A Companion to Mozart's Piano Concertos*, London 1947 (New York 1950)

JACKSON, F. J. F., *Social Life in England 1750–1850*, New York 1916

JACOB, H. E., *Johann Strauss: A Century of Light Music*, revised edition London 1949

——, *Joseph Haydn, his art, times and glory*, New York 1950 (German edition, Hamburg 1952)

JÄGER-SUNSTENAU, H., 'Beethoven als Bürger der Stadt Wien', in *Colloquium Amicorum*, Bonn 1967

JAHN, O., *Gesammelte Aufsätze über Musik*, 2nd edition, Leipzig 1867

——, see also under Abert

JALOWETZ, H., *Über einige Besonderheiten der melodischen Technik Beethovens und deren Wurzeln in den Werken von Mozart, Haydn und Philipp Bach*, Vienna 1908 (Dissertation)

——, 'Beethoven's Jugendwerke in ihren melodischen Beziehungen zu Mozart, Haydn und Ph. E. Bach', in *Sammelbände der Internationalen Musikgesellschaft* XII, 1910/11

JANCIK, H., *Michael Haydn, ein vergessener Meister*, Vienna 1952

JEAFFRESON, J., *Lady Hamilton and Lord Nelson* (2 vols.), London 1888

JERGER, W., *Die Haydndrucke aus dem Archiv der 'Theater- und Musik-Liebhabergesellschaft zu Luzern' nebst Materialen zum Musikleben in Luzern um 1800* (Freiburger Studien zur Musikwissenschaft, Band 7), Freiburg 1959

JOHANNSON, C., 'Publishers' addresses as a guide to the dating of French printed music of the second half of the eighteenth century', in *Fontes et Artis Musicae*, 1954

——, *French music publishers' catalogues of the second half of the eighteenth century, with an additional volume of catalogues in facsimile*, Stockholm 1955

——, *J. J. & B. Hummel Music-Publishing and Thematic Catalogues* (3 vols.), Publications of the Royal Swedish Academy of Music, Stockholm 1972

JOHNS, D. C., 'In Defence of Haydn: The "Surprise" Symphony revisited', in *Music Review* XXIV, No. 4 (Nov. 1963)

JOHNSTON, R. M. (ed.), *The Corsican: A Diary of Napoleon's Life in his Own Words*, Boston, Mass., 1910

JONAS, O., 'Musikalische Meisterhandschriften', in *Anthony van Hoboken, Festschrift zum 75. Geburtstag* (ed. J. Schmidt-Görg), Mainz 1962

JOVANOVIC, V., 'Joseph Haydn, die Esterházy und Eisenstadt', in *Haydn-Gedenkheft, Burgenländische Heimatblätter*, 1932

JUNKER, C. L., *Zwanzig Componisten, eine Skizze*, Berne 1776

——, *Einige der vornehmsten Pflichten eines Kapellmeisters oder Musikdirektors*, Winterthur 1782

KADE, O., *Die Musikalien-Sammlung des Grossherzoglich Mecklenburg-Schweriner Fürstenhauses*, Schwerin 1893

KAHL, W., *Selbst-Biographien deutscher Musiker*, Cologne 1948

KALAČIČ, V., *Untersuchungen über die Durchführungsgestaltung in den Symphonien, Streichquartetten und Klaviersonaten Joseph Haydns*, Vienna 1948 (Dissertation)

KALISCHER, A. C., *Beethoven und seine Zeitgenossen* (4 vols.), Berlin–Leipzig 1910

KANDUTH, E., 'Die italienische Libretti der Opern Joseph Haydns', in *Joseph Haydn und die Literatur seiner Zeit* (ed. H. Zeman), Eisenstadt 1976

KARAJAN, T. VON, *Joseph Haydn in London, 1791 and 1792*, Vienna 1861

KATONA, I., 'Fertöd Haydn Századában', in *Zenetudományi Tanulmányok* VIII (1960)

KEESBACHER, F., *Die philharmonische Gesellschaft in Laibach seit dem Jahre ihrer Gründung 1702 bis zu ihrer letzten Umgestaltung 1862. Ein geschichtliche Skizze*, Laibach 1862

KELLER, H., 'Zur Chronologie der Haydnschen Klaviersonaten, Klaviertrios, und Streichquartette', in *Neue Musikzeitung*, 1928

KELLER, HANS, 'The interpretation of the Haydn Quartets', in *The Score* 23 (1958)

KELLNER, A., *Musikgeschichte des Stiftes Kremsmünster*, Kassel–Basle 1956

KELLNER, D., *Treulicher Unterricht im General-Bass*, Hamburg, 4/1767

KELLY, M., *Reminiscences*, London 1826

KERMAN, J., *The Beethoven Quartets*, New York–London 1967

KERST, F., *Die Erinnerungen an Beethoven*, Stuttgart 1913

KIDSON, F., *British Music Publishers*, London 1900

KIER, H., *Raphael Georg Kiesewetter (1773–1850): Wegbereiter des musikalischen Historismus*, Regensburg 1968

KINDERMANN, H., *Theatergeschichte Europas*: Band IV, Band V (Von der Aufklärung zur Romantik), Salzburg 1961, 1962

KINKER, J., *De nagedachtenis van Joseph Haydn*, Amsterdam 1810

KINSKY, G., 'Haydn und das Hammerklavier', in *Zeitschrift für Musikwissenschaft* XIII, 1930/31

——, 'Eine frühe Partitur-Ausgabe von Symphonien Haydns, Mozarts und Beethovens', in *Acta Musicologica*, 1941

——, *Das Werk Beethovens: Thematisch-Bibliographisches Verzeichnis seiner sämtlichen vollendeten Kompositionen . . . nach dem Tode des Verfassers abgeschlossen und herausgegeben von Hans Halm*, Munich 1955

KIRKENDALE, W., *Fuge und Fugato in der Kammermusik des Rokoko und der Klassik*, Tutzing 1966

——, 'Beethovens Missa Solemnis und die Rhetorische Tradition', in Beethoven Number, Sitzungsberichte der Österreichischen Akademie der Wissenschaften, Philosophisch. historische Klasse, Band 271, Vienna 1971

KLAFSKY, A. M., 'Michael Haydn als Kirchenkomponist', in *Studien zur Musikwissenschaft*, 1915

——, 'Thematischer Katalog der Kirchenmusikwerke von Michael Haydn', in *Denkmäler der Tonkunst in Österreich*, XXX. Jg./vol. 62, Vienna 1925

KLEBEL, B., 'Oboe und Oboespiel zur Zeit des jungen Haydn', in *Der junge Haydn: Kongressbericht Graz 1970*, Graz 1972

KLIER, K. M., 'Haydn und das Volkslied seiner Heimat', in *Haydn Gedenkheft, Burgenländische Heimatblätter*, 1932

——, 'Das Volksliedthema eines Haydn-Capriccios', in *Das deutsche Volkslied*, Jg. 34, Vienna 1932

KLINGENBECK, J., [*Ignaz*] *Joseph Pleyel und seine Kompositionen für Streichquartett*, Munich 1928 (Dissertation)

——, 'Pleyels Streichquartette im Rahmen der Wiener Klassik', in *Festschrift Erich Schenk*, Vienna 1962

KLINKHAMMER, R., *Die langsame Einleitung in der Instrumentalmusik der Klassik und Romantik: Ein Sonderproblem in der Entwicklung der Sonatenform*, Regensburg 1971

KLOB, K. M., *Drei musikalische Biedermänner: Ignaz Holzbauer, Carl Ditters v. Dittersdorf, Michael Haydn*, Ulm 1911

KNAPE, W., *Karl Friedrich Abel: Leben und Werk eines frühklassischen Komponisten*, Bremen 1973

KNECHT, J. H., *Allgemeiner musikalischer Katechismus*, Freiburg 4/1816

KNIGHT, C., *Autobiography* (2 vols.), London 1861

KNIGHT, E. C., *The Autobiography of Miss Knight* (ed. R. Fulford), London 1960

KOBALD, K., *Joseph Haydn*, Vienna 1932

KOCH, H. C., *Musikalisches Lexikon*, Frankfurt 1802

KOCH, L., *Joseph Haydn ... Bibliographie als Festgabe der Budapester Stadtbibliothek*, Budapest 1932

KÖCHEL, L., *Chronologisch-thematisches Verzeichnis sämtlicher Tonwerke Wolfgang Amadeus Mozarts*, Leipzig 1862, 3rd ed. (edited by A. Einstein), Leipzig 1937; revised 3rd ed. with supplement by A. Einstein, Ann Arbor, Mich., 1947; 6th ed. (edited by F. Giegling), Wiesbaden 1967

——, *Die Kaiserliche Hof-Musikkapelle in Wien von 1543–1867*, Vienna 1869

KOLISKO, W., *Wenzel Pichls Kammermusik*, Vienna 1918 (Dissertation)

KOMORZYNSKI, E., 'Joseph Haydn's Messen', in *Neue Musikzeitung* XXX, 1909

KOPFERMANN, A., 'Zur Veröffentlichung des Haydnschen Flötentrios', in *Die Musik*, Jg. 8, No. 16 (1909)

KORABINSKY, J. M., *Geographisches-Historisches-Produkten Lexikon von Ungarn*, Pressburg 1786

KORCAK, F., *Luigi Tomasini (1741–1808), Konzertmeister der fürstlich Esterházyschen Kapelle in Eisenstadt unter Joseph Haydn*, Vienna 1952 (Dissertation)

KORNAUTH, L., *Die thematische Arbeit in Joseph Haydns Streichquartetten seit 1780 ...*, Vienna 1915 (Dissertation)

——, *Führer durch die Streichquartette Haydns*, Vienna 1919

KOSCH, F., 'Florian Leopold Gassmann als Kirchenkomponist', in *Festschrift, Beethoven-Zentenarfeier, Denkmäler der Tonkunst in Österreich*, 1927

KOZLIK, G., *Der Haydn'sche Streichersatz*, Vienna 1925 (Dissertation)

KRALIK, R. VON, 'Zu Haydns Kaiserlied', in *Musica Divina* V, 1917, Heft 2–3

KRAUSE, E., 'Ein interessantes Haydn-Autograph', in *Musikalisches Wochenblatt*, Leipzig, Jg. XL/9 (1909), No. 9

KREBS, C., *Dittersdorfiana*, Berlin 1900

KREBS, G., *Das Lied bei Haydn*, Innsbruck 1934 (Dissertation)

KREHBIEL, H. E., *Music and Manners from Pergolesi to Beethoven*, London 1898

KREMLJEW, J., 'Joseph Haydn und die russische Musikkultur', in *Bericht über die Internationale Konferenz zum Andenken Joseph Haydns, Budapest 1959*, Budapest 1961

KRETZSCHMAR, H., 'Haydns Jugendsymphonien', in *Jahrbuch der Musikbibliothek Peters*, 1908; (reprinted in Kretzschmar, *Gesammelte Aufsätze*, 1911)

——, *Führer durch den Konzertsaal* (I: Instrumentalwerke; II: Vokalwerke), Leipzig 1887/88 (numerous editions)

KRITSCH, C., and SICHROVSKY, H., 'Die Korrespondenz zwischen Karolina von Greiner, Lorenz Leopold Haschka und Johann Caspar Lavater', Appendix in *Joseph Haydn und die Literatur seiner Zeit* (ed. H. Zeman), Eisenstadt 1976

KUFFERATH, M., 'Les "Saisons" de Haydn', in *Le Guide Musicale* (Lüttich) XLII, 1896

KUHAČ, F., *Josip Haydn i Hrvatske Narodne Popievke*, Zagreb 1880

——, *Južno-slovjenske narodne popievke* (Chansons nationales des Slaves du Sud) III, Zagreb 1880

——, 'Ursprung der österreichischen Volkshymne', in *Kroatische Revue*, Agram, May 1886

KÜHNAU, R. E., *Quellenuntersuchungen zu Stendhal-Beyles Jugendwerken: Vie de Haydn 1814. Vie de Mozart 1814. Rome, Naples et Florence en 1817*, Marburg/Lahn 1908 (Dissertation)

KURTH, E., 'Die Jugendopern Glucks bis Orfeo', in *Studien zur Musikwissenschaft*, 1913

KÜTTNER, C. G., *Reise durch Deutschland, Dänemark, Schweden, Norwegen und einen Theil von Italien, in den Jahren 1797, 1798, 1799*, 4 vols., Leipzig 1801

LACHMANN, R., 'Die Haydn-Autographen der Staatsbibliothek zu Berlin', Sonderdruck from *Zeitschrift für Musikwissenschaft*, 1932

LA FAGE, J. A., *Notice sur la Vie et les ouvrages de Joseph Haydn*, Paris 1841 and 1844

LAMBALLE, PRINCESS, *Secret Memoirs of Princess Lamballe* (ed. and annotated by C. Hyde), St Dunstan Society, Akron, Ohio, 1901

LANDON, H. C. ROBBINS, 'On Haydn's Quartets of Opera 1 and 2', in *Music Review*, 1952

——, 'The original versions of Haydn's first "Salomon" Symphonies', in *Music Review* XV, No. I, (1954)

——, 'Die Verwendung gregorianischer Melodien in Haydns Frühsymphonien', in *Österreichische Musik-Zeitschrift* IX, 1954

——, 'Haydn and authenticity: some new facts', in *Music Review* 1955

——, 'Two orchestral works wrongly attributed to Mozart', in *Music Review* XVII, 1956

——, *The Symphonies of Joseph Haydn*, London 1955

——, 'La crise romantique dans la musique autrichienne vers 1770. Quelques précurseurs inconnus de la symphonie en sol mineur (KV 183) de Mozart', lecture given at the Sorbonne, October 1956; printed in *Les influences étrangères dans l'œuvre de W. A. Mozart,* ed. André Verchaly, Paris 1958, pp. 27–47

——, 'Mozart fälschlich zugeschriebene Messen', in *Mozart-Jahrbuch* 1957, pp. 85ff.

——, 'Ein neuentdecktes Bildnis Joseph Haydns' (the Dance portrait now in the Haydn Museum, Vienna), in *Wiener Schriften* 5 (1957), pp. 103ff.

——, 'The "Jena" Symphony', in *Music Review* XVIII/2, May 1957

——, 'Problems of Authenticity in Eighteenth-Century Music', in *Instrumental Music* (ed. D. G. Hughes), Cambridge 1959

——, *Collected Correspondence and London Notebooks of Joseph Haydn*, London 1959

——, 'Survey of the Haydn Sources in Czechoslovakia', in *Bericht über die Internationale Konferenz zum Andenken Joseph Haydns, Budapest 1959*, Budapest 1961

——, *Supplement to 'The Symphonies of Joseph Haydn'*, London 1961

——, 'Haydn's Marionette Operas and the Repertoire of the Marionette Theatre at Esterház Castle', in *Haydn Yearbook* I (1962)

——, *Joseph Haydn: Arien mit Orchester: Revisionsberichte*, Salzburg 1963

——, 'Haydn's newly-discovered "Libera me Domine"', in *Haydn Yearbook* IV (1968)

——, 'Haydniana (I)', in *Haydn Yearbook* IV (1968)

——, *Essays on the Viennese Classical Style*, London 1970

——, *Beethoven: a documentary study*, London and New York 1970

——, 'Haydniana (II)', in *Haydn Yearbook* VII (1970)

——, *The Piano Trios of Joseph Haydn* (Foreword to the Critical Edition), Vienna 1970

——, 'Haydns erste Erfahrungen in England', in *Beiträge zur Musikgeschichte des 18. Jahrhunderts* I/2, Eisenstadt 1971

——, 'A New Authentic Source for "La Fedeltà Premiata" by Haydn', in *Soundings* II (1971–2)

——, *Das kleine Haydnbuch*, 2nd edition, Salzburg 1972

——, 'Haydn's Pianos', in *The Listener*, 20 July 1972

——, 'Haydns Oper "La fedeltà premiata": eine neue authentische Quelle', in *Beiträge zur Musikdokumentation* (Franz Grasberger zum 60. Geburtstag), hrsg. Günter Brosche, Tutzing 1975

——, 'The newly discovered Autograph to Haydn's Missa Cellensis of 1776 (formerly known as the "Missa Sanctae Caeciliae")', in *Haydn Yearbook* IX (1975)

——, 'Auf den Spuren Joseph Haydns' [Haydn's Cantata for Davide, 1791], in *Österreichische Musikzeitschrift* XXXI/11 (1976)

LANDON, H. C. R., and CHAPMAN, R. E. (ed.), *Studies in Eighteenth Century Music: A Tribute to Karl Geiringer on his Seventieth Birthday*, London 1970 (see also under names of contributors)

LANDON, H. C. R., and LARSEN, J. P., 'Haydn', in *Musik in Geschichte und Gegenwart*, Allgemeine Enzyklopädie der Musik (ed. Blume, F.), Kassel 1947 et seq.; vol. V, 1956

LANDON, H. C. R., and MITCHELL, D. (ed.), *The Mozart Companion*, London 1956

LANDSHOFF, L., *Englische Canzonetten von Haydn*, Munich 1924

——, 'Haydn und Hasse', in *Münchner Neueste Nachrichten*, 1925

LANG, P. H., 'Haydn and the Opera', in *Musical Quarterly*, 1932

——, *Music in Western Civilisation*, New York 1941

——, 'Musicology and Related Disciplines', in *Perspectives in Musicology*, New York 1972

——, 'The Changing Portraits of Haydn', in *Haydnfest*, Washington, D.C., 1975

LA ROCHE, S. VON., *Sophie in London – 1786*, London 1933

LARSEN, J. P., 'Haydn und das kleine Quartbuch', in *Acta Musicologica* 1935; controversy between Larsen and A. Sandberger in *Acta Musicologica* and *Zeitschrift für Musik*, 1935–37

——, *Die Haydn-Überlieferung*, Copenhagen 1939

——, *Drei Haydn Kataloge in Faksimile*, Copenhagen 1941

——, Preface to Complete Edition of Joseph Haydn (first printed in Series I, vol. 9, 1950)

——, Article on Haydn in *Sohlmans Musik Lexikon* [1952]

——, 'Zu Haydns Künstlerischer Entwicklung', in *Fischer-Festschrift*, Innsbruck 1956

——, 'Eine bisher unbeachtete Quelle zu Haydns frühen Klavierwerken', in *Schmidt-Görg Festschrift*, Bonn 1957

——, 'Haydn und Mozart', in *Österreichische Musikzeitschrift*, 1959

——, 'Zur Bedeutung der "Mannheimer Schule"', in *Festschrift K. G. Fellerer zum sechzigsten Geburtstag*, Regensburg 1962

——, 'Probleme der chronologischen Ordnung von Haydns Sinfonien', in *Festschrift O. E. Deutsch zum 80. Geburtstag*, Kassel 1963

——, 'Sonatenform-Probleme', in *Festschrift Friedrich Blume*, Kassel 1963

——, 'A Challenge to Musicology: The Viennese Classical School', in *Current Musicology*, 1969

——, 'Zur Frage der Porträtähnlichkeit der Haydn-Bildnisse', in *Studia Musicologica Academiae Scientiarum Hungaricae* 12, 1970

——, 'Der Stilwandel in der österreichischen Musik zwischen Barock und Wiener Klassik', in *Der junge Haydn: Kongressbericht Graz 1970*, Graz 1972

——, 'Das Echtheitsproblem in der Musik des 18. Jahrhunderts', in 'Joseph Haydn und seine Zeit', *Jahrbuch für Österreichische Kulturgeschichte* II, Eisenstadt 1972

——, 'Haydn and the Classical Symphony' and 'The Haydn Revival', both in *Haydnfest*, Washington, D.C. 1975

LaRue, J., *Die Datierung von Wasserzeichen im 18. Jahrhundert* (paper), Vienna Congress 1956

——, 'A "Hail and Farewell" Quodlibet Symphony', in *Music & Letters* 37/3 (1956)

——, 'A new figure in the Haydn masquerade', in *Music and Letters* 40/2 (1959), pp. 132ff.

——, 'Three notes of non-authenticity', in *Haydn-Studien* II/1 (1969)

——, 'Haydn listings in the rediscovered Leuckhart supplements: Breslau', in *Studies in Eighteenth Century Music: A Tribute to Karl Geiringer on his Seventieth Birthday* (ed. H. C. R. Landon and R. E. Chapman), London 1970

——, *Guidelines for Style Analysis*, New York 1970

——, 'The Gniezno symphony not by Haydn', in *Festskrift Jens Peter Larsen*, Copenhagen 1972

Läufer, F., *Die Barmherzigen Brüder. Ein Buch über Entstehen, Werden und Wirken des Ordens*, Vienna 1931

Laurencie, L. de la, 'L'apparition des oeuvres d'Haydn à Paris', in *Revue de Musicologie*, 1932

Laurencie, L., and St. Foix, G. de, 'Contribution à l'histoire de la symphonie française vers 1750', in *L'Année musicale*, 1911

Lazarski, V. A., *Die Haydn-Hymne. Ihre melosophische Deutung*, Vienna 1972

Le Breton, J., 'Notice historique sur la vie et les ouvrages de [Joseph] Haydn', in *Le Moniteur*, Paris 1810, also separately (reprinted 1822 in *Bibliographie Musicale de la France et de l'étranger*).

Lecky, W. E. H., *A History of England in the Eighteenth Century*, New York 1891

Leichentritt, H., 'Joseph Haydn', in *Signale für die Musikal. Welt*, Berlin 1909

Lenneberg, H., 'A negative contribution to Haydn Iconography: The Longhi Portrait', in *Haydn Yearbook* II (1963/4)

Lepel, F. von, 'Josef Haydn als Opernkomponist', in *Zeitschrift für Musik* 88, 1921

——, 'Zwei unbekannte Haydn-Briefe', in *Signale* 92/41 (1934)

——, 'Unbekannte Briefe von Joseph Haydn und Gustav Mahler', in *Signale* 94/3 (1936)

Lessing, A., 'Zur Geschichte des Barytons', in *Beiträge zur Musikgeschichte des 18. Jahrhunderts* I/2, Eisenstadt 1971

Lesure, F., 'Haydn en France', in *Bericht über die Internationale Konferenz zum Andenken Joseph Haydns, Budapest 1959*, Budapest 1961

Levarie, S., 'The closing numbers of "Die Schöpfung"', in *Studies in Eighteenth Century Music: A Tribute to Karl Geiringer on his Seventieth Birthday* (ed. H. C. R. Landon and R. E. Chapman), London 1970

Levey, M., *Rococo to Revolution: Major Trends in Eighteenth Century Painting*, London and New York 1966

Levitschnigg, H. R., 'Biographische Skizze Haydns', in *Orpheus*, Mus. Taschenbuch II, Vienna 1841

Levysohn, S., 'Die Pflege der Haydnschen Musik in Dänemark', in *Haydn-Jubiläumsfeier, Kongressbericht*, 1909.

Library of Congress, *Report for the fiscal year ending June 30, 1939* – Divison of Music [printed separately], Washington, D.C.

Liessem, F., *Die Entwicklung der Klaviertechnik in den Sonaten der Wiener Klassiker Haydn, Mozart und Beethoven*, Innsbruck 1956 (Dissertation)

Lipsius, M. [pseudonym: La Mara], *Joseph Haydn* [reprinted from 'Musikalische Studienköpfe', vol. 4, Leipzig, 3/1890, 4/1899, 5/1913]

Liwanowa, T., 'Der frühzeitige Widerhall der Kunst Haydns in Russland', in *Bericht über die Internationale Konferenz zum Andenken Joseph Haydns, Budapest 1959*, Budapest 1961

Lodge, E., *The Peerage of the British Empire*, London 1834

Londonderry, Marchioness of, and Hyde, H. M., *More Letters from Martha Wilmot: Impressions of Vienna 1819–29*, London 1935

Lonsdale, R., *Dr Charles Burney, a literary Biography*, Oxford 1965

Lorenz, F., 'Josef Haydn und seine fürstliche Mäzene', in *Deutsche Musikzeitung* III, Vienna 1862

——, *Haydns, Mozarts und Beethovens Kirchenmusik*, Breslau 1866

Löw, H., *Joseph Haydn*, Basle 1907

Lowe, C. E., 'Centenary of Haydn's death, Brief biography', in *Monthly Musical Record* XXXIX, 1909

Löwenberg, A., *Annals of the Opera: 1597–1940*, Cambridge 1943; Geneva 1955

——, 'Lorenzo da Ponte in London. A Bibliographical Account of his Literary Activity', in *Music Review* IV/3, 1943

Lucam, J. R. von, 'Joseph Haydns Elementarunterricht bei Benedikt Gotschlig', in *Allgemeine Theaterzeitung*, Vienna 1852

Lùca, I. de, *Das gelehrte Österreich, Ein Versuch* (2 parts), Vienna 1776–8

Ludwig, C. A., *Joseph Haydn*, Nordhausen 1867

Luithlen, V., 'Haydn-Erinnerungen in der Sammlung alter Musikinstrumente des Kunsthistorischen Museums zu Wien', in *Anthony van Hoboken, Festschrift zum 75. Geburtstag* (ed. J. Schmidt-Görg), Mainz 1962

Lumsden, A., 'Haydn's "St. Anthony" Divertimento', in *Musical Times* 101/1407 (1960) (Landon's reply, *ibid.*, 1409)

Lunn, J., 'The quest of the missing poet', in *Haydn Yearbook* IV (1968)

MacArdle, D. W., 'Beethoven and Haydn', in *Monthly Musical Record* 89/996 (1959)

Macartney, C. A., *The Habsburg Empire 1790–1918*, London 1968

Mahling, C.-H., 'Verwendung und Darstellung von Volksmusikinstrumenten in Werken von Haydn bis Schubert', in *Jahrbuch des österreichischen Volksliedwerkes* XVII (1968)

——, 'Orchester, Orchesterpraxis und Orchester-musiker zur Zeit des jungen Haydn (1740–1770)', in *Der junge Haydn: Kongressbericht Graz*, Graz 1972

MAJOR, E., *Magyar táncdallamok Haydn feldolgozásában*, Zenei Szemle, 1928

——, 'Ungarische Tanzmelodien in Haydns Bearbeitung', in *Zeitschrift für Musikwissenschaft*, 1928/29

——, 'Magyar elemek a 18–19. századi európai zenében', in *Magyar muzsika*, 1936

——, 'Népdal és verbunkos', in *Zenetudományi Tanulmányok* I. kötet Akad. Kiadó, Budapest 1953

MALMESBURY, THIRD EARL OF (ed.), *Diaries and Correspondence of James Harris, First Earl of Malmesbury* (4 vols.), London 1844

MANN, A., 'Haydn as Student and Critic of Fux', in *Studies in Eighteenth Century Music: A Tribute to Karl Geiringer on his Seventieth Birthday* (ed. H. C. R. Landon and R. E. Chapman), London 1970

——, 'Beethoven's Contrapuntal Studies with Haydn', in *Musical Quarterly* LVI/4 (1970)

MANSFIELD, O. A., 'Haydn at Bath', in *Monthly Musical Record* 58/691 (1928)

MARCEL, H., 'L'iconographie d'Haydn', in *S. I. M. Revue musicale mensuelle*, Paris, January 1910

MARCO, G. A., 'A Musical Task in the "Surprise" Symphony', in *Journal of the American Musicological Society* X, 1958

MAREK, G. R., *Beethoven: Biography of a Genius*, New York 1969

MARGUERRE, K., 'Notationseigentümlichkeiten bei Haydn und Mozart', in *Musica* XIX/I (1965)

MARMONTEL, J. F., *Memoirs of Marmontel* (4 vols.), London 1806

MARPURG, F. W. [selection:]

——, *Der critische Musicus an der Spree*, Berlin 1749/50

——, *Die Kunst, das Clavier zu spielen*, Berlin 1750/51

——, *Abhandlung von der Fuge*, Berlin 1753/54

——, *Historisch-Kritische Beyträge zur Aufnahme der Musik*, Berlin 1754/62, 1778

——, *Handbuch bey dem Generalbasse und der Composition* ... (Berlin: Part I, 1755; Part II, 1757; Part III, 1758; Anhang, 1760; 2/1762)

——, *Anleitung zum Clavierspielen* ..., Berlin 1755

——, *Anfangsgründe der Theoretischen Musik*, Berlin 1757

——, *Anleitung zur Singcomposition*, Berlin 1758

——, *Anleitung zur Musik überhaupt und zur Singkunst besonders*, Berlin 1763

MARSHALL, D., *English People in the Eighteenth Century*, London 1956

——, *Eighteenth Century England* (in *A History of England*, 10 vols., ed. W. N. Medlicott), London 1962

MARX, A. B., *Gluck und die Oper*, Berlin 1863

——, 'Etwas über Joseph Haydn und seinen Standpunkt in der Kunstentwicklung', in *Mus. Schriften* I (2nd ed., L. Hirschberg, Hildburghausen 1913)

MARX, K., 'Über thematischen Beziehungen in Haydns Londoner Symphonien', in *Haydn-Studien* IV/1 (1976)

MASON, D. G., *The Quartets of Beethoven*, New York 1947

MATTHÄUS, W., 'Die Frühdrucke der Londoner Sinfonien Joseph Haydns', in *Archiv für Musikwissenschaft* XXI/3 and 4 (1964)

——, 'Das Werke Joseph Haydns im Spiegel der Geschichte des Verlages Jean André', in *Haydn Yearbook* III (1965)

——, *Johann André. Musikverlag zu Offenbach am Main. Verlagsgeschichte und Bibliographie 1772–1800*, Tutzing 1973

MATTHESON, J. [selection:]

——, *Das neu-eröffnete Orchester* ..., Hamburg 1713

——, *Critica musica* ..., Hamburg 1722

——, *Der vollkommene Capellmeister*, Hamburg 1739 (facsimile edition published by Bärenreiter Verlag, 1952)

MATTHEWS, B., 'Haydn's visit to Hampshire and the Isle of Wight, described from contemporary sources', in *Haydn Yearbook* III (1965)

——, 'George Polgreen Bridgetower', in *Music Review* XXIX/1 (1968)

MAYEDA, A., 'Nicola Antonio Porpora und der junge Haydn', in *Der junge Haydn: Kongressbericht Graz 1970*, Graz 1972

MAYER, E., 'Haydn in England', in *Musikalisches Wochenblatt* (Leipzig) XXXIII, 1902

MAYER, F. M., 'Die Franzosen in Steiermark', in *Geschichte der Steiermark*, Graz 1913

MAYR, G. S., *Brevi notizie istoriche della vita e delle opere di Giuseppe Haydn*, Bergamo 1809

McCALDIN, D., 'Haydn's First and Last Work: The "Missa Brevis" in F Major', in *Music Review* 28/3 (1967)

——, 'The "Missa Sancti Nicolai"; Haydn's long "missa brevis"', in *Soundings* III, 1973

McCORKLE, D. M., 'John Antes, "American Dilettante"', in *Musical Quarterly*, Oct. 1956

McGUIGAN, D. G., *The Hapsburgs*, New York 1966

MEAD, W. E., *The Grand Tour in the Eighteenth Century*, Boston and New York, 1914

MEE, J. H., *The Oldest Music Room in Europe*, London 1911

MEER, J. H. VAN DER, 'Die Verwendung der Blasinstrumente im Orchester bei Haydn und seinen Zeitgenossen', in *Der junge Haydn: Kongressbericht Graz 1970*, Graz 1972

MEIER, A., 'Konzertante Musik für Kontrabass in der Wiener Klassik', in *Schriften zur Musik*, Band 4 (1969)

MEISTER, M., *Souvenirs des mes Voyages en Angleterre. Seconde Partie (Voyage en 1792)*, Zürich 1795

MELKUS, E., 'Die Entwicklung der freien Auszierung im 18. Jahrhundert', in *Der junge Haydn: Kongressbericht Graz 1970*, Graz 1972

MELLO, A., 'Joseph Haydns Klavier-Sonaten', in *Die Musik* VIII, 1908/09

MENCIK, F., 'Einige Beiträge zu Haydns Biographie', in *Musikbuch aus Österreich*, 1909

——, 'Haydns Testamente', in *Die Kultur* (Vienna) IX, 1909

MENNICKE, C., *Hasse und die Brüder Graun als Symphoniker*, Leipzig 1906

MERZ, E., 'Zur Beurteilung Haydns', in *Die Musik* XX, 1927/28

Meyers Konversations-Lexikon (5th ed.), Leipzig and Vienna 1893

MICHEL, S., *La Sonate pour Clavier avant Beethoven*, Amiens 1907

MICHTNER, O., *Das alte Burgtheater als Opernbühne*, Vienna 1970

MIES, P., 'Joseph Haydns Singkanons und ihre Grundidee', in *Bericht über die Internationale Konferenz zum Andenken Joseph Haydns, Budapest 1959*, Budapest 1961

——, 'Anfrage zu einem Jos. Haydn Unterschobenen Werk', in *Haydn Yearbook* I (1962)

——, 'Textdichter zu J. Haydns "Mehrstimmigen Gesängen"', in *Haydn Yearbook* I (1962)

——, 'Joseph Haydns "Abschiedslied" – Von Adalbert Gyrowetz', in *Haydn Yearbook* II (1963/4)

MINGAY, G. E., *English Landed Society in the Eighteenth Century*, London 1963 (in *Studies in Social History*, ed. Harold Perkin)

MINTO, COUNTESS OF (ed.), *Life and Letters of Lord Minto, Sir Gilbert Elliott, 1st Earl of Minto, from 1751 to 1806* (3 vols.), London 1874

MITTMANN, P., 'Haydns Flötenmusik', in *Zeitschrift für Musik* IC, 1932, Heft 4

MOE, ORIN, JR., 'Texture in Haydn's early Quartets', in *Music Review*, 1975

——, 'Structure in Haydn's "The Seasons"', in *Haydn Yearbook* IX (1975)

——, 'The implied Model in Classical Music', in *Current Musicology* (in preparation)

——, 'Haydn's *Seven Last Words*: An Analysis', in *Revista Musical Chilena* (in preparation)

MOISSL, R. A., 'Haydn und sein Heimatland Niederösterreich', in *Musica Divina* XX, 1932, Heft 3

MOLL, A., *Deutschland, Deutschland über Alles – Das Lied aller Deutschen*, Leipzig–Vienna n.d. [1940?]

MOLNÁR, A., 'Der gestaltpsychologische Unterschied zwischen Haydn und Mozart', in *Bericht über die Internationale Konferenz zum Andenken Joseph Haydns, Budapest 1959*, Budapest 1961

MORATH, A., 'Die Pflege der Tonkunst durch das Haus Schwarzenberg', in *Das Vaterland*, 10 March 1901

MORITZ, C. P., *Travels of Carl Philipp Moritz in England in 1782* (reprint of English translation of 1795, with introduction by P. E. Matheson), London 1924

MÖRNER, C.-G. S., *Joseph Haydn*, Stockholm 1945

——, *Johan Wikmanson und die Brüder Silverstolpe*, Stockholm 1952

——, 'Haydniana aus Schweden um 1800', in *Haydn-Studien* II/1 (1969)

MORRISON, T. L., *The use of timpani and brass by Haydn, Mozart, and their predecessors*, Austin, Texas, 1947 (Dissertation)

MOZART, L., *Versuch einer gründlichen Violinschule*, Augsburg 1756 (2/1787; English translation by Knocker, E., with a preface by Einstein, A., London 1948 [2/1951])

MOZART, W. A., *Kritisch durchgesehene Gesamtausgabe*, 67 vols., Leipzig 1876–1907

——, *Mozarts Briefe, Gesamtausgabe* (Schiedermair, L.), Leipzig 1914

——, *The Letters of Mozart and his Family* (trans. E. Anderson), London 1938 (2/1966)

——, *Briefwechsel und Aufzeichnungen, Gesamtausgabe* (Mueller von Asow, H. and E. H.), Vienna 1949

——, *Neue Ausgabe sämtlicher Werke*, Kassel, etc., 1956 *et seq.*

MRAZ, G., 'Barock Frömmigkeit im aufgeklärten Staat', in 'Joseph Haydn und seine Zeit', *Jahrbuch für Österreichische Kulturgeschichte* II, Eisenstadt 1972

——, 'Bildungsanspruch und Bildungsmöglichkeiten im aufgeklärten Österreich', in 'Joseph Haydn und seine Zeit', *Jahrbuch für Österreichische Kulturgeschichte* II, Eisenstadt 1972

MULLER, J., 'Catalogue of Haydn's Portraits', in *Musical Quarterly* XVIII (1932), No. 2

MÜLLER, R. F., 'Heiratsbrief, Testament und Hinterlassenschaft der Gattin Joseph Haydns', in *Die Musik* 1929

——, 'Haydns letztes Testament', in *Die Musik* XXIV, 1931/32

MÜLLER-BLATTAU, J., 'Zu Haydns "Philemon und Baucis"', in *Haydn-Studien* II/1 (1969)

——, See also: 'Hohe Schule der Musik'

MÜNNICH, R., 'Haydn in Wagners Schriften', in *Musikalisches Wochenblatt* (Leipzig), LX, 1909, No. 10

MÜNSTER, R., *Die Sinfonien Toeschis*, Munich 1956 (Dissertation)

——, 'Wer ist der Komponist der "Kindersinfonie"?', in *Acta Mozartiana* XVI/3–4 (1969)

MÜNSTER, R., and MACHOLD, R., *Thematischer Katalog der Musikhandschriften der ehemaligen Klosterkirchen Weyarn, Tegernsee und Benediktbeuern*, Munich–Duisburg 1971

MÜRY, A., *Die Instrumentalwerke Gaetano Pugnanis*, Basle 1941

Musik in Geschichte und Gegenwart, Allgemeine Enzyklopädie der Musik [ed. Blume, F.], Kassel 1947 *et seq.*

NAFZIGER, K. J., *The Masses of Haydn and Schubert: A Study in the Rise of Romanticism*, Oregon University 1970 (Dissertation)

NAPOLEON, Katalog der Sonderausstellung *Napoleon in Österreich*, im Schloss Pottenbrunn, St Pölten, March–October 1973. Ergänzung zum Katalog (Mraz, Gerda): 'Die Franzosenkriege in Westungarn und die Rolle der Fürsten Esterházy'

——, *The Corsican: A Diary of Napoleon's Life in His Own Words* (ed. R. M. Johnston), Boston 1910

NAUMANN, H., *Strukturkadenzen bei Beethoven. Ein Beitrag zur Geschichte der harmonischen Sprachformen von Haydn, Mozart, Beethoven*, Leipzig 1929 (1931) (Dissertation)

NEF, K., 'Haydn-Reminiszenzen bei Beethoven', in *Sammelbände der Internationalen Musik-Gesellschaft* XIII [1911/12]

——, *Geschichte der Sinfonie und Suite*, Leipzig 1921

NETTL, P., 'The Czechs in Eighteenth Century Music', in *Music and Letters*, 1940

NEUKOMM, S., 'Dix-huit mois de la vie de Haydn' (*Revue et Gazette musicale de Paris*, vol. XLI), Paris 1874

——, *Bemerkungen zu den biogr. Nachrichten von Dies* (MS. formerly in collection O. Jahn; copy by C. F. Pohl, in possession of H. C. R. Landon): published in *Beiträge zur Musikwissenschaft* 3/1959

——, *Esquisse biographique de Sigismund Neukomm*, Paris 1859

NEURATH, H., 'Das Violinkonzert in der Wiener klassischen Schule', in *Festschrift, Beethoven-Zentenarfeier*, (*Denkmäler der Tonkunst in Österreich*), 1927

NEWMAN, W. S., *The Sonata in the Classic Era*, University of North Carolina 1963

NEWSTONE, H., 'The true Haydn', in *Music Survey* I (1947), pp. 26ff.

NIECKS, F., 'Haydn's string quartets' (abstract), in *Zeitschrift der Internationalen Musikgesellschaft*, 1909/10

NIEMETSCHEK, F. X., *Leben des K. K. Kapellmeisters Wolfgang Gottlieb Mozart, nach Originalquellen beschrieben*, Prague 1798

NIGGLI, A., *Joseph Haydn*, Zürich 1882

NISSEN, N. VON, *Mozart*, Leipzig 1828 (reprint, Hildesheim–New York 1972, with foreword by R. Angermüller)

NOÉ, G. VON, *Die Fuge bei Joseph Haydn*, Vienna 1954 (Dissertation)

NOHL, L., *Beethoven. Nach der Schilderungen seiner Zeitgenossen*, Stuttgart 1877

——, *Haydn*, Leipzig, 4/1931

——, *Musiker-Briefe*, Leipzig 1867

NORLÉN, G., *Joseph Haydn*, Uppsala 1926

NORTON, M. D. H., 'Haydn in America until 1820', in *Musical Quarterly*, 1932

NOSKE, F., *Le principe structural génétique dans l'œuvre instrumental de Joseph Haydn* (paper read at the Oxford Congress 1955)

NOTTEBOHM, G., *Beethoven-Studien*, Leipzig–Winterthur 1873

——, *Beethovens Unterricht bei J. Haydn, Albrechtsberger und Salieri*, Leipzig 1873

NOVÁČEK, Z., 'Haydns Kontakte zu der Stadt Pressburg', in 'Joseph Haydn und seine Zeit', *Jahrbuch für Österreichische Kulturgeschichte* II, Eisenstadt 1972

NOVELLO, V., *A Mozart Pilgrimage, Being the Travel Diaries of Vincent and Mary Novello in the year 1829, transcribed and complied by Nerina Medici di Marignano* (ed. R. S. M. Hughes), London 1955

NOWAK, L., *Joseph Haydn*, Vienna 1951

——, 'Ein Haydn-Autograph und sein Schicksal: Das Cello-Konzert in D-dur, op. 101' in *Biblos. Österreichische Zeitschrift für Buch- und Bibliothekwesen*, Jg. III [1954]

——, 'Haydns Cello-Konzert op. 101', in *Österreichische Musikzeitschrift*, 1954

——, 'Joseph Haydn und die Weltgeltung seiner Musik', in *Österreichische Musikzeitschrift* 25/4 (1970), pp. 210ff.

——, 'Die Skizzen zum Finale der Es-dur-Symphonie GA 99 von Joseph Haydn', in *Haydn-Studien* II/3 (1970)

NYS, C. DE, 'A propos du concerto pour deux cors et orchestre en mi bémol majeur', in *Bericht über die Internationale Konferenz zum Andenken Joseph Haydns, Budapest 1959*, Budapest 1961

OBSER, K., 'Josef Haydn und Abt Robert von Salem', in *Zeitschrift für die Geschichte des Oberrheins* XXV (1910)

OHMIYA, M., 'New Order for the "Lyra-Notturni" of Joseph Haydn', in *Tone and Meditation* (Festschrift for Prof. Nomura), Tokyo 1969

OLDMAN, C. B., 'Haydn's Quarrel with the "Professionals" in 1788', in *Musik und Verlag* (Bärenreiter Verlag, Kassel), 1968, pp. 459ff.

OLLESON, E., 'Gottfried van Swieten, Patron of Haydn and Mozart', in *Proceedings of the Royal Musical Association*, April 1963

——, 'Haydn in the Diaries of Count Karl von Zinzendorf', in *Haydn Yearbook* II (1963/4)

——, 'Georg August Griesinger's Correspondence with Breitkopf & Härtel', in *Haydn Yearbook* III (1965)

——, 'The Origin and Libretto of Haydn's "Creation"', in *Haydn Yearbook* IV (1968)

OMAN, C., *Nelson*, London 1947

——, *Sir John Moore*, London 1953

OREL, A., 'Katholische Kirchenmusik', in *Adlers Handbuch der Musikgeschichte*

ORTNER, M., 'Joseph Haydn in Kärnten', in *Carinthia* 1909

OTTLEY, D., *The Life of John Hunter*, in *The Works of John Hunter* (ed. J. F. Palmer), London 1835–37 (5 vols.)

PALM, A., 'Unbekannte Haydn-Analysen', in *Haydn Yearbook* IV (1968)

PANDI, M., and SCHMIDT, F., 'Music in Haydn's and Beethoven's time as reported in the Pressburger Zeitung', in *Haydn Yearbook* VIII (1971)

PAPENDIEK, C., *Court and Private Life in the Time of Queen Charlotte: being the Journals of Mrs. Papendiek, Assistant Keeper of the Wardrobe and Reader to Her Majesty* (ed. Vernon Delves Broughton), 2 vols., London 1886 and 1887

PARKE, W. T., *Musical Memoirs* (2 vols.), London 1830

PARRISH, C., 'Haydn and the Piano', in *Journal of the American Musicological Society* I, 1948

PÄSLER, K., Foreword to Joseph Haydn *Gesamtausgabe*, Series XIV, vol. I, Leipzig 1918

PASTON, G., *Little Memoirs of the Eighteenth Century*, London 1901

PAUER, M., 'Über Haydns zweite Londoner Symph.', in *Neue Musikzeitung* XLIII, 1922

PAUMGARTNER, B., *Mozart*, Zürich, 3/1945

——, P., 'Gesangsvorhalte', in *Musik-Erziehung*, 4 Jg./4 [1951]

Bibliography

PEČMAN, R., 'Der junge Haydn und die tschechische Musik des 18. Jahrhunderts', in *Der junge Haydn; Kongressbericht Graz 1970*, Graz 1972

PERGER, L. H., *Thematisches Verzeichnis der Instrumentalwerke von Michael Haydn* (Denkmäler der Tonkunst in Österreich, XIV. Jg., vol. 2 [1907]

PERGER, R. VON, 'Haydn und das Oratorium', in *Musikalisches Wochenblatt* XL (1909), Leipzig, Heft 9

PETRI, J. S., *Anleitung zur praktischen Musik*, Vienna 1782

PETRUCCI, G., 'Haydn e Beethoven', in *Musica d'oggi* VIII, 1926

PETZOLDT, R., 'Haydns Chorwerke', in *Die Musik* XXIV/6 (1932), pp. 408ff.

——, 'Fragen der Haydn-Forschung', in *Neues Musikblatt* XVI, 1937

PETZOLDT, R., and CRASS, E., *Joseph Haydn – Sein Leben in Bildern*, Leipzig 1959

PIERPONT MORGAN LIBRARY, *The Mary Flagler Music Collection: The Pierpont Morgan Library* (introduction by C. Ryskamp), New York 1970

PISAROWITZ, K. M., 'Mozarts Schnorrer Leutgeb', in *Mitteilungen der Internationalen Stiftung Mozarteum* XVIII/3–4 (1970), pp. 21ff.

——, 'Beitragsversuche zu einer Gebrüder-Stadler-Biographie', in *Mitteilungen der Internationalen Stiftung Mozarteum*, vol. XIX, 1/2 (1971)

PLATZ, N., and WALTER, H., 'Neukomms Bemerkungen über Haydns Grab', in *Haydn-Studien* III/2 (1974)

PLUMB, J. H., *The First Four Georges*, London 1956

POHL, C. F., *Mozart und Haydn in London* (2 vols.), Vienna 1867

——, *Denkschrift aus Anlass des 100-Jährigen Bestehens der Tonkünstler-Societät*, Vienna 1871

——, *Joseph Haydn* (Vol. I, Berlin 1875; Vol. II, Berlin 1882; Vol. III by H. Botstiber, Leipzig 1927; all three now reprinted)

——, Article on Joseph Haydn in Grove's *Dictionary of Music and Musicians* (1st to 4th editions)

POSTGATE, R., *Story of a Year: 1798*, London 1969

POŠTOLKA, M., 'Zur Methodologie der Forschung über die Beziehung zwischen der tschechischen und slowakischen Musikkultur des 18. Jahrhunderts und dem Schaffen Joseph Haydns', lecture held at the Haydn-Kongress, Bratislava, Sept. 1959

——, 'Joseph Haydn und Leopold Koželuh', in *Bericht über die Internationale Konferenz zum Andenken Joseph Haydns, Budapest 1959*, Budapest 1961

POTEMROVÁ, M., 'Haydns Musik in Košice', lecture held at the Haydn-Kongress, Bratislava, Sept. 1959

POWYS, P. L., *Passages from the Diaries of Mrs Philip Lybbe Powys of Hardwick House, Oxon., AD 1756 to 1808* (ed. E. J. Climenson), London 1899

PREISS, C., *Joseph Haydn in Graz*, Graz 1908

PROBST, F., *Beiträge zur Geschichte des deutschsprachigen Theaterwesens in Eisenstadt* (Burgenländische Forschungen, Heft 18), Eisenstadt 1952

——, 'Daten zur Geschichte des Hochfürstlich Esterházyschen Hoftheaters', in *Burgenländische Heimatblätter* XIV/1 (1952)

PULKERT, O., 'Über Aufnahme und Verbreitung der Werke Joseph Haydns in Böhmen in der zweiten Hälfte des 18. Jahrhunderts', lecture at the Haydn-Kongress, Bratislava, Sept. 1959

——, 'Dielo Josefa Haydna, Československo a cudzina', in *Slovenská Hudba* III/9 (1959), pp. 371ff.

PUTTMANN, M., *Haydn als Vokalkomponist*, Langensalza 1909

QUANTZ, J. J., *Versuch einer Anweisung die Flöte traversiere zu spielen*, Berlin 1752 (2/1780; 3/1789; facsimile of 3rd edition: Bärenreiter-Verlag 1953)

RAABE, F., *Baldassare Galuppi als Instrumentalkomponist*, Munich 1926 (Dissertation)

RACEK, J., 'Die Tschechische Musik des 18. Jahrhunderts und ihrer Stellung in der Europäischen Musikkultur', in *Colloquium Amicorum*, Bonn 1967

RÁCZ, E., *Schloss Esterházy in Fertöd [Eszterháza]*, Budapest 1972

RADANT, E. (ed.), 'The Diaries of Joseph Carl Rosenbaum (1770–1829)', in *Haydn Yearbook* V (1968), also in the original German as a separate publication

RADCLIFFE, P., 'The piano sonatas of Joseph Haydn', in *Music Review*, 1946

——, *Beethoven's String Quartets*, London 1965

RAJECZKY, B., 'Jegyzetek Haydn "Hat Nagy Misé"-Jéhez', in *Zenetudományi Tanulmányok* VIII (1960)

RANDALL, J. K., 'Haydn: String Quartet in D major, Op. 76, no. 5', in *Music Review* 21, No. 2 (May 1960)

RASMUSSEN, M., 'A Concertino for Chromatic Trumpet by Johann Georg Albrechtsberger', in *Brass Quarterly* V/3 (1962), pp. 104ff.

RATNER, L. G., 'Ars combinatoria: chance and choice in eighteenth-century music', in *Studies in Eighteenth Century Music: A Tribute to Karl Geiringer on his Seventieth Birthday* (ed. H. C. R. Landon and R. E. Chapman), London 1970

RATZ, E., *Einführung in die Musikalische Formenlehre*, Vienna 1951

RAUSCH, E., 'Haydn und die Klavier-Sonate', in *Musikwelt* (Hamburg) VI, 1926, Heft 4–5

RAYNOR, H., *Joseph Haydn: His Life and Work*, London 1961

REDFERN, B., *Haydn: a biography*, Hamden (Conn.) 1970

REICH, W., *Joseph Haydn: Leben, Briefe, Schaffen*, Lucerne 1946

——, *Joseph Haydn. Chronik seines Lebens in Selbstzeugnissen*, Zürich 1962

REICHARDT, J. F., *Briefe eines aufmerksam Reisenden, die Musik betreffend* (2 pts.), Berlin 1774/76

——, *Über die Pflichten des Ripienviolinisten*, Berlin 1776

——, *Vertraute Briefe geschrieben auf einer Reise nach Wien 1808–09*, Amsterdam 1810 (new edition by G. Gugitz, Munich 1915)

——, [Selbstbiographie] (ed. W. Zentner), Regensburg 1940 (cf. 'Periodicals')

REICHERT, E., *Die Variationsarbeit bei Josef Haydn*, Vienna 1926 (Dissertation)

REINECKE, C., *Meister der Tonkunst: Mozart, Beethoven, Haydn*, 1903

REINÖHL, F. VON, 'Neues zu Beethovens Lehrjahr bei Haydn', in *Neues Beethoven-Jahrbuch* VI, 1935

REISSMANN, A., *Joseph Haydn*, Berlin 1880

REUTHER, H., *Katalog der Haydn-Gedächtnisausstellung*, Vienna 1932 (with O. E. Deutsch, K. Geiringer, H. Kraus, etc.)

RHEINWALD, E., 'August von Griesinger', in *Schwäbische Lebensbilder* V (1950)

RIEDEL-MARTINY, A., *Die Oratorien Joseph Haydns. Ein Beitrag zum Problem der Textvertonung*, Göttingen 1965 (Dissertation)

——, 'Das Verhältnis von Text und Musik in Haydns Oratorien', in *Haydn-Studien* I/4 (1967)

RIEDINGER, L., 'Carl von Dittersdorf als Opernkomponist', in *Studien zur Musikwissenschaft*, 1914

RIEGLER, G., 'Die Kammermusik Dittersdorfs', in *Festschrift, Beethoven-Zentenarfeier* (*Denkmäler der Tonkunst in Österreich*), 1927

RIEHL, W. H., 'Haydns Sonaten' (separate print from *Musikalische Charakterköpfe* 2, 1860)

RIEMANN, H., Forewords to *Denkmäler der Tonkunst in Bayern: Symphonien der pfalzbayerischen Schule*, III. Jahrgang, vol. 1 (1902); VII. Jahrgang, vol. 2 (1907); and VIII. Jahrgang, vol. 2 (1908)

——, *Handbuch der Musikgeschichte*, Leipzig 1922

——, *Musiklexikon*, Berlin, 3/1929 (ed. A. Einstein)

RIES, F., and WEGELER, F. G., *Biographische Notizen über Beethoven*, Coblenz, 1838 (reprint Hildesheim–New York 1972)

RIESBECK, J. K., *Briefe eines reisenden Franzosen* [*sic*] *über Deutschland*, 2 vols., Zürich 1783

RIETSCH, H., 'Deutsche Klavier-Musik vom Haydn bis Reger', in *Der Auftakt* (Prague) VII, 1926, Heft 3

RIFKIN, J., 'Ein unbekanntes Haydn-Zitat bei Mozart', in *Haydn-Studien* II/4 (1970)

RINGER, A. L., 'The Chasse as a Musical Topic of the 18th Century', in *Journal of the American Musicological Society* VI (1953), No. 2

RITTER, H., 'Ein bisher unbekannter Brief Haydns', in *Allgemeine Musikzeitung* XXXI/21 (1904)

RITTER, W., 'Haydn et la musique populaire slave', in *Bulletin Sammelbände der Internationalen Musikgesellschaft* VI, 1910

RITTSTEUER, J., 'Die Beziehungen des Stiftes Lambach zu Burgenland' (*Burgenländische Forschungen*, Heft 19, Eisenstadt 1952)

ROBINSON, H. C., *Diary, Reminiscences and Correspondence* (ed. T. Sadler), 2 vols., London and New York 1872

ROBINSON, M. F., *Naples and Neapolitan Opera*, London 1972

ROCHEFOUCAULD, F. DE LA, *A Frenchman in England 1784* (ed. J. Marchand, trans. S. C. Roberts), London 1933

ROCHLITZ, J. F., *Für Freunde der Tonkunst* (4 vols.), Leipzig 1824/32

ROKSETH, Y., 'Manuscrits de Joseph Haydn à la Bibliothèque du Conservatoire', in *Revue de Musicologie* XIV/45 (1933)

ROMMEL, O., *Die Alt-Wiener Volkskomödie*, Vienna 1952

ROSCOE, C., 'Haydn and London in the 1780s', in *Music and Letters* 49 (1968), pp. 207ff.

ROSCOE, E. S., *The English Scene in the Eighteenth Century*, London 1912

ROSEN, C., *The Classical Style*, London and New York 1971

ROSENBAUM, J. C., see Radant, E. (ed.), *The Diaries* (1770–1829)

ROTHSCHILD, F., *Musical Performance in the Times of Mozart and Beethoven*, London 1961

ROY, K. G., 'The so-called violin sonatas of Haydn', in *Bulletin of the American Musicological Society*, 1948: (abstract)

RUBARTH, H., *Die Reprisengestaltung in den Symphonien der Klassik und Romantik. (Haydn, Mozart, Beethoven, Schubert, Mendelssohn, Schumann, Brahms, Bruckner)*, Cologne 1950 (Dissertation)

RUDÉ, G., *Revolutionary Europe 1783–1815*, London 1964

——, *The History of London: Hanoverian London 1714–1808*, London 1971

RUDOLF, M., 'Storm and Stress in Music', in *Bach* (Quarterly Journal of the Riemenschneider Bach Institute) III (1972), 1–28

RUNCIMAN, J. F., *Old Scores and New Readings . . .*, London 1899

——, *Joseph Haydn*, London 1908

RUNESTAD, C. J., *The Masses of Joseph Haydn: a stylistic study*, University of Illinois, Chicago 1970 (Dissertation)

RUPPRECHT, J. B., 'Joseph Haydns Geburtsstätte zu Rohrau a.d.L.', in *Allgemeine Theaterzeitung*, Vienna 1836

RUSHTON, J., 'The Theory and Practice of Piccinisme', in *Proceedings of the Royal Musical Association* 98 (1971–2)

RUTZ, H., 'Joseph Haydn in our Time', in *Music Review* 1950

——, *Joseph Haydn*, Munich 1953

RYCHNOVSKY, E. VON, 'Josef Haydn', in *Sammlung Gemeinnütziger Vorträge* No. 7 (1909)

RYWOSCH, B., *Beiträge zur Entwicklung in Joseph Haydns Symphonik 1759–1780*, Turbenthal 1934

——, 'Der Übergang zur Reprise in Haydns und Mozarts früherer Symphonik', in *Schweizer Musikpaedagogische Blätter* XXVI/1 (1937)

SACHS, C., *Handbuch der Musikinstrumentenkunde*, Leipzig 1920

SAINT-FOIX, G., 'Les manuscripts et les copies d'oevres de Joseph Haydn à la Bibliothèque du Conservatoire', in *Revue de Musicologie*, 1932

——, 'Les Sonates pour violon et alto de Haydn', in *La Revue Musicale* XIII (1932), pp. 81ff.

Bibliography

——, 'Histoire de deux Trios ignorés de Michel Haydn. Leur Influence sur Mozart', in *Revue de Musicologie*, 15 (1931)

——, 'Haydn and Clementi', in *Musical Quarterly*, 1932

——, *The Symphonies of Mozart* (trans. L. Orrey), New York 1949

——, (see also Wyzewa)

SAINT-SAËNS, C., 'Joseph Haydn et les "Sept Paroles"', in *École Buissonnière*, Paris 1913

SAKKA, K., 'Beethovens Klaviere: Der Klavierbau und Beethovens künstlerische Reaktion', in *Colloquium Amicorum*, Bonn 1967

SAN MARINO, FRANCESCO MARIA DA (Pater dei Frati Minori Cappucini), *Il Beato Bernardo da Offida*, Offida 1974

SANDBERGER, A., 'Zur Geschichte des Haydnschen Streichquartetts', in *'Altbayrische Monatshefte'* 1899; reprinted and revised in *Gesammelte Aufsätze zur Musikgeschichte*, Munich 1921

——, 'Zur Entwicklungsgeschichte von Haydn's "Sieben Worten"', in *Gesammelte Aufsätze zur Musikgeschichte*, Munich 1921 (originally in *Jahrbuch der Musik. bibliothek Peters*, 1904)

——, 'Neue Haydniana', in *Jahrbuch der Musikbibliothek Peters*, 1933

——, 'Zu Haydns Repertoir in Eisenstadt und Esterház', in *Jahrbuch der Musikbibliothek Peters*, 1933; resulting discussion between Sandberger and J. P. Larsen in *Acta Musicologica* VII and VIII (also in *Zeitschrift für Musik*), 1935–37

——, 'Zur Einbürgerung der Kunst Joseph Haydns in Deutschland', in *Neues Beethoven-Jahrbuch*, 1936

——, 'Zu den unbekannten Sinfonien von Joseph Haydn', in *Neues Beethoven-Jahrbuch*, 1937

——, 'Ein unbekannter Brief von Joseph Haydn', in *Zeitschrift für Musik*, 1938

——, 'Ein Lied-Autograph von Joseph Haydn', in *Zeitschrift für Musik*, 1942

SANDYS, W., and FORSTER, S. A., *The History of the Violin*, London 1864 (reprinted by William Reeves, London, n.d. [*c.* 1939])

SAN-GALLI, W. A. T., 'Haydns Streichquartetten', in *Musikalisches Wochenblatt* (Leipzig) XL, 1909, No. 9

SAUZAY, E., *Haydn, Mozart, Beethoven, Etude sur le quatuor*, Paris 1861

SCHAAL, R., *Verzeichnis Deutschsprachiger Musikwissenschaftlicher Dissertation 1861–1960*, Kassel 1963

——, 'Die Autographen der Wiener Musiksammlung von Aloys Fuchs', in *Haydn Yearbook* VI (1969)

——, 'Handschriften-Kopien aus der Wiener Musiksammlung von Aloys Fuchs', in *Haydn Yearbook* VII (1970)

SCHAFFRAN, E., 'Die niederösterreichischen Stifte', in *Österreichische Bücherei*, Sonderband I, Vienna [n.d.]

SCHANDORFER, E., 'Die drei Erzengel in Goethe's "Faust" und in Haydn's "Schöpfung"', in *Musica Divina* XXV (1937)

SCHANZLIN, H. P., 'Briefe des Haydn-Schülers Neukomm an den Schweizer Komponisten Schnyder von Wartensee', in *Anthony van Hoboken, Festschrift zum 75. Geburtstag* (ed. J. Schmidt-Görg), Mainz 1962

SCHARNAGL, A., *Johann Franz Xaver Sterkel*, Würzburg 1943

SCHAUFFLER, R. H., *Beethoven, the Man who Freed Music*, New York 1929 (reprinted 1946)

SCHEIBE, J. A., *Der critische Musicus*, Hamburg 1737/40 (1745)

SCHENK, E., 'Ist die Göttweiger Rorate-Messe ein Werk Joseph Haydns?', in *Studien für Musikwissenschaft*, 1960

——, 'Das Weltbild Joseph Haydns', in *Almanach der Österreichischen Akademie der Wissenschaften*, 109 (1959), Vienna 1960

——, 'Zur Genese der emphatischen None' [Haydn's *Stabat Mater* & *Salve Regina* in E], in *Beiträge zur Musikdokumentation* (Franz Grasberger zum 60. Geburtstag), ed. Günter Brosche, Tutzing 1975

SCHENKER, H., *Ein Beitrag zur Ornamentik*, Vienna 1908

——, 'Haydn: Klavier-Sonate Es-Dur Nr. 52', in *Der Tonwille*, I/3, Vienna and Leipzig 1922

——, 'Haydn: Klavier-Sonate C-Dur', in *Der Tonwille*, II/4, Vienna and Leipzig 1923

——, 'Haydns Kaiserlied', in *Der Tonwille*, IV/4 Vienna and Leipzig 1924

——, 'Die Chaos-Musik der "Schöpfung"', in *Das Meisterwerk in der Musik*, vol. 2, Munich 1925 *et seq.*

SCHERING, A., 'Künstler, Kenner und Liebhaber der Musik im Zeitalter Haydns und Goethes', in *Jahrbuch der Musikbibliothek Peters* XXXVIII, 1931

——, 'Bemerkungen zu Haydns Programmsinfonien', in *Jahrbuch der Musikbibliothek Peters* XLVI, 1939

SCHIEDERMAIER, L., 'Die Blütezeit der Öttingen-Wallerstein'schen Hofkapelle', in *Sammelbände der Internationalen Musikgesellschaft* IX (1907–8), pp. 83 ff.

——, *Der junge Beethoven*, Leipzig 1925

SCHILLER, J. C. F. VON, *Schillers Briefwechsel mit Ch. G. Körner* (ed. G. Goedeke), 2nd ed., Leipzig 1878

SCHINN, G., and OTTER, F. J., *Biographische Skizze von Michael Haydn*, Salzburg 1808

SCHLESINGER, T., *Wilhelm Cramer*, Munich 1925 (Dissertation)

SCHMID, A., 'Etwas über die Österreichische Volkshymne von Joseph Haydn', in *Wiener Allgemeine Musikzeitung* II, 1842

——, *Joseph Haydn und Nicola Zingarelli*, Vienna 1847

——, *Denksteine. Biographien von* [Seyfried, Eybler, Mosel, W. A. Mozart *fils*, Payer, Gänsbacker, Weigl, Várkony], Vienna 1848

SCHMID, E. F., 'Bemerkungen zu Haydns Nelson-Messe', in *Neue Musikzeitung* LIX, 1928

——, 'Ein neuentdecktes Requiem Haydns', in *Neue Musikzeitung* XLIX/2 (1928); also discussion with O. URSPRUNG in *Musica Divina* XVII/3 (1929)

——, *Carl Philipp Emanuel Bach und seine Kammermusik*, Kassel 1931

——, 'Joseph Haydn und Carl Philipp Emanuel Bach', in *Zeitschrift für Musikwissenschaft*, 1932

——, 'Joseph Haydns Heimat', in *Haydn-Festschrift, Monatsblatt des Vereines für Landeskunde und Heimatschutz von Niederösterreich*, Jg. 5, No. 4 [1932]

——, 'Joseph Haydn und Hainburg', in *Festschrift zur Haydn-Feier in Hainburg . . .*, 1932

——, 'Joseph Haydn in Eisenstadt, Ein Beitrag zur Biographie des Meisters', in *Burgenländische Heimatblätter, Haydn-Gedenkheft*, 1932

——, 'Joseph Haydn und die Flötenuhr', in *Zeitschrift für Musikwissenschaft*, 1932

——, 'Joseph Haydn und das Burgenland', in *Österreichische Kunst*, Heft 3/4 (1932)

——, *Joseph Haydn, Katalog der Gedächtnisausstellung in Eisenstadt, 1932* (with article by Schmid, facsimiles, reproduction of a march, etc.)

——, *Joseph Haydn, Band I. Ein Buch von Vorfahren und Heimat des Meisters*, 2 vols., Kassel 1934

——, 'Franz Anton Hoffmeister und die "Göttweiger Sonaten"', in *Zeitschrift für Musik*, 1937

——, 'Leopold Mozart und die Kindersinfonie', in *Mozart-Jahrbuch* 1951; also further in 1952

——, 'Gottfried van Swieten als Komponist', in *Mozart-Jahrbuch* 1953

——, 'Josef Haydns Jugendliebe', in *Innsbrucker Beiträge zur Kulturgeschichte*, Sonderheft 3 (*Festschrift W. Fischer*), Innsbruck 1956, pp. 110ff.

——, 'Mozart and Haydn', in *Musical Quarterly* XLII/2 (1956)

——, 'Joseph Haydn und die vokale Zierpraxis seiner Zeit, dargestellt an einer Arie seines Tobias-Oratoriums', in *Bericht über die Internationale Konferenz zum Andenken Joseph Haydns, Budapest 1959*, Budapest 1961

——, 'Neue Funde zu Haydns Flötenuhrstücken', in *Haydn-Studien* II (1970)/4

SCHMID, M. H., *Musikarchiv St. Peter, Salzburg: Katalog I: Mozart–Haydn*, Salzburg 1970

SCHMIDT, A., *Biographie Haydns* (*Orpheus musikalisches Taschenbuch*, 11. Jg., Vienna 1841)

SCHMIDT, G., *Die Musik am Hofe der Markgrafen von Brandenburg-Ansbach*, Kassel 1956

SCHMIDT, L., *Joseph Haydn*, Berlin 1898 (2/1905)

SCHMIDT, LEOPOLD, 'Joseph Haydn, Volksgesang und Volkslied', in *Joseph Haydn und die Literatur seiner Zeit* (ed. H. Zeman), Eisenstadt 1976

SCHMIEDER, W., 'Joseph Haydns Kopist und Bediensteter schreibt einen Brief', in *Allgemeine Musikzeitung*, Jg. 64 [1937]

SCHNAPP, F., 'Neue Mozart- [und Haydn-] Funde in Donaueschingen', in *Neues Mozart-Jahrbuch* II, 1942

SCHNAPPER, B., *The British Catalogue of Early Music*, London 1957

SCHNEIDER, C., *Geschichte der Musik in Salzburg von der ältesten Zeit bis zur Gegenwart*, Salzburg 1935

SCHNELLER, J., *Julius Schneller's Hinterlassene Werke* (ed. Ernst Münch), Leipzig and Stuttgart 1834

SCHNERICH, A., *Der Messen-Typus von Haydn bis Schubert*, Vienna 1892

——, 'Die Nelson-Messe von Haydn und die Theresienmesse von Haydn', in *Der Kirchenchor* (Bregenz) XXVIII, 1898, and XXIX, 1899

——, *Messe und Requiem seit Haydn und Mozart*, Vienna–Leipzig 1909

——, 'Die Mariazeller Messe', in *Die Musik* 1909

——, 'Die textlichen Versehen in den Messen Haydns und deren Korrektur', *Separatum* from the Vienna Congress of 1909

——, 'Zur Geschichte der früheren Messen Haydns', in *Zeitschrift der Internationalen Musikgesellschaft*, 1912/13

——, 'Zur Geschichte der späteren Messen Haydns', in *ibid.*, 1913/14

——, 'Das niederösterreichische Zeit- und Lokalkolorit bei Mozart und Haydn', in *Festschrift des Vereines für Landeskunde von N.-Ö.*, 1914

——, 'Zur Vorgeschichte von Haydns Kaiserhymne', in *Zeitschrift der Musikwissenschaft*, 1918/19

——, *Joseph Haydn. Leben und Wirken des grossen Meisters*, Vienna 1921

——, 'Haydns Orgelwerk', in *Wiener Almanach*, 1925

——, 'Die katholischen Glaubenssätze bei den Wiener Klassikern', in *Zeitschrift für Musikwissenschaft* 1925/26

——, *Joseph Haydn und seine Sendung*, Vienna 1922 (2/1926)

——, 'Zur Chronologie der Messen Haydns', in *Zeitschrift für Musikwissenschaft* 1935

SCHÖKEL, H. P., *Johann Christian Bach und die Instrumentalmusik seiner Zeit*, Wolfenbüttel 1926

SCHOLES, P. A., 'Burney and Haydn', in *Proceedings of the Royal Musical Association* LXVII, 1940/41, and *Monthly Musical Record* LXXI, 1941

——, *The great Dr. Burney* (2 vols.), London 1948

SCHOPENHAUER, J., *Erinnerungen von einer Reise in den Jahren 1803, 1804 and 1805* (2 vols.), Rudolfstadt 1813 and 1814

SCHORN, H., 'Neue Haydn-Funde', in *Neue Zeitschrift für Musik*, 1913, Nos. 34–35

SCHRADE, L., *Das Haydn-Bild in den ältesten Biographien*, Königsberg 1932

——, 'Joseph Haydn als Schöpfer der klassischen Musik', in *Universitas . . . XVII/7* (1962)

SCHREIBER, K. F., *Biographie über den Odenwälder Komponisten Joseph Martin Kraus*, Baden 1928

SCHUBERT, J. F., *Neue Singe-Schule oder gründliche und vollständige Anweisung zur Singkunst . . .*, Breitkopf & Härtel, Leipzig, n.d. [*c.* 1805]

SCHULZE-REIMANN, H., *Studien zur Formbildung in Haydns Klavier-Sonaten*, Erlangen 1943 (Dissertation)

SCHULTZ, D., *Mozarts Jugendsinfonien*, Leipzig 1909

SCHÜNEMANN, G., 'Ein Skizzenblatt Joseph Haydns', in *Die Musik* 1908/09

——, 'Joseph Haydns erste Symphonie', in *Allgemeine Musikzeitung*, vol. XXXVI, 1909, Nos. 20–21

——, 'Ungarische Motive in der deutschen Musik', in *Ungarische Jahrbücher* 1924

——, *Musikerhandschriften von Bach bis Schumann*, Berlin and Zürich 1936

SCHWARTING, H., 'Ungewöhnliche Repriseneintritte in Haydns späterer Instrumentalmusik', in *Archiv für Musikwissenschaft* XVII (1960)

——, 'Uber die Echtheit dreier Haydn-Trios', in *Archiv für Musikwissenschaft* XXII (1965)

SCHWARZ, B., 'Beethovens op. 18 und Haydns Streichquartette', in *Bericht über den internationalen musikwissenschaftlichen Kongress Bonn 1970*, Kassel 1971

SCHWARZ, V., 'Die Rolle des Cembalos in Österreich nach 1760', in *Der junge Haydn; Kongressbericht Graz 1970*, Graz 1972

SCHWEIKERT, F., 'Joseph Haydn und Luigia Polzelli', in *Neue Musikzeitung* XIII, 1892

SCOTT, M. M., 'Haydn's "83"', in *Music and Letters* XI (1930)

——, *Haydn Quartet Opus I No. I. Newly edited after the original editions*, London 1931

——, 'Relics and Reminiscences in England', in *Music and Letters* XIII (1932)

——, 'Some Haydn Portraits in England', in *Monthly Musical Record* LXII/738 (1932)

——, 'Haydn in England', in *Musical Quarterly* XVIII (1932)

——, 'Haydn's Chamber Music', in *Musical Times* LXXIII, 1932

——, 'Haydn's opus two and opus three', in *Proc. Royal Musical Association*, 1935/36

——, 'Mi-Jo Haydn', in *Monthly Musical Record*, 1939

——, 'Haydn: Thereabouts or There', in *Music and Letters*, 1940

——, 'Haydn, fresh facts and old fancies', in *Proceedings of the Royal Musical Association*, 1941/42

——, 'Some English Affinities and Associations in Haydn's Songs', in *Music and Letters*, 1944

——, 'Haydn and Folk-song', in *Music and Letters* XXXI (1950)

——, 'The Opera Concerts of 1795', in *Music Review* XII/1, 1951

——, *Analytical Notes to the complete string quartets of Joseph Haydn* (with K. Geiringer), Boston 1952 *et seq.*

——, Article on Joseph Haydn in 5th edition of Grove's *Dictionary of Music and Musicians* (with K. Dale)

SEEBURG, F. VON, *Joseph Haydn*, Regensburg 1882

SEEGER, H., 'Zur Musikhistorischen Bedeutung Albert Christoph Dies und seiner Haydn-Biographie von 1810', in *Bericht über die Internationale Konferenz zum Andenken Joseph Haydns, Budapest 1959*, Budapest 1961

SEMMELWEIS, K., 'Das Esterházy Schloss in Eisenstadt', in *Eisenstadt, 300 Jahr Freistadt*, Eisenstadt 1948

SHELLEY, LADY F., *The Diary of Frances Lady Shelley 1787–1817* (ed. R. Edgcumbe), London 1912

SHIELD, W., *An Introduction to Harmony*, London 1800

SICHEL, W., *Emma Lady Hamilton*, New York 1907

SIEBIGK[E], J. A. L. [C. A.?], *Joseph Haydn . . .*, Breslau 1801

SIEGMUND-SCHULTZE, W., 'Händels allegorisch-betrachtendes Oratorium und seine Weiterwirkung auf die Klassik, insbesondere auf Joseph Haydn', in *Zenetudományi Tanulmányok* VIII (1960), pp. 31ff.

——, 'Mozarts "Haydn-Quartette"', in *Bericht über die Internationale Konferenz zum Andenken Joseph Haydns, Budapest 1959*, Budapest 1961

SILBERT, D., 'Ambiguity in the String Quartets of Haydn', in *Musical Quarterly* XXXVI, 1950

SIMPSON, R., 'Observations of the "Jena" Symphony', in *Music Survey* II/3 (1950), pp. 155ff.

ŠIROLA, B., 'Haydn und Beethoven und ihre Stellung zur kroatischen Volksmusik', in *Kongress-Berichte der Beethoven-Zentenarfeier*, Bonn 1927

SMART, G., *Leaves from the Journals of Sir George Smart*, by H. Bertram Cox and C. L. E. Cox, London 1907

SMITH, C. S., 'Haydn's Chamber Music and the Flute', in *Musical Quarterly* XIX (1933)

SÖDERMANLAND, DUCHESS H. E. C., *Hedvig Elisabeth Charlottas dagbok* (ed. and trans. C. af Klercker), 6 vols., Stockholm 1927

SOLAR-QUINTES, N. A., 'Las relaciones de Haydn con la Casa de Benavente', in *Anuario Musical* II, Barcelona 1947

SÓLOYOM, G., 'A Klasszikus Századforduló', in *Zenetudományi Tanulmányok* VIII (1960), pp. 187ff.

SOMERSET, H. V. F., 'Joseph Haydn in England', in *Music & Letters* XIII/3 (1932)

——, 'Some Lesser Known Works of Haydn in Modern Editions', in *Music and Letters* XIV, 1933

SOMFAI, L., 'A Klasszikus Quartetthangzás megszületése Haydn Vónosnégyeseiben', in *Zenetudományi Tanulmányok* VIII (1960)

——, 'Ismeretlen Haydn-Kéziratok az Eszterházai Színház Opera-Repertorárjáböl', in *Zenetudományi Tanulmányok* VIII (1960), pp. 507ff.

——, 'Haydns Tribut an seinen Vorgänger Werner', in *Haydn Yearbook* II (1963/4)

——, 'Zur Echtheitsfrage des Haydn'schen "Opus 3"', in *Haydn Yearbook* III (1965)

——, 'Ein Authentisches Haydn-Bild aufgefunden', in *Österreichische Musikzeitschrift* XX/5 (1965)

——, 'Zur Authentizät des Haydn-Porträts von Loutherbourg', in *Österreichische Musikzeitschrift* XXIII/5 (1968)

——, *Joseph Haydn: Sein Leben in zeitgenössischen Bildern*, Kassel 1966

——, 'A bold enharmonic modulatory model in Joseph Haydn's string quartets', in *Studies in Eighteenth Century Music: A Tribute to Karl Geiringer on his Seventieth Birthday* (ed. H. C. R. Landon, and R. E. Chapman), London 1970

——, 'Ich war nie ein Geschwindschreiber', in *Festskrift Jens Peter Larsen*, Copenhagen 1972

——, 'Zur Aufführungspraxis der frühen Streichquartett-Divertimenti Haydns', in *Der junge Haydn: Kongressbericht Graz 1970*, Graz 1972

——, 'Vom Barock zu Klassik. Umgestaltung der Proportionen und des Gleichgewichts in zyklischen Werken Joseph Haydns', in 'Joseph Haydn und seine Zeit', *Jahrbuch für Österreichische Kulturgeschichte* II, Eisenstadt 1972

SONDERHEIMER, R., 'G. B. Sammartini', in *Zeitschrift für Musikwissenschaft*, 1920
——, 'Boccherini', in *Rivista Musicale Italiana*, 1920
——, 'Die Sinfonien Franz Becks', in *Zeitschrift für Musikwissenschaft*, 1922
——, 'Die formale Entwicklung der vorklassischen Sinfonie', in *Archiv für Musikwissenschaft*, 1922
——, *Die Theorie der Sinfonie im 18. Jahrhundert*, Leipzig, 1925
——, 'Die Entwicklung des Orchesters in der vorklassischen Sinfonie', in *Das Orchester*, 1927
——, *Haydn. A historical and psychological study based on his quartets*, London 1951
SOUPER, F. O., 'The Pictorial Element in Haydn', in *Monthly Musical Record* LVIII, 1928, No. 693
SOUTHEY, R., *Life of Nelson*, London 1813
SPITTA, A., 'Joseph Haydn in der Darstellung C. F. Pohls', in *Zur Musik*, Berlin 1892
SPOHR, L., *Lebenserinnerungen. Erstmals ungekürzt nach den autographen Aufzeichnungen herausgegeben von Folker Göthel*, Tutzing 1968; Eng. trans., *The Musical Journeys of Louis Spohr*, translated and edited by Henry Pleasants, Norman 1961
SQUIRE, W. B., *Catalogue of printed music published between 1487 and 1800 now in the British Museum* (2 vols.), London 1912
STADTLAENDER, C., *Joseph Haydns Sinfonia domestica . . .*, Munich 1963 (English trans., London 1968)
STEGLICH, R., 'Kadenzen in Haydns Klavier-Sonaten', in *Zeitschrift für Musik* IC, 1932, Heft 4
——, 'Eine Klaviersonate Johann Gottfried Schwanbergers in der Joseph Haydn-Gesamtausgabe', in *Zeitschrift für Musikwissenschaft*, 1932
——, 'Über Mozarts Adagio-Takt', in *Mozart-Jahrbuch* 1951
STEIN, F., 'Eine unbekannte Jugendsymphonie Beethovens?', in *Bulletin Sammelbände der Internationalen Musikgesellschaft* XIII (1911/12)
STEINBECK, W., *Das Menuett in der Instrumentalmusik Joseph Haydns*, Freiburg 1973
STEINBERG, L., *The Piano Trios of Joseph Haydn: Analysis of Style in Sonata-Form Movements*, New York 1973 (Dissertation)
STEINPRESS, B., 'Haydns Oratorien in Russland zu Lebzeiten des Komponisten', in *Haydn-Studien* II/2 (1969)
STENDHAL (pseud.), see under Beyle
STERN, I., *Formuntersuchungen an den ersten Sätzen der 6 'Russischen Streichquartette' op. 33 von Joseph Haydn*, Münster 1950 (Dissertation)
STERN, M., 'Haydns "Schöpfung": Geist und Herkunft des van Swietenschen Librettos. Ein Beitrag zum Thema "Säkularisation" in Zeitalter der Aufklärung', in *Haydn-Studien* I/3 (1966)
STOLLBROCK, L., 'Karl Georg Reutter', in *Vierteljahresschrift für Musikwissenschaft* VIII (1892)
——, 'J. G. Reutter, jun.', in *Vierteljahresschrift für Musikwissenschaft*, 1892
STRAKOVÁ, T., 'Josef Antonín Štěpán und Haydns Divertimento Es-dur', lecture delivered at the Haydn-Kongress, Bratislava, September 1959

STROMMER, R., 'Wiener literarische Salons zur Zeit Joseph Haydns', and 'Die Rezeption der englischen Literatur im Lebensumkreis und zur Zeit Joseph Haydns', in *Joseph Haydn und die Literatur seiner Zeit* (ed. H. Zeman), Eisenstadt 1976
STRUNK, W. O., 'Haydn's Divertimenti for Baryton, Viola and Bass', in *Musical Quarterly*, 1932
——, 'Notes on a Haydn autograph' [Piano Sonata No. 52], in *Musical Quarterly*, 1934
——, 'The London Symphonies of Haydn: a New Chronology', in *Bulletin of the American Musicological Society* XIV, 1948
STUBER, R., *Die Klavierbegleitung im Liede von Haydn, Mozart und Beethoven*, Berne 1958 (Dissertation)
SUCHALLA, E., *Die Orchestersinfonien Carl Philipp Emanuel Bachs nebst einem thematischen Verzeichnis sener Orchesterwerke*, Augsburg 1968 (Dissertation)
SUDER, A., *Die Coda bei Haydn, Mozart und Beethoven als Resultante verschiedener Gestaltungsprinzipien*, Munich 1951 (Dissertation)
SULZER, J. G., *Allgemeine Theorie der schönen Künste* (2 vols.), Leipzig 1771, 1774
SUMMERSON, SIR J., *Georgian London*, London 1962
SUMNER, F., 'Haydn and Kirnberger: A Documentary Report', in *Journal of the American Musicological Society* XXVII/3 (1975)
SVENSSON, S. E. E., *Joseph Haydn's stråkkvartetter*, Stockholm 1948
SWINBURNE, H., *Memoirs of the Courts of Europe* (ed. C. White), London 1840
SZABOLCSI, B., 'Haydn és a Magyar Zene', in *Zenetudományi Tanulmányok* VIII (1960), pp. 481ff.
——, 'Haydn, a jövö zenesze: az utolsö Menüettek', in *Zenetudományi Tanulmányok* VIII (1960), pp. 39ff.
——, 'Haydn und die ungarische Musik', in *Bericht über die Internationale Konferenz zum Andenken Joseph Haydns, Budapest 1959*, Budapest 1961
——, 'Ein melodiegeschichtlicher Beitrag zu Haydn', in *Studia Musicologica* II (1962)
——, 'Das Naturbild bei Händel und Haydn', in *Festschrift zur Händel-Ehrung der [D.D.R.] 1959*, Leipzig 1959
——, 'Der Zukunftsmusiker Haydn', in *Festschrift 1817–1967* (Vienna Music Academy), Vienna 1967
SZIGETI, K., 'Joseph Haydn zugeschriebene Orgelwerke in der Musicotheca zu Martinsberg (Pannonhalma) in Ungarn', in *Studia Musicologica* XIII (1971)

TANDLER, J., 'Über den Schädel Haydns', in *Mitteilungen der Anthropologischen Gesellschaft* XXXIX, Vienna 1909
TAPPERT, W., *Wandernde Melodien*, Berlin 1868 (2/1889)
——, 'Die österreichische Nationalhymne', in *Die Musik* XV, 1904
TAPPOLET, W., 'Haydn in unserer Zeit', in *Revue Musicale Suisse* CX/5 (1970)

TATNALL, A., *The Use of Symphonic Forms in the Six Late Masses of Joseph Haydn*, Northampton (Mass.) 1963 (Dissertation)

TAUSCH, H., *Benediktinisches Mönchtum in Österreich*, Vienna 1949

TENSCHERT, R., 'Joseph Haydn im Lichte seiner Zeit und der Nachwelt', in *Algemeine Musikzeitung* LIX/12 (1932)

——, 'Unbekanntes Autograph eines Canons von Joseph Haydn', in *Die Musik* XXI/4 (Jan. 1929)

——, 'Haydn der Künstler', in *Die Musik* XXIV/6 (1932), pp. 401ff.

——, *Joseph Haydn*, Berlin 1932

——, *Joseph Haydn – Sein Leben in Bildern*, Leipzig 1935

——, *Frauen um Haydn*, Vienna 1947

TERRY, C. S., *John Christian Bach*, London 1929; 2/1965 (ed. Landon)

THALER, J., *Die Klaviersonaten Joseph Haydns*, Innsbruck 1936 (Dissertation)

THAYER, A. W., *Ludwig van Beethovens Leben* (trans. and ed. by H. Deiters and H. Riemann; 5 vols.), Leipzig 1866/1908; 2nd edition (exclusively edited and revised by Riemann), 1970/17; [partly original] English version, New York 1921

——, *Life of Beethoven* (ed. and revised by E. Forbes), 2 vols., Princeton, N.J., 1967

THEMELIS, D., 'Violintechnik in Österreich und Italien um die Mitte des 18. Jahrhunderts', in *Der junge Haydn: Kongressbericht Graz 1970*, Graz 1972

THERSTAPPEN, H. J., *Joseph Haydns symphonisches Vermächtnis* (Kieler Beiträge zur Musikwissenschaft), Wolfenbüttel 1941

THIEME, U., and BECKER, F., *Allgemeines Lexikon der Bildenden Künstler*, Leipzig 1907–50

THOMAS, G., 'Griesingers Briefe über Haydn', in *Haydn-Studien* I/2 (1966)

——, 'Zu "Il mondo della luna" und "La fedeltà premiata": Fassungen und Pasticcios', in *Haydn-Studien* II/2 (1969)

——, 'Joseph Haydns Tanzmusik', in 'Joseph Haydn und seine Zeit', *Jahrbuch für Österreichische Kulturgeschichte* II, Eisenstadt 1972

——, 'Studien zum Haydns Tanzmusik', in *Haydn-Studien* III/1 (1973)

THOMAS, T. D., 'Michael Haydn's enigmatic "Clarino" Symphony', in *Brass Quarterly* VII/4 (1965), pp. 163ff.

THYSSE, W. H., *Joseph Haydn*, Haarlem 1948

TIBALDI CHIESA, M., *Cimarosa e il suo tempo*, 3rd edition, Milan 1949

TIERSOT, J., 'Le Lied, "Ein Mädchen, das auf Ehre hielt" et ses prototypes français', in *Zeitschrift der Internationalen Musikgesellschaft*, 12. Jahrgang, 1910–11

TIMBS, J., *Curiosities of London*, London 1855

TIRABASSI, A., 'Les œuvres inédites de Haydn d'après les manuscrits originaux conservés à la Bibliothèque royale de Belgique', in *Gazette Musicale de Belgique et Revue des tous les Arts* II/26 (1934)

TOBEL, R. VON, *Die Formenwelt der klassischen Instrumentalmusik*, Berne–Leipzig 1935

TOMASCHEK, J. W., 'Selbstbiographie', in *Libussa-Jahrbuch*, Prague 1845–50

——, 'Extracts from the Memoirs of J. W. Tomaschek', in *Musical Quarterly* XXXII/2 (1946), pp. 244ff.

TORREFRANCA, F., 'Le origini della sinfonia', in *Rivista Musicale Italiana*, 1913

TOSI, P. F., *Anleitung zur Singmusik. Aus dem Italienischen . . . mit Erläuterungen und Zusätzen von Johann Friedrich Agricola*, Berlin 1757

TOVEY, SIR D. F., 'Haydn['s String Quartets]', in *Cobbett's Cyclopedic Survey of Chamber Music*, London 1929

——, *Essays in Musical Analysis* (6 vols.), London 1935 *et seq.*

TOWNSEND, P. D., *Joseph Haydn*, New York 1884

TOYNBEE, A., *Lectures on the Industrial Revolution of the Eighteenth Century in England*, London 1928

TRAUNPAUR, A. H., Chevalier d'Ophanie – see above under ANONYMOUS, 'Excursion à Esterhaz . . . 1784'

TREVELYAN, G. M., *Illustrated English Social History*, vol. III: 'The Eighteenth Century', London 1966

TROMLITZ, J. G., *Ausführlicher und gründlicher Unterricht die Flöte zu spielen*, Leipzig 1791

TÜRK, D. G., *Klavierschule*, Leipzig 1789 (many other editions)

TUTENBERG, F., *Die Sinfonik Johann Christian Bachs*, Wolfenbüttel 1928

TYSON, A., 'Haydn and two stolen Trios', in *Music Review* XXII (1961)

——, 'One of Haydn's lost "Contrydances"?', in *Haydn Yearbook* I (1962)

——, 'New Light on a Haydn Trio (XV:32)', in *Haydn Yearbook* I (1962)

——, 'Clementi as an Imitator of Haydn and Mozart', in *Haydn Yearbook* II (1963/64)

TYSON, A., and LANDON, H. C. R., 'Who composed Haydn's Op. 3?', in *The Musical Times*, July 1964

TYSON, A., UNVERRICHT, H., and GOTTRON, A., *Die beiden Hofstetter*, Mainz 1968

UJFALUSSY, J., 'Egy Különös Formacsoport Haydn Zongoramüveiben', in *Zenetudományi Tanulmányok* VIII (1960), pp. 283ff.

ULRICH, H., 'Haydn and the String Quartet', in *Bulletin of the American Musicological Society* 11–13, 1948

UNGER, M., 'Haydn-Studien', in *Musikalisches Wochenblatt* (Leipzig) XL, 1909–10

——, 'Goethe und Haydn', in *Der Auftakt* (Prague) XII, 1931, Heft 3

——, 'Joseph Haydn und August Wilhelm Iffland', in *Die Musik* VIII/16 (1908–9)

——, 'Neues zur Lebensgeschichte Josef Haydns', in *Deutsche Musiker-Zeitung* LXIII/13–14 (1932)

——, 'Beethovens Unterricht bei Joseph Haydn. Ein bisher unbekannter Briefwechsel mit Erzherzog Max Franz', in *Kölnische Zeitung*, 27 Feb. 1936

UNVERRICHT, H., 'Die Simrock-Drucke von Haydns Londoner Sinfonien', in *Beiträge zur*

Rheinischen Musikgeschichte, Heft 52, Cologne 1962

——, 'Die gesammelten Briefe und Tagebücher Joseph Haydns', in *Die Musikforschung* XVI/1 (1963)

——, 'Unveröffentliche und wenig bekannte Briefe Joseph Haydns', in *Die Musikforschung* XVIII/1 (1965)

——, 'Die Kompositionen Johann Peter Salomons: Ein Überlick', in *Hüschen-Festschrift* (Beiträge zur rheinischer Musikgeschichte, Cologne 1965)

——, 'Zur Frage nach den Frühdrucken von Joseph Haydns Londoner Sinfonien', in *Archiv für Musikwissenschaft* XXIII/1 (1966)

——, *Geschichte des Streichtrios*, Tutzing 1969

——, 'Zur Chronologie der Barytontrios von Joseph Haydn', in *Symbolae Historiae Musicae (Federhofer Festschrift)*, Mainz 1971

——, 'Haydn und Bossler', in *Festskrift Jens Peter Larsen*, Copenhagen 1972

——, 'Ein unbeachteter authentischer Schattenriss Joseph Haydns von 1785', in *Österreichische Musikzeitschrift* 27 (1972)

——, (see also under Tyson)

URSIN, F., *Die Klavier [Cembalo] konzerte Joseph Haydns*, Vienna 1929 (Dissertation)

VALKÓ, A., 'Haydn Magyarországi Müködése a Levéltári Akták Tükrében', in *Zenetudományi Tanulmányok* VI (1957), pp. 627ff., and VIII (1960), pp. 527ff. (second instalment)

VANCEA, Z., 'Der Einfluss Haydns auf die rumänischen Komponisten des XIX. Jahrhunderts', in *Bericht über die Internationale Konferenz zum Andenken Joseph Haydns, Budapest 1959*, Budapest 1961

VÉCSEY, J., 'Az Országos Széchényi Könyvtár Haydn-Autográfjai', in *Zenetudományi Tanulmányok* VIII (1960), pp. 497ff.

VESTRIS, MADAME, *Memoirs of the Life, Public and Private Adventures of Madame Vestris* (anon.), London 1839

VIENNA, documents concerning:

AMT Hausannalen V. (Archives of the Piaristenkirche);

Annales Provinciae IV. (Archives of the Piaristenkirche);

Denkschrift zur 25 jährigen Jubelfeier der Gesellschaft der Musikfreunde des österreichischen Kaiserstaates durch Aufführung der 'Schöpfung' am 5. November 1837. Vienna 1840;

Hof- und Staats-Schematismus der röm. kaiserl. auch kaiserl. königl. und erzherzoglichen Haupt- und Residenz-Stadt Wien, [etc.] Vienna 1789 *et seq.*;

Verzeichnis aller nummerirten Häuser in der k.k. Haupt- und Residenz-Stadt Wien [&c] [with slightly differing titles], Vienna 1789 *et seq.*;

Wiener-Congress: Katalog der Wiener-Congress-Ausstellung 1896, Vienna 1896

Wiener Schriftsteller- und Künstler Lexikon, Vienna 1793

VIGNAL, M., 'L'œuvre pour Piano seul de Joseph Haydn', in *La Revue Musicale* (Carnet Critique), 1961, pp. 5–20

——, 'A side-aspect of Sigismund Neukomm's journey to France in 1809', in *Haydn Yearbook* II (1963/64)

——, *Franz Joseph Haydn*, Paris 1967

VINTON, J., 'The Development Section in Early Viennese Symphonies: a Re-valuation', in *Music Review* XXIV/1 (1963)

VIVENOT, A. VON, *Thugut, Clerfayt und Wurmser: Original-Documente aus dem k. k.Haus-, Hof- und Staatsarchiv und dem k. k. Kriegs-Archiv in Wien vom Juli 1794 bis Februar 1797*, Vienna 1869

——, *Vertrauliche Briefe von Freiherrn von Thugut . . . in den Jahren 1792–1801*, ausgewählt und hrsg. von . . ., Vienna 1872

VOIT, P., *Der Barock in Ungarn*, Budapest 1971

VOLKMANN, H., 'Ist Haydns Cellokonzert [D-dur 1783] echt?', in *Die Musik*, 1932

——, 'Das Haydn-Bildnis der Musikbibliothek Peters', in *Peters-Jahrbuch 1931* (1932)

VYSLOUŽWIL, J., 'Joseph Haydn und das tschechische Volkslied. Ein Beitrag zur Erläuterung von Haydns melodischen Denken', lecture delivered at the Haydn-Kongress, Bratislava, September 1959

WACKERNAGEL, B., *Joseph Haydns frühe Klaviersonaten. Ihre Beziehung zur Klaviermusik des 18. Jahrhunderts*, Tutzing 1974

WALDKIRCH, F., *Die Konzertanten Symphonien der Mannheimer im 18. Jahrhundert*, Ludwigshafen 1934

WALDSTEIN, W., 'Joseph Haydn und die Gegenwart', in *Österreichische Musikzeitschrift* IX, 1954

WALIN, S., *Beiträge zur Geschichte der schwedischen Sinfonik*, Stockholm 1941

WALKER, E., 'Haydn und das deutsche Lied', in *Die Musikerziehung* (Königsberg), IX, 1932

WALKER, F., 'Haydn at Seventy', in *Monthly Musical Record* LXII, 1932, No. 735

WALTER, H., 'Gottfried van Swietens handschriftliche Textbücher zu "Schöpfung" und "Jahreszeiten"', in *Haydn-Studien* I/4 (1967)

——, 'Haydns Klaviere', in *Haydn-Studien* II/4 (1970)

——, 'Die biographischen Beziehungen zwischen Haydn und Beethoven', in *Bericht über den internationalen musikwissenschaftlichen Kongress Bonn 1970*, Kassel 1971

——, 'Das Tasteninstrument beim jungen Haydn', in *Der junge Haydn, Kongressbericht Graz 1970*, Graz 1972

——, 'Ein Billett Haydns vom 6. November 1805', in *Haydn-Studien* III/1 (1973)

——, 'Das Posthornsignal bei Haydn und anderen Komponisten des 18. Jahrhunderts', in *Haydn-Studien* IV/1 (1976)

WANGERMANN, E., *Joseph II to the Jacobin Trials: Government Policy and Public Opinion in the Habsburg Dominions in the Period of the French Revolution*, London 1969

WAPPENSCHMITT, O., 'Die Durchführung ins ersten Satz von Haydns Militär Symphonie', in *Die Musik* 1908–9, XXXI, pp. 243–50

WATSON, J. S., *The Reign of George III 1760–1815*, Oxford 1960

WEBER, G., *Versuch einer geordneten Theorie der Tonsetzkunst . . .*, Mainz 1817

WEBSTER, J., 'Scorography: the music of Haydn', in *Musical Newsletter* III/2 (1973)

——, 'Haydn's String Quartets', in *Haydnfest*, Washington, D.C., 1975

WECZERCZA, W., *Das koloristisch-instrumentale Moment in Haydns Symphonien*, Vienna 1923 (Dissertation)

WEGELER, F. G., and RIES, F., *Biographische Notizen über Beethoven*, Coblenz 1838 (reprint Hildesheim–New York 1972)

WEINMANN, A., *Vollständiges Verlagsverzeichnis von Artaria & Comp.*, Vienna 1952

——, 'Verzeichnis der Musikalien aus dem K.-K. Hoftheater-Musik-Verlag', in *Beiträge zur Geschichte des Alt-Wiener Musikverlages* II/6

——, 'Kataloge Anton Huberty (Wien) und Christoph Torricella', in *ibid.* II/7

——, 'Die Wiener Verlagswerke von Franz Anton Hoffmeister', in *ibid.* II/8

——, 'Verlagsverzeichnis Tranquillo Mollo', in *ibid.* II/9

——, 'Verlagsverzeichnis Pietro Mechetti quondam Carlo', in *ibid.* II/10

——, 'Verlagsverzeichnis Giovanni Cappi bis A. O. Witzendorf', in *ibid.* II/11

——, 'Verzeichnis der Musikalien des Verlages Joseph Eder – Jeremias Bermann', in *ibid.* II/12

——, 'Wiener Musikverlag "am Rande"', in *ibid.* II/13

——, 'Verzeichnis der Musikalien des Verlages Maisch-Sprenger – Artaria', in *ibid.* II/14

——, (1) 'Verzeichnis des Verlagswerke des Musikalischen Magazins in Wien, 1784–1802', Vienna 1950; (2) 'Wiener Musikverleger und Musikalienhändler von Mozarts Zeit bis gegen 1860', Vienna 1956; (3) 'Verzeichnis der Musikalien des Verlages Johann Traeg in Wien 1794–1818', in *Studien zur Musikwissenschaft*, Band 23, 1956

——, 'Die Wiener Zeitung als Quelle für die Musikbibliographie', in *Anthony van Hoboken, Festschrift zum 75. Geburtstag* (ed. J. Schmidt-Görg), Mainz 1962

——, 'Bericht über ein Fund', in *Haydn-Studien* I/3 (1966)

——, 'Eine Variante zu einem Portrait Joseph Haydns', in *Haydn Yearbook* VI (1969)

——, 'Ergänzungen zum Verlags-Verzeichnis Tranquillo Mollo', in *Beiträge zur Geschichte des Alt-Wiener Musikverlages* II, 9a (1972)

——, 'Verlagsverzeichnis Ignaz Sauer, Sauer und Leidesdorf und Anton Berka & Comp.', in *ibid.* II/15

——, 'Verlagsverzeichnis Johann Traeg (und Sohn)'. in *ibid.* 11/16

——, 'Johann Traeg: Die Musikalienverzeichnisse von 1799 and 1804', in *ibid.* II/17/1

WEISSENBÄCK, A., 'Drei noch unveröffentliche Briefe Albrechtsbergers an Beethoven', in *Musica Divina* (Montsschrift für Kirchenmusik), IX. Jg., Vienna–Leipzig 1921

WELLESZ, E., and STERNFELD, F. (ed.), *The Age of Enlightenment 1745–1790* (New Oxford History of Music, volume VII, London 1973), with contributions by A. A. Abert, G. Abraham, M. Cooper, R. Fiske, K. Geiringer, G. Hausswald, R. Hughes, H. C. Robbins Landon, E. Olleson, P. Radcliffe, G. Seaman, F. Sternfeld and E. Wellesz

WENDSCHUH, L., *Über Joseph Haydns Opern*, Rostock 1895 (Dissertation)

WERNER, H., *Die Sinfonien von Ignaz Holzbauer*, Munich 1942 (Dissertation)

WERNER, J. G., *Lehrbuch für den ersten Unterricht im Klavierspielen*, Cursus I, Leipzig 1816

WESLEY, S., MS. Reminiscences, *c.* 1836, British Museum (Add. 27593)

WESSELY, O., *Musik in Oberösterreich*, Linz 1951

WESTPHAL, K., 'Die Formung in Haydns Sonaten', in *Die Musik* XXIV/6 (1932), pp. 419ff.

——, 'Der Begriff der Musikalischen Form in der Wiener Klassiker', in *Schriften zur Musik* Band 5 (1971)

WHITE, C. (ed.), *Letters Written at the End of the Eighteenth Century*, (part of a series: 'Secret Memoirs of the Courts of Europe'), reprint of the 1840 edition, Philadelphia, n.d.

WICHMANN, K., *Vom Vortrag des Recitativs und seiner Erscheinungsformen*: Ein Beitrag zur Gesangspädagogik, Leipzig 1965

——, *Der Ziergesang und die Ausführung der Appoggiatura*, Leipzig 1966

WILLEBRANDT, J. P., *Historische Berichte und Praktische Anmerkungen auf Reisen in Deutschland, in die Niederlande, in Frankreich, England, Dänemark und Ungarn*, ed. Gottfried Schütze, 3rd ed., Frankfurt/Leipzig 1761

WILLFORT, E. H., 'Haydn's compositions for mechanical instruments', in *Musical Times* LXXIII, 1932

WILMOT, M., *More Letters from Martha Wilmot: Impressions of Vienna 1819–29* (ed. Marchioness of Londonderry and H. M. Hyde), London 1935

WILSON, P. W., *William Pitt the Younger*, New York 1930

WINTER, L., *Joseph Haydns Klaviersonaten*, Vienna 1935 (Dissertation)

WIRTH, H., *Joseph Haydn als Dramatiker*, Wolfenbüttel 1941 (Kieler Beiträge zur Musikwissenschaft, Heft 7)

——, *Analytical Notes to Haydn's 'L'Anima del Filosofo'*, Boston 1951

WOLF, E. K., 'The Recapitulations in Haydn's London Symphonies', in *Musical Quarterly* LII/1 (Jan. 1966)

WOLFF, K., 'Johann Samuel Schroeter', *Musical Quarterly* XLIV/3 (July 1958)

WOLLENBERG, S., 'Haydn's Baryton Trios and the "Gradus"', *Music and Letters* 54/2 (1973), pp. 170ff.

WORBS, H. C., *Soziologische Studien an der Instrumentalmusik Haydns*, Berlin 1952 (Dissertation)

——, *Die Sinfonik Haydns*, Heidenau/Sa., 1956

WÖRNER, K., 'Joseph Haydn und die Programm-Musik seiner Zeit', in *Die Musik* XXIV/6 (1932), pp. 416ff.

WOTQUENNE, A., *Catalogue de la Bibliothèque du Conservatoire de Musique de Bruxelles* (2 vols.), Brussels 1902

——, *Table Alphabétique des Morceaux Mesurés contenus dans les Œuvres Dramatiques de Zeno, Metastasio et Goldoni*, Leipzig 1905

WRAXALL, SIR N. W., *The Historical and Post-humous Memoirs of Sir Nathaniel William Wraxall 1772–1784* (ed. H. B. Wheatley), 5 vols., London 1884

WROTH, W., *The London Pleasure Gardens of the Eighteenth Century*, London 1896

WÜNSCH, W., 'Zum Thema "Türkenoper und Allaturca Stil"', in 'Joseph Haydn und seine Zeit', *Jahrbuch für Österreichische Kulturgeschichte* II, Eisenstadt 1972

——, 'Das Volkslied als Thema der Zeit von Joseph Haydn', in *Der junge Haydn: Kongressbericht Graz 1970*, Graz 1972

WURZBACH, C., *Joseph Haydn und sein Bruder Michael*, Vienna 1861 (originally article in Wurzbach's 'Lexicon')

WYZEWA, T. DE, 'A propos du centénaire de la mort de Joseph Haydn', in *Revue des deux Mondes* 1909

WYZEWA, T. DE, and ST. FOIX, G., *Mozart*, Paris 1912 *et seq.*

——, 'Une Sonate oubliée', in *Bulletin de la société française des amis de la musique* IV/1 (1910); see also Päsler's reply in *Zeitschrift der Internationalen Musikgesellschaft* XI/6 (1910)

YORKE-LONG, A., *Music at Court*, London 1954

ZASTROW, C., 'Haydns erste Oper', in *Neue Musikzeitung* II, 1881

ZECHMEISTER, G., *Die Wiener Theater nächst der Burg und nächst dem Kärntnerthor von 1747 bis 1776*, Vienna 1971

ZEMAN, H., 'Die Österreichische Lyrik der Haydn-Zeit', in 'Joseph Haydn und seine Zeit', *Jahrbuch für Österreichische Kulturgeschichte* II, Eisenstadt 1972

—— (ed.), *Joseph Haydn und die Literatur seiner Zeit* (*Jahrbuch für Österreichische Kulturgeschichte*, VI 1976 [issued 1977]); contains articles by Zeman and others

ZIEGLER, B., *Placidus von Camerloher (1718–82)*, Freising 1919

ZIELINSKY, J., 'Joseph Haydn and his Time', in *The Musician* (Boston, Mass.) 1909, No. 10

ZINZENDORF, GRAF CARL VON, MS. Diaries by Count Carl von Zinzendorf, Haus-, Hof- und Staatsarchiv, Vienna

——, *Wien von Maria Theresia bis zur Franzosenzeit* (ed. H. Wagner), Vienna 1972

ZSCHINSKY-TROXLER, E. M., *Gaetano Pugnani (1731–98). Ein Beitrag zur Stilerfassung italienischer Vorklassik*, Berlin 1939

ZÜRCHER, J., 'Johann Gottfried Schwanenberger: Acht Sonaten für Cembalo', in *Die Musikforschung* 28 Jg., Heft 4 (1975)

Addenda

BADURA-SKODA, E., 'An unknown Singspiel by Joseph Haydn [*Der reisende Cerus*]', in *Report of the Eleventh Congress of the International Musicological Society*, Copenhagen 1972, I, 236ff.

——, 'The Influence of the Viennese Popular Comedy on Haydn and Mozart', in *Proceedings of the Royal Musical Association*, vol. 100, London 1974, pp. 185–99.

Index

Principal references are shown in bold type and references to illustrations in italics; references to artists, engravers etc. in captions to the plates are indicated parenthetically, e.g. (*pl. 2*). In documents cited in the text, variant forms (and misspellings) are frequently found; such variations are shown in parenthesis, e.g. 'Abukir (Aboukir)', as appropriate. For abbreviations of musical instruments, see p. 15.

473

INDEX OF COMPOSITIONS BY HAYDN

(HOBOKEN REFERENCES IN PARENTHESIS;
PRINCIPAL REFERENCES IN THE TEXT APPEAR IN BOLD TYPE)

Adagio (pf.), see Trios: No. 36 (2nd movement)
Alfred, incidental music to (XXX:5) 320; — Arie des
Schutzgeistes 326; — Chor der Dänen 316, 398;
Andante con variazioni (Sonata) in F minor (pf.; XVII:6)
303, 395
Ariadne (= *Arianna a Naxos*), see under Cantatas
ARIAS (mostly for insertion in operas by other
composers):
— 'Ah, come il core', see Operas: *La fedeltà premiata*,
below;
— 'Ah, tu non senti, amico' (XXIVb:10) 316, 320,
339;
— 'Chi vive, amante' (XXIVb:13) 316, 320;
— 'Da che penso a maritarmi' (XXIVb:16) 316, 320,
399;
— 'Dice benissimo' (XXIVb:15) 311, 319, 339, 342,
401;
— 'D'una sposa meschinella' (XXIVb:2) 316, 320,
399;
— 'Infelice sventurata' (XXIVb:15) 317, 320, 399;
— 'La moglie, quando è buona' (XXIVb:18) 312, 319,
401;
— 'Se tu mi sprezzi, ingrata' (XXIVb:14) 317, 320,
399;
— 'Signor, voi sapete' (XXIVb:7) 312, 319, 401;
— 'Sono le donne capricciose', see 'Dice benissimo',
above;
— 'Un cor si tenero' (XXIVb:11) 317, 320, 399;
Ave Maria (Hoboken *deest*?) 328

CANONS 77n., 283f., 294, 317, 327, 341, 401;
(a) miscellaneous (listed on p. 317): — 'Abschied'
(XXVIIb:13); — 'An Dorilis' (XXVIIb:9); — 'An
den Marull' (XXVIIb:5); — 'An einen Geizigen'
(XXVIIb:22); — 'A spettare e non venire (trelose)'
(XXVIIb:17); — 'Auf einen adelichen Dummkopf'
(XXVIIb:2); — 'Aus Nichts wird Nichts'
(XXVIIb:15); — 'Der Bäcker und die Maus'
(XXVIIb:37); — 'Das böse Weib' (XXVIIb:23); —
'Cacatum non est pictum' (XXVIIb:16); — 'Der Esel
und die Dohle' (XXVIIb:34); — 'Der Freygeist'
(XXVIIb:25); — 'Die Flinte und die Hase'
(XXVIIb:38); — 'Der Fuchs und der Adler'
(XXVIIb:42); — 'Der Fuchs und der Marder'
(XXVIIb:12); — 'Der Furchtsame' (XXVIIb:27); —
'Der Gänsewitz' (XXVIIb:4); — 'Die Gewissheit'
(XXVIIb:28); — 'Grabschrift' (XXVIIb:19); — 'Das
größte Gut' (XXVIIb:31); — 'Hilar an Narciss'
(XXVIIb:1); — 'Die Hofstellungen' (XXVIIb:14);
— 'Der Kobold' (XXVIIb:11); — 'Liebe zur Kunst'
(XXVIIb:40); — 'Die Mutter an ihr Kind in der
Wiege' (XXVIIb:6); — 'Der Nachbar'
(XXVIIb:39); — 'Phoebus und sein Sohn'
(XXVIIb:29); — 'Das Reitpferd' (XXVIIb:20); —
'Die Schallesnarren' (XXVIIb:35); — 'Der Spiess'
(Hoboken *deest*); — 'Das Sprichwort' (Hoboken
deest); — 'Tod und Schlaf' (XXVIIb:21); — 'Die

Tulipane' (XXVIIb:30); — 'Überschrift eines
Weinhauses' (XXVIIb:33); — 'Vergebliches Glück'
(XXVIIb:18); — 'Der Verlust' (XXVIIb:24); —
'Vixi' (XXVIIb:10); — 'Die Weld (Welt)' ('Frag'
und Antwort'; XXVIIb:41); — 'Der Wunsch'
(XXVIIb:43); — 'Zweyerley Feinde' (XXVIIb:36).
(b) other:
— 'The Ten Commandments' ('Die heiligen zehn
Gebote'; XXVIIa:1-10) 270, 282ff., 317
CANTATAS 413;
Applausus — (XXIVa:6) 142;
— *Arianna a Naxos* (XXVIb:2) 300, 303, 395, 413;
— *Lines from 'The Battle of the Nile'* (XXVIb:4) 313,
319, 327f., 401;
— *Scena di Berenice* (XXIVa:10) 268, 327f.
Cantilena pro Adventu (XXIIId:1?) 341
CANZONETTAS (see also *Lieder*; Songs) 310, 326,
327;
— First English Canzonettas (XXXVIa:25-30) 301f.,
395, 401;
— 'High on the giddy bounding mast'(Sailor's Song;
XXVIa:31) 310;
— 'In thee I bear so dear a part' (Sympathy; XXVI:a)
310;
— 'The Mermaid's Song' (XXVIa:25) 272;
— 'My mother bids me bind my hair' (A Pastoral
Song; XXVIa:27) 291n.;
— 'She never told her love' (XXVIa:34) 310
Capriccio (harpsichord, v., vc.), see Trios (pf., v., vc.):
No. 10
Cassatio in D (4 cor., str.; Hoboken *deest*) 129, 168
Cassations Stücke (various) 326, 327, 341
Catches and Glees, Twelve Sentimental (Earl of
Abingdon, pf. by Haydn; XXXIc:15) 302
Choruses, see *Alfred*; Madrigal, 'The Storm'
'Clock' Symphony, see Symphonies: No. 101
Concertante ('Sinfonia Concertante'; 'Concertino';
I:105) 312, 319, 400
CONCERTOS 341;
— baryton, 2v., basso (XIII:1-3) 326, 327;
— fag. and orch. (Hoboken *deest*) 325-7;
— cb. and orch. (VIIc:1) 326, 327, 341;
— flute and orch. (VIIf:1) 326, 327, 341;
— harpsichord and orch. (XVIII:2-4) 326, 327, 341;
— cor. and orch. (VIId:1, 3) 326, 327, 341;
— 2 cor. and orch. (VIId:2; lost) 294;
— lire organizzate and orch. 326, 327; — (VIIh:1, 2, 4)
311, 319, 399; — (VIIh:3 or 5) 309, 311, 318, 399;
— organ and orch. (XVIII:1) 207, 263, 266n., 282f.,
326, 327, 341; — (XVIII:1, 5, 8) 207; — (organ/
harpsichord; XVIII:6) 266n.;
— trumpet and orch. (VIIc:1) 59, 280, 341, 391;
— v. and orch. (VIIa:1-3) 326, 327, 341;
— v., harpsichord and orch. (in F; 'Double Concerto';
XVIII:6) 266;
— vc. and orch.: — (VIIb:1-3) 326, 327, 341; —
(VIIb:2) 423
Creation, The, see under Oratorios

487

DOUBTFUL AND SPURIOUS WORKS
(see also Pasticcio, *La Circe*, page 489)

(see also Pasticcio, *La Circe*, page 489)

ADDENDA AND ERRATA

Haydn in England 1791–1795

[page 38, letter to Prince Esterházy, line 10:]
For '. . . Mignotti . . .', read '. . . Mingotti . . .'.

[pages 59, 120, 122:]
Concerning Theresa Negri, we read in *The Times* of 3 March 1794: 'IL CAPRICCIO DRAMMATICO, a Burletta of one act, introduced Signora NEGRI, as well as DON GIOVANNI, to the Public. With the merits of the NEGRI, as an Orchestra [i.e. concert] Singer, the fashionable world are well acquainted; as an Actress, she possesses the powerful recommendation of a good stage figure and unembarrassed action. One of her arias in this piece was given with great taste, and received much applause. There was also a beautiful quintetto, in which NEGRI appeared to great advantage . . .'. In the announcement for this event, in *The Times* of 1 March, we read: 'The Music by GAZANIGA, FEDERICI, SARTI, and GUGLIELMI . . . Signora Negri, (being her first appearance on the stage) . . .'. Thus she cannot, in fact, have sung – as we suggested (p. 122) – in Guglielmi's Opera (p. 120), which was actually given, but probably appeared in Gyrowetz's Opera which (because of the fire) was not. A claque sabotaged this 1794 revival of what was basically Gazzaniga's *Don Giovanni* (see *The Times*, 10 March 1794).

[page 97, line 4:]
After '. . . in cash and', insert 'the capital from the sale of'.

[page 202, paragraph 2, line 5:]
This other Niemecz clock of 1793 has recently been rediscovered; it is owned by Baron and Baroness von Veyder-Malberg of Prien im Chiemgau and Merano. The clock, still in perfect playing condition, contains thirty pieces; of these, nos. 19-30 have been recorded, together with nos. 1-12 of the so-called 'Urban' clock of 1792, and issued on the Candide label (CE 31093) in 1975.

[page 242, before final paragraph insert:]
The concert on 10 March 1794 was reviewed in *The Times* of 12 March as follows:

SALOMON'S CONCERT

The fifth concert of this season was on Monday evening, and the room was crowded by all the amateurs. A more charming performance was never heard, and the Concert well deserves the very distinguished patronage it receives. The *Concerto* on the German flute by ASHE was heard with particular pleasure, and so was Madame MARA, who never fails to delight those who hear her, when she conducts herself with a becoming deportment. Impertinent behaviour in an orchestra shall never go unheeded by us. When a public performer cannot conduct him- or herself with respect to an audience, it is time to quit the stage.

[page 275, footnote:]
For confirmation of the story in Carpani of Haydn's *bon mot* concerning Elizabeth Billington, see Addenda (below) to *Haydn: the Late Years 1801–1809*, p. 340.

[page 288:]
The concert discussed in the last two paragraphs is patently the same event as that discussed on pp. 283f., including a newspaper quotation which is identical (the *Morning Herald* obviously reprinting the text of the *St. James' Chronicle*).

[page 301, last paragraph, line 5:]
For '. . . English copyist . . .', read '. . . a local copyist . . .'.

[page 350, musical example:]
In the orchestra, at bar 6 the first note (bass clef) should read *e* (not *d*) and the second notes (treble clef) should read *g* and *c* (not *g* and *d*); at bar 11, the first note in the bass line should read *c* (not *b*); in bar 12 the staccato should be deleted.

[page 358, at end of paragraph 2 add:]
A full autograph sketch of the *Third Commandment*, from the papers of F. H. Barthelemon, was sold in London at Sotheby's on 8 November 1976 (lot 103), together with a copy of the *First Commandment* (with the text added in Haydn's own hand); both are now in the Bodleian Library, Oxford.

[page 375, musical example:]
In the final bar, the note values in the soprano line should read: dotted crotchet; quaver.

[page 376, paragraph 2, line 5:]
For '. . . COZ . . .', read '. . . OCZ . . .'.

[page 379, first musical example:]
In bar 1 the lower note in the left hand should read *a* flat (not *g* flat), as in the following bar.

[page 404:]
Dr Harington's Compliment is published (in an edition by H. C. Robbins Landon based on the first edition published by Breitkopf & Härtel) by Broude Brothers, New York.

[page 413, paragraph 2, line 21:]
For '... five octaves, from *f'* ...', read '... five octaves, from *F*...'.

[page 420, musical example:]
At bar 100, for two sharps in piano left hand substitute two naturals.

[page 435, second musical example:]
In bars 1 and 2, add quaver rests in V. and Vc. parts, as in piano left hand.

[page 477, second musical example:]
In the final bar, add staccati to the third and seventh notes.

[page 478, paragraph 2, line 4:]
For '... The bracketed part at bars 14-15 and 18-19 (*c'*) seems ...', read '... Sections of bars 14/15 and 18/19 seem ...'.

[page 480, paragraph 2, lines 14-15:]
The piano arrangement in question was done by Haydn; the autograph of the concluding section was sold at auction in London by Bonham's on 23 February 1977 (lot 55; catalogue, p. 10). The page is also reproduced in *Apollo*, February 1977, p. 57.

[page 481, paragraph 2, lines 8-10:]
For '... the incredible chord ... bar eight – enough ...', read '... the incredible augmented chord (taken out of context the dominant of the wildly remote key of C major) in bar eight, marked *ff* and finely elaborated in the first violin part in the recapitulation – enough ...'.

[page 494, caption, line 3:]
For '... included in the ...', read '... included in this ...'.

[page 516, musical example:]
The time signature should read barred C, *alla breve*.

[page 526, second musical example:]
The sharp in the key signature should be deleted.

[page 530, musical example:]
In the final bar, a flat should be added before the flute's first note.

[page 553:]
After the first musical example, add:
(The relationship between the introduction and the slow movement's second subject is obvious and has often been noted.)

[page 557, paragraph 2, line 1:]
Beethoven, who in 1793 was a pupil of Haydn, actually made a copy of parts of the sketches for the Finale of Symphony No. 99; see L. Nowak in *Haydn-Studien* II/3 (1970).

[page 574, musical example:]
In bar 66, the last note in the bassoon part should read *g* (not *a*), as in bar 67.

[page 602, first musical example:]
The time signature of the Haydn melody should read barred C, *alla breve*.

[page 619, column 1:]
For 'Anderson, Betty ...' read 'Anderson, Emily ...'.

[page 628, column 2:]
After 'Mansfield, Orlando 268', insert new entry: Mara, Gertrud Elisabeth 25, 28, 30, 41, 44, 64, 92, 108, 131, 138, 152, 159-65, 171-4, 182, 189, 212f., 232-6, 239, 241-3, 245-7, 249f., 252, 278, 297f., 313; *pl. 4*; also Addenda to p. 242 [see above].

[captions to monochrome plates:]
12: in line 5, for 'autograph' read 'manuscript'.
13: in line 9, for '1764' read '1794'.

Haydn: the Years of 'The Creation' 1796–1800

[page 10, column 2:]
The information with reference to plate 32 and 33 should be transposed to conform with the captions to these illustrations.

[page 557:]
Add to footnote 1:
The original manuscript of Barbara Scheiger's marriage contract is now owned by a private collector in New Jersey.

[page 585:]
Under heading 'Selected Contemporary Reviews', in line 10, for '... infra, pp. 594f.', read '... infra, pp. 587f.'.

Haydn: the Late Years 1801–1809

[page 294:]
A lost letter of 14 September 1804 from Haydn to an unknown lady has been rediscovered just as this volume goes to press; the letter, in the possession of

an American private collector who wishes to remain anonymous, reads:

[To a Lady. *German*]
Gracious Lady
Accept, in your graciousness, this small and modest keepsake from your admirer, and may you ever prosper.

Joseph Haydn mpria.

From my house
14th September 1804
[not in CCLN except for mention on p. 233]

Since the letter is unpublished, we also include here the original German:

Gnädige Frau
Nehmen Sie diss kleine und schwache Ange-denken von Ihrem Bewunderer in Gnaden auf, und leben Sie

ewig wohl.

Joseph Haydn mpria.

Vom Hauß.
den 14:^m September 1804

The letter perhaps accompanied a fan or some other small present; there is no way at present of identifying the recipient.

[page 340:]
While reading an entertaining new book by Stella Musulin – *Vienna in the Age of Metternich*, London 1975 – we noted several references to the memoirs of an English physician, Dr Henry Reeve, who visited Vienna in 1805.[1] Since his account of life there, including references to the musical life of the city and an account of a visit to Haydn, are quite unknown to musical scholarship, we hasten to quote several important passages:

Tuesday, November 5.—Paid a visit to *Haydn*, the celebrated composer. He lives in a small house in the suburbs of Vienna at *Comptendorf*. I sent up my name and mentioned being a friend of Mr. G. Thomson's at Edinburgh, that we might have some medium of connection and something to talk about. He received me very civilly; he calls himself a very old man of seventy-five, but he has not at all the look of so many years. He has some of the infirmities of age; his head and his chest trouble him, and at present he is unwell, his nerves are so weak that he can do nothing. He cannot compose or write, which he finds very hard, and he is ordered not to make any such exertion by his physician. He speaks a little English, and about as much French and Italian, besides German. So we made a compromise; I spoke French, German, and English, and he spoke German. We managed to understand each other very well, and we talked a great deal in half an hour. He spoke with rapture of England; called it the

first and best country in the world; said he had been there twice, the last time in 1790 [*sic*], and had composed a great deal of his music while in London, amidst good eating and drinking. He related an anecdote of his dining in company with Mrs. Billington, at some house where there was a picture of her hanging in the room, representing her listening to an angel singing; Haydn said it ought to be reversed—she ought to have been drawn singing and the angel listening to her;[1] he got a kiss for this elegant compliment. Salomon was his interpreter in England. He spoke of the delight he took in composing symphonies for the Scotch songs, and said he should write music for some words Mr. Thomson sent to him lately, as soon as he was well enough to do anything. His last great work was the Oratorio of the Four Seasons. I thanked him in the name of Great Britain and all lovers of music for the pleasure he had afforded us by some of his fine compositions. His figure is about the common size, rather short in stature, his eyes dark, aquiline nose, and brown complexion, marked a little by the small-pox; he wears a nicely powdered tail wig; he was in excellent spirits, very glad to see me, and requested me to repeat my visit. [pp. 40ff.]

Thursday, November 21.—Went to the Wieden Theatre to the new opera 'Fidelio,' the music composed by Beethoven. The story and plan of the piece are a miserable mixture of low manners and romantic situations; the airs, duets, and choruses equal to any praise. The several overtures, for there is an overture to each act, appeared to be too artificially composed to be generally pleasing, especially on being first heard. Intricacy is the character of Beethoven's music, and it requires a well-practised ear, or a frequent repetition of the same piece, to understand and distinguish its beauties. This is the first opera he ever composed, and it was very much applauded; a copy of complimentary verses was showered down from the upper gallery at the end of the piece. Beethoven presided at the pianoforte and directed the performance himself. He is a small dark young-looking man, wears spectacles, and is like Mr. Koenig. Few people present, though the house would have been crowded in every part but for the present state of public affairs. [pp. 64f.]

Sunday, December 22.—This day may be noted as remarkable in this Journal, and in my life, for to-day I have seen BONAPARTE the EMPEROR NAPOLEON. I went to the chapel at

---

[1] This account provides us with the first authentic verification of the story about Haydn and the Reynolds portrait of Mrs Billington as St Cecilia (cf. *Haydn in England 1791–1795*, p. 275n.); in that context we doubted the truth of the story for which the only known evidence was provided by Carpani (pp. 230f.). The Reynolds engraving is reproduced in, *inter alia*, Geiringer (1947), pl. 34.

[1] Henry Reeve, M.D., *Journal of a Residence at Vienna and Berlin in the Eventful Winter 1805–6*, published by his son, London 1877.

Schönbrunn with Mr. Gräzenstein, and I had a complete view of him at mass. He was alone in the emperor's tribune on one side of the altar on high, his pages and attendants in adjoining seats. His countenance struck me as very remarkable, fuller, broader, and fatter than I had expected to have seen it, and his person stouter and older than usually represented. He has the usual marks of the sanguine melancholic temperament, dark hair, small dark eyes, rather fixed than animated, and a very piercing countenance; the forehead high, nose somewhat Grecian rather than aquiline, and cheek-bones and chin rather prominent; his physiognomy is striking, and there is a deal of character displayed in his countenance. His hair is cut short like the present mode. He was simply dressed in the regimentals of the guards or chasseurs à cheval, very dark green with red collar with gold epaulets, and a small star on his left side. After chapel he reviewed the Imperial and Royal Guards and an immense train of artillery. He came out of the palace, accompanied by four pages in scarlet and gold, eight servants in green and gold liveries, and many generals, officers, and attendants. Four grooms held a fine grey horse which he mounted, and every person uncovered. He galloped up to the line and then passed slowly along. His profile is very different from the front view of his face, and to me appeared more unfavourable; he sits badly on horseback, stooping, and is distinguished by the great simplicity of his dress – a simple small cocked hat without any lace, while his attendants are all glitter and gold. The pomps and equipage of the army is [*sic*] certainly great beyond all conception. The different regiments of guards are superb troops, consisting of eight or ten squadrons, the greater part of them mounted upon fine black horses, which seem to betray their birth and breed at Hanover! The Mameluke guard of about fifty or sixty men produces a striking effect; it attended General Berthier to-day. Prince Murat, Prince Borghese, General Berthier, General Clarke and all the principal officers were at the review. The whole sight was magnificent. Almost all the officers and many of the men wear the badge of merit; this red ribbon is the mark of their having signalised themselves, and as belonging to the 'legion of honour.' This honorary distinction is of infinite service: it gratifies particularly the national character.

The impression left on my mind, after looking at Bonaparte attentively for a considerable time, was that of increased admiration. There is a great deal of mental activity in almost every feature, though not vivacity; acuteness, quickness, and severity seem to be the predominant qualities. The lower part of the face appears constantly in action, revolving on itself and its complicated concerns; and Lavater would fix upon such a face in a crowd as bearing the marks of a superior and most

extraordinary man. To enable one to judge more accurately it is necessary to see him and observe him when speaking.

December 25, Christmas Day.—The weather is very mild, wet, and dirty from a gentle thaw which took place a few days ago; no snow or frost, dull, and joyless. I dined on roast beef and plum-pudding with Mr. Acklom, and in the evening went to hear the oratorio 'The Seasons,' composed by Haydn from subjects taken from our poet Thomson. The first overture is expressive of the passing over of the Winter and the opening of Spring; three characters are introduced: Simon a farmer, his daughter Jean, and a young peasant called Lucas, and these three personages recite and sing and are joined by a chorus of country people and huntsmen in the chace [*sic*]. Some of the airs are lively and pretty, and the choruses appear well arranged. The soprano parts were chiefly sung by boys. The foolish attempt to make the sound echo to the sense is too often made. Nothing struck me as particularly fine, and I should feel disposed to consider the 'Seasons' inferior to the 'Creation,' in having fewer fine passages and fewer beauties, and more faults of the same kind as in that composition. However, I cannot be allowed to judge, for I heard this performed to great disadvantage, an orchestra not well filled, and only Jean (Mademoiselle Laucher) who could sing; she has a good voice and good taste. The words are trumpery – a downright murder of poor Jemmy Thomson. By way of apology it may be mentioned that no concerts or places of amusement are open usually for the day of Christmas and the day preceding and following it; but as the French garrison remains here, an attempt was made to furnish some amusement and to increase the funds of the widows and orphans of decayed musicians. Few persons were present; chiefly military. Maret, minister and secretary to the French Emperor, we noted among *the most* distinguished characters present.[1]   [pp. 87ff.]

[page 397, item 271:]
Johann Philipp Samuel Schmidt, who visited Haydn at the turn of the century and gave him the work listed here. When Schmidt left Vienna, Haydn wrote his Canon 'Kenne Gott, die Welt und dich' in Schmidt's commonplace-book (*Stammbuch*). *MGG*, vol. 11, col. 1862.

1 [Original footnote:] Maret, afterwards Duc de Bassano, died in 1834.